The Stanford University
HEALTHY HEART COOKBOOK
& Life Plan

Over 200 Delicious Low-Fat Recipes
Plus the Revolutionary 25 Gram Plan
from the World-Renowned Medical Center

by Helen Cassidy Page, John Speer Schroeder, M.D.,
and Tara Coghlin Dickson, M.S., R.D.

CHRONICLE BOOKS
SAN FRANCISCO

Nutritional information for all foods listed in this book was compiled from two sources:

Nutritionist IV Food Product & Nutritional Labeling, Version 3.0, from N-Squared Incorporated

Bowes & Church's Food Values of Portions Commonly Used, Sixteenth Edition, Revised by Jean A. T. Pennington, PH.D, R.D., J. B. Lippincott Company, Philadelphia, 1994

Numbers taken from these sources have been rounded to the nearest decimal point.

Calculations listed for nutritional anaysis of the recipes are rounded as follows:
> 0.1 to 0.5 = Trace
> 0.6 to 0.9 = 1

We are grateful to reproduce the height and weight chart in Chapter 5. Joann Manson, M.D., 1987. Metropolitan Life Insurance Co., Build and Blood Pressure Study, 1959. The Journal of the American Medical Association 257: 353–358.

First paperback edition 1997.

Copyright © 1996 by Helen Cassidy Page and John Speer Schroeder.

Library of Congress Cataloging-in-Publication Data available.

ISBN 0-8118-1750-4

Printed in the United States of America

Cover photograph by Deborah Jones.
Cover Design by Barbara Vick.
Book Design by Laurie Szujewska.

Distributed in Canada by Raincoast Books
8680 Cambie Street
Vancouver, British Columbia V6P 6M9

10 9 8 7 6 5 4 3 2 1

Chronicle Books
85 Second Street
San Francisco, California 94105

Web Site: www.chronbooks.com

To my sister, Rita Jennings, who first taught me about heart; my brother,
Frank Cassidy, who first captured my heart; and above all to the memory of
my beloved mother and father, Mary and Jim Cassidy, and late brother,
Jack Cassidy, who will always live in my heart.
    —HELEN CASSIDY PAGE

With love for Jennifer, who is the epitome of eating for a healthy heart and body.
    —JOHN SPEER SCHROEDER, M.D.

To my family: Marilyn Elizabeth Coghlin and James Joseph Coghlin, III,
who started me on this at an early age, for their eternal strength and love;
Michael James Coghlin for his "fitness of the heart";
Alison Michelle Coghlin, who listens and speaks with her heart;
and my husband and chef, Peter Kiefer Newman Dickson,
with the biggest heart of all for his inspiration and passion.
    —TARA COGHLIN DICKSON, M.S., R.D.

CONTENTS

ACKNOWLEDGMENTS

The enormous undertaking of developing an institutionally approved life plan for a healthy heart evolved from years of research and the vision of large numbers of people at Stanford University. On the home front, the encouragement, loyalty and often unsung hard work of family and friends were crucial in sustaining us as well as helping us translate the scientific terminology of a medical program into a book for the lay person. We are pleased to have the opportunity to thank them properly and publicly.

At Stanford University Hospital, the initial strong support of Ken Bloem, and subsequently Malinda Mitchell along with Lewis Saksen, was essential to keeping the goals of this book alive over its four-year development stage. The support of the Nutrition Committee was crucial. As chair of the committee, Dr. Harvey Young and Diane Hester, Stanford Health Services Clinical Nutrition Manager, shepherded this book through the complex approval process to assure a work that represented the Stanford philosophy as well as the diverse opinions that always operate in an intellectually rich university environment. Many differences of opinion will always exist about the importance of one factor or another in the development of heart disease. However, we believe that the endorsement of this multidisciplinary group lends further credence and strength to the recommendations in this book.

We are especially grateful to Dr. John Farquhar, founder and head of Stanford's Center for Research in Disease Prevention and Dr. William Haskell, his colleague at the center. Dr. Haskell was pivotal in assuring scientific accuracy as new research came in and altered our views. His repeated reviews of the manuscript guaranteed that we always had the latest word in our fight against heart disease. Dr. Farquhar, a pioneer in efforts to educate and promote healthy lifestyles, not only offered many valuable suggestions for the manuscript, he made important contributions to Chapter Five, Assessing—and Eliminating—Your Risks, and helped tailor his Self-Assessment Risk Questionnaire for our use. He also wrote the Preface with its unqualified endorsement of the book, for which we are particularly thankful.

Without the generous efforts of the dietitians at Stanford University Hospital, this book could never have come to fruition. As the team that provides excellent nutritional support to Stanford's patients, they have not only given this book their endorsement, but their many excellent suggestions and their careful review of the final manuscript guaranteed the nutritional accuracy of our recommendations. Individually, they repeatedly made themselves available for curbside consultations to help Tara Coghlin Dickson assemble the mass of information that has been distilled into the consumer guidelines, nutritional charts and calculations throughout the book.

Dr. Victor Dzau, Chief of Cardiovascular Medicine and recent Chairman of the Department of Medicine, whose early enthusiastic support of the project was always appreciated. Jeanne Kennedy, Stanford Hospital's Director of Patient and Community Relations was another early supporter whose reviews and suggestions helped steer the formation of the book within Stanford's halls. We thank Cheryl Barry, who ably assisted Dr. Schroeder during the early drafts, and Deborah Bobrow, who helped Helen Page as well as Dr. Schroeder in many ways during the arduous process of formatting the chapters. Cheryl Ventimiglia came to the rescue to further assist as the book went to press.

How lucky we were to have an excellent crew of assistants who tirelessly cranked out page after page of manuscript, and who never (well, almost never) balked when drafts number 23, 24 and 25 showed up: first and foremost, Carol Cowen Moller, who steered us through the pitfalls of the entire first draft, offered discreet editorial comments and enthusiastic praise, each at the most needed moments; Jeffrey Swearingen, who showed up for the last stages with an impressive commitment that assured we would meet our deadlines; Joe Wachs, who stepped in with style at the right moment; Andrew Ettelson and Alex Von Below, who filled in as necessary to prevent the dam from bursting. When the task of proofreading threatened to crush the authors, an army of proofreaders, led by Fran Abenheimer, showed up and kept coming back for more chapters to scrutinize. We are indebted to Wendy Wood, Jeralyn Seiling and Neil Leiberman for the time they spent poring over the pages, and to Karen Morebeck for her keen editorial comments, careful reading and encouragement. Heartfelt thanks to Bernard Katz for his help with Chapter One, his careful eye and encouragement. We valued the support and suggestions of Betz Collins and Kira Kane of The Cook's Bookshop in San Diego.

A big thank you to the testers who gave thumbs up to the recipes: first to Lynn Brady, who tested repeatedly the dessert and bread chapters and gave excellent tips and insights; and to Chris and Phil Lee, Carolyn Federman, Carol Cowan Moller, Collette Rosenthal, Rachel Rosenthal, Gina Frye, Jill Rosenthal, Ken Aron and Linda Haggerty Holtzapple.

We will always remember the people who never lost faith, and in dark times, restored ours: Fran Abenheimer, Brian Cleary, Don Collins, Greg George, Linda Goldstone, Chris Hall, Carlin Holden, Shirley Ingalls, Chris Bennett Lee, Mary Murphy, Andrew Pelfini, Pam Perkins and Michael Skinner. A special, heartfelt thanks has to go to Jane Felder for her critical eye and unswerving belief, to Beeper Felder for his enthusiasm; to the Federmans, Irwin, Jaime Federman Greenberg, Eric, Alex and Carolyn, for their friendship and generosity of heart; to Sheila Federman, whose memory and spirit loom large over many pages; and to Helen Page's favorite brother-in-law, Hal Jennings, whose loyalty, humor and support exceeded at times even that of his wife's, a tall order in itself.

Praise for The Writing Group: Shoshanna Alexander, Barbara Austin, Nina Ham and Jane Ann Staw, the gifted, funny, remarkable women who ate the food, read the drafts, held the hand and lifted the spirits of Helen Page at every turn. The energy, friendship, love, wit and counsel of these writers was as mother's milk. In addition, Barbara and Jane served as developmental editors during the early formulation of The 25 Gram Plan; Shoshanna fine-tuned several of the recipe chapters and Nina lent a sensitive ear and astute eye when they were most needed. Thanks to Wendy Wood, not just a best friend, but the best a friend can be; to Heather Rourke, who kept all the moving parts working; to our friends at Farella, Braun & Martel, for their remarkable good will, especially Jon Hartung, Bruce Goldstein, Kathy Fotheringham and Dan Cohn; and our friends at Hanson, Bridgett, Marcus, Vlahos & Rudy, especially David Miller and Del Barbee.

From Helen Page, many, many thanks to the people who taught me to cook, whether they knew it or not: Julia Child, Madeleine Kamman, Robert Olney, the late Grace Ryan, and the late Randy Harvey, one of a kind, who encouraged me to do it with style. I am indebted to the people who taught me to write, from Homer to Barry Lopez and Tom Jenks, and I am grateful to Andrew Hill for making me believe I could. Harold McGee's remarkable book, *On Food and Cooking* (Scribners) proved an invaluable resource and delightful reading, and helped clarify for me oxidation, the structure of fat molecules and the browning process.

From the start, Felicia Eth, our literary agent, saw the book as larger than we could. She guided us until we got it right and the book had the depth, scope and acceptance it deserved. Our editor, the late Jacqueline Killeen, was simply the best of the best. She is sorely missed. Her intelligence, skill, perceptiveness, vision and thoroughness made this a better book; her warmth, humor, tact and enthusiasm were a personal comfort to Helen Page. We are beholden to them both.

The Buddhists say that even if we carried our parents on our backs for the whole of our lives, we could not repay them the gift of life. Helen Page is one parent who can never repay her daughter. The authors thank Allison Page for seizing the opportunity to speak up for the book when it mattered, during a chance encounter with Jay Schaefer of Chronicle Books. Because of Allison, the wheels started turning that eventually drove this book to market. Jay, thank you for your receptiveness. Our everlasting gratitude to Chronicle Books editor Bill LeBlond, not just for saying yes, but for saying it with such enthusiasm and warmth. Under Bill's leadership, the professionalism and style of everyone at Chronicle allowed the final blossoming. We were fortunate to be the recipients of Leslie Jonath's unflagging good will, efficiency and careful judgment as she steered the book through production. We are indebted to Jill Jacobson at Chronicle Books and Laurie Szujewska for their excellent book design, and to proofreader Carolyn Keating whose skill polished the final draft.

Finally, to our family and friends who have endured long absences, preoccupation, early-morning writing and faxing—to everyone who allowed this book to evolve in an energetic and scientifically correct way, we thank you.

This ambitious and marvelous book has a main message: Most heart attacks and surgeries that occur in this country to open or bypass the heart's arteries can be a thing of the past! The book has a personal message, as well: You don't have to suffer the grief, pain, disability and death caused by heart disease. The Stanford Life Plan gives you the knowledge, motivation and skills to live a longer, healthier life.

In this book, Helen Cassidy Page, author and food consultant, has teamed herself once again with Dr. John Schroeder, an eminent Stanford University Hospital cardiologist and research scientist. Their previous book, *The Whole Family Low Cholesterol Cookbook*, published in 1976, was ahead of its time in sounding the call for a heart-healthy diet. Tara Coghlin Dickson, versatile Stanford Hospital dietitian, joins them in this new book, which is also ahead of its time. In their "one stop shopping" approach, they have provided a complete resource book for heart attack prevention. Each of its four important sections—primer on heart disease prevention, nutritional sourcebook, meal planning and consumer guide to healthy foods, and cookbook—can stand alone. But together, they comprise a classic example of the whole being greater than the sum of its parts.

As Americans concerned about diet and heart attacks, we remain mystified by conflicting statements about the cause of heart disease. We ask ourselves, "Does the risk really apply to me and my family?" And we are certainly unhappy about the prospect of giving up the foods we like, believing, as someone once said, that "eating a healthy diet won't make me live any longer, it will only seem that way." Like so many of us, you might have searched yourself for the answer to the question, "What will it take to persuade me to suffer all the punishment that I anticipate if I change how I live and what I eat?" This book carries you across those barriers in gentle but convincing steps.

My words in this preface, of course, cannot convince you of the wisdom of this book. Perhaps, though, a personal tale from my own medical practice can help. Many of my patients have had heart attacks or have a high risk of developing one. After careful risk assessment, months of gradual lifestyle change, self education, and sessions with dietitians, they reduce their risks. Yet, if a patient who starts on this path to heart health answers "yes" to the question, "Are you on a diet," I know they haven't succeeded. Being "on a diet" connotes a feeling of being different. They must remind themselves to develop the harsh discipline to stay "on the diet." Some people definitely develop feelings of self-pity and of deprivation; their desire to continue wanes and their risk of heart attack once again climbs. This scenario is more likely to occur if a person switches overnight to an entirely new, demanding set of food rules that don't allow for individual tastes and preferences. However, when my patients can follow a heart-healthy program and say, "No, I am not on a diet, I eat whatever I want," I know they will succeed.

The Stanford Life Plan for a Healthy Heart provides the clear and pleasant path to become that second patient. In this book you will discover why the number 25 is one of the most important numbers in your life (but I won't give away the why here). The significance of the number 25 is only one of the new and innovative tools of The Stanford Life Plan to help you live a healthier life. In addition, in this book you will find new facts on women and heart disease, antioxidants in foods that can aid in the prevention of heart disease and cancer, healthy supermarket shopping, how to survive in restaurants, and even how to cope with fast foods.

Designed to keep you from becoming a heart attack patient, this book is for the entire family—for children, friends and neighbors. But if you or a family member has entered the health care system as a "patient"—with a positive treadmill test, a past history of heart attack, bypass operation or balloon angioplasty to open a blocked artery—then this book has extra meaning and relevance. The authors describe the special recommendations that can decrease the chances of any repeat heart attack or of an untimely death from coronary heart disease.

In addition to describing the role of diet in developing or avoiding coronary heart disease, Dr. John Schroeder, in his review of the best scientific evidence, provides clear explanations to all your questions and more. For example: What are the risk factors for coronary heart disease? What is the difference between cholesterol in food and cholesterol in the blood? What is "good cholesterol" and "bad cholesterol?" What is saturated fat and why is it bad? What about olive oil, calcium, dietary fiber and antioxidants such as beta-carotene, and vitamins C and E? And, crucial to anyone's health program, to bring home the story from abstract science, The Stanford Life Plan shows you how to score your own risk level and gives you ways to increase your personal motivation.

Helen Cassidy Page's lively writing and imaginative use of the material, for example, the informative and fun quizzes at the end of each chapter, has made crucial scientific information uniquely accessible to the lay reader. Because a heart-healthy diet becomes work without something good to eat, delicious food is at the heart of The Stanford Life Plan. Helen, in her dual role as writer and cook, brings healthy food into the mainstream with the best collection of imaginative, easily prepared recipes in print today. To complete the package, Tara Coghlin Dickson has supplied the numbers that will take the guesswork out of calculating how much fat is in the foods you eat. Every home needs both a dictionary and an encyclopedia to "keep up with the world." With this book as a resource, one volume instead of 15 can bring you and your family into a better, healthier world. And this knowledge will fill you with new optimism that you can avoid being part of the yearly statistic that puts heart disease as the most common cause of early death and disability.

JOHN W. FARQUHAR, M.D.
Director, Stanford Center for Research in Disease Prevention
Professor of Medicine
Professor of Health Research and Policy
Stanford University School of Medicine

INTRODUCTION

Put your hand over your heart. Rest it there for a moment and feel, once again, the familiar thrum, thrum, thrum of your own heartbeat. This gentle percussion announces the awakening of life while we are still in the womb; its silence will mark the close of life. That the heart will one day be silent adds an urgency and sweetness to our days. It is, perhaps, the music of life itself, this sound of the working heart. The mystery of feeling but not seeing so vital an organ, hints at larger mysteries. In the millennia before the advent of the science of anatomy, we could only imagine what this pulsating part of ourselves must look like — imagine its purpose, if it had one other than an insistent drumming to remind us that we were alive.

Perhaps because its gentle rhythm soothed us in the womb, or because its persistent ticking, like a marcher's cadence, has counted off every moment of our lives, the heart has captured our collective imagination as our most potent metaphor. We shun that which brings us heartache. We seek our heart's desire. Long before we knew the precise anatomical design of the heart or its physiological role in sustaining life, we celebrated in song, in poems, in the endearing names we gave to our loved ones, the heart as the core of life, its very center. The power of these metaphors helps us articulate those great mysteries symbolized by the heart—the confusion, pain and joy of life. The poet seizes upon the heart as an image to grapple with the complexities of life, while the medical scientist seeks a concrete vision to heal the heart. A desire to enhance life links them both, and it is the quality of life that concerns us in this book.

As you might expect, we are going to tell you about how the heart functions and the role dietary cholesterol plays in your health and well-being. We will discuss the merits of exercise and whole-grain foods. We will teach you how to make luscious, rich desserts that won't jeopardize your arteries, and we will help you determine your cardiac risk factors. But again, put your hand over your heart and listen to what we are really talking about—your very own heartbeat.

We usher in the next millenium with an ability to control and order life that a mere 50 years ago existed only in the science fiction imagination. The fields of genetics, biotechnology, immunology, microsurgery allow us to conceive an embryo in a test tube, rearrange DNA, transplant organs and even prolong life with an artificial heart. Yet for all these sophisticated techniques that provide a medical solution for wrenching human problems, the most persistent medical campaign has been the one against heart disease, our number-one killer.

Stanford University researchers have been at the forefront of the worldwide effort to decode the heart's physiological secrets. Like unraveling a great tangled skein, we and our colleagues have painstakingly pulled first one strand and then another until in the 1960s, 70s and 80s, order began to emerge from the confusion surrounding our understanding of the heart. We now know the human heart as never before — from the symmetry of its chambers to the electrical impulses that keep it throbbing and to the mechanical sophistication that allows it to pump and pump and pump over a lifetime a seeming ocean of nutrients to the farthest reaches of the body and back again. Much of what technology has revealed serves the surgeons as they repair defective valves and allows cardiologists to prescribe medications to calm an erratic beat. For a long time we considered the health of our hearts to be a matter of luck and a good doctor, but recent knowledge has added another dimension to our understanding of the heart: We know what keeps it healthy; we know what doesn't. We have learned that we must all become care-takers of our own hearts and those of our children, and that is the realm of the heart we will address in this book.

We at Stanford University Hospital have become frustrated with the campaign to end heart disease. Just a half century ago, no one believed you could prevent heart attacks. Now, coronary heart disease patients come to our clinics and into our hospital and operating rooms to undergo one of many miraculous treatments that have been developed to help the heart's cholesterol-clogged arteries. Balloon angioplasties, coronary bypass surgery, heart transplants are all daily procedures at Stanford Hospital and our patients leave with their lives improved. However, we have realized that these expensive miracles that go on here and at other hospitals frequently give only temporary relief and that much more needs to be done to prevent the problem. This book is therefore directed at preventing or slowing the process of coronary atherosclerosis by altering one of the major sources of the problem—the American diet. This book is not only for our patients who already have symptoms of heart disease, but for everyone who wishes to live a heart-healthy life from childhood to old age.

PART ONE

The Stanford Life Plan for a Healthy Heart

CHAPTER 1

Cholesterol and the Healthy Heart: A New Look

DO YOU FLINCH WHEN SOMEONE MENTIONS CHOLESTEROL? *Does the word raise images of heart attacks, blood tests, confusing medical data and complicated numbers you have to juggle before you can pick up your dinner fork? Does a low cholesterol diet make you think of food as medicine—something you have to eat because "it's good for you?" Do you think you have to deprive yourself forever of your favorite foods because "they're bad for you?" It's time to shine a new light on cholesterol, because, unfortunately, many people still think of cholesterol the old way—the signal for hard work, no fun and bad food. Perhaps the most serious misunderstanding about cholesterol is that only certain people need to worry about it, such as middle-aged men or those who have had heart attacks. It is time to change that perception.*

The Stanford Life Plan for a Healthy Heart takes a new look at caring for your heart and blood vessels. This book will help you view the level of cholesterol circulating in your bloodstream as an ally, the yardstick you can use to measure the health of your heart. We'll tell you exactly what cholesterol is, what it does and why maintaining a low blood cholesterol level is a cause for celebration—not deprivation. Research conducted at Stanford and other medical centers throughout the world proves that few heart attacks occur in people who have total cholesterol readings in the 160 range, while the risk of heart disease accelerates as the total cholesterol level creeps past the 200 mark. Achieving a low, even a very low, total cholesterol means you can prevent disabling heart disease as well as the number-one cause of death in America—heart attack. And the really good news is that most of us can achieve this goal by simply *limiting* saturated fat in our diets!

The comprehensive approach of The Stanford Life Plan for a Healthy Heart will guide you toward a lifestyle that stresses health, comfort and, above all, the joy of delicious food for you and for everyone. The cornerstone is The Stanford 25 Gram Plan and Fat Tracker's Guide, which gives you the simple, crucial key to keeping your cholesterol levels as low as possible: *eating less than 25 grams of saturated fat in a day.* If you are wondering why we are talking about saturated fat when the subject is cholesterol, you have hit on a major problem with the effort to prevent heart disease in America.

Today, now that the American public knows what causes heart disease, the cholesterol issue (like the weather, sports and politics) has become a standard topic of dinner conversation. But even though cholesterol is on everybody's mind (mostly giving a guilty prod when people eat something they think they shouldn't), heart disease is *still* the number-one killer in America. Dr. Stephen Fortmann, deputy director of the Stanford Center for Research in Disease Prevention, participated in a cooperative study called "Monitoring of Trends and Determinants in Cardiovascular Disease." Results revealed that even though our overall statistics have dropped in the last decade, the United States still ranks in the top third of countries with the most deaths from heart attacks worldwide! (In this book we refer to heart disease as the damage to the coronary arteries caused by the buildup of cholesterol deposits inside the coronary arteries that can lead to heart attacks, the same process that can clog the arteries that feed our brain and cause strokes. We are not talking about valve disease, murmurs or other heart problems. Atherosclerosis, coronary artery disease, heart disease and hardening of the arteries all refer to this same condition.)

❧ **Premature heart attacks unnecessarily kill almost one-half million of us every year.**

What do the statistics mean to you? Imagine yourself at a dinner table with the four people most central to your life—your spouse, your children, your parents, your favorite sibling or coworker. Maybe your business partner is there. Or your best friend. Include your own name on the guest list. Statistics prove that 25 percent of us will suffer a premature heart attack. So, which one of these people are you willing to sacrifice to heart disease? Now think of four other people you love and do the same thing. And then another four. Continue on with everyone you know. That's what the epidemic of heart disease is all about.

The Statistics Must Be Improved

In his book, *The American Way of Life Need Not Be Hazardous to Your Health,* Dr. John Farquhar, founder of Stanford's Center for Research in Disease Prevention, makes the point that if plane crashes killed the same number of people that die of heart attacks every year—*the equivalent of two full jet loads of passengers every day*—the federal government would shut down the airline companies until they guaranteed the public safety. Think of it: two jet loads of people every day. That equals the entire population of Vermont or Wyoming or Delaware every year! Yet if we know what causes heart attacks and we know how to thwart them, why don't Americans feel the same urgency about preventing heart attacks that we do about preventing plane crashes? Why aren't the statistics improving faster?

Our patients gave us the answer. Over and over they articulated the cloud of confusion and uncertainty surrounding the whole diet and cholesterol issue; and the fear of deprivation that people unfortunately assume is the price they must pay for a healthy heart. If our patients are confused about reducing their risk of heart disease, if they are groping for a way to understand this crucial health issue, we know you must be, too.

You can't prevent heart disease when you are confused about the basics—when you don't fully understand the difference between good fats and bad fats or why saturated fat is a greater dietary worry when the media emphasizes *cholesterol* as the problem. When doctors say eat less fat, you don't know how much is less and how much is too much. We find parents don't realize their children need a heart-healthy diet, and we all struggle to assemble meals that provide both good taste and good health. Nearly every month new medical studies show that *every heart—young or old, well or sick—benefits from limiting saturated fat.* Yet people still ask us, "Are you talking to me? I'm too young to begin worrying about preventing heart disease. Right?" Or, "Why bother? I'm too old to prevent heart disease, right?" Or, "It's too late for me, I've already had a heart attack. Right?"

We Provide the Missing Link

The Stanford Life Plan for a Healthy Heart provides the missing link in the public campaign against heart disease. It makes clear that heart disease prevention begins in childhood and continues throughout life, yet demonstrates that you don't have to sacrifice your whole way of life just to live a heart-healthy lifestyle. It concentrates on a simple key—minimizing the most harmful ingredient in your diet: saturated fat.

❦ **We suggest that along with your birthday, your social security number and your bank access code, you must make 25 the most important number in your life—because eating *less* than 25 grams of saturated fat a day may save your life by lowering your cholesterol to the safe levels that will keep your heart healthy.**

If you are not familiar with the metric system, you may have a hard time visualizing 25 grams of saturated fat. How much is it? If you could gather 25 grams of pure saturated fat together, you would have a walnut-sized nugget that weighed a little less than an ounce. Here's what it would look like:

One cup of sour cream, one-half cup of whipping cream and four ounces of chocolate each contains approximately 25 grams of saturated fat. How much does the typical American adult eat every day? More than twice that amount, a lump about the size of a small apple—and not the kind that keeps the doctor away!

The difference between the maximum, daily, walnut-size portion of saturated fat and the actual apple-size portion most Americans consume daily is one of the major reasons we have an epidemic of heart disease. Where does all this fat come from? Our daily bread—toasted and buttered, along with bacon and eggs for breakfast; a hamburger with fries and a chocolate shake for lunch; a lamb chop at dinner topped off with ice cream and a few butter cookies for dessert. Other factors, such as smoking, high blood pressure and lack of exercise contribute to heart disease, as we will discuss in the following chapters. But it is the American diet, with its overload of harmful fats—particularly saturated fat as well as cholesterol, found mainly in animal protein such as meat, poultry and whole-milk dairy products— that most dramatically raises blood cholesterol levels and causes heart disease. Our ceiling of 25 grams is based on the National Cholesterol Education Program's dietary recommendations released by the National Heart, Blood and Lung Institute in 1988 as well as its follow-up report in 1993. We will show why this crucial number will simplify every aspect of a heart-healthy diet, from giving you a maximum target to guide you as you read fat-content information on package labeling, to streamlining your menus by unloading them of harmful fats.

We want to reassure you that as a Stanford Fat Tracker, you can continue to enjoy delicious food, even as you reduce your risk of heart disease by restricting the amount of saturated fat you eat to 25 grams or less each day. But there is a lot more to The Stanford Life Plan for a Healthy Heart than this one crucial element and we want to tell you about all of it.

The Stanford Life Plan Is a Total Approach

The real secret to combating heart disease is an overall plan for reducing your risk of developing atherosclerosis that embraces all the sound medical, nutritional and lifestyle remedies, recommendations and healthy habits *you* need.

❦ **We have taken everything we know about preventing heart disease and put it where it will do the most good: in your hands.**

From giving you a picture of how the heart works, to explaining why the saturated fat in butter harms your arteries and why the monounsaturated fat in olive oil keeps them healthy, to the Stanford Heart Disease Self-Assessment Risk Questionnaire, which will help you understand your own personal risk of heart disease, The Stanford Life Plan for a Healthy Heart weaves all of this information into an overall approach that gives you all the data you need to make the choices that are right for you. Whether you are a man with low cholesterol levels who wants to keep them that way, a woman who has been advised to make changes in her diet as she approaches menopause, a person with symptoms of a cholesterol problem or heart trouble, or a parent who wants to give your children a head start on a healthy life, we will plug you into all the information you need to become an expert caretaker of your own heart. When you know the answers to the urgent questions and the basic principles that govern the care of your heart, you can protect yourself from heart disease. As you use this information, you can protect *your children* from heart disease. Then, as they grow, you can teach them how to protect *their children*. And that's when we will see the collapse of this epidemic.

❦ **We designed The Stanford Life Plan for a Healthy Heart to give everyone the chance for a healthier heart.**

But this valuable advice is just the beginning. Experience tells us that sound medical advice and recommendations for heart-healthy meals are only as good as the recipes that embody them and the ease with which they fit into your life. So after we help you finally make sense of all the information about heart disease that bombards everyone these days, we will then show you how to *use* this information every day of your life. The Stanford Life Plan for a Healthy Heart includes:

- The Stanford 25 Gram Plan that simplifies the concept of a healthy diet by teaching you how to limit all of the harmful types of fats in your food by restricting saturated fat to 25 grams a day or less.
- The Fat Tracking Guide that keeps your search on target for the healthiest and best-tasting meals.

- A collection of time-saving and worry-saving tools that complement the Fat Tracking Guide, such as The Fat Account, The Fat Tracker's Cooking Course, The Fat Tracker's Meal-Planning Guide and the guidelines for Nutrition for a Healthy Heart—all of which will help you implement easily a heart-healthy lifestyle.
- And, to cap off this proven eating plan for life, we give you more than 200 delicious recipes for food that is really worth living for.

The common denominator for everyone, however, must be a limit on the harmful dietary fats that *cause* heart disease, embodied in a plan for making heart-smart food choices throughout your life. Of all of the measures we will evaluate and recommend, though, we know that concerns about food always produce the most difficulty and anxiety for people. You worry that you can't continue to reap pleasure from a list of favorite foods that appears to dwindle with each new scientific study. And we worry that fear of culinary deprivation and hardship might convince you to ignore research that repeatedly shows the impact of diet, specifically the role of fats, on your heart. Rest assured that recipes such as Dried Blueberry Buttermilk Pancakes with Blueberry Honey Sauce, Persimmon and Chutney Muffins, Spiced Chicken Nuggets with Hot Mango Purée, Fettuccine with Smoked Salmon, Goat Cheese and Chives, Oven-Baked French Fries, Chicken Roasted with Pears, Fennel and Red Onions and Buttermilk Brandy Spice Cake will keep your meals in line with the recommended 25-gram limit on saturated fat with mouthwatering satisfaction.

The National Recommendations for Optimal Cholesterol Levels May Change

As researchers continue work to understand the role cholesterol plays in human chemistry, we will understand more about low, safe levels of blood cholesterol. Just as 225 was considered a healthy cholesterol level in the 1970s, and 200 was deemed safe in the '80s, the end of this century and the beginning of the next will very likely see a national target in the range of 160 to 200 milligrams, as we recommend currently in The Stanford Life Plan for a Healthy Heart. To achieve a new and lower cholesterol level, new recommendations will no doubt appear to urge healthy American adults to eat even less saturated fat—around 7 percent of their calories, as opposed to the 8 to 10 percent currently recommended for healthy persons. This will require even further changes in America's eating habits. You, as a follower of The Stanford 25 Gram Plan, will be ahead of the pack.

There Is No Short Cut to Heart Health

We know that everyone wants medical scientists to come up with a "magic pill" that will let them eat anything they desire and live as they wish without worrying about heart disease. As medical scientists *and* individuals who need to follow our own advice, we would love to produce that miracle. But unfortunately we just don't see it on the horizon. Medical technology allows cardiologists and cardiac surgeons at Stanford to perform miracles. We can prescribe lifesaving medications for people who have had a heart attack and do surgical procedures to bypass or open up blocked arteries. Under special circumstances, we can even consider the miracle of miracles, heart transplantation, to help the rare patient who meets the strict criteria. But everyone, especially the patients who undergo heart surgery or heart transplantation, agrees that the best way to deal with the coronary heart disease problem is to do everything you can to prevent it from getting started in the first place.

If You Can't Read the Whole Book in One Sitting…

You will use this book for the rest of your life, but you don't have to read every chapter thoroughly before you start making healthful sausages and toothsome desserts. For your convenience, we have made a list of all the recommendations for reducing your risk of heart disease that we will explain fully in future chapters. If you have to figure out what to have for dinner before you find out exactly why your food choices are so important to your heart, you can photocopy these guidelines and paste them on your refrigerator. Read them over and begin to take immediate steps to reduce your risk of heart disease by putting nonfat dairy products on your shopping list and committing to exercise for at least 30 minutes before you go to bed this evening. Then turn to the recipe section and plan a meal around, say, Pork Medallions with Two Marmalades (page 535), Stir-Fry of Green and White Beans with Ginger (page 402), followed up with Raspberry Sherbet (page 564) for dessert. After dinner, or over the weekend when you have more time to yourself, pick up the book again and turn to the Nutrition Section, where you will learn that eating less beef doesn't mean eating none at all. Then, by the time you get to the fat-tracking cooking lesson, you will have discovered how to beef up delicious recipes for stir-fries, stews and soups with smaller quantities of red meat that still leave you feeling fully satisfied and nourished.

We want you to give the book a careful reading, but if this is not the time, when convenient, sit down again at your leisure and give yourself the best chance for a long, healthy life by reading all the chapters to learn how to live well and eat healthfully. We have done everything we can to make sure that living a heart-healthy lifestyle is comfortable and delicious for you. The individual chapters are the essential building blocks that together form the structure for that lifestyle. It is only with *all* this information, which will begin to unfold systematically in the next chapter, that you can become that expert caretaker of your heart.

- Eat less than 25 grams of saturated fat per day
- Eat less than 300 milligrams of cholesterol* per day
- Eat at least 25 grams of fiber per day
- Eat less than 3,000 milligrams of sodium per day
- Adopt essential healthy lifestyle habits for optimal heart health by:
    - Quitting smoking
    - Keeping your blood pressure within the normal range
    - Exercising *a minimum* of 30 minutes daily
    - Maintaining your ideal weight
    - Reducing stress
    - Eating foods high in fiber and antioxidants every day
- After consulting with your physician, consider these other preventive measures:
    - One daily aspirin
    - Nutritional additives such as vitamins C and E, beta-carotene and calcium
    - Estrogen replacement therapy for postmenopausal women

Finally, we want to stress that, unless we state otherwise, *all of the recommendations we make throughout the book are for the average, healthy adult.* We will, however, specifically address the needs of particular groups who may require different guidance, such as children, women and people who already have heart disease.

*The scientifically accurate way of expressing cholesterol is in milligrams per deciliter, or mg/dL, for example, 300 mg/dL. For the sake of simplicity, we will just use the whole number throughout the text of the book.

CHAPTER 2

The Link Between Diet and Heart Disease

IN THE 16TH CENTURY, *when Leonardo da Vinci performed illicit autopsies to help him understand human anatomy, he discovered that the arteries in an elderly man were hardened with a strange substance that he compared to the rind of an orange. Though he had no name for it, Leonardo had witnessed the ravages of coronary artery disease.*

❧ Like the fire of Prometheus, cholesterol is both life-giving and life-threatening.

What you learn about cholesterol now can very likely lengthen your life and make you healthier, more productive and less susceptible to debilitating heart disease, heart attacks and strokes in your later years. The workings of the human body that Leonardo was trying to comprehend have become common knowledge to the typical TV viewer. But although everyone knows by now that "high cholesterol" is linked to heart disease and "low cholesterol" isn't, many people still have what we call a low CQ or cholesterol quotient. That is, they don't fully understand the cholesterol issue. We are going to take you back to the beginning and trace the history of heart disease research during this century that led to the recommendations of The Stanford Life Plan for a Healthy Heart.

Where Did the Problem Come From?

Today, with the word cholesterol stamped on nearly every food label (whether it belongs there or not), you run the risk of taking the current hoopla about heart disease for granted. But if you think back to the old days, when all any doctor could say to you about the prevalence of heart attacks was that's life—and death—in America, you can appreciate the tremendous accomplishments in modern cardiovascular research.

Investigations into the causes of heart disease began with an experiment on rabbits soon after the turn of this century in St. Petersburg, Russia. Two scientists— Ignatowski, and several years later, Anitschkow—fed rabbits raw meat, egg yolks and even raw cholesterol. Fatty streaks appeared in the animals' arteries. Anitschkow narrowed the offender down to animal fat, but despite these very convincing links between diet and heart disease, the scientific community either ignored or discounted the discovery. Rabbits are vegetarian, some said! You cannot compare them to humans. Valuable time was lost and more than half a century would pass before scientists would feel confident enough of the link between diet and heart disease to begin urging Americans to change their eating habits. Why did it take so long?

Though science has done a remarkable job of coming up with answers, successful research always depends on asking the right questions. It often takes a lot of digging to discover what you are really looking for, as was the case with cholesterol. Researchers attempted to duplicate the work of the Russians, using different species of animals, but the results of their studies were inconclusive. Not all types of animals showed fatty streaks when they were fed cholesterol, but if they didn't, their blood cholesterol levels didn't rise either. So the question became: What happens to animals whose cholesterol levels go up when they eat cholesterol? They developed the fatty streaks that led to heart disease. It appeared that artery disease only developed in the animals once the cholesterol levels started to climb. Experiments that manipulated blood chemistry to raise cholesterol levels showed that it didn't matter whether diet or other conditions caused the increase; once the cholesterol level began to climb, the development of plaque began.

The Search for a Single Cause

The next question was: Are human arteries similarly sensitive to dietary and blood cholesterol? As long as investigators focused only on cholesterol as a factor in coronary artery disease, results were shrouded in controversy. Scientists could not agree that high blood cholesterol levels caused cholesterol plaque or that eating cholesterol-rich foods played any part in the development of heart disease in humans. Coronary heart disease was revealing itself as a very complex process. To avoid misinterpretation of the data, a concern central to the integrity of the scientific process, researchers sought to find a single cause that would explain all the variables, just as the role of blood sugar and insulin explains diabetes. That one, single cause proved elusive. At the same time, other pieces of research were coming together as careful study of the heart in sudden death victims and the development of electrocardiogram machines helped diagnose heart attacks in patients complaining of angina—the chest pain that accompanies coronary artery disease—*before* they died. Work moved forward on early detection of heart attacks to prevent death.

Here at Stanford University Hospital, if you came to the cardiology clinic at the halfway mark of this century complaining of chest pain and shortness of breath, or landed in our hospital with a full-blown heart attack, we did the best we could for you. As time passed, what we could do for you got better and better. We learned how to use more powerful heart drugs and developed more sophisticated surgeries. Faced with many middle-aged patients otherwise healthy but dying from heart attack damage, Stanford researcher Dr. Norman Shumway paved the way for the establishment of Stanford's cardiac transplantation program. In 1968 Dr. Shumway and his team performed the first successful heart transplant in this country. But though we were learning how to repair damaged hearts, we still couldn't mobilize this burgeoning technology, medical skill and clinical experience until your heart literally had broken.

Heart Disease Prevention: A New Notion

So even as news of that first transplant surgery garnered headlines throughout the world, other Stanford researchers conducted quieter work to determine if heart disease could be prevented. The possibility of actually preventing heart disease before it ever got to the critical heart attack stage had intrigued many scientists, among them Dr. Ancel Keys, an epidemiologist from the University of Minnesota, who helped the medical community finally focus on the right questions. In the aftermath of World War II, as millions starved in war-torn Europe, Dr. Keys made the startling observation that in the midst of brutal food shortages, the incidence of heart disease in Europe plummeted during those terrible years. He began a campaign to find the link between the two events and in time gained the attention of researchers worldwide when he and his colleague, Dr. Henry Blackburn, launched the famous Seven Country Coronary Disease Study in 1958, the first of many major efforts to track the causes of heart disease.

❧ **This 10-year study showed an alarming trend for high rates of heart disease to cluster in regions with cuisines that favored rich, fatty food accentuating dairy products and meat, such as Finland and the United States.**

Countries depending on fish and grains for their food supply, such as Japan, and on monounsaturated fats, such as Italy, had much lower rates of coronary artery disease. This work provided the answer to one of the great ironies of post-war Europe noted by Dr. Keys: Though people suffered unspeakable hardships, the fact that they could not get meat and dairy products after the war apparently lowered their rate of heart disease. These results were published in 1970 and specifically showed several remarkable correlations:

- The first direct link between diet and heart disease finally showed that, as the percent of calories from saturated fats in the diet rose, so did the blood cholesterol. The link missing from modern research, first noted by Anitschkow in 1913, was that saturated fat, such as that found in animal products, not just cholesterol, caused blood fats to rise.

- In answer to the question, what happens when humans develop high cholesterol levels, the Seven Country Study showed that coronary heart disease rates were closely linked to the levels of cholesterol found in the blood. Here was the link that had also been suspected from the Russians' animal experiments, but which until now had been difficult to prove in humans.

❦ **The evidence was clear: All animal fat, not just cholesterol, caused blood cholesterol to rise, which then increased the risk of heart attack.**

But much more work had to be done to confirm and refine this information. The Seven Country Study set the stage for a number of important subsequent studies, such as the one begun in 1948 in Framingham, Massachusetts. Investigators from the National Heart, Lung and Blood Institute and Boston University followed the citizens of this small town over a 20-year period, performing blood tests and examinations every two years. They reported the same direct link between cholesterol and coronary heart disease first noted in the Seven Country Study—the higher the blood cholesterol, the higher the heart attack rate. This important epidemiological study also clearly showed that high blood pressure and smoking markedly increased the risk of heart attack even further.

Well, why didn't scientists recommend a change in our national diet as we learned about these links? Some researchers still were not satisfied with the evidence, and in fact to this day, a few doctors still discount the connection between diet and heart disease. But added to the lingering doubts in the medical community, another factor slowed a switch to a leaner diet—America's ingrained eating habits, which stemmed from 75 years of misguided nutritional advice.

A Century of Misguided Dietary Advice
As noted by Dr. Marian Nestle, dietitian at New York University, the United States government first encouraged Americans to "eat light" as far back as the late 19th century when it published nutritional guidelines similar to the ones currently set by the National Cholesterol Education Program. *It is interesting to note that in 1910, complex carbohydrates constituted 36 percent of the average diet; today that number has dropped to 17 percent.* However, political shenanigans and the efforts of agricultural lobbyists may have helped squelch that first campaign, because instead of those early recommendations for a diet that was low in fat and protein and high in complex carbohydrates, parents and school children of the 20th century ended up with the famous—or infamous as it turned out—four basic food groups.

❦ **The trouble with the four basic food groups was that they were the foods containing large amounts of the cholesterol and saturated fat that cause coronary heart disease!**

In the early part of the century, of course, few Americans knew the risks they were taking as they innocently insisted on bacon and eggs for breakfast and rare beef whenever they could get it. Children all memorized the same nutrition chart in school and parents dutifully followed it. Everyone tried to drain seven glasses of whole milk every day and no one blinked at pouring cream into coffee, or gorging on chicken fried in lard at dinner. For fiber, the obligatory two green vegetables and a potato—drowned in butter—usually made an appearance on the dinner plate. Mothers have often equated food with love, and in the 1920s, 30s and 40s, magazine ads stressed that motherly love meant plying the family with rich desserts. Concerned moms made their pie crusts with "pure" shortening out of a can *after* they piled high the cheese on their loved one's sandwiches.

As time passed, having conquered the technology that freed everyone from the drudgery that once accompanied mealtime, Americans began flocking to the supermarket to enjoy the rewards of an advanced new lifestyle: frozen foods, processed foods. In time, franchised fast-food outlets crisscrossed America, putting cheap, high-fat, assembly-line foods at our fingertips. As a nation, we couldn't get enough of them. But we did not know that we were processing ourselves toward disaster, because those foods were laden with saturated fat.

Following a long period of prosperity and mind-numbing technological advances in food production that contributed to the problem, we found ourselves the unwitting victims of strongly held but misguided notions about nutrition. For the better part of a century, experts urged upon us a diet glorifying all that was good in our way of life. Our national cuisine reflected our rich bounty, and we served up heaping portions of it. In addition, glossy ads extolled the presumed pleasures of smoking, while television and labor-saving devices made us ever more sedentary.

❧ **By the 1950s and 60s, Americans had become an underexercised people with a voracious national appetite for rich, fatty foods, while hypertension, strokes, cancer and heart disease loomed frighteningly over the national health scene.**

Meanwhile, physicians and scientists at Stanford and other medical centers across the country continued their commitment to understanding the link between diet and heart disease. Work progressed on many fronts and in many medical centers. The American Heart Association provided invaluable support for these research efforts and translated the findings into practical suggestions for the lay person. In the early 1960s, their recommendations for a "Prudent Diet," which reduced saturated fat and cholesterol for all Americans, was instrumental in bringing the link between diet and heart disease to the attention of the American public. Dr. Paul Dudley White (1886–1973), who is frequently referred to as the father of American cardiology, was cofounder of the American Heart Association and lived what he preached—bicycling daily to work and back home on the streets of Boston. By 1975, the American Heart Association had called for adoption by everyone of its "Prudent Diet," restricted in saturated fats and cholesterol. These calls grew louder as the scientific evidence linking fats to heart disease grew.

Does Reducing Harmful Fats Help?

Once we had established that high saturated-fat diets and high blood cholesterol levels were linked to coronary heart disease, we had to ask some new questions. Would changing to a low saturated-fat diet lead to a lower cholesterol count and eventually less heart disease? Investigators at Stanford and other centers across the United States performed the first, major, well-controlled studies demonstrating that, for average healthy adults, lowering your blood cholesterol level can reduce your vulnerability to coronary heart disease. Published in 1984, the results of these studies also showed that a program of low saturated-fat diets plus cholesterol-lowering medicines resulted in fewer heart-linked deaths compared to a group of patients with very high cholesterol counts who only followed a low-fat diet. Since then, other similar studies have confirmed that you can prevent heart attacks in high-risk patients by lowering their cholesterol counts.

But what about Americans who do not have excessively high cholesterol levels? Will changing their diets result in a lower blood cholesterol and less risk for heart attack? This has been much more difficult to prove, since it requires convincing healthy people to make major lifestyle changes, including altering their dietary habits and other risk factors such as smoking that they would not ordinarily choose. Dr. John Farquhar took on the task. He founded The Stanford Heart Disease Prevention Program in 1972, which expanded to become the Stanford Center for Research in Disease Prevention in 1984. He and his colleagues designed and launched the famous Three Community Study, a community-wide educational program in northern California. Aimed at determining the effectiveness of media campaigns to lower heart disease rates, the landmark study proved that people would make changes in their lifestyles if they had the right information.

Based on the success of that work, Dr. Farquhar launched an expanded Five City Project that monitored the health of entire cities. He and his colleagues analyzed the following four parameters: baseline cholesterol levels in the blood, blood pressure, resting heart rate and smoking habits. They then launched a community-wide education program and measured the changes in those four factors over a 30 to 64 month period. Their results showed a decrease of 2 percent in cholesterol, 4 percent reduction in blood pressure, 3 percent lowering in heart rate and 13 percent reduction in smoking. Despite these relatively small changes, total risk of fatal heart attack had decreased as much as 15 percent, and risk of developing serious coronary heart disease had dropped by 16 percent during the study period.

❧ **From what we already know, clearly, people who make even small, positive changes in their lifestyles significantly reduce the risk of heart attack and heart disease.**

Those who make even more aggressive changes show even greater reduction in risk. Larger scale studies, such as LRC–CPPT (Lipid Research Clinics–Coronary Primary Prevention Trial) have now confirmed the equation: *A 1 percent reduction in blood cholesterol equals a 2 percent reduction in coronary heart disease risk.*

Next Question: What Is a Normal Cholesterol Count?

The standard used to determine "normal" levels for many blood tests is the range found in 95 percent of the healthy population. Previously, the "normal" cholesterol level in the United States was in the 220 to 240 range. Along with the call for less saturated fat and cholesterol in the diet, Americans were urged to maintain this supposedly healthy cholesterol level. What was yet to be considered was that this "normal" range was determined from people who ate a high saturated-fat diet. They were healthy in the sense that they did not yet have symptoms of heart disease, but that did not mean they had healthy arteries. It was found that when cholesterol levels were measured in people living in countries where the diet is lower in saturated fats, the "normal range" was 175 to 200 *and* there was less heart disease. Consequently, it became clear that we had to lower the normal range in the United States and give people a healthier cholesterol target.

We now know, of course, that the lower the cholesterol, the better. The Multiple Risk Factor Intervention Trial (MRFIT) screened over 300,000 healthy men in the United States in an effort to determine whether making positive changes in risk factors (such as quitting smoking, lowering high blood pressure, and reducing fat and cholesterol in the diet) could lessen heart disease rates. MRFIT gave us important information, but it was not a perfect study. Some results were inconclusive partly because of the short length of the studies and the fact that the "control" group also reduced their risk factors for heart disease. The overall group, however, did show the same blood cholesterol–heart disease link as previous studies.

❧ **Using the results they did obtain, we see that when healthy men with blood cholesterol in the range of 221 to 244 reduce their cholesterol levels by 17 percent, they will show a 40 percent decrease in coronary heart deaths!**

This finding cinched the need to lower our previous "normal" levels to under 200.

The Result of All This Research

We know now that there is no single cause of heart disease. The reasons people suffer heart attacks range from genetic susceptibility—it runs in the family—to harmful habits. The cumulative effect of several of these genetic and environmental causes undermines the health of the heart and arteries. But the overwhelming contributor to heart disease is a diet high in saturated fat and cholesterol. An estimated 60 million Americans have cholesterol levels high enough to potentially jeopardize their hearts, and by the early 80s it had become clear to the medical community that people had to make *further* changes in their diets to prevent heart disease. Consequently, all of this research culminated in a call for a national campaign against heart disease. As a result of all of this work, the federal government revamped the national nutritional guidelines.

In 1986 the government sponsored a nationwide program to educate the public about heart disease prevention and urged that adults maintain a cholesterol level under 200. The National Cholesterol Education Program was formed and the media embraced "The Age of Cholesterol." Medical science had presented the evidence for dietary change, and Americans had been responding. Statistics released in early 1992 showed that the rates of heart disease had dropped 2.5 percent a year for the past 20 years. In Finland, which the Seven Country Study had shown to have the highest rate of heart disease, public information campaigns had also successfully lowered heart disease, proving, as Dr. Farquhar had in his first community-wide studies, that people do have control over the health of their hearts and will take action when they know what to do.

- Research has shown the link between high cholesterol levels and heart disease.
- Research has demonstrated that lowering cholesterol levels lowers your risk of heart disease.
- Research has shown the link between diet and heart disease.
- Eating foods low in saturated fat and cholesterol can lower your risk of heart disease.

The names of all of these researchers, their studies and statistics may blur in your mind. What is important to remember is that all of this research, in study after study, implicated cholesterol and in particular saturated fat in the development of heart disease, giving the question, "What's for dinner?" a new urgency. We are going to suggest some healthy alternatives for dinner, as well as all the other meals and snacks you eat, and we are going to help you understand all the facts about diet and heart health. First, however, take the folllowing quiz to see how often some popular high fat foods show up in your diet. You will have a new appreciation for the food choices you make for yourself and your family as you read on and discover the links between fat, food, cholesterol and your heart.

CHECK YOURSELF #1: HOW OFTEN DO YOU...?

	Seldom/Never	Sometimes	Frequently
1. Eat and serve pastries and baked goods made with butter or lard, instead of whole grain, low-fat items	3	2	1
2. Bake with butter or lard, instead of margarine and olive or canola oil	3	2	1
3. Season your vegetables with butter or bacon, instead of olive or canola oil, citrus juices or herbs	3	2	1
4. Buy packaged foods without looking at labels to avoid tropical oils, such as coconut, palm kernel or hydrogenated oils	3	2	1
5. Eat and serve gravy made from fatty pan drippings, instead of just serving meat "au jus"	3	2	1
6. Eat and serve deep-fried french fries and batter-fried vegetables instead of oven-roasted	3	2	1
7. Cook with pork fat or bacon drippings, instead of olive or canola oil	3	2	1
8. Eat and serve regular frozen entrées made with butter or gravy, instead of "diet" items	3	2	1
9. Snack on high-fat crackers, instead of fruit or vegetables	3	2	1
10. Add handfuls of grated cheese to a recipe, and nibble on what's left while you cook	3	2	1

Total

Circle the response that most nearly describes your habits and total your score.

25–30 = Excellent, try for a perfect 30.

15–24 = You have some problem areas. Set a goal to start cooking exclusively with olive oil or canola oil and strip whole-milk dairy products from your refrigerator.

10–14 = Whoops. Check The Fat Tracker's Shopping Lists before you shop and don't buy anything that isn't listed in the "Choose" column.

CHAPTER 3

The Link Between Cholesterol, Fat and Heart Disease

THERE IS CHOLESTEROL IN THE BODY, *cholesterol in foods, good cholesterol, bad cholesterol, high cholesterol, low cholesterol. No wonder people get confused. However, keep reading and you will discover the issue really isn't that hard to understand.*

What Is Cholesterol and Where Does It Come From?

Cholesterol is, in fact, one of the many miracles of human chemistry. The body manufactures many types of fats, referred to in scientific language as "lipids"; cholesterol, a waxy-looking substance, is one of them. Without it our bodies could not manufacture essential hormones, build cell walls and perform other vital tasks. Because it is a fat, cholesterol floats, the same way oil floats on water, and it cannot circulate in the bloodstream without help. Certain substances composed of fats and proteins called "lipoproteins" form a wrapping around the cholesterol molecule, providing ballast that allows it to travel easily.

Many forms of lipoproteins exist and perform various important functions; only two of them concern us here. The first is high-density lipoprotein (HDL), often called "good cholesterol" because it protects you from atherosclerosis. The second is low-density lipoprotein (LDL), commonly referred to as "bad cholesterol" because it is the cholesterol that is actually deposited in the artery wall. We will explain the significance of these cholesterol carriers shortly, but first it is important to understand cholesterol itself and learn how this crucial substance is formed.

THE BODY MAKES CHOLESTEROL Among its many important functions, your liver works as an efficient, cholesterol-making machine, constantly manufacturing all the cholesterol you will ever need from the food you eat.

CERTAIN FOODS SUPPLY CHOLESTEROL Because it is produced by the liver, cholesterol resides in *every* cell of *every* animal, whether it is mammal, fish or fowl. Therefore, every time you eat food derived from animal products—meat, fish, poultry, dairy products and eggs—you eat cholesterol, adding to your own already sufficient stores.

PLANT FOODS DO NOT PRODUCE CHOLESTEROL This distinction becomes important when you make food choices, because obviously you want to choose food with as little cholesterol as possible. Plants do produce their own substances, called "phytosterols," which perform the same vital functions in plant cells that cholesterol does in animals. These phytosterols are of great benefit to humans, however, because when we eat plant food, these phytosterols prevent the absorption of cholesterol.

Which Foods Contain Cholesterol?

Though some animal products have negligible saturated fat (for example fish and shellfish), *all animal products contain significant levels of cholesterol*. All meats, fish, poultry, eggs and dairy products such as milk, cream, cheese and butter give us a direct hit of cholesterol, though the amounts vary.

As you can see on the chart below, Foods High in Cholesterol, typical servings of eggs and organ meats such as liver, sweetbreads and kidneys, top the list of cholesterol-laden foods, with chicken livers as the worst offenders. Moving down the line, we find beef, pork products (such as bacon, sausages and cured meats), cream, butter, whole milk, cheeses and foods made with those ingredients burdening our diet with the most cholesterol.

FOODS HIGH IN CHOLESTEROL

	Serving	Mg Cholesterol
Chicken livers	3.5 ounces	631
Quiche Lorraine	⅛ of 8-inch pie	235
Custard, baked	1 cup	246
Egg yolk	1	213
Shrimp	3.5 ounces	152
Béarnaise or hollandaise sauce	1 cup	189
Yellow layer or sponge cake	1 slice	37
Soft-serve ice cream	1 cup	156
Chorizo, beef or pork links	3 links	150
Hamburger (Big Mac)	4 ounces	107
Ham and cheese sandwich (Hardees) with mayonnaise	4 ounces	65
Pound cake	1 slice	62
Chocolate cake with chocolate icing	1 slice	33

❦ **Stop reading for a moment. How often have you eaten these foods in the last week? Once? Twice? Daily?**

Of all the animal foods, fish, poultry, and lean meats have the lowest cholesterol counts. Shellfish, such as shrimp, crab and lobster contain much more cholesterol than even beef. However, even with their high cholesterol content, shellfish are so low in saturated fat that they don't raise blood cholesterol levels very much.

Stop reading for a moment. How often have you chosen fish or turkey over red meat in the last week? Once? Twice? Daily?

❦ **Do Foods Have Good and Bad Cholesterol?**

When we refer to "good" and "bad" cholesterol, we actually mean the types of cholesterol carriers that transport cholesterol molecules through the bloodstream. There is no such "good vs. bad" distinction in cholesterol found in food. None of it benefits us. Because our body manufactures sufficient cholesterol for our needs, no dietary cholesterol is necessary for health.

Saturated Fat Increases Cholesterol Production

In addition to the cholesterol the body naturally produces and the cholesterol you ingest in food, saturated fat interferes with certain receptors in the body and depresses their ability to recognize the LDL (think "lethal" cholesterol) that is circulating in the bloodstream. This sends to the liver a confusing message that says in effect: "We don't have enough cholesterol. Make more!"

The presence of saturated fat in your body causes your liver to make more cholesterol than you need.

❦ Even if you eat zero cholesterol, you can still damage your arteries by eating too much saturated fat, which causes your liver to pump out even more cholesterol. Thus, some cholesterol-free foods are still harmful due to their high amounts of saturated fat. Many processed foods in our supermarkets contain large amounts of saturated fat in the form of dried coconut and tropical oils.

	Serving	Grams Saturated Fat
Sour cream	2 tablespoons	3.2
Whole milk ricotta	½ cup	10.3
Half-and-half	1 tablespoon	1.1
Whipping cream, heavy	1 cup	56.0
Whipping cream, light	1 cup	46.4
Eggnog, nonalcoholic	1 cup	11.3
Tropical oils, i.e., coconut oil	1 tablespoon	11.8
Butter	1 tablespoon	7.6
Lard	1 cup	80.0
Lard	1 tablespoon	5.0
Blue cheese	1 ounce	5.3
Shredded Cheddar cheese	1 cup	24.0
Shredded Cheddar cheese	1 tablespoon	1.5
Hard cheese	1 ounce	6.0
Bacon, raw	3.5 ounces	19.8
Prime rib of beef, untrimmed	7 ounces	26.4
Béarnaise or hollandaise sauce	¼ cup	10.5
White sauce	1 cup	10.0
Cheese soup, condensed	1 cup	13.3
Cream of celery soup, condensed	1 cup	3.4
Quiche Lorraine	⅛ of 8-inch pie	23.0
Granola	1 cup	9.9
Cashew nuts	1 ounce	2.6
Dried coconut	1 ounce	16.3
Macadamia nuts	1 ounce	3.1
Milk chocolate–covered peanuts	10 pieces or 1.4 ounces	5.8
Chocolate candy bar, average	1 bar, 1.55 ounce	8.1
Semisweet chocolate chips	½ cup	14.9
Chocolate mousse	1 cup	37.2
Coconut cream pie	⅛ of 9-inch pie	11.1
Ice cream, 16% butterfat	1 cup	14.8
Ice cream, soft-serve from a machine, not frozen yogurt	1 cup	12.8

	Serving	Grams Saturated Fat
Jack in the Box		
Jumbo Jack with cheese	1	14.0
Jumbo Jack without cheese	1	11.0
Onion rings	1 bag	11.0
Taco Bell		
Taco salad	1	19.0
Tostada	1	4.0
Nachos Bell Grande	1	12.0
Burger King		
Bacon double cheeseburger	1	16.0
Double cheese burger	1	13.0
Croissant egg cheese	1	7.0
Hash Browns	1 serving	3.0
McDonald's		
DLT hamburger	1	11.5
McChicken burger	1	5.4
Quarter pounder	1	8.1
French fries	1 bag (large)	9.1
Pancakes with butter syrup	1 serving	3.7
Hamburger	1	3.6
Apple Snack pie	1 pie	4.8
Chef's salad, no dressing	1	5.9
Wendy's		
Big Classic	1	6.0
Pizza Hut		
Pepperoni pizza	2 slices	12.5
Cheese pizza	⅛ of 15-inch pie	6.8
Kentucky Fried Chicken		
Chicken sandwich	1	6.0
Crispy chicken	1 wing	4.4
Crispy chicken	1 thigh	7.7
Tartar sauce	1 packet	2.0
Trail mix with coconut	1 ounce	2.4
Trail mix without coconut	1 ounce	1.6
Granola bar, chocolate	1	4.3
Chocolate, vanilla, strawberry shake	10 ounces	6.0
Chile con carne	1 cup	8.0
Brownie	1	2.0
Devil's food cake with icing	1 slice	7.7
Banana chips	1 ounce	8.2
Whipped cream, pressurized	1 cup	12.8
Chop suey	1 cup	8.5
Pound cake	1 slice	2.3
Homemade pecan pie	1 slice	3.3

❧ How many times have you eaten any of these foods in the last week? How many times have you fed your children these foods in the last week? Remember, 25 grams total for the day can add up fast with these types of foods.

A *small* percentage, about 1 to 2 percent of the population, produces abnormally large amounts of cholesterol, regardless of how hard they try to eliminate fatty foods from their diets. However, some people use this hereditary factor as an argument to say, "It doesn't matter what I eat. It's all in the genes." Not true. Most of us have higher than healthy cholesterol levels simply because we eat too much saturated fat and cholesterol-laden food, we tend to be overweight and we don't get enough exercise!

Foods containing saturated fat contribute the largest source of *excess* cholesterol in your bloodstream. Since America's favorite foods are so high in saturated fat, comprising approximately 30 to 40 percent of all the calories the typical adult eats, you can easily understand why the average American has too much cholesterol circulating through the bloodstream. The Stanford 25 Gram Plan is aimed at reducing the saturated fat in your diet to lower your cholesterol.

If Cholesterol Is the Problem, Why Do We Target Saturated Fat?
From whatever dietary angle you choose to view the problem of heart disease — the cause or the cure — you have to contend with saturated fat. The campaign to prevent heart disease has centered on the link to cholesterol. Consequently, because people now vaguely understand that cholesterol somehow travels the route from their refrigerator to their arteries to cause heart disease and heart attacks, a dark cloud hangs over certain aisles in the supermarket. But most people don't realize that saturated fat is actually the most lethal element in your diet because it makes the liver manufacture a harmful type of cholesterol, LDL cholesterol, which over time damages the lining of your arteries and sets the stage for heart disease.

Since the media has focused on cholesterol as the key to a healthy heart, people look for reassurance that the products and foods they buy are free of, or at least low in, cholesterol. Consumers feel confident that they are taking adequate precautions to care for their hearts when they choose these items. But the focus is on the wrong fat. Saturated fat is even more harmful than cholesterol, and as we will show, simply focusing on reducing dietary cholesterol is a half-safe strategy that gives you a false sense of security.

Cholesterol and Saturated Fat Travel in the Same Foods
Because cholesterol travels with saturated fat in almost all of the same foods, mainly animal protein and whole-milk dairy products, these harmful fats often, *but not always,* come as a package deal. Buy an 8-ounce steak with up to 50 grams of saturated fat and you can also get 187 milligrams of cholesterol. However, if you are only focusing on cholesterol, the exception to the rule will allow too much

saturated fat to slip into your food and eventually show up in your bloodstream as harmful cholesterol. While all foods containing cholesterol also have saturated fat, *a food can be entirely free of cholesterol and still have lots of harmful saturated fat,* such as chips fried in lard or cereals and crackers containing hydrogenated and tropical oils. Hydrogenated oils contain harmful transfatty acids which also have been implicated in heart disease. The exceptions to this pairing system are organ meats and egg yolks. Because of their very high concentration of cholesterol compared to saturated fat, these foods require special limitations, which we will describe in the nutrition section. Just because a label says, "no cholesterol," doesn't necessarily mean it's good for you!

❧ **Stop reading for a moment. How often have you bought a product that says "no cholesterol," assuming, therefore, that it was heart healthy, but didn't check the label for saturated fat?**

So it's not that we want you to take the focus off cholesterol; you must restrict dietary cholesterol to less than 300 milligrams each day. *But because cholesterol travels with saturated fat, limiting foods high in saturated fat will automatically go a long way toward reducing your intake of cholesterol, as well.* Dangerous saturated fat serves absolutely no nutritional purpose that we know of and only causes damage to our bodies. Saturated fat is linked to a growing list of other serious illnesses, such as colon and breast cancer.

WHAT ARE WE SAYING?

- Cholesterol and saturated fat in foods can lead to the development of plaque and heart disease.
- Saturated fat causes the body to make excess LDL cholesterol.
- Saturated fat and cholesterol travel together in the same foods.
- When you limit foods high in saturated fat, you limit cholesterol as well, with the exception of eggs, shellfish and organ meats.
- We have designed The Stanford 25 Gram Plan specifically to help you keep both the saturated fat and cholesterol in your food to a healthy minimum so your body won't produce excessive cholesterol.
- By following this plan, you will also keep your total fat intake to the maximum of 75 grams daily.

You will learn how to become adept at finding both the obvious and hidden sources of cholesterol and saturated fat in food products when we introduce you to Fat Tracking in Part Three. How often does cholesterol and saturated fat sneak into your food? Take the quiz on the next page to test your "Cholesterol Quotient." Then we will take a look at the effect of all this cholesterol on your body.

CHECK YOUR CQ
Before you read more about cholesterol and your heart, take this little quiz to test your "cholesterol quotient."

1.	You must eat good cholesterol to protect your heart.	T	F
2.	To help lower your cholesterol level, eat fiber.	T	F
3.	Olive oil has less cholesterol than safflower oil.	T	F
4.	Fish is good for your heart because it has no cholesterol.	T	F
5.	The antioxidant, beta-carotene, which may help prevent heart attacks, is found only in fish.	T	F
6.	Too much sugar raises your cholesterol levels.	T	F
7.	Cutting out salt will lower your risk of a heart attack.	T	F
8.	You must never eat saturated fat.	T	F
9.	Foods with cholesterol cause heart attacks.	T	F
10.	Aspirin can lower your cholesterol levels.	T	F

Answers:
1. *False.* There is no such thing as good cholesterol in food. "Good" cholesterol, the kind that can protect your arteries from developing plaque, is produced by the body.
2. *Partly true.* To help lower cholesterol levels, eat water-soluble fiber, such as that found in beans and oat bran. Wheat fiber, which is not water soluble, may protect your colon from cancer and other diseases, but it has no effect on your cholesterol level.
3. *False.* They are both cholesterol free. No product in the vegetable kingdom contains cholesterol.
4. *False.* It contains approximately the same amount of cholesterol as meat. Fish is good for your heart because it contains very little saturated fat.
5. *False.* Antioxidants such as beta-carotene and vitamin E are found in some animal foods, but the major source is plant food, such as green and yellow vegetables and fruits. See the chart, Foods High in Antioxidants, on page 150–51.
6. *False.* Sugar does not affect cholesterol levels. It may, however, raise triglycerides, another blood fat.
7. *False.* Salt does not cause heart attacks directly, but reducing salt is important to people with high blood pressure, which is a risk factor for heart trouble.
8. *False.* Provided you don't have heart disease, small amounts of saturated fat in an otherwise low-fat diet will not harm you. In fact, it is almost impossible to eat meals without some saturated fat.
9. *Half true.* Both saturated fat and cholesterol in foods can lead to heart attacks.
10. *False.* Aspirin can prevent blood clots that cause heart attacks, but it does not affect your cholesterol levels.

CHAPTER 4

What Cholesterol Does to Your Body

REMEMBER, AS WE DESCRIBED IN THE PREVIOUS CHAPTER, *that the body can make all the cholesterol it needs. The saturated fat in cheeseburgers, toast slathered with butter, or hot fudge sundaes only helps to boost cholesterol production. Consequently, even though the body depends on cholesterol, it can end up with too much of a good thing. The human body is not capable of ridding itself of the excess cholesterol, so once it has used all the cholesterol it needs for maintaining itself, a storage problem arises. At first, excess cholesterol simply accumulates in the bloodstream. But in time, it begins to cause major trouble. As the saying goes, it hits you where you live—your heart.*

The Heart Depends on Healthy Arteries

Picture for a moment, the tubular network of arteries, veins and capillaries fanning out from the heart. The heart is a hardworking pump, sending fuel in the form of nourishing blood coursing through these vessels to the rest of the body. In addition, the heart needs its own supply of fuel because the heart is a muscle and, like any other muscle, it becomes damaged without a sufficient food supply. The heart receives its nourishment in the form of oxygen and nutrient-rich blood from a separate system called the coronary arteries. An organ with a voracious appetite, the heart must pump approximately 5 quarts of blood every minute just to provide the body with enough nourishment to perform its crucial work while we sleep! During strenuous exercise, the body requires as much as 20 quarts of blood flowing through its arteries each minute. To imagine that volume, that soaring need—which we take for granted as we run for a bus, play a game of tennis or chase after a child about to run into the path of oncoming traffic—is to appreciate the sheer power of the heart. Yet, it is totally dependent upon the health of the pencil-thin coronary arteries to keep it pumping. As Dr. William Haskell (of Stanford's Center for Research in Disease Prevention) points out, our lifeline is an opening one-quarter inch wide!

As you can see from the diagram above, it doesn't take much of an obstruction to block the path of blood flow through an artery. When you consider that the saturated fat in your food encourages the liver to produce a substance that can eventually close off that tiny opening, you realize the urgency on the part of the medical community to sound a health alert—to somehow convince Americans to make the relatively minor changes in their diet and overall improvements in their lifestyle that will help keep their arteries free of plaque.

How LDL and HDL Affect the Heart

When we study animals fed a high-cholesterol and high saturated-fat diet, we find that the levels of cholesterol in the bloodstream jump. We also know that as their cholesterol levels rise, deposits composed of cholesterol and other harmful substances invade the walls of the animals' arteries, building up over time into larger and larger clumps called plaque, which eventually block off the blood supply to the heart. This same process occurs in humans. The relative speed with which these cholesterol deposits form appears to be closely related to the blood cholesterol level and the amount of HDL and LDL cholesterol of each individual.

Earlier we said that cholesterol is wrapped in HDL and LDL particles that allow it to be transported through the body. When too much LDL-wrapped cholesterol—the so called "bad cholesterol"—accumulates in the bloodstream, the LDL dumps the cholesterol into the artery wall to form plaque. We mentioned earlier that LDL stands for low density lipoprotein, but it could just as easily mean *lethal* density lipoprotein, because LDL, as we currently understand it, is the most harmful type of cholesterol. Scientific research has found many variations or subforms of LDL cholesterol; *all* of them seem to be harmful. The most harmful may be the *oxidized* form of LDL, which simply means that oxygen bonds with the LDL, changing its behavior or properties, which makes it easier to establish a site for the development of plaque. This is important since foods containing *anti*-oxidants—substances such as beta-carotene and vitamins C and E contained in yellow and green leafy vegetables—may provide additional protective effects.

❧ **The saturated fat in the food you eat increases the production of harmful LDL.**

As these plaque deposits form in the walls of the arteries, with a patch here and a patch there, an uneven but ever-thickening mass builds up, like barnacles on the bottom of a boat. They cling there as a more or less permanent fixture. Sometimes graphically referred to as hardening of the arteries, doctors know this condition as atherosclerosis or coronary artery disease. By whatever name you call it, this means trouble. As one or more deposits grow in size, they can block off the blood flowing through the artery, just as debris will clog your plumbing and prevent water from flowing to or from your sink.

On the other hand, HDL—"good" cholesterol—actually *prevents* plaque from building up along the walls of the arteries. HDL carries the plaque-causing substances away from the artery lining to the liver, which can then eliminate them from the body. No plaque buildup—no heart disease. Think of high density lipoprotein, as *healthy* density lipoprotein.

❧ **"L" is for lethal: Keep lethal LDL low**
"H" is for healthy: Keep healthy HDL high

Over a period of years, if healthy habits do not interrupt or stop the process, layer upon layer of plaque accumulates until often, if you could peer inside the artery and down along its corridors to the heart, you wouldn't even see the wall of the artery any more, all you would see is plaque. The artery that was once healthy, flexible and wide enough to carry blood coursing vigorously to and from the heart in a life-sustaining flow, has become a narrow obstacle course, clogged with plaque, choking off the blood supply to the heart, starving it of nourishment.

Plaque and the Early Symptoms of Heart Disease

Angina, often the first symptom of heart disease a patient experiences, is chest pain following some form of exertion or psychological stress, indicating that a blockage in the artery is impeding blood flow to the heart. Millions of Americans suffer from angina, which only occurs when the coronary arteries are already severely diseased and obstructed by as much as 70 percent of normal. Sometimes this atherosclerotic deposit ruptures and the body responds as it does with any other injury. It causes a blood clot to form—in this instance, inside the artery. The clot can grow so large that it completely blocks the artery.

When the artery becomes totally obstructed either with plaque or a clot, the blood can't get to the heart, the heart does not receive the oxygen and nutrients it needs, and all or part of the muscle dies; the beat falters or it may stop altogether. We call this catastrophe a heart attack. If only a part of the heart muscle is affected and if the other arteries can continue to keep some blood flowing to the rest of the heart, or if treatment is administered immediately, the patient survives. Death occurs in almost 50 percent of cases—over 500,000 Americans die of heart attacks each year. *Approximately 30 percent of all first heart attacks are fatal.*

We know that some portions of an artery are more likely to attract these plaque deposits than others. Many researchers suspect that a microscopic injury of some kind causes tiny scars or inflammation to form in the wall of the artery, preparing a site that somehow invites cholesterol to begin the formation of atherosclerotic plaque.

What can cause the injury? We are not sure yet, but it is likely that smoking can cause damage at this cellular level or even high blood pressure pounding against a fragile artery wall. Once the artery lining is injured, from whatever cause, the cells in the wall try to repair the damage, in effect creating a scar in the same way one will form to protect a cut finger or scraped knee. This scarring, called proliferation, seems to attract LDL cholesterol deposits, which then attach to that spot. Most, if not all of us, have some degree of this type of artery damage.

Lengthwise section of a healthy artery showing an unimpeded flow of blood.

Lengthwise section of an artery with an early plaque deposit

Lengthwise section of an artery with a plaque deposit slowing down the flow of blood

Lengthwise section of an artery with a plaque deposit completely blocking the flow of blood

❧ Even if your arteries have experienced the type of injury that sets the stage for coronary artery disease, we believe that you can prevent plaque from forming and eventually clogging your arteries by boosting your HDL levels and lowering your LDL levels.

The Stanford Life Plan for a Healthy Heart is designed to promote the winning combination of the lowest possible LDL levels and the highest possible HDL levels. We will detail all the measures that promote optimum cholesterol levels in the following chapters on breaking the links to heart disease.

This description simplifies a very complicated process that we only partially understand. The development of plaque involves many types of cells, such as platelets, as well as various complex processes in the body. The final results, however, which we do understand with crystal clarity, are the consequences of atherosclerosis—strokes if the blockage occurs in an artery feeding the brain, heart attack or angina if it occurs in a coronary artery feeding the heart muscle.

Triglycerides and Heart Disease

Triglycerides, another blood fat, have been identified as the transporter that moves fat in the bloodstream from one location to another, for instance, to your liver when it needs it, to your muscles when you are exercising or to your waistline when you are not. High triglyceride levels are linked to coronary artery disease, though the connection is still not well understood. We do know that a study of 4,081 people in the Helsinki Heart Study found that not only did high LDL cholesterol predict heart problems, but also that when a high LDL and high triglycerides (levels over 200) were found together, the person's risk for subsequent heart attacks increased.

From what we know now, high triglycerides alone are not as strongly linked to heart disease as are the other risk factors. However, elevated triglyceride levels are usually seen with a low HDL, which *is* linked to increased risk for a heart attack. Weight loss and exercise are the most important approach to improving these elements of a worrisome cholesterol profile. It also appears that refined sugar causes triglycerides to rise, one of the reasons controlling excessive sugar is important to a heart-healthy diet.

The Process Starts at an Early Age

For decades after scientists began to understand the causes of heart disease, they assumed coronary artery disease only affected older people because the young almost never suffer from heart attacks or strokes. However, when researchers observed autopsies performed on presumably healthy children and adolescents who died accidentally, they found yellow streaks of cholesterol in their arteries. Researchers examining the bodies of young American soldiers killed in battle discovered that 70 percent of them had signs of plaque deposits in their arteries, and 15 percent of these young men had severe blockage in at least one coronary artery.

We know these deposits are not "normal" in the young because autopsies performed on Korean soldiers who eat a low-fat diet show no such deposits. With the important discovery that cholesterol deposits can, and too often do, begin developing silently at an early age, we see that prevention must start early before the disease gets a foothold, in the form of adopting a heart-healthy lifestyle for the whole family as we describe in The Stanford 25 Gram Plan.

Are There Warning Signs of a Heart Attack?

At first, the buildup of cholesterol plaque is ever so slight. No physical symptoms warn you that dangerous levels of cholesterol have begun to accumulate in your blood. However, the level of cholesterol circulating in your bloodstream will show up on a blood test. But, unless you have your blood cholesterol levels checked regularly, years and years can go by while you feel quite healthy. You can lead a very active life and still not know that you have plaque-choked arteries until the condition is quite advanced.

❦ **If you have not already done so, have your cholesterol checked now.**

Sometimes, though, the heart signals its distress, and you eventually experience some unexplained shortness of breath or perhaps angina, a pressure-like pain under your heart which can also travel down the inside of your left arm. At first these symptoms may occur only with exercise or exertion, but in advanced stages they may appear more frequently. If you experience these symptoms, count yourself lucky and seek medical attention immediately. You have been given a warning, and if you heed it, it may save your life.

❦ **If you ever experience a pressure or squeezing pain under your breastbone that goes into your neck or jaw or down the inside of your arm, you should seek medical attention immediately.**

All too often, though, you notice nothing out of the ordinary until the day disaster strikes, when one of two things can happen.

- You will suffer a sudden, fatal heart attack. (This book is dedicated to help avert this tragedy.)
- If you are lucky to receive immediate medical attention to reopen the blocked artery, you may live, but your heart may remain seriously and irreversibly damaged.

The Remedies for Cholesterol-Choked Arteries

When you seek medical help for your symptoms, your doctor will perform tests that will show if plaque has severely narrowed your arteries. Testing might include a stress test where the electrocardiogram is monitored during exercise for signs of insufficient blood flow through the coronary artery as the heart works harder and demands more blood. More complex scanning tests using radioisotopes can also be useful. These tests can track the blood flow through your coronary arteries to see if they are supplying sufficient quantities of blood to the heart muscle.

If a severe blockage is suspected, your doctor may order a coronary angiogram (a movie X-ray of the inside of the coronary arteries) to help analyze the location and severity of the obstruction. The treatment plan may include:

- Medicines to improve the blood flow to the heart, such as calcium blockers, and a daily aspirin to prevent blood clots from forming inside the arteries.
- A diet *extremely low* in cholesterol and saturated fats to help control further production of plaque. If you have received this recommendation to change your diet, use our Fat Tracker's Guide (pages 169–256) to help you choose foods that will eliminate these harmful fats from your meals and snacks.
- If the blockage is severe, coronary angioplasty may be performed. Known as balloon treatment, this is a procedure in which a very small balloon is inserted through a catheter or tube into the coronary artery and inflated. The balloon compresses or flattens the plaque deposits against the artery wall and when it is removed, adequate blood flow is usually restored. Heart surgery may be necessary in some cases, such as coronary artery bypass which uses a graft from a leg vein or a small artery behind the breastbone to detour the blood flow around the blocked artery. In rare cases an endarterectomy is performed, in which the cholesterol is pulled out of the artery. However, this is not as successful as other measures.

Unfortunately, most of these dramatic treatments are only temporary, as the buildup of plaque continues unless the patient breaks the links to heart disease.

Drugs That Lower Your Cholesterol

By improving health habits and diet, notably by eating limited amounts of saturated fat, 99 percent of Americans can remain healthy and reduce their risk of heart disease without cholesterol-lowering medicines. As the links between elevated cholesterol and coronary heart disease have become more firmly established, however, it is clear that certain people are at very high risk. For them, eating less fat, quitting smoking, and so forth, won't do the job alone. People in these high risk groups need to be considered for drug therapy: those with a genetic tendency to produce too much cholesterol, those with diagnosed coronary heart disease, and those who have a high LDL cholesterol despite decreasing the saturated fat in their diet.

Drugs and the Person Without Known Heart Disease

It is estimated that about 1 percent of Americans have a genetic defect that causes their liver to produce too much cholesterol (hypercholesterolemia), even when they follow the recommendations of The Stanford Life Plan for a Healthy Heart. The NCEP has developed guidelines for drug treatment in these cases. Called "primary prevention," the goal is to do everything possible to avoid the *first* cardiovascular event in these high-risk persons, including reducing all risk factors such as smoking, lack of exercise and a high-fat diet, as well as adding cholesterol-lowering drugs.

We urge everyone to use The Stanford Life Plan for a Healthy Heart as the primary line of defense against coronary heart disease, but if your LDL cholesterol has remained high despite your best efforts to lower it, your physician may recommend the addition of certain drugs. Large clinical research studies have shown they can make a difference and lower the risk for a heart attack. However, concern about the possible cumulative side effects of these medicines taken over many years has raised some controversy about when physicians should give these drugs to otherwise healthy individuals. Your doctor will explain any potential side effects.

Drugs and the Coronary Heart Disease Patient

If you have had a diagnosis of coronary heart disease established by your physician because of symptoms such as angina, that is generally a clear signal that the coronary arteries are already badly clogged with cholesterol. You will have to work doubly hard to avoid another heart attack or bypass surgery, if you have already had one. You not only have to attack any coronary disease risk factors, such as smoking, lack of exercise and so forth, but also you must achieve the lowest possible blood cholesterol levels in an attempt to prevent future layering of cholesterol in the already clogged arteries. Clinical studies at Stanford and elsewhere have shown that these efforts do pay off and can stabilize the disease process and can even dissolve some of the deposited cholesterol. *However, to achieve this ideal result, blood cholesterol levels need to be lowered to the 160 milligram range.* To help you reach this goal, your physician may add drugs to the other recommendations in the Stanford Life Plan for a Healthy Heart. This concept is called "secondary prevention"—in other words, the coronary problem has become obvious and is being treated, but the patient and the physician work hard to avoid any new or recurring problem.

High Cholesterol Is Not the Only Risk Factor

We have just described the chain of events that begins with a microscopic injury in the wall of the artery that allows the development of cholesterol plaque, which can then cause heart disease and heart attacks. We have shown how blood clots further complicate this scenario. Clearly, high blood cholesterol levels are the key to plaque development. But there are other factors that play a role, as well. Clinical researchers and epidemiologists don't all agree, but the following appear to be the major indicators of and links to heart disease.

The Links to Heart Disease

- High total blood cholesterol levels
- High LDL levels
- Low HDL levels
- High total/HDL cholesterol ratio
- High blood pressure
- Smoking
- Family history of heart disease
- Lack of exercise
- Obesity (more than 30 percent over ideal weight)
- Loss of estrogen in postmenopausal women
- Diabetes mellitus
- Oral contraceptives
- Excessive stress

Physicians call the links to heart disease risk factors. Are we saying that if you have one of these risk factors or even two or three, that you will definitely have a heart attack? Certainly not everyone who eats saturated fat or resists daily exercise will suffer a heart attack. Estimating risk is not that simple; most people have other factors working in their favor that offset some of their risks. Computing an individual's actual risk of heart disease is a task for a sophisticated statistical computer program, but if you take the Stanford Risk-Assessment Test on page 50 you will have a reliable indication of where you stand.

However, if you think of heart health as a bridge to a desirable quality of life and well-being, then your risk factors whittle away at that bridge. As you accumulate risk factors in your health profile, unless you take measures to reduce their effect, that bridge may narrow until you find yourself walking a tightrope. Many factors are interconnected, and the idea is not so much to reduce the potency of one element of risk, but to maintain heart-smart habits that continually defuse all risk throughout your life. The best course of action is to keep saturated-fat foods to a minimum by following The Stanford 25 Gram Plan and Fat Tracker's Guide.

- Lethal LDL cholesterol causes plaque to form that can cause heart disease and heart attacks.
- Healthy HDL cholesterol reduces plaque and keeps the arteries healthy, protecting the heart from coronary artery disease.
- Most people have some signs of cholesterol plaque and no one can take a healthy heart for granted.
- There is no magic bullet: We must live and eat responsibly to prevent heart disease.
- We will show you all the ways to keep your HDL high and your LDL low.

If you have not already done so, now is the time to have your cholesterol levels checked. On the following pages you will learn what your results mean. You will also find a chart that will help you compare them to the ideal levels, giving you healthier targets to aim for if you need them.

Your Cholesterol Blood Test

A cholesterol blood test is a barometer of your heart health and will give you the one piece of crucial information upon which you can base your future heart-smart decisions. If you have not had a recent blood (serum) cholesterol test to determine all of your cholesterol levels, we suggest that you launch your heart-healthy lifestyle by obtaining one from your doctor's office or a reliable testing center.

A cholesterol test involves having a small amount of blood drawn from your arm, which is then analyzed in a laboratory. Or, ask if a newer finger-stick test is available in your area; it can get a reading with a drop of blood from your fingertip. The finger-stick method may not be as reliable, so if the result is elevated, it is best to have the test repeated by a more complicated method which can be done by most laboratories. It is also possible to purchase a kit at your pharmacy that will allow you to test your total cholesterol at home. Approved by the FDA, this home method has been shown to have the same accuracy as laboratory tests. One limitation of the over-the-counter home test is that it shows only the total cholesterol level, which is only a small piece of your cholesterol picture.

Whichever medically supervised test you have, make sure that a Total Lipid Panel is done. This measures your total, HDL (high-density lipoprotein) and LDL (low-density lipoprotein) levels, in addition to the total/HDL–cholesterol ratio. Without a Total Lipid Panel you will have an incomplete measurement, because the total number alone does not tell the whole story (even though it is the number most people are eager to know). As you learned in the preceding chapter, HDL and LDL play separate and crucial roles in determining heart health and only a complete panel will determine if your healthy HDL levels are working for you or if your lethal LDL levels are working against you. This may sound like alphabet soup, but these four numbers shown on your test will help you best implement The Stanford Life Plan for a Healthy Heart.

What the Numbers on Your Test Results Mean

1. YOUR TOTAL CHOLESTEROL gives you an overall picture of the amount of cholesterol circulating in your bloodstream. The recommended level is under 200 mg, but as we have said, studies show that heart attacks almost never occur when the cholesterol level drops to the 160 mg range. These lower values are not as important for premenopausal women, who usually have a much higher protective HDL making up their total cholesterol. (See Chapter 9: Women and Heart Disease.) In order to prevent further plaque development in your arteries, this ideal reading of 160 is also the number to target when you have symptoms of atherosclerosis or have a combination of other risk factors.

2. THE LDL (LETHAL) READING indicates how much of the harmful cholesterol (the type that *promote* development of plaque) you have. The recommended reading is below 130 and the ideal reading is under 100. In fact, we recommend that it be under 80 if you are at high risk for or already have coronary heart disease (see Stanford Self-Assessment Risk Questionnaire on page 50).

3. THE HDL (HEALTHY) READING indicates how much good cholesterol (the type that *prevents* plaque from forming) you have. This number should at least be above 45 for men and 55 for women—and the higher the better.

4. YOUR RATIO OF TOTAL CHOLESTEROL TO HDL will be the last figure. This figure should be between 3.5 and 4.5. Studies show that ratios above 4.5 double your risk of suffering a heart attack. The ideal ratio is below 3.5 and ideally as low as you can get it.

	Recommended Range	Ideal Levels	Your Levels
Total cholesterol level	Below 200 mg	160 mg	_____
HDL level (men)	Above 45 mg	Above 45 mg	_____
HDL level (women)	Above 55 mg	Above 55 mg	_____
LDL level (men and women)	Below 130 mg	Below 100 mg	_____
Total cholesterol/HDL ratio (men)	Below 4.5	The lower the better	_____
Total cholesterol/HDL ratio (women)	Below 3.5	The lower the better	_____

Test results can vary from laboratory to laboratory, so it is best to have any abnormal results rechecked—your physician's office can easily arrange this. Once you have your test results in hand, refer to them as you read the next several chapters, which explain in detail the significance of all these numbers. But first, we have a very important but simple test for you to take, The Stanford Heart Disease Self-Assessment Risk Questionnaire (page 50), which will point out how your lifestyle and medical history stack up against the risk factors that influence the health of your heart. With both of these test results in hand, you will be able to use The Stanford Life Plan for a Healthy Heart and The Stanford 25 Gram Plan to reduce *all* risks to your heart.

CHAPTER 5

Assessing—and Eliminating—Your Risks

SO FAR, WE HAVE GIVEN YOU SOME OF THE GRIM NEWS *about heart disease and how it can alter your life in all the ways no one would ever willingly choose. Now we come to the good news: You can break your links to heart disease. You can minimize, and in some instances, completely eliminate every risk to your heart by following the recommendations of The Stanford Life Plan for a Healthy Heart, and in particular by using The Stanford 25 Gram Plan and Fat Tracker's Guide to reduce saturated fat in your diet. The key is to start making changes now, before a heart attack does irreparable damage. However, we know that sometimes change appears to come with a price tag, perceived as deprivation or a loss of comfort. People need incentives to curb lifelong behavior, even when they know it is in their best interests. It is human nature that we become motivated only when we know what change is worth.*

What Is Prevention Worth?

What is it worth to you to lower your risk of coronary heart disease? A better way of framing the question is to focus on the cost of heart disease. It is hard to measure the physical suffering of heart disease and heart attacks, but on a national level we count the monetary costs of preventable heart disease in the billions of dollars spent yearly in doctor bills and costs of surgery, hospital stays, rehabilitation programs, medications, lost wages and increased insurance premiums. When it comes to your own heart, however, statistics about billions of health-care dollars don't begin to measure the personal cost.

You must balance the value of heart disease prevention against the plans you have for your future—the career you want to continue, the trips you want to take, the friends you want to visit, the books you want to write, the pictures you want to paint, the parties you want to give, the furniture you want to build, the garden you want to tend, the grandchildren you want to love.

In short, no amount of money puts a price on the life you want to lead. What is it worth to eat less saturated fat and take the other steps we will recommend to protect yourself from heart disease? Well, we can only tell you what our patients at Stanford tell us: everything.

Will You Live Longer?

Studies have tracked the longevity of patients as they reduced harmful dietary fats for a period of years. A statistical analysis of those results shows only a small impact on death rates. Some calculations indicate that a person who follows a heart-healthy lifestyle may only live an average of four additional months. When this finding hit the news, the predictable response on the part of the public was, "Four months? Why bother?" We have a strong answer to "why bother."

First of all, in our experience, most people want to live as long as they can. When the four months in question is *their* four months, they welcome any additional time they can get. However, the point of the extension of life span, brief as it seems to be in these preliminary studies, is that lowering dietary fats *does* extend longevity. We want to point out that the length of these studies is relatively short—four, five and six years. While this may seem like a long time to a lay person, in terms of following the effects of lifestyle changes on heart disease, scientists need to observe people who restrict saturated fat in their diets over the course of their entire lives. Current and future research projects will eventually give us that information. We believe that the longer positive health habits are maintained, the stronger their effect on the health of the heart. We strongly suspect that in future decades the data will reveal that a lifetime of avoiding deadly fats can yield far greater benefits in terms of extended life span than the mere four months that the short-term studies currently show.

Longevity Is Not the Issue; Quality of Life Is

But longevity is not the only reason we urge all Americans to eat a healthier diet. A heart attack always comes unannounced when you are least prepared for it, least want it. If you survive a heart attack you may have to live with disabling symptoms. Statistical calculations of longevity cannot measure the decline in quality of life before death, such as the impact on a person's life when dealing with the effect of heart disease becomes the major focus; when recovering from a heart attack takes every ounce of commitment and confidence; when the pain of angina demands daily medication, decreased activity, a complete reordering of life's priorities and even the possibility of surgery, including, at the extreme, heart transplant.

Martin C., for example, once claimed he lived just to be with his three grandchildren. He took an early retirement from his union job in part to participate in their care while his daughter and son-in-law worked. Heart disease was rampant in Martin's family. For most of his life he had bacon and eggs for breakfast, steak and thoroughly buttered potatoes for dinner. He smoked. Upon retirement in his early 60s, a series of progressively worsening heart attacks rearranged his plans to "bounce his grandkids on his knee," as he had hoped. He spent his last several years alternating between hospitalizations, doctor visits and explaining to his eldest granddaughter why he couldn't roughhouse as he once had. If you have had one heart attack and survive, it is very hard to dispel the fear that you will have another. Martin lived with the worry that lifting a child, walking through the neighborhood to visit relatives or eating the wrong foods would bring on another attack. We don't know how Martin would have responded to the news that he could have lived an extra four months if he had taken earlier measures to ward off his heart attacks; he didn't live long enough to read about the statistics. But we do know he wished he could have changed the quality of the last seven or eight years that he lived with disabling heart disease.

❧ **No one can guarantee you longer life, but we know that The Stanford Life Plan for a Healthy Heart will help you live *healthier*.**

No matter how many habits, hereditary factors or medical conditions endanger your heart now, even if you have severe plaque deposits, dietary changes can still improve the health of your arteries. They did for Lucas R. He was 70 when a series of tests uncovered a cholesterol level of 270 and severe narrowing of his coronary arteries due to cholesterol plaque. He immediately altered his diet and all but eliminated saturated fat. Though he never smoked, he had led a sedentary life so he began exercising 30 minutes each day. At his one-year checkup following his health alert, his performance on the treadmill showed tremendous improvement in his heart function and his blood cholesterol was down to the 200 range. He was out of the woods, enjoying his life and committed to dietary changes and an exercise program that restored health to his heart.

What we are really stressing in this book is the quality of life, regardless of its length. The Stanford 25 Gram Plan is designed to help you skim the saturated fat from your diet, along with encouraging you to incorporate all the other aspects of a healthy diet into your daily meals, such as sufficient fiber and nutrients. But in particular, people who eat minimal amounts of saturated fat and smaller portions of total fats than Americans typically eat, have less risk of developing the host of known health problems related to dietary fat in addition to heart disease—cancer, obesity, strokes. Researchers studying the bridge between good nutrition and good health expect to find confirmation that saturated fat is linked to other ailments as well. Based on all medical evidence, it is highly likely that a permanent reduction in saturated fat over the course of an entire lifetime will show dramatic results in not just a longer life, but a healthier one as well.

Risk Factors Predict Likelihood of Heart Attack

Yet even with all we have just said about heart disease risk, you may wonder, "Are you talking to me?" Well, yes we are. The majority of health agencies in the United States advise all Americans, including children over the age of two, to eat less fat to protect themselves from a number of diseases. That is why we say, yes, whatever age group you are in, whatever state of overall health you enjoy, The Stanford 25 Gram Plan is for you and your family. However, some people have a higher risk of developing heart disease than others. How do you know if you are one of them?

We would need a crystal ball to say for sure who will and will not suffer a heart attack, but it doesn't take any magic to estimate the *chances* of your developing coronary artery disease. You can play medical sleuth and estimate your own risk of premature heart attack, the first step in preventing heart disease. To do this, you simply assemble the necessary information that can give you a glimpse of the future, at least as it relates to the relative health of your heart and your arteries. You can then use this information to help you discuss clearly your medical needs with your physician, and, of course, to make the choices that will keep your risk at a minimum. But we are getting ahead of ourselves.

❧ **The first step is to take The Stanford Heart Disease Self-Assessment Questionnaire, which will indicate the factors in your life, your health habits and certain aspects of your medical and family histories that may link you to heart disease.**

We hope there are very few. However, if you do find your score higher than you would like, remember that no matter what the final tally adds up to, we will help you break *all* your links to heart disease. We suggest that you take the test now, and begin following our recommendations. Repeat the questionnaire every six months, more often if your score is in the high-risk range, as a gauge to check your continued progress. The formula is simple: As the number of risk factors increases, so do your chances of developing coronary artery disease.

We are grateful to Dr. John Farquhar and Addison Wesley Publishers for permission to use the self-assessment test he designed for his book, *The American Way of Life Need Not Be Hazardous to Your Health.* With Dr. Farquhar's help, the questionnaire has been modified from the original version for our purposes. Before you take the test, it will help to do a little bit of homework in preparation.

Your Homework for the Self-Assessment Risk Questionnaire

First, as discussed earlier, if you have not done so, have your blood cholesterol level checked. Next, think about your family's experience with heart disease for a moment, to recall whether any of your family members such as parents, grandparents, aunts and uncles developed heart disease *before* age 65.

THINK ABOUT YOUR LIFESTYLE You can easily answer whether or not you smoke. But think about your diet in the past several months. No one will see your test score, so consider honestly whether you eat a lot of rich, fatty foods and snacks. What level of stress do you live with consistently? What are your exercise patterns? The answers to these questions will indicate whether or not your personal habits and ways of dealing with the complex world we all inhabit are helping you stay healthy or pitching you toward the high-risk statistics.

EXAMINE THE STATE OF YOUR GENERAL HEALTH If you don't know your blood pressure, have it checked. If it is high, what steps are you taking to lower it? If you have not weighed yourself recently, do so on a reliable scale. Compare your weight to the ideal weight chart below.

IDEAL WEIGHT FOR MEN AND WOMEN

Height*		Men's Weight*	Women's Weight*
Feet	Inches		
4	9	-	94–106
4	10	-	97–109
4	11	-	100–112
5	0	-	103–115
5	1	111–122	106–118
5	2	114–126	109–122
5	3	117–129	112–126
5	4	120–132	116–131
5	5	123–136	120–135
5	6	127–140	124–139
5	7	131–145	128–143
5	8	135–149	132–147
5	9	139–153	136–151
5	10	143–158	140–155
5	11	147–163	-
6	0	151–168	-
6	1	155–173	-
6	2	160–178	-
6	3	165–183	-

*Height measured in stocking feet without shoes. Weight in pounds without clothing. These figures are not broken down according to age and they refer to persons of medium frame.

DO YOU HAVE ANY OTHER MEDICAL PROBLEMS? Some diseases, such as diabetes mellitus, appear to raise cholesterol levels and promote the development of plaque. Also, some medications will raise cholesterol levels, particularly diuretics and beta blockers. If you are not sure, ask your doctor whether you are taking any medication or have a medical condition that can account for a higher than normal cholesterol. Do not take a random guess or let well-meaning friends give you advice about whether or not certain medications help or harm your heart. Only your physician can tell you whether or not your other medical problems and medications will contribute to a higher cholesterol level. If you have other ailments, you should discuss their effects on your cholesterol levels and overall heart disease risk with your doctor.

Once you have all of this information in hand, complete the answers to the questionnaire. The test cannot diagnose heart disease, of course, but it will give you valuable information and serve as the starting point for a longer and healthier life.

How to Use the Results of the Self-Assessment Risk Questionnaire

As you continue reading this book, the questionnaire will take on added meaning when you discover the significance of smoking, exercise, cholesterol levels and the other indicators of heart health. As you begin each new chapter, you can refer back to the questionnaire to refresh your memory about the factors that increase your personal risk, as well as the ways you can break your links to heart disease.

If your score is higher than you want it to be, follow the measures we describe in The Stanford Life Plan for a Healthy Heart to lower it to a safer range. If your score is satisfyingly low, follow these same measures for added insurance that it will stay that way. If your score is above 20, you should see your doctor immediately. You may require further testing and close medical supervision. Obviously, if you discover that your cholesterol is high and you have been having symptoms of heart trouble, you should put this book down, call your doctor and get medical attention *now*.

- The cost of heart disease is high: to the nation, to you personally.
- Lowering your risk of heart disease may extend your life.
- Lowering your risk of heart disease will improve the quality of your life.
- When you know your blood cholesterol level and your personal risk of heart disease, you will have the two most important pieces of information you need to embark upon your new heart-smart lifestyle.
- Encourage the other adults in your household to take the test.
- Show it to your friends and suggest they take it as well, so that everyone close to you can become more aware of ways to live longer and healthier by following The Stanford Life Plan for a Healthy Heart.

THE STANFORD HEART DISEASE SELF-ASSESSMENT RISK QUESTIONNAIRE
Simplified Self-Scoring Test of Chronic Disease Risk

Risk habit or factor		Increasing risk ⟶			
1. Smoking cigarettes	None per day	Up to 5 per day	10 to 15 per day	16 to 24 per day	25 or more per day
Score	0	1	2	3	4
2. Body weight	Ideal weight	Up to 19 pounds excess	20 to 29 pounds excess	30 to 39 pounds excess	40 pounds or more excess
Score	0	1	2	3	4
3. Blood pressure upper reading (if known)	Less than 110	110 to 129	130 to 139	140 to 149	150 or over
Score	0	1	2	3	4
4. Blood cholesterol level (if known)	Less than 160	160 to 179	180 to 209	210 to 229	230 or over
Score	1	2	3	4	5
5. Physical activity	Vigorous exercise 4 or more times/week, 20 minutes each	Vigorous exercise 3 times/week, 20 minutes each	Vigorous exercise 1 to 2 times/week	U.S. average, occasional exercise	Below average, exercises rarely
Or walking rating	Brisk walk 4 times/week, 45 minutes each	Brisk walk 3 times/week, 30 minutes each	Brisk walk 2 times/week, 30 minutes each; or normal walking 4½ to 6 miles daily	Normal walking 2 miles daily	Normal walking less than 1 mile daily
Score	0	1	2	3	4
6. Stress and tension	Rarely tense or anxious	Calmer than average	U.S. average feel tense 2 to 3 times/day	Quite tense, usually rushed	Extremely tense
Or	Yoga, meditation, or equivalent 20 minutes 2 times a day	Feel tense about 3 times/week	Frequent anger or hurried feelings	Occasionally take tranquilizer	Take tranquilizer 5 times/week or more
Score	0	1	2	3	4

Subtract 1 point if you have any of the following:

Dietary fiber intake is high

You are a female taking estrogen

Your HDL is over 50

You take daily vitamins and anti-oxidants
  (beta-carotene, vitamin C and E)

You take a daily aspirin

Add 2 points if you have any of the following risk factors:

You have diabetes

You have a family history of heart attacks under age 60

Your LDL is over 150

Add 1 point for each 10 points of systolic blood
  pressure (top number) above 150

Add 1 point for each 30 points of cholesterol above 230

ENTER YOUR FINAL SCORE HERE _____

Interpretation of The Self-Assessment Risk Questionnaire

Risks are given for cardiovascular disease. They apply, but with less precision, for adult-onset diabetes and diet-related cancers of the breast and colon. For smoking-related cancer of the lungs, the predominant risk is duration and amount of smoking.

SCORE

20 OR ABOVE The probability of having a premature heart attack or stroke is about four to five times the United States average. You must take urgent action. Try to drop four points within a month and three more within six months. If your score is as high as 30, you should seek immediate medical attention.

16 TO 19 Incidence of heart attack or stroke is about twice the United States average. Action is urgent. Try to drop four points within six months and continue reduction.

12 TO 15 The United States average is 13, an uncomfortable score considering the rates of heart disease in this country. Begin The Stanford Life Plan for a Healthy Heart and aim for a five- to six-point reduction within a year.

8 TO 11 The likelihood of having a heart attack or stroke is about one-half the United States average. Most people with a score currently between 19 and 12 can rather easily drop down to this healthier level within a year. At this level, and with a commitment to The Stanford Life Plan for a Healthy Heart, most people can achieve a further four- to six-point reduction within a year.

4 TO 7 Incidence of heart attack or stroke is about one-quarter of the United States average. This goal is achievable for many people. It often takes one or two years to reach, but have patience. This is a plan for life and each drop in your score will benefit you throughout your life.

0 TO 3 Incidence of heart attack or stroke rates very low, averaging less than one-tenth the rate in the United States for the 35 to 65 age group. This goal requires diligent effort, considerable family support, and often takes three to four years to reach. Individuals in this range should be proud and gratified—and will serve as models and teachers for their children, friends and family.

CHAPTER 6

Breaking the Saturated Fat Link

THE LINK BETWEEN SATURATED FAT AND HEART DISEASE *is not a difficult concept for people to grasp, but it has gotten buried under the avalanche of media information put out as a response to The National Cholesterol Education Program's (NCEP) efforts to help America halt the spread of heart disease. The NCEP, a coalition of 38 health agencies, in its nutritional guidelines has given us a formula for calculating a healthy diet. However, these scientific recommendations are so complex that the American public has trouble understanding how to apply them on a daily basis to maintain a heart-healthy diet. It is difficult to know what these calculations mean in real food without doing some sophisticated math every morning, and yet no one can afford to ignore them, because these equations will keep blood cholesterol levels low and arteries clear of the plaque that causes coronary artery disease.*

The Stanford 25 Gram Plan has taken a bold step by simplifying these complicated calculations and translating them into a simple number everyone can understand and live with: 25 grams—the daily limit on saturated fat for the normal adult. It may seem that we are adding yet one more number to the endless digits that seem to define modern life. However, slipping a new number, 25 grams, into your nutritional thinking is easy by comparison, especially when you realize what it replaces.

We took this:

GUIDELINES OF THE NATIONAL CHOLESTEROL EDUCATION PROGRAM FOR DIETARY CONTROL OF HIGH BLOOD CHOLESTEROL

	Recommended Intake	
Nutrient	*Step One Diet**	*Step Two Diet**
Total Fat	Less than 30% of total calories	
Saturated fatty acids	8 to 10% of total calories	Less than 7% of total calories
Polyunsaturated fatty acids	Less than 10% of total calories	
Monosaturated fatty acids	10% to 15% of total calories	
Carbohydrates	50% to 60% of total calories	
Protein	10% to 20% of total calories	
Cholesterol	Less than 300 mg/day	Less than 200 mg/day
Total calories	*To achieve and maintain ideal weight*	

*Step One and Step Two Diets are discussed in Timetable for Change, Chapter 12

and made it look like this:

THE STANFORD 25 GRAM PLAN DIETARY RECOMMENDATIONS

Eat LESS than 25 grams of saturated fat each day.

The Stanford 25 Gram Plan Simplifies the National Recommendations

This exciting breakthrough simplifies the complicated cardiac math previously required and gives you the single, most important piece of information that will finally help you implement a heart-healthy diet. We based the 25 gram figure on a typical adult diet of approximately 2,300 calories a day. The ideal diet as defined by the national guidelines limits all fat to 30 percent of those calories and saturated fat to a *maximum* of 10 percent. (In 1993, the report first released in 1988 further recommended that the maximum level for an average healthy person should ideally be between 8 percent and 10 percent for Step One.) The guidelines also stress that you limit cholesterol to a concrete number: 300 milligrams. That part is easy. Figuring out your saturated fat allotment is another matter, however.

The recommendations require that people know how many calories they eat in a day before they can figure out what percentage of which fats to restrict. Next, you must translate those percentages into a whole number and then divide by nine (the number of calories in a gram). Without knowing the number of grams you have budgeted for yourself, the package labeling information and recipe nutritional calculations that list fat content in grams of fat won't make sense.

For example, if you don't know what number to use as your limit, you can't figure out if a package of crackers that has four grams of saturated fat per serving is a nutritional bargain or a fatty excess. Things get trickier when several family members have different calorie needs and you have to keep track. This whole mathematical process prevents people from understanding what it takes to eat and not eat for a healthier heart.

By going directly from calorie counting to fat tracking, The Stanford 25 Gram Plan helps you easily achieve the end product of the guidelines—a sensible portion of saturated fat. Using the NCEP guidelines as our standard, we estimated that 10 percent of the typical 2,300 calorie diet equals approximately 25 grams of saturated fat, the foundation of our fat-stripping approach to a healthy heart. Since fat has 9 calories per gram, our calculation looks like this to give you an answer you can easily understand.

> *Recommended fat ratio for 2,300 calorie diet:*
> *2,300 x 10 percent (saturated fat) = 230 ÷ 9 = 25.55 grams.*

We Make Sure You Don't Get Too Much Saturated Fat

While not everyone restricts calories to 2,300, everyone must, however, limit saturated fat to 25 grams or less per day. For some people, the 10 percent of total calories rule in the National Cholesterol Education Program guidelines may actually permit *too much* saturated fat. For example, the activity levels of large-framed, active men and women and the growth requirements of athletic adolescent boys may require up to 3,000 calories or more each day to adequately fuel their bodies. But they don't need 10 percent of them or a whopping 33 grams as saturated fat, which, as you can see below, the current formula would allow.

> *Recommended fat ratio for 3,000 calorie diet:*
> *3,000 x 10 percent (saturated fat) = 300 ÷ 9 = 33 grams.*

We recommend that all normal, healthy adults stay under 25 grams of saturated fat and use foods low in or free of saturated fat to make up additional needed calories. Recommendations for children follow.

How to Calculate *Your* Personal Saturated Fat Target

For persons who are small, older, less active, very slender, or who have evidence of heart disease, 25 grams may still be too much saturated fat. Since our example is based on 2,300 calories per day, the health of thin women and activity level of elderly adults may require they eat only 1,900 calories each day, or even less. It is easy to calculate your personal, daily target for saturated fat by using the following equation:

> Ideal weight x 15 calories per pound = _____ calories per day
> _____ calories per day x 10 percent = _____ calories of saturated fat
> _____ calories of saturated fat ÷ 9 = _____ grams of saturated fat

For example, for a woman with an ideal weight of 124 pounds, the equation would look like this:

> 124 pounds x 15 calories/lb. = 1860 total calories
> 1860 x 10 percent = 186 calories of saturated fat
> 186 ÷ 9 = 21 grams of saturated fat

If you don't want to do the math, use the following table from The American Heart Association to approximate your target.

ESTIMATED DAILY CALORIE NEEDS (AGE 19 TO 50)

Activity Level	Men (157 lbs.) Calories	Women (125 lbs.) Calories
Very Light	2,200	1,700
Light	2,600	2,000
Moderate	2,800	2,100
Heavy	3,500	2,500

Locate your estimated daily calorie level on the following chart to find your personal daily saturated fat target. (For an explanation of a Step Two diet, see page ooo.)

DAILY SATURATED FAT TARGETS (AGE 19 TO 50)

Calorie Level	Total Fat Grams (30 percent)	Step One Saturated Fat Grams (8 to 10 percent)	Step Two Saturated Fat Grams (7 percent)
1200	40	13	9
1500	50	17	12
1800	60	20	14
2000	67	22	16
2200	73	24	17
2500	75	25	19
3000	75	25	23

❧ **Notice that we recommend you *never* eat more than 25 grams of saturated fat per day, even if you consume and burn more than 2,250 calories per day.**

Here are the recommendations for children, computed per pound of body weight. As you can see, growing children need many more calories per pound compared to adults, who require only about 15 calories per pound.

ESTIMATED CALORIE NEEDS, TOTAL FAT AND
SATURATED FAT TARGETS FOR CHILDREN AND TEENAGERS

Age	Calories per lb.	Total Fat	Saturated Fat
All children			
1 to 3	46 calories/lb.	43	14
4 to 6	41 calories/lb.	60	20
7 to 10	32 calories/lb.	66	22
Males			
11 to 14	25 calories/lb.	75	25
15 to 18	20 calories/lb.	75	25
Females			
11 to 14	21 calories/lb.	73	24
15 to 18	18 calories/lb.	70	23

Go Lower Than Your Target If You Wish

Just as some people normally eat more than 2,300 calories in a day, many others eat fewer, and still many more have cardiovascular problems that require even more stringent restrictions on saturated fat. The Stanford 25 Gram Plan places a *ceiling* on this harmful fat; that is, you must not eat more than that amount each day. However, the lower you go, the more protection for your arteries. Regardless of the number of calories you consume each day, you can follow the Step Two Diet in the National Cholesterol Education Program's guidelines. As we explain in Chapter 12, Timetable for Change, Step Two limits saturated fat to 7 percent of calories, or a maximum of about 17 grams.

What About Total Fat?

In addition to reducing saturated fat, most experts believe it is best to limit your total daily intake of every kind of fat to less than 30 percent of calories, because high-fat diets have been linked with other serious diseases such as cancer of the colon and possibly other types of cancer. For example, some researchers believe that the putrefaction bacteria in the colon that feed on animal protein (containing saturated fat) react with cholesterol and bile salts to produce carcinogenic agents that cause colon cancer, while fermentation bacteria, the kind that feed on carbohydrates (containing unsaturated fat) do not. Consequently, just as we recommend that you limit saturated fat to 25 grams or less each day, we also urge you keep your total fat intake to less than 75 grams (i.e., 30 percent of calories) each day. In a later chapter, we will talk more about how The Stanford 25 Gram Plan will also help you maintain this limit on total fat, and how you can lower the fat target for people who must eat a more restricted diet. But for now, we want to mainly stress the need to limit saturated fat.

WHAT ARE WE SAYING?

- One of the major ways to prevent heart disease is to limit saturated fat to 25 grams or less each day.
- For overall good health, limit total fat to 75 grams or less each day.
- If you wish to or need to, place even lower ceilings on your intake of saturated fat, total fat and cholesterol.

How well do you control the major sources of saturated fat? Take the Fat Traps quiz on the next page to find out where harmful fats creep into your diet.

FAT TRAPS

Fat sneaks up in the most unexpected places and it wears many disguises. Do you know where the fat is? Take this little quiz. You may be surprised at the ways fat traps you when you least expect it—when you are at a picnic, a party or a restaurant and it seems you have to choose the lesser of two or more evils. Circle the item with the *least* saturated fat per serving.

1. Butter
   Margarine
   Old-fashioned peanut butter

2. Grilled chicken breast with skin
   Grilled regular hamburger patty
   Grilled lean ground round

3. Lobster
   Fish sticks

4. Salad with cheese, croutons and
      bleu cheese dressing
   Grilled lean hamburger patty

5. Peanuts
   Potato chips

6. Croissant
   Sweet roll

7. Nondairy cream
   Half-and-half

8. Baked potato
   Pasta with cheese

9. Butter-fried catfish
   Grilled lean ground round

10. Guacamole
    Sour cream dip

11. Sunflower seeds
    Pretzels

12. 1 peanut butter cup candy bar,
       1.8 ounces
    Marshmallows, 1.8 ounces

Answers:

1. Old-fashioned peanut butter wins hands down. Butter and margarine have at least twice as much saturated fat. In addition, butter has cholesterol and none of the others do. Compare a tablespoon serving.

	Saturated Fat (g)	Total Fat (g)
Butter	7.6	12.2
Margarine	2.0	11.0
Old-fashioned peanut butter	1.7	8.0

2. In this fat test, it is almost, but not quite, a dead heat. The saturated fat is the same, but in terms of total fat, chicken loses to beef. You are actually slightly better off with lean, grilled ground round than a chicken breast with skin, provided you don't add cheese or other fatty items to the beef. (Of course, you are heart-smarter when you choose the chicken and toss the skin.) Compare a 3.5-ounce serving.

Grilled chicken breast *with skin*	2.2	7.6
Grilled regular hamburger patty	8.2	21.0
Grilled lean ground round	2.2	6.2

3. No contest. Choose any shellfish cooked without butter over fried anything. Commercially made breaded fish products often have saturated fat and whole eggs added. (When we take you on a fat-tracking tour of the supermarket you will learn that shellfish is higher in cholesterol, though, and an even better choice is grilled or broiled fish.)

	Saturated Fat (g)	Total Fat (g)
3 ounces broiled lobster	0.1	0.5
3 ounces breaded fish sticks	2.7	12.0

4. Salads are one of our Crunchy Lunch selections (see Chapter 13); the croutons cooked in fat, mountain of shredded cheese and creamed salad dressing are not. If these are your only alternatives, go with the lean beef.

Salad with 1 ounce cheese, and 1 tablespoon salad dressing	8.0	19.0
3-ounce grilled lean hamburger patty	6.2	16.0

5. If you are just comparing total fat, potato chips win. However, peanuts have no saturated fat, so they are a better fat-tracking choice. Look around for the pretzels or air-popped popcorn, though. They have almost no fat. Compare a 1-ounce serving.

Peanuts, 1 ounce	1.9	14.0
Potato chips, 1 ounce	2.6	10.0
Pretzels, 1 ounce	0	0
Air-popped unbuttered popcorn, 1 cup	0	0

6. In this choice between two tantalizing fat traps, the croissant is the winner. Although the croissant is crammed with butter, the saturated fat in a Danish can range from 4 grams per serving to 23! Fast-food restaurants are more likely to serve the hefty pastry, while your market will probably stock lower-fat versions. However, if it is a shot of sugar or richness you want in the morning, have raisin toast instead, and smear it with honey or Blueberry Honey Sauce, page 306. This treat won't cost you even one of your 25 grams of saturated fat.

Danish pastry	up to 23.0	36.0 (14.0 on average)
Croissant (large)	4.0	20.0

7. Nondairy cream products made with tropical or hydrogenated oils (and many of them are!) can out-fat real cream.

1 ounce liquid nondairy cream	5.2	6.4
1 ounce half-and-half	2.2	3.4

8. We didn't say baked potato with butter, sour cream and bacon. A plain, steaming baked potato has no fat, saturated or otherwise. Pasta, on the other hand, can have olive oil and a smattering of low-fat cheese and still be a fat-tracking winner compared to the saturated fat toppings that usually drown the innocent baked potato.

	Saturated Fat (g)	Total Fat (g)
Baked potato, plain	0	0
Baked potato with 3 tablespoons each butter and sour cream and 1 teaspoon crumbled bacon	28.0	45.0
Pasta with 1 tablespoon each olive oil and Parmesan cheese	2.8	15.0

9. Don't kid yourself. Fish is never good for your heart—when it is drowned in butter, that is. If you have no choice, order the beef. If you have an accommodating chef, request the catfish grilled and served with salsa or tartar sauce (mayonnaise has a trace of cholesterol but no saturated fat) and your fish entrée will triumph over the beef. Compare these 3.5-ounce portions.

Catfish, grilled	0.9	4.2
Catfish, breaded and fried in butter	3.3	13.2
Grilled lean ground round	2.2	6.2

10. Yes, avocados have fat. But it is monounsaturated and perfectly acceptable to your heart, if you can stand the calories. If you don't add sour cream to the guacamole, it is a far better choice than a sour cream dip. Compare a 3-ounce serving.

Guacamole	2.3	15.0
Sour cream onion dip	6.0	10.0

11. Neither snack has much saturated fat, but sunflower seeds, like all seeds, contain unsaturated fat. Pretzels, except the ones doctored with cheese or other high-fat flavorings, have none. Some seeds, though, are roasted in tropical oils and then salted, so if you snack on sunflower seeds occasionally, check the package and choose dry-roasted or raw seeds.

1 ounce sunflower seeds	1.5	14.1
1 ounce pretzels	0	0

12. Go easy on the chocolate bars. But just because something is sweet doesn't necessarily mean it has fat. When it is time to roast marshmallows, you don't have to hang back. Made from an egg-white base, they are just one example of sweet treats that won't hurt your heart.

1 peanut butter cup candy bar, 1.8 ounces	6.0	17.0
Marshmallows, 1.8 ounces	0	0

CHAPTER 7

Your Cholesterol Targets

THE PURPOSE OF ADOPTING *The Stanford Life Plan for a Healthy Heart is to maintain optimal cholesterol levels. Here are the numbers you want to achieve.*

Target: Total Cholesterol 160
Heart attacks generally only begin to occur when total cholesterol levels rise above 160, with the risk becoming significant as total cholesterol levels move over the 200 mark.

Statistics show that half the people with total cholesterol levels in the 200 to 240 range will suffer a heart attack at some point.

We now recognize that a doubling effect occurs, boosting even higher the percentage of risk as the total cholesterol level rises. For example, if you start with a cholesterol reading in the 150 to 160 range, every percentage point increase in total cholesterol doubles the percent increase in risk: A 10 percent increase in total cholesterol, say from 200 to 220, equals a 20 percent increase in your chance of dying of a heart attack. Increase the actual number by 15 percent and your risk jumps 30 percent. This is a two-for-one deal no one can afford. As cholesterol levels shoot up to 250, 275 and higher, your risk of suffering a fatal, premature heart attack becomes very great. This increase in risk holds true regardless of sex, age or race. Clearly, then, to break your link to heart disease, you must keep your total cholesterol levels low.

How Low Is Low?
Cholesterol readings are like golf scores: the lower the better. Heart attacks almost never occur in people whose total cholesterol levels are 160 and under. But that's not all the good news. Studies show a reverse doubling as you lower your cholesterol. For each 1 percent drop, you will *decrease* your risk of heart disease by 2 percent. Lower it by 10 percent and your odds go down 20 percent. Does it pay to reduce your blood cholesterol levels? Does it pay to scrutinize your eating habits to eliminate as much cholesterol-producing saturated fat from your meals as posssible? Figure it out!

If your cholesterol is 226 and you lower it to just 221, you chop 4 percentage points off your risk for heart disease. As you continue your efforts and reduce it by 10 percent, to 203, close to the healthy range, your risk of heart disease sinks by 20 percent. When a cholesterol reading of 226 drops by 25 percent, to 170, you have cut your risk of heart disease in half and entered the comfort zone. Now this is a two for one offer that no one can afford to refuse. These results hold true for all age and racial groups. The point of this math exercise is to show that every decrease you make in your total cholesterol counts, even in the smallest increments. By getting your total cholesterol level low, you can not only prevent the development of plaque, but by achieving total cholesterol levels of 160 and lower you can even reverse the buildup of cholesterol plaque that may have already begun, a feat that was once thought possible only with surgery.

❦ **Very low cholesterol levels can actually help you reverse heart disease!**

Keeping your saturated fat and cholesterol intake low, as we describe in The Stanford 25 Gram Plan, generally can lower your cholesterol by 30 percent or more. For people requiring greater decreases, certain medications can bring the total cholesterol down dramatically. Remember that positive changes have cumulative effects: Lowering your cholesterol levels *and* controlling blood pressure *and* staying away from cigarettes *and* exercising at least 30 minutes a day all add up tremendously to increase the health of your heart and lower your risk of heart disease.

If the NCEP Guidelines Say Less Than 200, Why Do We Recommend 160?

The guidelines established by the NCEP, though they seemed radical to people used to frequent rations of steak, bacon, butter and cream, actually may turn out to be quite conservative. New information about heart disease prevention has emerged since the guidelines' first publication in 1988 and the follow-up report in 1993, and every indication points to a need to set our national cholesterol target lower. Moreover, recent studies have shown that some patients with heart disease can actually *reverse* the cholesterol-plaque process by working very hard to get total cholesterol levels down toward the 160 range. We recognize that everyone must maintain a cholesterol reading of no higher than 200. However, since many researchers believe that *everyone* in this country has some degree of artery damage, it is even better to aim for as low a reading as possible, in the hope that this lower target will attack any atherosclerotic plaque already building up in your coronary arteries. The recommendations of The Stanford Life Plan for a Healthy Heart will help you keep your cholesterol levels as low as possible.

Can Your Cholesterol Be Too Low?

You may have read news reports that indicate people with extremely low cholesterol levels have a higher mortality rate. As a result, many people became confused, believing that low cholesterol levels *caused* the problem, and consequently they shied away from low-fat, low-cholesterol diets. It is more likely that this higher death rate reflects people who are already ill from other serious diseases that cause changes in cholesterol metabolism.

Some investigators have also suggested that other problems, such as aggression and suicide, may be linked to very low cholesterol levels. Recent studies have found no evidence to support this connection. Since it is very difficult for most healthy people to achieve cholesterol levels lower than 120 to 130, the concern about having a cholesterol reading that is harmfully low is misguided and no reason to ignore recommendations to eliminate harmful fats from your diet. Because the body can make all the cholesterol it needs, scientists have discovered no harmful effects of maintaining a diet and lifestyle that will keep excess cholesterol to a minimum.

❧ **Even though the National Cholesterol Education Program guidelines recommend that you maintain a cholesterol level *below* 200, we recommend you keep it as far below that number as possible.**

It is presumed that over 95 percent of Americans have cholesterol readings above 150, and 60 million have levels over 200, as opposed to the Japanese, for example, whose average cholesterol level is around 160 and whose national incidence of heart disease is very low. We see many patients, colleagues and friends who have achieved total cholesterol levels in the 160 to 190 range with a low saturated fat diet and who remain completely healthy.

Target: LDL Cholesterol Less Than 100
Many researchers, among them Stanford's Dr. Peter Wood and Dr. John Farquhar, believe that LDL (lethal cholesterol) readings are a much more accurate predictor of heart disease than even total cholesterol levels. How low do you want your LDL reading to be? As low as you can possibly get it. The Framingham study (discussed on page 16) showed that the risk of heart disease jumps with a high LDL, with readings above 160 posing the most serious risk.

❧ **However, an LDL reading above 130 still shows a strong likelihood that an individual will develop heart disease, even if the total cholesterol level is below 200!**

How can this be when we have just advised you that 200 is the current advice of the NCEP for a cutoff point of total cholesterol for increased risk? If the total cholesterol level is 200, but most of it is comprised of lethal LDL rather than helpful HDL, the relatively low total cholesterol number is misleading. The ratio of HDL to LDL is imbalanced, without enough HDL to carry cholesterol away from the artery wall off to the liver before a frenzy of high LDL activity deposits it in the artery wall.

However, as you decrease the level of LDL in the bloodstream, there is less and less of it to be deposited in the artery wall to fuel plaque formation. With less plaque formation, the risk of heart disease plummets. We urge you to make every attempt to maintain an LDL reading of 100 or less.

Target: HDL Above 45 for Men and 55 for Women

HDL(healthy cholesterol) may be compared to the horsepower of an engine, the higher the number, the more power you have to do the job. The level of protective HDL your body can produce may be genetically determined, so it is extremely important to make sure that you do nothing that interferes with the highest HDL level you can achieve. The Stanford Life Plan for a Healthy Heart will help your body produce that maximum output. As many as 25 percent of all Americans may have low HDL readings. Results from the Framingham study have indicated that when your HDL level drops below 35, your risk of heart disease increases markedly. In addition, a report from the National Institutes of Health issued in the spring of 1992 concluded that, based on all the available studies, a low HDL level augured the same risk of heart disease as a high total cholesterol level.

As we said in an earlier chapter, HDL protects your heart by carrying away harmful cholesterol from the artery wall. Without enough HDL to carry unused cholesterol to the liver, destructive LDL works unimpeded to keep feeding existing plaque formations more cholesterol. How much HDL is enough? As much as you can produce, but studies seem to indicate that even if you have lots of good HDL cholesterol, it can't overcome the effects of a large amount of LDL. So, again, if your LDL is high, even if you have a very healthy HDL reading, you have a higher risk of developing heart disease. HDL readings seem to be most crucial in the midrange of cholesterol readings. If your total cholesterol level is extremely high— over 290 or 300—you may not be able to manufacture enough good HDL to protect you from plaque-building harmful LDL. And if you have very low total cholesterol, around 150 to 160, it doesn't take much HDL to clear away the relatively small amount of excess cholesterol circulating in the arteries, so at those low levels, even a little HDL goes a long way.

Studies also show that high levels of HDL can protect against heart disease even if the total cholesterol is higher than normal, as the following discussion of the importance of a favorable ratio between the two will show. Women tend to have higher HDL levels than men, presumably because estrogen during child-bearing years helps keep HDL high. This may account for the low rate of heart attacks among younger women.

Low Ratio of Total Cholesterol to HDL

The ratio of total cholesterol to HDL appears to give a more accurate reflection of your risk of heart disease, since your total cholesterol affects both LDL and HDL. A low ratio indicates that you have a healthy quantity of HDL to combat harmful LDL and a high ratio alerts you to an increased risk of coronary heart disease, even if your total cholesterol is in a "safe" range. Dr. William Castelli, head of the Framingham study, believes that the ratio of total cholesterol to HDL is one of the most important indicators of heart health, more accurate than just the total cholesterol number. Dr. Castelli's statistics indicate that people with a ratio of 4.5 or higher are twice as likely to have a heart attack as those with a ratio of 3.5. To determine your ratio, simply divide your total cholesterol by the HDL level.

We must examine HDL and LDL separately to get an accurate picture of your risk of atherosclerosis. But as you begin to understand the various components of cholesterol, you see that HDL and LDL are inextricably linked to the health of your heart, the protective effects of good HDL offsetting the destructive LDL. Obviously, because you can never totally eliminate the harmful effects of LDL, you want to maintain the most favorable balance between the two. Compare the following total cholesterol/HDL ratios, noting that the lowest number is most desirable.

RATIO OF TOTAL CHOLESTEROL TO HDL

Total Cholesterol	÷	HDL	=	Ratio
175	÷	60	=	2.9
200	÷	56	=	3.6
240	÷	56	=	4.3
200	÷	35	=	5.7
235	÷	40	=	5.8

As you can see from our examples, you are most likely to achieve the most favorable ratio results with lowest possible total cholesterol and highest possible HDL, but note that the recommendation for a total cholesterol of 200 may not protect you sufficiently if your HDL is low, as the 35 in our example.

How to Maintain Ideal Cholesterol Levels

You can achieve the ideal cholesterol levels by following The Stanford Life Plan for a Healthy Heart which contains *all* the measures that are known to raise health ful HDL and lower lethal LDL and total cholesterol levels, whether you need minor adjustments in your eating habits or major modifications because of signs that you are already headed for cardiac problems. People who have already been diagnosed with coronary artery disease, however, may need to more aggressively limit all sources of saturated fat, such as the 17 Gram Plan described in Chapter 12. In addition, they may need to take drugs that block the body's own production of cholesterol by the liver.

The following positive measures appear to influence the various components of cholesterol differently, some boosting favorable HDL levels, others acting to decrease the harmful LDL.

Type of Cholesterol	Factors that Worsen Levels	Factors that Improve Levels
Good HDL	Smoking	Stop smoking
	Lack of aerobic exercise	Exercise at least 30 minutes per day
	Anabolic steroid use	Replace saturated fats with monounsaturated fats
	Low estrogen postmenopause	Estrogen replacement therapy
	Obesity	Achieve and maintain ideal weight
		Moderate alcohol use (see following note)
Bad LDL	Saturated fat in the diet	Limit saturated fat to 7 to 10 percent of calories
	Obesity	Achieve and maintain ideal weight

Note About Alcohol Use

The media has given a lot of attention to the news about alcohol protecting the heart. It is true that small daily doses of alcohol raise HDL. But this finding has to be accompanied with strong warnings about a recommended dose and who should take it. Alcohol does raise your good HDL slightly. A limit of 12 ounces of beer, one glass of wine or one shot of hard liquor is sufficient, and more is not better. It also makes no difference which drink you choose. Many people cannot tolerate alcohol; some find it makes them ill, others find it addicting. We do not recommend that you start drinking since alcohol is not crucial to a heart-healthy lifestyle. Abstaining from alcohol, if you must for any reason, will not harm your heart. We want to caution you that it makes no sense to try to prevent one disease by overindulging in alcohol, which can then contribute to another—alcoholism, cirrhosis, cancer— or cause accidents.

What If You Already Have Coronary Heart Disease?

Once angina or a heart attack has occurred, is it too late to do anything about it? Study after study has shown that heart attack victims can improve their chances of avoiding a *second* heart attack and/or death by changing their risk factors, particularly those related to diet, smoking and blood pressure. Coronary arteriograms, which actually can measure the degree of blockage in the coronary arteries, have now shown that patients with coronary heart disease can prevent progression of the cholesterol plaque process by reducing their blood cholesterol.

At Stanford, Dr. Edwin Alderman, Dr. William Haskell and their colleagues reported to the American Heart Association on two groups of coronary artery disease patients. One group began a program to reduce their cholesterol levels by following a total heart-healthy program, including changing their diets, maintaining an exercise program and using cholesterol-lowering medication when indicated. The other group made only minor lifestyle changes. Four years later, the first group, who had made major positive changes, not only had the biggest drop in cholesterol levels, but repeat coronary arteriograms showed much more beneficial effects on their arteries and sometimes even partial reduction of the plaque deposition process. The second group did not do as well on any of the tests.

What about patients who have had heart surgery or coronary angioplasty? There is a common misconception that they are "cured," and that the arteries have been "cleaned out," meaning they can go back to their old ways. Nothing could be further from the truth. While these measures can return adequate blood flow to the heart, most of the cholesterol plaque remains in the artery and will simply continue to grow and cause new blockages unless major changes are made to break the links that cause cholesterol deposits. You must break these links and keep them broken, or you will reconnect your arteries to the heart disease process. Dietary change is the cornerstone of any program to break these links.

At Stanford University Hospital, we have worked very hard to remind our patients that the modern miracle of angioplasty or heart surgery simply provides a *second chance* to change their lifestyles dramatically in order to *remain* heart-healthy—not permission to return to their old habits.

Prevention—The More the Better
You can use an ounce of prevention to guide most of the decisions in your life, but when it comes to heart disease, you want to take every precaution possible. We don't suggest you pick and choose specific recommendations to effect one aspect of your cholesterol reading; we urge you to adopt all of them. The Stanford Life Plan for a Healthy Heart is a total package, and the more of these preventive measures you employ, the better chance your heart has to withstand the development of heart disease.

WHAT ARE WE SAYING?

We are saying, follow The Stanford Lifeplan for a Healthy Heart and The Stanford 25 Gram Plan to get as close as possible to these targets:

- Total cholesterol = 160
- LDL cholesterol = under 100
- HDL cholesterol (men) = over 45
- HDL cholesterol (women) = over 55
- Ratio of total cholesterol to HDL = under 3.5

In the next chapter we'll take a look at the other steps you can take to keep your heart healthy. But first, are you aware of how often you eat high-fat meat and poultry items? Take the quiz on the next page and you will begin to see some of your high-fat patterns.

CHECK YOURSELF #2: HOW OFTEN DO YOU EAT...?

	Seldom/Never	Sometimes	Frequently
1. Bacon, sausage or ham for breakfast	3	2	1
2. Hot dogs, regular lunch meats like salami or bologna	3	2	1
3. Organ meats, including liver, brains, kidney and sweetbreads	3	2	1
4. Regular hamburger, including meat loaf; meat sauces for pasta	3	2	1
5. Beef steak, ribs or stew meat not cut from the round	3	2	1
6. Pork chops, ribs, pork BBQ	3	2	1
7. Meat without trimming the visible fat before and after cooking	3	2	1
8. Meat servings larger than a pack of cards	3	2	1
9. Poultry skin	3	2	1
10. Deep-fried fish and poultry	3	2	1

Total

Circle the response that most nearly describes your habits and total your score.

25–30 = Excellent, try for a perfect 30.

15–24 = You have some problem areas. Broil and grill more often; choose skin-less poultry breast and fish more often; eat whole grain cereals for breakfast instead of meat items and make hefty salads a lunch habit.

10–14 = Whoops. Read The 25 Gram Plan Meal-Planning Guide and start insisting on Better Breakfasts, Crunchy Lunches and 2 + 2 Dinners.

CHAPTER 8

Breaking the Other Links
to Heart Disease

ALTHOUGH THE MAIN PURPOSE OF THIS BOOK *is to break your link to heart disease by focusing your attention on reducing the amount of saturated fat and cholesterol you eat, we know a great deal about other factors that can compound the risk. We will briefly review these factors, since they are just as important as your diet for maintaining overall heart health.*

Do Not Smoke

Roughly 50 million Americans smoke, slightly less than the number of Americans with elevated cholesterol levels. This habit benefits no one but the tobacco interests. No health professional has anything good to say about smoking; it is one of the worst things you can do to your body. The list of ailments made worse by smoking gets longer as researchers uncover more and more tobacco-related evils. In addition to increasing the risk for coronary heart disease, smoking is a major cause of lung cancer and emphysema. It seriously aggravates ailments such as respiratory disease, and also causes low birth weights in infants whose mothers smoked during pregnancy. Smoking doesn't make you look good, either. Many physicians have become adept at recognizing smokers by what they describe as an unhealthy "smoker's pallor." The habit also seems to accelerate the aging process, doing part of the damage on a cellular level throughout the body, as well as surface damage showing as increasingly wrinkled skin.

In addition, persons in the vicinity of smokers become passive smokers as they unwittingly breathe secondary smoke and suffer unhealthy reactions to it. Spouses of smokers have a 30 percent higher risk of lung cancer than spouses of nonsmokers. In particular jeopardy are young children who demonstrate health problems in increasing numbers after exposure to secondary smoke inflicted upon them by adults. Children of smokers are hospitalized at twice the rate of children of nonsmokers for pneumonia, bronchitis and asthma. Also, children of smokers take up the habit at twice the rate of children of nonsmokers, perpetuating the problem.

The media emphasizes the role of cholesterol in the heart disease epidemic. What you don't hear enough about in the headlines is the harmful effect of smoking on your arteries, which statistics from the Framingham study over the past 20 years have confirmed.

❦ **Smokers double their risk of heart disease and have a 70 percent greater chance of dying of a heart attack than nonsmokers.**

The risk increases with the number of cigarettes smoked daily. The chance of dying in any given year for men who smoke more than a pack a day is almost double that of men who smoke half a pack. While smoking has dropped substantially in the United States overall, women and teenagers continue to smoke at an alarmingly higher rate. It is estimated that half of all heart attacks in women under 55 are related to smoking, and smoking "light" cigarettes does not appear to lower the mortality rates. In addition, smoking aggravates other risk factors you may have, increasing your chances of developing heart disease.

Although we are not sure how smoking affects the arteries, it is likely that smoking releases into the bloodstream a substance that damages the lining of the coronary arteries, making them more susceptible to cholesterol deposits. We do know that smoking decreases helpful HDL and also aggravates hypertension, which in itself increases your risk of coronary artery disease, trapping your heart in a vicious cycle. Women who both smoke *and* use oral birth control, increase their risk 39 times the rate of nonsmokers who don't use oral contraceptives.

However, we have great news for ex smokers. While studies show that active smokers die from heart disease at a faster rate than do nonsmokers, within two to three years of quitting, ex smokers have no more risk of heart disease than people who never smoked. In fact, by quitting, smokers can decrease their risk of heart attacks 50 to 70 percent compared to people who continue to smoke. In addition, stopping smoking can increase your HDL by 10 to 15 percent. This is significant, because a 1 percent increase in HDL equals a 3.5 percent lowering of coronary heart disease risk.

The easiest way to handle smoking, of course, is don't ever start. However, if you do smoke, it pays to quit, though we don't want to minimize the difficulty of actually abandoning a smoking habit that has you in its grip. If you find it hard to kick the habit, help is available. For many people, the buddy system works, and statistics show that support groups have a high rate of success in helping people quit smoking permanently. Many people find the patch method effective. However, in one study that followed ex-smokers, 90 percent reported they quit without treatment or group support, and the smoking rate in the United States continues to drop, proving that many approaches work. Stick with your determination to quit; even if it takes several attempts. Make a daily resolution to keep looking until you find the support and motivation to give up smoking for good. Your physician can assist you.

There are new medications available that can help supply nicotine to your system during the difficult transition period. If you are one of those who smoke because you believe it calms you, remember that many other stress-reducing measures provide a more healthful relaxation response, such as biofeedback, relaxation/visualization exercises, physical exercise, yoga and meditation. Seek diversion in creative outlets such as art, gardening or some other consuming interest. If you believe smoking helps you control your weight, realize that many, many slender people do not smoke. Look for a weight-control support group to help lose unwanted pounds, rather than depending on cigarettes for weight control. If you are a smoker with children, and quit, you will serve as an important role model in helping them resist any temptation to take up the habit.

Maintain a Normal Blood Pressure

Because it can persist without symptoms, hypertension, or high blood pressure, is called the silent epidemic. More than 60 million Americans have high blood pressure, and many of those persons do not know it. Have your blood pressure checked regularly. The greatest risk of high blood pressure is the potential for stroke as well as heart disease, but it can also lead to kidney failure if it is not brought under control. The link between high blood pressure, high cholesterol levels and a high risk of heart disease is clearly demonstrated in every study done to track this dangerous combination. The numbers show that cholesterol levels tolerable in nonhypertensive individuals can be lethal in those with high blood pressure. The risk of stroke from high blood pressure is even greater than that for heart disease, though reducing blood pressure seems to give you a statistically better chance of heading off a stroke than heart disease.

Your blood pressure shows how hard your heart has to work to keep blood flowing through the arteries, much the way rpms indicate the efficiency of an engine. A comfortably low blood pressure taken at rest indicates that the heart is neither straining itself as it does its work, nor damaging the arteries with overly powerful surges of blood. Generally, a blood pressure higher than 140/90 is a cause for concern because it adds to the risk of developing early coronary heart disease, presumably by damaging the lining of these coronary arteries, which then sets the stage for plaque to develop.

Evidence seems to indicate that even when treatment to lower blood pressure is effective, the risk of heart attack does not always return to the level of someone with normal blood pressure. Side effects of blood pressure medications may partly offset the benefit of lowering blood pressure by additionally increasing the risk of heart disease. Drugs known as beta blockers and thiazide diuretics, which have commonly been used in the past to treat high blood pressure, have been shown to raise blood cholesterol and LDL cholesterol and/or to lower HDL cholesterol. Newer blood pressure medicines, such as calcium blockers and ACE inhibitors, do not have these same adverse effects on cholesterol and appear less likely to promote coronary heart disease.

Consult your physician to determine your target blood pressure. When blood pressure is brought under control, the risk of heart attack drops approximately 2 to 3 percent for each 10 point decrease in the systolic or diastolic blood pressure. Also, studies seem to indicate that when total cholesterol is maintained at lower than 160, the potential for hypertension to accelerate coronary artery plaque deposits is lessened. This is another example of the way these risk factors are interconnected, and underscores the fact that the cumulative effect of reducing as many risk factors as possible gives you the best protection against heart disease.

Pass the Salt?

Every cook worth his or her salt knows the power of those sodium crystals, but everyone has heard warnings to cut out salt. Consequently, many people pass on salt because they believe it causes heart trouble. Actually, there is no direct relation between salt and cholesterol blockage. Salt does not cause heart disease. But if you have high blood pressure will salt make it worse? That depends. Of the more than 60 million Americans with high blood pressure, only approximately 25 percent are salt sensitive; that is, salt or, more accurately, sodium, will cause their blood pressure to rise. The other 75 percent of hypertensive patients suffer little effect from salt used in moderation. Most blood pressure–lowering drugs are so effective now that these lucky individuals can control hypertension without having to eat a salt-free diet.

Why, then, is salt under attack if it does not *cause* disease? Because excessive sodium can have harmful effects for some people, and there is a lot of it sneaking into commercial foods. We should make the distinction here that salt and sodium are not the same. Salt contains sodium as well as other minerals. Sodium, however, the element that triggers problems for some people, is found in many foods, not just salt. If you are one of the 25 percent with hypertension, or if hypertension runs in your family and you are salt sensitive, then salt in excessive or even moderate quantities (e.g., eating salted chips every day) may cause your blood pressure to rise. As we have just shown, if your blood pressure stays elevated above this level, your risk for stroke and heart attack increases. Lowering your blood pressure by medication, weight reducing, exercise and, if you are salt sensitive, cutting down on salt, lowers your risk for these problems. Salt may also hurt patients with advanced heart disease, especially if they suffer heart failure after one or more heart attacks. In this situation, salt can cause fluid accumulation in the lungs, making it harder to breathe and causing the feet and legs to swell. Although medicine such as diuretics can help to remove the fluid, sodium restriction also helps these persons.

❧ **The American Heart Association recommends healthy individuals limit sodium to 3,000 milligrams per day.**

As a rule, sensible salting of food to enhance the flavor will cause no problems and allow you to stay within this recommendation. So what about all the no-salt warnings for healthy people? Even people with normal blood pressure readings, however, experience water retention, uncomfortable bloating or unpleasant thirst when they consume too much salt. However, the salt shaker on the table isn't the culprit.

Where Does the Excess Salt Come From?

Too much salt in the diet usually equals too many processed foods, which are overloaded with salt. If you want to keep excessive salt to a reasonable minimum and still enjoy your food, pass up packaged foods, the salty snacks, soups and convenience items. Then, unless your physician has recommended that you limit salt, at mealtime you can feel free to say, "Pass the salt." As a convenience, we have indicated sodium content of our recipes for salt-sensitive individuals. In addition, always check the sodium content on packaged foods, particularly if it is a problem for you.

Maintain Your Ideal Weight

When you look at the scientific evidence, obese people—those who are 30 percent or more over their ideal weight—suffer heart attacks at a much higher rate than lean folks. In addition, extreme obesity leads to hypertension and diabetes, both of which increase the risk of heart disease, and all three form a deadly web that threatens the individual's general health. In addition, recent research from Harvard shows that even modest weight gain early in life can increase the risk of heart disease in women. Finally, it goes without saying that everyone feels better when they believe they look trim. Research shows that for every two-pound increase of excess body fat, you experience an average of one milligram increase in total cholesterol.

Dr. Peter Wood of Stanford has demonstrated that maintaining normal weight also helps to keep healthy HDL levels normal, and losing excess pounds drives low HDL levels up, adding further protection from heart disease. Overweight men who lose weight either by dieting or exercising consistently show up to a 15 percent or approximate six-point increase in HDL levels. Weight loss also lowers the harmful LDL to safer levels. Dr. Wood states that dieting and exercise are equally effective; it is the weight loss that lowers LDL, not the method you use to achieve it.

❧ **People who maintain an ideal body weight can lower their risk of heart disease 35 to 55 percent compared to people who are 20 percent or more over their desirable weight.**

If you have trouble losing unwanted pounds, consult a weight-loss professional, such as a registered dietitian, your physician or a weight-loss clinic sponsored by a reputable health maintenance organization. Be wary of quick-loss schemes that will definitely slim your wallet, but not necessarily your waistline. People on weight-loss regimens are almost doomed to regain lost pounds if they do not include regular exercise as part of the program. If you struggle to maintain your optimal weight, take encouragement from the fact that most people say that the combination of losing pounds and keeping them off is the hardest enterprise they undertake, but one of the most worthwhile. In addition, keep reminding yourself that the goal is possible. With the right approach, millions do lose weight and keep it off.

We recommend that you use The Stanford 25 Gram Plan initially to switch from high-fat foods to low-fat, high-fiber foods, rather than focusing on eliminating calories and suffering the feelings of deprivation that inevitably drive people to seek comfort in the refrigerator. Embark on an exercise program and once you have become used to eating lower-fat foods, with sufficient calorie intake to guard against constant hunger pangs, you may notice that these two measures will have begun to whittle away the pounds without drastic dieting.

Exercise Regularly

The connection between regular exercise and good health grows stronger with every study that investigates this crucial component of a healthy lifestyle. People who exercise reduce their risk of heart disease by approximately 45 percent, while over 30 studies performed in the past 40 years indicate that lack of exercise predisposes people to heart disease.

❧ **In fact, the American Heart Association has included lack of exercise as a definite risk factor for coronary heart disease.**

A sedentary lifestyle contributes to obesity, compounding the problem because obesity also increases your risk of heart disease. Moderate exercise at frequent and regular intervals controls weight, develops muscle strength, increases endurance and reduces stress. But this exercise also seems to offer added protection from heart disease by raising healthy HDL cholesterol levels. Exercise builds muscle, which is metabolically active, as opposed to fat, which is not. This means that muscle requires—and burns up—calories that might otherwise get stored as fat. In addition:

- Exercise activates the enzymes that increase HDL production as the muscles contract. The more exercise performed, the more enzyme is produced and the greater the welcome hike in the HDL level.
- Exercise also helps control high blood pressure, important for the hypertensive patient.
- Exercise keeps the heart muscle strong and also seems to decrease the stickiness of platelets, which makes them less likely to form dangerous blood clots.
- Exercise not only burns calories to help you lose weight, but as you exercise over time and increase muscle mass, your body's metabolism will burn more calories even while resting, making weight control easier.
- Exercise encourages the brain to produce more endorphins, the substances responsible for our ability to experience pleasure, giving you a natural high.

You don't have to train for a marathon to boost your HDL. Moderate exercise will increase these important levels, though for the average healthy person more is better. Elderly persons and those with special medical problems should only pursue more vigorous exercise under the supervision of their physicians. Almost any exercise will do, as long as it is done continuously for 30 minutes every day. From a daily walk, bike ride or tennis game to a rigorous aerobic and weight-training program, all exercise benefits your heart, lungs, muscles, nerves, curves and overall feeling of well-being. If you prefer, choose an inside exercise such as riding on a stationary bike or walking on a treadmill. Start slowly and commit to a daily routine, such as a brisk walk, a fast-dance session with your favorite partner or an aerobic tape workout.

Initiating an exercise program is sometimes harder than maintaining it, once you get into the habit of taking your daily walk or aerobic class. Many people say, even as they are walking out the door to take their daily hike, "I don't want to do this." But as they get lost in thought while jogging or bike riding, the momentum keeps them going. Even if they experience some resistance to getting a session started, *no one* finishes a workout complaining, "I wish I hadn't done that. I didn't need to feel this good today!" If you doubt it, notice how people brag about how far they walked or ran over the weekend, or how fast they cycled compared to the previous week. Become one of them.

Other Risks
Certain people have other risks shown to be linked to heart disease, and may need to:

CONTROL DIABETES MELLITUS Studies show a link between diabetes and heart disease, though the cause of the relationship is not altogether clear. Diabetics must follow their physicians' recommendations for diet and medication to keep diabetes under control. Juvenile and adult-onset diabetics have evidence of more plaque development and a higher rate of heart attacks than individuals without diabetes. Diabetics also show consistently higher total cholesterol levels and higher rates of lethal LDL than otherwise normal individuals. Dr. Gerald Reaven at Stanford has demonstrated that, in a highly complex process, insulin resistance and higher insulin levels are linked to development of atherosclerotic plaque. This is particularly important, since some of the medications used to treat high blood pressure, such as thiazide diuretics and beta blockers, tend to raise insulin resistance in patients with high blood pressure, possibly aggravating the tendency to plaque development.

MINIMIZE EXCESSIVE STRESS Studies indicate that too much stress can raise cholesterol levels in people with documented evidence of heart disease, though it does not appear actually to cause atherosclerosis in an otherwise healthy person. Excessive stress definitely contributes to high blood pressure, which increases risk, to say nothing of diminishing the quality of life. For people with evidence of heart disease, a more relaxed lifestyle appears to act as a protective buffer for your heart. We recognize that stress is hard to measure and harder to do anything about. If stress is hard for you to control, adopting a healthier diet is doubly important. Bear in mind also, that one of the many benefits of our recommendation to exercise regularly is that it is a proven stress reducer. In addition, you may want to investigate biofeedback, meditation, relaxation exercises and/or yoga as aids to a calmer state of mind.

What About Genes?

All studies show that genetics play a big role in heart disease risk, positively and negatively. For example, if your close family members—parents, aunts, uncles and grandparents—tend to have heart attacks before age 65, then your risk of a premature heart attack is greater than someone who has no family history of this type of heart disease.

Genetic factors that we don't fully understand seem to predispose certain individuals to develop plaque, in part by influencing the levels of LDL and HDL. A small number of families with low heart disease rates, for example, have been identified with abnormally high (in the 200 range) levels of HDL. These groups are of great interest to researchers because their chemistry may hold the clue to understanding how we can help everyone produce more of this valuable component. On the other hand, among the inheritable genes appears to be one that may predispose you for hypercholesterolemia or abnormally high LDL cholesterol. If you have a genetic predisposition to heart disease, then the presence of any other risk factor compounds the threat.

You can't reach into the past and change your genetic coding. People who are genetically susceptible to high cholesterol levels and heart attacks at an early age, though, represent a relatively small number of those of us who are at risk. Even if your genes work against you, you can neutralize this risk as much as possible by following all the other measures we recommend to combat the production of plaque.

Estrogen Replacement Therapy for Postmenopausal Women

As we have discussed earlier, premenopausal women have a much lower risk for coronary heart disease than men, apparently because the female hormones raise HDL cholesterol and lower total and LDL cholesterol. Estrogen may also exert other stabilizing effects on the artery wall. Many observational studies have shown a link between estrogen replacement and increased protection from heart attack. Recent reports from the Nurse's Health Study, a ten-year study of almost 49,000 nurses in the United States, reported a 49 percent lower risk of coronary heart disease in women using estrogen replacement. These impressive results showing that estrogen provides additional preventive therapy have been nearly universally accepted and will be discussed in the following chapter on Women and Heart Disease.

What About Medications to "Cure" Atherosclerosis?

Researchers have worked diligently to understand the mechanisms that damage arteries and to find new ways to keep the heart healthy. Everyone hopes there will someday be a medication that effectively dissolves cholesterol plaque. But scientists point out that medications or other welcome measures may help relieve some symptoms of heart disease and future research may even explain its cause and effect. But these advances will *not* relieve us of the necessity of promoting healthy arteries or controlling the spread of the disease once it has started by monitoring our diet, giving up smoking and the other heart-healthy measures that we will discuss in following chapters.

Daily Aspirin

Although most of us think of aspirin as a minor pain or headache medication, we have known for many years that aspirin affects blood clotting. Research has shown that in adults even a small child's dose (80 milligrams) of aspirin daily makes the platelets (an essential piece of our blood clotting machinery) less sticky and therefore less likely to form clots. The final event in the sequence that ends in a heart attack is the blood clot forming on top of an atherosclerotic plaque deposit and blocking off blood flow to the heart. Therefore aspirin's anticlotting properties may be important in preventing heart attacks. The United States Physicians Health Study of 22,071 men aged 40 to 84 years reported a dramatic 44 percent reduction in risk of a first heart attack in those who took daily aspirin. Since the publication of this research in 1988, most researchers now believe that anyone over 50 years of age with a risk of developing cardiovascular disease should consider taking a daily aspirin. In fact, if you have other cardiovascular risk factors for heart disease, we recommend aspirin to those under 50—after consulting your physician.

Aspirin also may have important preventive effects on other serious diseases. A recent study in the *New England Journal of Medicine* reported on a prospective study of 662,424 adults and found that the death rate from colon cancer was 40 percent less in both men and women who reported taking aspirin 16 times a month or more. Several other studies have reported similar reductions in colon rectal cancer. How the aspirin prevents the cancer isn't clear; however, the results are very impressive!

❧ **What is the correct aspirin dose? No one is sure yet, but most researchers recommend an adult aspirin (325 milligrams) every other day or a baby aspirin (80 milligrams) every day.**

You should check with your physician first, since bleeding tendencies, ulcers or other medical conditions may preclude your taking aspirin. We recommend the enteric coated aspirin, the type with an outer shell that lessens the chance of irritation to the stomach.

Antioxidants and Fiber

Recent research has shown what many people throughout the world have known all along. Plant food is good for us. The benefits of fiber and antioxidants, disease-fighting substances in green and yellow vegetables, are clearly documented. In fact, this aspect of diet-related heart disease prevention is so important, we have devoted a full chapter (beginning on page 145) to a full discussion of its merits.

Who Is Most At Risk—Men, Women, Children or the Elderly?

When it comes to heart disease risk, are all men, women and children created equal? Let's take a look.

Men

Men continue to have the greatest risk of developing premature heart disease under the age of 60. In addition, if a man's father, grandfathers and uncles had heart attacks before the age of 65, then the chances are even greater than average that he is heading for a heart attack, too.

Children

In September 1992, The American Academy of Pediatrics recommended that all children over the age of two years follow the low-fat diet recommended by the NCEP (and endorsed by The Stanford 25 Gram Plan) to prevent heart disease and obesity. This is a change from the diet containing 30 to 40 percent fat previously recommended for children. The academy warned, however, against any fat restrictions in the diets of infants and children under two. Such restrictions in very young children could result in an unhealthy overload of protein and minerals, and they may not get enough calories to maintain normal growth. This means that everyone else in the family should follow The Stanford 25 Gram Plan. Why the attention to children's diets?

As we have already mentioned, autopsies of children and young adults killed in accidents have shown that cholesterol buildup begins in the arteries of even very young children. Recent studies indicate that teenage boys with high cholesterol levels show evidence of early plaque deposits. This tells us that even though the problem may not appear as damage to the heart and arteries until much later in life, the plaque that causes coronary artery disease can and often does begin early and just gets worse with age.

Also, it seems the apple doesn't fall far from the tree. Children whose parents and/or grandparents suffered heart attacks or other symptoms of heart disease before age 55, and whose parents have blood cholesterol levels above 240 milligrams, appear to have an increased risk of heart disease. These children should receive careful monitoring of their cholesterol levels, as well as dietary counseling to limit saturated fat and cholesterol in their foods. Eventually we expect to see the development of national recommendations for children of high-risk adults that will help track early signs of cardiovascular disease, allowing these vulnerable children to develop diet and lifestyle habits that will curb the progress of the disease. Unfortunately, those national recommendations do not yet exist.

The Elderly

Tufts University performed studies that seem to indicate that certain fats remain in the bloodstream twice as long in people over the age of sixty, than in younger folks. This sluggish fat-elimination system may allow components of plaque more time to build up in the arteries and may explain one risk that is age related, since older people do have a higher risk of developing coronary artery disease. However, the beneficial effects of lowering risk factors know no age barrier, and people in their 60s, 70s and 80s just as certainly can reduce their risk and improve the health of their hearts as their younger family members and friends.

Women

So much research recently has focused on women and heart disease, that we have devoted the following chapter to this important subject.

WHAT ARE WE SAYING?

We are saying that, in addition to limiting saturated fat and cholesterol, you can break your other links to heart disease by:

- Not smoking.
- Maintaining a normal blood pressure.
- Maintaining an ideal weight.
- Exercising regularly.
- Increasing dietary fiber and antioxidants.
- Controlling diabetes.
- Minimizing excessive stress.
- Taking a daily aspirin, after consulting with your physician.

TAKE A GUESS

1. How many Americans check the fat content on food labels?
2. How many Americans make sure they only eat the amount of the serving size?
3. How many Americans were aware in 1989 that the Surgeon General had singled out fat as the major problem in the American diet?
4. How many were aware of the above in 1991?
5. How many Americans believe you lower cholesterol by eating less cholesterol?
6. How many believe you lower cholesterol by eating less saturated fat?
7. How many Americans claim to be very careful about their fat consumption?
8. How many know that the National Cholesterol Education Program recommends a maximum total fat intake of 30 percent of calories and a maximum saturated fat intake of 10 percent of calories?
9. What are the four leading sources of total fat in the diets of American women?
10. What are the four leading sources of saturated fat in the diets of American women?
11. What are the four leading sources of cholesterol in the diets of American women?
12. What percentage of Americans know that high LDL cholesterol levels indicate a high risk of heart disease?
13. What percentage of Americans think that food labels list ingredients by weight, from most to least?
14. What percentage think that food labels list ingredients by nutritional importance, from most to least?
15. Which group is correct?
16. How many grams of saturated fat in a Burger King Double Whopper with Cheese?

Answers:

1. 52 percent
2. 1 percent
3. 17 percent
4. 39 percent
5. 34 percent
6. 21 percent
7. 45 percent
8. 7 percent
9. Salad dressing, margarine, cheese and ground beef
10. Cheese, ground beef, whole milk, and beef cuts
11. Eggs, poultry, ground beef, and beef cuts
12. 20 percent
13. 36 percent
14. 37 percent
15. Ingredients are listed by weight
16. 25 grams

CHAPTER 9

Women and Heart Disease

RITA J. APPEARS TO LEAD A CHARMED LIFE. *A fashion model in her 20s, this mother of four and grandmother of six remains a beauty and has to show her driver's license before anyone will believe she is 66. Instead of graying and dulling it with time, nature burnished Rita's coppery hair with glints of gold. Though she has high blood pressure, she controls it with medication. Fit and slender, she has never smoked, and she takes a daily one-hour aerobic walk upon rising before she begins to play—tennis daily, golf two to three times a week and always an evening swim. Her easy smile lights up a room, and the glow in her warm green eyes fairly trumpets good health.*

When she and her husband Hal retired, she convinced him to quit smoking, lose some weight and lower a dangerously high cholesterol level. Worried about Hal's health and his lifelong devotion to rare steaks, ripe cheese and anything made with chocolate, Rita stocked low-fat treats for him and pulled him onto the tennis court with her. As far as her own diet was concerned, she was a calorie counter, but had otherwise always eaten a typical American diet with lots of satu-rated fat. As long as her exercise program kept her weight in check, she allowed herself to eat what she wished. If her weight climbed, she would cut down on calories. Rita's determination to help Hal improve his health habits prevailed. He hasn't had a cigarette in five years, and he shed some extra pounds. When Hal had his cholesterol checked as part of a routine exam, on a whim, Rita did too.

Fifteen years earlier, when Rita last had her cholesterol tested, it was comfort-ably low. Her body was just beginning to shut down the production of estrogen, and at the time any doctor would have predicted that in time she would sail easily into a healthy old age. With Rita's then-normal cholesterol level, their concern would have been for Hal because of his risky eating habits and sedentary lifestyle. In those days, the majority of doctors believed that women just didn't have to worry about heart attacks. When the test results came in, Hal was elated. His cholesterol level had plummeted from 300 to 230. Rita's cholesterol, on the other hand, had soared from the normal 200 range of her early 50s to 270, the range that predicts heart disease and heart attacks. We now understand that Rita's situation is more common than we once thought, though not all women experience her same pattern.

Shortly before her 51st birthday, Sheila F. had a physical that showed no evidence of heart disease. She received regular treatment for asthma, but was in otherwise excellent health. Energetic, involved in her community, she was also an educator of educators. Sheila developed landmark programs at the university level to train teachers in the field of parenting, and she spearheaded training programs for incarcerated mothers to prepare them to resume family life with their children upon their release from jail. In line with that work, she developed advocacy programs to protect children whose parents were in prison. She was herself a devoted wife and mother. While accompanying a youngster in one of her programs to an appointment, she suffered severe pain that seemed to drive a wedge between her shoulder blades. She had noticed more shortness of breath than usual in the days before this episode and had attributed it to her asthma. The pain was intermittent during the day. After dinner with her husband and friends that evening, the pain returned and she retired. She suddenly experienced a massive heart attack and died in her husband's arms. What happened to these women?

Women's Risk of Heart Disease Is as Great as Men's

We used to think that heart disease was primarily a man's disease, since relatively few women have heart attacks prior to menopause. However, the reality is that half of all persons who die of heart disease are women. Statistics show that a 50-year-old woman has a 46 percent chance of developing heart disease. At age 65, cancer typically kills as many women as does heart disease, but at age 75 and up, heart disease exacts the highest toll. In 1991, findings were published from The Nurses Health Study, performed by researchers at Brigham and Women's Hospital in Boston who followed approximately 48,000 female nurses over a period of 10 years.

❧ **Results indicated that the chances a white woman between the ages of 50 and 94 will die of heart attack are 31 percent. The risk of death during these same years from breast cancer, on the other hand, is only 2.8 percent!**

Mainly white women volunteered for the nurses study, but the researchers assume that heart disease risks for all women, regardless of color, are equally high. As shown in the following chart, there is a steady increase in percentage of deaths of women due to coronary heart disease beginning at age 30 to 34 years.

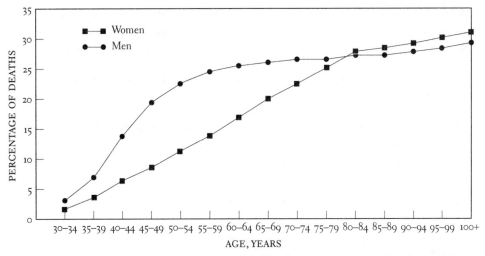

Percentage of male deaths due to ischemic heart disease during 1988 compared with percentage of female deaths due to ischemic heart disease. National Center for Health Statistics.

Why It Took So Long to Uncover Women's Risk

The answer is clear. For decades we didn't know women were at risk simply because we didn't study women. Men show up in emergency rooms with symptoms of heart disease at a much earlier age than women, so we focused on studying heart disease in men. Studies tracking various aspects of the prevention and treatment of heart disease either used men exclusively as subjects or typically observed people of both sexes under the age of 60. Since few women get heart attacks at that age, those studies also seemed to confirm that women had an immunity to heart disease. Now we know that women rapidly "catch up" with men beginning at menopause. More importantly, the concern about breast cancer has diverted attention away from heart disease. Yet, as we see in the chart, at age 50, risk for breast cancer starts falling, whereas risk of heart disease climbs and outnumbers breast cancer.

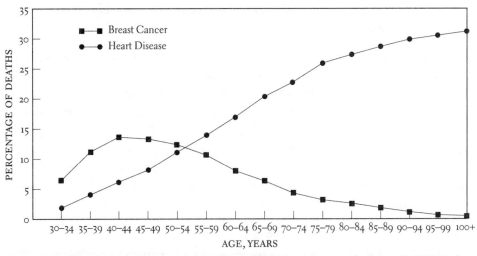

Percentage of deaths due to breast cancer or heart disease in US women during 1988. National Center for Health Statistics.

When Sheila turned 50, like most women, she was not attuned to the fact that she had entered the high-risk zone for heart disease. When she first experienced symptoms, she did not recognize them as the warning signs of heart attack.

❧ The risk of heart disease is the same for men and women—only the timetable differs.

We now know that far too many women experience symptoms of heart attack, some at a relatively early age, and go untreated past a critical point. Heart attacks strike women later in life, and sometimes the symptoms can follow a different pattern, confusing physicians accustomed to the way heart attacks behave in men. Some researchers have reported that women are less likely to have constant chest pain, although for both men and women, it can be in the back, chest and/or shoulder, as well as radiate down the inner arm, the common heart attack warning in men. In addition, both men and women can experience indigestionlike discomfort, nausea and shortness of breath. We already know that some people can suffer heart attacks even though they have normal cholesterol levels. Perhaps if Sheila's pain had followed the pattern commonly known to occur in men (a sudden crushing pain in the chest instead of intermittent pain between the shoulder blades), she might have recognized what was happening to her and called for help.

Unfortunately, as a consequence of the difference in symptoms, studies show that until recently, even when a woman had more severe symptoms than a man, she was less likely to receive the same diagnostic screening, such as an angiogram, that would determine the severity of the situation. Now that the alarm bell has sounded, the National Institutes of Health has acted to make disseminating information to the public about women and heart disease a priority for the future.

Risk Factors for Women
We will get a head start here, by discussing what we do know about women and coronary heart disease: Many of the same risk factors that predict heart disease in men apply to women as well.

SMOKING Smoking is the leading contributor to heart disease in younger women. One study has shown that in women aged 25 to 64 years, smokers were 3.6 times more likely to have a heart attack than nonsmokers, and female hormones no longer seem to be protective in these cases. The good news is that within two to three years after quitting, this increased risk for women disappears. Smoking also aggravates other risk factors for women. *Oral contraceptives increase a woman's susceptibility to heart disease only slightly, but if she smokes and takes the pill, it soars!* Smoking also aggravates any other risk factors a woman may have, such as family susceptibility to heart disease, high cholesterol levels or diabetes.

DIABETES In the United States, over 2 ½ million women have diabetes, and studies have reported that these diabetic women have a greater risk of developing heart disease than men with diabetes. Controlling their diabetes becomes an even more urgent important health issue for these women, because female diabetics have been shown to have high levels of lethal LDL cholesterol in their blood-streams—thus making them even more susceptible to coronary heart disease.

HIGH BLOOD PRESSURE As it is for men, high blood pressure is a very powerful predictor of coronary heart disease and stroke in women. This raises a double concern because strokes are the third leading cause of death in the United States. While the overall death rate from strokes has declined by 33 percent, thanks to better monitoring and treatment, the death rate among women stroke victims is increasing. Each 10 point rise in blood pressure leads to a 20 to 30 percent increase in risk of death from stroke and heart disease. Rita did one thing right. She knew that maintaining a normal blood pressure was crucial for her.

MAINTAINING NORMAL WEIGHT Recent studies have confirmed the need to maintain normal weight. Researchers at Harvard have reported that even modest weight gain early in a woman's life will pose an increased risk for heart attack later in life.

High Cholesterol: How the Message Differs for Women

Rita was also rightly concerned about her husband Hal's high cholesterol. But because research studies have focused primarily on the risk of heart disease in men (especially in the under-65 age group), many questions about the links between women and heart disease remain unanswered. However, there are at least nine studies that point to elevated cholesterol levels as a predictor of coronary heart disease in women. The strongest link is a total cholesterol over 260—much higher than we recommend for anyone—while there is much less risk for women with cholesterol levels under 200, a better target for everyone.

Some of the difficulty in assessing risk for women with cholesterol levels between 200 and 260 is due to the fact that, while a high total cholesterol level in men automatically raises a red flag, the same number can be misleading in women. In general, women tend to have higher levels of the protective healthy HDL cholesterol, and this adds to their total cholesterol score. For example, a woman might have total cholesterol levels of 260 in part because of an HDL reading as high as 100, giving that person an enormous ability to carry harmful cholesterol away from the artery wall. A man, on the other hand, with that same cholesterol reading of 260, is less likely to have as much protective HDL (usually less than 60), and so his high total level would strongly increase the risk of cholesterol plaque in his arteries.

This situation underscores the argument for obtaining a total lipid panel that computes the HDL/total cholesterol ratio, rather than relying on a single number to give a complete picture of an individual's risk of heart disease as we discuss on page 64. We expect future studies to document this crucial relationship. The Framingham study already backs up the importance of high HDL in determining the health of a woman's arteries. It has shown that women with an HDL level of

40 instead of 50 have nearly double the risk for heart problems. In the meantime, we believe there is ample evidence to encourage all women to keep their cholesterol counts under 200 by following The Stanford 25 Gram Plan.

Menopause and the Risk of Heart Disease

From puberty to the onset of menopause, a woman's ovaries produce estrogen at very high levels. Researchers now believe that this output of the female hormone shields her during her reproductive years from the dangerous buildup of plaque in her arteries. They believe that estrogen increases the levels of HDL, the good cholesterol in the bloodstream, and decreases the levels of LDL, the bad cholesterol. However, upon reaching menopause, estrogen levels drop sharply, and we see that women lose this built-in protection. Many researchers and clinicians believe this turning point in a woman's life alters her previously low risk for coronary heart disease.

In fact, The Nurse's Health Study reported that even women who experience early menopause after a hysterectomy that includes removal of the ovaries have a risk for coronary heart disease 1.7 times higher than other women of the same age who have not had the surgery. We pointed out that Rita maintained a safe cholesterol reading as she entered menopause, at a time when research studies had not yet begun to track heart disease in women. Thirteen years later, when she next had her blood lipids checked, we can see clearly what happened when her natural protection deserted her: Her cholesterol climbed into the 270 range, too high for anyone no matter how much protective HDL they carry.

Rita's case points out the importance of regular monitoring of cholesterol levels, especially after menopause. She assumed that once a low cholesterol level, always a low cholesterol level. Cholesterol levels can change over time, especially if there is a major change in lifestyle or general health. As in Hal's case, the change was a positive reflection of healthier habits. Rita, on the other hand, was simply unaware that her low estrogen levels increased her risk of heart disease, and she didn't change her own diet when she changed her husband's. She did most of the right things: She didn't smoke and she exercised regularly. When Rita realized that her father and his brother and sister had died of heart attacks and that her own brother also had an elevated cholesterol level, she knew that her family history also put her at risk. Had she checked her cholesterol routinely after menopause she would have been aware of its gradual rise and taken measures to control it much sooner, certainly before it reached the range where it caused anxiety. By following The Stanford 25 Gram Plan, Rita lowered her cholesterol to safe levels in the course of a few months.

How Estrogen Replacement Reduces Risk

The good news for women is that the increased risk of heart disease no longer exists for women who use estrogen replacement for symptoms of menopause! Several studies have shown the protective effect of estrogen replacement ranging from 10 to 90 percent. In studies evaluating the effect of estrogen replacement on a woman's total health picture, we now see that women who take estrogen also reduce their risk of osteoporosis (thinning of the bones) and show a 60 percent reduced chance of hip fracture. Combined with the benefit to the arteries, this reduction in aging damage to a woman's body makes a strong case for estrogen replacement therapy. By the way, men with high cholesterol levels show no similar benefit from hormone treatment.

It is important to note that a few reports show some women may experience serious side effects from estrogen therapy; among the most talked about is an increased risk for certain cancers. However, most of the reported studies to date have shown little or no increased risk for breast cancer in women who use estrogen. On the other hand, the risk for uterine cancer appears to be increased compared to that of women who don't take estrogen. With this information, you might think it strange that we encourage estrogen replacement.

However, analysis of these studies have clearly shown that the *benefits* of estrogen therapy in reducing your risk for coronary heart disease and preventing hip fractures far outweigh the slightly increased chance of ending up with cancer of the uterus.

Are we saying all women should run to their physician and demand replacement hormone therapy when they reach menopause? As we have stated, the issue is not that simple. However, on the basis of what we know, we do recommend that all women talk to their physicians about the option of long-term estrogen replacement after menopause, and after discussing the ramifications for their own health profiles (including the prevalence of uterine and breast cancer in their families), make an informed decision. If you are a menopausal woman who cannot or prefers not to take estrogen, you must choose other options for protecting yourself from heart disease and osteoporosis: Keep the saturated fat in your diet to a minimum to keep your cholesterol levels low, maintain an exercise program and take calcium supplements to protect your bones. We recommend you follow these measures throughout your life.

Important questions remain for women. If estrogen protects during their reproductive years, does that mean they can indulge in fatty foods before menopause, holding off diet modifications until they know they have stopped manufacturing estrogen? If estrogen therapy reduces a woman's chances of developing heart disease, why do we still encourage premenopausal women to follow The Stanford 25 Gram Plan? Why not just enjoy the natural immunity during your reproductive years and then take hormones? First of all, not all women are candidates for estrogen therapy. As we said earlier, those who do not take hormones must follow a low-fat diet when they reach menopause, and it is harder to change habits at 50 than if they have been established early. It's equally important to remember that diets high in fat have also been strongly linked to increased risk for colon and breast cancer. Therefore, even if you have a low blood cholesterol level and few risk factors in coronary heart disease, these dietary changes we recommend in The Stanford 25 Gram Plan is important for your overall health.

The Future

The medical research community has received a mandate from the National Institutes of Health to ensure that women are equal participants in future studies of disease. This will virtually guarantee that we will have a clearer understanding about the links between women and heart disease in the next decade. As part of the focus on studying heart disease in women, the NIH is studying estrogen replacement therapy as part of the Women's Health Initiative. However, it will be years before we have definitive answers. In the meantime, we will make recommendations for staying healthy based on our best current information.

The Woman as a Role Model

With change and upheaval defining the times, one thing remains constant: In most homes, the woman remains the food buyer and the food preparer, and thereby influences the eating habits and food preferences of her family. As we have stated, the American Academy of Pediatrics now urges all children—boys and girls, over the age of two—to eat a low-fat diet and to continue this program throughout life. As a woman chooses a heart-healthy diet for herself, to guard against developing cholesterol plaque in her own arteries, her children watch and learn from her. As she refuses to stock the cupboard and refrigerator with high-fat snacks and offers the healthy alternatives we recommend, she takes a leading role in the war against heart disease by steering her children away from the major cause of heart attacks—too much saturated fat in the American diet.

WHAT ARE WE SAYING?

- Women's hormones protect them from heart disease during their reproductive years.
- After menopause, a woman's risk of developing heart disease is equal to or possibly even greater than a man's.
- Smoking greatly increases a woman's risk of heart disease.
- Symptoms of heart disease differ between men and women.
- Estrogen replacement therapy after menopause reduces a woman's risk of heart disease and osteoporosis.
- For total health women need to follow The Stanford Life Plan for a Healthy Heart and The Stanford 25 Gram Plan throughout their lives.
- Women must learn to monitor their own risk of heart disease by having their cholesterol tested every five years and more frequently upon reaching menopause. We urge every woman to take the Stanford Heart Disease Self-Assessment Risk Questionnaire and become familiar with her risk factors.

PART TWO

The Stanford 25 Gram Plan

CHAPTER 10

Nutrition for a Healthy Heart: Carbohydrates and Protein

"WHAT'S FOR DINNER?" *When it seems that, every day, more and more of everyone's favorite foods end up on the "bad for you" list, this question can unnerve anyone concerned with maintaining a healthy heart and enjoying mealtime. However, The Stanford 25 Gram Plan looks at mealtime from a different vantage point—the number of delicious and healthy dishes actually stretches much, much longer than the list of items we urge you to restrict. The Fat Tracker's Guide (Part Three) will help you learn how to choose those healthy foods in the healthiest proportions, and as a Fat Tracker you will discover that cutting down on foods with saturated fat doesn't mean cutting them out! You were born with a need to eat, but choosing what you eat is a learning process that begins with the first bite of solid food. Fat-tracking will help you strengthen your link between good food and good health, but first we have to address a question basic to the diet–heart health issue.*

What Kind of Diet Are Humans Supposed to Eat?

Did Mother Nature really have meat in mind when she designed the human diet? Though we know more about the evolution of the human diet today, the question is not new. For almost 2,000 years, "it was generally believed that all foods supply one basic nutriment," as Harold McGee tells us in his excellent book, *On Food and Cooking*. Then in the early 1800s, when mystery and quack theories shrouded our understanding of human nutrition, a researcher named William Prout became the original Fat Tracker, making dietary history by identifying fat as one of the basic nutrients in food. Prout advanced our understanding of nutrition by actually identifying *three* basic nutritional elements, calling them *oleosa*, *albuminosa* and *saccharina*—what we now know as fat, protein and carbohydrates.

In the latter 1800s, arguments raged over what constituted the most healthful diet for humans. Dr. James H. Salisbury believed humans were carnivorous because they had what he called "meat teeth." He also argued that starchy foods "fermented" in the stomach and caused a frightening array of ailments from heart trouble to mental derangement. Meat and more meat (at least he recommended it be lean), followed by lots of hot water to flush out unfermented food products, became his prescription. Salisbury steak, which originated as his formula for a mixture of lean ground meat, endures as the culinary legacy of his protein-packed beliefs. We shudder at what large-scale cholesterol testing of his followers would have revealed.

Several decades later, Dr. John H. Kellogg scorned the Salisbury approach by stating that meat was *not* the food of early man. He reasoned that since many animals didn't eat meat, but instead fed on grains and plants, meat was essentially a predigested end product of vegetable food, contaminated with the animals' own toxins. He stoutly advanced a high-roughage diet and encouraged the population to forego meat. Instead, he insisted, they should take their nourishment directly from the source, the vegetable kingdom and its "chlorophyll grain," to prevent what he also saw as fearsome putrefactive processes from taking place in the intestine, which could apparently produce the same host of physical maladies and mental disorders that concerned Salisbury about starch! A century later, fiber and carbohydrates remain crucial to a healthy diet, but today we don't have to make wild guesses about their role.

And the evolutionary question? Did we start out as meat eaters or plant eaters? What we do know is that we have neither the massive jaws nor the long, sharp, fang-like incisors that carnivorous animals need to tear apart and chew their prey. Nor do we have the body metabolism to handle large amounts of fat. Our teeth and jaw structures instead resemble those of creatures who don't eat meat. To further bolster the argument that the human engine was not designed to run on animal fuel, other primates, such as monkeys, rarely eat meat and have much lower cholesterol levels and rates of heart disease. Yet, if we feed those monkeys a typical American diet with large amounts of saturated fat and cholesterol, their cholesterol levels rise dramatically and lead to the same plaque deposits found in humans.

❦ **Perhaps an urgent food shortage at some point in our evolutionary journey made us hunters as well as gatherers; maybe it was simple curiosity.**

In any case, many researchers conclude that whatever evolutionary detour led us to the first barbecue, we went astray when we began gnawing on meat, because the average human body, in particular the heart and arteries as we have shown, cannot cope with the high concentration of saturated fat we cram into it. As far as heart disease was concerned, it didn't really matter whether meat was part of the prehistoric human diet since overnutrition (taking in more calories than you expend) was never a problem. Before any sort of technology came along, the demands of mere survival worked off everyone's excess fat-calories. As far as the modern diet is concerned, the answer to this evolutionary speculation may help us pinpoint the start of our trouble with dietary fat. But as we struggle today to find healthful and pleasurable ways of nourishing ourselves amidst complex health issues and deeply ingrained food habits and traditions, to eat meat or not to eat meat is not a simple question. Environmentalists raise a legitimate concern that dependency on food harvested from animals drains the earth's resources, while some people have deeply held convictions that prevent them from using animals for food. Both camps fortify their arguments with the ample evidence that humans can live successfully on vegetarian nutrition.

We may never be able to read nature's original intent for us. But at Stanford we recognize that at this point in time, the Western world — with its diverse tastes and carefully defined culinary histories — will most likely never totally purge its diet of this major food source and revert, if indeed we ever were herbivores, to strictly vegetarian delicacies. Evidence shows that even though some people in this country do not choose to eat animal protein, a meat-free diet simply doesn't mesh with the way most Americans, indeed most Westerners, like to live and eat. Any successful approach to maintaining a healthy diet therefore has to maintain the important links between food, ritual and pleasure that all people need when they sit down to break bread.

❧ Tearing people away from favorite foods and labeling them "bad" has not proved a successful tactic in any long-term dietary program dedicated to either prevention of heart disease or weight control.

Our intent is to provide you with a framework for choosing foods that are as enjoyable and familiar as they are healthy. That means that we must find a place for meat and dairy products on the menu, yet find a balance between the diverse food preferences that we find in this country and the medical imperative of cutting out saturated fat. To help Americans curb excessive consumption of meat and whole-milk dairy products, we developed The Stanford 25 Gram Plan and Fat Tracker's Guide, an eating plan for life with food truly worth living for.

The Stanford 25 Gram Plan and Fat Tracker's Guide

Though the core of our plan is the 25-gram limit we place on the saturated fat you consume each day, The Stanford 25 Gram Plan and Fat Tracker's Guide gives you more than just a target; we tell you how to reach it. If the task is to restrict saturated fat, you have to know what it is, where you find it, how to measure it and how to find alternatives to it, before you can begin stripping it from your meals. And that brings us up against the real challenge in a heart disease prevention program: meshing lifestyle concerns with the need for a healthy diet.

After all, almost everyone is on a fast track these days. And even though everybody wants to stay healthy, we understand that nobody wants to change cooking styles to accommodate a new "diet" or to sift through mountains of low-fat cookbooks for one or two good recipes that they and their families *might* enjoy eating. Children want tasty after-school snacks, *now*, mom. Teenagers — whose growth spurts, energy levels and athletic commitments can consume thousands of calories every day—are hungry for food that will keep them from complaining, "There's never anything good to eat in the house." People have birthday parties to attend, holidays to celebrate, vacations to take and occasional chocolate-driven impulses to satisfy—the normal dietary peaks and valleys of a lifetime. The Stanford 25 Gram Plan and Fat Tracker's Guide will help you maneuver around all of your concerns by providing you with the equipment to stay anchored to *our* heart-healthy recommendations and enjoy meals and snacks based on *your* choices and needs.

We Will Teach You to Become a Fat Tracker

If the term "fat tracking" conjures up images of Sherlock Holmes sleuthing his way through a maze of clues with an oversized magnifying glass, that is only part of what we intend. Our world is becoming more and more fat conscious. But not everything we eat comes with a label that indicates exactly how much saturated fat the food contains. We have to learn to trim down and count up saturated fat for ourselves by relying on nutritional tables, ingredients and fat content per portion listed on product labels and dietary information that is sometimes included with recipes. Whether you follow The Stanford 25 Gram Plan or struggle to limit fat on your own, you have to find some way of tallying up the fats in your food every day so you can keep them to a minimum. When nutritional information is available to you, you can simply add up the grams of saturated fat you eat and stop at 25.

But accurate information isn't always handy when you are making a food choice. As yet, fresh meat, poultry and fish don't come with product labels that list healthy portions; not all recipes calculate their fat and cholesterol content for you. Product labels are better at telling you how much fat a serving contains, but restaurant menus rarely even try. When you are reaching for peanuts at a party, you can't see any fat, but you know they have them. On the other hand, some of the fat in well-marbled meat and poultry is visible, but not all of it. And how do you identify hidden fats, such as the fat in prawns or a scoop of cottage cheese or a slice of cake? How do you determine if the fat you are eating is harmful or healthy? Even if you have the best dietary information on hand, it doesn't help you turn a smaller and therefore healthier portion of red meat into a delicious and satisfying meal for your family.

This is where The Fat Tracker's Guide comes in. First we simplified the nutritional guidelines for you, then we designed the Fat Tracker's Guide to help you identify, track down and tally every gram of saturated fat you eat to stay under the 25-gram limit. The Fat Tracker's Guide will help you move easily and deliciously in the world of low saturated-fat eating by teaching you to become a fat expert. You will learn how to manage every aspect of dietary fat—from understanding the urgency of controlling the fat in your diet as you learn the relationship between protein, carbohydrates, fats and your heart to discovering how to bake the best chocolate cake that contains the fewest harmful fats. We will show you how to calculate the amount of fat in each portion of that cake and count up the grams of saturated fat you eat during the day so you can stop before you reach 25. The

Stanford 25 Gram Plan and Fat Tracker's Guide leads you step by step to a healthier diet by keeping you focused on all the routes fat can use to gain entry into your arteries. Then you can regulate the amount of fat, both harmful and helpful, that creeps into your food as you buy, cook, order and eat it, and keep fat to the maximum 25 grams we recommend. You will learn to:

- Fat track nutritional information
- Fat track with your Fat Account
- Fat track your meal plan
- Fat track in the supermarket
- Fat track in restaurants
- Fat track your kitchen
- Fat track your favorite dishes
- Fat track our recipes

Fat tracking starts with understanding the building blocks of a healthy diet.

Fat Tracking Nutritional Information

Modern dietetic science has led us out of the nutritional dark ages. Although quack theories about health and diet still abound — witness diets that insist we not mix foods or allow only fruit or only raw food or, in the case of the obscure breathetarians, apparently no food at all — we understand a great deal about the intricate relationship between our food and the health of our bodies.

Prout's original classifications of carbohydrates, protein and fat still hold up, of course. Just as red, yellow and blue (the primary colors of the spectrum) form all other colors, we now know that carbohydrates, fat and protein are the primary building blocks of the human diet. Scientists have enlarged upon Prout's breakthrough, determining the role of this nutritional big three in human health and making important discoveries about amino acids, nitrogen, oxygen and vitamins. Researchers have long debunked lopsided notions about nutrition such as those inspired by Salisbury and Kellogg. The dietary challenge everyone faces today comes down to a simple balancing act: eating the healthiest ratio of fat, protein *and* carbohydrates. The Stanford 25 Gram Plan, following the guidelines of the National Cholesterol Education Program, defines that daily ratio as follows:

An Ideal Diet Equals:

- 20 to 30 percent fat
- 15 to 20 percent protein
- 50 to 60 percent carbohydrates

The Stanford 25 Gram Plan will now help you use these numbers to design healthy and appetizing meals. The first step is to understand what a healthy diet means. Designing a healthy diet would be a simple matter if you could just take the percentage chart to the supermarket and ask for a pound of complex carbohydrates and a few ounces of unsaturated fat and lean protein, please. But we rarely consume those nutrients in straight doses. Most foods contain a combination of these crucial nutritional elements. Legumes, for example, have a trace of fat along with protein and carbohydrates, and beef contains both protein and fat. A few foods, sugar for instance, are composed of pure carbohydrate. Prepare any recipe, your favorite dessert, soup, snack, salad or entrée, for example, and you will see further combinations of protein, fat and carbohydrates.

In addition, humans add a level of complexity by demanding a high percentage of pleasure from their food, as well as good nutrition. So you fill your shopping cart on one day with beef, soy sauce, chicken, cookies, white wine, lima beans and bread; on another with pretzels, broccoli, cottage cheese, pasta, frozen fish sticks and beer; while another time you might shop for canned soup, salad makings, apples and a chocolate bar. All of these foods will nourish you, and even perhaps add (in the case of the pizza and pretzels) a rallying point for a gathering of good friends — certainly as much an ingredient for good health as a proper diet.

But how do all these foods measure up to the ideal ratio? Do you have too much protein, not enough fiber? Will you transform these foods into meals low enough in overall fat so you can munch on the occasional chocolate bar without fear of sabotaging your arteries? If you are a healthy adult, you don't have to scratch any of your favorite foods off your shopping list. But you do need to know how often they should show up in your shopping cart to give you the healthiest ratio of nutrients. We will begin your fat tracking education by explaining how each of the three basic elements — fat, carbohydrates and protein — contributes to your overall health, so you can begin to understand the significance of all your food choices.

Carbohydrates

The fuel from carbohydrates is what makes the body feel most alive and energetic. Carbohydrates are the starches and sugars found in vegetables, fruits and grains; the lactose in milk, a sugar, is the only carbohydrate found in animal products. Carbohydrates provide bulk in our diet, which gives us in turn a satisfying sense of fullness as we eat. Then the body converts carbohydrate calories into our main source of fuel, primarily glucose, and sends it through the bloodstream to feed every last cell.

Without sufficient carbohydrates, your body would convert protein into energy, the cause of malnutrition in regions plagued by famine. Like a high-performance engine, the body burns carbohydrate fuel so efficiently that few of those calories end up as fat. The runners of the 60s and 70s, who made jogging such a popular sport today, experimented with diets that would boost their endurance. They quickly recognized the energy potential of carbohydrates to give them stamina and coined the term "carbo loading," the practice of minimizing fat and protein in favor of eating a big meal of pasta and potatoes the night before a long run.

SIMPLE CARBOHYDRATES These include fruit, honey, table sugar processed from cane or beet sugar, molasses and corn syrup, and contain mostly sugar and little other nutrition. The body doesn't have to work very hard to break down simple carbohydrates and convert them into glucose, and can send these aptly named "empty calories" into the bloodstream for a quick burst of energy. As we indicated in an earlier chapter, sugar concerns the Fat Tracker because when sugar reaches the bloodstream rapidly, it calls forth an increased amount of insulin from the pancreas, and the insulin in turn increases the liver's production of triglyceride-rich lipoproteins, a form of lethal LDL cholesterol. Though we are unsure about the exact mechanism, we do know that triglycerides play a role in coronary artery disease, and because of their connection to blood sugar, we recommend eliminating any unnecessary sugar from the diet. However, as you will see in our recipes, we will sometimes add a bit of sugar to increase the appeal of a fat-reduced dish, because it does not have the same harmful consequences as fat and adds few calories. It is the copious additions in processed foods and sweets that seriously jeopardize the teeth, waistlines and other parts of the human body.

COMPLEX CARBOHYDRATES Found in vegetables and grains, these are starches that also contain fiber and many other nutrients, as well. Because of the fiber content and makeup of these carbohydrates, the body has to work harder to break them down. Thus the glucose from these calories feeds into the bloodstream more slowly, allowing a more stable blood sugar, which you experience as a steady flow of energy. The brain and nervous system rely solely on fuel from carbohydrates; other organs can use fuel from fats. The body accepts and burns up all carbohydrates, whether in the form of cooked vegetables or fresh salad, whole wheat bread or pasta made from white flour, an apple or a doughnut. But as with all foods, some carbohydrate foods have more to offer us than others. For example those with high amounts of processed sugar, such as candy, don't help us. However, those complex carbohydrates, such as grains and produce, with high ratios of fiber, less processed sugar and more vitamins and minerals are essential to our health.

Carbohydrates, long considered to be a major source of calories, have been given a bad name among dieters for decades. On the surface, it would seem that because weight control is important to the health of your heart, we might recommend that you go easy on carbohydrates. However, as we have just pointed out— and the long distance runners discovered through experience—calories from complex carbohydrates get burned first, fast and efficiently.

❧ But equally important to a heart-healthy diet, carbohydrates are the only source of the fiber, vitamins and other nutrients the body needs for all its functions, including heart disease prevention.

If you don't eat enough plant food, you may suffer deficiencies in the B vitamins (found in grains, bread and pasta), vitamin C (in citrus fruits), the A vitamins (in green and yellow vegetables), and the antioxidant properties of a variety of fruits and vegetables.

Because the carbohydrates in processed foods, such as cereals, cookies and pastries, may be sugar coated and drenched in hydrogenated fat, and because so much fiber and nutrition is stripped from vegetables, grains and fruits during processing, modern Americans eat almost half the complex carbohydrates and twice the fat as their turn-of-the-century counterparts!

For many Americans, sugar now comprises up to 70 percent of their carbohydrate intake, while in many European countries, on the other hand, people maintain healthy diets that are upwards of 75 to 80 percent complex carbohydrate. The Stanford 25 Gram Plan reverses the American trend, making low-fat, high-fiber foods such as pasta and breads (especially those made from whole grains, vegetables and fruits) the cornerstone of a heart-healthy diet. We place no actual limit on complex-carbohydrate foods provided they are not mixed with fat, as in potato chips and chocolate bars. If you are on a reduced-calorie program for weight control, make sure that your vegetables do not have oil added, that your bread is not coated with butter or margarine, and that your pasta is not richly sauced.

Protein

Its very name (from *proteios*, the Greek for primary) signals the importance of protein to the human body. All organs, tissues and bodily functions depend on protein. Yet of all the nutritional components of food, none is as misunderstood by the general public. Protein in all living things is formed from a combination of various amino acids. Many amino acids exist, with names such as lysine, leucine, tryptophan. But to make a complete protein, the human body uses 22 amino acids, 9 of which are essential and must come from our diet because our bodies cannot manufacture them. All 22 are found in animal products. Various plant foods contain some, but not all, the essential amino acids humans need, so they are incomplete proteins. However, when fed a meal of the correct combinations of complementary vegetable and grain proteins, the body can demonstrate its superb adaptability by making complete protein from the sum of those parts. Otherwise, people from lands with limited supplies of animal protein would not survive. Otherwise, strict vegetarians would not survive. Otherwise, children who refuse at times to eat nothing but peanut butter and jelly sandwiches would not survive, since the peanut butter and bread form a complete protein.

❧ That protein is "muscle food," capable of providing energy and muscle mass, is the American protein myth.

As a result, misguided athletes—both professional and weekend varieties—consume protein powders and supplements and load up on red meat in the belief that protein will build muscles and make them stronger. Athletes also often assume a big steak will help them perform better, providing extra energy during competition or a workout. But protein is an inefficient energy source, like asking a five-horsepower motor to haul a two-ton trailer. Many people, athletes and couch potatoes alike, erroneously believe that they need to pile on the protein in order to stay strong and healthy.

Without going into the biochemical details, protein literally keeps you alive. From growing nails, hair and tissue, to controlling fluid balance in the cells, to keeping nerve endings functioning, protein is involved in every aspect of tissue building, repair and maintenance. But it won't make muscles bigger. Muscles get their bulk from exercise that pumps them up, not from eating a huge steak for dinner every night. Protein will provide some energy, but it won't give that boost you want when you exercise or compete. Carbohydrates, as we have just explained, do that. So why do people think they must load up on protein to stay fit? Because some of the myths surrounding nutrition and fitness have been around so long that people regard them as gospel. As a result, and because Americans in general just eat more of everything, many people consume 90 to 100 grams of protein per day, almost twice as much as they need.

Figuring Your Protein Quota

To determine how many grams of protein you need each day, multiply your body weight by 0.36. For example, a 180-pound man needs 64.8 grams of protein (180 x 0.36 = 64.8). A 120-pound woman needs 43.2 grams. Women who are pregnant or nursing, because they are providing for themselves and the baby, need about 30 grams more protein every day than nonpregnant women. Nursing mothers should add an extra 20 grams of protein to their diet every day until their children are weaned. Children, because they are growing and building tissue, also need more protein.

What's wrong with eating a protein-rich diet? For starters, many protein foods are often high-fat foods. In addition, the body stores excess protein as fat. You need adequate protein daily, but once the body uses what it needs, it will not store what's left over for its protein needs tomorrow. If you are not an athlete, or otherwise very active individual, and don't burn off excess protein, a high-protein diet will contribute to weight gain. Feeding yourself excess protein is an example of forcing the body to turn gold into straw. So eating an extra serving of steak because you think it helps your workout won't give you bigger muscles, but it can give you bigger hips, thighs and belly, and boost your risk of heart disease because that steak comes loaded with saturated fat.

❧ **If you eat a variety of low-fat foods, protein deficiency is the least of your worries.**

In addition to providing all the essential amino acids, animal protein offers critical vitamins and minerals that nonmeat sources do not provide as easily or abundantly. So we don't suggest you give up meat products. *However, removing fat from animal foods does not remove protein, so choose low-fat protein foods.* For example, one cup of nonfat milk has as much protein as one cup of whole milk, but without the fat. Chicken without skin contains nearly as much protein as chicken with skin, without the extra fat and cholesterol. Top round, one of our four choices for beef, is as protein-rich as a well-marbled steak, but with half the fat. The Stanford 25 Gram Plan assures you get enough protein, but it doesn't couple it with extra fat.

The Best Protein: Meat or Vegetable?

A myth exists that vegetarian foods do not provide enough protein and that vegetable/grain sources are not as "good" as animal sources. Since the body doesn't store protein, it wants those 9 essential amino acids, and it doesn't care where they come from, as long as they are available at the same time. In other words, your body cannot differentiate between protein from a hefty steak and protein from our White Bean and Tomato Soup with White Bean Pesto (page 366) and a Connemara Scone (page 334), which, when eaten at the same meal, provide a complete protein.

Even those who are not practicing vegetarians derive much of their protein from mixtures of legumes and grains without realizing that many of their normal food choices boost their intake of protein. If your optimum protein quota is, for example, 65 grams per day, you don't have to run out and buy a half pound of steak, the equivalent of 65 grams of protein—and many grams of saturated fat. Many foods disguise their protein content. The bread for your morning toast may contain eggs, also a source of protein. If you order a steaming bowl of vegetable soup containing red beans and some pasta to keep you warm on a cold day, you also get a complete protein, which is as healthy as a hamburger. Spinach lasagna made with nonfat cottage cheese and part skim mozzarella or Parmesan cheese can give you 15 or 20 grams of protein per serving, with much less fat than if you had added ground beef and high-fat cheeses. If you snack on peanut butter and crackers or ice milk or frozen yogurt to satisfy your sweet tooth, you also increase your protein. When you add 75 to 80 grams of pure animal protein to your meals (forgetting that other foods may have already contributed as much as 25 grams or more of hidden protein), you are running on protein (and fat) overload by the time you sit down for dinner.

Is a Vegetarian Diet Better?

If humans can survive on plant foods, does that mean that a vegetarian diet is the path to heart health? Historically, we know that many cultures have survived and even thrived on largely vegetarian fare. From ancient times up to the present, feast and famine have always played a role in determining whether a meal is centered on meat or grains. And of course, philosophical considerations have always led some people to abstain from meat and choose solely vegetable foods.

As we will discuss in The Fat Tracker's Meal Planning Guide, the Stanford solution is to become a twice-a-week vegetarian as a means of cutting excess fat, as well as excess protein, from your meals. If you prefer to eat meatless meals exclusively, here are a few pointers for you. If you don't get your protein from animal products, the only source of *all* 9 essential amino acids, then you must eat complementary protein, that is, combinations of foods that provide them.

Complementary Proteins

The following complementary proteins, or food combinations, must be eaten at the same meal to make a complete protein. You may also consider investigating various protein substitutes, such as soy products, to enhance your diet.

- Grains + legumes, i.e., Miniature Black Bean Burritos (page 360) in a tortilla
- Nuts + grains, i.e., peanut butter and crackers
- Legumes + seeds, i.e., Curried Red Lentil Soup (page 364–65), tahini (sesame butter) and raw vegetables
- Legumes + nuts, i.e., Red Bean Stew with Basil Purée (page 433–34) and roasted pears sprinkled with ¼ cup pistachio nuts for dessert

LEGUMES INCLUDE adzuki, black beans, fava, lima, kidney, pinto, white beans, Great Northern, cannellini, flageolet, Scarlet Runners, mung, navy, pea, soy or tofu, lentils, black-eyed peas, chickpeas (garbanzos), cowpeas, field peas and split peas, among others.

WHOLE GRAINS INCLUDE barley, corn, cornmeal, hominy, polenta, oats, rice, wild rice, rye, wheat (bulgur, sprouts, wheat germ, cracked wheat), couscous, quinoa, amaranth, among others.

NUTS AND SEEDS INCLUDE almonds, beechnuts, Brazil, filberts, pecans, pinenuts (pignolia), walnuts, sunflower seeds, soybean seeds, pumpkin seeds, sesame seeds, chestnuts, peanuts (peanut butter), cashews (cashew butter), pistachio, macadamia, corn nuts, among others.

While making a choice to follow a vegetarian diet is a personal and legitimate decision, you must follow the same care in monitoring cholesterol and foods laden with saturated fat as those who eat conventional diets. If you prefer a vegetarian regimen, do not rely solely on cheese and eggs for your protein. Choose your protein from nonfat and low-fat dairy products and the long list of complementary proteins, such as grains and beans, that enhance meat-free meals. You will find The Stanford 25 Gram Plan's soups, breads, desserts, salads, vegetables, grains and bean dishes deliciously satisfying to the vegetarian palate.

Portion Control = Protein Control

You can't always sit down with a calculator and a book of nutrition tables to compute the hidden protein in your meals, but you can practice portion control: Eat smaller portions of concentrated, animal protein, and you will meet your protein needs without packing in unwanted calories and saturated fat.

The following table shows the most common sources of protein. As you scan the list, you can see that choosing low-fat protein foods, such as low-fat and nonfat dairy products and lean meats provides the same amount of protein as their higher-fat cousins.

Food	Serving Size	Grams Protein	Grams Saturated Fat	Grams Total Fat
Nonfat milk	8 ounces	9	0.3	0.4
Low-fat milk	8 ounces	9	2.9	4.7
Instant breakfast drink	1 package	7	0	0
Nonfat dry milk powder	½ cup	11	0.2	0.3
Nonfat evaporated milk	4 ounces	9	0	0.4
Whole evaporated milk	4 ounces	9	5.8	9.5
Nonfat yogurt**	8 ounces	13	0.3	0.4
Low-fat yogurt**	8 ounces	12	2.3	3.5
Whole-milk yogurt	8 ounces	8	4.8	7.4
Frozen yogurt, regular	4 ounces	8	3.0	4.6
Nonfat cottage cheese	¼ cup	6	0.1	0.15
Low-fat (2%) cottage cheese	¼ cup	7	0.7	1.1
Cheese, hard	1 ounce	7*	6.0	9.4*
Egg white	1 large	3	0	0
Egg yolk	1 large	3	1.7	5.6
Egg substitute, liquid	¼ cup	7	0.4	2.0
Poultry, white meat	1 ounce	9	0.3	1.1
Fish, white, lower fat	1 ounce	7	0.1	0.2
Beef, extra-lean ground	1 ounce	7	1.8	4.8
Tofu, uncooked ½ cup	1 ounce	10	0.9	5.9
Dried beans, lentils, peas, cooked	½ cup	9	0.1	0.7
Peanut butter	1 tablespoon	4	1.7	8.0
Pasta, dry	4 ounces	14	Trace	2.0
Rice, cooked	½ cup	2	Trace	0.2
Tortilla, corn	1	2	Trace	0.6
Potato, with skin	1	5	0	0.1
Broccoli, cooked	¼ pound	4	0	0
Soda crackers	10	3	0.9	3.7
Oatmeal, cooked	4 ounces	3	Trace	1.0
Nuts	1 ounce	5*	1.0 to 4.5*	13 to 22*

* Varies with type
** Nonfat dry milk added

We are saying that you don't have to give up your favorite foods. Just fit them into a diet that includes:

- 20 to 30 percent fat
- 15 to 20 percent protein
- 50 to 60 percent carbohydrates

Before we turn our attention to examining fat, do you know how to recognize a Fat Tracker?

WHAT A SUCCESSFUL FAT TRACKER LOOKS LIKE

What does a Fat Tracker look like? The Fat Tracker is the person who keeps saturated fat to a minimum by carefully reading each label before putting a processed food product in the grocery cart, passing up those that contain tropical oils, a source of saturated fat. She is the diner asking the waiter to serve her sauce or salad dressing on the side so she can apportion just enough to flavor her food without overdrawing her Fat Account for the day. The Fat Tracker is the family cook who controls cholesterol by substituting two egg whites for a whole egg in a muffin recipe; who knows onions don't have to be cooked in the three, four or five tablespoons of oil called for in most conventional recipes. The Fat Tracker substitutes water or stock in a skillet to save fat grams, but also to keep the pan from drying and to control the temperature of the cooking surface as good cooks have always done.

The Fat Tracker is aware of every gram of saturated fat in his or her food and adjusts meals as necessary to stay under the 25-gram limit. The Fat Tracker is the person who has completed an accurate saturated fat target (page 55) and knows if even 25 grams of saturated fat per day is too much. But the successful Fat Tracker is also the person who can eat a gooey chocolate dessert *without guilt* for knocking the day's allotment of fat askew, because the rest of the day's meals were kept low enough in fat to provide good nutrition and also allow the *planned* indulgence.

- The successful Fat Tracker has made fat awareness a part of life, like flossing, recycling newspapers, using consumer reports—because it is the smart thing to do.
- The successful Fat Tracker has a large collection of delicious, low-fat recipes that keeps mealtime interesting and appetizing.
- The successful Fat Tracker teaches children how to find nutrition and pleasure in low-fat foods.
- The successful Fat Tracker sits down with morning coffee and a bagel (1 gram total fat) rather than a croissant (10 grams total fat) or an apple fritter (15 grams total fat).
- The successful Fat Tracker knows how to select the low-fat beef cuts (cut from the round), rather than a sirloin or a T-bone.

- The successful Fat Tracker orders the nonfat frozen yogurt rather than higher fat regular on a Saturday afternoon outing to the mall (0 grams vs. 2 grams per 4 ounces). The successful Fat Tracker also passes up the high-fat toppings for fresh berries.
- The successful Fat Tracker knows that consistent, daily, heart-smart, low-fat food choices in the supermarket and restaurants keep everyone under the 25-gram ceiling.

The successful Fat Tracker also:

- Reads all packaging information on food labels.
- Checks recipe ingredients to choose those with leaner ingredients.
- Looks for ways to reduce the fat in his/her own favorite recipes.
- Makes lean substitutions at one meal to make room for an indulgence at another.
- Orders leaner foods in restaurants; requests that dressings and sauces be served separately.
- Stocks the kitchen cupboards with low-fat staples and snacks.
- Keeps track of the grams of saturated fat eaten each day.
- Keeps a chart of the content of saturated fat in foods tacked on the refrigerator.
- Uses the nutritional calculations at the end of each of our recipes to balance fat in individual meals.
- Teaches his/her children fat tracking techniques.
- Orders a low-fat meal in advance when making a plane reservation.
- Doesn't agonize about eating "bad" foods. There are no bad foods, only foods that need to be eaten infrequently and in reasonable portions.
- Passes up cookies, candy and processed foods and reaches for fresh fruit or vegetables instead.
- Keeps low-fat snacks such as dried fruit, low-fat crackers, pretzels and mini-bagels on hand in the desk or locker at work instead of lining up at the vending machines for high-fat temptations.
- Eats slowly and allows a feeling of fullness to develop before deciding he or she is still hungry and needs a second helping of an item containing fat, especially saturated fat.
- Selects seconds from low-fat items, such as bread and vegetables, instead of second helpings of meats.
- Knows some sugar in a sauce, fruit preserve, hard candy, fruit-based cookie or dessert is a better alternative to making meals and snacks satisfying than cutting out all flavor and pleasure in favorite foods. Too much deprivation eventually will send you screaming for some fat-intensive food relief.
- Orders free reference publications from the government to have on hand as a reference for the cholesterol and saturated-fat content of all foods, such as: *Nutritive Value of Foods,* Home and Garden Bulletin #72 ($3.75), or the most recent edition of *Composition of Foods, Handbook #8.* (Order from Superintendent of Documents, U.S. Government Printing Office, Washington, DC 20402.)

CHAPTER 11

Nutrition for a Healthy Heart: Fat and Fads

CLEARLY AMERICANS LOVE FAT. *In a typical year, each of us will consume 15 gallons of it—about two-thirds of a cup every day, a conservative estimate. If the sheer volume of this fatty indulgence doesn't give you pause, consider that the body needs just two teaspoons of essential fatty acids every day, such as those found in unsaturated fats. Two teaspoons equals about 3 percent of the calories the average American consumes in a day, yet some people eat as much as 50 percent of their daily calories in fat!*

Where Does All That Fat Come From?

You don't need *any* saturated fat. Although hard to do, your body, and especially your heart, would benefit tremendously if you cut out *saturated* fat altogether. Our national fat consumption looks like this:

FAT CONSUMPTION IN AMERICA: WHAT WE NEED VS. WHAT WE EAT

	Americans Need	*Americans Typically Eat*
Unsaturated Fat	10 grams to approximately 14 grams a day (2 teaspoons to 1 tablespoon)	150 grams a day (⅔ cup)
Saturated Fat	-o-	50 to 75 grams a day (¼ to ⅓ cup)

How can anybody eat that much fat? Well, think about it. How many times a year do you stop at a fast-food place for a quick meal on the run? The typical order of burger, fries and a shake adds up to a staggering 57 grams of fat, almost half of it saturated, the type of fat most harmful to us. Make that a cheeseburger or a double burger, add bacon and grilled onions, and you can easily consume *several days'* ration of saturated fat in that one convenient lunch.

If burgers are not your thing, consider how often you exchange a few coins at your favorite vending machine for a quick shot of chocolate-laden energy. Do you know that the average 1-ounce candy bar has 8 grams of saturated fat? If a daily limit is 25 grams, that's nearly *one-third* of your saturated fat allotment, with no other nutrients to justify the expense. How about ice cream? Did you have one scoop last year? One a week? One a day? That's 4 grams of saturated fat for each ½-cup scoop. The creamier and usually more expensive the ice cream, the more saturated fat (up to 7.5 grams per scoop) with cholesterol locked in every luscious spoonful.

You find fat in your dinner steak, the pats of butter on your toast, the dressing on your salad, the frosting on your birthday cake. It's packed into the sour cream you pile on your baked potato and the mayonnaise that's spread on your sandwich. It's in the little bag of potato chips that comes with your sandwich, as well as in the healthy bran muffin you munch on with your morning coffee. And about your coffee. Do you give it a shot of half-and-half? A tablespoonful barely lightens a cup of coffee. Two spoons? Or do you just pour until it turns the pale caramel color you love? *Every tablespoon of half-and-half contains almost 1 gram of saturated fat.* Or do you use nondairy creamers, made with tropical oils, because you think you are conserving calories or fat? That's approximately 2 grams of saturated fat per tablespoon for powdered creamers or 1 gram saturated fat per tablespoon for liquid creamers. Multiply by the number of cups you drink in a day, and you get an idea of how quickly and unobtrusively your fat count can add up.

If you dine out often, consider how much butter and oil the chef in your favorite restaurant ladles on all your favorite dishes to make them taste so good you will come back another day begging for more. Or does eating out for you usually mean a congenial meal at the home of a friend that starts with a tray of cheese and crackers, creamy dip with chips, bacon-wrapped tidbits or pâté?

❧ **With the exception of raw fruits, grains and vegetables, can you think of anything you eat that *doesn't* have some fat in it?**

Why would anyone eat so much fat when everybody knows it threatens our health? The answer is simple: Because fat tastes so good! Fat makes meat tender and flavorful, pastries light and flaky. And what's a salad without dressing? Fat smoothes sauces, keeps foods from sticking to the pan and scorching, and makes cakes moist. Let's face it. Americans are hooked on fat because it adds mouth-watering richness to everything it touches.

Some Fat Is Necessary for Good Health

Fat yields more than just flavor. Aside from pleasing your palate, fat also makes you feel satisfyingly full after a meal and slows down the digestive process so you don't suffer the pangs of an empty stomach for a while. It is the absence of fat that makes reducing diets so painful. But, of course, it is the absence of fat that also makes them work. Fat contains over *twice* as many calories per serving as anything else you eat. For example, a tablespoon of sugar has less than *half* the calories of a tablespoon of butter. The half-and-half that lightens your coffee does more dam-age to your heart *and* your waistline than does the lump of sugar that sweetens it.

In addition to providing taste and hunger-satisfying calories, fat is part of the fuel that keeps the body running. But nobody needs two fried eggs, a side of bacon, and several pieces of toast slathered with butter just to crank up their engine in the morning. Since fat—both the fat in your food and any excess fat on your body—can cause so many problems, you may be tempted to ask if nature goofed in making humans such fat-intensive creatures. To answer that question, we must examine a fat molecule's reason for being. Though fat is maligned as a dietary villain, you could not survive without some fat. Fats aid central nervous system function and your metabolism, for example, and fat wraps many of your organs in a protective buffer. Fat allows you to absorb essential fat-soluble vitamins and helps to keep your hair, skin and nails healthy. Without adequate fat in your diet you would have to feed hourly, like a ferret, or collapse from hunger, because, most importantly, fat stores energy.

❧ You store fat because Mother Nature didn't anticipate the supermarket.

The body breaks down food, using some of its nutrients for building and rebuilding, and for converting calories into your maintenance level of energy. If you eat more food than your normal activity level burns in a day, the body stores the excess as fat. The two sources of energy or fuel, carbohydrates and fat, serve you well. When you rev up your engine to play a few sets of tennis, for example, your body first draws energy from the carbohydrates you have most recently eaten. When that supply is exhausted, your body turns to your fat stores for the necessary boost of energy. Without the ability to store energy in fat cells, you would suddenly drop on the court exhausted as soon as you had used up the fuel from your most recent meal—the way a car stops when the gas tank runs dry.

Think of a fat cell as nature's ingenious response to the long, hard winters, drought, game shortage, crop failure, empty fish nets, blight and other catastrophes that can threaten the human species with starvation and extinction. Perhaps if nature had anticipated neighborhood supermarkets, fast-food franchises, modern refrigeration and microwave ovens—all of which afford you an ample and quick food stream—your body would burn fat more effectively and not need to store it so efficiently. But when food is in short supply, the body draws on its fat reserves to keep us going, much like a car that uses a reserve gas tank.

Diets and exercise help you slim down because there are fewer calories available to get converted to fat, and the increased level of activity forces the body to burn fat. Eating fat makes you fat, because the body immediately stores the fat component of any food eaten, the way an animal stores nuts for the winter, burning off the carbohydrate calories first. This accounts for the first principal of weight control—eat less fat! From the perspective of a healthy heart, the body can convert many excess nutrients into the fat it needs. Therefore, you don't need to feed yourself large quantities of *dietary* fat, saturated or unsaturated, in an attempt to maintain adequate *body* fat.

You Need Fat-Balanced Meals, Not Fat-Free Meals

No one argues about the need for fat, or the unique design that allows our body to store fat to make energy available when we do need it. You run into trouble, though, when you eat too much fat and don't burn off the calories you take in each day and when you eat unhealthy fats, specifically the saturated fat that leads to cardiovascular disease. The challenge for all of us is to select the healthy types of fats, such as olive oil, and eliminate the harmful ones found in animal foods; to eat enough healthy fats to make our food tasty and enjoyable without overdoing it; and to burn off excess fat before it becomes our most unattractive and unhealthy feature.

Healthy fat? Harmful fat? Isn't all fat the same? Not by a long shot. All fats have the same calorie count: a tablespoon of butter, a tablespoon of margarine, a tablespoon of olive oil or a tablespoon of beef fat has between 100 to 125 calories each. But the similarity ends there. A difference in chemical structure and a difference in the way our bodies handle them distinguishes the various fats. And for many, the difference is deadly.

The one thing you already know about saturated fat is that you are saturated with warnings about it. But what is it saturated with? How does it differ from unsaturated fat, monounsaturated fat and polyunsaturated fat? What difference do they make to you? And how can you tell what foods have which fat? Without a chemistry degree, these terms make a crucial health issue unnecessarily complicated and hard to understand. To help you understand a little more about the makeup of these fats so that you will know what to look for when you are reading labels and putting together your dinner menu, we offer you a quick course in fat chemistry.

Saturated and Unsaturated Fat

In the simplest of terms, the storm surrounding diet and heart disease is contained in an atom, specifically a hydrogen atom. Saturated fat is packed or saturated with hydrogen. Unsaturated fat is not. The many different types of fats—the ones you can see, such as the oil in your salad dressing and the marbled fat on your steak, as well as the ones you can't see, such as the oil in soybeans and the fat in a scoop of cottage cheese—all have one thing in common: they are made up of molecules containing chains of carbon and hydrogen atoms. Like a row of dancers lined up in an unbroken chain, each carbon atom bonds with two hydrogen atoms in a saturated fat molecule, as shown in this diagram:

```
      H  H  H  H  H  H  H  H
      |  |  |  |  |  |  |  |
   H-C- C- C- C- C- C- C- C-COOH
      |  |  |  |  |  |  |  |
      H  H  H  H  H  H  H  H
```

You can see that this symmetrical pattern has a pair of hydrogen atoms attached
to each carbon atom or, as a chemist would say, the molecule is saturated with
hydrogen. An unsaturated fat molecule is missing some hydrogen atoms, the symmetry is broken and as a result, the carbon forms different bonds, as the following
diagram shows.

```
     H  H   H  H   H  H  H  H
     |  |   |  |   |  |  |  |
  H-C- C = C- C = C- C- C- C-COOH
     |                |  |  |
     H                H  H  H
```

Unsaturated and saturated fat molecules behave differently inside and outside
the body. We have described at length the damage that hydrogen-packed saturated
fat can cause, primarily by encouraging the liver to crank out more cholesterol.
However, unsaturated fat, with hydrogen vacancies on the chain, allows, among
other things, oxygen to enter the molecule, which has consequences for you in the
supermarket. The oxygen can speed up the process that causes rancidity. Producers
of packaged foods, therefore, often add saturated fats, such as tropical oils, butter
and lard, which do a better job of resisting spoilage to give their foods a longer
shelf life. They also manipulate an unsaturated fat molecule for the same purpose,
by putting some hydrogen back in and making it more saturated.

More saturated? Yes, saturation is not an all or nothing deal. All fats are actually
a combination of saturated and unsaturated fat molecules, and we will show you
how to choose those that have more healthy unsaturated-fat molecules and less
harmful saturated-fat molecules. As you will discover in Fat Tracking in the Supermarket, Chapter 17, finding the key words, "hydrogen" and "hydrogenated," on a
package label helps you sort out healthy from less healthy products.

❧ The word "hydrogen" on a food label always means trouble.

There is one more piece of fat chemistry that is of concern to the consumer—monounsaturated and polyunsaturated fats. If you have followed the discussion this far, you can see in these two sketches that these terms simply refer to the number of hydrogen vacancies on the chain, which allows the carbon to form what is called a double bond, indicated by the = sign. When only one double bond is present (count the = signs), it is monounsaturated.

$$
\begin{array}{c}
\text{H H H H H} \quad \text{H H H H} \\
\text{H}-\text{C}-\text{C}-\text{C}-\text{C}-\text{C} = \text{C}-\text{C}-\text{C}-\text{C}-\text{COOH} \\
\text{H H H H} \qquad \text{H H H}
\end{array}
$$

The more double bonds (our example has two) the more polyunsaturated the oil. These subtle changes in the chemical composition of fats signal vastly different properties, which we will begin to explain.

$$
\begin{array}{c}
\text{H H} \quad \text{H H} \quad \text{H H H H} \\
\text{H}-\text{C}-\text{C} = \text{C}-\text{C} = \text{C}-\text{C}-\text{C}-\text{C}-\text{COOH} \\
\text{H} \qquad\quad \text{H H H}
\end{array}
$$

The presence or absence of the hydrogen molecule determines the melting point of saturated and unsaturated fats, which does help identify which type predominates in various foods. A fat molecule saturated with hydrogen remains solid at room temperature, as in butter and chicken fat, as well as in hydrogenated vegetable oils. On the other hand, a fat molecule that is *unsaturated* with hydrogen produces oils that remain liquid at room temperature. The visible difference is really that simple, and you can use texture as a rule of thumb even when you are eating butter or salad oil in a restaurant and don't have a list of ingredients to remind you which is which.

❧ Unsaturated fat can actually reduce the cholesterol in our bloodstream.

In moderation, unsaturated fats are heart healthy because they don't trigger the liver to manufacture excessive amounts of cholesterol. Studies have shown that simply substituting unsaturated fats for saturated fats lowers both total cholesterol and the lethal LDL cholesterol.

Polyunsaturated vs. Monounsaturated Fats: Which Are Better?

While we know for sure the importance of limiting saturated fat, there is still some controversy about what other types and amounts of unsaturated fat you should eat during the day. Everyone agrees that your total fat intake (saturated *and* unsaturated) should be less than 30 percent of calories or 75 grams per day, because of the studies linking cancer as well as heart disease to high-fat diets. This recommendation is 10 times more than you actually need for good health. Some researchers also feel a cap of 30 percent fat may still allow too much total fat. On the other hand, some scientists point to the Mediterranean region, where there is a much lower incidence of heart disease, and whose population eats between 30 to 40 percent of their daily calories as fat, mostly in the form of monounsaturated fat, primarily olive oil. This camp believes the *type* of fat is more crucial than the *amount* of fat.

The term "Mediterranean Diet," in fact, has gained popularity recently because of observations such as a recent study of 600 heart attack victims. Half of the participants ate a diet composed of fresh fruits, vegetables, grains and olive oil typical of the foods in this part of the world. Compared to the control group, they showed a dramatic reduction in their risk for a second heart attack. How does the so-called Mediterranean Diet differ from The Stanford 25 Gram Plan? In one significant way: Mediterranean dishes are not the only foods that will keep you healthy. As we will demonstrate in The Fat Tracker's Guide, and throughout our collection of recipes, you can stay healthy by eating a wide range of foods from all parts of the globe. In addition, you will find streamlined versions of traditional American favorites, such as fried chicken, hash browns and our own Stanford Salad that are just as kind to your arteries as is pasta.

Where does all this leave you? As we stated on the first page of this chapter, the human body requires only about 14 grams of fat per day, total. *Approximately 1 tablespoon of safflower oil or other vegetable oil will satisfy your entire daily requirement.* (While olive oil should have center stage as a cooking oil, it does not provide linoleic acid, the essential fatty acid. Even on a low fat diet, a tablespoon of safflower or other vegetable oil, 1% to 2% of your total calories, is needed to supply sufficient linoleic acid.) So after you supply your minimum daily needs, the question becomes: How much *more* can you safely eat without harming your body? Future generations may chuckle at dietary recommendations that turn out to have little or no effect on the body. However, they will greet with horror, and rightly so, too liberal recommendations that took liberties with human health and, in fact, caused harm.

Until we understand more clearly the role of the types and amounts of unsaturated fats in the body, The Stanford 25 Gram Plan places a conservative limit on fat—30 percent total fat (or 75 grams) and 10 percent saturated fat (or 25 grams for healthy persons). You can use either monounsaturated or polyunsaturated fats as you wish, although we recommend using predominately the monounsaturated form of oil, such as olive, canola or peanut. It is possible that future research may require that we even adjust *this* ceiling downward. We look forward to uncovering more about the links be-tween food and health, but for now we recommend that you take no risks with your health and follow The Stanford 25 Gram Plan.

Hydrogenated Fats: Turning Gold into Straw

Saturated fat resists rancidity because there is no room for oxygen compounds to attach to the tightly packed chain and alter the chemical composition, which produces the unmistakable foul taste of rancid fat. We have already explained why manufacturers concerned about long shelf life prefer to douse their products with saturated rather than unsaturated fat: Saturated fat makes them stay fresher, longer. (You can compensate for vegetable oils' susceptibility to turn rancid by storing them in a darkened cupboard or in the refrigerator.) But when they put the missing hydrogen atom back in healthy, unsaturated oils to make *hydrogenated or partially hydrogenated fats,* they turn gold back into straw as it were, making the previously unsaturated, healthy oils partially saturated, and therefore harmful. As you shop for food, you don't have to remember everything we have said about fat molecules and hydrocarbon chains. But when you read the label on a package of microwave popcorn, a can of soup, a box of crackers or cereal, in fact the label on any processed food, stop when you see hydrogenated or partially hydrogenated oils on the list of ingredients. *Remember that hydrogenated oils mean saturated fat, and that means bad news for your arteries.*

Omega-3 Fatty Acids and Fish

Epidemiologists have found that Greenland Eskimos have a very low incidence of heart disease despite the fact that 40 percent of their calories come from animal fat in the form of seal and whale blubber. Further analysis of their diet revealed that they eat large amounts of oily cold-water fish that are known to contain highly unsaturated omega-3 fatty acids. These substances not only have a favorable effect on cholesterol levels, but alter the stickiness of platelets in the bloodstream. These observations and other potential beneficial effects have made fish consumption, in addition to the low saturated-fat and cholesterol content, an even more important part of the heart-healthy diet.

Some scientists have advocated taking fish oil (omega-3) capsules in order to mimic the beneficial effects in Eskimos. These efforts have had mixed results, so we do not currently advocate them for the average person.

Stearic Acid Fats

Recently a type of saturated fat called stearic acid, found in beef and chocolate, has been found to lower cholesterol levels slightly. Naturally chocolate and beef lovers celebrated this discovery. We hate to dampen their spirits, but unfortunately the amount of harmful saturated fats in these foods far outweighs any possible benefit from the stearic acid fats, and so beef and chocolate remain on the limited indulgence list.

Sources of Fat

Now that you know the difference between saturated and unsaturated fat, let's take a look at where they show up in your food.

ANIMAL FAT The animal kingdom contributes the largest concentration of fat to the human diet, most of it saturated: fish, chicken, chicken skin, beef, lamb, egg yolk, milk fat, pork, game (both wild and domestic), veal, liver, venison, rabbit, quail, mussels, octopus and on and on. Much of this fat is visible as the excess fat, skin and marbling on meat and poultry. However, much also remains hidden in the tissues. Even when you buy one of our recommended cuts of lean top round without any visible fat or marbling, saturated fat still remains in the cells, though the quantity is much lower than in other, fattier, cuts.

VEGETABLE FAT (UNSATURATED) Few true vegetables, fruits or grains contain fat in significant quantities. Some, such as corn, sunflower seeds and soybeans, have very small concentrations of unsaturated fat, small enough that they appear essentially fat-free when they show up at mealtime as corn on the cob or sunflower seeds. Food manufacturing processes, however, can extract this fat to produce the unsaturated vegetable oils so important to a healthy diet. In the vegetable kingdom, avocados, olives, seeds and nuts contain relatively large amounts of fat, which is mainly unsaturated.

VEGETABLE FAT (SATURATED) There are a few plants, however, with high amounts of saturated fat. Coconut and its oils and palm and palm kernel oils all contain a large percentage of saturated fat, while other items, such as avocados, have smaller amounts. These harmful oils are used primarily by commercial companies in the manufacture of various food products and are not available to the consumer, but they pack a wallop in the prepared and processed foods we've come to rely on. Diligent Fat Trackers must check package labels for these harmful oils and avoid those products that contain them, otherwise they will unwittingly sabotage their fat-reduction efforts. Coconut oil is a whopping 86 percent saturated fat. Compare its 16 grams of saturated fat per tablespoon to the comparatively meager 2 grams per tablespoon or 15 percent in olive oil. Or consider that palm oil contains about 50 percent saturated fat, and you can see why there is such a push for manufacturers to cut down on these oils in commercial products. A dousing with these oils can make even innocent sounding "health" foods positively lethal. Granola, for instance, which many choose for its seeming health-giving vitamins and fiber, gets bumped from the health food list when manufacturers toast it heavily in coconut oil (as they often do). Popcorn vendors in places like movie theaters turn a healthy food, corn, into a harmful food by popping it with butter or tropical oil/hydrogenated oil flavoring. Never ask for butter on your popcorn.

PROCESSED FOODS Processed foods (including those served at fast-food restaurants, canned foods and soups, packages of microwaveable foods, and other manufactured products) often contain large amounts of fat, usually in the form of hydrogenated fats and highly saturated tropical oils, but other fats, such as butter and lard also find their way into these foods. Some food manufacturers are beginning to use vegetable oils in place of saturated fats. We welcome this trend, of course, though for the Fat Tracker, these healthy fats must be tallied to meet the total fat limit of 75 grams a day. Fat Tracking in the Supermarket (page 171) will help you learn to read labels to determine what kind of fat your favorite products contain.

MAJOR SOURCES OF SATURATED FAT The Stanford Life Plan for a Healthy Heart limits saturated fat in your diet to 7 to 10 percent of calories or 19 to 25 grams daily. This will allow you to enjoy the advantages of *some* saturated fat without harming your heart. Here are the most common, general sources of saturated fat:

- Animal fat, such as beef, pork, veal, lamb, lard and suet
- Whole-milk dairy products, such as cream, cheese and butter
- Hydrogenated/partially hydrogenated vegetable oils, such as margarine and canned shortening
- Tropical oils, such as coconut oil, palm and palm kernel oil

The tables of Foods High in Saturated Fat, Foods High in Cholesterol and Saturated Fat in Fast Foods (page 235) gave you an idea of where saturated fat materializes in popular foods. Take another look at them. You can see how easily these high-fat items can sneak into your diet almost unnoticed and put you over The Stanford 25 Gram Plan limit if you are not a careful Stanford Fat Tracker.

HIDDEN FAT IS HARMFUL FAT Finally, remember that just because you can't see fat, doesn't mean it isn't there. Hydrogenated fats hide in processed foods, such as packaged sauces, cereals, cookies, doughnuts, margarine, creamy peanut butter and all manner of frozen, microwaveable, canned and dried processed foods, allowing saturated fat to sneak into your diet unless you read labels carefully. Saturated tropical oils also hide in processed foods. Even though it is hidden, the fat in these products is still harmful. Perhaps even more so, because, unlike the highly visible marbling on beef, you cannot see these hydrogenated fats and you may not realize you are consuming harmful saturated fat and possibly exceeding your 25-gram limit. The Fat Tracker's Guide will help you weed out these hidden fats from the food you buy and prepare.

Tracking the Right Fats, the Right Foods
In a nutshell, to choose the right foods, first track the texture of the fat. Remember that dietary fat comes in two forms: the kind you pour from a bottle and the kind you slice with a knife.

- Hard (saturated) fats hurt hearts. Avoid fats you can cut with a knife.
- Pourable (unsaturated) fats protect hearts. Choose oils you pour from a bottle.

Reach for liquid oils instead of butter, lard, canned vegetable shortening, bacon fat, chicken fat, salt pork, fat back, and even margarine (see below our further discussion of concerns about margarine). Limit firm fats and this step alone will go a long way toward making your food choices kinder to your heart. The following table will help you remember which fats to buy and use.

HEART HEALTHY GUIDE TO OILS AND FATS

Bad Fats (Hard) Saturated	Better Fats (Liquid) Polyunsaturated	Best Fats (Liquid) Monounsaturated
Coconut oil	Vegetable oils	Olive oil
Palm and palm kernel oil	Corn oil	Canola oil
Margarine	Safflower oil	Peanut oil
Butter	Soybean oil	
Animal fat		
Lard		
Hydrogenated/partially hydrogenated vegetable oils and shortening		

What About Margarine?

Margarine has come a long way since World War II when it was called "oleomargarine" and hailed as a butter substitute during those years of rationing and scarcity. First it appeared on the market in white, lardlike bricks that had to be beaten into softened oleo, at which time powdered food coloring was added to give it a more appetizing hue. The next advance delivered it in sealed plastic bags with a distinctive little button of coloring in one corner. After softening and massaging the contents until the "marg" turned a pale gold, you cut away the plastic and had "pretend" butter.

Margarine still does its best to imitate butter, but for different reasons. Margarine hung on in the markets long after butter was again available, first because it was cheap and, in later years, because it was believed to be healthier than butter. Some people misguidedly think even today that margarine will keep them thin, when in fact, a teaspoon of margarine and a teaspoon of butter have the same number of calories—and they are both saturated fats. What they don't have in common is cholesterol. Butter is loaded with it; margarine has none.

Margarine and Transfatty Acids

Margarine may not have cholesterol, but it does have saturated fat. Manufacturers hydrogenate the vegetable oil to create the firmness of butter, so in terms of saturated and unsaturated fat, margarine straddles both worlds. Researchers are also discovering that other elements in margarine may push up cholesterol levels. Discoveries about substances called "transfatty acids," a byproduct of hydrogenation, have cast doubt about the benefits of substituting margarine for butter as a means of lowering saturated fat in the diet. In the past, some studies done on these compounds raised concern that they increased cholesterol levels in the blood. But other studies showed no effect. Further investigations conducted in Holland indicated that transfatty acids significantly lower HDL, the good cholesterol, sounding the alarm once again about margarine.

🌿 **And remember, transfatty acids are a product of hydrogenation, a process occurring in many foods, not just margarine.**

The news hasn't gotten any better, just clearer. Recent work shows that transfatty acids get you coming and going. Not only do they deplete good cholesterol, but they also raise the lethal type of cholesterol, LDL. And we still don't have the full picture. It is clear (as reported in *The American Journal of Cardiology* in 1993) that high levels of transfatty acids are found in patients with coronary heart disease. In a study of 90,000 women reported by Dr. Walter Willett of Harvard, those who ate the most foods with the highest transfat counts increased their risk of heart disease by 50 percent.

Every time you read a label and see a word resembling hydrogen, you know that in addition to saturated fat, the product contains transfatty acids. If you frequent fast-food chains, chances are high that before freezing they precook their food in hydrogenated shortening, which contains transfatty acids. Always remember, transfatty acids are *in addition to*, not just another name for, saturated fat.

Margarine vs. Butter and Butter Flavorings

So what's a Fat Tracker to do? Go back to butter? Absolutely not. If the total intake of saturated fat in your diet remains low, a pat of butter on your toast every morning will not harm you. But if you find too much saturated fat and cholesterol creeping into your diet, then avoid butter whenever possible, even if you occasionally have to use margarine as a stand-in. For the present, margarine still remains a better choice than butter. A vegetable-based fat, it still contains less saturated fat than butter *and* it has no cholesterol. But we give this advice cautiously. These questionable strengths may pale if future studies reveal more harmful effects from transfatty acids. Or, if the current labeling requirements catch up with the research and demand that the amount of transfatty acids in a product be listed with the saturated fat and cholesterol totals revealing that excessively high levels occur in margarine. Some researchers report values as high as 60 percent in some items! Presently, the consumer has no way of knowing how much of this harmful stuff they are buying and eating because the manufacturer doesn't have to disclose that information.

🌿 **Our bottom line on margarine: It is definitely better than butter, but certainly not as good as monounsaturated oils, such as olive oil.**

Treat margarine as you would any other high-fat product. A little once in a while isn't going to hurt you, but don't make a habit of it. With so many food choices out there, you don't have to eat dry toast. The Breakfast chapter will introduce you to creamy substitutes for butter and margarine. Or, reach for fresh fruit purées instead of any fat. Better yet, buy dense, flavorful breads that don't require any topping at all.

State-of-the-art food producing has given us a range of whipped and tub margarines and butter. Air and water whipped into some of these products, replacing some of the fat, make them even lower in both fat and cholesterol. Powdered butter flavorings, vegetable sprays flavored with butter and olive oil, and blends of butter and vegetable oils also offer fat reduction while retaining some butter flavor. By all means, use these and any new products that come along if they help you reduce the harmful fats in your diet. When it comes to margarine, the softer the better because that means less hydrogenation, therefore fewer harmful fats. In addition to the softer tub margarines, try liquid margarines. The healthiest ones list vegetable oil as the first ingredient rather than a partially hydrogenated oil. Whichever product you use, don't rely on it to flavor your food on a daily basis and make sure you incorporate it into your 25-gram plan.

Fake Fats

We have come a long way from the 1790s, when a recipe for syllabub, a rich mixture of cream and wine, advised you to sweeten cider with sugar and nutmeg, and "then milk your cow into it." These days we have synthetic "dairy" products that have never even been close to a cow!

A peek into our crystal ball reveals, if not a fat-free future, a fat-freer future, thanks in part to work of food chemists reproducing fatlike substances with many of the textural and flavorful charms of dairy fats, but with none of the hazards. Made from milk and eggwhite proteins, the first of these products successfully imitates butterfat in fat-free ice cream and sour cream and we eagerly await more fat-free delicacies from food producers who use them. Fat-free sandwich spreads that mimic mayonnaise are already available to the consumer. Use them or not as you prefer. We will discuss these products further as we steer you toward healthful food choices in Fat Tracking in the Supermarket, Chapter 17.

Low-Fat Dairy and Meat Products

In response to the public's concern about the link between heart attacks and diet, manufacturers have developed low-fat and nonfat counterparts for our favorite cheeses, creams and butter. We wholeheartedly endorse the concept of dairy and meat products containing less fat and cholesterol. And we welcome the appearance of all of these products, even the ones that still need perfecting before they approximate the flavor and texture of their high-fat counterparts. Reading labels will help you choose the products with the least fat; experimentation will help you choose the ones with the most flavor.

We predict that public demand for low-fat dairy products will continue to motivate the food technologists and manufacturers to break through the food technology frontiers and produce truly flavorful and healthy cheeses, creams and butter substitutes. You will see throughout our recipe section that we use these products at every opportunity, though it is *not* our policy to endorse any particular manufacturer. However, we do urge our readers to buy and use these products and to write letters of appreciation to their manufacturers. Likewise we urge you to write critical letters to food producers who have not yet gotten the word that we are in a new age of health awareness and that they must make healthy products available to us.

No Fad Remedies

Over and over again, you read throughout The Stanford 25 Gram Plan about the virtue of well-balanced meals that come from a variety of low-fat foods. To those who respond to words like *super, mega, newer, instant, better, painless, improved,* those who want detours to health and vitality, the words *well-balanced meals* may sound like a splash of ice water.

However, we see no value in nutritional shortcuts, such as eating any one food to the exclusion of many others. Oat bran and fish oil have had their share of the media spotlight as antidotes to heart disease. We have explained the value of these items, and yet we continue to favor a program of moderation as the path to good health, choosing from a wide variety of low-fat foods and eating them in well-balanced meals. We see no evidence to the contrary; if we did, we would recommend it.

Not only is dietary moderation nutritionally sound, but it tastes better! Rather than take fish oil capsules, enjoy Poached Salmon with Spiced Melon Sauce (page 490–91). Eat water-soluble fiber to help keep your cholesterol level low, but you don't have to swallow oat bran all day to do it; instead have an apple or a peach or hummus and warmed pita bread or black bean soup or a stir-fry with broccoli, onions and water chestnuts. These foods are just as good for you and they make a much better match with a glass of red wine!

We also urge you to practice a healthy skepticism when you read about "miracle cures" for atherosclerosis, or claims that what you eat doesn't matter.

What About the "French Connection?"

Since its media hype in the early 1990s, the "French Connection" is raising new questions about diet and heart disease. The traditional French diet—high in cheese, butter and other high-fat foods—seems to flout The Stanford 25 Gram Plan recommendations for a heart-healthy diet. And it poses a new riddle to the medical community: Why don't the French have high rates of heart disease? The tendency for some people who are reluctant to make changes in their diet is to say, "See, it doesn't matter what you eat."

Well, it does matter, and we don't have a scientific explanation for the French Connection—yet. Very likely, since the French diet is becoming more "Americanized" as they succumb to fast foods and other high saturated-fat items, the expected rise in heart disease rates from eating these foods, which can take a generation or two to show up in the statistics, simply hasn't appeared yet. Large-scale studies are underway to investigate the French diet and the role of daily wine consumption. The results will definitely help us understand more about diet and heart disease. But the news we have heard so far does not change The Stanford 25 Gram Plan or The Stanford Life Plan for a Healthy Heart.

The human body has complex nutritional needs. You do not live by bread alone, nor oat bran, nor fish oil, rice bran nor any of the other natural remedies that sometimes take off as health fads. Man, woman and child—each needs apples and chicken and potatoes and broccoli and tomatoes and lentils and strawberries, and on and on and on. It is the entire food chain that supplies the human body with the subtle combination of nutrients that keeps it healthy and vibrant and keeps your spirits soaring from the sheer pleasure of eating this bounty.

WHAT ARE WE SAYING?

- Your body needs some healthy fat every day.
- Your body never needs saturated animal fat.
- Don't put yourself at risk by falling for so-called miracle cures for atherosclerosis.
- There is no substitute for a heart healthy diet; in other words, there is no substitute for The Stanford 25 Gram Plan.

Perhaps some of these recommendations have already become part of your eating style. Check the next food quiz to see how closely your current eating habits match The Stanford 25 Gram Plan.

CHECK YOURSELF #3: HOW OFTEN DO YOU...?

	Seldom/Never	Sometimes	Frequently
1. Order low-fat items on restaurant menus	3	2	1
2. Pack a low-fat snack for work rather than get stuck with only high-fat items in the snack bar or vending machine	3	2	1
3. Buy low-fat snacks instead of high-fat ones to have on hand for your kids	3	2	1
4. Eat tofu, dry peas, legumes or beans instead of meat	3	2	1
5. Remember to count the egg yolks in bread and other baked goods as part of your weekly allowance of three	3	2	1
6. Reach for raw vegetables or fruit instead of a high-fat snack	3	2	1
7. Drink fruit or vegetable juice instead of a high-fat shake	3	2	1
8. Order low-fat or nonfat frozen yogurt instead of the high saturated-fat soft-serve ice cream	3	2	1
9. Head for the salad bar in a fast food franchise instead of the burger bar	3	2	1
10. Refuse to buy butter, cheese and whole-milk dairy products so you won't be tempted to snack on them	3	2	1

Total

Circle the response that most nearly describes your habits and total your score.

24–10 = Excellent, try for a perfect 10.

25–30 = Consider these questions as the first 10 of many low-fat, low-cholesterol commandments that you and your family will try to live by.

CHAPTER 12

Timetable for Change

DO YOU HAVE TO UPROOT YOUR ENTIRE LIFESTYLE *to protect your heart?
That depends. If you have high cholesterol levels, you smoke and you have other
risk factors, then you need to take quick action to lower your risk by eating as little saturated fat as possible and by addressing the other risks under your control.
People without this worrisome health profile, however, can take a more gradual
approach. Dietary habits are formed one meal at a time, one change at a time. It
is wise to make one or two changes, such as cutting down the number of times you
eat red meat during the week and switching from butter to margarine, and allowing them to become habit before incorporating another change into your diet.*

❧ **If you overload your circuits with too many drastic changes, chances are
you will begin to feel deprived and be tempted to give up in frustration.**

Remember that The Stanford 25 Gram Plan is an eating program for life—for
the length of your life and the quality of your life. As you make alterations in the
types of foods and quantity of high-fat items you eat, you are beginning to form
what will become lifelong heart-healthy habits. But unless your blood test reveals
LDL cholesterol levels above 100 and HDL levels below 40, and your Stanford Heart
Disease Self-Assessment Risk Questionnaire score is 16 or higher, then you don't
have to make these changes overnight. (If you do fall into these parameters, we
will discuss your best plan of action shortly.)

There even will be times when you will find it hard to stick to the plan. After all,
while we want you to take the best possible care of your heart, we know that people
have birthday parties to go to, holidays to celebrate, vacations to take and occasional chocolate-driven impulses to satisfy—the normal dietary peaks and valleys
of a lifetime. We say, enjoy them. If you make The Stanford 25 Gram Plan your
daily eating program year in and year out, you can succumb to an occasional delicious, guilt-free temptation. This flexibility will work because you will have established habits that make returning to The Stanford 25 Gram Plan the following day
an automatic reflex.

We know that the prospect of dietary change raises all sorts of unpleasant visions of deprivation. But realize that The Stanford 25 Gram Plan changes the types of food you eat, not necessarily the amount. Unless you must lose weight, you need not feel hungry. As we explain in Chapter 16, Will Counting Calories Help Your Heart?, you can continue to eat the same number of calories you eat now. Simply choose more of them from complex carbohydrate foods, and less of them from fat and protein. To help you embrace these important dietary changes, consider this: If you were vacationing out of the country, you would enjoy foods different from the typical American diet. However, if you were to travel to Italy or other Mediterranean locales, your style of eating would resemble The Stanford 25 Gram Plan—lots of pasta, produce and foods prepared with olive oil. In either case, you would continue to enjoy good food. You need have no more sense of deprivation following our heart-smart approach to eating than if you were taking a holiday to a different land.

Timetable for The Stanford 25 Gram Plan

We have outlined a timetable for change to serve as a two-month guideline for transforming your current eating patterns into The Stanford 25 Gram Plan and adopting the other aspects of The Stanford Life Plan for a Healthy Heart. You can certainly speed up your timetable, if you wish, but don't slow it down.

Weeks 1 and 2
- Switch from whole milk products to low-fat milk products.
- Use olive oil or canola oil exclusively in cooking and dressings.
- Select lean cuts of all meats, trim off all visible fat and use only beef cut from the round.
- Bake, broil, grill, stir-fry more frequently; deep-fat fry, braise, panfry in large amounts of fat less frequently.
- Begin taking daily doses of aspirin and vitamin E and beta-carotene supplements (with your physician's approval).
- Increase your intake of yellow and green vegetables and fruits to at least 5 servings per day.
- If you are sedentary, begin exercising 30 minutes a day at least three times a week.
- If you smoke, quit.

Weeks 3 and 4
- Switch from butter and margarine to low-fat alternative spreads.
- Limit eggs to less than three or four per week.
- Switch to Better Breakfasts (page 136).
- Switch to 2 + 2 Dinners (page 140).

Week 5

- Cut down on highly sugared desserts.
- Switch to more fruits and low-fat milk desserts.
- Cut down on egg breads and rolls, sweet rolls, pastries and croissants.
- Switch to more fruits and vegetables, especially yellow and green vegetables high in antioxidants, both at mealtime and snack time.
- Switch to Crunchy Lunches (page 138).
- Increase exercise to at least 30 minutes a day four to five times per week.

Week 6

- Switch to 1 percent and nonfat milk, nonfat yogurt and cottage cheese.
- Use lower-fat cheese; eat smaller portions of cheese.
- Broil, grill, stir-fry even more frequently.
- Order low-fat meals and snacks when you eat out.

Week 7

- Use more peanut butter, dried peas, beans, in place of cheese, eggs and meat.
- Use more whole grain dishes and breads.
- Add more fruits and vegetables up to 10 or more servings a day.
- Switch from ice cream and ice milk to sherbets and low-fat and nonfat frozen yogurt.

Week 8

- If you need to lose weight, begin to decrease your serving size of higher-fat foods; don't take second helpings.
- Limit hard cheese to four ounces per week.
- Up your exercise program to at least 30 minutes every day.

The Stanford 17 Gram Plan

If you need to make immediate changes to your diet, The National Cholesterol Education Program recommends what they call a "Two Step Eating Plan." Step One closely parallels The Stanford 25 Gram Plan. For people who have moderate to high elevations of blood cholesterol, or people who have not been able to lower cholesterol by following Step One, they recommend Step Two, which contains even more restrictions in saturated fat and cholesterol. For Fat Trackers, that translates into The Stanford 17 Gram Plan, with a maximum of 17 grams of saturated fat and 200 milligrams of cholesterol daily. To help you make this downward shift in saturated fat, we suggest you follow the timetable and other guidelines for The Stanford 25 Gram Plan with the following changes:

- Eat one egg yolk per week.
- Eat only nonfat diary products, low-fat cheeses, low-fat and nonfat frozen yogurt and fruit ices instead of ice cream or ice milk.
- Use cheese as a seasoning, not as a food.
- Eat less than two tablespoons of margarine or vegetable oil per day.
- Eat no butter or hydrogenated shortening.
- Eliminate red meat or eat it only once a week and remove all fat.
- Eat fish, turkey and chicken breast, no dark meat and no skin or fat, three times a week.
- Eat meatless entrees at least three times a week.

Putting The Stanford 25 Gram Plan to Work for You

As you begin to amass a store of fat-tracking tools, you want to include a strategy that will make The 25 Gram Plan work best for you. Incorporate the following tips into your timetable to ease your transition to healthier foods.

Keep the Dietary Goals in Mind
- Limit saturated fat to 25 grams or less each day.
- Limit cholesterol to 300 mg or less each day.
- Limit total fat to 75 grams or less each day.
- Eat abundant grains and antioxidant fruits and vegetables, up to 10 or more servings each day.
- Limit salt to 3,000 mg each day.
- Eat at least 25 grams of fiber each day.

Remember that Limiting Saturated Fat Reduces All Harmful Fats

Remember, your goal is not merely to minimize fat: You can reduce the grams of total fat in your diet by simply eliminating the oil in your salad dressing. But if you butter your bread and eat large portions of red meat, each of which contains high levels of saturated fat *and* cholesterol, you haven't accomplished your goal of reducing all harmful fats.

Keep the emphasis on reducing *saturated* fat because with the exception of hydrogenated or partially hydrogenated oils in processed foods, saturated fat always has two traveling companions: other *unsaturated* fats, and cholesterol. Cut out foods high in *saturated* fat and you automatically reduce your intake of those harmful fats, as well.

Learn to Spot Sources of Saturated Fat

You don't have to memorize the nutritional content of every variety of food to protect your heart. But you should learn to spot quickly foods high in saturated fat. The Fat Tracker's Guide, pages 169 through 256, gives you this information in depth, but generally speaking, the following foods contain the most harmful fat:

- *Red meat products*, such as beef, lamb, pork products, veal; high-fat poultry such as duck; dark meat of chicken and turkey; and organ meats.
- *Whole-milk dairy products*, such as butter, cheese, milk, cream, cottage cheese and yogurt.
- *Egg yolks.*
- *Commercial products containing partially hydrogenated or hydrogenated oils*, such as margarine, baked goods and packaged snack and convenience foods.

Learn to Spot the Healthiest Foods as Well

Always reach for these foods first: fish and shellfish, white meat of chicken and turkey, low-fat and nonfat dairy products, vegetable oils, fruits, vegetables and grains, which contain little or no saturated fat.

Use More Than One Approach to Reducing Saturated Fat

You can achieve your fat-tracking goals more comfortably if you have more than one approach to eating leaner meals. For example, instead of striking all high-fat foods from your meals, follow these tips:

- *Eat Smaller Portions of Favorite High-Fat Foods* You don't have to banish high-fat items from your pantry, just cut down on the serving size and you can have your cake and eat it too, or a hamburger, if you prefer.
- *Eat Only the High-Fat Foods You Really Love* Saturated fat sneaks into your diet in the form of mouthwatering, rich, hard-to-resist temptations, but most likely you eat some foods simply out of habit. Make a list of the five highest-fat foods you most enjoy. Now turn to the fat-tracking chapters to find the totals and jot down the saturated fat in each serving, calculating the portion size you actually eat.

FIVE HIGH-FAT FAVORITES

		Saturated Fat Grams Daily	Saturated Fat Grams Weekly	Saturated Fat Grams Monthly
1				
2				
3				
4				
5				
Totals				

You don't want to give up these foods entirely, so you look for a way to fit them into your 25-gram plan. Start by making another list. This time, write down five high-fat foods that you eat, not because you love them, but because they are available, or they have become a habit. These are foods you consume without really being aware of the taste, without being startled by the pleasure of eating them. You order a cheese sandwich at lunchtime, not because it is your favorite sandwich, but because it has become an automatic response when a counterperson asks, "What will you have?" Then you wolf it down without really tasting it because you're on the run. You absentmindedly snack on stale potato chips that come with your lunch order. You put half-and-half in your coffee at work simply because your office supplies it. You spread cream cheese on your bagel because you thought you were supposed to, but it's not your favorite spread.

FIVE HIGH-FAT HABITS

	Saturated Fat Grams Daily	Saturated Fat Grams Weekly	Saturated Fat Grams Monthly
1			
2			
3			
4			
5			
Totals			

Add up the numbers and you have an idea where some of the easily dispensable saturated fat appears in *your* diet. Remember, this list contains only five foods. It is a safe bet that you eat many other nonessential saturated fat foods during the day, every day.

Now compare your two lists. Given the choice between say, a chocolate chip cookie (substitute your own favorite food) and the same old cheese or bologna sandwich or whatever high-fat food habit you have, which would you pick? Eating only the higher-fat foods that are important to you can make a big difference in your total saturated-fat intake for the day and leave more room for serious eating pleasure.

Tailor Your Fat Quota to Suit the Eating Patterns You Already Enjoy

Mealtime eating patterns are as important, varied and individual as the foods people enjoy eating. Use your own eating patterns as clues for apportioning higher-fat foods. For example, if you like to eat three full meals every day with little or no in-between snacking, start by simply dividing your maximum saturated fat quota by three. On the other hand, if you are a snacker, make low-fat tradeoffs throughout the day, such as using only nonfat milk or low-fat protein to allow for a cookie at breaktime. As far as your heart is concerned, you can keep the eating patterns that are most comfortable for you. It doesn't *matter* so much when during the day you eat saturated fat, as long as you don't go over your daily limit.

Or, Design Your Plan Around Your Favorite Foods

If a recommended serving size of a favorite food, such as red meat, seems more like an appetizer than an entrée, use food choices rather than meal size as your guide to budgeting saturated fat. Eat lower-fat foods during the day and come dinner time, you will still have a major portion of your 25 grams left so you can dig into a larger portion of meat. However, if meat has been at the center of your meals all your life, you need to break up that daily pattern with fish, poultry and vegetarian entrées, because if you devote all of your 25 grams to meat (or any other high-fat food that you love) each day, you won't have enough diversity in your meals for health or pleasure. But on the days you do eat meat, you can budget your food choices so that you can push yourself away from the table feeling satisfied and well fed.

- We're saying that the speed with which you make changes depends on your overall heart health.
- If you have evidence of heart disease, make changes to your diet immediately by following the Stanford 17 Gram Plan.
- Others can adopt a gradual program of change that takes no longer than two months to incorporate all the recommendations of The Stanford Life Plan for a Healthy Heart and The Stanford 25 Gram Plan.
- Adopt a strategy for implementing change and incorporate it into your timetable.
- Use many approaches to cutting fat.
- Learn to identify high-fat foods.
- Use your own eating patterns to fashion your personal 25-gram plan.
- Eat small portions of your favorite high-fat foods.
- Eat these high-fat foods less frequently, interspersing them with lower-fat versions of the same dish or other low-fat foods.
- Eat only your favorite high-fat foods.
- Pass on high-fat foods you eat out of habit, not for pleasure.

To help you and your family keep track of the fat in your meals each day, we have designed The Fat Tracker's Fat Account, which you will find on the following pages. You may wish to make copies of it to keep handy for tallying your fat intake each day until fat-tracking high-fat foods becomes automatic.

THE FAT TRACKER'S FAT ACCOUNT

Your Fat Tracker's Fat Account can help you decide where to spend your grams of fat each day. Before long, as you familiarize yourself with the sources of saturated fat, healthy choices will become automatic. But until then, the Fat Account will help you control saturated fat and spread your 25 grams evenly throughout your meals. A double cheeseburger at the local fast-food franchise, for example, has a whole day's (or more!) allotment of fat, saturated and otherwise. If you choose our low-fat salads and vegetable recipes for the rest of your meals, you can indulge yourself and still stay within your allowance.

On occasion, blowing your allowance at one meal doesn't do any harm. But if you have one huge, saturated-fat blowout daily, such as barbecued spareribs or a hot fudge sundae, even if you stay within your fat budget for the day, you would have to pass up many healthy foods that supply needed vitamins and minerals because they also contain saturated fat. Your Fat Account will help you manage your daily allotment of fat and cholesterol, so you aren't reduced to nibbling on celery at dinner when your stomach is rumbling for something more substantial. It doesn't matter if you keep a written record or mental tally. You start each day with 25 grams in your Fat Account and subtract the saturated fat in your meals and snacks from that total.

To avoid overdrawing your Fat Account, become aware of all the foods with saturated fat (as well as total fat and cholesterol items) you eat during the day. When you have used up 25 grams of saturated fat, (75 grams of total fat and 300 milligrams of cholesterol), begin choosing foods such as grains, green vegetables and fruits that contain no fat.

You will notice as you become familiar with balancing your Fat Account that you may use up your allotment of *saturated* fat grams for the day, but still be able to choose foods flavored with olive oil or your favorite salad dressing, or delicious fish and turkey entrées because you still have *unsaturated* fat grams left to spend. The Fat Account is a boon when you know you have a party, vacation or other festive occasion coming up. Choose low-fat items for breakfast and lunch, and then use your unspent saturated fat grams to enjoy yourself when your favorite foods are passed at dinner or as snacks. For those of you with families to feed, we suggest you keep everyone's fat allotment posted in a prominent place in the kitchen to teach your children the value of "less is better" when it comes to saturated fat.

The Fat Tracker's Fat Account is especially crucial if you already have cardiovascular disease and must be very precise about limiting saturated fat to give your arteries every chance of healing the atherosclerotic lesions. Guessing the amount of fat in your food may be too risky for you. Refer to the nutritional tables throughout this book, as well as the recipe calculations, to determine the amount of saturated fat in your meals. Though we want to keep the emphasis on reducing saturated fat, if you wish, you can also track the amount of cholesterol in your meals as well. By referring to the nutritional tables in this book and writing down all sources of fat in the food you eat, you will guard against grams of saturated fat slipping unnoticed into your diet. When you reach the daily fat limits set in consultation with your doctor and/or dietitian, simply switch to other, fat-free foods that you enjoy. Whatever your needs, use The Fat Tracker's Fat Account to help you stay on the low-fat track.

THE FAT TRACKER'S DAILY FAT ACCOUNT

Date:

GRAMS OF SATURATED FAT AND MILLIGRAMS CHOLESTEROL EATEN AT:

Sources of Fat	Breakfast Saturated Fat/ Cholesterol	Lunch Saturated Fat/ Cholesterol	Dinner Saturated Fat/ Cholesterol	Snacks Saturated Fat/ Cholesterol
Milk				
Cheese				
Yogurt				
Cream				
Eggs				
Butter				
Margarine				
Cooking and salad oil				
Fish				
Poultry				
Red meat				
Snack and packaged foods				
Totals:				

CHAPTER 13

The Fat Tracker's Meal-Planning Guide

THE PATH TO THE TYPICAL AMERICAN DINING TABLE *is littered with good intentions about healthful eating. The Fat Tracker, on the other hand, knows how to maintain a commitment to healthy eating and enjoy fabulous food by following The Stanford 25 Gram Plan. But before we explain how to implement this plan, let's take a look at previous nutritional strategies. For many years the bible of healthful eating was the four basic food groups, which started out as an aid to ensure that people ate sufficient quantities of the right foods. What we didn't know hurt us, because that list unwittingly encouraged Americans to eat many high-fat foods. The four-food-group approach to nutrition has finally been tossed out. Let's examine its replacement before we give you The Stanford 25 Gram Plan's even more precise approach to choosing healthy foods.*

The Food Guide Pyramid and Why It's Not Enough

In an attempt to help the consumer figure out what to eat and how often, the U.S. Department of Agriculture and the U.S. Department of Health and Human Services collaborated on the design of the now famous Food Guide Pyramid. This logo illustrates how to build on a foundation of complex carbohydrates to compose a diet of healthy foods. The harmful fats, as well as other oils and sugars, are shown in smaller portions at the top, almost like icing on a cake. Suggested servings for each food category also help the consumer make healthier choices. Unfortunately, some patients have told us that when they first tried to interpret the pyramid they assumed that the most important foods were at the top and not the bottom.

The Food Guide Pyramid urges you to eat the same types of foods that we recommend in this book. It is a welcome addition to anyone's nutritional library and has been adopted by many food companies to augment the nutritional information they are now required to list on all products. We suggest you use the pyramid as the important visual aid that it is, as one way of helping you conceptualize the framework of your diet. Eat the many breads, cereals, fruits and vegetables that you find at the bottom of the pyramid; eat the few fats and sugars that you can squeeze into the top. In the middle, however, the pyramid lumps all cuts of meats together in its serving recommendations, rather than pinpoint those lowest in saturated fat, and it does not distinguish between whole-milk, low-fat and nonfat dairy products, nor other saturated-fat vs. unsaturated-fat items.

The Stanford 25 Gram Plan

The concrete information in the Stanford 25 Gram Plan and the meal-planning and fat-tracking information in this and the following chapters go several steps further to help you select the leanest version of the foods in the pyramid.

Let's recap what we have covered so far. You know that saturated fat is one of the major villains in coronary heart disease. It is also one of the most insidious—because, unlike smoking, you can't always tell when you are taking the substance into your body. Fat Trackers solve that problem by becoming expert at uncovering and controlling the sources of saturated fat.

❧ **Fat tracking begins with meal planning. The goal is to keep high the pleasure and satisfaction you deserve from mealtime, while keeping low the amount of harmful fats.**

Fat tracking allows you many options for controlling fat. The most obvious one consists of simply keeping a running tally of every single gram of saturated fat that you eat and stopping when you reach 25 grams each day. Unhappily, given America's breakfast tradition, that stopping point can occur by the time you are ready for a midmorning snack! But fat tracking doesn't just mean you have to put a laptop computer on your knee instead of a dinner napkin. You can achieve your dietary goals by fat tracking your food choices, in addition to counting each gram of fat you eat. Mealtime fat tracking helps you plan menus for breakfast, lunch and dinner that include a high percentage of filling and satisfying complex carbohydrate foods with a lower percentage of saturated-fat foods spread over the course of a day.

But the successful Fat Tracker doesn't stop at planning meals one day at a time. We want you to eat complex carbohydrates several times every day, in our mouth-watering dishes such as White Bean and Chicken Salad with Basil and Fennel (page 395), Minestrone (page 378–79), Roasted Winter Vegetables with Persillade (page 420–21), Oven-Baked French Fries (page 412–13), and Black Bean Breakfast Cakes with Salsa Ranchera (page 302–3). However, you must put a weekly cap on other foods, such as egg yolks and items made with coconut oil, as well as limiting the portion size and number of weekly servings of meat, fish and poultry that contain saturated fat and cholesterol. Obviously then, the successful Fat Tracker thinks ahead—way ahead—by planning a week's worth of meals, all 21 breakfasts, lunches and dinners, to include all food options for the week. We will give you guidelines for those meals and show you how to turn our recommendations for Better Breakfasts, Crunchy Lunches and 2 + 2 Dinners into a healthy scheme for a week's worth of exciting eating. But first let's discuss what we mean by serving size and the frequency that you eat—or don't eat—certain foods.

The Fat Tracker's Serving Size

We have told you to fill your shopping cart with foods that are 25 to 30 percent fat, 15 to 20 percent protein, 50 to 60 percent carbohydrates. Okay, you answer, but how do I make a meal out of numbers? You begin by determining what this ratio means in terms of serving size and number of servings of your favorite foods. The concept of serving size has different meanings for different people. Your neighbor's idea of a single serving of rich lasagna might feed you for a week. However, if the lasagna is heavy on pasta and tomato sauce and light on meat and cheese, you can both help yourself to the portion size you prefer.

Though it is difficult to be exact without listing all possible combinations of foods and dishes, you may find the following chart helpful for estimating serving sizes of these foods. In addition, each of our recipes indicates the number of servings or serving size, and we have calculated the grams of total fat, saturated fat, cholesterol, calories, fiber and sodium for each serving. As you become familiar with the serving size for the ingredients in our recipes, you can use these concepts to estimate more accurately the ideal serving size for your other recipes that do not provide this important information. Use the following sketch as an estimate of the recommended 3.5-ounce portion of meat, fish and protein, roughly the size of a deck of cards.

SERVING SIZE OF FOODS

Meat, poultry and fish	3 to 4 ounces (cooked)
Fats and oils	1 tablespoon
Low-fat or nonfat milk, yogurt, cottage cheese	1 cup
Hard cheese or cream cheese	1 ounce
Egg yolks	3 per week
Grains and pasta	1 cup (cooked)
Cold or cooked cereals	1 cup
Breads	1 slice
Vegetables	1 cup (raw)
Fruits	1 medium
Juice	½ cup

Frequency

How often should you eat these foods? As we have discussed, The Stanford 25 Gram Plan helps you design 21 menus, with the goal of spreading fat and cholesterol items more or less evenly over seven days' worth of meals. The Stanford 25 Gram Plan's Frequency Table will help you stay on target by suggesting how often to include these items. In The Stanford 25 Gram Plan, we have spelled out the limits for fat and cholesterol in your diet. In addition, we recommend that you include a minimum of 3 to 5 servings of vegetables, 2 to 4 servings of fruit and 6 to 11 servings of breads and grains each day. A rigid daily schedule is not as important as tracking your intake of these foods over time. For example, when you are on vacation or are partying during the holidays you may eat more rich foods than normal. But if, throughout the year, you use these recommendations to balance your meals on a daily basis, those welcome, occasional indulgences will not cause you any harm.

Use the flexibility of The Stanford 25 Gram Plan to help you with food selection. For instance, we list hard cheese and partially skim-milk cheese in the "Twice a Week" column, but you may prefer to have a small amount of Parmesan or Romano cheese grated on pasta four to five times a week, rather than have a larger serving in a cheese sandwich once or twice a week. Organ meats stand alone in the "Almost Never" column, not only because they contain a great deal of fat, but because they have astronomically high cholesterol levels. Limit liver, liver pâté, kidneys and other organ meats to very infrequent occasions. As yet, we have not found any food that falls into the "Never, ever let it cross your lips" category, but we do have an extensive list of foods under "Rarely." While you can fit small amounts of these foods into The Stanford 25 Gram Plan on occasion when you are designing your own menus, some of the items are simply hard to avoid in the outside world. For example, dinner at a friend's home may include more butter, chocolate or high-fat meat than you had bargained for, so we suggest you reserve these high-fat items for the rare times when you simply can't avoid them.

Use this table as a handy general guideline, but remember that the daily limits of 25 grams of saturated fat and 75 grams of total fat will actually determine the portion size and the frequency with which these foods appear on your menus. You will find yourself referring to this table frequently at first, but before long you will recognize the precise serving size for your favorite foods and you will only need to check it for foods you eat occasionally. Until you become familiar with the foods you can eat regularly and those to enjoy only on an infrequent basis, you may want to photocopy this chart and keep it handy in your kitchen.

THE STANFORD 25 GRAM PLAN'S FREQUENCY TABLE

Almost Never	Rarely (Once a month)	Occasionally (Twice a week)	Often (4 to 5 times a week)	Always (Daily)
Organ meats	Cream	Lean meat	Fish	Fruits
	Butter	Dark meat of poultry	Chicken and turkey breast	Vegetables
	Duck	Chicken and turkey hot dogs	Low-fat or nonfat cheeses and dairy products	Grains, breads and pasta
	Poultry skin	Shellfish		Nonfat milk, yogurt, cottage cheese and other nonfat cheese and cream products
	Sausage	Egg yolks (3 per week)		
	Bacon	Whole-milk cheeses and dairy products		
	Lard			
	Canned shortening	Avocados		Olive oil and canola oil
	Palm and coconut oils	Nuts		
	Chocolate	Seeds		
	Cold cuts			
	Hot dogs			
	Spareribs			
	Rich desserts and pastries			

Now that you know what to eat, let's take a look at how to transform these foods into heart-healthy meals.

Better Breakfasts

A friend who traveled extensively in rural parts of Asia thrilled at discovering local foods. However, despite his adventurous appetite at lunch and dinner, he missed his American-style coffee, toast and eggs for breakfast. His experience, shared by many travelers, illustrates our deeply ingrained breakfast rituals. We resist altering whatever combination of fat, protein and carbohydrates that helps us make the transition from peaceful slumber to the rigors of the day. People have strong opinions about the best way to start the day, whether it is simply black coffee on the run; a bacon, sausage and egg extravaganza or any of the toast/juice/muffin/cereal/fruit combinations. We can explain that a steaming bowl of vegetable soup with tofu will nourish you at breakfast as fully as a cheese omelet. However, we know that many of you will gladly trade a roast beef sandwich for a bowl of nonfat yogurt at lunch before you would let anyone tinker with your favorite breakfast menu.

❦ **The first meal of the day remains the most challenging one to alter because so many Americans are introduced to the world of high-fat breakfasts at a tender age.**

Food rituals and preferences evolve from the choices parents make for their children. But even as they mature and eventually expose themselves to ethnic foods, new friends and travel opportunities that exert new influences and broaden their appetites for different foods, *everybody* in America seems to eat the same limited fare at breakfast. Even restaurants that feature diverse foods during the rest of the day usually offer a variation on the bacon and egg routine at breakfast. You can see that without a concerted effort to break away from these lethal breakfasts, there is very little inspiration to change. It would almost seem that we are ordained to stuff ourselves with saturated fat early in the morning—or doomed to.

Your most important fat-tracking exercise, therefore, may be to recall on a daily basis, until it becomes part of your personal philosophy, that food preferences are merely learned. We gently suggest to those of you who cling to the typical American breakfast—complete with a combination of butter, cream, cheese, eggs, fried ham, bacon and sausage—that these items, depending on the size of your servings, can contain more than a day's maximum allotment of harmful fats. A hearty weekend brunch for example, could use up several days' allowance of saturated fat or cholesterol. In addition, because many people are hooked on breakfast pastries, you can consume a high concentration of saturated-fat calories with very little in the way of real nutrition before the day has begun. For example, an old-fashioned glazed doughnut has 3.5 grams of saturated fat and 242 calories, while a thick slice of whole grain pumpernickel toast topped with ¼ cup cinnamon-laced nonfat cottage cheese and drizzled with a teaspoon of orange or sage honey contains only a trace of saturated fat and about 140 calories plus crucial calcium and B vitamins. Since honey contains mostly fructose (fruit sugar), which is almost twice as sweet as sucrose (table sugar), you get a bonus of more sweetness per calorie—good news for those of you with a sweet tooth.

Even people who are health conscious, but don't scrutinize the ingredients in their choices, may assume that a bran muffin or bowl of granola is giving them a healthy edge. But careful label-reading shows how high in fat some of these items can be. Remember that because of the new labeling laws, producers can't hide high-fat items behind meaningless claims such as "low in cholesterol," anymore. As we explain further in Part Three, however, supermarkets stock these impostors in the health food section, giving them an aura of fat-tracking respectability they may not deserve. But just as we learned to enjoy high-fat breakfast foods when we were toddlers, we can also learn to enjoy Better Breakfasts composed of less fatty, less health-threatening but equally delicious foods as adults.

🌿 **It may also help to realize that not all humans breakfast on a glut of fatty food; in many countries rice, cereal, breads, fish and vegetables are the preferred first meal of the day.**

The Stanford 25 Gram Plan Better Breakfasts include moderately low-protein and low-fat foods, such as our enriched fruit shakes. We replace whole eggs with liquid egg substitute to create yolkless Pasta Omelet with Fresh Tomatoes and Basil (page 317–18) or French Toast with Orange and Dried Cranberry Sauce (page 310). And we use low-fat and nonfat milk products such as buttermilk, yogurt and cottage cheese in familiar delicacies such as Dried Blueberry Buttermilk Pancakes (page 305) and Whole Grain Buttermilk Waffles (page 307), which have zero fat, and top them with fresh fruit or Dried Blueberry Honey Sauce (page 306) and Strawberry-Peach Sauce (page 308) instead of butter and syrup. In addition to being fat free, these sauces require little sugar to bring out their natural sweetness. We choose liberally from whole grain cereals, muffins and breads, fresh fruit or yogurt spreads on toast.

For hearty appetites, we suggest lean Canadian bacon or easy-to-make, wonderfully seasoned homemade or commercial low-fat sausages (take a close look at our easy-to-make collection starting on page 321). Instead of conventional hash browns and a breakfast steak containing a punishing 11.6 grams of saturated fat, try our Jalapeño Hash Browns with Cilantro Cream and a broiled chicken breast weighing in at under 2 grams saturated fat per serving. For the adventuresome, try soup, bean dishes, tortillas filled with hot salsa and chicken. Why not reheat any remaining chicken stew, stir-fried vegetables or low-fat lasagna? They are as nourishing the next morning as they were the night before. And since many dishes age well, you might find some of them even more robustly flavored.

When you are on the run, stick a potato in the microwave before you jump in the shower, then top it with some yogurt and a dash of piquant Tellicherry, lemon or Malabar pepper for a quick, filling, low-fat start to your busy day. Use weekends or evenings to bake our low-fat pastries, such as Plum Focaccia (page 318–19), and freeze them in individual servings. They will defrost by the time you get to work, and, on your coffee break, you can replace the usual cheese Danish or greasy apple fritter with your own home-baked, low-fat pastry.

Remember that breakfast is the ideal place to start your goal of 25 grams of fiber for the day. In Chapter 17: Fat Tracking in the Supermarket, you will learn how to read labels to find high-fiber cereals, breads and muffins. We could go on and on. And we will, giving you detailed recipes for low-fat, high-enjoyment breakfast options without the cholesterol and saturated-fat booby trap that too many people think of as their breakfast birthright.

The Crunchy Lunch

A creamy, fatty lunch is usually a quiet affair: Saturated fat slips almost silently into your body if you chew softly on a hamburger and fries during the noon hour, or sip cream of broccoli soup, made with real cream. Fat Trackers do away with the quiet, creamy, fatty lunch and celebrate the healthy, noisy, crunchy lunch packed with crackling, crispy complex carbohydrates. Yes, *we* know potato chips announce themselves loudly as you dip into the little bag that often accompanies a cheese sandwich from the local deli. But *you* know that is not the kind of crunch that will help your heart or keep you under your 25-gram saturated-fat target.

Whether you brown bag it in the lunchroom at work, eat on the run so you can stop at the bank on payday or treat yourself to a linen napkin lunch at a terrific restaurant now and then, saturated-fat foods are a constant lure. At noontime they offer portability (cheese sandwich from home), availability (hamburger and fries from the nearest franchise) and pure luxury in fine restaurants (creamed soups du jour, hollandaise and butter sauces on vegetables, gooey desserts).

❧ **Don't give up convenience, portability or elegance. Just make your selections heard—literally.**

If your lunch doesn't have a crunch, at least make sure it doesn't have cream. When you crave something smooth, make it icy sherbet, nonfat frozen yogurt or fruit sorbet. Save the cheese-laden, creamy sauces, soups and dressings for dinnertime when you can control the richness by preparing them from our heart-smart recipes. Reach for the cruets of oil and vinegar at the salad bar instead of ladling on big globs of creamy and fatty cheese or ranch-style dressings. Yes, an oil and vinegar dressing has fat and calories, but the fat is easier on your arteries compared to the saturated fat and cholesterol hidden in rich cream and cheese dressings. Pass on the trays of potato, macaroni and chicken salad if they appear drenched in mayonnaise, and choose instead strips of turkey or chicken breast, lean roast beef, sushi and all the beans and vegetables you like.

Find a Mexican restaurant that serves whole black beans, instead of refried beans that may harbor lard. Order a bean and vegetable burrito rather than a deep-fried taco. Say "no" to cheese and guacamole, but "yes" to extra beans, salsa and even hot sauce if you like. Frequent any Asian restaurant and ask for the chicken or fish specialties they don't deep-fry. Go to a fish house and ask them to grill the day's catch, rather than drown it in the deep-fat fryer. When you join the gang at a fast-food restaurant use the eating-out guidelines on page 240 to stick to your 25-gram allotment of saturated fat.

Get the idea? Just because you have to rush, doesn't mean you can't turn heads at noontime—as neighboring diners strain to identify that crunch that sounds so good in your lunch.

Choose the Low-Fat Crunch in:

Crunchy salads—in a bowl, in a pita pocket, in a sandwich

Crunchy fruits and fresh vegetables (raw or lightly steamed) from the salad bar

Crunchy whole grain rye, wheat, raisin or pita breads, French rolls, bagels, cracker bread and crisp, low-fat crackers

Crunchy soups made with vegetables, pasta, legumes and grains

Crunchy relishes, such as salsas and chutneys

Crunchy air-popped popcorn (no butter) or pretzels

Grilled skinless chicken breast on a whole wheat bun

Smoked turkey on a whole grain roll

Tuna or chicken salad (hold the mayo please) with lots of celery, apples or grapes

Shrimp,* crabmeat,* tofu or low-fat cheese sandwiches with salsa, vegetable relishes, cranberry, curry or low-fat yogurt sauce instead of mayonnaise or cheese dressings

Old-fashioned-style peanut butter (without hydrogenated oils) and unsweetened fruit purée sandwich on whole grain bread

Homemade vegetable-filled burritos

Bean, lentil or grain salads and soups

Pasta, bean, rice and grain salads with vegetables

Taco salads with lots of beans

Low-fat leftovers tucked into a sandwich or added to a salad

Crunchy gingersnaps

*Not as a daily selection, though, because of the high cholesterol count

Instead of the Soft, Creamy Items in:

Meat and cheese sandwiches

Beef or processed meat sandwiches, such as bologna or salami

Soft, white bread

Creamy soups

Creamy sauces

Creamy salad dressings such as ranch, Roquefort or bleu cheese

Shakes and ice cream

2 + 2 Dinners = A Healthy Heart

As you can see from the fat-tracking tables in Part Three, ounce for ounce, *in addition to lots of cholesterol* red meat packs more saturated fat than any other food. Typical portions of beef, pork and lamb feed a minimum of 7 or 8 grams of saturated fat into your body, and the richer cuts, such as a (not uncommon) 7-ounce serving of prime rib, can have 27 grams of saturated fat. You have exceeded your daily total before you even put butter and sour cream on the baked potato! Taking in a slug of fat and cholesterol at the end of the day, except for festive occasions when it is very carefully budgeted into your eating plan, doesn't leave you any options for eating a few higher-fat items, intermingled with many filling and delicious complex carbohydrates at your other meals.

The Fat Tracker's answer to the red meat dilemma consists of some simple arithmetic: 2 + 2 Dinners, a frontal attack on the typical protein-rich American dinner. No one has to swear off all red meat or *any* food that contains saturated fat unless your doctor has advised you that your cholesterol levels or other symptoms are warning you of heart trouble. In that case, you must consider removing nearly all red meat from your diet. However, for those of you who enjoy red meat and don't require such drastic reductions in saturated fat, we have the solution: Just eat no more than two red meat entrées each week. The other half of the 2 + 2 equation turns you into a fat-tracking, twice-a-week vegetarian by calling for *at least* two meatless dinner entrées each week that focus on complex carbohydrates. Choose fish, chicken or even another meatless entree for the remaining meals.

❧ **2 + 2 = no more than 2 red meat dinners each week + at least 2 vegetarian dinners.**

The typical adult needs in the neighborhood of six to eight ounces of protein each day, but it doesn't have to be in the form of red meat. By striking large and frequent servings of red meat from your diet, you rid your meals of excess grams of fat *and* cholesterol in one swift stroke. As 2 + 2 Dinners reduce both saturated fat and total fat calories from your diet, they also keep the amount of protein you eat in check.

On days when you eat your meatless main meal, plan to include low-fat cottage cheese and/or yogurt, egg whites, tofu, legumes, nuts, grains or small amounts of cheese in your menus to provide adequate low-fat protein. If you find yourself unexpectedly having a red meat lunch on a day you planned a meat entrée for dinner, remember to change your plans and substitute chicken, fish or a meatless entrée for your evening meal instead.

The section Is a Vegetarian Diet Better? (page 100) contains tips on combining nonanimal protein foods to provide adequate complete protein in your meals. Our recipes, those with and without meat, will also supply plenty of inspiration for satisfying meals using small amounts of meat or no meat at all. We will also show you how you can turn some of your own red meat recipes into leaner, healthier versions.

Meal Planning in Action

Keep the follow fat-tracking rules in mind as you plan your meals:

- Do not serve red meat more than once a day. On days you have bacon for breakfast, don't fix a roast beef sandwich for lunch or grill lamb for dinner. Have chicken, fish or a vegetarian entrée instead.
- To control calories as well as fat, and keep protein levels in line, limit meat, fish and poultry portions to approximately 3 cooked ounces. A 4-ounce lean, uncooked portion usually yields a 3 to 3.5 ounce cooked serving.
- Do not eat more than one food high in cholesterol, such as eggs and shellfish, on the same day.
- As you limit egg yolks to 3 per week, don't forget to count the eggs in mayonnaise (if you use it frequently), baked goods and other cooked products.

The following table illustrates The Fat Tracker's Meal-Planning Guide in action. Your tastes may differ from ours entirely, but you can use the fat-tracking principles to design your 21 healthy and delicious meals each week to include your own favorite foods. The recipes for the items in italic type are listed in the index. The other lunch items represent a cross section of quick and take-out lunch menus. This sample illustrates how to include the major items in your meals. During the course of the day, have a glass of low-fat milk now and then or a dish of nonfat yogurt with berries, add a roll at dinner or some breadsticks at lunch, snack on a mix of raisins, sunflower seeds and almonds from the vending machine at break time, and otherwise satisfy yourself with favorite foods that would provide all the protein, fiber and nutrients your body needs.

	Better Breakfast	Crunchy Lunch	2 + 2 Dinner
Monday	Breakfast Fig and Banana Split, whole wheat toast and honey, coffee	Chicken salad with whole wheat roll, frozen yogurt	Spaghetti with Meat Sauce, green salad
Tuesday	Whole Grain Butter-milk Waffles with Strawberry-Peach Sauce, coffee	Minestrone, bread-sticks, fruit salad, Gingerbread with Ginger Cream	Sea Bass Grilled with Cilantro and Jalapeño Marinade, Brussels Sprouts with Lemon and Garlic, whole wheat rolls, Roasted Pears with Anise Crumbs
Wednesday	Cold cereal with 1% milk and fresh berries, bagel with low-fat yogurt cheese and marmalade, tea	Stuffed grape leaves, Heart-Healthy Hum-mus and whole wheat pita bread, apple and sherbet	Curry-Spiked Turkey with Mango Chutney Sauce, brown rice, grilled eggplant, red peppers and zucchini with balsamic vinegar, Fresh Plum Pastry Cake
Thursday	Orange juice, Cran-berry Bran Muffin spread with part skim milk ricotta cheese and strawberry jam, low-fat hot cocoa	Spinach salad, Potato and Red Pepper Soup, Fig Newton	Grilled salmon, Linguini with Quick Roasted Tomato Sauce, Pear Mousse with Blueberries
Friday	Orange juice, Break-fast Cheese Pizza, coffee	Turkey sandwich, Stanford Shake	Couscous With Simmered, Spiced Vegetables, breadsticks and White Bean Pâté, low-fat or nonfat frozen yogurt
Saturday	French Toast with Orange and Dried Cranberry Sauce, coffee	Low fat cottage cheese, fresh fruit salad, breadsticks with sesame seeds	London Broil Teriyaki, rice, grilled vegetables, fresh pineapple and gingersnaps
Sunday	Fresh melon, Jalapeño Hash Browns with Cilantro Pesto, coffee	Onion soup, hard roll, fresh pear, iced tea with lemon	Black Bean Chili with Cilantro Pesto, Whole Wheat Corn Muffins, sliced tomato salad

*Note: Italics indicates recipe is listed in the index.

Following the Fat Tracker's Meal-Planning Guide will ensure that you reduce the fat and cholesterol in your diet. Remember that a maximum of 25 grams of saturated fat is only one side of the coin in the Stanford Plan. The other side is a minimum of 25 grams of fiber. In the following chapter we will tell you how to raise your intake of fiber along with all the vitamins, minerals and antioxidants for a healthy heart.

- The specific infomation provided by The Stanford 25 Gram Plan in its meal-planning and fat-tracking information helps you select the leanest versions of your favorite foods.
- Fat tracking depends on meal planning and controlling portion size and frequency.
- There are no forbidden foods, but some foods should be eaten infrequently.
- Plan ahead and over the course of a week you can include any food in your 25-gram plan.
- Plan your meals around Better Breakfasts, Crunchy Lunches and 2 + 2 Dinners, and you can stick to your 25-gram plan without having to give it much thought.

Check Yourself #4: How Often Do You Eat...?

	Seldom/Never	Sometimes	Frequently
1. Salads with cheese and creamy dressings	3	2	1
2. Pies, cakes, cookies	3	2	1
3. Chocolate candy	3	2	1
4. Snack chips, potato chips, corn chips, pork skins or cheese puffs	3	2	1
5. Buttered popped or microwaved popcorn	3	2	1
6. Snack crackers, like Ritz or Wheat Thins	3	2	1
7. Sour cream and mayonnaise dips	3	2	1
8. French fries, fried potatoes or hash browns	3	2	1
9. Rice, potatoes or noodles with butter, sour cream, whole cream	3	2	1
10. Doughnuts, sweet rolls, croissants	3	2	1

Total

Circle the response that most nearly describes your habits and total your score.

25–30 = Excellent, try for a perfect 30.

15–24 = You have some problem areas. Acquaint yourself with more low-fat snack foods; don't automatically reach for familiar salads, sauces and dips; look for low-fat alternatives—they are plentiful.

10–14 = Whoops. Your best strategy is to choose whole grains, fresh fruit and vegetables and no "white" sauces and dips until new low-fat habits take root.

CHAPTER 14

Finding Fiber and Antioxidants: Produce, Legumes and Grains

EVE'S TAMPERING WITH THE APPLE NOTWITHSTANDING, *there is no forbidden fruit. Nor is there a vegetable, legume or grain that isn't good for you, except of course for coconut with its unfortunate slug of saturated fat. Otherwise, unless you adulterate plant food with butter or cream, you will find most of the healthful nutrients your body needs in the garden. And that is only the beginning. These foods are not only nutritious, they are proving to be disease fighters. So much so that every mother's urging to "eat your vegetables" may in fact be a medical imperative. Nature's bounty is our only source of phytosterols, which we have already discussed in Chapter 3 as playing a role in preventing the absorption of cholesterol. We depend on vegetables, fruits and grains to provide essential nu-trients, low-fat or fat-free complex carbohydrates and healthful oils, all of which are crucial to a sound body. But it is also the heavy concentration of fiber and antioxidants in plant food that has excited the medical community. These two important dietary elements have featured roles in The Stanford Life Plan for a Healthy Heart.*

Finding Fiber

It has become clear that including at least 25 grams of fiber in your diet every day is as important as limiting saturated fat to 25 grams. Most Americans eat fewer than 25 grams of fiber, and studies have consistently linked a low-fiber intake with increased risk for coronary heart disease and colon cancer. On that basis, the National Research Council has recommended that everyone consume at least 25 to 35 grams of dietary fiber a day, a goal that the guidelines of The Stanford 25 Gram Plan will help you reach. Fruits, vegetables (including the skins and seeds) and whole grain products contain two distinct types of fiber: insoluble and soluble. It is helpful to appreciate their differences and recognize the foods that contain them.

INSOLUBLE FIBER England's Dr. Denis Burkitt and others pursued landmark research showing that insoluble fiber (indigestible roughage that does not dissolve in water) adds bulk to the stool and appears to protect against diseases of the colon, such as diverticulitis and cancer. Of all the foods that provide this crucial type of fiber, the most important are grains.

SOLUBLE FIBER Soluble fiber, which does dissolve in water, has been shown to bind with cholesterol when it circulates into the gastrointestinal tract, thereby lowering your cholesterol count. Studies at Stanford University Hospital have also shown that, in addition to eating a diet high in fruits and vegetables, when commercial products with soluble fiber such as Metamucil® or Citrucil® are taken for the purposes of adding bulk to the stool, they also can lower cholesterol levels. The finding that 15 to 45 grams of soluble fiber daily can lower blood cholesterol by as much as 6 to 19 percent started the oat bran boom. You may have also noticed that you can buy fiber capsules over the counter. However, we recommend that you steer clear of supplements or schemes that depend on a single food or item to shore up a diet. While oat bran does supply this important fiber, keep in mind that nature does not hoard its bounty in one or two foods, but deliberately spreads it around, and we suggest you do, too.

Finding Fiber in Legumes

Oat bran may have gotten the media blitz, but one of the best places to look for soluble, heart-saving fiber is in the legume family. For example, one cup of uncooked oats or two-thirds cup oat bran adds up to more cooked oat bran cereal or muffins than most people enjoy eating in a day. But approximately the same amount of soluble fiber is found in one cup of legumes (dried beans and peas that are among the most nutritious of foods), a volume quite palatable in a bowl of our Black Bean Chili with Cilantro Pesto (page 428–29). Sop up the chili with our Whole Wheat Corn Muffins—a combination that also makes an excellent, protein-rich, meatless entrée for one of your 2 + 2 Dinners. Then munch on a piece of fresh fruit to cool the chili's fire, and you will have increased your fiber totals even more. Sample the whole family of dried legumes, from tiny white beans to giant black runners to delicate flageolets to hardy split peas to elegant French green lentils to robust garbanzos (chickpeas), as well as the humble navy bean. You don't have to give up oat bran muffins for breakfast if you don't want to, but for lunch, dinner or just plain noshing, don't forget about Pinto Beans with Carmelized Onions and Thyme (page 432–33), Flageolets with Tarragon (page 435–36), White Bean and Vegetable Chili with Grilled Chicken (page 436–37), Curried Red Lentil Soup (page 364–65) or lemon-tinged White Bean Pâté (page 345) from our collection of recipes that showcases all the dried beans.

Finding Fiber in Grains

If you read a 1950s vintage cookbook, you would think only one grain ever appeared in an American market—white rice. And the only thing that ever topped it was a white sauce made with butter and whole milk or cream. The influx of ethnic cuisines and the easy access to many of the ingredients they require has created an explosion of grain dishes available across the country. Track down several different varieties of rice in Asian markets and health food stores or look for the newly popular aromatic rices such as basmati (Hindi for "queen of fragrance" and our favorite), Texmati (an American hybrid), wehani and jasmine. A California grower has produced delicious strains of brown rice variously called Christmas rice and red rice. If you think brown rice has to replace white to get sufficient fiber, you are succumbing to a food myth. The total fiber in unmilled rice is high enough that even a serving of milled white rice has the equivalent fiber of two slices of raisin toast. Choose a rice, white or brown, because it has complex carbohydrates and because you like its flavor and the way it complements your dish.

Look for new grains, at least new to our markets, such as healthful quinoa and amaranth (try popping amaranth kernels in a hot, dry skillet for a fiber-filled crunchy addition to cereals, vegetables and poultry). Experiment with cornmeal in breads and coatings for oven-baked or grilled dishes, as we do in Herb Crusted Oven-Fried Chicken (page 500–1). Try Whole Grain Buttermilk Waffles (page 307) to sample the successful combination of millet for sweetness and buckwheat for texture that also works in breads and muffins. Add whole wheatberries, softened slightly in water, to oatmeal cookies or breads. Use whole grains and extra unprocessed bran in your cereals and baking whenever possible.

Remember that you need both kinds of fiber for optimum health, so eat a mix of foods that will give you a total of at least 25 grams of soluble and nonsoluble fiber every day. Cooking decreases the amount of fiber in foods, so canned fruits and vegetables are not ideal sources. Some brands of cereals and breads have fiber added for totals even greater than our examples. Read all product labels to find those with the most fiber and least fat.

HIGH-FIBER FOODS

Food	Grams Fiber	Serving Size
Cereals (100% bran or concentrated bran cereals are generally higher and can contribute as much as 15 grams per ½ cup serving)	2–3 grams	1 ounce or ½ cup
Unprocessed bran (for baking)	6 grams	1½ ounces
100% whole wheat, whole grain breads and crackers	2 grams	1 slice
Fresh or dried fruit, *not* canned, cooked, processed or peeled	2 grams	1 piece fresh; approximately 3 tablespoons dried depending on type
Fresh or frozen vegetables, *not* canned, cooked, processed or peeled	2–3 grams	½ cup
Dried beans, cooked	7–9 grams	½ cup
Split peas and lentils, cooked	4 grams	½ cup
Whole potatoes, brown, wild or white rice, bulgur wheat, cooked	3 grams	1 cup
Nuts and seeds	1 gram	1 tablespoon

❧ **Always leave skin on fresh fruit and vegetables for higher fiber content.**

The following sample menu demonstrates how to add sufficient fiber to a typical day's meals. The totals will vary with individual products and portion sizes.

SAMPLE ONE-DAY MENU OF HIGH-FIBER FOODS

	Fiber Content
Breakfast: A bowl of whole grain oat cereal (3g) a small sliced fresh peach (2g) and a toasted piece of multigrain bread (2g)	7 grams
Lunch: Bowl of split pea soup (8g), green salad (2g) and a small unpeeled apple (2g)	12 grams
Dinner: Small baked potato (3g), carrots (2g), whole wheat roll (2g)	7 grams
Total for day	26 grams

Antioxidant Foods and Supplements

The diversity of foods that supply both types of fiber also provide many other essential nutrients, including the important antioxidants. Scientific evidence is mounting that these compounds found in plant food are associated with lessened risk for coronary heart disease, as well as cancer. Among the more than 20 known antioxidants are vitamins C, E, and beta-carotene. We recommend you eat freely of foods containing antioxidants and supplement your diet with antioxidant vitamin supplements when necessary. The table on page 150 lists the foods highest in these important elements.

❧ **How might these simple vitamins ward off something as serious as heart disease or cancer?**

Free radicals, substances that form within a cell as the body transfers food into energy, have been implicated in many diseases, including atherosclerosis. Free radicals lack a crucial electron and will rob one from neighboring compounds within the cell, changing their structure and damaging the cell. This process can occur thousands of times in each cell over the course of the day and is considered to be one of the factors that contribute to the aging process and tissue damage. Antioxidants are substances, such as vitamins C and E and beta-carotene, that may protect against heart disease by rendering these harmful free radicals inactive. As we discussed earlier, we currently believe that it is the oxidized form of LDL that gets into the artery wall to deposit cholesterol and contribute to plaque development. Antioxidants, therefore, may prevent the oxidization of LDL from occurring, and thus lessen deposition of cholesterol in the artery wall.

How do you know if you are eating enough antioxidants? Hefty daily servings of the foods on page 150 will help. Baby Pumpkins with Apple, Grape and Walnut Stuffing (page 408–9), Spiced Sauté of Broccoli Stalks, Carrots and Potatoes (page 401) and Garlic Roasted Chicken with Wilted Greens (page 510–11) are just a few of our recipes high in antioxidants. However, many scientists believe that it is difficult to get adequate antioxidants from food sources alone. Vitamin supplements are now being recommended as preventive therapy for people who want to do everything possible to maintain optimal health and to prevent heart disease and cancer. It will be many years before we understand fully the role of vitamins in preventing heart disease. However, we believe the evidence is strong enough to make the following daily recommendations for adults, in addition to including vegetables and fruit in your diet:

Daily Recommendations for Vitamin Supplements

- Vitamin C 500 mg
- Vitamin E 400 I.U.
- Beta-carotene 25,000 I.U.

Are these the right doses? As researchers continue to investigate these intriguing substances, only time will tell if, in terms of health awareness, antioxidants will become to the 90s what cholesterol was to the 80s. In the meantime, we believe that these supplements are safe for you and may help you with your goal for a healthy heart and body.

No capsule or single food can provide the adequate nutrition or pleasure that comes from eating a variety of foods. If you do take a supplement, though, such as the vitamin E we recommend, or a daily vitamin pill, make sure it is in addition to, not instead of, well-balanced meals, which the Stanford 25 Gram Plan will supply. We are grateful to Patricia Schaaf, R.D., of Stanford Hospital's Nutrition Department, for permission to use the following chart of foods high in antioxidants which she prepared for Stanford's patients.

Foods	Serving	Beta-carotene	Vitamin C	Vitamin E
Apple	1 each		*	
Almonds	1 ounce			**
Apricot	3 each	**	*	
Asparagus	½ cup each		*	**
Avocado	½ each		*	*
Broccoli	1 cup	*	**	
Brussels sprouts	1 cup	*	**	*
Cantaloupe	1 cup	**	**	
Carrot	1 each	**	*	
Cauliflower	½ cup		**	
Celery	3 each	*	*	
Cornmeal	1 cup			*
Endive	1 cup	*		
Filberts	1 ounce			**
Grapefruit, pink	½ each	*	**	
Green beans	½ cup		*	
Greens, beet	½ cup	*		
Greens, collard	1 cup	**	**	
Greens, mustard	1 cup	**		*
Guava	1 cup	*	**	
Kale	½ cup	**	**	**
Leek	½ cup		*	
Lettuce, romaine	1 cup	*	**	
Mango	1 each		**	**
Oat Bran	2 cups			**
Oils	¼ cup			**
Orange	1 each		**	
Parsley	½ cup	**	**	
Peach, dried	10 halves	**	*	**
Peanuts (butter)	1 ounce			*
Pepper, green bell	½ cup		**	
Pepper, red bell	½ cup	*	**	
Plum	1 each		*	
Pumpkin	1 cup	*	**	*
Rice, brown	1 cup			**
Soy flour	1 cup			**
Spinach	1 cup	**	**	*
Squash, summer	½ cup		*	
Squash, winter	1 cup	**	**	*
Sunflower seeds	1 cup			**

Foods	Serving	Beta-carotene	Vitamin C	Vitamin E
Sweet potato	1 medium	**	**	**
Swiss Chard, raw	1 cup	**	**	*
Tomato products	½ cup	*	**	*
Tomato, raw	1 each		**	
Tomato, sun-dried	1 cup		**	
Wheat germ	1 cup			**
Wheatena 1 each	1 cup			**

* Good Source = 10–19% Daily Value
** Excellent Source = 20% or greater Daily Value

For optimum health, help yourself to all the delicious, fresh apples, cherries, lettuce, broccoli, potatoes, carrots, pineapple, grapefruit, yams, persimmons, parsley, asparagus, peaches, eggplant, grapes, hot peppers, sweet peppers and corn your shopping cart can hold.

❧ **We recommend from five to nine servings of produce a day with only one limitation: Avoid the processed, high-fat items you find in cans, microwave-ready meals, and frozen dinners.**

These processed foods may contain too much saturated fat and transfatty acids to justify the convenience. When fresh produce is simply not available to you, sharpen your fat-tracking skills and seek out frozen vegetables that don't have added butter or cheese sauces (save the two to three grams of saturated fat and season plain frozen vegetables with some olive oil and herbs), and look for canned beans without pork or chicken fat added.

WHAT ARE WE SAYING?

- Eat your vegetables! And grains and legumes, as well. For flavor, for fiber, for antioxidants.
- Choose fresh produce whenever possible and season fruits and vegetables without butter, cream and cheese.
- Help yourself to all produce that is frozen, canned in natural juices and unsweetened, dried fruits and vegetables; all dried or canned (without saturated fat) legumes, such as split peas, lentils, garbanzo beans, tofu, kidney beans, white beans, vegetarian and fat-free refried beans and refried black beans; and any whole grain, such as rice, wheat berries, quinoa, millet, cornmeal, barley and oats.
- Avoid packaged items processed with saturated fat or hydrogenated oils, such as canned beans with pork or bacon, frozen and for-the-microwave vegetables prepared in butter and cream, as well as grain or rice mixes with added cheese, butter or other saturated fat.

Check Yourself #5: How Often Do You...?

	Seldom/Never	Sometimes	Frequently
1. Assume you have to serve your guests rich food.	3	2	1
2. Peel and discard the skin from fruits and vegetables, forgetting it has lots of fiber.	3	2	1
3. Assume that if a product contains sugar or salt, it is automatically bad for your heart.	3	2	1
4. Assume a "health food" product is low-fat without checking the label.	3	2	1
5. Pass up salmon and other cold fish because you think their fat is bad for your heart.	3	2	1
6. Buy a product because it says "No Cholesterol" on the front label without checking for saturated fat on the ingredients list.	3	2	1
7. Eat granola because you think it is healthy.	3	2	1
8. Pass over starches, such as rice, potatoes and whole grain breads, because you are worried about your waistline.	3	2	1
9. Choose a high-fat processed or packaged food because you think preparing low-fat food takes too much time.	3	2	1
10. Buy processed or packaged high-fat foods because you think low-fat food is too expensive.	3	2	1

Total

Circle the response that most nearly describes your habits and total your score.

25–30 = Excellent, try for a perfect 30.

15–24 = You have some problem areas. Often, all people need to begin heart-healthy eating is to become heart-smarter. As you finish reading about The Stanford 25 Gram Plan and study The Fat Tracker's Guide, any misconceptions will fall away about where fat is, how to avoid it and how easily you can plan and enjoy low-fat meals.

10–14 = Whoops. Maybe you should turn off the TV for the next several nights and finish reading *The Stanford Life Plan for a Healthy Heart*, to answer all your questions about taking care of your heart.

CHAPTER 15

Reduced-Fat Dairy Products: The Link between Strong Bones and a Healthy Heart

ASK US HOW TO STRENGTHEN YOUR BONES *and we'll tell you to go take a hike. And when you return home, fix a sardine sandwich for lunch. Or dance the night away and then for a nightcap have a Stanford Shake (page 566). After a set of tennis, snack on your favorite fruit-flavored nonfat yogurt. Why are we concerned about your bones when the subject of this book is your heart? Because bones need calcium and gentle weight-bearing exercise to grow strong when we're young and to prevent (or at least slow down) osteoporosis as we age. And Americans are not getting enough calcium or exercise.*

❧ Heart-conscious eaters risk sabotaging their bones if they avoid dairy products for themselves and their children because of their fear of fat.

Calcium is the stuff of bones—and muscle contraction, nerve transmission and other important body functions. The body needs sufficient calcium to regulate its heartbeat, and there are even indications that calcium plays a role in lowering blood pressure. But it is our calcium-hungry skeletons that absorb 99 percent of this crucial mineral from the foods we eat to develop, maintain and repair bone. Yet evidence points to a calcium crisis in this country. Part of the reason may be our priorities: In 1990, Americans spent $16.7 billion on milk; $47.3 billion on soft drinks and $86.7 billion on alcohol. In addition, people following a heart-healthy diet unknowingly increase the risk of osteoporosis if they toss out bone-strengthening dairy products because of their fear of fat. Reduced-fat dairy products belong on a well-balanced heart-conscious diet not only because they are our most important source of calcium, but because calcium-enriched low-fat and nonfat versions can provide even more calcium than the regular products, benefiting both hearts and bones.

We Never Outgrow Our Need for Calcium

People who complain about their old bones are not quite accurate—at any age we have some new bone and some older bone. Throughout our lives, bone goes through cycles of dissolving, then replenishing itself. Women lose bone at a greater rate after menopause due to hormone loss. Sufficient calcium and vitamin D throughout our lives minimize bone thinning (the vitamin D allows the body to absorb calcium). Heart-healthy low-fat and nonfat dairy products provide an ample supply of both. However, if we have allowed bone loss to go unchecked, we may discover with a shock, or more accurately with a break, that our bones can no longer hold us up.

Osteoporosis Is Not Just a Woman's Problem

Typically we think of the osteoporosis patient as a fair-skinned, elderly woman, fearfully groping her way through life terrified of a broken hip, stooped and shrunken from the deformity we call dowager's hump (a crippling of the spine caused by collapsed vertebrae). But despite assumptions to the contrary, men as well as women—and people of color as well as Caucasians—suffer from osteoporosis. Because men are living longer, consuming less calcium and not getting enough exercise, they too are suffering from the effects of osteoporosis at increasing rates.

In addition, people who diet frequently, particularly teenage girls and women, associate dairy products with calories and typically scrap calcium-rich foods such as nonfat milk, for a can of diet pop. Over time these chronic dieters lessen their intake of calcium and increase their chances of unnecessarily fracturing bones later in life. Adolescents' bodies produce almost half of the bone they will carry on their skeletons for the rest of their lives. In the old days, ensuring that kids drank enough milk to grow strong bones and teeth was a national mission. It still should be a mission—this time with low-fat and nonfat milk—but it isn't.

Children Are Drinking Less Milk

These days soft drinks and sugar water masking as fruit juice flood our markets, and our children guzzle it down instead of reduced-fat milk. Parents concerned about milk allergies and feeding too much fat to their families consequently have shortsightedly switched their children from milk to other drinks. As a result, studies show that our children may not be getting enough calcium in their diets to protect them adequately against fractures as young adults, much less ward off the effects of osteoporosis in their later years. And as adults, we need to continue taking in calcium in our later years as much as we did in our younger years, not to build bones, but to preserve them, the way we add extra oil to a leaky engine to keep the level up.

The following chart shows our elemental calcium requirements as we age. Elemental refers to the calcium actually absorbed by the body. You have to take 2,500 mg of calcium carbonate to get 1,000 mg of elemental calcium.

The following are the calcium requirements for a healthy body.

ELEMENTAL CALCIUM REQUIREMENTS

	Male	Female
Age 1 to 10	800 mg	800 mg
From 11 to 24	1,200 mg	1,200 mg
Pregnant women	—	1,200 mg
Nursing women	—	1,200 mg
Age 25 to 50	800 mg	800 mg
Age 51 on	800 mg	1,500 mg

Boning Up: Get Your Calcium from Reduced-Fat Dairy Foods

While you *could* chew on chalk, limestone, marble, bones and Great Aunt Minnie's pearls—all high in calcium—the following chart lists tastier ways to get your recommended daily dose of calcium without sabotaging your heart. Down the list, from nonfat milk to ice milk, the low-fat/nonfat dairy products have more calcium. Since calcium does not reside in the fat cells, extracting fat does not leach calcium from these foods, but it does make them less appetizing. So producers of dairy products often add nonfat dry milk solids, which contain calcium, to their low-fat products to improve texture and taste. You can identify these fortified products by looking on the nutritional label for "NFDM added" or "nonfat dry milk solids added." If they are available in your market, choose fortified dairy products for a bonus in lower fat content *and* higher calcium levels. If you are concerned that you or your family are not getting enough calcium, you can also add—as we have in several of our baking recipes—nonfat dry milk to your baked goods, cereals and sauces. So reach for the reduced-fat milk products. They are better for you in every way. Better for your waistline. Better for your bones. And better for your heart.

	Calcium	Calories	Grams Total Fat	Grams Saturated Fat
1 cup nonfat yogurt	450 mg	130	Trace	Trace
1 cup low-fat yogurt	400 mg	140	4.0	2.0
1 cup 1% milk	300 mg	102	2.6	1.6
1 cup 2% milk	297 mg	121	4.7	2.9
1 cup nonfat milk	302 mg	86	0.4	0.3
½ cup tofu	130 mg	94	0.6	0.9
1 ounce Parmesan cheese	336 mg	111	7.3	4.7
1 cup nonfat cottage cheese, dry curd	46 mg	123	0.6	0.4
1 cup 1% cottage cheese	138 mg	164	2.3	1.5
1 cup 2% cottage cheese	155 mg	203	4.4	2.8
1 ounce part skim mozzarella cheese	183 mg	72	4.5	3.0
1 cup ice milk	176 mg	184	5.6	3.6
1 cup calcium-fortified orange juice	270 mg	120	0	0
Broccoli, ½ cup chopped	55 mg	25	0	0
Collard greens, ½ cup cooked	148 mg	27	0	0
Spinach, ½ cup cooked	122 mg	25	0	0
Kale, ½ cup cooked	47 mg	21	0	0
Chard, ½ cup cooked	51 mg	18	0	0
Kidney beans, 1 cup cooked	50 mg	225	0.9	0.1
Lima beans, 1 cup cooked	32 mg	217	0.7	0.2
Lentils, 1 cup cooked	37 mg	231	0.7	0.1
Garbanzo beans, 1 cup cooked	80 mg	269	4.3	0.4
Hummus, 1 cup	124 mg	420	21.0	3.1

Though we include calcium levels for vegetables, the body does not absorb as much as it does from dairy products, which are a much better source.

Calcium Supplements
Supplements are fine, but we don't recommend that you rely solely on calcium tablets or antacids for your daily dose of calcium unless you are on a medically supervised special diet or are unable to tolerate dairy products. Foods high in calcium also have other necessary nutrients and you need those other vitamins and minerals that supplements don't provide. Also, since we applaud good food and the hearty enjoyment thereof, we hate to think about a futuristic diet that offers a plateful of pills instead of delicious, healthy meals.

❦ **2,500 grams of calcium carbonate supplement daily provides the recommended daily dose of 1,000 milligrams of elemental calcium.**

Do not take large doses of antacids containing aluminum to supplement your calcium reserves. They actually promote calcium loss. Also, do not use bone meal or dolomite supplements as they may contain lead. Antacids with calcium carbonate, however, are excellent. If you do take supplements, don't overdo it because more is *not* better. Studies indicate that doses over 1,500 milligrams do not offer any increase in protection, and too much calcium throws off the balance of minerals in the body, as will too much of anything.

Exercise: The Other Half of the Strong Bone Equation

Use 'em or lose 'em: It's as true for bones as it is for muscles. In addition to calcium, our bones need weight-bearing exercise that opposes the force of gravity to remain dense and strong. People who are bedridden due to illness cannot help the price their inactivity exacts on their bones. But consider the amount of time kids spend watching TV rather than engaging in bone-enhancing exercise. Add the alarming trend toward including less calcium in their diets and you can see why studies predict that in the coming decades cases of osteoporosis will increase. Additionally, we may see bone problems occurring 10 to 20 years earlier than normally expected for men and women. The Stanford Life Plan understands that heart healthy is bone healthy—its recommendation of a minimum 30-minute daily exercise routine benefits both.

Exercise that Strengthens Bones	*Exercise that Doesn't**
Dancing	Yoga
Swimming	Stretching routines
Aerobics	Isometrics, such as weight lifting
Sports	
Walking	
Jogging	
Bicycling	
Jumping rope	
Hiking	

*These are great exercises, but don't rely on them to keep your bones or your heart strong. Add walking or some other weight-bearing activity to these routines.

Estrogen and Osteoporosis

As we have discussed in Chapter 9, Women and Heart Disease, we recommend that postmenopausal women investigate estrogen replacement therapy as a protective measure against heart disease. Remember as well that in yet another crossover benefit of the recommendations of The Stanford Life Plan for a Healthy Heart, estrogen also signficantly reduces the risk of osteoporosis for women.

- You can help your heart while you help your bones.
- Don't skimp on calcium-rich foods when you or your children are young or as you get older. Then you and they will have strong bones for life.
- Take supplemental calcium in the form of calcium carbonate 2,500 milligrams per day.
- Calcium-fortified low-fat and nonfat dairy products may have even more calcium than whole-milk dairy products so they are good for your heart as well as your bones.
- Use 'em or lose 'em. Daily vigorous exercise is good for every part of your body, especially your bones and heart.
- Postmenopausal women should discuss with their physicians the possibility of estrogen replacement therapy for their hearts and their bones.

Check Yourself #6: How Often Do You Drink And Eat...?

	Seldom/Never	Sometimes	Frequently
1. Whole milk	3	2	1
2. Milkshakes made with whole milk and ice cream	3	2	1
3. Hard cheese, such as Cheddar, jack and American; creamy cheeses, such as cream cheese, Brie, Camembert, double and triple crème cheeses	3	2	1
4. Puddings made with eggs and whole milk	3	2	1
5. Regular, premium or gourmet ice cream	3	2	1
6. Whipped cream desserts	3	2	1
7. Cream, half-and-half, or powdered creamers in coffee or tea	3	2	1
8. Cream sauces and white sauces	3	2	1
9. Whole-milk or creamed cottage cheese, whole milk yogurt	3	2	1
10. Fruit salads with whipped cream or sour cream	3	2	1

Total

Circle the response that most nearly describes your habits and total your score.

25–30 = Excellent, try for a perfect 30 by switching to all fat-free and low-fat dairy foods.

15–24 = You have some problem areas. Look for ways to replace whole-milk products with more low-fat and nonfat dairy products; switch from ice cream to frozen yogurt and ices; select fruit desserts over creamy pies, cakes and puddings.

10–14 = Whoops. Become better acquainted with the reduced-fat dairy section of your supermarket and switch to fresh fruit instead of desserts made from whole milk and cream.

CHAPTER 16

Will Counting Calories Help Your Heart?

THE STANFORD 25 GRAM PLAN *is an eating plan that can help you reduce your risk of heart disease and enhance your general health, but it is not a "diet" in the sense of a Spartan weight-loss program. Dropping pounds can help lower cholesterol levels if you are overweight. So long as you don't exceed your ideal weight, when we talk about reducing fat and cholesterol in your diet we are not suggesting that you limit the amount of food, but that you pay attention to the kinds of foods you eat. A medium banana has about 100 calories; a thick slice of cooked bacon has about 75. Even though the banana has more calories, we will tell you to choose it every time, because none of its fat-free calories will cause heart disease, while all of the calories in the fat-intense bacon potentially can.*

❦ **We will teach you to become a Fat Tracker rather than a calorie counter.**

Sometimes this calorie confusion occurs when people equate cholesterol with calories. They assume that thin people don't have to worry about diet-related heart disease because only overweight people have high cholesterol levels. However, slender folks can have cholesterol levels soaring off the scale. And though it is not as common, overweight people can have perfectly healthy cholesterol levels. Perhaps they eat healthy but hefty meals and don't exercise enough to burn the extra calories. Maybe they have genetic factors that protect them from high cholesterol. Whatever the reason, these individuals refute the common but erroneous myth that high cholesterol levels go hand in hand with excess weight. You cannot determine from your bulk, or lack of it, whether or not your cholesterol is too high.

As we said in the beginning of the book, you can only know the relative health of your arteries by having your cholesterol levels checked. However, since fat contains more calories than any other food, reducing fat will naturally help you lose weight *if* you don't replace the fat calories with other high-calorie foods, such as sugary desserts. A recent study at Stanford by Dr. Peter Wood also showed that fat tracking is more important to weight loss than calorie counting: The proportion of fat in the diet, rather than number of calories, is more directly related to obesity. If you need to reduce your calorie intake to shed unwanted pounds, the nutritional calculations for each recipe will help you to select dishes that have less fat *and* fewer calories. Let's take a look at your new dietary balancing act.

Change High-Fat Calories to Low-Fat and Carbohydrate Calories

The Stanford 25 Gram Plan limits total intake of fat for the average adult to 75 grams or 30 percent of the total daily calories, with less than 25 grams or 10 percent of those calories coming from saturated fat. *A gram of fat, whether saturated or unsaturated, equals 9 calories.* So on the Stanford Plan, your limit would be 225 calories from saturated fat (25 grams x 9 calories). If you are accustomed to eating roughly 2,300 calories in a day, and you eat the usual foods in the American diet, this is approximately what your breakdown of foods would look like before and after starting The Stanford 25 Gram Plan:

TYPICAL DAILY CALORIE CONSUMPTION OF THE AVERAGE AMERICAN ADULT

	Fat Calories (45%)	Protein Calories (25%)	Carbohydrate Calories (30%)	Total Calories
50 grams saturated fat	450			
65 grams unsaturated fat	585			
Totals	1,035	575	690	2,300

TYPICAL DAILY CALORIE CONSUMPTION: STANFORD 25 GRAM PLAN

	Fat Calories (30%)	Protein Calories (15%)	Carbohydrate Calories (55%)	Total Calories
25 grams saturated fat	225			
50 grams unsaturated fat	450			
Totals	675	365	1,260	2,300

Okay, what does this arithmetic mean in real food? In the following charts, we have listed two sample meals for breakfast, lunch and dinner containing typical foods that millions of people enjoy every day. We haven't overloaded the menus with fast foods, alcohol, junk food or other items that would tip the scale toward items high in calories, fat or cholesterol. The second example contains roughly the same number of calories, but the proportions of fat, carbohydrates and protein have changed. These second menus are typical of The Stanford 25 Gram Plan. Here's how they add up.

CALORIES IN A TYPICAL AMERICAN BREAKFAST

	Total Calories	Grams Total Fat	Grams Saturated Fat	% Calories from Fat*	Mg Cholesterol
1 small Danish	274	23.0	14.0	76	10
4 ounces orange juice	56	0	0	0	0
1⅔ ounces granola	199	13.0	8.0	59	0
½ cup whole milk	80	4.0	3.0	48	18
Total for Meal (360 calories from fat)	609	40.0	25.0	59%	28

*In our chart, we show the percentage of fat in each food, but the total number (59% in the above chart for instance) represents the percentage of fat in the entire meal.

This typical American breakfast contains 609 calories. But 360 of them are fat calories (59 percent), using up an entire day's allotment of saturated fat. On the other hand, consider our Stanford Plan breakfast.

CALORIES IN A STANFORD PLAN BREAKFAST

	Total Calories	Grams Total Fat	Grams Saturated Fat	% Calories from Fat*	Mg Cholesterol
2 pieces whole grain toast	175	2.0	Trace	Trace	0
1 teaspoon diet margarine	25	2.5	0.8	90	0
2 tablespoons honey	122	0	0	0	0
1 cup Wheaties	101	0.5	0	0	0
½ cup nonfat milk	43	0.2	0	4	2
1 large banana	116	0	0	0	0
Coffee or tea with 2 tablespoons low-fat milk	20	Trace	Trace	Trace	Trace
Total for Meal (47 calories from fat)	602	5.2	0.8	8%	2

The Stanford breakfast provides almost the same calories (629) with only a scant 7 percent total fat (47 fat calories) and a negligible amount of saturated fat. Let's see what happens at lunch.

CALORIES IN A TYPICAL LUNCH

	Total Calories	Grams Total Fat	Grams Saturated Fat	% Calories from Fat*	Mg Cholesterol
1 ham and cheese sandwich with mayonnaise, lettuce and tomato	660	34.0	18.0	46	102
1 chocolate chip cookie	100	4.0	1.5	41	10
Coffee with 2 tablespoons half-and-half	40	3.4	2.2	77	12
Total for Meal (373 calories from fat)	800	41.4	21.7	47%	124

Compare those numbers with . . .

CALORIES IN A STANFORD PLAN LUNCH

	Total Calories	Grams Total Fat	Grams Saturated Fat	% Calories from Fat*	Mg Cholesterol
Large green salad with 3 ounces turkey breast, steamed vegetables	115	1.5	0.5	12	45
2 tablespoons salad dressing	162	18.0	2.6	100	0
2 slices whole wheat French bread	200	2.0	Trace	2	0
½ cup nonfat chocolate frozen yogurt	80	0	0	0	0
1 apple	80	0	0	0	0
Total for Meal (194 calories from fat)	637	21.5	3.1	30%	45

Here we dropped from a total of 42 percent fat (372 fat calories) to approximately 14 percent (194 fat calories), and the saturated fat total is only one-fourth of the first menu. The dinner menus show a similar picture.

CALORIES IN A TYPICAL DINNER

	Total Calories	Grams Total Fat	Grams Saturated Fat	% Calories from Fat*	Mg Cholesterol
2 pieces fried chicken with skin	350	21.0	6.0	54	163
Mashed potatoes, ½ cup with butter and milk	111	4.4	1.1	36	13
Corn with butter	112	11.0	6.0	88	35
Green beans	25	0	0	0	0
Pound cake	160	10.0	5.9	56	68
Total for Meal (418 calories from fat)	758	46.4	19.0	55%	279

Look how those numbers go down when you make a few switches.

CALORIES IN A STANFORD PLAN DINNER

	Total Calories	Grams Total Fat	Grams Saturated Fat	% Calories from Fat*	Mg Cholesterol
Lemon roast chicken, no skin	206	5.6	2.0	24	99
Potatoes sautéed in butter	150	9.0	1.3	54	0
Gingered carrots	50	0	0	0	0
Green bean salad with vinaigrette canola oil dressing	75	3.6	2.0	43	0
4 whole wheat breadsticks	100	2.4	0	22	0
Strawberries and angel-food cake, with scoop of vanilla nonfat yogurt	230	0	0	0	0
Total for Meal (185 calories from fat)	811	20.6	5.3	23%	99

Again, by switching the types of food but not the amount of food, we significantly reduce the intake of cholesterol and saturated fat, while still enjoying appetizing and satisfying meals. Look at how the day's totals add up.

DAILY CALORIE TOTALS FOR TYPICAL MENUS AND STANFORD PLAN MENUS

	Total Calories	Grams Total Fat	Grams Saturated Fat	% Calories from Fat*	Mg Cholesterol
Typical Menu	2,167	127.8	65.7	53%	431
Stanford Plan Menu	2,050	47.3	9.2	20%	146

See how quickly fat and cholesterol add up, even when the total number of calories remains the same. Our selection of foods weighs in at considerably less than the 25-gram limit on saturated fat, giving you plenty of room to make your own favorite healthy but slightly richer substitutions if you like.

- You don't have to go hungry to have a healthy heart.
- By substituting foods high in complex carbohydrates (such as fresh vegetables and fruits, whole grains, pastas, whole grain breads and rolls) and fish, fowl and lean meats rich in protein but low in fat you can fill up on heart-healthy foods without sacrificing calories.
- Choose healthy calories, not just fewer of them, unless you step on the scale and go, "whoops!"

LITTLE THINGS ADD UP

It's easier to incorporate small switches and substitutions in your eating habits than to initiate radical changes. These simple suggestions for a more healthful diet can reduce your saturated fat and cholesterol intake considerably while still satisfying your appetite. To put these numbers in perspective, if you consume 2,000 calories a day, you should eat no more than about 66 grams of fat—so that fat will contribute less than 30 percent of your daily calories.

Instead of Eating This	Have This	To Save Milligrams of Cholesterol	To Save Milligrams of Saturated Fat
8 ounces whole milk	8 ounces nonfat milk	31	5
8 ounces whole milk yogurt	8 ounces nonfat yogurt	29	5
1 butter croissant	1 plain bagel	31	7
1 cup cooked egg noodles	1 cup cooked pasta	53	1
1 egg yolk	1 egg white	213	2
1 ounce Cheddar cheese	1 ounce part skim mozzarella	14	3
1 ounce cream cheese	1 ounce nonfat cream cheese	31	6
1 tablespoon unwhipped whipping cream	1 tablespoon pressurized whipping cream	19	3
3.5 ounces skinless duck, broiled	3.5 ounces skinless chicken breast, broiled	5	3
3.5 ounces shrimp, raw	3.5 ounces scallops, raw	116	0
3.5 ounces choice beef tenderloin, untrimmed, broiled	3.5 ounces choice beef tenderloin, trimmed broiled	4	4
1 ounce regular bacon, cooked	1 ounce Canadian bacon, cooked	5	5
1 ounce pastrami	1 ounce extra-lean ham	13	2
1 glazed yeast donut	1 slice angelfood cake	4	3
1 fast food large French fries	1 baked potato	0	10
1 ounce potato chips	1 ounce roasted chestnuts	0	2
1 tablespoon sour cream dip	1 tablespoon salsa	6	2
1 ounce corn chips	1 ounce plain air-popped popcorn	0	4
3 macaroons	3 fat-free fig bars	0	8
1 ounce unsweetened chocolate	3 tablespoon cocoa powder	0	5
1 cup premium ice cream	1 cup sorbet	100	15
2 shortbread cookies	2 vanilla wafers	20	4
2 peanut butter cookies	2 ginger snaps	8	2

PART THREE

The Fat Tracker's Guide

CHAPTER 17

Fat Tracking in Supermarkets: Reading the Labels

UNLESS YOU GROW ALL OF YOUR OWN FOOD, *the supermarket has a direct line to your heart. A shopper aimlessly circling the aisles of the modern supermarket is easy prey for food companies that would like you to fill up your shopping cart with as many of their products as you can cram into it, whether or not they are good for you. The successful Fat Tracker must become a supermarket skeptic, because even with new labeling laws, a food supplier can seduce you with a few well chosen words: healthful, wholesome, real, old-fashioned. But they don't always mean what they say, or in the case of "no cholesterol," what they imply.*

Some food advertisers will do almost anything to get you to buy their products: they enclose their food in brightly colored packaging that is hard for you and your children to resist, then they use labels that trumpet every assurance of superior quality, flavor and value, using their way with words to disguise or downplay actual harmful ingredients or quantities of fat. Markets may show off their produce in the best light (sometimes quite literally, using bulbs that artificially heighten color). And irresistible smells waft through the aisles from in-house bakeries that offer a steady supply of cookies, cakes and breads to take home or munch on while you shop, and you can bet these delicacies are not fat-free or adequately labeled.

The existence of the nutritional land mines lining the shelves of your food market is not news. The media has done a fine job of focusing on labeling and packaging excesses, and new labeling laws set standards for the nutritional information listed on products.

But truth-in-labeling laws won't cure all of your food shopping woes. They force more of the hidden fat out into the light of day so you can spot it, but only if the item is packaged—over-the-counter baked goods are a notable exception. Labels also don't stop the flood of high-fat products or make it any easier to resist their temptation. You will still have to figure out how to navigate through the visual and sensual feast displayed in the supermarket and track down, not just your favorite foods—they rush out at you on every advertising poster and package—but the foods that are best for you, as well. How does the Fat Tracker resist supermarket seduction? With information from the following Fat Tracker's shopping lists and a low-fat shopping strategy that has you ask two questions of the food you buy: What's in it for me, and do I need it or want it?

What's in It for Me? Read the Label—*Every* Label—to Find Out!
Whenever you go shopping, keep in mind that your goal is to keep the saturated fat in your day's meals under 25 grams, your total fat under 75 grams and your cholesterol to 300 milligrams or less. To uncover the packaged foods that contain those harmful fats, the label is the obvious place to look. The labeling laws that took effect in May 1994 are a boon to Fat Trackers because nutrition facts are now on every packaged food product. Fresh meat, poultry and fish, fresh produce and fresh bakery items as yet require no labeling at all, but your grocer should display this information in the area where these products are sold. Read *every* label before you buy a food product. Here is a sample nutrition facts label and a survey of what the categories mean and how to use them to free your meals of excess and formerly hidden fats.

Nutrition Facts		
Serving Size 1/2 cup (114g)		
Servings Per Container 4		
Amount Per Serving		
Calories 90	Calories from Fat 30	
		% Daily Value*
Total Fat 3g		**5%**
Saturated Fat 0g		**0%**
Cholesterol 0mg		**0%**
Sodium 300mg		**13%**
Total Carbohydrate 13g		**4%**
Dietary Fiber 3g		**12%**
Sugars 3g		
Protein		
Vitamin A 80%	Vitamin C 60%	
Calcium 4%	Iron 4%	

*Percent Daily Values are based on a 2,000 calorie diet. Your daily values may be higher or lower depending on your calorie needs:

	Calories	2000	2500
Total Fat	Less than	65g	80g
Saturated fat	Less than	20g	25g
Cholesterol	Less than	300mg	300mg
Sodium	Less than 2400mg		
Total Carbohydrate		300g	375g
Fiber		25g	30g

Calories per gram
Fat 9 • Carbohydrate 4 • Protein 4
g = grams (about 28g = 1 ounce)
mg = milligrams (1,000 = 1g)

Serving Size

This is an estimate of the number of servings per package, which manufacturers use to calculate the nutritional information. The serving size is a real boon to the Fat Tracker, *if* you pay close attention to what the manufacturer considers a serving size. It may *not* be the actual serving size you choose to eat. For example, one-half cup of cereal, a typical serving size, may be adequate for a 50-year-old moderately active woman, but a 17-year-old high school basketball center may need two or three times that amount for breakfast. On the other hand, a two-year-old child may only be able to down one-fourth cup of cereal before reaching his or her capacity. In healthful cereals and breads, the difference between *their* serving size and *your* serving size may not cause any real problems. However, if you don't consider what the serving size really means in terms of the human appetite you can get hoodwinked into thinking you can indulge in a dessert or snack and seriously undermine your fat tracking efforts.

Let's say a package of small cookies lists 1.5 grams of saturated fat per serving and you decide that is a reasonable fat expenditure. Before you pay for those cookies, take a look at what the manufacturer considers to be a serving size: one small cookie at 80 calories each, no bargain in anyone's kitchen. Would you or your six-year-old be willing to stop at one cookie? Humans have been known to eat three or four small cookies at a sitting. At 80 calories each and 1.5 grams of saturated fat, this dessert will take a 6-gram chunk out of your 25-gram allotment. You would be offering your child almost one-third of a daily ration of saturated fat in that treat. Can you afford it? Or should you look for another brand? Adjust all the calculations to the realistic serving size you and your family actually eat before you make your decisions about packaged foods. Refer to Chapter 13, The Fat Tracker's Meal-Planning Guide, for our recommended serving sizes of various foods.

Calories

Actual calories and calories from fat *per serving size listed* help you gauge how well an item fits into a weight-control plan, if that is a concern to you or a family member. You can also now determine whether the item contains too many calories in fat. Though items such as olive oil and salad dressings by definition derive most of their calories from fat, try to choose food items that limit calories from fat to 30 percent or less, as does our example.

Total Fat, Saturated Fat and Cholesterol

The listing most crucial to a Fat Tracker, these are the numbers that, in conjunction with the nutritional information at the end of each of our recipes, will help you stick to your 25-gram plan. These three numbers should be the first you look for every time you pick up a packaged food. Notice, as we have pointed out throughout the book, that in most cases saturated fat and cholesterol travel together. In our example, the product has no saturated fat, therefore it has no cholesterol. It does have unsaturated fat, however, included in the total fat number. The only way to tell if an item contains harmful transfatty acids, unfortunately, is to check the ingredient list.

🌿 **If it lists hydrogenated or partially hydrogenated oils, realize that in addition to saturated fat, the product contains harmful amounts of transfatty acids.**

You won't know how much, though the total may be lumped in with total fat.

Sodium

With a reminder that the American Heart Association recommends limiting sodium from 2,400 to 3,000 milligrams or less each day, this listing is an important aid in tracking high-sodium processed foods. These are items that Fat Trackers try to keep to a minimum, of course, choosing fresh foods whenever possible.

Total Carbohydrates

As a Fat Tracker, you know that you are looking to substitute carbohydrate calories for fat calories at every opportunity. Unfortunately, this listing does not distinguish between simple sugars, such as added white sugar and corn syrup, and complex carbohydrates, some of which also have a lot of natural sugar, such as fruit sugar and the milk sugars in milk and yogurt. Therefore, a listed 8-ounce serving of apple juice with 26 grams of sugar seems excessively high. But if the label specifies no added sweeteners, then you know all 26 grams are natural sugars found in apples. Nor does the listing include *all* types of sugars, so the product may actually contain more sugar in real life than the label is required to indicate. A careful reading of ingredients, as we will describe shortly, will help here.

Protein

As we discuss in Part Two, protein and fat often travel together, and you want to choose lean protein as often as possible. Many foods provide protein and this listing will help you gauge what we might call beneficial but hidden protein, so you don't have to rely solely on the obvious sources in meat and other animal products.

Dietary Fiber

The listing of dietary fiber is an important addition to labeling information. When choosing between brands, go for the items with the highest fiber count. Though the labels do not break down water soluble and nonsoluble fiber, remember that we recommend choosing foods with both kinds for a minimum of 25 grams of total fiber per day. (Refer to Chapter 14, Finding Fiber and Antioxidants: Produce, Legumes and Grains, for the foods that contain both essential types of fiber). Some foods that might seem like obvious high-fiber choices, such as cereals and breads, may actually be low in fiber, comprised of (in the case of some high-sugared cereals for example) more sugar than fiber. Read this item carefully, rather than assuming a bread or product is high in fiber.

Vitamins and Minerals

The percentage of a recommended number of selected important vitamins and minerals are listed. You want to eat a variety of foods to reach 100 percent each day. In addition to calcium, vitamin C, a good source of antioxidants, is listed here.

Daily Value

The Percent Daily Value is useful for estimating how much essential nutrition you are getting in each serving of the product. Remember, of course, that you eat many foods over the course of a day, each one contributing to your daily totals. Some foods, such as sugar and protein, do not have FDA established daily values and are not listed.

❧ **Look for foods that have a low percentage of fat, cholesterol and sodium, and a high percentage of fiber, vitamins and minerals.**

Now that you can interpret the nutrition facts on a label, don't stop there. Sometimes, label reading means knowing how to read between the lines. For example, while a product label must contain nutrition facts, that does not mean it can't try to draw your attention away from less than beneficial ingredients. Here are some important tips for interpreting label subterfuge.

Be Wary of "No Cholesterol" or "Cholesterol Free" Products

Every supermarket offers a staggering array of cholesterol-free products these days. Are they the answer to a Fat Tracker's prayer? Maybe, but many of those products, such as margarine or vegetable oil, have never contained cholesterol. The claim is actually misleading, giving the impression that cholesterol has been cleared out of a once forbidden food, or that perhaps a competitor's version is packed with cholesterol.

❧ **Remember, cholesterol is found only in animals—plants can't produce cholesterol.**

Whenever you read a label it is by definition cholesterol-free if *none* of the contents comes from an animal, in other words, it has no meat, fish, poultry, eggs or other dairy items added. Proclaiming a vegetable product as "cholesterol-free" is like a farmer boasting his potatoes have no pits! What is the harm in a labeler steering you toward cholesterol-free products? On the surface, nothing. But the real problem is that many marketers lure you into reaching for a product with the words "no cholesterol" so you won't read any further. In fact, the item may be loaded with saturated fat, which can make a cholesterol-free item every bit as lethal to you and your children's arteries as if it contained egg yolks. The "no cholesterol" banner may also divert your attention away from the fact that the product contains large amounts of salt or sugar (so-called empty calories), which is *never* printed in large type, as you will discover only if you read the nutrition facts.

So, do not automatically reach for a bottle of cooking oil or a cereal box or any other product because the label proclaims "no cholesterol." Choose naturally cholesterol-free, vegetable-based foods because you like the brand, the price is competitive, the shape of the bottle appeals to your aesthetic sensibilities or because you have a discount coupon from the Sunday newspaper. Choose them as you would all other products, but *not* just because they are cholesterol free.

The Dilemma of Incomplete Labels

All domestic processed food products *must* have the Nutrition Facts printed prominently on the package. But many imported products arrive from countries that do not have our strict labeling requirements, and these items give no indication of their contents. When you come across a product that does not list ingredients or nutritional content, the best course is to choose another brand. Persons with heart disease, who must follow a 17-gram or less limit on saturated fat, should not buy anything unless they know what is in it. Keep looking, you will find a similar product that won't have any unhealthy surprises for you.

To followers of The Stanford 25 Gram Plan, passing up these items in favor of a similar, labeled product is also good advice. It never hurts to assume they have high counts of saturated fat. However, based on your new knowledge of where saturated fat usually lurks, you might find clues that will help you decide whether you can buy an unlabeled product comfortably, or use it sparingly, perhaps for parties or holiday entertaining only. Some imported items list ingredients, even if they don't have specific fat or cholesterol amounts. Check first for ingredients, looking for butter or other saturated fats. Perhaps the name will help. Butter cookies, imported pastries, creamed soups and sauces are obvious clues to the presence of harmful fats, for example.

In addition, if listed on the label, look for these ingredients: beef fat, lard, meat fat, bacon fat, pork fat, chicken fat, turkey fat, shortening, chocolate (real or imitation), milk chocolate, hydrogenated oil, hydrogenated or partially hydrogenated oil or fat, vegetable fat or oil as shortening, hydrogenated whole milk solids, egg, egg yolk, egg yolk solids, butter, cocoa butter, cream, cream sauce, coconut, coconut oil, palm oil, palm kernel oil. When a product lists chicken, unless it specifies only white meat, it usually includes higher-fat dark meat and very often skin. Assume beef and other meats are the high-fat varieties, unless specifically denied.

Check the First Five Ingredients

In addition to the nutritional information, all labels must include the ingredients, which are listed according to weight. A good rule of thumb is to assume that the first five ingredients comprise the bulk of the product, with small amounts of any other items listed. This feature is most helpful for determining the value of an item such as cereal, which may not have fat or cholesterol, but contributes essential fiber. Some cereals will list a gram or less of fiber, and very high amounts of carbohydrates or sugar. A quick scan of the label reveals that the first five, six or even seven or more ingredients are sugars, corn syrups and sweeteners of some kind. Serious, healthful complex carbohydrates are way down at the bottom, letting you know that you are getting little nutrition here. If wheat, corn, rye, oats or other grains were present in significant amounts, they would be among the first five listed. The cereal in this case is truly more of a snack treat than breakfast food.

You may also come across imported products or items that have been sitting in a warehouse since the days before the new labeling was required. These might, if mentioned at all, list fat but do not break it down into saturated and unsaturated fat. Check the ingredients: If you see animal or dairy products listed or hydrogenated or partially hydrogenated oils, you know it has saturated fat. If they are listed among the first five ingredients, put these foods on your "only occasionally" list.

Label Lingo

New labeling standards don't mean you can drop your fat-tracking shopping skills. Food suppliers will continue to use appealing label lingo to steer you toward their products. For example, a billboard promoting eggs claims, "22 percent less!" Less than what—liver, beef steak, shrimp? Unless you know precisely what higher calorie, fat or salt item is being compared to a product, less is, well, meaning-less. Regard descriptive words as a come-on. For example, vegetable oils and olive oils promote themselves as "lite," and it simply means light in flavor. Forget lighter or "liter" labeling. Go for the grams. The following are the claims food makers can make only if they can back them up with sound nutrition.

IF IT SAYS	IT HAS TO MEAN
Fat Free	Less than 0.5 grams of fat per serving
Low Fat	3 grams of fat (or less) per serving
Lean	Less than 10 grams of fat, 4 grams of saturated fat and 95 milligrams of cholesterol per serving
Light (Lite)	⅓ less calories or no more than ½ the fat of the higher-calorie, higher fat version; or no more than ½ the sodium of the higher-sodium version
Cholesterol Free	Less than 2 milligrams of cholesterol per serving

And if an item is promoting its healthful attributes, remember this:

TO MAKE CLAIMS ABOUT . . .	THE FOOD MUST BE . . .
Heart Disease and Fat	Low in fat, saturated fat and cholesterol
Blood Pressure and Sodium	Low in sodium
Heart Disease and Fruits, Vegetables and Grain Products	A fruit, vegetable or grain product low in fat, saturated fat and cholesterol, that contains at least 0.6 grams soluble fiber per serving

Words to Watch Out for

And finally, take a food manufacturer at its word. When a product boasts rich, butter-flavored, smoked, premium, gourmet, or traditional on the front, you know what to expect from the information on the back. These adjectives signal high-fat ingredients.

Avoid all products with descriptions such as, butter, buttery, butter sauce, sautéed, fried, pan-fried, crispy, nutty, braised, creamed, in cream sauce, gravy, in its own gravy, cheese-flavored, cheese sauce, bacon-flavored, hollandaise, au gratin, Parmesan-flavored, marinated in oil, oil-packed, chocolate, chocolatey.

Words to Live By

"Fat free *and* cholesterol free," "No salt or sodium," "Sugar free," "Sweetened with natural juice," "No hydrogenated oils," "No tropical oils," mean what they say, or the food manufacturer is breaking the law. Go for packages that list some combination of cocoa, canola oil, olive oil, corn oil, safflower oil, nut oil, avocado oil, grape seed oil, sesame oil, soybean oil, sunflower oil, cottonseed oil (generally any vegetable oil *not* hydrogenated or partially hydrogenated), nonfat milk solids, skim/nonfat milk and egg whites, in addition to other healthy ingredients such as vegetables, fruits, grains and flour.

Reach for products that are promoted as steamed, broiled, baked, oven baked, poached, with tomato juice, in its own juice, roasted, garden fresh, dry broiled, in natural juices packed in water.

The Fat Tracker's shopping strategy is based on heart-smart food choices and awareness of the fat in all foods. We hope the new labeling laws will clear up all the confusion that surrounds nutritional information, but still be skeptical. If some labeling obstacles remain, think in terms of wise choices and you will always make the right choice. That means you have to ask . . .

Do I Need It or Do I Want It?

Many of the foods you need are easy to recognize: fish, chicken and turkey breast, low-fat meats, low-fat and nonfat milk products, all fresh fruits and vegetables, all whole grain products and legumes sold in bulk, such as wild rice, brown and white rice, wheatberries, flour, cornmeal, oats, millet, quinoa, dried peas, beans and lentils. These complex carbohydrates and low-fat, low-cholesterol foods must be at the center of your diet. You can also buy many of these foods canned and frozen; whether you need those versions depends on what the labeling on the package says. Does the list of ingredients include added fat or cholesterol? If so, then you have to ask yourself, "Do I want it?"

Suppose your children clamor for a popular breakfast cereal because they see it advertised on television. Or, you want to buy some hearty canned soup for dinner, because you're too tired to fix an elaborate meal. The cereal has a bright banner across the front, "no cholesterol," but the label indicates it is high in saturated fat and total fat. Realize that if you have served your children eggs and bacon more than once for breakfast in a week, you don't want them to have cereal loaded with saturated fat on the other mornings. Once a month as a treat? Sure, buy them the cereal if you want to indulge them. But don't let them eat it on any regular basis.

And before you fill your basket with a variety of canned soups, take a look at the contents. These soups usually have little cholesterol, but look at what they do have: The pea soup could have coconut oil and hydrogenated (saturated) vegetable oils, the minestrone might contain chicken fat and clam chowder often lists non-dairy creamers made with tropical oils. You wonder if you are holding a can of trouble. Ask yourself if you want to spend any of your 25 grams on a canned product. Occasionally, for convenience sake, and if the product does not contain an excessive amount of fat, you may say, "yes." Certainly, you can enjoy a creamed soup once in a while. But for the days you have a hamburger for lunch or an omelet for breakfast, after you read the list of ingredients you may want to put the soup back and head for the canned tuna instead.

As you can see, we are not saying you should permanently boycott these items. But realize that most processed foods with their overload of fat and sodium can be habit-forming. You can also be seduced by convenience. When you get pressed for time, try not to trade convenience for regular doses of high-fat foods.

❧ **We don't know any heart attack patients who say they are glad they cut nutritional corners and saved time by eating high-fat, labor-saving, overly processed, fiberless foods.**

The key to choosing any high-fat product is "Do I want it enough to give up another high-fat item?" If you do, fine. One time-saving device we do recommend, is that you become familiar with the packaged foods that will keep your 25-gram plan balanced. Heart-smart choices are out there and we are going to help you find them. When you make an initial investment in time to become adept at reading labels, before long you will reach for the fat-tracking specials as quickly as you do your favorite brand of toothpaste or detergent.

While fat, cholesterol and calorie contents for all foods vary from manufacturer to manufacturer, nowhere is this more evident than in the dairy section of your market. In all of our tables we have attempted to simply give you a representative sample, rather than a complete listing, of the products available to you in all of the food groups and show you the differences in fat between high-fat, low-fat and nonfat versions. We have not done a scientific analysis of these products, but rather used nutrition tables compiled by other experts to complete our own charts.

Rarely have we found two tables that list exactly the same calculation for the same item, whether it is a type of cracker or a cut of meat. You, in fact, may find brands with slightly more fat or slightly less than we list. We don't expect you to hunt obsessively for the leanest product all the time. Buy the product with the most flavor and the least fat. If your favorite brand of a reduced-fat product has a slightly higher fat content than a competitor's, stick with the one you prefer. In the course of a lifetime, eating an extra gram of saturated fat here and there is not going to harm you. However, the consistent switch from whole-milk products to low-fat versions, and from low-fat to nonfat items, will make a huge difference to your heart, not the minor variations from brand to brand.

CHAPTER 18

Fat Tracking Meat, Poultry and Fish

EATING LESS RED MEAT *doesn't mean you can't eat any at all. Packed with protein, vitamins and minerals, red meat is also an excellent source of iron. Unfortunately, large amounts of saturated fat and cholesterol can fill out the package. Seek out the cuts with the least saturated fat—we recommend that you stay under 4 grams of saturated fat per 3.5 ounce serving, but don't waste your time hunting for the cuts with the least cholesterol. Except for organ meats such as liver and kidneys, all meats and poultry—chicken, beef, veal, even a slice of bacon—have approximately the same amount of cholesterol, about 20 to 25 milligrams per ounce, or about 85 milligrams for the 3.5 ounce servings we recommend. Fish, on the other hand, has less cholesterol and less saturated fat.*

Ranchers have been quite successful in breeding and feeding animals that produce leaner meat; look for these products to arrive in your area. Be aware that fat content in meat and poultry may vary according to breeding practices in different parts of the country. Though fresh meat, poultry and fish products do not have labels, by law there should be a highly visible "point of purchase" in markets listing the nutrient analysis of these products for the consumer. Ask your market to point it out to you if it is not easily visible. Also, consumers can call the FDA directly for information regarding meat and poultry (800) 535-4555, and they can be reached by fax at (202) 690-2859. For questions about seafood and shellfish, call 800 332-4010; FAX (202) 401-3532.

Fat Tracking Beef

Don't give meat the center stage at mealtime. The fat tracking trick is to do a lot with a little. Use it to flavor dishes and to accent a meal that is mainly designed around complex carbohydrates. In the old days, before fat tracking, a trencherman could easily put away a 6- to 8-ounce or even a 16-ounce steak! Today, you can stir-fry one-half pound of thinly sliced top round with a variety of vegetables in a quick gingery sauce and serve it with steamed rice to feed three or four comfortably. Though the meat section of the supermarket holds a confusing array of beef cuts, the Fat Tracker's choice is easy: Stick with those cut from the top round (located in the hind leg), which will give you a 3.5 ounce cooked serving with less than 4 grams of saturated fat. Meat from the leaner round is tender enough to tolerate dry-heat cooking (roasts and grilled or broiled steaks) and will hold up in moist-heat cooking (braised pot roasts and stews) without shredding. Top round cuts also are less expensive than the other cuts.

Fat-tracking lean meats is made a little easier when you understand the difference between grades and cuts. Federal regulations have standardized the fat content of the various grades of meats, rating the quality of meat in terms of flavor, juiciness and tenderness. This grading system will help you track the leanest cuts. The presence of fat tenderizes meat, so these grades, which can vary from animal to animal, give an indication of the fat content. The highest grades cost the most and have the largest concentration of fat. Grades are typically listed as prime, choice, select and good, in that descending order. We recommend that you look for select and good grades, which are the leanest—and cheapest. Realistically, though, good grades of beef are not always easy for the consumer to find. Some chains may sell "good" as "commercial grade" and occasionally some independent markets will stock it.

How much difference does the grade make? A 3.5 ounce serving of prime top round can contain 10 grams of total fat and 4 grams of saturated fat, while a serving of good top round shrinks the total fat to 7 grams and the saturated fat to 2.5 grams, with select and choice grades falling in between. And no, you won't be gnawing on shoe leather. These leaner grades remain remarkably tender when you approach them with the proper cooking method. Be aware that there is some inconsistency in the way some markets refer to grades. We have found that some markets do not adhere strictly to the accepted definition of grade in their advertising and you may want to quiz your butcher about the cuts he or she considers to be leanest. Some markets also make up their own names for various grades, especially those that may not be as marketable if precisely labeled. Whenever you are pondering a meat selection with an unusual description, just ask your butcher how the fat content compares to the commonly known grades.

Cuts, in contrast to grades, define the location of the meat on the animal and are available in all grades. In general, cuts from the top loin, rib, chuck, plate, shoulder and flank sections have too much fat for a Fat Tracker, because, on the hoof, their muscles don't get worked enough. (Sound like any humans you know?) Hind cuts (from the round), however, come from the part of the steer that moves the most. You may notice that the names of particular cuts vary in some regions of the country. Denver pot roast, wafer steaks, breakfast steaks, London broil, Swiss steak and butterball steaks are all cut from the round. Ask your butcher to steer you (oops) toward beef cut from the round and your choices will always be lower in fat.

The fat content of ground beef can range from a relatively meager 10 to 14 percent for extra-lean ground beef to 66 percent for regular ground beef. Though not an accepted practice, some butchers may add fat to ground beef to add flavor and tenderness. To make sure you don't have too much extra fat, grind your own lean round in a food processor. Choose either ground round or extra-lean ground beef (10 to 12 percent fat) for all of your meat loaf, burger or other ground beef dishes.

❧ **Approximately 4 to 5 ounces of boneless, uncooked meat will yield a 3.5 ounce cooked serving. Cuts with bones can require up to 16 ounces of uncooked meat to yield a similar cooked, lean portion.**

TOP ROUND, ALSO PACKAGED AS LONDON BROIL Choose top round for your next barbecue or grind it for hamburgers and meat loaf. Cut it into chunks for stew, as it will also hold together in a long simmer without shredding. Slice it thinly for your stir-fry dishes. If you grill or panfry top round, don't overcook it or it will toughen (but then, so will the more tender, fattier cuts). But if you cook it rare or medium rare, you are in for a delicious, lean, tender treat.

RUMP ROAST Cut from the leanest portion of the top round, a standing (with bone) or rolled (without bone) rump makes an ideal oven roast.

BOTTOM ROUND A less tender cut that is perfect for stews. Swiss steak comes from the bottom round.

ROUND TIP Cut from the top round, it is very tender. Roast a whole round tip for a crowd.

EYE OF ROUND Not as tender as rump or top round, the eye is often found cut into minute steaks. Ideal thinly cut and quick cooked as in grilled fajitas, panfried dishes and stir-fries.

Fat tracking lean beef means you don't let your hand wander over the selection of fat-wrapped, well-marbled cuts in the meat counter; instead you consistently choose the leanest cuts and grades with as little visible fat streaks or marbling as possible. Before cooking, you trim as much remaining fat as you can. The following table of 3.5 ounce portions of choice, broiled beef demonstrates how many grams you shed when you follow this strategy.

FAT CONTENT OF TRIMMED VS. UNTRIMMED BEEF

3.5 ounces	Calories	Grams Total Fat	Grams Saturated Fat	% of Calories from Fat	Mg Cholesterol
Tenderloin					
Untrimmed	304	21.8	8.6	64	86
Trimmed	222	11.2	4.2	45	84
Top Round					
Untrimmed	224	10.6	3.9	42	85
Trimmed	194	5.9	2.0	28	84

By simply switching from tenderloin to top round, the saturated-fat content of untrimmed meat can drop by more than half! In addition, when you trim the fat from the round, you cut the fat by almost two-thirds. But even if you left the visible fat on, the leaner cut (with less fat in the tissues) still has less fat than the trimmed tenderloin. The fat-tracking lesson here is to select red meat with not just the least *visible* fat, but go for the cuts and grades with the least *invisible* fat.

The tables on pages 26 and 135 give a good idea of the meats highest in saturated fat. Here is a breakdown on the leanest cuts of 3.5-ounce portions of trimmed, broiled beef. For the sake of comparison, remember that one of America's favorites, beef short ribs, can have from 8 to 18 grams of saturated fat for each cooked 3.5-ounce portion and between 18 and 42 grams of total fat! Unless otherwise noted, all of the calculations for meat, poultry and fish are for 3.5 ounce, trimmed, broiled servings. In some cases, however, where noted on the tables, only uncooked calculations were available.

LOW AND HIGH SATURATED-FAT BEEF

Low Saturated-Fat Beef

3.5 ounces	Calories	Grams Total Fat	Grams Saturated Fat	% of Calories from Fat	Mg Cholesterol
Top round	191	5.9	2.0	28	84
Eye of round	175	5.7	2.1	29	69
Round tip	190	7.3	2.6	34	81
Bottom round	193	7.8	2.6	36	78
Rump roast	197	7.8	2.7	36	73

High Saturated-Fat Beef

T-Bone	214	10.2	4.2	43	80
Porterhouse	218	11.0	4.3	45	80
Rib roast	233	14.0	5.8	54	79
Flank	207	10.1	4.4	44	67
Ground beef, extra lean	250	16.0	6.3	58	82
Ground beef, lean	268	18.3	7.2	61	87
Ground beef, regular	287	21.0	8.2	66	90
Brisket	263	16.0	5.9	55	91
Chuck, braised	363	27.8	11.0	69	101

Fat Tracking Lamb

As you can see from the table below, the leanest lamb is still fattier than lean beef round. You can see on a lamb breast, for example (though not listed on our table), the thick, hard-to-remove coating of fat covering the small portions of meat that cling to the bones. However, you can still enjoy the distinctive flavor of leg of lamb and loin chops as an entrée at one of your twice-weekly 2 + 2 dinners. Roast vegetables and a lean leg of lamb for a crowd and load the buffet table with white bean and eggplant dishes to fill up hungry guests. Lamb stew, thoroughly skimmed and stretched with barley and vegetables, is another possibility for cheaper cuts of lamb. Or, use these cuts for our outstanding Grilled Lamb Kabobs with Skordalia (page 531–32).

LOW AND HIGH SATURATED-FAT LAMB

Low Saturated-Fat Lamb

3.5 ounces	Calories	Grams Total Fat	Grams Saturated Fat	% of Calories from Fat	Mg Cholesterol
Leg	191	7.7	2.8	36	89
Loin chop	216	9.7	3.5	40	95
Lamb shank	180	6.7	2.4	44	87
High Saturated-Fat Lamb					
Shoulder chop	203	10.0	5.6	44	90
Rack of lamb	230	13.0	4.7	51	87

Fat Tracking Pork

Pork is the most maligned and misunderstood of meats. You have probably had an experience with greasy pork dishes afloat in fat. A smoked ham conceals many grams of fat under its honeyed and mustard-tinged skin. Bacon can't even hide its fat while sausages spluttering in the frying pan ooze fat. And barbecued pork spareribs—dare we even mention their name in the same book that urges a heart-healthy diet? The pork industry has worked hard to convince us that it is "the other white meat." Is it? Well, it is getting closer.

In recent years the pork industry has been under the gun to bring leaner pork to market. They have worked at streamlining feed, among other things, and have had very good success. In some cases, pork, especially tenderloin, is closer to poultry in terms of fat than the leanest beef. You will find several dishes that highlight this leanest of the pork cuts, such as Island Stew with Pork (page 534–35), brimming with flavor and short on fat, as well as Pork Roast with Prunes (page 532–33), a delicious loin cooked with port. But most people like their pork in the morning. Bacon, ham, sausage, please, with scrambled eggs and buttered toast. Note that just one strip of bacon has slightly more saturated fat than a 3.5-ounce serving of pork tenderloin. Break the breakfast meat habit. Turn to the Breakfast chapter to find suggestions for stoking your engine with carbohydrates and lean poultry sausages instead of pork products.

3.5 ounces	Calories	Grams Total Fat	Grams Saturated Fat	% of Calories from Fat	Mg Cholesterol
Pork tenderloin, top loin, roasted	166	4.8	1.7	26	93.0
Canned ham, roasted, 4-5% fat	136	4.9	1.6	32	30.0
Pork center loin	231	10.5	3.6	41	98.0
Fresh ham, roasted	221	10.7	3.7	43	96.0
Bacon, 1-ounce only, panfried	163	14.0	4.9	77	24.0
Pork chop, meat and visible fat	237	13.5	5.0	51	79.3
Pork, Italian sausage, cooked	370	31.0	10.7	75	81.0
Pork spareribs, braised	397	30.0	11.8	69	121.0

Fat Tracking Veal

As with all animals, including humans, the younger and friskier, the less fat. But while veal is lean, its delicate white meat is also tender and desirable, and an all-around good choice. Yes, we still limit veal to twice a week, because though it is lean relative to other meats, it is not as lean as fish and fowl. All cuts are acceptable with the exception of the fatty breast, featured in many Italian dishes. To accent its delicate flavor, cooks have traditionally adorned veal with rich, creamy and cheesy sauces. Fat Trackers quick-grill it (taking it off the heat before it toughens), or roast it or panfry it in a small amount of oil. Grilled Lemon Veal with Green Bean and Basil Purée (page 525–26), will prove that you do not have to disguise veal in a glut of saturated fat to appreciate its appeal.

Note that free-range veal is making a comeback, in part due to the pressure brought to bear by consumer groups and some high-profile chefs such as Berkeley's Alice Waters of Chez Panisse fame, who object to the husbanding of animals in unsanitary conditions and the heavy doses of antibiotics in their feed. The meat has more color than milk-fed (white) veal and a more robust flavor, which is suitable for any recipe. Ask your market to stock it.

3.5 ounces	Calories	Grams Total Fat	Grams Saturated Fat	% of Calories from Fat	Mg Cholesterol
Leg of veal	150	3.4	1.2	20	103
Veal rib chop	177	7.4	2.1	38	115
Veal cutlet, sirloin	175	6.9	2.6	35	106
Loin of veal	175	6.9	2.6	35	106
Breast of veal	304	21.0	10.2	62	90

Fat Tracking Organ Meats

A serving of chicken liver has 630 milligrams of cholesterol, more than twice the daily recommended allowance! Need we explain any further why we put liver and the pâtés that use them on the "almost never" column of our What to Eat When list? When you crave the taste and texture of pâté, try White Bean Pâté (page 345).

ORGAN MEATS

3.5 ounces	Calories	Grams Total Fat	Grams Saturated Fat	% of Calories from Fat	Mg Cholesterol
Chicken livers	157	5.5	1.8	32	631
Pork kidney	151	4.7	1.5	28	480
Beef liver	161	4.9	1.9	27	389
Beef sweetbreads	232	15.0	6.8	58	397
Beef kidney	144	3.4	1.1	21	387
Beef heart	175	5.6	1.7	29	193
Tongue	283	21.0	9.0	67	107

Fat Tracking Poultry

Of all poultry, skinless turkey breast (with chicken breast a close second) has the least fat, and we encourage you to include it on your menus often. We showcase it throughout our recipes—grilled, stir-fried, roasted, broiled, sautéed and turned into homemade sausage. When you cook dark meat of chicken or turkey, consider it as one of your 2+2 entrees, because per calorie it contains less protein and twice as much fat as white meat. More fat per serving also means more calories, as well. Though you no doubt know this by now, it bears repeating for novice chefs: *Always remove and discard the skin and any visible fat from poultry.* Though wild fowl is low in fat, domestic duck is not, as the comparison below of a 3.5-ounce serving of skinless roasted duck breast shows. There is no way to prepare goose, a holiday favorite, to eliminate all of its fabled fat. So enjoy it once during the holiday season, if you like, but never make it a regular entree. Game hens have little fat and you can enjoy them regularly. Whole volumes have been written about the virtues of poultry. However, we narrow the focus to one important point.

❧ Poultry fat is in the dark meat and the skin.

A word about ground poultry. It would seem that turkey burgers, chicken sausage and ground poultry would be ideal choices for the Fat Tracker, because poultry comes up so lean on the fat charts. However, grinding up good lean white meat, the most expensive cut, drives the price up, and the lack of fat in the breast meat makes ground poultry dry. To compensate, the producers often dump dark meat and skin or fat into the mixture, for a moist, economical, but hardly leaner product. When you select one of these items, read the label for the grams of saturated fat in each serving. If the calorie or total fat gram count is high, you know fat has been added in some form, and you might be better off with lean, ground beef round. Our recipes will show you how to grind poultry in a food processor and turn commercial or homemade ground breast meat into flavorful sausages that rely on canola or olive oil and apple to keep them moist.

The following table illustrates the fat and cholesterol equivalents for a 3.5-ounce portion of the most popular types of poultry. Because turkey has the least fat, we highlight it first.

TURKEY

3.5 ounces	Calories	Grams Total Fat	Grams Saturated Fat	% of Calories from Fat	Mg Cholesterol
Turkey breast, no skin	109	1.6	0.5	13	41
Turkey breast with skin	197	8.3	2.3	38	76
Turkey, dark, with skin	221	11.5	3.5	47	89
Turkey, dark, no skin	187	7.2	2.4	35	85
Ground turkey, dark and light meat, no skin	183	10.5	3.6	52	72

CHICKEN

3.5 ounces	Calories	Grams Total Fat	Grams Saturated Fat	% of Calories from Fat	Mg Cholesterol
Chicken breast, no skin	165	3.6	1.0	20	85
Chicken breast with skin	193	7.6	2.2	35	83
Chicken, dark, no skin	205	9.7	2.7	42	93
Chicken, dark, with skin	253	15.8	4.4	56	91

GAME

3.5 ounces	Calories	Grams Total Fat	Grams Saturated Fat	% of Calories from Fat	Mg Cholesterol
Domestic Game					
Game hens, no skin	238	14.0	1.0	53	52
Duck, domestic, breast, no skin	201	11.2	4.2	50	89
Goose, no skin	238	12.7	4.6	48	9
Wild Game					
Pheasant, uncooked, no skin	133	3.6	1.2	24	96
Duck, wild, breast	122	4.2	1.3	31	79
Quail, uncooked no skin	134	4.5	1.3	30	90
Squab, uncooked	142	7.4	2.0	47	90

Fat Tracking Fish and Shellfish

Healthy in all respects, a portion of fish usually contains less than one gram of saturated fat per serving. Clearly, you can't go wrong by including fish on as many dinner menus as possible. Although shellfish is well known for its high levels of cholesterol, it is so low in saturated and total fat that it is still an important fat-tracking food. In addition, fish is high in omega-3 fatty acids, news, by the way, that spawned an advertising campaign for fish-oil capsules. However, these capsules are not necessary for a healthy heart. First of all, the capsules add extra oil and calories to your diet. Secondly, the omega-3 fatty acids are not as beneficial in capsule form as in the fish sources, which provide many other important nutrients, as well.

Note that the cold water fish, such as salmon and tuna, have 6 to 7 grams of fat per 3.5-ounce serving, though they are quite low in saturated fat. The fat, however, is in the form of the healthier monosaturated oils and omega-3 fatty acids. Canned tuna in water is on our Crunchy Lunch and sandwich menus for obvious reasons. Just remember not to ruin this by adding too much regular mayonnaise! Grill and poach fish, and forego the rich sauces and deep-fat fried breading that hikes up the grams of saturated fat per serving.

Here are some examples of cholesterol and saturated fat in a 3.5-ounce serving of fish and shellfish. With the exception of crayfish, shrimp and squid, shellfish contains approximately the same amount of cholesterol as a serving of egg noodles. By the way, always weigh shellfish without any shells or you will cheat yourself of a delicious morsel.

3.5 ounces	Calories	Grams Total Fat	Grams Saturated Fat	% of Calories from Fat	Mg Cholesterol
Anchovies, raw	129	4.8	1.3	33	51
Catfish, raw	115	4.2	0.9	33	57
Halibut, cooked	139	2.9	0.5	19	41
Monkfish	96	2.0	Trace	18	67
Orange roughy	88	0.8	0.1	10	26
Salmon, coho, cooked	183	7.5	1.4	37	49
Sea bass, cooked	122	2.6	0.7	19	52
Snapper, cooked	127	1.7	0.3	12	47
Sole, baked	80	1.0	0.2	11	46
Squid, raw	91	1.4	0.3	14	231
Swordfish, cooked	154	5.1	1.4	30	50
Trout, rainbow, cooked	150	4.3	0.8	26	72
Tuna, bluefin, cooked	183	6.2	1.6	30	49
Clams, cooked	147	2.0	0.2	12	66
Crab, Dungeness, raw	85	0.9	0.1	10	58
Crayfish, cooked	113	1.4	0.2	11	176
Lobster	98	0.6	0.1	5	72
Mussels, cooked	171	4.4	0.8	23	56
Oysters, raw	80	2.3	0.5	26	55
Scallops, raw	87	0.7	0.1	7	33
Shrimp, cooked	98	1.0	0.2	10	194

Canned fish and shellfish are as low in fat as their fresh or frozen varieties, *provided* they are packed in water, as the following comparison table shows.

CANNED FISH AND SHELLFISH

3.5 ounces	Calories	Grams Total Fat	Grams Saturated Fat	% of Calories from Fat	Mg Cholesterol
Water-packed tuna, light	129	0.5	0.1	3	23
Clams, canned, drained	147	2.0	0.2	12	66
Oil-packed tuna, light	197	8.2	1.5	37	17
Salmon, pink, with bone	137	6.0	1.5	39	51
Anchovies, in oil	210	9.5	2.0	41	17

Fat Tracking Processed Meats

Many people enjoy these deli items for breakfast and lunch. You don't have to give them up, but you may have to do some careful menu juggling and label scanning to make sure that your selection fits into your 25-gram plan. Some bacon, pork strips and sausages contain up to 80 and 90 percent fat calories! Make sure that the serving size listed on the package corresponds to your appetite for the product. Certain brands sometimes list 1 gram of fat per serving, which is an unrealistic paper-thin slice. We have listed a selection of some favorites, and as you can see, Canadian bacon and very lean Danish ham stand out as the lean choices in this pack of mostly high-fat meats. Some people choose "imitation" meats made from soy, rather than forfeit so many saturated-fat grams to a beef frank or an ounce of bacon, but they, too, have their drawbacks, as we will discuss next.

PROCESSED MEATS

	Calories	Grams Total Fat	Grams Saturated Fat	% of Calories from Fat	Mg Cholesterol
1 ounce extra-lean Danish ham, 5% fat	37	1.4	0.5	34	13
1 ounce Canadian bacon, grilled	51	2.3	0.8	41	16
1 ounce regular roasted ham, 11% fat	52	3.0	1.0	52	16
1 slice head cheese	60	4.5	1.4	68	23
1 Vienna sausage	45	4.0	1.5	80	8
1 slice pimento loaf	74	6.0	2.2	73	10
1 ounce Polish sausage	92	8.1	3.0	79	20
1 ounce bologna	88	8.0	3.4	82	16
1 ounce hard salami	115	9.5	3.4	74	42
1 ounce regular bacon, panfried	161	13.9	4.9	77	24
1 link bratwurst	256	22.0	8.0	77	51
1 corn dog	330	20.0	8.4	55	37
1 link chorizo	265	23.0	8.6	78	52

However, take a look at the following table comparing 3.5-ounce portions of some of the popular processed turkey products—much better fat tracking choices.

TURKEY COLD CUTS

3.5 ounces	Calories	Grams Total Fat	Grams Saturated Fat	% of Calories from Fat	Mg Cholesterol
Breast meat, turkey loaf*	94	1.4	0.3	13	35
Barbecued breast slices	100	1.4	0.5	13	43
Turkey ham, thigh (dark) meat	110	4.4	1.5	36	51
Turkey pastrami	120	5.3	1.5	39	45
Turkey salami	111	7.8	2.2	63	68
Turkey bologna	120	9.0	2.8	68	40
Turkey frankfurter	222	18.0	6.0	73	86

*Note: Synthetic and processed meats may also contain fillers, which may decrease the fat and calorie content because the fillers often have less fat and protein. Terms such as "loaf," in ham loaf and turkey loaf, for instance, is a clue to the presence of these fillers.

Meatless Meats

What about those meatless meats? Known as "analogues," they are products (often made with foods such as soybeans) to simulate other (usually more expensive) foods. Look for this word to become more popular as food producers work to provide nourishing alternatives to saturated-fat foods. Obviously, they have no cholesterol, and the saturated fat count is way down also. But when producers start adding oil, hydrogenated fats and flavorings (sometimes including MSG, a problem for many people) to mimic the taste of beef franks, salami and turkey, some products reach 70 percent total fat and the hydrogenation process will add dangerous transfatty acids, as we discussed in Chapter 11, Nutrition for a Healthy Heart: Fat and Fads. However, do sort through the offerings of these analogues in the deli case. Some "veggie" burgers have only 8 percent total fat. How can you tell which is which? Read the label.

MEAT, POULTRY, FISH AND SEAFOOD SHOPPING LIST

Food	Choose	Instead of
Beef	Lean cuts with fat trimmed, such as top round, beef round, 10 percent fat hamburger, loin	Prime cuts, corned beef brisket, regular ground, short ribs, T-bone, sirloin, chuck
Lamb	Loin, leg, shanks	Breast, shoulder
Pork	Tenderloin, Danish ham, Canadian bacon	Spareribs, blade roll, fresh, picnic ham, canned ham
Veal	Tenderloin, leg	Ground (may contain fat) and breast
Poultry	Turkey and chicken, especially breast meat, game hens, wild birds (remember to remove the skin)	Duck, goose, chicken and turkey dark meat, all skin
Fish and shellfish	All fish, all shellfish canned in water frozen fish, not breaded or deep-fried	All fish canned in oil, any deep-fried or breaded fish with saturated fat
Processed meat	Turkey breast, low-fat and fat-free luncheon meats	Regular luncheon meats, frankfurters, sausage
Miscellaneous		Organ meats such as liver

CHAPTER 19

Fat Tracking Dairy Products

WE, TOO, LOVE THE CREAMY, BUTTERY GOODNESS *of dairy products, but if you use sweet cream, whole milk, premium ice cream and rich cheeses on a regular basis, your saturated fat and cholesterol intake will skyrocket. You can eliminate red meat from your diet, but then turn around and offset that healthy gain by indulging in one of the most abundant sources of saturated fat and cholesterol—the cheese, butter and cream which has been the core of American cooking for most of this century.*

Glutted with fat, these products beckon from every ice cream shop, restaurant menu and dairy case. They seem to sauce or coat almost every favorite food. Food producers use butter to seduce the consumer into buying crackers, popcorn, canned sauces, packaged noodle and rice mixes and other hard-to-resist items. Almost every dessert recipe seems to require cream. Can you remember the last time you attended a social event and didn't find cheese the focal point of the appetizer tray? If you are a milk drinker and down three or four glasses of *whole milk* a day—on your cereal, with your sandwich at lunch, as an afternoon snack, with some cookies while you relax in the evening—the 5 grams of saturated fat in each glass will almost put you over your 25-gram limit without eating anything else.

🌿 **And remember that cholesterol travels with the saturated fat in that glass of whole milk, as it does in all animal products.**

Obviously, these high-fat dairy products simply do not fit into The Stanford 25 Gram Plan on a regular basis, and people with heart disease must *always* pass them by. However, you don't have to give up milk and cookies, macaroni and cheese, potatoes au gratin, an omelet, frozen desserts or even sour cream on your baked potato to keep your saturated fat under the 25-gram limit. The key is to make *enlightened* dairy choices.

The dairy industry has done a lot of valuable footwork to eliminate fat from milk products, and some low-fat switches don't require very much effort at all. You don't have to change everything overnight. Start using 1 percent milk immediately in your baking instead of whole milk or 2 percent low-fat milk. Also switch from drinking whole milk to 2 percent low-fat milk and in two or three weeks it will begin to taste rich and creamy. After a month or so, start drinking 1 percent milk exclusively. For a further reduction in fat, if you desire you can mix 1 percent milk with nonfat milk in equal portions. With these small changes you will have taken a step almost imperceptible to your taste buds, but a giant leap toward maintaining healthy arteries.

Rearrange your omelet ingredients, adding more spinach, mushrooms, onions and egg whites and substituting all or part of the egg yolks with liquid egg substitute; they will taste as good as the original. Keep the lower-fat cheeses such as Parmesan, part-skim mozzarella, Swiss (part or skim-milk versions) and sapsago in your refrigerator to accent sauces and toppings, and you can still enjoy cheese as a delicious supplier of calcium, protein and flavor.

Dairy Substitutes

With the restrictions the Fat Tracker must place on dairy products, are substitutes the answer? Some shoppers view the low-fat and nonfat substitutes for eggs, butter, cream and cheese with disdain, while others reach for them with unabashed enthusiasm. Whether you choose to use them depends on your taste and need. If your doctor places very tight restrictions on the fat and cholesterol in your diet, liquid egg substitutes and fat-free cheese may take on a new luster. The wonderful diversity of foods and ethnic seasonings available in American supermarkets definitely broadens the options for heart-healthy meal planning by decreasing the cook's dependency on dairy products in general. Imagination and creativity also play a part in making mealtime pleasurable *and* healthy.

For example, many people prefer to make a sauce with real cream or a pat of butter only occasionally, rather than use substitutes frequently. They will choose from a variety of salsas, tomato or other vegetable-based sauces, as well as olive oil marinades and dressings to flavor foods on a daily basis. However, rather than use a fat-free brand, some folks prefer to juggle a menu, for example, by choosing the lower-fat, skinless turkey breast instead of the roasted ham for a sandwich, to allow for the extra grams of fat and milligrams of cholesterol in homemade mayonnaise. On the other hand, many people find nonfat sour cream, made with acceptable vegetable products, tastes just fine as the base for a vegetable sauce or dip. Many parents wisely introduce their children to low-fat products early, when they will have a much easier time accepting them. Or they may take another tack entirely and demonstrate with various food choices that good food doesn't always require either a glut of dairy products or substitutes.

❧ **It is up to you to decide your own dairy approach, but since dairy products do provide good sources of protein and calcium, make sure you get a minimum of reduced-fat or nonfat milk and cheese.**

We have experimented with every reduced-fat and nonfat dairy product currently available. Many do a good job of approximating the familiar creamy texture and flavors of the original. We have our own biases. For instance, we give a thumbs down to reconstituting powdered butter substitutes and using them as "butter" on steamed vegetables. But we do like to use this product in baked goods where it blends with other ingredients to give a hint of buttery goodness in an otherwise low-fat item. We will show you how to jazz up your vegetables with more flavorful vinaigrettes and by using lemon and herb and olive oil and garlic mixtures, as well as other low-fat or fat-free sauces. Though we include fat-free mayonnaise in some sauces and spreads, for flavor's sake, we pan it for use straight out of the jar as a sandwich spread, preferring the tastier flavored yogurt cheese and other ideas you will find throughout the book.

Because individual tastes vary so much, you might pass up products we favor, and you may rave over ones we don't like. In time, we believe food technology will refine these items, and we hope that the ones that consumers now find marginal in quality will soon be indistinguishable from the original. Just as you would not compare yogurt to cottage cheese, but use them for different effects, it helps to think of dairy substitutes as additions to the roster of dairy products, not replacements. For instance, you may feel nonfat sour cream does not exactly duplicate the original. But you may find that it provides a taste and texture that pleases nonetheless when you blend it into Cilantro Pesto (page 293).

We find that combining other ingredients with *all* reduced-fat dairy products enhances their flavor and texture. You will notice in several of our recipes, for instance, that we use nonfat yogurt and add a small amount of 1 percent or low-fat milk to sweeten it and smooth the texture, rendering the yogurt very low in fat but greatly improved in flavor. While nonfat cottage cheese makes a healthy alternative to sour cream as the base for a dip, adding a blend of low-fat sour cream, yogurt and cream cheese in some of our dessert and breakfast creams is a more flavorful alternative with only a slight increase in fat. You can improve nonfat sour cream by mixing it with pesto, salsa or homemade mayonnaise.

We are not pushing any of these products. Use them or not as you wish. But if you select any of them, make sure they fit into your entire nutritional scheme. Take the same label-reading precautions for these substitute items that you do with any food. Don't assume that because it is "nondairy" that it has been cleansed of all traces of saturated fat or cholesterol. Nondairy creamers, for example, often contain highly saturated tropical and/or hydrogenated oils to make them creamy and tasty. Obviously, those substitutions are not a sensible alternative to real cream; instead learn to lighten your coffee with milk—better yet, low-fat milk. It is a tough market out there. Advertisers will write on a box anything they can get away with to get your attention. Just don't believe everything you read.

Fat Tracking Milk
With few exceptions, you can scratch whole milk from your shopping list. With as much or more calcium (producers add extra calcium), low-fat and nonfat milk products are as nutritious as the whole milk versions, but with much or all of the fat and cholesterol removed. What low-fat, 1 percent and skim milks *do* retain, how-

ever, is the natural sweetness of milk, so as you become accustomed to their lighter taste, you will discover that they still have the familiar delicious appeal of milk.

Reduced-Fat Milks

What about the differences among reduced-fat milks? If low-fat milk is only 2 percent fat, why do we tell you to pass in favor of 1 percent or nonfat milk? Are we just being picky, or can the difference between 1 percent and 2 percent be that significant? Most definitely, because those percentages refer to the weight of the fat, a number that always looks more appealing on a label. If you put a glass of low-fat milk on a scale, fat would only account for 2 percent of the weight compared to the water and other nutrients. A Fat Tracker, though, only cares about fat in terms of grams or percent of calories. The following table lists the actual fat content of milk, and proves that a simple maneuver such as choosing 1 percent over 2 percent milk saves 2.1 grams total fat and 1.5 grams saturated fat per 8-ounce glass of milk. If you drink 3 or 4 glasses a day, that can mean a difference of up to 6 grams of your maximum 25 grams of saturated fat, or more than one-fifth of your daily total!

Buttermilk

Despite its name, the fat is largely absent from buttermilk. Made from low-fat or fat-free milk, it makes it an excellent choice for cooking and drinking. As you will see in our baking recipes, we combine its unique properties with olive oil or canola oil to produce a delicate crumb in several of our muffins and scones. Low-fat buttermilk also makes an excellent base for our creamy buttermilk and Roquefort Shallot Dressing (page 382). In addition, buttermilk is an excellent tenderizer for turkey and chicken breast, as we demonstrate in Turkey Piccata (page 512). Do not buy churned or sweet cream buttermilk, which is much higher in fat.

MILK

8 ounces	Calories	Grams Total Fat	Grams Saturated Fat	% of Calories from Fat	Mg Cholesterol
Whole milk (3½ percent milkfat)	150	8.0	5.0	48	34
Low-fat (2 percent milkfat)	121	4.7	2.9	35	18
Low-fat (1 percent milkfat)	102	2.6	1.6	23	10
Nonfat (skim) milk	86	0.4	0.3	4	4
Buttermilk, low-fat	90	2.5	1.5	20	9
Churned or sweet cream buttermilk	160	8.0	5.6	25	35

Whole Milk

While you can enjoy all the milk you want if you make it nonfat, whole milk does have its advantages. Use it to lower the fat content of a rich and creamy favorite recipe by substituting it for cream or half-and-half when reduced-fat milk simply won't work. When you do use whole milk, buy it in half-pint or one-pint containers, rather than quart or half-gallon cartons, so you are not tempted to drink what you don't use in your recipe.

Tricks with Milk

Do you know that you can freeze milk and even cream? Pour it into small containers or even ice cube trays, freeze, and then pop them into a plastic bag to have on hand to add these very small amounts to soups and sauces for an occasional rich fillip. You can also make your own half-and-half. You can adjust the richness of available milks if you like, by blending half 2 percent milk and half 1 percent milk for an 8-ounce glass that contains 2.3 grams of saturated fat. Or you can blend 4 ounces each of 1 percent and skim milk for an 8-ounce glass with less than 1 gram of saturated fat. On the page these differences may seem insignificant, but as your palate becomes accustomed to leaner foods, these slight adjustments can help make your transition to low-fat dairy products easier. You will also have saved a few grams of fat to spend on some other indulgence during the day.

Nonfat Powdered Milk

You can mix powdered milk with water for an economical drink. This mixture also makes a terrific calcium booster in baking recipes, and adds an extra richness in those that call for low or nonfat milk.

Canned Milk

Sweetened condensed milk gained popularity during the 30s, 40s and 50s as a base for many desserts. The process removes half the water and adds sugar to stabilize it, producing a very high-fat, very sweet product. With more water and fat removed, but no sugar added, evaporated low-fat or skim milk is a better choice when you want a sweet and rich tasting milk for baking. Read labels carefully to avoid confusing these various canned milks.

CANNED MILK

3 ounces	Calories	Grams Total Fat	Grams Saturated Fat	% of Calories from Fat	Mg Cholesterol
Sweetened condensed milk	369	9.9	6.3	24	39
Evaporated milk, whole	126	7.2	4.5	51	27
Evaporated low-fat milk	83	2.3	1.5	24	8
Evaporated skim milk	75	0.3	0	4	3

Fat Tracking Cream and Half-and-Half

Large quantities of cream or half-and-half should not appear with any regularity on a Fat Tracker's shopping list. However, on occasion you may choose to spend some of your fat grams on a small creamy addition to a sauce or dessert. Again, the temptation to use the whole carton might be strong, so when you do purchase cream, buy the smallest quantity possible, use only what you need for your recipe and freeze the remainder in ice cube trays. An "ice cube's worth" will vary in size depending on the size of your ice tray, but one cube may be just enough to give a satiny finish to a recipe, and when divided among your family and friends, will give each person only a very small addition of saturated fat.

From the following table, you can see why we place tight restrictions on cream products. Even though your recipe may call for heavy cream, half-and-half should provide ample creaminess. See our alternatives to whipped cream, such as Ginger Cream, Ricotta Cream, and Grand Marnier Cream in the Desserts chapter and Sweet Cheese (page 309) in the Breakfast chapter. By now, you are beginning to see how easily saturated fat grams add up over the course of a day. However, wise substitutions that save even one or two grams allow you a wider choice of foods. For example, by switching from heavy to light cream or better yet, light cream to milk in a sauce or soup at dinner, you still have creaminess where you want it. And then you can also enjoy another spoonful of low-fat Parmesan cheese sprinkled on your pasta or an extra muffin containing some margarine at breakfast—a choice that would also add filling and healthful carbohydrates and fiber.

CREAM

Per Tablespoon	Calories	Grams Total Fat	Grams Saturated Fat	% of Calories from Fat	Mg Cholesterol
Whipping cream, heavy	52	5.6	3.5	97	21
Whipping cream, light	44	4.6	2.9	94	17
Half-and-half	20	1.7	1.1	77	6

Fat Tracking Cottage Cheese, Cream Cheese and Sour Cream

As with the sweet creams, sour cream and creamy cheeses do not make regular appearances in a Fat Tracker's shopping cart. However, from time to time you can include in your recipe reduced-fat cream cheese (often packaged as Neufchâtel), part-skim ricotta and reduced-fat or low-fat sour cream over the whole milk versions. Compared to the whole milk versions, the difference in flavor is negligible, and the savings in fat is considerable, as you can see in the following table. Note that whipped cream cheese has almost a third less fat than regular cream cheese. Fat-free cream cheese is available, though it does not deliver the same flavor that low-fat versions do.

Strike whole milk (4 percent) cottage cheese, as well as creamed cottage cheese from your shopping list, and use uncreamed, low-fat or nonfat exclusively. You can add to cottage cheese small amounts of low-fat milk to give a creamier texture if you like. As a general rule, the cottage cheeses flavored with chives, pineapple and fruit salad are made with the higher-fat cottage cheeses. They are also more expensive, although low-fat versions are beginning to appear in response to the call for more low-fat dairy products. Buy low-fat and nonfat cottage cheese, add your own fruit or herbs and save money and saturated fat!

Ricotta

Ricotta cheese has two to three times the fat of whole milk cottage cheese, but it is much lower in fat than cream cheese. Selecting part-skim over whole milk ricotta reduces the fat by almost a third. An even lower-fat ricotta is available that is leaner, yet has more richness than fat-free ricotta, and we use it successfully in our recipes. Nonfat ricotta, while definitely the healthiest, does not deliver as much flavor as the higher-fat versions. Ricotta's pronounced flavor is ideal in our sumptuous Chocolate-Crusted Raspberry Cheesecake (page 550–51), where we combine it with cottage cheese and Neufchâtel. In Pasta Shells Stuffed with Winter Squash and Four Cheeses (page 470–71), we stuff pasta shells with a cheesy mix of skim-milk ricotta, Parmesan and nonfat cottage cheese. Look for ways to blend these soft, low-fat cheeses into your own recipes. Even though they do contain some saturated fat, by comparison they are so much lower than the whole milk versions that you still have many options for creating rich dishes.

Nonfat Sour Cream

If you have not tried it already, give nonfat sour cream a try. Made of natural ingredients, with the fat replaced by vegetable gums acceptable to nutritionists and cooks alike, this product has many virtues. The flavor and texture are quite light, almost airy, which in many cases is delightful; for example, spread on a minibagel and topped with salsa or pesto. Quick Black Bean Dip (page 355) puts nonfat sour cream to work to create the smoothness that was once only achieved with lard! While a purist may prefer to substitute yogurt rather than this "doctored cream," you don't always want the tartness of yogurt in your dish and this creamy product offers a happy alternative.

Per Tablespoon	Calories	Grams Total Fat	Grams Saturated Fat	% of Calories from Fat	Mg Cholesterol
Whole-milk sour cream	26	2.5	1.6	87	5
Imitation sour cream	27	2.4	2.0	80	0
Reduced-fat sour cream	20	1.8	1.1	81	6
Nonfat sour cream	9	0	0	0	0
Whole-milk cream cheese	49	4.8	2.7	88	14
Reduced-fat cream cheese	31	2.4	1.4	70	8
Whipped cream cheese	37	3.6	2.0	88	11
Per 1 Cup					
Whole-milk cottage cheese	217	9.5	6.0	39	31
Low-fat cottage cheese (2 percent)	203	4.4	2.8	20	19
Low-fat cottage cheese (1 percent)	164	2.3	1.5	13	10
Nonfat cottage cheese	70	0	0	0	0
Dry curd cottage cheese	123	0.6	0.4	4	10
Per ½ Cup					
Whole-milk ricotta cheese	216	16.1	10.3	67	63
Part skim ricotta cheese	171	9.8	6.1	52	38

Are Fat-Free Creams and Cheeses the Answer?

As far as taste is concerned, you have to decide how much fat of your daily fat allowance you want to spend on dairy products. If you have a very sensitive palate, you probably won't like the substitutions and will juggle your fat ration accordingly. On the other hand, you may not notice much of a difference and be happy with the fat-free product. Most of these products do not perform well in cooked foods, though that could change. New, improved items are appearing all the time and the technology will only get better as demand for these foods increases.

If you are trying to make the downward shift in dairy products, comparing the fat-free version to the original product probably won't help you, for it will almost always come up short. On the other hand, while fat-free cream cheese does not have the smoothness or precise delectable tang of whole milk cream cheese (and will not make a superior cheesecake), it does not have an objectionable flavor. If you spread fat-free cream cheese on a slice of delicious toasted bread with your favorite marmalade, hot pepper jelly or a smear of chutney, it can be delicious in its own right and far better for your heart on a daily basis. Save the real cream cheese for a bagel and lox at brunch on occasion. Not all products hold up equally well. Try all brands and you may find a fat-free sour cream, yogurt or ricotta cheese you can live with, and, who knows, maybe even enjoy.

Be aware that just because a dairy product is fat-free, it is not necessarily lower in calories. Often the fat is replaced with carbohydrate substances that may be kind to your arteries, but still hard on your waistline. If you are trying to lose weight, read the labels and choose a brand with a calorie count that fits into your overall weight-reducing plan.

❧ **Note the difference between "imitation" and "reduced-fat" dairy products. Imitation products do not necessarily have less fat.**

Individuals with milk allergies can enjoy imitation milk-free products, but as you can see from the preceding table, they may still contain as much or more saturated fat than whole milk versions. Look for "reduced," "low-fat" or "fat-free" products, with or without dairy ingredients—the only guarantee that you are getting less harmful fat.

Fat Tracking Yogurt

This cultured milk product has long been an important food in Middle Eastern cooking. Yogurt gained ground in American markets several decades ago as a "diet" food, and now has become one of our staple snacks and quick meals when we have to eat on the run. Pass up the whole milk yogurts and choose the low-fat and nonfat versions. Follow our trick of adding the sweetness of a few tablespoons of low-fat or skim milk to smooth the flavor and texture of nonfat yogurt before you cook with it. Flavorings from coffee, chocolate, vanilla, and every variety of fruit make low-fat and nonfat yogurt ideal for snacks and simple desserts. Plain yogurt smoothes pestos and soups (as Melon and Cucumber Soup, page 377, demonstrates), and adds creaminess to dessert toppings.

Sample several brands of yogurt to find the one you prefer. Some nonfat yogurts taste quite pallid, while others are rich, creamy and satisfying without any additional fat. In some recipes we specify creamy-style yogurt, which contains gelatin and has a smoother texture that does not separate or become watery as regular yogurt often does. The nutritional content of creamy-style yogurt is identical to that of yogurt without gelatin. This type of yogurt does not work for Drained Yogurt (page 290–91), however. We give you a comparison of plain yogurts; check the label to get a calorie reading on the flavored brands you prefer.

YOGURT

Per 8 Ounces	Calories	Grams Total Fat	Grams Saturated Fat	% of Calories from Fat	Mg Cholesterol
Whole-milk yogurt	139	7.4	4.8	48	29
Low-fat yogurt	140	4.0	2.0	26	14
Nonfat yogurt	130	Trace	Trace	Trace	4

Fat Tracking Cheese

No doubt about it, cheese is a difficult item for the Fat Tracker. Riddled with harmful fats, various cheeses and cheese products are a major source of saturated fat and calories, even in households that otherwise limit fat. Those who need or want to limit sodium may also want to curb their intake of salty cheeses such as Roquefort and Parmesan. We need to get rid of the "cheese as a snack or sandwich filling" concept, which the Crunchy Lunch (page 138) addresses. Though you or your children may promise to limit it, a block of cheese sitting in the refrigerator can tempt a hungry soul looking for a quick snack, so if you don't keep it around, no one can eat it. Find a deli or cheese shop that will cut just the specific amount you need for your dish, then you won't have to worry about the remains of a big block of cheese luring you—or your family when you are not around to monitor their snacks. You can also store many cheeses in the freezer. Take advantage of strong-flavored cheeses by grating an ounce or so into a sauce or dip. A 1-ounce cube of Cheddar has 6 grams of saturated fat and is hardly a mouthful on an appetizer tray. But take an ounce of grated Parmesan or Romano, stir it into a cup of roasted and puréed red pepper and add some garlic and minced fresh basil. Four or five people can happily dunk crisp breads or steamed vegetables into this pesto-style dip without loading up on saturated fat before dinner is even served.

Think of cheese as a condiment that enlivens a dish, rather than a major food source. For instance, instead of letting cheese dominate a pizza, as it often does, try Eggplant and Red Onion Pizza (page 477), an easy crust topped with tomato sauce and just enough Parmesan to add excitement. Use lower-fat mozzarella, domestic or imported Parmesan and imported Regianno as a matter of course, rather than whole milk cheeses such as Swiss or Monterey Jack. Whenever your budget can stand it, buy imported varieties of low-fat cheeses for maximum flavor. Instead of an appetizer cheese tray at your next party, serve a variety of marinated vegetables, olives, crisp low-fat breads and crackers, then offer Onion Cream (page 353), which uses only a trace of cheese. Cheeses are a real boon to the cook and an acceptable fat-tracking choice when you use them merely to flavor dishes, not to overpower them.

Double and triple crèmes, such as Camembert and St. André, are irresistible because they are almost pure butterfat. When the cheese appetizers are passed at a party, it is hard to keep track of how many times you have reached for a crackerful of Brie or Camembert—precisely the reason these high-fat cheeses belong in the "almost never" column of our what to eat Frequency table on page 135. Processed cheeses, American cheese and cheese spreads usually are a blend of high-fat cheese and, as you will see on the labels, very high in fat. Don't buy them. Ideally, try for reduced-fat type of cheeses such as low-fat Swiss with two grams or less of fat per ounce or less than 10 percent butter fat. When you buy higher-fat cheeses, plan to limit the number of weekly portions.

Cheese Substitutes

We include reduced-fat cheeses here because many of them have vegetable oil and other ingredients added to make up for the saturated fat stripped away in the manufacturing process. We believe low-fat cheeses will get better in the future as the technology improves. As far as currently available products are concerned, some work, some don't. Since fat adds a smooth texture to cheese, the lowest-fat products (reduced by as much as 50 percent) and those that are actually fat free, are often rubbery and relatively tasteless as an eating cheese, though they might add some interest stirred into a creamy sauce. The best-flavored reduced-fat cheese substitutes have the most fat, though they are still a bargain, relatively speaking. Regular cheese can have from 0 to 27 milligrams of cholesterol, yet contain over 80 percent fat calories. A reduced-fat product may not be fat free but still a better choice, giving you less fat than regular cheese and more flavor than a fat-free tasteless cheese substitute. Remember to read the labels carefully and work these products into your daily totals.

Because people enjoy cheese so much, and will no doubt juggle their 25-gram plans to accommodate servings of their favorite cheese now and then, we have provided a detailed listing to help you select cheeses with the lowest fat. You will see that we often call for grating cheese coarsely in recipes to produce volumes of ¼ or ½ cup. This trick makes the cheese easier to manage, and sometimes large shreds of a favorite cheese will linger on the palate to give you a feeling of satisfaction that you would normally get only with larger quantities. Note that most cheeses have 5 to 9 grams of saturated fat per ounce, which could be just one thin slice! That's why using a few sprinkles as a condiment is the heart-healthy way to enjoy cheese.

CHEESE

Per 1-ounce Serving	Calories	Grams Total Fat	Grams Saturated Fat	% of Calories from Fat	Mg Cholesterol
American	106	9.0	5.6	76	27
Bleu	100	8.0	5.3	72	21
Brick	105	8.4	5.3	72	27
Brie	95	8.0	6.0	76	28
Camembert	85	6.9	4.3	73	20
Cheddar	114	9.0	6.0	71	30
Processed American spread	82	6.0	3.8	66	16
Colby	112	8.7	6.0	70	29
Cream cheese	99	10.0	6.2	91	31
Neufchâtel (low-fat cream cheese)	74	7.0	4.2	85	22
Edam	101	7.9	5.0	70	25
Feta	75	6.0	4.2	72	25
Fontina	110	8.8	5.4	72	33
Havarti	121	10.4	6.5	77	34
Gouda	101	8.0	5.0	71	32
Gruyère	117	9.0	5.4	69	31
Jack	106	9.0	6.0	76	25
Mozzarella, whole milk	80	6.0	3.7	68	22
Mozzarella, skim milk	72	5.0	2.9	63	16
Parmesan	111	7.3	4.7	59	19
Ricotta, whole milk	54	4.0	2.5	67	16
Ricotta, skim milk	43	2.5	1.5	53	10
Roquefort	105	9.0	5.5	69	26
Swiss	107	8.0	5.0	67	26

Fat Tracking Eggs and Egg Substitutes

Egg substitutes, both frozen and liquid types, retain the whites of eggs and replace the yolks with a variety of acceptable vegetable, often soybean, ingredients. Most, but not all, brands are fat free and none contain cholesterol. We use the nonfat liquid egg products exclusively because we don't have to wait for them to thaw (though of course they do need refrigerating). You can decide whether you prefer the fat-free substitutes or, for the sake of perfectly reproducing a favorite recipe, you would rather use the product that adds a small amount of fat. We have employed both of these substitutes liberally in muffins, cakes, pastries, breads, pancakes, cheesecakes, waffles and soufflés. To give you an idea of their range, we have even made smooth, delicate Heart-Healthy Pastry Cream (page 553–54) and a satiny, egg-yolk-free custard sauce using liquid egg substitutes.

You can substitute two egg whites for a yolk in most standard recipes and forego the substitutes entirely. This does not always produce the desired result, however; in an omelet, for example, the texture tends to be slightly rubbery. As far as baked goods are concerned, only one trusted recipe in our testings—a puffed oven-baked pancake—would not reproduce satisfactorily with liquid egg substitute. Otherwise, we found egg substitute virtually indistinguishable from whole eggs in baked goods, especially when used with other reduced-fat products. The comparatively long (refrigerated) shelf life allows you to keep it on hand without worrying about spoilage if you do not use it all at once. Though at times you may still prefer to eat whole eggs, when you have used up your weekly allotment of egg yolks, you will find these egg substitutes a boon, certainly an acceptable alternative to no baked treats or egg dishes at all.

EGGS

Egg Equivalent	Calories	Grams Total Fat	Grams Saturated Fat	% of Calories from Fat	Mg Cholesterol
Whole egg	79	5.6	1.7	64	213
Egg yolk	63	5.6	1.7	80	213
Egg white	16	0	0	0	0
Egg substitutes, frozen, ¼ cup	96	0	0	0	0
Egg substitutes, liquid, ¼ cup	53	2.1	0.4	36	0
Egg substitutes, fat-free, ¼ cup	30	0	0	0	0

Fat Tracking Ice Cream and Frozen Dairy Desserts

Ice cream is the quintessential summer food (except in China where it is eaten in winter because it matches the frosty weather during the ice sculpture festivals!). The richer the better everyone used to believe, and so ice cream companies, eager to please the consumer, began offering premium or gourmet grades with 16 percent butterfat. When Americans started balking at all that fat, a new strain of goodies appeared in the freezer case: frozen dairy desserts such as frozen yogurt, frozen tofu, nondairy desserts and ice milk. "Hallelujah," everyone said, envisioning a fat-free heaven. But before you start licking that tofu ice cream cone (a better choice than a chocolate-covered bar on a stick, by the way), we have to tell you that not all low-fat frozen desserts are created equal.

Read the labels for these desserts and choose those with 1 gram or less of saturated fat per 100-calorie serving. Some have a lot more. A fat-free ice cream made with a synthetic fat has come to market and is available in many flavors. Of course, some fruit-based frozen favorites, such as popsicles, fruit gelato, sorbet and sherbet are almost entirely fat free. Do you know the difference between these fruity concoctions? Many chefs and cookbooks use sorbet and sherbet interchangeably, but in fact they are quite different. Sorbet is a mixture of fruit purée and or juice mixed with sugar syrup, sometimes egg whites and possibly other flavorings. It does not contain egg yolks, cream or milk. Sherbet, however, always contains some milk or cream, though not nearly as much as ice cream. Gelato, the Italian entry, is always made with milk, and ices are a blend of fruit juice and sugar syrup. Popsicles are similar to fruit ices but, depending on the brand, may be fruit flavored, rather than made with pure fruit juice. Popsicles rarely contain milk or cream.

If you are an ice cream lover, you may want to wean yourself away from the high-fat treats gradually. At first, switch to low-fat frozen yogurt or from premium to regular ice cream or from regular to ice milk. When the substitutes taste rich and creamy to you, try nonfat frozen yogurt and in time you will find it satisfying as well. Better yet, make your own fresh fruit ices or Raspberry Sherbet (page 564) with no or very little fat. Be aware that the calorie count and fat content in the frozen desserts listed below may vary slightly depending on the flavor.

FROZEN DESSERTS

½ Cup Serving	Calories	Grams Total Fat	Grams Saturated Fat	% of Calories from Fat	Mg Cholesterol
Ice cream, rich, 16 percent butterfat	175	11.9	7.4	61	44
Standard ice cream regular, 10 percent butterfat	135	7.2	4.5	48	30
Ice milk	92	2.8	1.8	28	9
Low-fat frozen yogurt	130	4.0	2.0	28	4
Nonfat frozen yogurt	80	0	0	0	2
Sherbet	127	1.7	1.0	12	4
Popsicles, ounces	42	0	0	0	0
Fruit gelato	70	0	0	0	0
Fruit ice	90	0	0	0	0
Sorbet	110	0.1	0	Trace	0

Food	Choose	Instead of
Milk	Skim (nonfat) milk, 1 percent milk, low-fat buttermilk, low-fat and nonfat chocolate milk; low-fat eggnog, nonfat evaporated milk	Whole milk—regular evaporated, condensed, sweetened condensed; whole milk chocolate drinks;
Cream	Low-fat and nonfat sour cream and sour cream substitutes, low-fat and nonfat yogurt	Whole cream, half-and-half, whipping cream, nonfat dairy creamers and imitation milk or cream products that contain tropical oils or saturated fat, sour cream
Soft Cheese and Yogurt	Low-fat and nonfat yogurt; low-fat and nonfat soft cheese, such as cottage cheese, farmer and pot cheese; part-skim-milk ricotta; reduced-fat cream cheese and Neufchâtel	Whole-milk yogurt; whole milk ricotta; soft cheeses such as Brie, double and triple crèmes, cream cheese
Cheese	Reduced-fat hard cheeses, such as part skim mozzarella, skim Swiss, low and nonfat cheeses	Hard cheeses such as American, Cheddar, Jack, Muenster
Eggs	Liquid, cholesterol-free egg substitutes, eggs (discard the yolks, use the fresh egg whites)	Packaged foods containing whole eggs
Frozen Dairy Desserts	Nonfat frozen desserts, such as sherbet, sorbet, Italian ice, frozen yogurt, popsicles, fruit gelato	High-fat frozen desserts, such as whole-milk or premium ice cream; frozen tofu; nondairy frozen desserts made with tropical or hydrogenated oils; milkshakes; eggnog

CHAPTER 20

Fat Tracking Fats and Oils

"THEY GO TOGETHER LIKE BREAD AND BUTTER," "*buttery skin*," "*smooth as butter*"—*this high-priced spread—butter—doesn't just reign supreme in traditional American kitchens, but has insinuated itself into our national consciousness. At this point, you can imagine what we have to say about this storehouse of saturated fat and cholesterol.*

❧ **One tablespoon of butter has 7 grams of saturated fat! One tablespoon of butter has 30 milligrams of cholesterol!**

Spread butter on two pieces of toast at breakfast and a baked potato at dinner and you can't eat any saturated fat in between without completely derailing your fat-tracking efforts. Of course, canned vegetable shortening and lard are no saturated-fat bargains, either (how could they be—they are solid at room temperature), but nobody longs to smother a hot muffin with them. However, even if you don't buy shortening and lard for kitchen or table use, careful label readers know that food producers, especially bakers, love them. They insert lard and canned or hydrogenated shortening into countless packaged foods and franchised fast foods, quietly hiking up the saturated-fat and transfatty acid count for the unsuspecting consumer. For example, the creamy, chocolate frosting on packaged cakes and cupcakes (those that aren't true buttercreams made according to French pastry traditions with butter *and* cream) is nothing but canned shortening and sugar. In the old days, when home baking was the rule rather than the exception, lard was the favored medium for producing flaky, tender pastries, as well as for frying potatoes, chicken and some vegetables. Lard is still widely used today by commercial bakers and cooks, and unless you read the label, you may not know you are eating it. In sauces, soups, vegetables and desserts, uninformed cooks are used to anointing every part of a meal with these harmful, highly saturated fats. But since these are the same fats that produce the flavor and texture of foods, is the Fat Tracker doomed to a life of tasteless meals with the approximate juiciness of sawdust? Hardly.

❧ Just as those of us who are concerned about the health of your heart will urge you to say "no" to butter, imaginative chefs interested in creative, healthful food will say, "amen."

Contemporary cooks eager to minimize the fat in American food have been re-thinking cooking fats and oils. Thanks to their innovations—as well as to the influences from Mediterranean and Asian cuisines that have never relied on butter—your recipes don't have to sacrifice flavor and texture on the altar of good health.

The substitution solution to the highly saturated butters and shortenings in baking is a mixture of unsaturated vegetable oil and other ingredients that add moisture and a desired texture. These might include buttermilk and yogurt, which tenderize; fruit purées, which provide moisture and lightness; and low-fat and nonfat sour cream and butter-flavored granules, which in various combinations approximate the full-bodied flavor of butterfat.

Need a good breakfast spread? We have the answer for that too, and it isn't always margarine, which has its own brand of trouble—transfatty acids. Instead of using butter, you will find that breakfast toast thickly spread with Stanford Breakfast Cream (page 315), Sweet Cheese (page 309) or White Bean Pâté (page 345) both satisfies and fortifies hungry bodies in the morning. And these spreads also give an innocent reward to an adolescent snacker in the afternoon. In an earlier chapter, we discussed the health benefits of cooking with vegetable oils. Now we will focus on their cooking properties, as well.

In choosing oils, select those with the least number of saturated fat molecules and the most monounsaturated and polyunsaturated molecules. Basically, you want oils that can tolerate high cooking temperatures without breaking down, as well as those with good flavor. They don't necessarily come in the same bottle. Just as you keep a variety of herbs, spices and other seasonings for your food, we suggest that you acquire a small collection of oils to add excitement to your dishes. Choose oils such as olive, walnut, Asian sesame and hazelnut to flavor your food, and others, such as canola oil or peanut oil, to tolerate high cooking temperatures without burning. Experiment with our suggestions for flavoring your oils to have instant seasoning always at hand.

Olive Oil: Nature's Gift to Your Heart—and Your Food

Some food connoisseurs prize a fine olive oil as highly as they do a fine wine. And to continue the analogy, if you find an olive oil that seems wildly overpriced to you compared to, say, garden-variety canola oil, ask yourself how often you purchase an expensive wine for a party that is consumed in an evening. A similarly priced olive oil will last for months and enhance your meals just as significantly. The variety and quality of olive oils you keep at your disposal actually give you a greater range of flavors than butter does, without the saturated fat and cholesterol. In addition, they provide a surplus of beneficial monounsaturated fatty acids. In fact, olive oil has the highest mono count of all fats (read good for your heart). But all olive oils are not the same. How do you choose an oil when you can't taste it or smell it first? Buy olive oil in small quantities until you find a brand you like.

Spanish and Greek olive oils, which tend to be more strongly flavored, work well in hearty, full-bodied dishes. But for baking, or for delicately seasoned salads and sautés, or for a table oil to replace butter, you would be happier with oils from France and northern Italy. Many cooks prefer the exceptionally fine olive oil from Lucca, though small producers in other regions of Italy also create exceptional oils. We are also happy to report that California wine growing regions have entered the olive oil market and produced some wonderful olive oils. With a little experimenting, you can find the oil and price you desire. The success of a dish can hinge on the quality and flavor of a good olive oil, and as with so many other aspects of cooking, the subtleties of flavor that appeal to one cook may disappoint another.

To give you an idea of how to distinguish among the many available olive oils, remember that the terms *extra-virgin, virgin,* and finally, just *plain olive oil* denote the number of pressings and the process used to extract the oil. The finest and most expensive are extra-virgin and virgin. These are the first to be extracted and both are cold pressed, that is, with mechanical presses. Processes that use heat or chemicals to extract the oil more efficiently offend some palates, though these heat-pressed oils are as healthy as the cold-pressed. Plain olive oil is a blend of refined and virgin oils and is a good cooking oil. Pomace, a lower grade used mostly in restaurants, though occasionally available in markets, is produced by chemical extraction of the residue of crushed and pressed olives, with virgin oil added to improve the flavor.

In general, olive oil has a low smoking point, which means it will burn at relatively low temperatures, making it a superb oil for long, slow cooking or quick sautéing. Oils with higher smoking points such as canola oil or peanut oil, are more desirable for stir-frying, a method that uses high heat.

SMOKE POINTS OF VARIOUS COOKING OILS

Sunflower	450° F
Soybean and canola	440° F
Corn	430° F
Peanut	420° F
Olive	390° F

Reserve your best extra-virgin olive oil for salads and lightly cooked food so the flavor will come through unaltered by heat; use virgin oil or plain olive oil for general use if you need to economize. Store all oils, especially expensive oils, in the refrigerator and they will stay fresher longer. Remember that unsaturated fat doesn't have the same protection against rancidity as saturated fat. Even polyunsaturated oils have a longer shelf life than the more heathful monounsaturated oils, such as olive oil and canola oil.

Canola Oil—The Heart-Healthy Windfall

Unknown almost a decade ago in the United States, canola oil, bred by genetic engineers from a strain of the rape plant (from the Latin *rapum* for turnip), is now a household word. Canadian marketing strategists gave their country a plug and named it canola oil because Canada was its largest producer. Health experts discovered that canola oil is very low in saturated fat and second only to olive oil in monounsaturated fatty acids, and in 1985 the FDA approved it for use in this country. This healthful oil is inexpensive, light tasting and excellent as a salad and cooking oil. If you wish, you can use canola oil exclusively, a cheaper alternative to olive oil, but your food will not have the distinctive flavors that good olive oils impart. You can increase the appeal of canola oil with garlic, herbs and other flavorings as we suggest on page 296–97.

Nut and Specialty Oils for Flavoring

Often used in Asian cooking, especially for stir-fries, peanut oil is a good monounsaturated cooking oil with a heavier flavor than canola oil, but a slightly lower smoke point. For salads, though, use only cold-pressed peanut oil, which is tastier.

Asian (dark) sesame seed oil has a distinctive flavor crucial to many Asian dishes. Use it sparingly as a seasoning—not for cooking unless, of course, you desire its strong flavor. And don't substitute any other oil when a recipe calls for it; the flavor cannot be duplicated. The light cold-pressed sesame oil (usually sold with health or organic foods) does not have the same desirable pungency.

The wonderfully aromatic and healthy nut oils—walnut, almond and hazelnut—have delicious and distinctive tastes, but use them sparingly as flavor accents. They will overpower a salad or other dish if used in excess, and (unlike peanut oil) are not suitable for prolonged cooking over heat. Again, sample them in salads and marinades and keep a small bottle of your favorites in the refrigerator. Grapeseed oil has a sweet flavor that we find useful in baking. Avocado oil is a mild-flavored, monounsaturated, good all-around oil with a high smoking point, but too expensive for daily use. Hazelnut is perhaps the queen of the oils, richly flavored and royally priced. But you need just a teaspoon or so of this monounsaturated oil in chocolate desserts or delicate salad dressings to capture its elegant toasted hazelnut flavor. Walnut oil, mostly polyunsaturated, is a favorite addition to light-flavored composed salads. These oils can impart a remarkable depth of flavor to your food that will elevate your dishes from the merely "good for you" to the "and can you believe its also good for you" class of fine cooking.

Polyunsaturated Vegetable Oils

You are probably familiar with the wide selection of polyunsaturated vegetable oils available in your market, from the generic vegetable oil, to corn, soy, safflower and sesame. We discuss them at length in Chapter 11, Nutrition for a Healthy Heart. We do not use these oils because they don't have the character or flavor we like, and they are not as high in monounsaturated fats as olive and canola oil. However, if they are the only oils available to you, they are far superior to butter and animal fats, and you should use them by all means. You can enhance their flavors by adding garlic and herbs, if you wish, as we suggest in Flavored Oils (page 296–98).

Butter—The Fat Tracker's Downfall

Real butter aficionados can tell the difference between butter and margarine, but many people raised on oleo, margarine's early name, don't mind the difference. We restrict our use of butter to the very few pastries that absolutely require it, and occasionally stir a tablespoon or two into a sauce. Also, we don't make those dishes very often. For those rare occasions, you might keep a stick of butter in the freezer and shave off a tablespoon or so as you need it. Otherwise, *never* use butter; it is a total saturated-fat and cholesterol package. If butter is your downfall, do not keep it on hand at all until your palate has gotten used to (and learned to enjoy) other low-fat spreads. Sometimes people reach for butter out of habit, when in reality, alternatives such as those in our recipes are just as satisfying.

For cooking purposes, many pastries and baked goods adapt easily to canola oil, olive oil, margarine, low-fat sour cream, low-fat cream cheese, low-fat buttermilk and nonfat yogurt—alone and/or in combinations with other higher-fat ingredients that still work out to healthier numbers than butter. When we do use butter, it is just enough for a buttery flavor or texture, and we add fruit purée, oil, juice or other liquids to do the bulk of the work in the recipe. Also, we carefully calculate the butter into the fat totals for the day. Whipped butter is a better lower-fat choice than stick butter, with almost one-third less fat, depending on the brand. Though even with that reduction, butter is still *not* an everyday spread.

Margarine and Vegetable Oil Spreads

When stick margarine was the only alternative to butter, the choice of a cholesterol-free spread was clear. Today, though, you not only have to sort your way through a variety of diet tubs, squeeze bottles and butter blends, but margarine look-alikes that are defined merely as "spreads." The common denominator is the absence of cholesterol. But as for the presence of fat, finding the leanest brand takes some diligent fat tracking.

In general, tubs and diet margarines have air or water blended into them which replaces some of the fat, though the amount differs from brand to brand. If you remember that liquid fats have less saturated fat, you might think that margarine in a squeeze bottle is the best choice. However, the labels of most brands list saturated fat as equal to that in sticks, approximately two grams per tablespoon, give or take a decimal point, although there are some brands with less than a gram per serving. A squeezable dairy spread (nonmargarine), on the other hand, has only one gram per tablespoon of saturated fat.

The best course is always to read the label and check the saturated fat in each brand, rather than just assume that all types, such as tubs or liquids, are the same. The label won't indicate the level of transfatty acids, of course, so just be aware that it is part of the hydrogenated package and you would be wise to curb other fats in the meal when you indulge in margarine. The Fats and Oils table on page 218 is a survey of some of the products available, not a definitive list. Margarine, of course, is a much better alternative to butter in your cooking, and we demonstrate that you can successfully use oil or margarine exclusively in your kitchen, even for baking, if you wish. Though as you will see in our recipes, we resort to using margarine rarely. Soft, tub, liquid and diet margarines are not as easily interchangeable with stick margarine or butter in cooking, although they make acceptable table spreads. Blend softened, unsalted margarine with puréed fruits or juices to make a creamy but lower-fat spread for special occasions.

Some stick substitutes claim a resemblance to butter, using buttermilk and a measure of cream for a buttery flavor, or a mixture of margarine and butter, but their success is a matter of opinion. We don't use them.

Butter-Flavored Powders

We have used butter-flavored powders with some success in our Basic Polenta recipe (page 445), blending the powder with skim milk to give it a richness we could not otherwise achieve. We have also used powders occasionally in muffins that call for nonfat milk products. However, we put them to limited use. Some people lightly coat air-popped popcorn with vegetable spray (a natural product) and then toss it with powered "butter." Although this is basically a fat-free milk product and not a composite of chemicals, using powdered butter substitutes frequently to give food the aura of real butter can blind you to the delicious qualities of other flavorings, such as a good fruity olive oil, flavored vinegars, fresh herbs, citrus juices and fiery chiles. Instead of a butter crutch, seek out ingredients that can offer a more invigorating range of flavors that are free of saturated fat.

❧ Consider this radical possibility: Some foods don't need any enhancement!

There are people who actually do enjoy air-popped, unbuttered popcorn. Who knows? You might be one of them and not know it, if you haven't tried it. When a green bean, ear of corn, spear of broccoli or stalk of asparagus is absolutely fresh at the peak of its season, it is almost criminal to keep the unique flavor under wraps— of salt, butter or anything else, for that matter. If you can't immediately recall the taste of your favorite vegetable without a buttery garnish, you are in butter-overload and need desensitization treatment immediately. Forego anything on your vegetables, if only to reacquaint yourself with their true flavors, which really is why we like them in the first place. The "they're good for you" line is accurate and never more important since the discovery of vegetables' antioxidant potency. But let's face it, we don't anxiously await the appearance of fresh corn in July, or view slender stalks of asparagus as the "right" of spring just for a hit of vitamins, do we?

Dense, sweet, grainy breads have wonderful complex tastes that get lost under the weight of heavy oil-based spreads. Toast them and add a spoonful of honey and Drained Yogurt (page 290–91), a touch of marmalade or enjoy as is. Our taste buds are designed to pick up nuances of flavors that fatty additions can blunt. These "pretend" products may give your arteries a break, but give your palate a break as well and use them sparingly.

Other Animal Fats and Saturated Fats

Do not buy lard, pork fat or use bacon for fat. Always substitute oil in any recipe that calls for them. We demonstrate in the chili and soup recipes and significantly in baked goods, that you can use various seasonings to give intense flavor and pleasing texture to food without resorting to animal fat.

Also do not buy canned shortening, which is a vegetable oil highly saturated with hydrogen and, in addition, contains harmful transfatty acids, which we discuss at length in Chapter 11, Nutrition for a Healthy Heart. Use oil combined with a sour-milk product as we describe in our muffin and scone recipes.

Per Tablespoon	Calories	Grams Total Fat	Grams Saturated Fat	Grams Poly-unsaturated fat	Grams Mono-unsaturated fat	Mg Cholesterol
Butter, stick	108	12.0	8.0	0.5	4	33
Butter, whipped	81	9.0	6.0	0.3	3	24
Butter, margarine blend	100	11.0	2.0	5.0	4	5
Margarine, stick						
corn oil	102	11.0	2.0	1.0	7	0
soybean oil blend	102	11.0	2.0	2.0	6	0
Margarine, tub						
diet	90	10.0	1.0	2.0	6	0
reduced-calorie	50	6.0	1.0	2.0	2	0
25-calorie	25	3.0	0.4	1.0	1	0
Margarine, liquid	80	9.0	1.0	5.0	3	0
Vegetable oils						
Corn oil	120	14.0	2.0	8.0	4	0
Soybean oil	120	14.0	2.0	8.0	4	0
Safflower oil	120	14.0	1.0	10.0	3	0
Canola oil	120	14.0	1.0	4.0	9	0
Olive oil	120	14.0	2.0	1.0	11	0
Peanut oil	120	14.0	2.0	4.0	8	0

These figures are taken from a sampling of various brands. There may be some slight variations depending on the manufacturer.

Fake Fats

While you cannot purchase for home use the new synthetic "fats" now used in some dairy products and frozen desserts, they provide a broader range of foods with some surprisingly good results, both in taste and texture. As far as affecting your cholesterol levels, any overall reduction in fat is a plus, but no evidence shows that fake fats lower blood levels, as do unsaturated fats. Nevertheless, these products help lighten a high-fat diet and make rich, fat-free desserts more available to the Fat Tracker.

Fat Tracking Mayonnaise

Mayonnaise is not a threat to a reduced saturated-fat diet, but whole egg mayonnaise adds cholesterol and jacks up the total fat count of any food it dresses. Fat-free mayonnaise is a good choice if you can't imagine life without mayonnaise on your lunch sandwich and you have to skim as much fat as possible from your food. But low-fat varieties of mayonnaise cut saturated fat and cholesterol by as much as 50 percent and taste more like the original. These leaner mayonnaises work best in recipes that call for other, highly flavored ingredients, such as tuna salad. Try them and if no one notices the difference, you've just achieved another saturated-fat reduction! However, look for our outstanding spreads and appetizer recipes that combine reduced-fat mayonnaise with nonfat yogurt and sour cream with delicious, lean results.

MAYONNAISE

Per Tablespoon	Calories	Grams Total Fat	Grams Saturated Fat	% of Calories from Fat	Mg Cholesterol
Mayonnaise	100	11.2	2.1	100	51
Reduced-fat mayonnaise	35	2.9	1.6	75	4
Fat-free mayonnaise	12	0	0	0	0
Miracle Whip	69	6.9	1.1	90	6
Miracle Whip (light)	44	3.9	0.6	80	3

Fat Tracking Other High-Fat Foods

Nuts, seeds, avocados and olives contain a large amount of unsaturated fat, which is actually not harmful to your heart. But as we have already demonstrated, it is also important to limit total fat. In large quantities, these high-calorie foods can also deal a fatal blow to your efforts to achieve and maintain an ideal weight. Eat small amounts only as snacks or flavorings. Chestnuts, however, have almost less than half the fat of regular nuts and make a delicious snack and flavoring ingredient. Look for them at holiday time. If you use chestnut purée, check the label to find brands that don't add extra fat.

FATS AND OILS SHOPPING LIST

Fats	Choose	Instead of
Oils	Monounsaturated oils: olive, canola, peanut, sesame and nut oils, grapeseed oil	Saturated fats and oils: butter, coconut oil, palm and palm kernel oil, lard, bacon fat
Butter	Polyunsaturated vegetable oils: corn, cottonseed, safflower, soybean, sunflower oil	Margarine or canned shortening made from animal fats or hydrogenated oil
Margarine	Margarine products made from unsaturated fats: liquid, tub, stick, diet versions	

CHAPTER 21

Fat Tracking Baked Goods, Cereals and Pasta

FOODS MADE FROM GRAINS *add cholesterol-lowering fiber, important nutri-ents, such as the* B *vitamins, and a satisfying crunch to meals. Here are our tips for choosing the healthiest of the grain-based foods in the supermarket*

Fat Tracking Breads and Rolls

Almost by definition, breads and rolls can be a high-fiber, low-fat plus on anyone's diet. The only breads you need to limit are those made with butter, egg yolks and cheese. How often can you include these rich breads and stay under 300 milligrams of cholesterol a day? Obviously, that depends on what other foods you eat. If you buy a loaf of fresh, egg-rich brioche from your local bakery, you may want to freeze it and enjoy a slice occasionally. Or, if your family plans to finish off a loaf of cheese bread while it is fresh, adjust your other fat choices to accommodate this luxury. A slice of rich bread now and then certainly won't harm your arteries. However, when so many delicious varieties of breads and rolls are available without harmful fats, it is usually wiser to spend your cholesterol quota elsewhere.

Many people believe that breads made solely with white flours are nutritionally deficient. Not necessarily, though they may have less fiber than whole grain breads. Fat Trackers can freely enjoy French, Italian, potato and other white breads and feel confident that they are adding fiber to their diet. Intersperse these choices with whole grain breads and rolls, but limit the spongy processed breads, which often do have less fiber and more questionable additives than whole or coarser-grained breads.

Nibble on crisp breadsticks and serve them with soup, pasta or with dips or on any occasion that calls for bread. Even though breadsticks coated with seeds may have more unsaturated fat than the plain variety, they still make a heart-healthy snack. Dunked in our fat-free Quick Black Bean Dip (page 355), Hot Mango Purée (page 359) or one of the yogurt creams (pages 292–93)—all recipes from our collection of appetizers—breadsticks will fill up hungry teenagers on the prowl for a quick snack.

Choose brands of breads with less than 2 grams of saturated fat per serving and at least 2 grams of fiber per serving.

BREADS

Per Slice or Roll	Calories	Grams Total Fat	Grams Saturated Fat	% of Calories from Fat	Mg Cholesterol	Grams Fiber
Raisin bread	71	1.0	0.3	13	3	0.6
Multigrain (7-grain bread)	70	1.0	Trace	13	0	1.1–1.7
Rye bread with seeds	69	0.8	Trace	10	0	1.3
White dinner roll	85	2.0	Trace	23	0	0
Breadsticks, 2	39	0.3	Trace	7	0	0
French bread	81	1.1	Trace	12	0	0.6

Fat Tracking Crackers

Crackers require a word of caution: As with potato chips, cookies and nuts, it is hard to stop at one soda cracker. Ignore the claims of "no cholesterol." You know this only exists in animal products. Most rich, buttery, cheese-flavored, bacon-flavored, homestyle and smoked varieties of cracker will overdraw your Fat Account, even if they don't have eggs, because they do have hydrogenated vegetable oils and possibly harmful transfatty acids. Some companies have started offering delicious reduced-fat and fat-free cheese crackers and seasoned crackers. Check the labels carefully and choose brands with the least fat. But be forewarned many of these products have negligible fiber, even though they are grain based. Like many imported products, your favorite brand of imported crackers might not have any nutritional information on the label; assume that since you don't know what you are getting, these products are probably higher in fat and use them on special occasions only.

Choose brands of crackers with less than 1 gram of saturated fat per 100 calories and at least 2 grams of fiber per serving.

CRACKERS

½ Ounce Serving	Calories	Grams Total Fat	Grams Saturated Fat	% of Calories from Fat	Mg Cholesterol	Grams Fiber
Ritz Bits Sandwiches (14)	160	10.0	2.5	56	5	0.4
Ak mak (2½)	58	1.1	Trace	17	0	1.7
Rykrisp (2 triples)	45	0.2	Trace	5	0	2.5
Soda cracker (5)	60	2.0	Trace	30	0	0
Triscuit (3)	60	2.0	0.6	30	0	2.0
SnackWell's (7)	60	1.0	Trace	15	0	Trace

Fat Tracking Breakfast Pastries

Need we say more about these butter-rich, cheese-filled, deep-fried, sugar-coated temptations than approach them with care? A croissant once a month? No problem. A cheese Danish or deep-fried apple fritter once in a great while? Sure. But choose low-fat breakfast treats on all the other mornings.

❧ **Watch out for the bran muffin or granola bar that you think shrieks good health. Many of them contain coconut, butter and/or tropical oils and are no better for you than a greasy doughnut!**

Before you pat yourself on the back for a healthier choice and sink your teeth into your morning muffin, check the label or ask your bakery to find out the ingredients. Pick breakfast pastries as you would any other prepared item: by searching the label for the grams of saturated fat. Some commercial bakers have successfully reproduced breakfast muffins and pastries with little cholesterol and no fat. Try them. Note that many companies tout their baked products as "healthful" because they contain only organic ingredients and whole grains. Don't let the "health food" label lull you into overlooking "organic butter and eggs" on their list of ingredients. Select "health-food" brands that get rid of both fat *and* chemicals.

Choose brands of pastries with less than 2 grams of saturated fat and at least 2 grams of fiber per serving.

	Calories	Grams Total Fat	Grams Saturated Fat	% of Calories from Fat	Mg Cholesterol	Grams Fiber
Croissant	365	19.0	10.5	47	67.6	0
Apple Fritter	250	15.0	5.0	54	6.0	0
Doughnut, cake, 2 ounces	200	11.0	1.8	50	18.0	0
Doughnut, yeast, glazed	242	14.0	3.5	52	4.0	0
Blueberry muffin, from mix, 2 ounces	220	4.0	2.0	16	0	0
Bagel plain, 2 ounces	163	1.4	0	8	0.6	0.6
Oatmeal bread	71	1.2	0	15	0.5	0.6
Bisquick biscuit, 4 ounces	240	8.0	2.0	30	0	Trace
White bread, 1 slice	64	0.9	0	13	5.0	0.8
Light white bread, 1 slice	40	0	0	0	0	Trace
Whole wheat bread, 1 slice	60	1.0	0	15	Trace	1.6
Corn muffin, from mix, 1 piece	189	6.0	1.6	29	37	0.7

Fat Tracking Cake, Cookie and Muffin Mixes

Read the labels on packaged mixes for baked goods to find those without butter, hydrogenated oils or saturated fat. Instead of adding butter, as some instructions say, add oil or applesauce; instead of adding whole eggs, add two egg whites for each egg or liquid egg substitutes. Do not buy frozen or chilled cookie dough without checking the label for fat content and ingredients. These tend to be as high in fat as regular packaged or butter-rich cookies.

Fat Tracking Cereals and Breakfast Foods

Instead of making breakfast a high-fat meal with the traditional fried eggs, buttered toast and a side of bacon, make it a high-fiber meal and get your day off to a healthier start. Select cereals with a minimum of two grams of fiber per serving and check the labels for products without hydrogenated vegetable oils, whole eggs, egg yolks or excess sugar. Bear in mind that a shortcoming of the nutrition facts label is that it lumps together all sugars (including fruit) in one number. It is unfair to assume that a cereal that lists on its label large amounts of sugar is delivering empty calories when it's full of corn, raisins or other dried fruit, which have lots of perfectly acceptable natural sugar. We hope future revisions of the label will address that dilemma. Until then, always check ingredients as well as nutrition facts for a clearer picture of what you are getting. We have compared some typical cereal labels to demonstrate that just because a cereal is crunchy and has words like "provides important nutritional. . ." prominently displayed on the package, it doesn't necessarily qualify as a Fat Tracker's first choice.

- General Mills Cocoa Puffs proclaims in bold type on the front of the box that it is "High In 7 Essential Vitamins & Iron." In very small print that took a few minutes to find we discovered that it is not a significant source of fiber. Though it has no cholesterol, a 1-ounce serving does have 14 grams of sugars and 1 gram of saturated fat. The first ingredient listed, which signifies the greatest quantity, is sugar. Next (in the listing and in quantity) come cornmeal, corn syrup, cocoa processed with alkali, wheat starch and hydrogenated oils. You have to ask yourself if you want to squander even 1 gram of your 25-gram daily allotment of saturated fat for less than 1 gram of fiber that is buried in so many empty calories. And is this any way to start your day, or, more to the point, your children's day?
- Honey Bunches of Oats, from Post, sounds like a healthier choice: Oats have water-soluble fiber that may lower cholesterol levels. But this cereal also has 6 grams of sucrose and other sugars and only 1 gram of fiber per serving.
- Kellogg's Frosted Flakes lists only 5 ingredients, but look at what they are: corn, sugar, salt, malt flavoring and corn syrup, adding up to 13 grams of sugars in each ¾ cup serving. Oh yes, we were looking for fiber. Well, keep looking. It doesn't have any!
- The same company's Low Fat Granola with Raisins highlights its lean qualities on the box, but for its 3 grams of fiber per serving you also get 3 grams of fat, 16 grams of sugars (most, of course, from raisins) and 200 calories.
- An ounce of Post Grape Nuts manages to include 5 grams of fiber from wheat, malted barley, salt and yeast, but it also has 7 grams of maltose and other sugars adding up to 200 calories in every ounce.
- Wheatena, on the other hand, from American Home Food Products, has 5 grams of fiber and no sugars, containing only whole wheat, wheat bran and wheat germ in each ⅓ cup. The wheat germ most likely contributes the 1 gram of saturated fat.
- However, General Mills Fiber One contains only 1 gram of fat and a satisfying 14 grams of fiber per ½ cup serving, no sugars and only 60 calories!

We mention these products, not to endorse any, but merely to show the range and variety available, often from the same manufacturer. Only when you flip over the box can you know what it contains. We also noted that in the products we have discussed, the lighter the box, the more empty calories it had and the more expensive it was. Although we have to admit, the cartoon characters were cute!

There are many options. Choose carefully. Does your brand of hot cereal include added butter or milk with the nutritional information? If not, add the amount you use on to per serving count. Most cold cereals list nutritional information per serving with and without added milk. Make sure you check both. The first listing may make the product seem healthier, but the more realistic totals are those that include milk. You can subtract 4 grams of total fat (or 2.5 grams saturated fat), though, because you will substitute nonfat or 1 percent-fat for their ½ cup of whole milk. Won't you?

Waffles and pancakes provide another opportunity for including the grains that provide energy yet don't add excessive fat to your breakfasts. If you don't make them from scratch with liquid egg substitute, buy mixes that allow you to add your own liquid ingredients. Add oil instead of butter or margarine and liquid eggs or two egg whites in place of whole eggs or egg yolks. Buy frozen waffles made without egg yolks and top these treats with unsweetened fruit purée. And instead of using butter or margarine, cook them on a griddle coated with a light film of vegetable spray. Better yet, make our fat-free Whole Grain Buttermilk Waffles (page 307) and drown them in one of our fresh fruit toppings.

Fat Tracking Pasta

Everybody hails pasta, made almost entirely of high-protein (14 grams per 4-ounce serving) durum wheat, as the solution to bulking up a low saturated-fat diet. Though low in fiber, pasta is chock-full of complex carbohydrates. However, few people tuck into a bowl of plain, boiled noodles. Much of the allure of this popular dish is what goes on top. Creamy sauces and many supermarket sauces are very high in both saturated and total fat, and numerous fresh sauces line the deli case. A welcome sight to the pasta lover, these deli sauces can almost duplicate the flavor of homemade simmered sauces. However, "fresh" means they can have fresh cream, fresh butter and fresh cheese added. And with as much as 40 to 50 grams of fat per serving, they can seriously erode your fat rations for the day. Bottled sauces tend to be a better choice; always choose a red sauce over a white one. Better yet, make your own. It isn't hard to make the sauce itself as low in fat as the pasta; just do some careful fat tracking when you are pairing them up. Sauces can include lots of steamed vegetables with a little olive oil, lemon juice and hot pepper flakes for a simple pasta primavera, or fish, shellfish, or chicken for a more substantial entrée. As you can see in the following chart, a homemade pasta can save you many grams of saturated fat. Quick Roasted Tomato Sauce (page 453) is a good example of a fat saver and also saves time. You can save even more time if you seek out a pasta boutique that sells fresh tomato-based and vegetable sauces and homemade pasta, as well as a variety of flavorful breads that don't need butter added.

	Calories	Grams Total Fat	Grams Saturated Fat	Mg Cholesterol
Packaged macaroni and cheese, 1 cup	430	22.2	11.9	30
Pasta, 1 cup with 1 tablespoon olive oil and 1 tablespoon grated Parmesan cheese	341	15.9	2.9	4

Many varieties of noodles find their way into the markets these days. Asian noodles—soba, bean threads, udon and somen, for example, are made with combinations of wheat, rice, buckwheat and other grains. Also, you can find pastas made with amaranth and quinoa (pronounced keenwa), two highly nutritious grains appearing more frequently in breads, cereals and baked goods. Sample the delicious pastas seasoned with corn, spinach, herbs, carrots and other flavorings. Avoid butter and cheese noodle mixes. They really don't offer any savings to the Fat Tracker. You still have to cook, stir and mix ingredients into them, so why not just boil noodles, coat them with a little olive oil and toss with a little grated Parmesan or Romano cheese? Same preparation time and much less fat.

It's better not to use egg noodles, but if you do, don't forget to calculate the yolks as part of your weekly limit of three each week. An average four-ounce serving of egg noodles contains about 140 milligrams of cholesterol.

Food	Choose	Instead of
Breads, Rolls, and Crackers	Whole grain breads	Croissants
	Pumpernickel bread	Butter rolls
	Rye bread	Egg and cheese breads
	Pita bread	Sweet rolls
	Breadsticks	Danish pastries
	English muffins	Doughnuts
	Sandwich buns	Fritters
	Dinner rolls	High-fat snack crackers
	Rice cakes	Cheese crackers
	Low-fat or egg-free	Butter crackers and any made
	biscuits	with saturated-fat
	Muffins	
	Corn bread	
	Ak mak	
	Melba toast	
	Matzo	
	Saltines	
	Zwieback	
	French bread	
	Rolls	
	Water bagels	
	Cracker bread	
	Rykrisp	
	Soda crackers	
	Oyster crackers	
	Rice cakes	
	Saltines	
	Reduced-fat and	
	fat-free/cholesterol-	
	free crackers	
Cereals, Breakfast Foods	Hot cereals	Granola cereals made with
	Dry cereals low in saturated fat	coconut or saturated fat
	Whole grain cereals	Commercial waffle and
	Granola and cereal mixes	pancake mixes with egg
	without coconut, butter or	and milk fats, hydrogenated
	saturated fat added	oils or butter fats added
	Packaged waffles	Cereals with excessive sugar
	Waffle and pancake mixes that	and fat and little fiber
	allow you to add your own	
	egg or egg substitute and oil	
	Whole grain waffles and pancakes	
	made without eggs or butter	
Pasta, Noodles	Pasta	Egg noodles
	Whole wheat and vegetable	Packaged pasta or noodle
	pasta and noodles	mixes with cheese, butter,
	Rice, bean and other	cream sauces and saturated
	Asian noodles	fat added
	Buckwheat noodles (soba)	

CHAPTER 22

Fat Tracking Desserts and Snacks

ONCE YOU HAVE NEGOTIATED YOUR WAY *through the meat and dairy-food sections of your market, you have triumphed over the most challenging part of your shopping trip. Desserts and snacks are a piece of cake (as long as it is low-fat) by comparison. Many folks lump sweet foods in with the heart-stopping, high saturated-fat items, but while you don't want to overload on sugar, a little sweetness is better than a lot of fat. This leaves you with a lot of scrumptious choices at dessert and snack time. For example, a handful of totally fat-free hard candy or gummi bears is better than a chocolate bar. A few dry roasted peanuts are better than a few potato chips. But a handful of pretzels is even better.*

While a Fat Tracker always passes up premium or gourmet (translation: packed with saturated fat) ice cream, you can succumb to the lure of fruity sherbets, low-fat and nonfat frozen yogurts and frozen juice bars. If you occasionally like to drizzle a gooey topping on your ice milk (also a good choice), buy a can of chocolate syrup instead of a jar of fudge sauce or pick up the ingredients for Hal's Hot Fudge Sauce (page 565–66). Stuff fat-free fruit Newtons or Walnut Brownies (page 539) with almost zero fat into your children's lunch box instead of chocolate chip cookies. And at a special dinner, serve Summer Fruit Tart (page 552) with our rich cholesterol-free and almost fat-free Heart-Healthy Pastry Cream (page 553–54) instead of a commercially baked, high-fat cream pie. Here are some specific suggestions to appease your sweet tooth and hunger for snacks.

Fat Tracking Snacks

Obvious choices of snacks for Fat Trackers include vegetable sticks and fresh fruit, but most people have richer tastes. Here's how to satisfy them. Choose snacks without added fat, such as air-popped popcorn, oven-baked chips, raw nuts (only a few at a sitting—they have no harmful fats, but are high in unsaturated-fat calories). Several food producers are on the fat-free bandwagon and have marketed delicious tortilla chips, pretzels and other nibbles that will please the Fat Tracker, but check the labels. Some products also are more expensive than the fat-logged brands, but if your budget can swing them, they are worth the price. Snack-chip makers are starting to use more monounsaturated fats and we predict their numbers will increase if we show our support by buying them.

Raw trail mix is a good, low saturated-fat choice, providing the mix doesn't have tropical oils or coconut added. Many do, so check the label. However, mixes with nuts and seeds will boost your total fat count, so be aware of the serving size. Nuts are a better choice over potato chips as far as saturated fat is concerned, as long as they are dry roasted—check the package. A half cup of oil-roasted almonds (about two or three dips into the bowl) has 45 grams of fat! You know how easily and quickly they disappear as you nibble in front of the TV. Nut for nut, cashews have less fat, but a seasoned rice cake has only a trace of fat. Instead of nuts, look for cereal snack mixes made without added fat. When they are in season, enjoy low-fat chestnuts. Fat Trackers don't have to give up the munchies, they just have to head for the ones with the least fat. Read the labels. Good ones are out there.

Fat Tracking Cookies, Cakes, Pies and Other Desserts

The best choice is to make your own healthful desserts. If that is not an option for you, choose commercial products that have three grams or less of fat per ounce or per 100 calories and those made without butter or hydrogenated oils. Buy open-faced fresh fruit tarts instead of cream pies or those fatty single-serving individual pies wrapped in plastic. If you have the willpower, sample the crust on an open-faced tart (which most likely will contain lard or butter), but don't finish it. If you must use packaged mixes, buy those that allow you to add your own liquid ingredients and substitute additional egg whites or a liquid egg substitute for egg yolks and oil for butter. If you buy a dessert that contains eggs, don't forget to subtract the cholesterol from your daily allowance of 300 milligrams or less.

Cookies present a problem, because many of them pack a lot of fat in a bite-sized serving. We found one popular toffee munchie offering in two small cookies 4 grams of fat, 3 of them saturated, for each 60 calories. The same manufacturer makes a chocolate chip cookie with 5 grams of fat, 2 grams of saturated fat, in each small 80-calorie cookie. These numbers are no worse and no better than those of any other cookie maker. A typical advertising ploy is to show how quickly the cookie jar empties out, because their product is so good, no one can leave them alone. Well, for once these ads are based on real life. Cookies and other small munchies *are* good. And it *is* hard to leave them alone.

If you have room in your Fat Account at the end of the day for a dessert with two grams of fat, can you trust yourself, or your children, to dip into the cookie jar for just one small cookie? A better choice is the ever-widening range of reduced-fat and fat-free cookies and baked goods, many of them thoroughly laced with chocolate flavor. If you are trying to wean yourself, or your family, away from rich desserts, fill the cookie jar with this type of reduced-fat product and alternate with an even leaner cookie. In time, reduce the number of times you buy rich chocolate and butter cookies, and increase your purchases of raisin bars, molasses cookies, fig, apple and other fruit Newtons, ginger snaps and oatmeal cookies.

A dessert that is dusted with powdered sugar or a sugar glaze is better than one topped with whipped cream or a butter frosting. Note that many frostings are made with canned vegetable shortening, which is loaded with saturated fat. Avoid them. Keep mousses, cream pies, filled cupcakes, whipped cream or frosted cakes and yellow cakes (the yellow often comes from egg yolks, not food coloring) and anything with butterfat chocolate to a minimum and substitute one of our luscious desserts that begin on page 537.

Fat Tracking Chocolate

In recent years a new word has crept into our vocabulary—"chocoholic," a term used with light-hearted seriousness. Are you one of these people who place chocolate at the head of the food chain? While it is hard to find commercial chocolate ice creams, desserts and candies made without huge amounts of saturated fat, you can enjoy chocolate treats to your heart's content if you make them at home with powdered cocoa. After adding butterfat to cocoa to turn it into chocolate, manufacturers then begin adding coconut, nuts, peanut butter and shortening, which all cause the fat content to rise precipitously. However, as you will discover in the dessert chapter, you can make Walnut Brownies (page 539), Chocolate-Crusted Raspberry Cheesecake (page 550–51) and other confections with cocoa and a mix of other low-fat ingredients that will bring a contented smile of satisfaction to the fiercest chocoholic's face.

Another way of introducing chocolate into your desserts without bankrupting your daily Fat Account is to shave a teaspoon or two of good baking chocolate onto a bowl of ice milk, into nonfat vanilla frozen yogurt or over an orange-filled crêpe. Like cheese, a lump of chocolate doesn't go very far for its many grams of saturated fat (six grams in a one-ounce square of baking chocolate). For serious chocolate lovers, an ounce is merely an appetizer. But if you grate or shave it, you can get delicious chocolate chip-style mileage from only a teaspoonful or two, even spreading an ounce's worth over five or six servings.

Fat Tracking Candy

Choose hard candies to satisfy your sweet tooth, from butterscotch balls to sour balls. Fruit leathers, jelly beans, licorice and mints will all give you a tasty jolt of sugar without adding any fat to your day's totals. But, as we have pointed out, too much sugar can affect triglyceride levels, so use heavily sugared sweets only occasionally as a change from fresh fruit and dried fruit tasties such as raisins or dates. One of the sweetest treats we can think of is dried pineapple and it doesn't have a grain of added sugar. Avoid sweets that use coconut, butterfat (chocolate) or hydrogenated or partially hydrogenated fat added (peanut butter cups). And beware of dried banana chips, which are actually fried in oil! Don't buy them. Here is a comparison of some popular snacks and desserts. In compiling this list we have used brand names when their values were available.

Instead of:	Grams Saturated Fat	Grams Total Fat	Choose:	Grams Saturated Fat	Grams Total Fat
1 ounce oil-roasted peanuts	1.9	14.0	1 ounce dry-roasted chestnuts	0.1	0.3
1 ounce potato chips	2.6	10.1	1 ounce thin pretzels	0	0
1 ounce potato sticks	2.5	9.8	2 cups plain air-popped popcorn	0	0
1 slice cheesecake	8.0	12.9	1 slice angel food cake with fruit sauce	0	Trace
1 slice devil's food cake with icing	7.7	15.0	1 slice gingerbread	1.1	4.2
4 chocolate sandwich cookies	2.4	9.0	4 ladyfingers	1.0	3.4
4 oatmeal-raisin cookies	2.1	8.0	4 gingersnaps	0.6	2.4
1 ounce unsweetened chocolate	10.1	15.7	3 tablespoons cocoa powder	0.2	3.0
1 cup premium ice cream	14.7	23.7	1 cup sherbet	2.4	3.8
4 chocolate chip cookies, 2 ¼ inch-diameter	6.0	16.0	4 Fig Newtons, 2 ounces	Trace	4.0
4 small shortbread cookies	3.0	8.0	8 graham crackers, 2 ounces	Trace	4.0
5 Ritz crackers	0.5	4.0	4 Rykrisp crackers, 1 ounce	Trace	2.0
Mr. Goodbar, 1.85 ounces bar	8.0	20.0	1.5 ounces Sugar Babies	Trace	2.0
M&M's 1.69 ounces package	6.7	12.0	1 ounce gum drops	Trace	Trace
1 ounce chocolate-covered peanuts	3.0	12.0	2 ounces fruit roll	0	1.0
2 cups buttered popcorn	7.6	12.2	2 ounces jelly beans,	0	0.2
2 tablespoons fudge topping	2.9	5.1	2 tablespoons chocolate syrup	0.2	0.4
1 cheese and peanut butter cracker sandwich	Trace	2.0	1 seasoned rice cake	0	Trace

Choose:

Fruit (fresh, frozen, dried)
Water or juice-packed canned fruit
Marshmallows
Candy corn
Caramel (no nuts)
Fondant
Nougat (no nuts)
Gum drops
Licorice
Peanut brittle (note that nuts have a
    higher total fat content)
Jellied and hard candies
Mints
Taffy
Jelly beans
Fruit rolls and leathers
Butterscotch hard candies
Hard mints
Dinner mints (not chocolate coated)
Sugar-free gum and candy
Corn chips made with canola oil or
    other unsaturated nonhydrogenated oil
    (homemade oven-baked tortilla, bagel
    and potato chips are best)
Popcorn (air-popped or made with
    canola or olive oil)
Pretzels
Rice cakes
Cookies
Plain graham crackers
Vanilla wafers
Fig/fruit bars

Gingersnaps
Animal crackers
Molasses cookies
Frosted and whipped or buttercream
    layer cakes
Gingerbread
Angel food cake
Popsicles
Fudgsicles
Fruit pops
Juice bars
Ice milk
Frozen yogurt (nonfat and low-fat)
Sherbet and sorbet
Fruit, Italian and water ices
Jello or gelatin with or without fruit
Puddings or custards made with nonfat or low-
    fat milk and egg; substitute if egg is required
Trail mix, raw and without
    chocolate or coconut added
Raw or dry roasted nuts and seeds
Cereal snack mixes without hydrogenated fats
Raw vegetable sticks with salsa or low-fat
    salad dressing

Beverages

Iced tea and coffee
Fruit juices/vegetable juices
Carbonated fruit-flavored drinks
Lemonade
Cocoa or commercial cocoa mixes
    (check label for calories/added fat)
Low-fat or fat-free chocolate milk

Instead of:

High-fat butter cakes
Whipped cream
Creamy frosted products
Packaged cakes, pies and cookies
Chocolate candy
Potato chips
Buttered and saturated-fat flavored
    snacks such as cheese-flavored potato
    chips, corn chips or popcorn

High-butterfat ice cream
Chocolate-covered nuts, dried fruits, cookies
Whole-milk puddings, custards, cream desserts
Fried tortilla, potato or corn chips
Chocolate malts
Milkshakes
Floats
Eggnog

CHAPTER 23

Fat Tracking Fast Foods: Take-Out and Processed Foods

TV COMMERCIALS HAVE ALMOST CONVINCED US *that when we have more hunger than time, our only choice is to drive to the nearest fast-food place. Fast food in one form or another is a fact (and, let's face it, one of the boons) of modern life. You don't want to spend hours nurturing a delicate soup after a long day, or worry over a complex sauce when you need to chauffeur a houseful of kids in opposite directions after school. Unfortunately, though, fast food has come to mean fatty food in this country: grabbing a burger and fries that fill you up quickly on the way to a movie; popping a frozen Mexican dinner in the microwave after you've worked late. And what family doesn't welcome the occasional pizza and soda pop for dinner. But clearly, a steady diet of these choices will snooker anybody's commitment to good health.*

So what do you do when you are hungry and tired, hungry and rushed, hungry and lazy or just plain hungry? One answer is to turn to our collection of recipes and choose one of our delicious quick chicken, fish, pasta or vegetable dishes. But when you can't face even one of those jiffy recipes at the end of the day and you are tempted by the ad from a neighborhood pizzeria for a special that includes free delivery, try one of our take-out ideas that follow.

Instant Meals from the Deli

Head for the deli section in your local market and select from an assortment of mixed greens, fresh vegetable and bean salads in oil and vinegar dressings, sliced turkey, spit-roasted chicken, fruit medleys, olives, peppers, breads, rolls, breadsticks and salad bar items to assemble an instant meal with more character than the usual burger or TV dinner. Or visit the fish counter and pick up some cooked shrimp or crab to have with a salad and crusty bread. Avoid high-fat cheeses, ham and processed meat and "white" salads, since those potato and macaroni concoctions are made with excessive amounts of mayonnaise, cooked egg yolks and sour cream. Here are a baker's dozen of our favorite deli combos:

CHICKEN AND FRESH FRUIT SALAD Pick up a barbecued chicken, fresh fruit salad without dressing and whole wheat rolls at the nearest deli. Strip and discard the skin from the chicken. Remove the meat from the carcass, dice and toss it with the fruit salad and your favorite olive oil dressing or blend of nonfat yogurt and low-fat mayonnaise. Serve with the rolls.

APPLE AND TURKEY SANDWICH Instead of chicken, have the deli slice turkey breast for you and choose a large crisp apple. Make a sandwich of turkey and apple slices, sweet mustard and a dash of chutney on crunchy, whole grain toast.

ANTIPASTI PLATTER Pick up some raw vegetables from the deli salad bar and a selection of spicy olives and Italian sweet and hot peppers. Include them in a meal of antipasto items that also offers an arrangement of canned water-packed tuna, a slice of low-fat mozzarella or some feta cheese. Sprinkle with fresh basil, balsamic vinegar and olive oil, if you like. Munchies can include hard rolls, breadsticks, low-fat crackers or your favorite bread.

FROZEN ENTRÉE Choose a low-fat or diet frozen entrée. Add bulk to the meal with some fruit or crusty bread, and a huge salad from the salad bar tossed with some of your favorite low-fat or nonfat dressing.

PESTO CHICKEN Buy baguettes, mixed fresh salad greens and a spit-roasted chicken. Discard the skin. Stir fresh or commercial pesto into a mixture of half nonfat yogurt and half mayonnaise and spread it on the chicken. Toss the greens with your favorite low-fat dressing, heat the baguettes and enjoy.

TURKEY AND TRIMMINGS Buy some sliced turkey breast, hard rolls, three-bean salad, roasted sweet or hot peppers and one baking potato per person. Microwave the potatoes and smother them with nonfat yogurt, dill and chopped green onions. Heat the rolls, coat with sweet mustard and top with the turkey breast and peppers. Serve the three-bean salad separately and dig in.

MANGO CHICKEN Buy a fresh fruit salad and a green salad from the deli, as well as a spit-roasted chicken. Pick up a ripe mango from the produce department. Purée it with a tablespoon or two of your favorite flavored vinegar and a diced green onion. Spread on skinless chicken and microwave 30 seconds or until heated through. Serve with chutney and the two salads.

EAST INDIAN CHICKEN SALAD Cut up any available fruit, add some diced and skinned spit-roasted deli chicken. Mix in equal amounts mayonnaise and nonfat yogurt and stir in a spoonful of chutney, a little curry powder, raisins and a few dry roasted nuts to taste. Mound on lettuce leaves and serve.

OPEN-FACED SHRIMP SANDWICH Pick up cooked baby shrimp at the deli or fish counter. Make open-faced sandwiches by blending the shrimp with nonfat yogurt, dill and chopped onion. Spoon onto slices of pumpernickel or other good, dark bread.

NIÇOISE SALAD SANDWICH Open a jar of roasted peppers and layer them on slices of French or Italian bread with olives, tuna, sweet onion and a small sprinkling of feta cheese. Serve cold or lightly broiled.

CHICKEN BURRITOS LIGHT Fill corn tortillas with a mixture of skinned, diced deli chicken or shrimp, chopped tomato, minced onion, canned chilies and canned fat-free vegetarian refried beans. Microwave on high for one minute. Add hot sauce or salsa and top with nonfat yogurt.

CRACKED CRAB FEAST Pick up cooked, cracked crab at the fish market when it's in season. Serve with a green salad, sliced tomatoes, French bread and dip the crab in a nonfat yogurt and low-fat mayonnaise blend.

PITA PIZZA Shred low-fat mozzarella onto pita rounds, add sun-dried tomatoes, marinated artichoke hearts, snips of fresh basil and a bottled red pepper or, if you have the energy, thinly slice a fresh one. Broil until hot and bubbly.

Fat Tracking Processed Foods

When the deli is closed and your only alternative is packaged foods, we have some guidelines to help you choose the leanest. We recommend that you eat fresh vegetables and entrées as often as possible, but realistically that doesn't always fit real life. Processed foods beckon from every aisle when you need quick solutions at mealtime. Here are some ideas for taking advantage of the convenience of packaged foods, without paying too high a price in fat. *Always* read the label before you make your selections.

CANNED SOUPS Buy those made with broth or stock, such as minestrone or lentil. Skim off any visible fat from the surface before you heat the contents. Pass on canned cream soups, which are loaded with fat. Also check the label and choose low-fat, low-sodium soups.

CHILI Buy canned or frozen vegetarian chili or chili with beans instead of beef chili. Skim all fat from the surface before you heat the contents.

CHOCOLATE BARS Buy energy bars, but check the labels to avoid those with hydrogenated oils or saturated fats. Watch out for saturated-fat-laden coconut, a popular ingredient in "health" snacks.

FROZEN BREAKFAST ENTRÉES Pass on "sandwiches" made with eggs, ham, bacon or sausage, as well as the full-course, typical frozen breakfast banquets, which offer as much as 28 grams of total fat per serving! Buy egg-free frozen waffles or pancakes and top them with unsweetened fruit purées or fresh fruit and nonfat yogurt instead of butter and syrup. Pass on frozen sausages and breakfast meats, even if they say "lean," and choose white meat turkey or chicken sausages.

FROZEN DESSERTS Find the sweets in the diet section and choose Weight Watchers Boston Cream Pie or Carrot Cake with 4 and 5 grams of fat per serving over desserts such as the pecan coffee cakes (up to 16 grams per serving) or plain pound cakes at 11 grams of fat per serving. Again, read the labels and compare fats.

FROZEN DINNERS Read labels and choose healthy and convenient entrées for an occasional quick meal (but not too often, since you will deprive yourself of high-fiber, fresh produce). Regular frozen entrées tend to be high in fat and/or sodium. We found chicken parmigiana with 51 grams of total fat and a Salisbury steak listed 42 grams of fat. Choose "diet" or low-fat frozen entrées and low-fat "fried" fish and chicken entrées. Choose "diet" baked potato entrées instead of fried or hash browns that you must cook in oil (these potatoes have often already been cooked in oil before factory freezing). Toss out any packages of extra sauce (read "extra fat") in the package. Choose the entrée according to the least fat per serving. They can range from 9 grams for steak Diane to 2 grams for the same producer's sweet and sour chicken.

FROZEN MEXICAN DINNERS Finding low-fat frozen Mexican food is a challenge. You are better off with diet varieties, some of which offer a generous portion of bean and chicken enchiladas and burritos with minimal fat and only 300 calories.

FROZEN VEGETABLES Use *plain* frozen vegetables without butter or cheese.

PASTRIES Check the labels and buy the fat-free pastries available now.

PIZZA The best solution is to buy a shell and make your own. Coat it with jarred low-fat marinara sauce, canned white beans, a smear of pesto, a sprinkling of low-fat Parmesan or nonfat mozzarella cheese and bake.

SALAD DRESSINGS Choose vinaigrettes, Italian or oil-free dressings. Avoid ranch-style, cheese or creamy dressings unless the label specifies low-fat or fat-free.

SAUCES Buy meatless, mushroom or vegetable sauces without cream or cheese containing 1 gram of saturated fat and 3 grams of total fat or less per 100 calorie serving. Add very lean ground round, chicken or turkey. Pass on sauces containing meat or sausage or cheese. If you add a little Parmesan cheese to pasta, add dressing on a salad, spread margarine on your bread or need to fill up on a second helping now and then, these fatty sauces (with up to 9 grams of fat per serving) can force your total fat intake to climb. When you are in a rush, buy unbuttered frozen mixed vegetables, steam briefly and toss into cooked noodles with a little olive oil, garlic and grated Parmesan cheese. Finish with a spritz of fresh lemon juice. Pass on white sauce, hollandaise, béarnaise, canned gravies and cheese sauce for noodles, vegetables and entrées. Sprinkle cooked food with a little olive oil, one of our Flavored Oils (page 296), lemon juice, fresh pepper, hot pepper and/or grated Parmesan cheese when you are too busy to prepare more elaborate, low-fat sauces.

STUFFINGS AND STOVETOP MIXES These are often repositories for harmful fats in the form of hydrogenated vegetable oils. To stretch your dish, buy seasoned bread or corn bread stuffing mixes without added butter or hydrogenated oil.

CHAPTER 24

Fat Tracking in Restaurants

WHAT DOES A FAT TRACKER DO *when someone says, "Let's eat out"? Grab your coat and use your fat-tracking skills to enjoy a healthy meal and a good time. When it is your turn to pick the restaurant, stick with those famous for their seafood, grills or salad bars, and you will have no trouble keeping saturated fat in check. Many ethnic restaurants also get high ratings, as do steak houses. Steak houses? Absolutely. Their streamlined menus almost always feature grilled chicken and fish, as well as a variety of baked potatoes, rice, vegetables, salads and breads — all great fat-tracking choices. Reserve one of your weekly 2 + 2 red meat entrées for a night out and split a steak with your dining partner. If the portion is still larger than the Fat Tracker's preferred three to four ounces, ask for a doggie bag for the remainder and let a family member enjoy it for lunch the next day.*

If you have used up your red meat entrées for the week and don't see a suitable alternative, forego an entrée and say yes to both when the waiter asks, "Potato or rice?" Skip the butter and sour cream, but ask for a side serving of vinaigrette to moisten your potato. Then help yourself to the salad bar. Fortunately, these days, many restaurants would rather accommodate a few special requirements of a customer than lose that customer, so ask for your entrée to be prepared without butter, or grilled or poached. When all you can see are high-fat items on a menu, ask your server which ones are lowest in fat. If all the entrées are high in fat, choose one and share it with a friend. Fill up on dinner rolls and an extra salad, if necessary.

The "save now to spend later" approach works for Fat Trackers as well as money trackers. When you make a Saturday night date for dinner with friends, you can use your Fat Account to help you monitor a low-fat breakfast and lunch. When you pick up the dinner menu, you can indulge more freely without fretting, "Oh, I shouldn't."

A word of caution about "health food" restaurants: People have many concerns about the food they eat these days, and restaurants promising meals made with organic and chemical-free ingredients have a large following. We love them too, except when *we* say health food, we focus on food low in saturated fat. Many chefs gain a reputation for cooking with the freshest of seasonal, pesticide-free produce and for buying poultry and meat from farmers that raise their livestock on special, organic feed. However, these chefs often add to their dishes enormous amounts of butter, cheese and eggs from these organically fed animals, and we have to ask, "What do they mean by *health food*?" Yes, by all means eat chemical-free and pesticide-free food at every opportunity. But huge numbers of people die because their arteries are clogged with cholesterol from a lifetime of eating too much saturated animal fat. And it doesn't matter if the animal is organically fed or not or if you eat pesticide-free vegetarian meals loaded with high-fat dairy products. Don't forget the larger issue that truly defines an item as "health food" when you select a restaurant: low in saturated fat. These are general issues. Now we will get specific about fat tracking various menus, taking on the toughest challenge first, the fast-food chains.

Fat Tracking Fast-Food Restaurants

Notorious heartbreakers, the fat-laden burger, fries and shakes sold in fast-food franchises appear to glorify saturated fat. Take a peek at what most people have on their trays as they search for a table or counter space where they can bolt down their quick meal at the mall: a cheeseburger, French fries, chocolate shake and apple pie has approximately 67 grams of total fat and 26 grams of saturated fat— an entire day's limit. In addition to burgers, you can find chains that specialize in Mexican food, fish and chips and fried chicken, with most of these foods pre-cooked in harmful fats and lots of sodium before they even leave the factory. They are given a second dousing of one or both after you give your order so the company can boast that their food is served to you "freshly cooked"! Some of these chains claim that they use healthy oils. That may be true for the final heating while you are waiting at the counter. But what happens at the factory before freezing and shipping? Behind the scenes, so to speak, may be another kettle of fish—more likely another kettle of fat—containing highly saturated shortening or lard.

Why would a Fat Tracker patronize these places? That's not the right question. All of us are likely to find ourselves in one of these fat emporiums at some time or another. That's where the crowd is headed, you're on the road, and they are the only restaurants available—or you simply succumb to temptation. Some people visit this type of restaurant once or twice a year, if that often. They keep their meals lean on a regular basis and the rare double cheeseburger, cheesy burrito or deep-fried chicken or fish entrée won't do any damage to their arteries. But let's face it. These fast-food restaurants are part of the American scene, indeed even the international scene. The National Restaurant Association has estimated that 45 million people eat at one of these chains every day! Many of those folks are our teenagers.

So rather than ask why anybody eats chain-cooked food, a better question is: How

So rather than ask why anybody eats chain-cooked food, a better question is: How often do you find yourself at their doorsteps? Once a year? Go ahead and enjoy yourself. Once a month may be okay if you juggle your Fat Account carefully and choose your selections wisely. Once a week is probably far too often. If you habitually eat at these chains we ask, as we did in the preface, for you to put your hand on your heart and feel your heartbeat. That is what you are jeopardizing by eating regularly at these places. Do you take your children with you on these fast-food excursions and let them choose whatever they want? If your answer is yes, their well being is the best argument we can think of to encourage you to change your habits. On the occasions when you do find yourself at the fat food/fast-food counter, we do have a strategy that can help you make healthy, or at least healthier, choices.

Among the worst offenders at these restaurants are the deep-fried chicken entrées, sandwiches, nuggets and batter-coated chicken parts that hide low-fat breast meat under a thick, breaded mantle which clings to crisped skin dripping with saturated fat. You can strip the coating and skin away before digging in, but such draconian measures will only work for those with superhuman willpower. If possible, of course, order nonfried fish, chicken or lean beef. In general, always skip the shakes. Save creamy desserts for mealtimes at home when you can choose your favorite brand of nonfat frozen yogurt or make a dessert using one of our recipes.

Franchises don't encourage substitutions; they slow down the assembly-line operations that make these restaurants hugely profitable. But don't let that stop you from at least asking for your cheese toppings and sauces on the side. On the other hand, many franchises now feature low-fat items. Look for them. If you don't see any heart-smart choices, let the restaurant owner know there is a market for healthy, quick food, and if you can, walk out without buying anything. Trust us. When it happens often enough, your exit will be noticed. Do these new low-fat items really make a difference? Take a look.

A TYPICAL FAST FOOD MEAL

	Calories	Grams Saturated Fat	Grams Total Fat	% of Calories from Fat	Mg Cholesterol
Double cheeseburger	480	13	27	51	100
French fries (medium)	340	3	16	42	28
Chocolate shake	350	6	10	26	31
Apple pie	310	4	14	41	4
Total	1460	26	67	41	163

A FAT TRACKER'S FAST-FOOD MEAL

	Calories	Grams Saturated Fat	Grams Total Fat	% of Calories from Fat	Mg Cholesterol
Grilled chicken sandwich on whole wheat bun	380	3	18	43	53
Low-fat chocolate milk (2%)	180	3	5	25	17
Fresh apple	80	0	0	0	0
Total	640	6	23	32	70

The best fat-tracking strategy is to steer clear of these restaurants, at least until your taste buds have learned to savor the freshness of the crisp greens at the salad bar more than the greasiness of fried potatoes. It will happen, if you don't put too much temptation in your path, such as hanging out regularly at the fast-food chains.

Fast-Food Fat Traps	Order	Instead of
Special sauces	Grilled fish or chicken fillet on bun	Beefburger
Breaded or deep-fried coating on fish and chicken	Roast beef sandwich on whole grain bread with mustard	"Pocket" sandwiches with mayonnaise or a special sauce in a high-fat crust with cheese added
Batter-fried crusty chicken skin		
Fried potatoes and onions	Green salad (Don't add chicken, turkey, tuna or shrimp if you are also having a burger)	French fries
Shakes		
Cheese toppings	Coleslaw	Onion rings
Creamy salad dressings	Mustard, ketchup or pickle relish	Special sauces
	Iced tea, low-fat chocolate milk or orange juice	Shakes
	Soft-serve desserts	Pies, brownies or cookies
	Chicken or shrimp salads	Chicken or fish nuggets
	Cereal, fresh fruit	Breakfast sandwiches, hash browns or sweet rolls
	Toast and jelly	
	English muffin and jelly	

Fat Tracking Salad Bars

The concept of the salad bar—helping yourself to crisp greens while you wait for your entrée—has become a fixture on the restaurant scene. The concept has expanded in recent years. Salad bars in downtown metropolitan areas cater to the take out lunch crowd, and large shopping malls often have one or two "green" restaurants that answer the needs of hungry shoppers. You can find a smorgasbord of potato items, mixed vegetable, bean and pasta salads, roast chicken, turkey and tuna. And some of the larger places also provide steamed and stir-fried low-fat entrées, a choice of soups, chili and even hot pastas to accompany your salad.

Use our whiteness test to find the prepared salads with too much fat: When lots of white, mayonnaise or sour cream-based dressing mask chicken, celery, tuna or potato, make another choice, such as salads in an oil-based dressing. When you can see mostly chicken or potato, and very little white dressing, you can sample the salad. Some restaurants prepare these salads with vinegar and oil dressings, always a better low saturated-fat choice. Fortunately, at the salad bar you can help yourself to a small portion of dressing as an accompaniment to a large bowl of greens and vegetables.

For a convenience salad, don't pass up the old standby, three-bean salad. It may not have a place in a gourmet's salad paradise, but you can't argue with its enduring popularity, or the fact that the dressing is oil free, usually a blend of vinegar and sugar. A large portion accompanied with breadsticks and a whole wheat bagel or roll provides fiber, filling carbohydrates and complete protein. And it leaves room for frozen nonfat yogurt with fresh berries for dessert. Note that hearts of palm, a favored salad ingredient, does not contain the palm kernel oil we advise you to avoid and it contains no saturated fat. While we suggest you skirt the high-fat temptations—the mountains of grated cheese, fried bacon and prepared salads made with far too much mayonnaise, sour cream and cheese dressings—the salad bar was designed with Fat Trackers in mind.

Salad Bar Fat Traps	Order	Instead of
Grated and sliced cheese	Pasta salads with vegetables in oil and vinegar dressing	Potato, macaroni and chicken salads in heavy mayonnaise dressings
Fruit salads in whipped or sour cream		
Salami and other lunch meats	Slices of roast chicken and turkey breast	
Hard-cooked eggs	Tuna salad	
Whole-milk cottage cheese	Tuna chunks, packed in water, if possible	
Crumbled bacon		
Cheesy, fried croutons	Fresh vegetables, greens, beans, tofu, pickled vegetables	
Cheese and ranch-style dressings	Vegetables marinated in oil	Grated cheeses, cheese cubes
Nuts and coconut toppings for fresh fruit	Grain salads, such as tabbouleh	
	Bean salads	
	Vinegar and oil dressings	Creamy, ranch-style or cheese dressings
	Lemon juice	
	Low-calorie dressings	
	Fresh fruit	Fruit salads with whipped cream or sour cream
	Olives and pickles	Fried croutons
	Sprouts	
	Sautéed vegetable medleys	
	Stir-fried or steamed entrées	
	Any pasta, soup or chili made without cream or obvious saturated fat	
	Whole grain breads, breadsticks and rolls	French fries or hash browns
	Low-fat or nonfat cottage cheese and yogurt	Whole-milk cottage cheese and yogurt

Fat Tracking Sandwich Shops

The spirit of Dagwood Bumstead must have hovered over the creator of the contemporary sandwich shop. Just don't get carried away and order your own towering skyscraper on whole wheat. The sandwich shop is a real boon when you don't feel like brown-bagging it at noontime; you can find excellent Crunchy Lunch selections, unless the shop is staffed with generous-minded sandwich makers. While a double- or triple-decker may seem like a lot of sandwich value for the buck, the fat and calories you might consume at some of these places are no bargain (some sandwiches come with upwards of four or five ounces of meat and/or cheese).

Before you enter the establishment, practice saying, "Hold the mayo," and "No, no butter either." You can try asking for just a little bit of mayo, if that is what you like on your bread, but some sandwich makers don't always understand what "little" means to a Fat Tracker. So it is wise to keep an eye on the production end of things to make sure your sandwich doesn't get slathered with a high-fat dressing. What can you moisten a sandwich with if not mayo? Mustard, ketchup, cranberry sauce, vinaigrette, plain low-fat or nonfat yogurt, horseradish, pickle relish, chutney.

Definitely pass on ham, beef, salami and other high-fat meat sandwiches. And if they insist on putting two or three inches of filling between your choice of whole grain bread or roll, ask for half a sandwich instead and also order a huge green salad. If necessary, reach for an extra roll to fill you up. Grilled sandwiches are really misnamed; they are actually fried sandwiches. On a sourdough roll, a grilled chicken breast, cooked over an open grill, comes off deliciously smoky and reduced in fat. But a grilled cheese, Reuben, grilled ham and cheese, Monte Cristo and other high-fat variations are cooked in butter or may even be deep-fried in an egg batter. Rather than purchasing from the deli case the plastic-wrapped versions that will have more high-fat ingredients, order a custom-made sandwich so you can choose the fillings and specify no added cheese, mayonnaise or butter. And when you get to the cashier, resist the tray of pastries, brownies and cookies placed there as a last-minute temptation and look around for the fresh fruit basket instead. Oh, yes, don't forget to say, "No thanks," to the complimentary bag of potato chips.

Why are we spending so much time on the lowly sandwich? Many working people visit a sandwich shop daily and the owners often do a good job of making a humdrum lunch meal interesting. Unfortunately, they do it with large amounts of high-fat foods. At lunchtime, if you habitually eat one of these monster sandwiches, such as a grilled ham and cheese (15 grams of saturated fat for 2 ounces of cheese and 2 ounces of ham), you will go through your 25-gram allotment of saturated fat before you are ready for an afternoon snack, much less dinner.

Alternatives? Ask for one slice of chicken or turkey or tuna and triple the lettuce, tomato and sprouts. Split a sandwich and a bowl of crunchy (vegetable packed) soup with a friend, and have a second piece of fruit if you are still hungry. Use the whiteness test (see Fat Tracking Salad Bars preceding) to determine whether tuna or chicken salads might have too much mayonnaise. Ask for a filling of marinated vegetable salad instead of meat or cheese. Choose roast breast of chicken or turkey or even a thin slice of rare beef over salami and other high-fat or high-sodium fillings.

Sandwich Shop Fat Traps	*Order*	*Instead of*
Grated and sliced cheese	Lean, roasted chicken, turkey and beef	High-fat luncheon meats, such as pastrami, bologna, salami, mortadella
Salami and other lunch meats		
Hard cooked eggs	Vegetables and/or beans in a pita pocket	Egg salad sandwich
Bacon		
Butter, mayonnaise, margarine	TLT (turkey, lettuce and tomato)	BLT (bacon, lettuce and tomato)
Cheese and ranch-style dressings, special sauces	Peanut butter and jelly	Grilled cheese
		Meat and cheese melts
Tuna, chicken or turkey salads with too much mayonnaise	Tuna salad	Ham salad
Hot dogs	Any vegetable combo	Any meat and cheese combo
Grilled cheese and meat sandwiches	Lean roast beef	Ham and cheese

Fat Tracking Asian Restaurants

Korean barbecue, spicy and hot Thai noodles, Chinese stir-fried vegetables, Japanese clear soups and sushi! Is it any wonder that rates of heart disease in Asian countries lag behind the West? Though we might seek out a Japanese restaurant for its delicious sukiyaki (a mix of beef and vegetables cooked in broth) or a Thai restaurant for its fiery spiced vegetables or its *pad thai* (the seasoned noodle dish) or a Korean house for its kimchee (marinated vegetables) and tabletop barbecue, we also know these entrées have little saturated fat and are usually cooked with monounsaturated peanut oil. While beef and pork may show up on these menus, they are rarely in the guise of a thick steak riddled with marbling or barbecued ribs that have more fat than meat. More often meat is added in small portions to season the broth or vegetable mix that accompanies it. Most of the fried dishes on these menus use peanut oil. If you can stand the calories, they won't hurt your saturated fat count.

Japanese tempura (thinly sliced vegetables and fish deep-fried in a batter) may seem like a dish to avoid. But in traditional Japanese restaurants, the batter does not contain egg yolks, and the brief immersion in hot peanut oil contributes very little saturated fat to the dish and far less total fat than American-style fried chicken with skin cooked in canned vegetable shortening or lard. Indonesian and Vietnamese cuisines have been influenced by the Dutch and French respectively, and some of their dishes may contain more saturated fat than other Asian foods. Asian soups are almost always a good choice, except for Thai soups with coconut milk. But watch out for "Americanized" restaurants that use lard or tropical oils for deep-frying. How would you know? Ask.

One added caution about Asian restaurants: While many restaurants pride themselves on MSG-free food, the battle for healthier food doesn't end there. Heavy doses of soy sauce and similar items may lace some items with excessive sodium, and some places may drench their items with extra oil. When a dish comes to your table floating in oil, it is your signal not to order it again. A welcome sign of the times, however, is that more and more restaurants, including Asian houses, are switching to canola oil and olive oil.

Asian Fat Traps	Order	Instead of
Sweet-and-sour chicken, pork, shrimp and duck dishes, especially those that include fried skin	All steamed rice and boiled noodle dishes	Fried rice and fried noodles
	Broiled, steamed and barbecued lean meats, poultry and fish	Spareribs and pork
Deep-fried chicken, shrimp, pork and beef spareribs	All stir-fries	Fried chicken and duck skin. Anything cooked in an egg yolk batter
Pot stickers filled with pork		
Thai dishes with coconut and coconut milk in sauces and soups	Whole steamed fish	Fried fish
	Vegetarian pot stickers	Fried wontons
Indonesian dishes with coconut	Steamed buns (not pork)	Spring rolls, lumpia
Vietnamese dishes with French cream sauces	Clear soups with vegetables, fish and poultry	
	Dim sum (check the items/ingredients)	
Egg dishes, such as fried rice & fried food coated with batters	Frozen ice desserts	Ice cream
Dishes excessively laced with high-sodium chicken stock and soy sauce	Fruit desserts	Fried desserts
	Fortune cookies	Thai coffee (heavy cream)
	Mints, hard candy	

Fat Tracking Mexican and Southwestern Restaurants

Most people would not think to use Mexican food and low-fat food in the same sentence—and with good reason. "Heartbreakers" include super nachos piled with beef, sour cream, cheese and guacamole, a meal that contains enough saturated fat for the whole family—and the family at the table next to you! Dunking fried tortilla chips in salsa (a free perk at all Mexican places) will break your fat bank for the day, even before your entrée arrives. A meal at most large Mexican fast-food chains is about as bad as it gets, nutritionally speaking. Even rice and beans—the staple duo that nourished people in the American tropics probably long before there was an America to speak of—becomes in the hands of the assembly line food producers merely sponges that soak up a glut of sodium-enriched chicken stock and saturated fat. And with cheese, sour cream and guacamole on top of everything, need we say more?

But the fast-food bad news is not the whole story on this versatile *cocina*. Though often heavy on cheese, meat, refried beans and fried entrées, this delicious cuisine can still offer delicious heart smart options. Mexican food is a favorite throughout the Southwest and California, though the culinary definition of this style of cooking is becoming increasingly blurred in the United States. For example, gazpacho, the chilled, tomato-based vegetable soup from Spain, shows up on many Mexican menus and is a definite yes for Fat Trackers. Many fine neighborhood taquerias that cook to order have switched to using canola oil and olive oil instead of lard. And they offer whole black beans that, even if they are cooked in oil, do not have as much clinging to them as they are scooped onto your plate as do refried beans.

Tex-Mex and Southwestern food have healthy entrées in the low-fat arena: vegetables, meats, chicken and fish, grilled over mesquite, oak or applewood and accompanied with innovative fruit and vegetable salsas that take the place of rich sauces. You can also find an intriguing blend of low-fat Native American and Mexican foods to sample, such as dishes featuring corn, pumpkin and nopales (cactus). Avoid *flautas* and *chimichangas* (high-fat ingredients wrapped in a flour tortilla and deep-fried), and ask for crab enchiladas without cheese or snapper entrées prepared with tomato salsa. A bean burrito at popular chains can weigh in between 10 percent and 26 percent fat, and a beef taco can range from 45 to 54 percent fat, depending on the restaurant's recipe.

However, we have had, within walking distance of our own kitchen, *tacos pescado* in a family-owned, popular and inexpensive Mexican restaurant. On many menus that cook to order (as opposed to serving up batches of prefried frozen entrées from a chain's central processing plant), *tacos pescado* is a tantalizing blend of mesquite-grilled snapper, naturally sweet black beans containing a small amount of olive oil and a sensational mouth-singeing mole wrapped in a corn tortilla (unfried because we asked for it that way). Healthwise and tastewise, it doesn't get much better than that. Beans also can show up in white tablecloth Mexican houses in every spicy, healthy variety (just make sure to ask for the beans without lard).

Ask your server to remove the basket of tortilla chips (48 percent fat), the perk on every table. An electric salsa is just as sizzling on warm unfried corn tortillas (each has a meager one gram of total fat and just a trace of saturated fat), which every Mexican restaurant offers (if you ask). If your entrée is wrapped in a flour tortilla, which can have approximately three grams of total fat and one gram of saturated fat per tortilla, include it in your daily totals. Also encouraging to the lover of Mexican food, many kitchens are switching to canola oil and olive oil instead of lard. If your favorite restaurant hasn't, let the owner know that you will come back when lard is no longer in their larder. And while you are at it, ask to have low-fat and nonfat yogurt as an option to sour cream, or at least ask them to offer a half and half blend. Flex your consumer muscle and restaurateurs who want to stay in business will respond.

Mexican Fat Traps	Order	Instead of
Refried beans, chicken, beef and pork cooked in lard	Refried beans made with canola oil or olive oil	Refried beans with lard
Sour cream	Refried and whole beans without oil	
Grated cheese added by the handful	Warm corn tortillas and salsa	Tortilla chips or nachos
Cheese-stuffed burritos, enchiladas and tacos	Vegetarian burritos and tostadas filled with beans, rice, vegetables and salsa	Burritos filled with beef, pork cheese or lard
Pork		
Stuffed, deep-fried tortillas		*Flautas* or *chimichangas*
Tortilla chips	Hot sauce, salsa	Shredded cheese
Heavy, fatty meat	Guacamole	Sour cream
Deep-fried entrées such as *chimichangas*	Tostadas without sour cream or cheese	Quesadillas
		Tacos
	Vegetarian chili	Beef or pork chili
	Steamed rice (not fried or cooked in oil with meat)	Beans cooked in lard
	Chicken, shrimp or lean beef fajitas (not fried meats)	Barbecued beef ribs
	Salads (watch the ingredients)	
	Vegetarian bean soups	Pork and bean soups
	Snapper Veracruzana and other fish and chicken house specialties that use tomato-based sauces	
	Tropical fresh fruits	Flan

Fat Tracking Italian Restaurants

Fat Trackers love Italian food. Not just because of its delicious minestrone, marinara sauces, linguine with clams and garlic, veal with peppers and fabulous bread, but because Italian cooks use olive oil almost exclusively. Of course, they also put meatballs in their spaghetti and sausage and pepperoni on their pizza, but what is life without its challenges here and there to make it interesting. Fortunately, your favorite trattoria will have a surplus of fat-tracking triumphs. *Buon appetito!*

Italian Fat Traps	Order	Instead of
Pizza with extra cheeses and meats	Vegetable antipasto with peppers and olives	Cheese, dried meat plates
Sausage	Minestrone	Cream soups
Dried meats such as salami, coppa, pepperoni	Italian bread	Buttered garlic bread
	Focaccia	Pizza
Pasta sauces made with butter, cheese and cream	Pasta in tomato sauce, marinara or clam sauce	Cream sauces, meat sauces
	Grilled veal and chicken	
	Chicken and fish in olive oil-based sauces	
	Grilled scampi, anchovies, clams, eel, calamari or catch of the day	Fried fish
	Insalata (salad) with calamari, broccoli, cauliflower or beans	
	Italian dressing	Gorgonzola and creamy Italian dressings
	Polenta (without butter or cheese)	
	Risotto with vegetables	Risotto with cheese or butter
	Pastas and soups that combine beans and vegetables	
	Marinated eggplant and artichokes	Deep-fried vegetables
	Vegetable pizza with mushrooms, peppers, onions, garlic, vegetables, clams, anchovy	Pizza with salami, extra cheese, hamburger, pepperoni, sausage
	Frozen ice	Italian creams
	Fruit	Italian pastries
	Fruit gelato	Zabaglione
	Neapolitan nougat	Zuccotto
	Biscotti	
	Espresso	
	Cappuccino and *latte* with low-fat milk	Coffees with steamed whole milk

Fat Tracking Middle Eastern and Mediterranean Restaurants

Stuffed grape leaves, couscous, vegetable *tagines*, barley, pita, garlic, onions, eggplant, yogurt, honey, cucumbers, hummus, tomatoes, feta, raisins, lemon, olive oil and olives! Jewels of the ancient cuisines that ring the Mediterranean, these are the foods that also nourish the heart. Dishes from this region often use meat sparingly, blending it with vegetables and grains. Cooks rely on olive oil and richly flavor their food with garlic, lemon and herbs. They use feta cheese in modest amounts. Restaurants specializing in Greek and what is loosely called Middle Eastern cuisines are not as prevalent in this country as Italian and Chinese, but well worth seeking out. Their intriguing dishes celebrate many fat-tracking principles.

Because the dishes vary greatly depending on the country of origin, our "order this instead of this" list is short. In general, order eggplant and chickpea purées (baba ghanouj and hummus) spooned on pita. Look for dolmas, grapes leaves stuffed with rice. Try currant-flecked couscous, the whole grain steamed to an almost creamy texture; or a lemon-scented vegetable *tagine* filled with carrots, greens and basil. You will find many chicken dishes cooked in fragrant broths, but they will probably include the skin, and the fat from the chicken will have dissolved into the sauce. Lean roast lamb or grilled chicken would be a better choice.

Middle Eastern Fat Traps	Order	Instead of
B'stilla, a pastry filled with chicken and eggs	Grilled eggplant	Eggplant fried or in cheese sauce
Avgolemono, the Greek lemon and egg soup	Roast lean lamb (leg or loin chop)	Fatty lamb shank stews
Lamb, fried or cooked in large amounts of oil	Roast vegetables	
Deep-fried pastries	Grilled meat, chicken and fish	Fried meat, chicken and fish
Filo coated with butter	Fish stews	Fatty gravies and sauces
	Couscous and other grains	
	Garbanzo beans (Chickpeas)	
	Vegetable stews	
	Fresh fruit	Fried pastries

Fat Tracking European Restaurants

It is hard to pigeonhole European food. To some, it is epitomized by Frence soufflés and cream sauces, while to others it means German pancakes and Viennese pastries. Much of America's food preferences are rooted in the regional cuisines that European emigrants brought with them, and consequently these restaurants are very popular. Since these cuisines cover a large terrain from Scandinavia to the Mediterranean, we certainly can't advise you on every Continental menu choice, but these are the restaurants most likely to serve rich portions of meats, butter, cheese and eggs. If you go to an eastern European restaurant that features dumplings and sausages, select a small order for everyone to sample. Ask how the dish is prepared and choose a wine sauce over a cream sauce. Instead of rich coffees with cream and liqueurs added, ask for coffee with low-fat milk and a dusting of powdered chocolate and cinnamon, and consider it dessert.

European Fat Traps	Order	Instead of
Sauces made with eggs, butter, cream and cheese, such as hollandaise, béarnaise, mornay	Poached, steamed or broiled fish and chicken	Meunière (dishes cooked in butter)
	Wine or tomato sauces	Cream sauces and soups
	Ratatouille	Buttered vegetables
Meats wrapped in pastry	Lean grilled meats without sauces	
Quiches		
Whipped cream desserts	Appetizers such as steamed mussels or a vegetable soup	
Mousses (savory and dessert)		
Soufflés (savory and dessert)	Beef ragouts or chicken stews with the fat skimmed	Braised beef dishes, which absorb during cooking a great deal of fat that may be part of the sauce
Chocolate		
	Fruit coupes, compotes, sorbets and ices, or fresh fruit	Whipped cream and chocolate

Fat Tracking Other Ethnic Restaurants

Throughout the United States, you can find restaurants that specialize in foods from just about every part of the world—India, Ethiopia, Brazil, Guatemala, the Caribbean. Many of these foods originated in traditions that valued economy and depended on local, seasonal produce rather than high-fat items, which were often not readily available. Though some of these foods use red meat, many are by definition healthy, if the recipes have not been tampered with to appeal to Western tastes (by adding butter, etc.). However, when you peruse a menu with unfamiliar foods, or you are not sure which foods fit into The Stanford 25 Gram Plan, use the first principal of fat-tracking restaurants: Ask what's in a dish and in what kind of oil it was cooked.

By now you know that Fat Trackers avoid deep-fat-fried foods and foods with rich sauces. But don't forget to seek out the grain and vegetarian specialties; the meats, chicken or fish that may be grilled with an interesting marinade or basting sauce that has little fat. Ask for a rundown on the types of vegetables and salads the restaurant offers. If a name sounds unfamiliar, like tandoori on an Indian menu, ask what it means. When you find a low-fat cooking method, you can adapt it to your fat-tracking recipes at home, as we have with Curry-Spiked Turkey with Mango Chutney Sauce (page 517–18).

Fat Tracking Coffee and Dessert Cafés And Ice Cream Shoppes

The Fat Tracker's downfall? Not necessarily, though if you have a sweet tooth, these places will definitely put you to the test. Let's start with the cafés. Instead of a rich dessert, order a flavored coffee with whole milk or a touch of half-and-half, an indulgence with much less fat than a cream pie or richly frosted cake. Biscotti, often made with olive oil, and oatmeal cookies supply sweetness without too much fat, and a fruit tart is better than a chocolate mousse or a torte made with butter.

When you find yourself in an ice cream shoppe, remember that premium ice creams mean saturated fat in fat-tracking language. Eggs, cream high in butterfat, nuts, chunks of cookies and candy bars, chocolate and other rich ingredients keep this dessert at the high end of the fat and cholesterol spectrum. But in recent years, thankfully, the modern ice cream store has added sherbet, fruit ices, sorbets and fruit gelatos, as well as low-fat and nonfat frozen yogurt to their roster of frozen desserts.

Which is the best choice? Well, fat contents vary with each ice cream maker, but obviously, a scoop of anything that says low-fat or nonfat is better than a scoop of anything billed as regular, creamy, rich or premium. Go for fruit-based ices, rather than milk or cream based. Pass on toppings, except for those made with fresh fruit or jam or those specified as fat free. Also watch out for some frozen desserts made with cookies and candy that were high in fat before they ever hit the ice cream. If you walk into your favorite ice cream store, and your knees buckle at the sight of someone licking a triple scoop of your favorite, richest flavor; or, as you are trying to choose between lemon and pineapple ice, your resolve fails when you catch the clerk passing over the counter a hot fudge sundae with extra sauce, nuts and whipped cream, put your hand over your heart, quickly find your heart beat and repeat, "lemon ice is good for my heart, lemon ice is good for my heart!" If that doesn't work, how about ordering just a small scoop of high-fat ice cream and sharing it with a friend?

In a more serious vein, remember that the American Pediatric Association has recommended that all children over the age of two follow a low-fat diet, so encourage your children to ask for frozen nonfat yogurt instead of high-fat ice creams. Turn to the desserts and snacks section of Fat Tracking in the Supermarket for a comparison of these frozen favorites.

- Make the run to the nearest fast-food chain the exception rather than the rule.
- Don't pass up the chance to eat at a good restaurant; just take your fat-tracking principles with you.
- Pass up deep-fried, creamed and buttered dishes.
- Choose broiled, steamed, roasted, grilled and stir-fried dishes over those that are fried and deep-fried.
- Choose ethnic restaurants that serve cuisines that don't rely on animal products, such as Asian and some Middle Eastern traditions.
- When you have no choice and are held captive at a sumptuous banquet, enjoy yourself and resolve to lower your saturated fat intake for the following few days to balance out unavoidable extravagances.
- Ask what type of oil is used before you order an unfamiliar dish.
- Ask to have your sauces served on the side.
- Split a meat entrée with a friend and order extra rice or potatoes, bread, vegetables and salad.

PART FOUR

The Stanford Fat Tracker's Cookbook

Feeding Many Hungers

THE FOOD WE EAT FEEDS MANY HUNGERS, *with choices based as much on nostalgia and a yearning for comfort as on taste. Ask ten people to describe the perfect meal, and you will receive ten different menus. Food preferences are as personal as fingerprints and almost as traceable. Think of the people you know best, and chances are you can name their favorite foods. Life's celebrations center around rituals of food, and disappointment weighs heavy over the holiday table that lacks the traditional dishes. We offer comforting soups as a consolation in times of trouble; we reward ourselves with delicious bites of this or that for good reason or no reason. Cultural identities are defined in part by food, and except perhaps for music, the foods we love can evoke memories and emotions like no other stimulus.*

The need for food as nourishment is as urgent as the need for air, but surely the need for food as a source of pleasure and contentment is just as insistent. It is true that some people regard food merely as fuel, and once they have brushed away the crumbs from one meal, hardly give thought to the next. Perhaps for them the need to impose a new dietary order is an easy burden, but most people regard it as an exercise in deprivation. Yet, knowing the importance of food at the center of your life, here we are, asking you to make changes in the foods you love to eat. The bitter pill here is not dietary change, but the epidemic of heart disease. Rethinking food choices is a major part of the solution. In the preceding chapters, we have discussed the fine points of incorporating the 25-gram principles in your daily life. As a preface to our recipes, we will outline the best cooking methods to use for delicious, healthy meals. As you begin using the recipes and embracing a healthier style of eating, we want to leave you with some food for thought, a point of view to further ease this transition.

First of all, by dietary change we do not mean deprivation, but a widening of perspective. A researcher has speculated that most families eat the same eight or ten dishes over and over, year in and year out. But then look at America today. Consider the abundant quantity, quality and dazzling assortment of foods available to the American consumer; the ethnic diversity that has introduced a wide variety of cuisines to neighborhood restaurants; the recent emphasis on innovative cooking with fresh ingredients; the bookstore shelves groaning with cookbooks of coffee-table quality; the endlessly exciting food magazines, as well as food columns and articles featured in even the most rural newspapers. Consider all this, and it would seem that anyone who eats a mere dozen dishes over and over is in the grip of severe culinary deprivation, a famine of the imagination. Underscoring all this is the fact that, despite the glut of fat in the American diet, the majority of the foods available in your supermarket are perfectly healthy, and many of the world's most respected cuisines are ideal models for healthy as well as delicious food. Clearly, the challenge of heart-healthy cooking is not, "What is left to eat," but what to choose from a dizzying array of healthful possibilities.

Anyone who appreciates good food can still look forward to a lifetime of eating pleasure. However, we know you have ingrained food preferences, food habits and strong opinions about what makes food taste just the way you like it. We don't ask you to change your mind about these notions, but to open your mind to expand the possibilities. Keep your treasured, family recipes on file for special occasions. And keep sampling the great variety of innovative dishes in this book to find the recipes that will become the new family favorites, ones you will not have to ration at all. Just as you wouldn't cook chicken the same way every time you serve it, try to discard rigid notions that there is only one right way to cook anything.

No one who understands the cooking of China criticizes it because it doesn't have enough cream and butter. It's not supposed to. Chinese cooks valued products made from soybeans, chicken, fish and vegetables, so they did not become butter churners or cheese makers. Yet Chinese cooking is regarded as one of the world's great cuisines. Chinese chefs approach cooking with the care of an artist and their food shows flair, imagination, inventiveness, taste and diversity. And by the way, it is also some of the healthiest food served on the planet.

Low-fat food doesn't taste exactly like high-fat food. However, it doesn't have to in order to qualify as delicious and satisfying. Learn to appreciate every dish for its own attributes, its freshness of flavor, delicacy of texture, complexity of taste— not whether it exactly duplicates some other recipe. This suppleness of mind will reward you for the rest of your life by opening the door to exciting opportunities to savor wonderful, healthy food.

Remember that your choice of food is not a moral issue. Everyone has said at least once as they headed for the cookie jar, "I'm being bad." Sadly, some people mean it. Hungering after a thick steak, a hot fudge sundae or some other food that contains an abundance of fat or calories doesn't make you "bad." It means you are human, otherwise the cookie jar wouldn't have such universal appeal. When you are confused about what to eat, go back to the first words of our introduction and put your hand on your heart to remember the real purpose behind this book. Let your heartbeat guide you to the smart choices as often as possible, and when you eat any foods, even if on occasion they are high-fat ones, enjoy them.

CHAPTER 26

The Fat Tracker's Cooking Course

TO FRY OR NOT TO FRY? *We see it as an option, not a question, because "low-fat" cooking does not mean "no-fat" cooking. Steaming, poaching and grilling may be ideal cooking methods from a health standpoint because they don't use any added fat. But eventually even a healthful fish fillet, grilled to perfection, will cause the most committed Fat Tracker's spirit to sag if it is the only entrée that ever appears on the dinner plate. When your taste buds hunger for an occasional fried morsel, follow our advice for healthy frying and indulge yourself. French fried potatoes, in fact, cooked in a healthy, monounsaturated oil and well drained are better for your arteries than a baked potato oozing butter, sour cream and bacon. Of course, even better are our Oven-Baked French Fries (page 412–13).*

You can include almost every cooking method in your repertoire if you trim excess fat each step of the way. By excess fat we don't mean the fat needed for flavor and texture, but rather those extra tablespoons that only add unnecessary calories and saturated fat without enhancing the flavor of the dish. We describe tips for removing excess fat in each recipe, either by reducing the amount of fat you use or by substituting ingredients, and throughout this book, we give you ideas for adjusting your favorite dishes to use fewer eggs, oil instead of butter, and smaller portions of red meat.

In this chapter we will show you how to trim excess fat to allow room in your 25-gram plan for soups, sweets, soufflés, for fried, steamed, baked and grilled food—all cooked in the healthiest way possible, whether you use our recipes or your own. Whether you are a novice or a practiced chef, you will learn to recognize when to substitute a quarter cup of oil in a stew instead of the half cup the recipe calls for; or switch the butter in a pasta sauce to the more authentic and healthier olive oil. Indeed, many of the recipes in your personal collection might not need much altering because they are already low in fat—grilled foods and roasted meats, for example.

How Much Fat Should You Put in Your Recipes?

The healthiest cooking methods produce moist, flavorful food with the least amount of fat in general, but especially saturated fat. Is the least amount of fat a teaspoon? A tablespoon? A quarter cup? There are no set rules. You have to take into consideration the needs of the recipe, the number of people it will feed and your personal fat-reducing goals. The results you want to achieve will dictate how much fat to use. Fat enhances the taste and texture of foods and provides moisture, especially in baked goods. But there are many ways to achieve these same results with no fat or less fat.

If, in the interest of trimming fat from your diet, you sauté a cup of chopped onions in a teaspoon of oil, you will end up with a scorched mess. If you simply slash the fat in a muffin recipe, you may find no one will eat them because they are too dry or tasteless. Fruit purées can provide needed moisture *and* flavor to cakes in place of some or all of the fat you normally use. On the other hand, adding a few tablespoons of cream may make all the difference to an otherwise low-fat but not quite perfect sauce; divided among several people, the slight addition of saturated fat would be minimal, paying handsome rewards in smoothness and overall satisfaction. Healthful recipes have to taste good, too; nutritious, bland foods can't help anyone's heart if the meal ends up in the trash.

The best guideline for adding fat is to use what you need for a successful dish — and no more. You will realize a tremendous overall reduction in your fat intake by following the Fat Tracker's commandments we have already discussed: Always reach for lower-fat snacks, enjoy Better Breakfasts, Crunchy Lunches, 2 + 2 Dinners (see Chapter 13), stick to your maximum fat limits for the day, select lower-fat cooking methods, follow the fat-tracking tips for each recipe, substitute lower-fat ingredients whenever possible and routinely use lower-fat dairy products and leaner cuts of red meat. When you use these guidelines on a regular basis to gain control of the major sources of fat in your diet, you will have more leeway to adjust the fat in individual recipes to make them satisfying as well as healthy.

Heart-Healthy Cooking Don'ts

Following is a matchup of heart-healthy cooking methods and the foods best suited for them. Our recipes give explicit instructions for using these various methods, but you can use these general guidelines to lower the fat in all of your cooking. We will start with a very short list of cooking "don'ts," techniques to avoid because they add very high concentrations of saturated fat to a dish. While you may decide to enjoy these types of foods on rare occasions, including them on a regular basis will make it very difficult if not impossible to keep harmful fats under control.

- Don't fry foods in rendered animal fat, such as bacon, chicken fat or lard.
- Don't deep-fry foods that are dipped in a whole egg batter; the cholesterol is higher and a rich batter allows fat to seep into and cling to the coating.
- Don't lard meat by threading fat into the center of a cut of meat or by wrapping it in a layer of pork fat or bacon.
- Don't braise meats and poultry, such as pot roast, in which food is partially immersed in liquid. Fat melts into the liquid at first, but the meat reabsorbs some of these fatty juices at the end of the cooking period.
- Don't prepare sauces and gravies with the fat rendered from roasted meat or poultry.

How Much Cheese Should You Use in Your Recipes?

To a Fat Tracker, the term grated cheese is woefully inexact for purposes of measuring calories and grams of fat. Nutritional content is determined by weight but recipes usually list cheese by volume—a tablespoon or a cup or something in between. For example, a tablespoon of coarsely grated cheese weighs more than a tablespoon of finely grated cheese, which has more air incorporated into it. In addition, a tablespoon of packaged grated cheese is drier and more compact, and consequently weighs more than a tablespoon of cheese you grate yourself. For convenience, we measure by volume as we assume you do, and cheese is usually listed by spoonful or cupful, rather than ounces. However, we have used freshly grated cheese in our recipes. If you use commercially grated cheese, be aware that your recipe may have a little more fat than the amount we list in the calculations. We specify coarsely grated cheese or shaved cheese in some recipes because a few large shreds of cheese satisfies the palate more than a larger amount of finely grated cheese. However, if you are on a severely fat-restricted diet, we suggest that you weigh the cheese instead of measuring by volume, and for that reason we have supplied the weights as well.

What really matters over a lifetime of eating is not that you measure every last shred of cheese in every recipe, but that in your cooking you use cheese somewhat sparingly as an accent to improve the flavor of your food and not as a main ingredient. Also, make it a practice to snack on lower-fat or nonfat cheeses to keep this major source of saturated fat to a minimum.

Fat-Free Cooking Techniques

What's left? Everything else. Here are some general tips that will help you match foods with the best cooking methods, starting with the preparations that require no added fat.

Grilling

Our partiality to cooking foods directly over an open flame shows in the extensive collection of grilled recipes throughout the book. The high temperatures reached on a grill melt away saturated fat. But there are other reasons to praise grilled food. The coals impart a delectable, smoky aroma to everything on the grill, from fish and chicken to bread and vegetables, producing a complexity of flavors simply not possible with any other method. Here are some tips to follow:

- The high temperatures and flames that occasionally leap up and dance on meat, chicken and fish unfortunately also will draw out their moisture. Enter low-fat marinades. Use them to help keep your foods juicy as well as tasty.
- Pay close attention to timing and check the food frequently so it doesn't over-cook, which will toughen meat and poultry and generally dry out all foods. Grilled food can burn quickly.
- Turn the food frequently, moving it closer to the coals or further away as necessary to keep the outside deliciously crusty and the interior sufficiently cooked. The outward appearance of grilled foods does not accurately signal a cooked center. A chicken breast too close to the coals can char quickly and appear done, but the center may need more time.
- Experiment with cooking times and distance from the coals to produce moist, flavorful entrées, and you won't need to mask their natural succulence and aromas with rich sauces.
- Add sugary marinades sparingly at first or the foods will scorch beyond recognition; then add more liberally in the last few minutes of cooking.

We recommend all manner of grilling equipment: stovetop grills that catch fat in ridges and carry it into trays of water below, tabletop electric grills and outdoor barbecues from the simple hibachi to elaborate, electric, spit-roasting, automatic fire-starting, dome-covered smoking wonders. Acquire a grill basket or grid to hold small pieces of chicken, fish or vegetables so they don't fall through the rack. Also, coat your barbecue or grill with vegetable spray for easy cleanup and to prevent food from sticking. Although general rules for grilling are the same for most foods, the temperature of the coals, their distance from the grill and timing varies depending on the item you are cooking. Each of our grilling recipes indicates the proper timing.

> FOODS BEST SUITED FOR GRILLING: *tender meats, fish, poultry, vegetables, fruit, bread.*

Broiling

The chief difference between broiling and grilling is that broiled food is cooked *under* the flame and you can't use the variety of coals and wood chips that add distinctive flavor to grilled foods. Otherwise broiling is an excellent method when you don't have access to a grill. The fat melts away, producing moist, tender and flavorful meat, fish and poultry. You can substitute broiling for grilling in most recipes, following the same general guidelines, although foods may cook slightly faster, especially if you place the rack directly under the heat source. Broiled foods need close attention during cooking so they don't overcook and dry out. Turn foods frequently and if they begin to scorch, lower the rack. Marinades and basting sauces intended for grilling will also work their magic on broiled foods.

FOODS BEST SUITED FOR BROILING: *tender meats, fish, poultry, some pulpy vegetables such as eggplant.*

Oven-Roasting

In the oven, currents of heat circulate around food to cook it slowly. Roasting meat and poultry releases fat (which you then skim away and discard) and produces flavorful juices, which you can turn into a low-fat sauce, rather than a high-fat gravy. If you want a succulent outer crust, first sear roasts on all sides briefly in a hot, heavy-bottomed skillet coated with a thin film of olive oil. For the juiciest interior, however, forego this step. Always place meats and poultry on a rack. This way they do not absorb any of the fat that accumulates in the roasting pan and the bottom will not cook faster than the rest of the roast. Do not cover roasts (the sealed-in steam does not favor the best-tasting roast). Nor should you salt a roast as it cooks.

Roasting works best for large, tender cuts of meat, such as rump roast. Though not necessary, you can baste roasts with small amounts of olive oil, if you like, but don't use the saturated fat that melts from the roast. If possible, baste with just the cooking juices, though it is hard to separate them from the rendered fat until after you remove the roast from the oven. Lower temperatures and longer cooking times release more fat, which can be skimmed away; you also get less shrinkage, more pan juices, and a slightly drier roast, but with good flavor. Higher temperatures and shorter cooking times allow the meat to retain slightly more fat; this combination also produces maximum juiciness and flavor, but with little or no pan juices. Herbs, flavored mustards, slices of orange or lemon and other fat-free ingredients can also be inserted under the breast skin to flavor poultry further.

Roast whole squash, carrots, peppers, parsnips, turnips, eggplant, onions, garlic, yams, unpeeled beets, and pears on a baking sheet following the directions in the individual recipes.

FOODS BEST SUITED FOR OVEN-ROASTING: *meat roasts, poultry, root and fibrous vegetables, such as potatoes, squash, peppers and onions.*

Steaming

The technique of cooking food over simmering water in a covered container produces moist, high heat that cooks food rapidly with no added fat. The fat in chicken or fish melts away. Because no evaporation occurs to concentrate the flavors, however, you get a moist but rather bland-tasting result when you steam unseasoned poultry and fish. An exception is a class of Chinese dishes that are coated before steaming with a mix of Asian flavorings. Many of these entrées are so deeply flavored that they do not require any further enhancement.

Steaming is particularly suitable for both root, tuber and tender green vegetables. Potatoes, yams and carrots emerge incredibly moist, and tender green vegetables retain the most nutrients, color and flavor. Note the timing of your steamed foods, and when you have discovered your preferred ratio of doneness, pot size and cooking time, don't vary it, even if you come across a recipe that instructs you differently. If broccoli steams to your own standard of perfection in seven minutes, for instance, then always cook it for seven minutes, unless a recipe suggests giving vegetables a quick steaming before you stick them on a grill.

To find the equipment that works best for you, investigate steamers and steaming inserts, as well as grids and baskets that fit inside a wok. Place food in a steamer or basket and set it over at least an inch of boiling water. Do not allow the food to sit in the water as it cooks; if the water level spills into the basket, drain off the excess. Reduce the heat until the water returns to a lazy bubble and keep the pot tightly covered as it steams. Remove the food from the steamer as soon as it is done. Otherwise, if you merely set it aside and keep it covered, the contents will continue to cook, and overcook, in the intense, trapped heat. You can even arrange thick celery stalks, lengthwise quartered carrots and zucchini in a crisscross pattern on the bottom of a large saucepan or stockpot to form a steaming platform for fish or chicken breasts, add water or diluted stock so that only the vegetables are immersed in it, bring to a boil, then reduce the heat to a simmer. Serve the steamed vegetables as a flavorful garnish to your entrée. Don't forget to set a timer when you steam foods. The water can evaporate (especially if the heat is too high), badly scorch your pot and ruin your food.

❧ **When steaming green vegetables such as broccoli or string beans, don't remove the lid to check if they are done, then recover them, or they will lose their bright color. Once covered, they should stay covered or they will turn army-blanket green.**

FOODS BEST SUITED FOR STEAMING: *fish, poultry, vegetables, fruits, grains.*
DO NOT STEAM: *meat.*

Microwaving

Microwaving is in many cases, though not all, even quicker than steaming and a more heart-healthy way to prepare green vegetables without losing their rich store of vitamins. An obvious advantage of microwaved vegetables is that you can cook and serve them in the same container if you wish. However, we have found that, depending on the power of your microwave and the degree of doneness you prefer, actual cooking times for green vegetables do not always vary that much from steaming times. The microwave also offers many excellent low-fat options for cooking foods other than vegetables which do slash cooking times and we will discuss several of them in specific recipes. We offer a few general tips for microwaving. However, their requirements are so essentially different from conventional cooking methods that we suggest you refer to a microwave cookbook to learn the finer points of preparing food in this oven.

Use only containers made from materials suitable for a microwave oven: glass, hard plastic, ceramic, paper, plastic wrap for the microwave. Do not use metal or enamel products with metal centers or metallic decorations that will not only cause a startling arc inside the oven, but prevent the microwaves from penetrating and cooking your food. Also, soft (bendable) plastic will melt. Certain ceramic glazes are not designed for microwave use so it is wise to check the manufacturer's instructions or with the seller before using a questionable container. Rounded shapes seem to work best with tightly fitting covers. As with all types of cooking, use a size that will hold the food comfortably in a single layer—not too large to waste energy, not too small to cook unevenly. Arrange food in a circle as much as possible with the thickest portion on the outside rim and the most tender or thinnest parts in the center. Rotate foods during the cooking period manually, or place them on a carousel, so the microwaves will bombard (and thus cook) the food evenly. Salt vegetables only after cooking or they will shrivel. You will no doubt find that food cooked in liquids, such as soups and sauces, require less salt. The microwave can play havoc with the proportion of certain seasonings, such as herbs and spices, either blunting or accentuating them. When you are adapting a conventional recipe for the microwave, be prepared to make adjustments with ingredients such as garlic, cinnamon, chilies, pepper and so forth. If you are experienced using a microwave, your own experiments will be your best guide. Novice microwave cooks should consult their owner's manual or a microwave cookbook for more specific guidelines.

Boiling and Simmering

Although it does not use any fat, boiling (immersing food in boiling liquid) has limited use. This method produces sustained, intense heat ideal for softening pasta, cereals and grains, but it leaches nutrients in other foods. Boiling is often used to break down the fibers in root vegetables, such as potatoes and yams, but steaming and microwaving accomplish the same end with a healthier result. *Don't ever boil any vegetable*, in fact; always use a steamer or microwave to preserve vitamins and minerals. If you cook meat, fish and poultry in violently churning water, you will not only ruin their texture, but they will emerge essentially flavorless and inedible. Some recipes recommend bringing a sauce, soup or stew to a boil, but then you should always immediately reduce the heat.

Simmering (a very gentle boil), however, cooks at a lower heat that is much kinder to foods such as legumes. Many recipes utilize simmering, which can range from an almost imperceptible rippling on the surface to a regular, insistent but slow bubble. Soups and stews, for example, rely on slow simmering (never boiling) to cook tough or fibrous ingredients uncovered so the liquids evaporate and concentrate the flavors deliciously.

FOODS BEST SUITED FOR BOILING: *pasta, grains.*
DO NOT BOIL: *vegetables, meat, chicken, fish.*
FOODS BEST SUITED FOR SIMMERING: *soups, stews, sauces.*

Poaching

In this classic technique, food is immersed in a very gently simmering liquid — usually a fat-free blend of chicken or fish stock, water, wine, vegetables and herbs, and in the case of fruit, a flavored sugar syrup. The food takes on the character of the poaching liquid. Use a low-sided pan with a tight-fitting cover that will hold the food in one layer for even cooking.

FOODS BEST SUITED FOR POACHING: *fish, chicken breasts, fruit, vegetables.*
DO NOT POACH: *meat.*

Low-Fat Cooking Techniques

Cooking methods familiar to all cooks, such as sautéing and stir-frying, produce intensely flavored food through the addition of fat. With the fat-trimming modifications that follow, these techniques can continue to work their culinary wizardry on the Fat Tracker's meals.

Browning

Cooking techniques that add fat require an understanding of the process called browning. At very high temperatures (310 degrees F), complex chemical changes occur in foods that produce incredibly delicious flavors. Boiling does not release these desirable essences because the temperatures cannot rise above 212 degrees F. Oven-roasting without added fat produces a browning effect. But stovetop cooking at high heat requires adding fat, which prevents scorching but causes problems for Fat Trackers. Many recipes instruct you to brown onions, garlic, potatoes or a chicken breast in numerous tablespoons of fat, often butter, bacon or the like. But we will show how to control the type and amount of oil, the size of the pan, the cooking temperature and the time to produce deliciously browned foods with a minimum of harmful fat.

- Use the smallest possible pan that will hold your food in one layer. If you cook a clove of minced garlic in a large skillet, you will have to add a lot of oil to cover the pan so it won't scorch. In a small skillet, however, you need only a small amount of oil to achieve the same result. But if you put too much food in a small pan, the temperature will take longer to rise to the browning point, allowing the food to absorb the oil so you will have to keep adding more. You need just enough room so that the food is continually in contact with the hot surface of the pan.
- Use the least amount of the healthiest fat. Remember that browning is necessary to transform internal flavors at high heat, and you don't need a large pool of oil for those changes to occur. The fat requirements are the same for whatever you are browning. Even if a recipe specifies a half cup of oil, you merely need enough oil—preferably olive oil or canola oil instead of bacon or lard—to coat the bottom of the skillet and keep things from scorching and sticking to the pan as the temperatures rise and begin to perform their wonderful alchemy. If necessary, you can add more oil, though it will lower the temperature and slow down the browning process.
- Lower the heat if you use less oil; it may take slightly longer but you will be happier with the result. A small amount of oil (especially in an overly large pan) reaches high temperatures quickly and may scorch before the food browns properly. Stir the food frequently so it doesn't stick.
- Brown meat and poultry without added oil by broiling them briefly, then proceed with your dish.
- Use our favorite technique of adding browned vegetables to a dish by oven-roasting onions, garlic and other aromatic foundations. Then add the fat-free but deliciously browned item to your dish.

Sautéing, Panfrying, Pan-Broiling

Based on the preceding browning technique, these terms refer to tender cuts of meat, fish, poultry or vegetables cooked quickly in a small amount of oil. Use an uncovered skillet following the general directions for browning. After skimming off excess fat, you can make flavorful sauces by deglazing the pan juices. Or drain the meat or poultry and add a fat-free sauce. Our best sautéing trick is to place the food in an ovenproof skillet with a very small amount of oil. Stir it briefly over medium heat on top of the stove, then place it in an oven preheated to 400 degrees F for 10 to 20 minutes until browned. This reduces the likelihood of the food scorching, as it can in the intense heat of a pan placed directly on a burner.

Nonstick cookware allows you to sauté, panfry and pan-broil without any fat at all. The Fat Tracker in us loves these pans because they really do live up to their fat-free billing. You can fry an egg (or better yet, liquid egg substitute) without a drop of oil. However, the cook in us is far less enthusiastic; these pans (except for one or two of the most expensive brands) rarely produce satisfactory results. Foods don't brown, color or taste as well as those cooked in conventional cookware. Use these products only if your fat-tracking goals require that you cook with absolutely no fat.

FOODS BEST SUITED FOR SAUTÉING: *tender cuts of meat, poultry, fish, tender vegetables.*

Deglazing

Deglazing preserves the browned pan juices from sautéed or panfried meat and poultry by adding liquid (wine, stock, and/or fruit juice) to the congealed juices to transform them into a flavorful, easy sauce that's very low in fat. If a great deal of fat has accumulated in the pan after frying, skim it away first, then over moderately high heat, pour in the liquid and stir constantly until the juices loosen and the liquid evaporates, usually by a third or half. Spoon the deglazed juices over your entrée, or incorporate them into another sauce.

Sauté-Reduction

A technique we call "sauté-reduction" achieves the wonderful flavors of browning onions and garlic with the barest minimum of fat. Our method takes a little more time than the traditional browning technique, and somewhat resembles cooking risotto—you stir in small amounts of flavorful liquid over an extended period of time. The following instructions are for cooking one-half cup of chopped onions, shallots, garlic or leeks. For larger or smaller quantities, make the necessary adjustments in the amount of oil you use initially, skillet size, cooking time and liquid added. For the liquid use water, wine, stock, fruit juice or whatever best complements your dish.

Use a heavy-bottomed skillet, which will retain the heat and cook slowly without scorching. Keep a half cup or so of water (or, even better, stock) close by. Add a coating of vegetable spray or ½ tablespoon of olive oil or canola oil to the pan. For a larger volume, double the oil. Heat the pan over low-medium heat and add the onions or other vegetables when a spray of cold water dances on the surface. Toss the onions quickly to coat them with the oil. Add 1 tablespoon of liquid and stir. Keep the heat low enough so that the liquid does not immediately evaporate when it hits the hot pan. Stir the onions and as the liquid cooks down, add another spoonful. Cook as slowly as possible, constantly stirring and adding liquid until the onions turn limp, golden and fragrant, 15 to 25 minutes. As the onions cook, they release some of their own moisture and you will add liquid a little less frequently.

Sauté-Sweat

This is a variation of the preceding sauté-reduction method. For more sweetness, after adding the initial ¼ to ⅓ cup of water, wine or stock to your onion mixture, cover the skillet. Simmer on very low heat for 20 to 30 minutes. Check the pan from time to time to make sure that the liquid has not evaporated. If the liquid begins to dry up, add more in small amounts to keep the onions sweating (releasing their own liquid), which greatly enhances their flavor. If you like, you can also place the covered pan in an oven preheated to 300 degrees F (no hotter or the liquid may evaporate and scorch the onions) for this final cooking.

Stir-Frying

The technique of stir-frying is the cornerstone of many Asian cuisines, and we cannot do justice to all of its subtleties in a quick paragraph. We do give stir-frying a fat-tracking gold star because it achieves an amazing variety of effects with a minimum of oil. Small pieces of food are tossed continually in very hot oil against the tall, sloping sides of a wok. They don't scorch, but cook quickly each time they hit the hot surface of the pan. In addition to requiring less oil, stir-frying allows you to stretch a smaller portion of meat by slicing it thin and adding it to a mix of vegetables. You can also coat your wok with a nonstick vegetable oil spray to cut down on some of the oil in your recipe. Though woks are ideal, you can stir fry in any skillet with sides high enough to keep the food from spilling out when you toss the ingredients.

FOODS BEST SUITED FOR STIR-FRYING: *meat, poultry, fish, vegetables.*

Deep-Fat Frying

Though it is usually discouraged on low-fat diets, frying foods in several inches of oil, when done properly, can remain part of a Fat Tracker's cooking repertoire. Use monounsaturated oils only and base your decision to deep-fry foods on how much total fat you want to add to your meal.

- Use healthy oils (not animal fats), such as peanut, canola, olive.
- The temperature of the oil is critical. If it is too low, food will absorb more oil, take longer to cook and have a soggy rather than crisp texture. Use a cooking thermometer and preheat the oil to 370 to 375 degrees F; it will drop to the actual cooking temperature (approximately 350 degrees F) when you add the food.
- Cut pieces no larger than two inches or they will take too long to cook and absorb more oil.
- Timing will depend on the type of food your are cooking. Fish, for example, will cook faster than potatoes. Test the food frequently. Many foods will drop to the bottom of the pot and when they are almost done, pop to the surface.
- Do not coat the food with egg batters, which add cholesterol and also act as sponges to soak up fat. Use flour and water, or flour and beer mixtures instead. Or, use bread or cracker coatings rather than whole egg batters; use beaten egg whites or liquid egg substitute in place of whole eggs in the batter. Batters that are too rich will absorb too much oil and taste greasy and/or disintegrate in the oil.
- Dry food thoroughly and have it at room temperature before deep-frying. This will prevent the oil from bubbling up precipitously and overflowing the pan when you add it (causing a fire) and also will prevent the temperature from dropping too low.
- Deep-frying is safe when you're careful. But keep a lid and salt close by to douse a fire, and follow these safety rules: Never pour water on burning oil or it will spatter and explode. Always move the pot slowly to prevent oil from sloshing over the sides. Stir or turn foods with tongs or slotted spoon; do not agitate them by shaking the pan. Use a deep frying basket to hold food so you can lift it all at once as soon as it is done.
- Have many sheets of paper towels ready and drain the food immediately. Place just a few pieces on several thicknesses of paper, otherwise the paper will become saturated and the fat will remain on the food. Cool the food slightly before salting and enjoy.

FOODS BEST SUITED FOR DEEP-FRYING: *root vegetables such as yams and parsnips, potatoes, breaded fish, shellfish, poultry and vegetables.*

Stewing and Braising

Stewing and braising are moist-heat cooking methods that challenge most cooks to define their differences. Both methods are ideal for tougher cuts; for the Fat Tracker that translates into lean meat. True braises call for large cuts (whole roasts, for example, which might comprise the major part of a meal), use less water and are tightly covered while cooking. Stews employ bite-sized pieces (a better choice for stretching meat as a 2 + 2 entrée), use a larger amount of liquid and are cooked uncovered. A good stew eases the pinch on the budget and stretches a portion of meat to feed several people. But best of all, stewing allows the creative cook to devise imaginative combinations of meat, poultry, fish, wines, herbs and vegetables. Moroccan Beef with Couscous (page 528–29) and Island Stew with Pork (page 534–35) exemplify this principle most delectably.

In a stew, leaner but tougher cuts of meat are first browned, then simmered in hot, flavorful liquids until they are tender. As the liquid evaporates, the flavors imparted from the meat concentrate into a mouthwatering, low-fat sauce. Fat may rise to the surface, which you can then skim away. Reserve choice cuts of meat for grilling or broiling; they will become stringy in the extended cooking time necessary to marry the diverse flavors of a stew. Browning the meat or chicken first as we have described above is essential to give the stew a full-bodied flavor; if you have a favorite recipe that calls for an initial cooking in bacon or pork fat, use Canadian bacon or olive oil instead. Add beef stock as part of the liquid to enrich the meaty flavor, if you like. Limit the meat in the recipe to four uncooked ounces per serving, and if this reduces the quantity of the dish significantly, double the vegetables or serve the stew with couscous, rice or other grains.

Though we don't recommend braising red meat, such as pot roast, because the meat reabsorbs the fat that is released into the cooking liquid, you can use a braising technique for lean chicken breasts, fish and vegetables such as leeks. Brown the foods first in a small amount of oil, add flavored stocks, juices and other seasonings, cover them with a piece of aluminum foil or oven parchment paper, pressing it around the food, then cover the pot. Place in a preheated 400 degrees F oven or cook over low-medium heat on top of the stove. The food absorbs the seasoned liquid for a tender, delicious effect. Double-covering the food intensifies the heat around the food and allows tender foods to cook quickly and produce a true braise. Food merely covered allows too much moisture to circulate, resulting in steamed or boiled food that can produce off tastes.

FOODS BEST SUITED FOR STEWING AND BRAISING: *meat, poultry, fish, vegetables.*

The 25 Gram Plan's Fat-Tracking Recipe Aids

The recipes that follow offer a wide range of options for meal planning. The Stanford 25 Gram Plan's recipe fat-tracking aids will help you meet your own goals, whether you need to follow an extremely restricted-fat diet or can include up to the maximum limit of 25 grams in your food.

Fat-Tracking Nutritional Calculations

Found at the end of each recipe, these calculations make gram counting at mealtime easy. When you are planning a menu, flip to the recipes that follow. If a maximum of 8 grams of saturated fat is your goal for dinner, for example, choose an entrée that appeals to you, such as Spaghetti with Chicken, Garlic and Salsa (page 465), a very low 2 grams of saturated fat, 74 milligrams of cholesterol and 12 grams of total fat. Simply scan through the recipes for other dishes on which to spend your remaining 6 grams of saturated fat. Look first for dishes that appeal to your taste buds, then select the ones that will safely balance out the saturated fat in your meal.

If 5 or even 8 grams of saturated fat sounds like a meager portion around which to plan a meal, here are some delicious possibilities. A green salad with oil and vinegar dressing and a sprinkling of Parmesan cheese will add 2 grams of saturated fat to the meal. Warmed French bread dipped into the pasta sauce contributes no extra saturated fat. You can grill a selection of baby potatoes and seasonal vegetables, brushed lightly with a fruity olive oil and balsamic vinegar, for an additional gram. If you started with a budget of 8 grams, you still have 2 or 3 grams of saturated fat left to spend. If you feel like a rich, chocolatey finale, consider Walnut Brownies (page 539) and Mocha Torte (page 542–43), each of which will keep you within your 8-gram limit for the meal.

On the other hand, if you don't have a sweet tooth, start the meal with a cream soup, such as Curried Broccoli Soup (page 372–73), and use some of the remaining grams of fat to add a spoonful of half-and-half for extra richness, or crumble some goat cheese over your grilled vegetables. You may even decide that the menu is filling enough with an appetizer or dessert and choose to eat less than 8 grams of saturated fat for the meal. Any of these options will keep you with your day's limit of fat: It's up to you to decide—with the help of the fat-tracking nutritional calculations. Gram counting to control fat is the wave of the future, and The Stanford 25 Gram Plan covers all the bases to help you remain at the forefront of this important new direction in disease prevention and health promotion.

The Fat-Tracking Tip

Located at the end of many of the recipes is an optional reduction in fat or cholesterol. We have developed these recipes using the least amount of saturated fat needed to deliver the best flavor. The fat-tracking tip suggests ways to remove some additional fat, if necessary. While the optional fat reduction may slightly alter the flavor, texture or moistness, we have not recommended a change to the standard recipe that would result in an inedible dish. Use these suggestions routinely if your physician has recommended that you make significant reductions in your intake of saturated fat and cholesterol; or use them occasionally when you need to shave some fat from your menu to stay under your fat target. You can also use them when you want to make a slight fat reduction in one recipe to accommodate another higher-fat item in your menu.

Guidelines for Nutritional Calculations

Since many of these recipes contain sauces or marinades, it is helpful that you understand the guidelines we followed for calculating the fat and sodium in the ingredients. The total amount of fatty and salty ingredients in a given recipe may be high, but we have estimated the amount of sauce or marinade that would actually be eaten. Yakitori Marinade, for example, contains a great deal of sodium from the soy sauce, but most of it remains in the bowl after marinating and cooking the chicken. In these instances we have attempted to estimate realistic portion sizes. However, you may brush a little more or a little less of a particular marinade, dressing or sauce on your entrée than we calculated, and so there may be some small variation between the numbers we list for a serving size and the actual amount you consume. When serving instructions call for passing an item separately, we specify the serving size of the passed ingredient as follows: Per serving: (Includes 1 tablespoon sauce).

Remember you are tailoring The Stanford 25 Gram Plan to suit your needs and tastes. Where we specify serving sizes—1 tablespoon of Cilantro Pesto, for example—we are not limiting you to that amount. The nutritional information is designed to help you determine the effect on your meals of larger or smaller servings.

Grams of Fat in Cooking Oils, Fats and Dairy Products

At the end of this chapter, an invaluable table will help you monitor fat in several ways. First, you can scan favorite recipes that do not list nutritional calculations to get an idea of the fat content per serving. Look for the ingredients in your dish that contain the most fat—dairy products, fats and oils—find the items and quantity on the Table of Cooking Oils, Fats and Dairy Products and tally the fat in those items. Divide the total by the number of servings and you will have a rough estimate of where the recipe fits into your 25-gram plan. You can also use the chart to see how much fat you will add or subtract from a dish if you make adjustments in your recipes, for example, by switching from whole-milk dairy products to low-fat or nonfat versions, or using heavy cream instead of half-and-half.

When You Want to Increase the Fat in These Recipes

By using as little animal fat as possible in these recipes, we are giving you two options. You have a framework of low-fat meals around which you can add other higher-fat items, such as a midafternoon cookie from your favorite bakery or a second helping of an entrée. On the other hand, if you have had a fat-free breakfast and low-fat lunch, you can boost the fat in our recipes if you wish, by adding some extra olive oil, a second helping of meat or chicken, a little cream instead of low-fat milk or a spoonful of butter to a sauce. Remember, as long as you don't exceed your personal target, you can spend your 25 grams any way you like, even by adding some more fat to our recipes.

Where Do Rules About Percent of Fat fit into the 25 Gram Plan?

The Stanford 25 Gram Plan is based on the National Cholesterol Education Program's guideline to restrict saturated fat to 10 percent of calories and to restrict all fat (saturated and unsaturated) to 30 percent of calories. Our cap of 75 grams of all fat equals 30 percent of 2,300 calories, a typical daily intake. The Stanford gram-based plan means you don't have worry about calculating percentages, a formula that has confused every lay person we have interviewed. Still, many people misunderstand the emphasis on the 30 percent rule, assuming it means they have to limit every item and every meal to the 30-percent fat test. The recommendation to eat no more than 30 percent of calories as fat, whether it is healthy or unhealthy fat, refers to a *daily total*. It is almost impossible to restrict all food items or individual meal totals to a 30 percent fat limit. However, when you add up all the foods you eat during a day, you want your average percent of all fat, good and bad, to be no higher than 10 percent saturated fat and 30 percent for all fats, saturated and unsaturated combined.

If you eat very low-calorie meals and need to eat fewer than 25 grams of saturated fat to stay within the 10 percent/30 percent guideline, refer to the gram/percent of calories conversion table on page 56 to find your target number of fat grams. You can also refer to that section any time you want to review the formula for computing the percent of fat-calories you eat during the day.

❧ **Remember that the 25 Gram Plan limits the upper range of fat in your diet. You are not locked into 25 grams, however. You can eat as *little* saturated fat as you wish.**

This chart will help you estimate the fat and calories you use in your personal collection of recipes. To get a sense of how much fat you add with each portion size of commonly used cooking oils, fat and whole or low-fat dairy products, add up the quantities for a total recipe and divide by the number of servings. Note that the top number is the total fat and the bottom number is saturated fat. For example, if you add ¼ cup of butter to a recipe for four people, you increase the total fat by 46 grams (11.5 grams per serving) and the saturated fat by 28 grams (7 grams per serving).

TABLE OF COOKING OILS, FATS AND DAIRY PRODUCTS

Ingredient	Tsp.	Tbsp.	⅛ Cup	¼ Cup	⅓ Cup	½ Cup	⅔ Cup	¾ Cup	1 Cup
Total Fat / Saturated Fat									
Olive Oil	4.5	13.5	27.0	54.0	72.0	108.0	144.0	162.0	216.0
	0.6	1.8	3.6	7.2	9.6	14.4	19.2	21.6	28.8
Canola Oil	4.7	14.0	27.0	55.0	73.0	109.0	145.0	164.0	218.0
	0.3	1.0	1.9	3.9	5.2	7.8	10.3	11.6	15.5
Corn Oil	4.5	13.6	27.0	55.0	73.0	109.0	145.0	164.0	218.0
	0.6	1.7	3.5	6.9	9.2	13.9	18.5	20.8	27.7
Peanut Oil	4.5	13.5	27.0	54.0	72.0	108.0	135.0	162.0	216.0
	0.8	2.3	4.6	9.2	12.3	18.4	23.0	27.6	36.8
Sesame Oil	4.5	13.6	27.2	54.4	73.0	109.0	136.0	163.0	218.0
	0.6	1.9	3.8	7.6	10.1	15.2	19.0	22.8	30.4
Safflower Oil	4.5	13.6	27.0	55.0	73.0	108.0	145.0	164.0	218.0
	0.4	1.28	2.6	5.1	6.8	10.0	15.4	15.4	20.5
Butter	3.8	11.4	22.8	46.0	61.0	91.2	122.0	137.0	182.4
	2.4	7.1	14.0	28.0	38.0	56.5	75.4	84.8	113.1
Margarine	3.8	11.3	22.8	46.0	61.0	91.2	122.0	137.0	182.4
	0.7	2.2	4.2	8.4	11.2	16.8	22.4	25.2	33.6
Mayonnaise	4.0	12.0	24.0	48.0	64.0	96.0	128.0	144.0	192.0
	0.7	2.0	4.0	8.0	11.0	16.0	21.3	24.0	32.0
Whole Milk	0.2	0.5	1.0	2.0	2.7	4.0	5.4	6.1	8.1
	0.1	0.3	0.6	1.3	1.7	2.6	3.4	3.8	5.1
Low-Fat Milk	0.1	0.3	0.6	1.2	1.6	2.4	3.1	3.5	4.7
	0.06	0.2	0.4	0.7	1.0	1.5	1.9	2.2	2.9
1% Milk	0.06	0.2	0.3	0.7	0.9	1.3	1.7	2.0	2.6
	0.03	0.1	0.2	0.4	0.5	0.8	1.1	1.2	1.6
Yogurt	0.3	0.9	1.8	3.7	5.0	7.4	7.3	11.0	14.7
	0.2	0.6	1.2	2.4	3.2	4.8	6.3	7.1	9.5
Low-Fat Yogurt	0.13	0.4	0.9	1.9	2.5	3.7	4.9	5.6	7.4
	0.1	0.3	0.5	1.2	1.6	2.4	3.1	3.5	4.7
Sour Cream	1.0	3.0	6.0	12.0	16.0	24.0	32.0	36.0	48.0
	0.6	1.9	3.8	7.5	10.0	15.0	20.0	22.5	30.0
Light Sour Cream	0.23	0.7	1.4	2.8	3.7	5.6	7.0	8.4	11.2
	0.17	0.5	1.0	2.0	2.67	4.0	5.0	6.0	8.0
*Whipping Cream	1.8	5.5	11.0	22.0	29.4	44.0	58.7	66.1	88.1
	1.1	3.4	6.9	13.7	18.3	27.4	36.5	41.1	54.8
*Light Cream	1.5	4.6	9.2	18.5	24.6	37.0	49.0	55.4	73.9
	1.0	2.9	5.8	11.6	15.4	23.1	30.8	34.7	46.2

* Unwhipped

Ingredient	Total Fat/ Saturated Fat								
	Tsp.	Tbsp.	⅛ Cup	¼ Cup	⅓ Cup	½ Cup	⅔ Cup	¾ Cup	1 Cup
½ and ½	0.6	1.7	3.5	7.0	9.3	14.0	18.5	20.9	27.8
	0.4	1.1	2.2	4.3	5.8	8.7	11.5	13.0	17.3
Cream	1.7	5.0	10.0	20.0	27.0	40.5	54.0	60.8	81.0
Cheese	1.0	3.0	6.1	12.2	16.2	24.3	32.4	36.5	48.6
Light Cream	0.8	2.3	4.7	9.4	12.5	18.8	23.5	28.2	37.6
Cheese	0.5	1.4	2.8	5.6	7.5	11.2	14.0	16.8	22.4
Whole-Milk	0.7	2.0	4.0	8.0	10.7	16.1	20.0	24.0	32.2
Ricotta	0.4	1.3	2.6	5.1	6.9	10.3	13.0	15.6	20.6
Skim-Milk	0.4	1.2	2.4	4.9	6.5	9.8	12.2	14.7	19.5
Ricotta	0.2	0.8	1.5	3.0	4.0	6.1	7.6	9.2	12.2
Whole-Milk Cottage	0.4	1.3	2.6	5.2	6.9	10.4	13.9	15.6	20.8
Cheese	0.3	0.8	1.6	3.2	4.3	6.4	8.5	9.6	12.8
Low-Fat Cottage	0.09	0.3	0.5	1.1	1.4	2.2	2.8	3.4	4.4
Cheese(2%)	0.06	0.2	0.3	0.7	1.0	1.4	1.8	2.2	2.8
Low-Fat Cottage	0.05	0.1	0.3	0.6	0.7	1.1	1.4	1.7	2.3
Cheese(1%)	0.03	0.09	0.2	0.4	0.5	0.7	1.0	1.1	1.5
Grated Parmesan	0.5	1.5	3.0	6.0	8.0	12.0	15.0	18.0	24.0
Cheese	0.3	1.0	2.0	4.0	5.3	8.0	10.0	12.0	16.0

CHAPTER 27

Kitchen Basics

GOOD FOOD IS NOT A HIT OR MISS PROPOSITION; *even the simplest dish begins with a reliable foundation. For the Fat Tracker that means stocks, sauces and flavoring agents that do not depend on large quantities of fat and sodium. We have gathered together in this opening chapter certain basic preparations that you will use over and over as you prepare our recipes. Additionally, as you adapt your own favorites to meet heart-healthy standards, you will discover that you can substitute our fat-free roasted peppers, tomatoes and onions whenever heavily oiled sautéed versions appear in a recipe; keep our fat-free and low-sodium stocks on hand in your freezer to add gusto to any soup made with fresh ingredients; and use our yogurt-based creams in place of rich sauces laced with saturated fat. Use Cilantro Pesto and Cilantro Cream as examples of how to make other herb-infused and vegetable-based sauces. Subtract saturated fat from a favorite recipe at every opportunity and use instead our flavored oils and vinegars to perk up the flavor in an effortless stroke. Make these basics the foundation of all your cooking. But use them as well as kindling for your own imagination as you declare your kitchen the proving ground for delicious, heart-healthy cooking.*

The Big Three: Peppers, Tomatoes and the Onion Family

This flavorful triumvirate (which includes leeks, shallots and garlic) can appear mellow and full bodied in Mediterranean dishes, zesty and keenly spiked with pepper in Mexican and Island food or crisp and quick-cooked in Asian recipes. Healthful as well as versatile, these three vegetable groups are the jumping off point in every cuisine for countless soups, sauces and stir-fries. We begin by showing you how to reap the fullest flavor from this essential kitchen triad using little or no fat.

Preparing Peppers: Sweet and Hot

As a rich source of vitamins, fiber and flavor, we use fresh sweet bell peppers and hot chili peppers at every opportunity. Note that commercially canned and bottled sweet and hot peppers can have up to 700 milligrams of sodium added — another good reason for using fresh produce as often as possible.

PEELING AND SEEDING FRESH PEPPERS For salads, stir-fries and nibbling, you can leave the skin on fresh peppers for additional fiber. Slice them in half and scrape out the seeds with a spoon and trim away the white ribs that run the length of the pepper. Use a vegetable peeler if you do want to peel peppers before cooking. Use the following methods for preparing peppers for purées and other uses. Handle cooked peppers carefully or cool before peeling.

ROASTING PEPPERS Roasted red, yellow, green, orange, purple or any other hybrid sweet pepper adds color, sweet flavor and a delicious, smoky quality to foods. Prepare peppers in batches, when the harvest is bountiful and the market price is low, and store them for future use. You can place prepared bell peppers in a tightly sealed jar with just enough olive oil to cover them, adding basil leaves and whole garlic cloves for a rich infusion of flavor if you like. The roasted peppers will keep up to a month in the refrigerator, but when you add them to a dish, be sure to decrease the other oil in your recipe slightly to compensate. You can also cover and refrigerate batches of roasted peppers without oil for several days before use.

To roast, preheat the oven to 425 degrees F. Place whole peppers on a rack or a flat sheet of aluminum foil set on a baking sheet and roast 30 to 40 minutes or until blistered and slightly scorched. Reduce the time if you want crisper peppers. Place the peppers in a bowl and set aside to cool slightly. Pull away and discard the skin. Allow the juices to drain off and scrape away the seeds and any stringy membrane. They are ready to prepare for immediate use or storing covered in the refrigerator. If you find peeling roasted peppers a chore, instead of letting the peppers cool in the open air, cover the bowl, sealing it tightly. Set aside to steam for 4 to 5 minutes, or until cool enough to handle, then slip off the skins and scrape away the seeds and ribs. Be aware however, that the steaming effect from covering the peppers may slightly blunt the desirable smoky flavor. You can also follow these instructions for whole peppers using a grill instead of an oven, grilling them for 8 to 12 minutes depending on size.

MICROWAVING PEPPERS Though you won't get the intense aroma of roast peppers, you can microwave peppers to speed up the softening process for purées and other dishes. Place whole, washed peppers in a microwave-safe dish with a small amount of water, cover tightly and microwave on medium high for 5 to 8 minutes, depending on the size and quantity of the peppers. Allow to stand, covered, for an additional 5 minutes, slip off the skins, halve and scrape away the seeds and ribs.

CHILI PEPPERS We use a variety of hot chili peppers, both fresh and dried, in our recipes. You can add or subtract hot peppers as you desire. Hot peppers mixed with other companionable seasonings can enliven a low-fat dish so that its interest centers on complexity of flavor rather than on fat calories. Island Stew with Pork (page 534–35), a pleasantly spicy mix of pork with vegetables and yams, is a case in point. If you are not used to cooking with chili peppers and other lively condiments, add hot seasonings to your food *en pointe*, as French cooks do. Dip a knife into the spice jar and use whatever clings to the very tip. As your palate becomes accustomed to spicy food, dip deeper.

HANDLING FRESH CHILIES You can peel, seed, roast and purée hot chilies as you do sweet bell peppers, but you must take some fire-fighting precautions. Capsicum, the fire element in chilies, resides in the veins of the peppers and inflames everything it touches. If you can't stand the heat, first get rid of all the seeds (they don't actually produce the heat but do absorb it as they come in contact with the pulp). Capsicum also seeks out papercuts and small nicks in your fingers that you never knew were there. Try rubbing a little vegetable oil on your hands before handling chilies. For more complete protection (if your hands are rough and raw or if your skin is especially sensitive), wear rubber gloves (the thin painting gloves work well) whenever you handle chilies. Remember that your eyes are always sensitive to capsicum, even if your hands are not. The substance stays on your skin for a time even after washing your hands, so be careful not to rub your eyes when you have been handling chilies. Also, if you taste other food as you work with chilies, the food will pick up heat from your fingertips. Barbara Karoff (our chili pepper expert who also contributed her recipe for Seafood Soup-Stew on page 380), tells us that she has suffered burning eyes when she has worked with chilies for an entire day. Though few home cooks spend that much time with fresh chilies, if you do large-scale chili cooking, work in a well-ventilated room.

POWDERED ANCHO CHILI Our recipes do not call for generic chili powder, a musty mix of spices that is merely hot, but without a distinct flavor. We prefer to use our mild homemade powder of dried ancho chilies, or any of the Hungarian varieties of sweet and hot paprikas, or a mix of peppercorns or even exotic varieties such as the pungent, sweet-scented African bird pepper. To make powdered ancho chili, use a dried ancho pepper (a particularly fragrant variety) or other dried hot chili pepper. Preheat the oven to 350 degrees F, place the dried chilies on a baking sheet and roast for 5 to 8 minutes or until the skin becomes brittle. Cool slightly, crack open the chilies and remove and discard the stems and seeds. Grind the outer shell to a fine powder in a blender or with a mortar and pestle, then store in a covered jar. Use whenever chili powder is required.

Preparing Tomatoes: Fresh and Dried

Home gardeners know the treasure of a vine-ripened tomato, but anyone fed only the glassy, dare-you-to-find-a-blemish, ripe-all-year-round, bet-you-can't-tell-them-from-plastic, red globes sold in the supermarket may wonder what's so special about a tomato. We don't have time to wax poetic about the joys of reaching into the garden for a fat beefsteak, of nudging away a ladybug before surrendering to the sweet juicy flesh still scented and warm from the summer sun. But suffice it to say, sometimes, canned is better than fresh, when fresh is darn near tasteless. Many canned tomato products, whole, chopped, tomato sauce and purées, have more flavor than out-of-season fresh fruits (yes, technically, the tomato is a fruit). Buy canned tomatoes without citric acid whenever possible; the flavor is more rounded, less tart. You may prefer to use a blend of fresh and canned tomatoes at times; even adding one or two fresh hothouse tomatoes can cut the acidity of a sauce made with all canned tomatoes.

TO PEEL, SEED AND CHOP TOMATOES In French cooking the term *tomates concassees* simply means "peeled, seeded and chopped." Use this method to prepare just one tomato or several pounds. Store them covered in the refrigerator for up to 24 hours, if necessary. Dice the tomatoes finely for sauces and salad dressings, coarsely when you want to add them to long-cooking recipes.

Plunge one or more whole, washed tomatoes into a pan of rapidly boiling water for 10 to 45 seconds or until the skins just begin to crack. The time will vary with the size and ripeness of the tomato. Turn them with a long handled spoon so they will heat evenly. Remove them as soon as the skin breaks or they will become mushy and overcooked. Immediately immerse them in a bowl of ice cold water for a minute or two until the skin blisters and peels off easily. Remove the stems and slice in half through the middle, not from the top down. Squeeze out the juice and seeds, chop the pulp and the tomatoes are ready for action.

ROASTING TOMATOES Roasting tomatoes is the easiest way to impart an extra dimension of flavor. Remove the stems from fresh tomatoes but do not pierce the skins. Place the tomatoes in a small baking dish or on a piece of aluminum foil under the preheated broiler on the lowest rack, approximately 3 inches from the heat source. Roast them for 10 to 15 minutes or until the skins are scorched and have begun to shrivel. Turn them once or twice. Don't worry if the tomatoes blacken in spots, the flavor will be rich and smoky, rather than burned. Cool slightly and slice in half through the middle; then with a spoon, gently scrape away the seeds and slip off the skins. You can also grill whole tomatoes briefly for the same delicate smoky effect. Add to sauces, dressings or any recipe calling for chopped tomatoes.

SUN-DRIED TOMATOES Recipes in this book that call for sun-dried tomatoes assume you will use dried tomatoes (usually packed in plastic bags or sold in bulk) rather than those bottled in oil. If you do use oil-packed tomatoes, realize that you are adding extra oil to your menu and, if necessary for your personal fat targets, make other adjustments to reduce the oil in your recipes. If desired, soak dried tomatoes in hot water to cover for 10 minutes or until softened, or add a few tablespoons of water, cover and microwave on high for 30 seconds.

Onions, Leeks, Shallots and Garlic
Close cousins in the lily family, onions, leeks, shallots and garlic are used in most savory recipes, typically sautéed in oil. You can eliminate the oil most recipes call for and add a dimension of flavor by roasting them in the oven.

ROASTED ONIONS, LEEKS AND SHALLOTS Slice an onion or leek in half and brush with balsamic vinegar or a few drops of olive oil and place cut side down on a baking sheet; use a whole shallot bulb or individual cloves, peeled or unpeeled. Roast in a preheated 375 degree F oven until soft. Set aside until cool enough to handle, remove and discard the outer layer of skin, slice or dice and use as directed by your recipe.

COOKING GARLIC You can prepare cooked garlic in several ways; each with its own distinctive character. Peel the cloves from a whole bulb and simmer them until tender in a cup of low-fat or nonfat milk and puree the mixture in a blender. Use it to add zest to pureed vegetables or soups. Stick a whole bulb of garlic on the grill along with other foods you are barbecuing. Or—one of the easiest—roast whole bulbs (see below) to serve with grilled foods, roasted meat or poultry or to toss in a salad.

ROASTED GARLIC WITH HERBS Use sprigs of fresh basil, thyme, oregano, marjoram or savory, as you like or omit the herbs altogether. Preheat the oven to 400 degrees F. Slice whole bulbs of garlic in half, brush with balsamic vinegar or a few drops of olive oil and wrap in aluminum foil. Or, separate the cloves and smash them lightly with a mallet just to break the skin. Use a garlic roaster or place the individual garlic cloves on a large piece of aluminum foil and add the herbs if you wish. Seal the ends of the foil to make a tightly wrapped package. You can roast unpeeled individual cloves with the skins broken, but do not put peeled cloves on a baking sheet without a covering of some kind or they will shrivel. Roast the packet in the oven for 30 to 40 minutes or until the garlic is creamy and soft; individual cloves will take less time. Unwrap and cool the garlic just until you can handle it comfortably. Slip off the skins before serving. Add individual cloves to your recipe. Cover and store remaining cloves in the refrigerator for several days, or cover them with a layer of olive oil and they will last up to a month.

Garlic Purée

MAKES APPROXIMATELY 3 TABLESPOONS, SERVING SIZE 1 TABLESPOON

A PURÉE OF ROASTED GARLIC *may be one of your most valued fat-tracking allies. Each bulb of garlic contains dozens of cloves, each of which mellows and sweetens into a creamy purée which bears little resemblance to its raw state. You can further perfume the purée with fresh or dried herbs. Spread the purée on a baguette instead of butter or oil at dinner, coat grilled fish or poultry with it in place of a high-fat sauce, enrich baked potatoes with a spoonful in place of butter and sour cream or swirl it into soups or sauces as a final flourish. Each enrichment adds barely a trace of added oil. You can also stir a tablespoon or so of garlic purée into a roasted puréed pepper, eggplant or tomato to use as a spread or topping and smooth any of them with a little olive oil, if you like. You can roast the garlic with the herbs for subtle flavor or add them after for more contrast between the mellowed garlic and fresh herbal taste.*

> 4 whole bulbs garlic
> Olive oil
> Sprigs of fresh basil, thyme, oregano, marjoram or savory, optional

1. Preheat the oven to 400 degrees F. Cut the bulbs of garlic in half crosswise and brush the cut sides with a few drops of olive oil. Place the fresh herbs on the garlic if desired, fit the two halves together and place the bulb on a large piece of aluminum foil. Seal the ends of the foil to make a tightly wrapped package.

2. Roast the packets in the oven for 40 to 45 minutes or until the garlic is creamy and soft. Unwrap and cool the garlic just until you can handle it comfortably. Over a small bowl, squeeze the halves of garlic as you would a tube of toothpaste, using a spoon to coax out any resistant garlic. If you wish, add the herbs now and with a spoon, mash the garlic until smooth. Use warm or cold. Store in a covered container in the refrigerator for up to a week. You can add more olive oil to the purée and it will last longer, though be sure to calculate the added oil into your fat totals.

❇ PER SERVING *Calories: 97, Cholesterol (mg): 0, Saturated fat (g): Trace, Total fat (g): Trace, Sodium (mg): 11, Total fiber (g): 1*

The Stock Pot

Why go to the trouble of making your own stocks when you can pick up a can or two in the market? Because the canned version is loaded with sodium—unless you buy low-sodium broth, which, depending on the brand, can also be quite pallid. In our book, homemade always tastes better, and at very little expenditure of your time and energy. Freeze the stock in ice cube trays, then pop into a plastic bag to have on hand when you need small amounts to finish a sauce. Or freeze it in larger containers for soup making. Note that the first cardinal rule of stock making is to keep the heat at a simmer so the action of the boiling liquid does not pull the foamy material that rises to the surface back into the stock and make it cloudy. Skim frequently to remove the foam as it accumulates. The second cardinal rule is to defat the stock thoroughly. Defatted chicken stock contains no saturated fat or cholesterol and only a trace of other fats.

Chicken Stock

MAKES APPROXIMATELY 10 CUPS, SERVING SIZE 1 CUP

WHAT WOULD COOKS DO WITHOUT CHICKEN STOCK? *Use this most basic of ingredients as the foundation for soups or in any recipe that calls for chicken stock or broth. If you use reserved chicken bones, instead of a whole chicken, you may oven-roast the bones and vegetables first to intensify the flavor.*

> 1 chicken (2 to 3 pounds) or equivalent chicken parts
>   (bones, neck, etc.)
> 1 medium-size onion, quartered
> 1 whole clove
> 1 small bay leaf
> 1 carrot, chopped
> 1 stalk celery
> 3 to 4 bunches parsley
> 1 tablespoon fresh thyme or 1 teaspoon dried
> 5 to 6 peppercorns
> ¼ teaspoon salt
> Pinch of freshly ground pepper
> 12 cups water

1. Place the chicken in a large stock pot with the remaining ingredients. Bring to a boil and *immediately* reduce the heat.

2. Simmer the stock uncovered for 1 to 1½ hours, skimming the surface as necessary to remove the foam. Taste for seasoning, adding salt and pepper as desired. When the stock has reached the desired strength, cool and strain it. Cover and allow it to stand, preferably overnight in the refrigerator, until the fat congeals or at least rises to the surface.

3. Skim all fat from top of stock and reheat. Strain 2 or 3 times through successively finer sieves or cheesecloth until very clear. Use immediately or reboil every 3 days if you store stock in the refrigerator. Freeze the stock if you have not used it within a week.

❋ PER SERVING *Calories: 9, Cholesterol (mg): 0, Saturated fat (g): 0, Total fat (g): Trace, Sodium (mg): 10, Total fiber (g): 0*

Rich Fish Stock

MAKES APPROXIMATELY 4 CUPS, SERVING SIZE 1 CUP

VARIOUSLY CALLED FISH FUMET, *fish broth or court bouillon, fish stock is easy to make, and a wise sauce maker keeps a batch in the freezer and adds one or two ice cube's worth to enrich fish sauces such as the Red Pepper Sauce for Fish (page 463). Fish stock is invaluable as a poaching liquid. Save and freeze fish trimmings such as shrimp peels, fish heads, tails or bones and toss them into the stock to make it richer and more full bodied. You can use this stock to make a quick soup by adding diced red potatoes, carrots, a leek and a pound or so of your favorite firm-fleshed fish or shellfish. Always freeze any leftover stock to add to a future batch. Note that the wine adds calories, but if the stock is used only as a poaching liquid they do not contribute significantly to the total for your dish.*

> 4 cups water or water mixed with any leftover poaching liquid
>   to make 4 cups
> 1 cup white wine
> 3 green onions or 1 leek or 2 shallots, coarsely chopped
> 12 peppercorns
> 2 to 3 whole cloves, optional
> ½ bay leaf
> Handful of parsley leaves
> 1 tablespoon fresh herbs or 1 teaspoon dried (such as thyme,
>   oregano, marjoram, chervil or dill)
> 1 pound fish bones
> Salt and freshly ground pepper

1. Place all the ingredients in a large nonreactive saucepan and bring to a boil. Immediately reduce the heat and skim any foam that accumulates on the surface. Simmer uncovered for at least 20 to 30 minutes.

2. Strain thoroughly. If you don't plan to use the stock immediately, store it covered in the refrigerator for 1 to 2 days or freeze for future use.

✽ PER SERVING *Calories: 47, Cholesterol (mg): 0, Saturated fat (g): 0, Total fat (g): Trace, Sodium (mg): 9, Total fiber (g): 0*

Beef or Veal Stock

MAKES APPROXIMATELY 8 CUPS, SERVING SIZE 1 CUP

KEEP THIS FULL-BODIED, CLASSIC STOCK ON HAND *for soups and sauces. Add an ice-cube's worth to stir-fry dishes or sautéed vegetables to deepen their flavor. If you follow the instructions to skim all the fat from the surface of the cooked, cooled stock, and strain it several times, the stock will be essentially fat free.*

1 veal knuckle (use for both beef and veal stock)
10 pounds beef or veal bones
2 carrots, chopped
5 stalks celery, chopped
3 onions, peeled and coarsely chopped
2 leeks (white part only), coarsely chopped
3 to 4 quarts cold water
2 bay leaves
5 or 6 black peppercorns or 1/4 teaspoon freshly ground black pepper
Large bunch of fresh parsley
Large sprig of fresh thyme or 1 teaspoon dried
2 egg whites and shells, optional

1. Preheat the oven to 350 degrees F. Place the bones and vegetables in a roasting pan and roast uncovered for 1 hour.

2. Add 4 cups of the cold water and stir to loosen the meat particles. Transfer the entire mixture to a very large stockpot. Scrape every shred of meat and every last drop of the cooking juices into the stockpot. Add the remaining ingredients except the salt and the optional egg whites and shells. Bring to a boil, then reduce the heat immediately.

3. As the foam accumulates, skim as much as possible from the surface of the stock. Simmer at a slow bubble. Partially cover the pot with a lid or piece of aluminum foil. Do not completely cover it or the liquid won't evaporate and concentrate the flavors, and you will have boiled soup bones, not stock. Simmer for 6 to 7 hours, checking occasionally to make sure the surface bubbles very gently. If it cooks too quickly, the stock can't achieve the concentration that occurs with long, slow cooking and the stock will be weak.

4. Add a pinch of salt during the last half hour of cooking. Cool and strain into a very large bowl or another large saucepan. Discard everything but the liquid. Refrigerate overnight or long enough to allow the fat to congeal. Skim off and discard the fat from the jelled stock and reheat the stock. For crystal clear stock, add 2 egg whites and their shells (no yolks) and boil rapidly for 10 minutes. The whites draw out the impurities that can cloud the stock. Line a colander with

cheesecloth or a coffee filter and strain the stock several times until it is clear. Use immediately or cover and store it in the refrigerator. Reboil stock every 3 days. If you have not used it within a week, freeze in covered containers.

❋ PER SERVING *Calories: 9, Cholesterol (mg): 0, Saturated fat (g): 0, Total fat (g): Trace, Sodium (mg): 10, Total fiber (g): 0*

Vegetable Stock

MAKES APPROXIMATELY 8 CUPS, SERVING SIZE 1 CUP

TO ENRICH FUTURE STOCKS, *reserve a cup of the finished stock, freeze it, then add it, thawed or unthawed, to your next batch.*

> 1 teaspoon olive oil
> 2 onions, coarsely chopped
> 1 leek (white part only), cut into 2-inch lengths
> 1 to 2 garlic cloves, chopped
> 1 pound carrots, cut into 2-inch lengths
> 2 small stalks celery, cut into 2-inch lengths
> 1 red or green bell pepper, seeded and chopped
> 2 tomatoes, stems removed
> ½ cup red or white wine
> 10 cups cold water
> Pinch of thyme or *herbes de Provence*
> ¼ bay leaf
> Salt and freshly ground pepper

1. Preheat the oven to 350 degrees F. Brush a nonreactive roasting pan with the olive oil and add all the vegetables. Roast for 45 minutes, turning them every 15 minutes. Add a tablespoon or two of water if the vegetables appear to scorch. Remove the tomatoes and bell pepper.

2. Add the wine to the pan and stir over high heat until the liquid has reduced to about 2 or 3 tablespoons. Transfer everything into a stockpot and add the water, herbs and ½ teaspoon of salt. Bring to a rolling boil. Reduce the heat and simmer for 1 hour. Taste and add a bit more salt if necessary and a pinch of pepper. Continue to cook for 45 minutes or until the flavor is rich and full bodied.

3. Remove from the heat and when cool, cover and refrigerate for at least 1 hour, or overnight. Skim any fat from the surface, strain and taste for seasoning. Use immediately or store in the refrigerator. Cover and reboil every 3 days. If you have not used it within a week, freeze in covered containers.

❋ PER SERVING *Calories: 15, Cholesterol (mg): 0, Saturated fat (g): 0, Total fat (g): 1, Sodium (mg): 1, Total fiber (g): 0*

Creams and Sauces

You will find many versatile sauces throughout the cookbook. However, we have highlighted the following for you to pair with other favorite recipes or use as the basis for creating some of your own dishes. While they are lean from the outset, if necessary, you can use the following fat-tracking tip for any pesto, cream or similar sauce that contains oil.

In a bowl, stir the finished pesto or sauce into an equal amount of nonfat plain yogurt to reduce the total fat per serving. You can further reduce the fat per serving by reducing some of the oil in the master recipe, if homemade, or adding even more yogurt to a commercial sauce. Note that while diluting pesto with large amounts of nonfat or low-fat yogurt will produce a nicely flavored sauce for vegetables, dips, fish and poultry, it may not contain enough oil to coat pasta without the noodles becoming gummy. Test a small amount of pasta with a yogurt pesto for consistency and texture; you may need to coat the pasta with a small amount of oil before adding the rest of the pesto.

Drained Yogurt

MAKES 2 CUPS, SERVING SIZE ¼ CUP

A MIDDLE EASTERN TECHNIQUE FOR DRAINING YOGURT *and turning it into a type of fresh cheese is variously referred to as* lub'n, lubn, luben, labani, *yogurt cheese, fresh cheese or simply—by those who call a thing what it is— Drained Yogurt. This soft, tangy, spreadable cream is not as silky in texture as sour cream, but it's smoother than cottage cheese and quite delicious in its own right. Salt it, add garlic, onion and/or herbs, or sweeten it with some sugar or honey. Use plain on toast with unsweetened preserves, marmalade or fresh fruit. Replace sour cream with Drained Yogurt in such recipes as toppings for bean dishes, lentils, soups and vegetable casseroles. You can also use it in many of our sauce or dip recipes that call for plain yogurt. Make it in large or small quantities and store, covered, in the refrigerator. When making Drained Yogurt, you end up with about half the amount you started with. As it drains, the whey (liquid) separates from the curd, which will remain in the strainer. You will vary the amount of time you allow it to drain depending on the yogurt's final use. It will release sufficient moisture in an hour or two for most of our yogurt cream recipes. For a consistency almost like cream cheese, allow it to drain for at least 8 and up to 24 hours. Read the ingredients when you buy yogurt for this purpose: Do not use yogurts with gelatin, for they will not separate and clot properly. Drained Yogurt will last as long as the date on the yogurt carton.*

4 cups low-fat or nonfat plain yogurt, less if desired

1. Place a coffee filter in its cone and set it over a large measuring cup or bowl. (This is the easiest draining device, but you can put the yogurt in a cheese-cloth-lined strainer or a fine-meshed plastic strainer.) Make sure the sides of the measuring cup or bowl are high enough so that the cheese does not sit in the liquid as it accumulates.

2. Place the yogurt in the filter and refrigerate 2 to 4 hours. As noted above, the longer the yogurt drains, the thicker it will get, though much of the liquid will have drained off during the first hour if you want a thinner consistency. When it has reached whatever consistency you desire, discard the liquid. It requires absolutely no other attention. Place the Drained Yogurt in a covered container and keep refrigerated between uses. Drained Yogurt will last as long as the date on the yogurt carton.

❀ PER SERVING *Calories: 60, Cholesterol (mg): 2, Saturated fat (g): 0, Total fat (g): 0, Sodium (mg): 80, Total fiber (g): 0*

Spiced Yogurt
MAKES 1 CUP, SERVING SIZE 1 TABLESPOON

YOU CAN USE NONFAT PLAIN YOGURT *but Yogurt Cream makes this heavenly sauce incredibly smooth. We use this as the base for several quick and sensational dips, sauces and soups, such as Poached Salmon with Spiced Melon Sauce (page 490–91) or Oven-Fried Yams with Spiced Yogurt (page 414). Spiced Yogurt is excellent on steamed new potatoes, carrots, grilled poultry and fish and as a dip for crisp vegetables and fruit, especially summer fruit such as nectarines and peaches.*

> 1 cup Yogurt Cream (following) or nonfat plain yogurt
> ½ teaspoon ground cumin
> 1 teaspoon curry powder
> Scant ½ teaspoon salt
> Generous pinch of cayenne

Stir the Yogurt Cream in a small bowl. Add the remaining ingredients and blend thoroughly. Taste for seasoning, adding more curry or cayenne to suit your taste. Cover and chill until serving time.

❀ PER SERVING *Calories: 24, Cholesterol (mg): Trace, Saturated fat (g): Trace, Total fat (g): 2, Sodium (mg): 79, Total fiber (g): Trace*

Yogurt Cream

MAKES APPROXIMATELY 1 CUP, SERVING SIZE 1 TABLESPOON

NONFAT YOGURT MAY BE VERY GOOD FOR YOUR HEART *and its calcium strengthens your bones, but for many recipes it is too thin-tasting and tart to serve as a truly satisfying substitute for cream or sour cream. On the other hand, whole-milk yogurt just has too much saturated-fat to use on a daily basis. To come up with an acceptable alternative, we employed a little kitchen chemistry to create a lovely, creamy mixture that you can keep on hand to stir into puréed vegetables, drizzle over grilled fish, mound on bean or lentil salads or just eat out of the container for a quick, creamy snack. We start with healthful nonfat plain yogurt. The addition of nonfat milk sweetens it, a little monounsaturated oil smoothes the texture and gives it an appealing sheen, a little vinegar flavors and emulsifies it, and a pinch of salt smoothes the tartness—all of which transforms ordinary yogurt into a very creamy sauce. Yes, Yogurt Cream has more total fat than undoctored nonfat yogurt, but it is still very low in saturated fat compared to regular creams because we use healthy olive oil or canola oil. We use our Vanilla Oil and our Apple Cinnamon Vinegar in the basic recipe, you can experiment with your own stock of flavored vinegars and oils. Unflavored oils do not add much interest, but you could use garlic-flavored oil instead of Vanilla Oil and any fruit-flavored vinegar, though we think our mix produces the superior cream. Use Yogurt Cream in place of mayonnaise to strip your favorite creamy salad dressing recipes of a great deal of fat and cholesterol, or use it as a sandwich spread.*

> 1 cup Drained Yogurt (page 290–91), made with nonfat plain yogurt
>   and drained for only 1 hour
> ¼ cup nonfat milk
> 2 tablespoons Vanilla Oil (page 298)
> 2 teaspoons Apple Vanilla Cinnamon Vinegar (page 298)
> Pinch of salt

1. In a small bowl, stir the yogurt and milk together and blend until smooth. Stir in the oil. You may find a few small lumps or curds forming, but they will smooth out as you proceed. Next, add the vinegar and stir until the mixture thickens slightly; make sure the cream is well blended at this point. Smooth out any small lumps by pressing them against the side of the bowl with the back of your spoon. Taste and add salt in very small increments just until the flavors are harmoniously blended.

2. Cover and refrigerate the cream until you need it. It will remain fresh up to the date on the yogurt carton.

❋ PER SERVING *Calories: 24, Cholesterol (mg): Trace, Saturated fat (g): Trace, Total fat (g): 2, Sodium (mg): 12, Total fiber (g): Trace*

Cilantro Pesto

MAKES APPROXIMATELY ½ CUP, SERVING SIZE 1 TABLESPOON

AS A FLOURISH FOR HUMBLE BEAN DISHES, *poached or grilled fish, steamed or grilled vegetables, and baked potatoes, this pesto has no peer. Prepare it at least 30 minutes before serving to let the flavors concentrate. We use mild canola oil, but you can substitute a fruity extra-virgin olive oil if you prefer.*

1 cup fresh cilantro leaves, include soft part of stems
3 fresh basil leaves
1/4 teaspoon ground cumin, optional
2 large garlic cloves
1/2 cup canola oil
Salt and freshly ground pepper

1. Place the cilantro leaves, basil leaves and cumin in a blender or food processor. With the machine running, drop in the garlic and when you have a coarse purée, dribble in the oil.

2. Add salt and pepper to your taste, but don't oversalt. Use immediately or cover and refrigerate until serving time. This will last several days.

❋ PER SERVING *Calories: 124, Cholesterol (mg): 0, Saturated fat (g): 1, Total fat (g): 14, Sodium (mg): 2, Total fiber (g): 0*

Cilantro Cream

MAKES APPROXIMATELY 1½ CUPS, SERVING SIZE 1 TABLESPOON

ONE OF OUR MOST POPULAR CREAMS. *You can use it as a dip and spoon it on Black Bean Chili (page 428–29), but don't stop there. The freshness of this sauce complements scallops and salmon, and even a simple poached fillet of sole will come to life if you nap it with this cream. You can make this in larger or smaller quantities and store it covered in the refrigerator up to the expiration date on the yogurt. For a more delicate flavor, add just 1 cup of cilantro leaves; increase to 1½ cups for a pronounced cilantro taste.*

> 1 to 1½ cups fresh cilantro leaves, including soft part of stems
> 3 fresh basil leaves
> ½ teaspoon ground cumin
> 2 large garlic cloves
> ½ cup canola oil
> 1 cup nonfat plain yogurt
> Salt and freshly ground pepper
> Grated lime zest, optional

1. Place the cilantro leaves, basil leaves and cumin in a blender or food processor. With the machine running add the garlic and then dribble in the oil until you have a smooth purée.

2. Fold in the yogurt and season to your taste with salt and pepper. Grate a few shreds of lime zest into the cream if desired, taste and chill thoroughly before serving.

FAT TRACKING TIP: Reduce the oil to ¼ cup and add ¼ cup nonfat sour cream.

❀ PER SERVING *Calories: 47, Cholesterol (mg): Trace, Saturated fat (g): Trace, Total fat (g): 5, Sodium (mg): 8, Total fiber (g): 0*

Apple Jelly with Garlic

MAKES 1 CUP, SERVING SIZE 1 TABLESPOON

THE GARLIC GIVES THIS VERSATILE SPREAD A SURPRISING KICK, *which is excellent with grilled slivers of pork tenderloin or chicken breast. Or, for a rich and complex spread far different from the usual jams and preserves served with brunch menus, use it as a spread for muffins or Curried Corn Fingers (page 333). In place of mayonnaise, spread our apple jelly on one side of a French roll and top with thin slices of cold turkey breast and leftover grilled onions for a super open sandwich.*

> 1 cup apple butter or apple jelly
> 3 garlic cloves, minced
> ½ cup minced fresh parsley

Combine all the ingredients in a saucepan and bring to a boil. Reduce the heat immediately and simmer about 10 minutes or until the garlic has softened and mellowed. Stir frequently to make sure it doesn't scorch. Serve hot or chilled. This will keep, covered, in the refrigerator for at least a week.

❊ PER SERVING *Calories: 39, Cholesterol (mg): 0, Saturated fat (g): Trace, Total fat (g): Trace, Sodium (mg): 1, Total fiber (g): Trace*

Flavored Oils and Vinegars

Seek out ways to maximize the flavor in your food, as you limit harmful fats. One easy way is to make the most of the fat, more specifically oil, that you do use by flavoring it with herbs, spices, garlic or even vanilla. Recipes follow for our specialties, Asian Spiced Oil and Vanilla Oil. But you can dress up olive, peanut and even canola oil with the suggestions below. You can make these oils in larger or smaller quantities as fits your needs. Store them in a cool, dark place and discard when they lose their special pungent or herbal aroma. Vinegars such as balsamic and sherry can make a bold statement in a dish while light and refreshing fruit vinegars add sparkle to salads. Also seek out flavored oils and vinegars in your markets.

Hot Pepper Oil

You can make this as hot as you like by adding more dried pepper. This is an oil you want to add by drops sparingly as an accent, in addition to other oil in your recipe.

> 2 cups peanut oil
> 3 to 4 teaspoons dried crushed red peppers

Warm the oil and dried crushed peppers in a small saucepan. Remove from the heat and cool. Pour into a bowl and cover for 3 to 4 days. Strain the oil into a bottle and discard the pepper. Or for continued heating power, do not strain the pepper but store the oil with the pepper. The oil will last for 6 months, stored in a cool, dark place.

❀ PER SERVING *Calories: 120, Cholesterol (mg): 0, Saturated fat (g): 2, Total fat (g): 14, Sodium (mg): 0, Total fiber (g): 0*

Garlic Oil

> 1 cup extra-virgin olive oil
> 3 cloves garlic, crushed

Warm the oil with the garlic as directed for Hot Pepper Oil. Cool and transfer to a covered jar with the garlic. For a more subtle flavor, remove the garlic before storing.

❀ PER SERVING *Calories: 120, Cholesterol (mg): 0, Saturated fat (g): 2, Total fat (g): 14, Sodium (mg): 0, Total fiber (g): 0*

Basil Oil

Substitute ½ cup coarsely chopped fresh basil leaves for the garlic in the Garlic Oil.

❀ PER SERVING *Calories: 120, Cholesterol (mg): 0, Saturated fat (g): 2, Total fat (g): 14, Sodium (mg): 0, Total fiber (g): 0*

Garlic Basil Oil
Add 2 crushed garlic cloves to the Basil Oil.

✻ PER SERVING *Calories: 120, Cholesterol (mg): 0, Saturated fat (g): 2, Total fat (g): 14, Sodium (mg): 0, Total fiber (g): 0*

Asian Spiced Oil

MAKES 2 CUPS, SERVING SIZE 1 TABLESPOON

INSTEAD OF BLANKETING STEAMED VEGETABLES *and other simply prepared foods with buttery sauces, cheese or other saturated-fat ingredients, transform them with this fragrant, hot oil. One of our most popular kitchen aids, this oil requires careful attention to the time the flavorings sit in the oil. If you get the oil too hot or let it steep too long, the ginger will cloud the oil, though it will settle and clarify somewhat in time. This will not disturb the flavor, however. Otherwise, this oil is foolproof and absolutely fantastic. You can make this in half or double batches and store it covered almost indefinitely. At holiday time, do as our testers have done and bottle Asian Spiced Oil for your friends.*

> 2 cups peanut oil
> 2 tablespoons Asian sesame oil
> 2 tablespoons dried crushed red peppers
> 10 garlic cloves, chopped
> 2 tablespoons minced fresh ginger
> Zest from ½ lemon
> ½ teaspoon Tellicherry or other black peppercorns

1 Warm the oils in a saucepan over low-medium heat, but do not allow them to boil. Stir in the remaining ingredients and immediately remove the saucepan from the heat. Set aside for ½ hour.

2. Place a strainer or cheesecloth over a measuring cup, strain the oil into the cup and discard the flavorings. Pour the oil into a clean bottle, cover and store in a cool, dark place. It will last several months, if you can keep it around that long.

✻ PER SERVING *Calories: 129, Cholesterol (mg): 0, Saturated fat (g): 2, Total fat (g): 14, Sodium (mg): 0, Total fiber (g): 0*

Vanilla Oil

MAKES 2 CUPS, SERVING SIZE 1 TABLESPOON

THIS IS AN EXQUISITE OIL *that adds an almost buttery smoothness to sauces, steamed vegetables, fish and dressings. Try it in Vanilla-Scented Butter Beans with Orecchiette (page 458–59), for example, or just use its exotic flavor to dress up white beans, steamed rice or artichokes.*

    1 vanilla bean (3 to 4 inches), split lengthwise to expose the seeds
    2 cups olive oil or canola oil

Place the bean in a small saucepan with the oil. Warm over low-medium heat until either the bean floats to the surface or the oil *just* begins to bubble. Immediately remove the pan from the heat and cool for 6 to 8 hours. Remove the bean and pour the oil into a clean bottle. Store in a cool, dark place. This will keep for 2 to 3 months.

❇ PER SERVING WITH CANOLA OIL *Calories: 120, Cholesterol (mg): 0, Saturated fat (g): 1, Total fat (g): 14, Sodium (mg): 0, Total fiber (g): 0*

❇ PER SERVING WITH OLIVE OIL *Calories: 120, Cholesterol (mg): 0, Saturated fat (g): 2 Total fat (g): 14, Sodium (mg): 0, Total fiber (g): 0*

Apple Cinnamon Vinegar

MAKES 4 CUPS, SERVING SIZE 1 TABLESPOON

A DELIGHTFUL VINEGAR *to use with canola oil or Vanilla Oil to dress fruit sal- ads, a light mix of greens and cooked chicken, or steamed vegetables. Easy and unbeatable, use it whenever your recipe calls for a fruit vinegar.*

    2 Granny Smith apples, peeled, cored and sliced
    4 x 1-inch strip lemon zest
    2 sticks cinnamon
    1 vanilla bean (4 to 6 inches), split lengthwise to expose the seeds
    4 cups distilled white vinegar

1. Place all the ingredients in a nonreactive saucepan. Warm over medium heat just until the first bubble appears but do not allow it to boil. Remove from the heat immediately and cool for 8 hours.

2. Strain and funnel the vinegar into a pretty bottle. Store covered in a cool, dark place.

❇ PER SERVING *Calories: 2, Cholesterol (mg): 0, Saturated fat (g): 0, Total fat (g): 0, Sodium (mg): 0, Total fiber (g): 0*

Blackberry Vinegar

MAKES 4 CUPS, SERVING SIZE 1 TABLESPOON

A FRUITY VINEGAR *with just enough spice added to make a simple oil and vinegar dressing special. If you wish, you can substitute another summer berry for the blackberries. As an example of the distinctive quality this recipe can add to a salad, try it in Melon Chili Salad with Blackberry Vinaigrette (page 388–89), which we developed as an excuse to showcase this delightful vinegar.*

> 1 pint blackberries, thoroughly mashed
> 3 cups distilled white vinegar
> 1 cup red or white wine vinegar
> 3 tablespoons sugar
> 1 strip orange zest (about 3 inches long)
> 2 whole cloves
> 1 stick cinnamon

1. Place the berries in a saucepan and add the remaining ingredients. Bring to a gentle simmer over medium heat and remove from the heat immediately.

2. Pour into a wide-mouthed, clean bottle and seal tightly. Store in a cool place for 3 weeks, shaking the bottle gently from time to time.

3. Strain into a clean, decorative bottle, cork or seal.

❋ PER SERVING *Calories: 4, Cholesterol (mg): 0, Saturated fat (g): 0, Total fat (g): 0, Sodium (mg): 0, Total fiber (g): 0*

Toasting Nuts, Seeds and Spices

Toasting nuts and seeds, such as sesame and walnuts, before adding them to a recipe, accents their flavorful oils. With heightened flavor, you can also use less of these high fat ingredients. This small effort is one of the tricks that makes food flavorful and distinctive, regardless of how much or how little oil you use.

Nuts

Place the nuts on an unoiled baking sheet and place them in a hot (at least 450 degrees F) oven for 3 or 4 minutes or until fragrant. Remove immediately before they scorch and use as your recipe directs. If you are adding them to a warm salad or similar dish, you can heat the nuts in the oil you will use for the dressing, for a wonderful burst of flavor.

Seeds

Place the seeds on an unoiled baking sheet and place in a hot oven (at least 450 degrees F) for several minutes until they turn a light golden brown. Watch them very carefully (especially if you use higher temperatures to speed up the process). Once they begin to color, as in the case of sesame seeds, they can scorch very quickly. Remove from the oven as soon as they are toasted and use as your recipe directs.

Spices

While ground spices are convenient, you miss out on the wonderful aromas wafting up from the skillet as whole spices such as cumin, peppercorns, mustard seeds and coriander toast. Add the spices to a dry skillet (preferably cast iron) and stir them continuously over high heat for a minute or so until the mustard seeds pop and the spices release their fragrance. Remove the skillet from the heat and with a mallet or the back of a large wooden spoon immediately crush the spices against the bottom and sides of the pan or grind them in a spice grinder.

CHAPTER 28

Breakfasts

ADMONITIONS TO START THE DAY WITH A GOOD MEAL *are as numerous as good intentions. The reality is that the typical morning scene in most households is too hectic for most people to sort out the best nutritional choices at the crack of dawn. And it's another stretch to expect them to roll up their sleeves and whip up something well balanced, low in fat and tasty while getting the kids off to school, the dog walked and themselves out the door on time. Which explains the allure of egg and muffin sandwiches at fast-food restaurants, sugary, fatty pastries and buttery croissant ham and cheese breakfast sandwiches picked up on the way to work. We offer a better prescription: Breakfast Fig-and-Banana Split (page 315–16), assembled in minutes and full of fiber and flavor; saturated-fat-free Almond Blueberry Granola (page 311–12) made on a weekend to get your weekdays off to a healthy start. And when it's time to settle down for a leisurely breakfast or brunch, enjoy waffles, pancakes, hash browns, fritters, sausages, omelets, pastries, sweet creamy spreads and button-popping burritos and black bean cakes. Hard to believe all this food is good for your heart? But that's what the Stanford 25 Gram Plan is all about—a plan for life with food worth living for!*

Whether you like your first meal sweet or savory, a few tips will aid all of your breakfast cooking. Certain items require the proper cookware to produce the best results with the least fat. Cast-iron skillets or griddles provide the best surface for pancakes, fritters, hash browns and bean cakes. Instead of a butter-slicked omelet pan, a good nonstick skillet allows omelets to slide easily onto your plate. To heighten the flavor of all of your reduced-fat breakfast desserts or sweet recipes (such as pancakes and waffles), in addition to adding vanilla extract, reserve a canister of sugar for baking and flavor it with orange or vanilla as described on page 538. Note that in waffles, pancakes and baked goods that call for baking powder, the sodium content may increase significantly. None of our recipes is excessively high in sodium. However, persons who wish to or need to curb their sodium intake can use the total in the list of nutritional calculations as a guide to choose whether to make the dish infrequently, or when included in a menu, to avoid table salt or other salted items during the meal or reduce or eliminate any added salt in the recipe.

🌿

Black Bean Breakfast Cakes with Salsa Ranchera

SERVES 4, APPROXIMATELY 2 CAKES EACH

THESE CAKES ARE TERRIFIC WITH SALSA RANCHERA, *but you can use Tomato Orange Salsa (page 350) as well. For a real wake-up call in the morning, make a spicier cake using canned black beans jazzed up with one or more minced hot chili peppers, such as dried guajillo or fresh serrano, or a slightly milder fresh jalapeño or poblano. Remember that eaten together, beans and grains form a complete protein and these cakes served with Whole Wheat Corn Muffins (page 332) or grilled Basic Polenta (page 445) make a particularly satisfying combination. For a brunch party, add Grilled Fruit Kabobs with Stanford Breakfast Cream (page 314–15).*

> 2 cups Basic Black Beans or Jazzed-Up Canned Black Beans
>   (page 427)
> Generous pinch of powdered ancho chili (page 281)
>   or cayenne, optional
> 1 tablespoon minced fresh cilantro
> 2 teaspoons olive oil
> ½ cup creamy-style nonfat plain yogurt mixed with
> 1 tablespoon nonfat sour cream or 1% milk
> 2 cups Salsa Ranchera (recipe follows)

1. Make sure the beans are well drained or they will not form patties easily and hold together as they cook. Chop the beans with the powdered chili (if using) and the cilantro in a food processor or blender until they are very chunky, but not puréed. If you use a blender, use a stop and start approach. Every few seconds, chop the beans briefly and stir up the mixture to prevent it from becoming puréed. If they remain beanlike and do not thicken at all, simply mash a ¼ cup of the beans, return them to the machine and continue to process the beans until they have a consistency that holds together. This is not difficult to achieve.

2. Form the beans into 8 cakes approximately 3 inches in diameter and ½ inch thick. Heat the oil in a skillet large enough to hold the cakes without crowding or make them in batches and keep warm until ready to serve. (They should not sit too long, though, before serving.) Cook the cakes for 2 or 3 minutes or until they are heated through and slightly crusted on the bottom. Turn and cook briefly on the other side. Instead of pressing the cakes down with a spatula (as you might with a hamburger patty), press the edges toward the center to help them hold their shape. Serve immediately with a spoonful of the yogurt mixture on top of each. Pass the Salsa Ranchera separately.

FAT TRACKING TIP: Use olive oil–flavored vegetable spray instead of olive oil.

❋ PER SERVING (INCLUDES ½ CUP SALSA RANCHERA) *Calories: 158, Cholesterol (mg): 1, Saturated fat (g): Trace, Total fat (g): 3, Sodium (mg): 241, Total fiber (g): 5*

Salsa Ranchera

MAKES APPROXIMATELY 3½ CUPS, SERVING SIZE ½ CUP

YOU CAN USE THIS CLEAN-TASTING, *easy and versatile relish to perk up Breakfast Burritos, add zest to Black Bean Breakfast Cakes, sauce yolkless huevos rancheros or give a piquant finish to grilled chicken or fish. And if that's not enough, Salsa Ranchera, which freezes well, by the way, can double as a cooked salsa served cold on the appetizer tray with Oven-Baked Tortilla Chips (page 348) or steamed red potatoes.*

> 1 can (16 ounces) chopped tomatoes with juice
> 2 large tomatoes (about ¾ pound), unpeeled, diced
> 1 medium-size onion, diced
> 2 ounces canned chilies (mild or hot), diced
> 1 garlic clove, minced
> Salt and freshly ground pepper to your taste
> 2 tablespoons minced fresh cilantro

Place all the ingredients except the cilantro in a medium-size nonreactive saucepan and bring to a boil. Reduce the heat and simmer for 25 to 30 minutes or until the onion is very soft and translucent and the sauce has thickened. Stir in the cilantro and taste for seasoning. Serve hot or cold.

❋ PER SERVING *Calories: 17, Cholesterol (mg): 0, Saturated fat (g): 0, Total fat (g): 0, Sodium (mg): 109, Total fiber (g): 1*

Breakfast Burritos

SERVES 4

BEANS, POTATOES, CHEESE—*rib-sticking food for a high-energy breakfast. Sleek Cilantro Pesto and tangy Salsa Ranchera make these filling breakfast packets special. For ease in preparation, this recipe assumes you will use canned vegetarian refried beans, which typically have a small amount of unsaturated fat and good flavor, but you can also substitute canned fat-free refried beans. Or fill the burritos with one of our chilies in Chapter 34, such as White Bean and Vegetable Chili with Grilled Chicken (omitting the chicken if you and your family don't have gargantuan appetites), Black Bean Chili with Yellow Pepper Purée with Cilantro and Ginger (instead of Cilantro Pesto), or simply homemade, full-of-flavor mashed Basic Beans, Basic Black Beans or Jazzed-Up Canned Black Beans.*

1 tablespoon olive oil
¼ cup diced onion
1 small garlic clove, minced
½ pound raw russet potatoes, peeled and finely diced
Salt and freshly ground pepper
4 large flour tortillas, warmed
¼ cup Cilantro Pesto (page 293), optional
2 cups vegetarian refried beans, heated
¾ ounce low-fat Monterey Jack cheese, shredded (about ¼ cup)
1 cup Salsa Ranchera (page 303)

1. Heat the oil in a medium-size skillet and add the onion and garlic. Stir over medium heat until softened slightly, about 1 minute, and add the potatoes, salt and pepper to your taste. Toss frequently until the onions are translucent and the potatoes cooked through and lightly browned. Allow them to settle into the hot skillet for 30 seconds or so between turns so they will brown nicely.

2. To assemble, coat a warm tortilla with the Cilantro Pesto, then fill the center with the refried beans, the potato mixture and the cheese. Fold the edges toward the center, then tuck the ends under. Spoon Salsa Ranchera on the side and serve immediately.

❀ PER SERVING *Calories: 352, Cholesterol (mg): 13, Saturated fat (g): 2, Total fat (g): 8, Sodium (mg): 728, Total fiber (g): 8*

Dried Blueberry Buttermilk Pancakes
with Blueberry Honey Sauce

SERVES 4, MAKES APPROXIMATELY 1 DOZEN 4-INCH PANCAKES

TYPICAL PANCAKES ARE OFTEN DOUGHY SPONGES *that are an excuse to soak up butter and sugar syrup. Not these elegant blueberry-flecked beauties. Our combination of pancakes and Blueberry Honey Sauce has very little sugar compared to the usual stack, and barely any saturated fat because they are so flavorful you don't need to drench them in butter. But if you want to guild the lily just a bit, top them with a spoonful or two of Yogurt Cream (page 292–93). You can make the batter for these the night before, reserving the berries, then cover and refrigerate. Thin the batter with a little buttermilk if necessary, and stir in the berries.*

1 cup Dried Blueberry Honey Sauce (recipe follows)
1 cup unbleached, all-purpose flour
½ cup whole wheat flour
1 tablespoon granulated sugar
1 tablespoon packed brown sugar
2 teaspoons baking powder
¼ teaspoon baking soda
½ teaspoon ground cinnamon
½ teaspoon salt
¼ cup liquid egg substitute
1½ cups plus 2 tablespoons low-fat buttermilk
1½ teaspoons vanilla extract
2½ tablespoons canola oil
⅓ cup dried blueberries

1. Prepare Blueberry Honey Sauce and set aside. In a large bowl, stir the flours, sugars, baking powder and soda, cinnamon and salt until they are well blended. Add the remaining ingredients except for the blueberries and beat lightly until smooth. Fold in the berries.

2. Heat a nonstick griddle or skillet until a spray of water dances on the surface. Ladle on ¼ cupfuls of batter spaced far enough apart to give you turning room. Cook about 45 seconds to a minute or until they look set on the bottom, flip each one and press it lightly with your spatula. Cook the underside a minute or so until golden as well and the pancake looks done in the center. Prepare them in batches, keeping the finished pancakes warm until you are ready to serve. Drizzle with the Blueberry Honey Sauce and serve immediately.

❈ PER SERVING (INCLUDES 3 PANCAKES AND ¼ CUP BLUEBERRY HONEY SAUCE) *Calories: 433, Cholesterol (mg): 4, Saturated fat (g): 1, Total fat (g): 11, Sodium (mg): 670, Total fiber (g): 4*

Dried Blueberry Honey Sauce

Makes approximately 1 cup, serving size 1 tablespoon

This special sauce uses no added sugar for a surprisingly sweet result. It relies on honey, with twice the sweetening power of sugar, and dried blueberries, which are packed with natural sugar. The result will transport you to blueberry heaven. When you want to substitute honey in place of sugar in your recipes, experiment with varieties such as lavender, clover, sage and orange blossom, for each has a special characteristic. Use the sauce on frozen yogurt or slices of angel food cake. You can substitute frozen berries for fresh when they are out of season.

> 2 cups fresh blueberries
> 1 tablespoon fresh orange juice
> ¼ teaspoon grated orange zest
> 1 tablespoon honey
> 3 tablespoons dried blueberries

1. Place 1 cup of the fresh berries and the remaining ingredients in a small nonreactive saucepan and stir over medium high heat until the honey has dissolved. Reduce the heat to a simmer and cover. Cook 3 to 4 minutes just until the berries soften and the juices thicken slightly.

2. Remove from the heat and stir in the remaining cup of berries. Serve hot or chilled. Thin cold sauce with a little water or orange juice before serving.

❋ PER SERVING *Calories: 15, Cholesterol (mg): 0, Saturated fat (g): 0, Total fat (g): 0, Sodium (mg): 1, Total fiber (g): Trace*

Whole Grain Buttermilk Waffles
with Strawberry-Peach Sauce

SERVES 6, MAKES APPROXIMATELY 1 DOZEN WAFFLES, 4½ INCHES SQUARE

THERE IS NO MISTAKE IN THE RECIPE; *these tender waffles are practically fat free. The butter granules add richness but negligible fat. In repeated testings, we found them to be crisper, lighter and more flavorful than the same recipe made with a tablespoon or two of oil. Make the waffles tart by adding one-half cup dried cherries to the batter and serve with Orange and Dried Cranberry Sauce (page 311); or sweeter with one-third cup dried blueberries and serve with Dried Blueberry Honey Sauce (page 306).*

Strawberry-Peach Sauce (recipe follows)
¼ cup millet
⅔ cup unbleached, all-purpose flour
2 tablespoons whole wheat flour
⅓ cup rolled oats
¼ cup buckwheat flour
1 tablespoon baking powder
1 tablespoon butter granules
¼ teaspoon salt
Pinch of baking soda
Pinch of ground cinnamon
3 tablespoons firmly packed brown sugar
½ tablespoon granulated sugar
1½ cups low-fat buttermilk
¾ cup liquid egg substitute
½ teaspoon vanilla extract
Vegetable spray for coating waffle iron

1. Prepare Strawberry-Peach Sauce and set aside. Grind the millet in a blender until the kernels are at least half their original size. Place them in a large mixing bowl with the other ingredients except the buttermilk, egg substitute and vanilla, and stir until completely blended. Add the buttermilk, egg substitute and vanilla and stir until thoroughly blended.

2. Coat the waffle iron with a light film of vegetable spray. Heat the waffle iron and cook the waffles according to the manufacturer's directions. Between each batch stir the batter and spray the grids of the iron to prevent the waffles from sticking. Keep each batch warm and when they are all cooked, serve immediately with the Strawberry-Peach Sauce.

❋ PER SERVING (INCLUDES 2½ TABLESPOONS SAUCE) *Calories: 302, Cholesterol (mg): 3, Saturated fat (g): 1, Total fat (g): 3, Sodium (mg): 395, Total fiber (g): 6*

Strawberry-Peach Sauce
> *Makes approximately 1 cup, serving size 1 tablespoon*

We have made this sauce sweet, but compared to pancake syrups the sugar content is negligible. Depending on the sweetness of your fruit, however, you may want to reduce the sugar.

> 1 cup sliced strawberries
> ½ pound fresh peaches, peeled, pitted and sliced over a bowl
>   to collect as much juice as possible
> ¼ cup fresh orange juice
> 1 tablespoon sugar
> 1 teaspoon vanilla extract
> ½ teaspoon ground cinnamon
> Pinch of ground ginger

Blend all the ingredients together in a mixing bowl. Place half of the mixture in a blender and purée until smooth. Stir this back into the sliced fruit and refrigerate until you are ready to serve.

❀ PER SERVING *Calories: 23, Cholesterol (mg): 0, Saturated fat (g): 0, Total fat (g): 0, Sodium (mg): 0, Total fiber (g): 1*

Fried Apples with Sweet Cheese
SERVES 4

A FRIEND CALLS FRIED APPLES "COUNTRY FOOD." *Thank goodness we live in that country. Simple and rich, serve these luscious apples with their sweet, creamy, cheese topping for brunch or even a casual supper menu. Be sure to turn them constantly; with so little oil, they may scorch otherwise.*

> ½ cup Sweet Cheese (recipe follows)
> 2 teaspoons canola oil or Vanilla Oil (page 298)
> 4 medium Gravenstein apples, cored and sliced but not peeled
> 1½ tablespoons firmly packed brown sugar
> ½ teaspoon ground cinnamon

1. Prepare the Sweet Cheese. Heat the oil in a medium-size skillet. Add the apples and turn them constantly over medium heat for 4 to 5 minutes or until they begin to soften. Adjust the heat as necessary so they don't scorch as they cook.

2. When the apples are soft, sprinkle on the sugar and cinnamon and continue turning for another minute or so until they are glazed. Serve hot topped with the Sweet Cheese.

❋ PER SERVING (INCLUDES 2 TABLESPOONS SWEET CHEESE) *Calories: 184, Cholesterol (mg): 5, Saturated fat (g): 1, Total fat (g): 8, Sodium (mg): 53, Total fiber (g): 2*

Sweet Cheese

Makes approximately ½ cup, serving size 1 tablespoon

In most recipes we advise against putting yogurt in a blender. However in this topping it actually helps to smooth the texture. The quantity is small enough that it does not liquefy, as larger amounts do. You can make the topping ahead and also double it for larger crowds. It is delicious on any cooked fruit or as a rich, but relatively low-fat, spread for toast with fruit preserves or unsweetened fruit purées on special occasions. Compared to butter (with 12 grams of fat, 7 of them saturated) or creamy whole-milk cheeses, this blend of low-fat cheeses with barely a trace of harmful fat per serving gives a welcome, luxurious touch to fruit desserts or unfrosted cakes. Serve it also as a butter replacement for toast or muffins at a weekend brunch.

> 1 tablespoon nonfat plain yogurt
> 3 tablespoons low-fat cottage cheese
> 3 tablespoons low-fat cream cheese
> Juice of ½ orange
> ½ teaspoon vanilla extract
> ½ teaspoon grated orange zest
> 1 tablespoon canola oil or Vanilla Oil (page 298)

In a blender or with a hand processor, mix the yogurt, cottage cheese and cream cheese. With the machine running, pour in the orange juice, vanilla extract, orange zest and oil and blend until completely smooth. Cover and refrigerate until serving time.

FAT TRACKING TIPS: Use nonfat cottage cheese. Use nonfat cream cheese.

❋ PER SERVING *Calories: 36, Cholesterol (mg): 3, Saturated fat (g): Trace, Total fat (g): 2, Sodium (mg): 25, Total fiber (g): 0*

French Toast with
Orange and Dried Cranberry Sauce

SERVES 4

CREATE A CHOLESTEROL-FREE BATTER *for this perennial favorite with egg whites or egg substitute. Instead of lathering the toast with butter and the usual syrup, offer a fresh fruit topping that supplies you with antioxidants and vitamins, in addition to sugar. Because there is no cholesterol and very little saturated fat in this French toast, a spoonful of butter or margarine smoothes the Orange and Dried Cranberry Sauce and still keeps the saturated fat low per serving. (You can also serve with Blueberry Honey Sauce, page 306, or your favorite fruit topping.) As with all French toast recipes, bread that is not very fresh works best. If you don't have any sitting around, dry it out slightly in a low oven or lightly toast it.*

> Orange and Dried Cranberry Sauce (recipe follows)
> 4 egg whites or ½ cup of liquid egg substitute
> 2 tablespoons fresh orange juice
> 2 tablespoons skim milk
> ½ teaspoon ground cinnamon
> 8 slices dried bread
> Vegetable spray for coating skillet

1. Prepare Orange and Dried Cranberry Sauce and set aside. In a shallow bowl, combine the eggs, orange juice, milk and cinnamon and blend well. Dip the bread in the batter quickly, turning it once to coat each side. Transfer to a separate dish.

2. Lightly coat a large skillet or griddle with a thin film of vegetable spray. Heat it over medium-high heat until a spray of cold water dances on the surface. Add half the bread slices in one layer. Cook 3 to 4 minutes or until golden brown on each side. Turn several times and check the underside frequently to make sure the toast doesn't scorch. When golden, place the toast on a serving platter and keep warm.

3. Repeat for the second batch. Serve immediately with Orange and Dried Cranberry Sauce.

✻ PER SERVING (INCLUDES 6 TABLESPOONS ORANGE AND DRIED CRANBERRY SAUCE) *Calories: 230, Cholesterol (mg): 8, Saturated fat (g): 2, Total fat (g): 5, Sodium (mg): 354, Total fiber (g): 2*

Orange and Dried Cranberry Sauce
Makes 1½ cups, serving size 1 tablespoon

Tart fresh cranberries require a lot of sugar to keep your mouth from puckering. Dried cranberries, on the other hand, have concentrated sweetness that requires less sugar, ideal for sweetening your breakfast menu and helping to keep your triglycerides low, as we describe in Chapter 40. Make this in double or triple batches to keep in the refrigerator if morning cakes are your daily habit.

> 1 cup fresh orange juice
> 1 tablespoon firmly packed brown sugar
> ½ cup dried cranberries
> 1 tablespoon butter

1. Combine all ingredients in a small nonreactive saucepan and bring to a boil. Reduce the heat and simmer for 20 minutes. The sauce will thicken slightly.

2. Serve immediately or store covered in the refrigerator.

❁ PER SERVING *Calories: 13, Cholesterol (mg): 1, Saturated fat (g): Trace, Total fat (g): Trace, Sodium (mg): 5, Total fiber (g): Trace*

Almond Blueberry Granola
MAKES 4½ CUPS, SERVING SIZE ½ CUP

THOUGH CLASSIFIED AS A "HEALTH FOOD," *commercial granola cereals often contain excessive amounts of saturated fat because they are processed with tropical or hydrogenated oils. You can make your own easy, high-fiber, fruity mix yourself with essentially no saturated fat. Serve it for breakfast, snacks or use it to make our Crunchy Crust (page 548). A few granola-making tips: Add dried fruits such as dried blueberries and raisins after roasting, or you will get hard, little scorched balloons instead of sweet, moist fruit. The nonfat dried milk gives only a small calcium boost, but it is an important addition because it extends the shelf life of homemade granola. Make double or triple batches and freeze it for future use. You can also divide the granola into three or four portions and use a different fruit in each batch.*

3 cups rolled oats
1 cup whole bran cereal (not flakes)
1/4 cup slivered or chopped almonds
1/2 cup nonfat dry milk
1/4 cup whole wheat flour
1/4 cup sunflower seeds
1/4 cup firmly packed brown sugar
1 teaspoon ground cinnamon
1/2 teaspoon ground allspice
1/4 cup frozen apple juice concentrate, thawed
3 tablespoons maple syrup or honey
1 tablespoon canola oil
1/2 cup dried fruit (such as raisins, chopped dates, dried blueberries,
    currants, cranberries or mixed dried fruit)
Vegetable spray for baking sheet

1. In a large mixing bowl, add in the order given all the ingredients except the apple juice, syrup, oil and dried fruit. Toss until completely mixed.

2. Blend together the apple juice concentrate, syrup, and oil in a measuring cup. Pour it over the dry ingredients and toss until the granola is thoroughly coated.

3. Preheat the oven to 350 degrees F and lightly coat a baking sheet with a film of vegetable spray. Spread the granola in a thin layer on the sheet and place it in the oven for 20 to 25 minutes. Do not crowd the mixture or it will not toast properly. (Toast it in 2 or more batches if you have only a small baking sheet.) Stir it from time to time so it will toast evenly without scorching.

4. When the granola mixture is toasty and golden, remove it from the oven and stir it once more. Allow it to cool for a few minutes. Place 3/4 cup on a pie pan, and return to the oven to bake for another 8 minutes. It should be dark and crunchy, but not scorched. (You can omit this step, but this extra toasting gives the granola a richer flavor.) Stir this into the granola, cool and add the dried fruit, blending everything thoroughly. Place the granola in plastic bags or containers and store it in a dark, cool place or freeze until needed.

FAT TRACKING TIP: To reduce the total fat, omit or reduce the almonds and canola oil by half.

❋ PER SERVING *Calories: 372, Cholesterol (mg): 1, Saturated fat (g): Trace, Total fat (g): 7, Sodium (mg): 97, Total fiber (g): 9*

Corn and Chive Fritters
with Southwest Sausage

SERVES 6, MAKES 12 FRITTERS

FOR A WEEKEND BRUNCH, *make these cloudlike fritters, which are lightened with beaten egg whites instead of whole eggs. With the savings in cholesterol, you can add Parmesan cheese and still keep these delicate puffs low in harmful fats. High in fiber, they will give a nutritious start to your day. You can also serve them as a first course for an outdoor supper accompanied with Tomato Orange Salsa (page 350) and nonfat yogurt, or Yellow Pepper Purée with Ginger and Cilantro (page 430) or Cilantro Cream (page 294). Additionally, as a light weekend luncheon entrée, they would complement a salad filled with steamed vegetables and white beans or garbanzos (chickpeas). A cast-iron skillet works best. Don't be impatient to turn fritters and pancakes; they need time to set on the bottom before you can flip them easily. Lightly oil the tip of your spatula to facilitate turning them.*

> 1 pound (½ recipe) Southwest Sausage (page 322)
> ¼ cup cornmeal
> 2 teaspoons unbleached, all-purpose flour
> 1 tablespoon baking powder
> Salt and freshly ground pepper
> 2 cups freshly grated corn kernels with juice
>   from scraping cobs (about 4 ears)
> 4 egg whites
> 2 tablespoons minced fresh chives
> ¾ ounce Parmesan cheese, freshly grated (about ¼ cup)
> Vegetable spray for skillet
> Tufts of fresh cilantro or small blossoms for garnish

1. Prepare the sausage, form into patties and cook as directed in the recipe. Keep warm while preparing the fritters.

2. Place the cornmeal, flour, baking powder and salt and pepper to your taste in a food processor or blender and pulse until thoroughly combined. Add the corn kernels and juice to the dry ingredients. Add 1 egg white and pulse several times again until you have a coarsely blended mixture. Turn the batter into a medium-size bowl.

3. In a separate bowl, beat the remaining egg whites until they form soft peaks. Fold about ⅓ into the corn mixture to lighten the batter. Fold in the remaining egg whites, chives and grated cheese. Work quickly at this point so the batter doesn't deflate too much.

4. Coat a large skillet or griddle with a light film of vegetable spray. When a spray of water dances on the surface spread 3-inch circles of batter onto the hot surface. Use only a scant 3 or 4 tablespoons of batter or the fritters will be too thick and they won't cook through. Cook approximately 1 minute on each side or until golden. Arrange the fritters on one side of a serving platter and the cooked sausage patties on the other. Garnish with fresh cilantro or small blossoms and serve while still hot.

❋ PER SERVING: (INCLUDES 2½ OUNCES SOUTHWEST SAUSAGE) *Calories: 232, Cholesterol (mg): 53, Saturated fat (g): 2, Total fat (g): 6, Sodium (mg): 348, Total fiber (g): 2*

Grilled Fruit Kabobs
with Stanford Breakfast Cream
SERVES 4

THIS SURPRISING FRUIT PRESENTATION *delights children as well as grown-ups. Serve your own favorite fruit assortment, including apples, pears, grapes and melon according to the season. Or use the bright summer medley we assemble here.*

½ cup Stanford Breakfast Cream (recipe follows)
2 teaspoons honey
⅓ cup fresh orange juice
Pinch ground cinnamon or ground ginger
1 small nectarine, pitted and cut into eighths
8 strawberries, stems removed
1 small peach, pitted and cut into eighths
8 pineapple chunks
4 apricots, pitted and halved
2 fresh plums, pitted and cut into eighths
8 wooden skewers, soaked in cold water

1. Prepare Stanford Breakfast Cream, cover and refrigerate until serving time. Place the honey, orange juice and cinnamon in a small saucepan and stir over medium heat for a few minutes until the honey has melted and the juice bubbles slightly. Or, place in a microwave-safe bowl, and cook on high for 20 seconds or until heated through. Stir until smooth and toss with the fruit. Set aside for at least 15 minutes.

2. Thread the fruit onto skewers, alternating the varieties in the order listed. You can assemble the skewered fruit ahead of time, cover and refrigerate the kabobs until you need them.

3. Prepare a grill or preheat the broiler. Grill or broil the kabobs for 1 minute or so until they are heated through. Turn them several times to prevent scorching and brush them with the remaining marinade. Arrange them on individual plates and spoon 2 tablespoons of Stanford Breakfast Cream on the side of each.

✿ PER SERVING (INCLUDES 2 TABLESPOONS STANFORD BREAKFAST CREAM) *Calories: 130, Cholesterol (mg): 5, Saturated fat (g): Trace, Total fat (g): 2, Sodium (mg): 92, Total fiber (g): 3*

Stanford Breakfast Cream
Makes 1 cup, serving size 1 per tablespoon

Not only does this luscious breakfast cheese turn fresh or broiled fruit into a dessert, you can use it as a replacement for butter on toast, muffins, waffles and pancakes. When fresh berries are plentiful, make a breakfast shortcake with Connemara Scones (page 334), Stanford Breakfast Cream and your favorite sweet berries.

½ cup nonfat cottage cheese
¼ cup low-fat cream cheese
1 teaspoon honey
¼ cup creamy-style nonfat vanilla yogurt

In a blender or with a hand mixer or processor, beat the cottage cheese and cream cheese with the honey until smooth and fold in the yogurt by hand. Place the mixture in a serving bowl, cover and refrigerate until ready to use.

✿ PER SERVING *Calories: 17, Cholesterol (mg): 3, Saturated fat (g): 0, Total fat (g): 1, Sodium (mg): 46, Total fiber (g): 0*

Breakfast Fig-and-Banana Split
SERVES 2

IF YOU ARE IN A MILK AND CEREAL RUT, *give yourself a naturally sweet, calcium-loaded, practically fat-free treat with this quick, nourishing breakfast. Dried blueberries, while not exactly economical, are so chock full of sweetness, that less than a tablespoon per serving provides ample flavor. For the best price, search for them in a bulk food store. Don't make the cream ahead of time; it will separate and the blueberries will turn the cream purple. It is easy enough to assemble at the last minute.*

½ cup nonfat creamy-style vanilla yogurt
½ cup nonfat cottage cheese
4 teaspoons dried blueberries
2 large bananas
2 ripe figs
⅔ cup Almond Blueberry Granola (page 311–12)
   or other low-fat or nonfat granola

1. In a small bowl, blend the yogurt, cottage cheese and dried blueberries. If you are not going to serve immediately, add blueberries last.

2. Peel and slice the bananas and figs lengthwise and arrange them on a serving plate. Sprinkle with the granola and top with the blueberry cream. Serve immediately.

❀ PER SERVING *Calories: 495, Cholesterol (mg): 4, Saturated fat (g): 1, Total fat (g): 6, Sodium (mg): 242, Total fiber (g): 12*

🌿

Jalapeño Hash Browns with Cilantro Cream
SERVES 6

IF YOU HAVE EVER SEEN HASH BROWNS *made on a restaurant griddle, you know that they are flooded with either bacon fat or butter. Hash browns and potato pancakes made with raw potatoes need large amounts of oil, or the pan will scorch before they are cooked. Use Walla Walla, sweet red or cipolline onions to sweeten these contemporary hash browns and reduce the fat by baking them in the oven for a spicy and lower-fat version of this heartland favorite. Leave some of the seeds in the jalapeños for extra heat if desired.*

2 pounds russet potatoes, peeled and grated
½ cup finely diced sweet onion
½ cup seeded and finely diced red bell pepper
1 large egg white
½ to 1 tablespoon seeded (optional) minced jalapeño pepper
¾ teaspoon salt
Freshly ground pepper to your taste
2 teaspoons extra-virgin olive oil
⅓ cup Cilantro Cream (page 294)

1. Preheat the oven to 425 degrees F. In a large mixing bowl, combine all of the ingredients except the olive oil and Cilantro Pesto. Blend thoroughly.

2. Liberally coat a 9-inch cast-iron skillet with the olive oil. Pour the potato mixture into the skillet and bake for 10 minutes. Reduce the heat to 425 degrees F and continue to cook for another 15 to 20 minutes or until browned and tender.

3. Loosen the sides of the cake and gently slide a spatula underneath, carefully releasing the cake from the bottom. With thick potholders protecting your hands, place a platter over the skillet, carefully invert the skillet onto the platter and slide it onto the counter. Gently shake the skillet until the cake falls free, nudging it from underneath with the spatula if necessary. An alternative method is to serve from the skillet; before bringing it to the table, brush the top of the

potatoes with a bit of olive oil and brown under a preheated broiler for 15 or 20 seconds. Cut into wedges and serve piping hot. Pass the Cilantro Cream separately.

FAT TRACKING TIP: Coat the skillet with a film of olive oil–flavored vegetable spray instead of olive oil.

❉ PER SERVING (INCLUDES APPROXIMATELY 1 TABLESPOON CILANTRO CREAM) *Calories: 230, Cholesterol (mg): Trace, Saturated fat (g): Trace, Total fat (g): 5, Sodium (mg): 300 Total fiber (g): 4*

Pasta Omelet
with Fresh Tomatoes and Basil

SERVES 1

THIS IS THE WAY TO HAVE AN OMELET WITH CHEESE *without a huge hike in your cholesterol intake, adding fiber (in the pasta) as well. Make this in high summer when tomatoes are fat and mellow and basil is sweetest. Timing is everything here. Have the tomatoes ready, garlic minced and the pasta cooking when you begin. The tomatoes should be briefly sautéed over high heat just before they are ready to go in the omelet. If they cook slowly or sit in a hot pan too long they will become watery, a good start for a sauce maybe, but bad news for an omelet. If you can manage it, have the tomatoes finishing up just as you are stirring the eggs. As with any omelet, a nonstick surface is crucial to the final presentation. A well-seasoned omelet pan allows you to slide the perfectly set egg mixture from fire to plate in a heartbeat. A nonstick skillet coated with vegetable spray will also do the trick. And be sure to use short pasta only, long strands won't work.*

> 1 teaspoon olive oil
> 1 small garlic clove, minced
> 3/4 cup peeled, seeded and chopped tomato
> 1 generous tablespoon finely chopped fresh basil leaves
> 1 1/2 ounces dried fusilli pasta, cooked and drained
> 1/4 ounce Parmesan cheese, freshly grated (about 1 1/3 tablespoon)
> Salt and freshly ground pepper
> 1/2 cup liquid egg substitute lightly beaten with 1 egg white

1. Reserve a few drops of oil for the omelet pan. Heat the remaining oil in a small nonreactive skillet over medium heat. Add the garlic and stir briefly until fragrant. Add the tomatoes and basil and toss just until warmed through. Don't overcook them or they will release too much liquid. Stir in the drained pasta and half the cheese, and season to your taste with salt and pepper. Remove from the heat immediately.

2. Brush a medium-size nonstick skillet or seasoned omelet pan with the remaining oil to make the surface as slick as possible. Quickly heat the pan until a spray of water dances on the surface. Pour the egg mixture into the pan and stir vigorously as you rotate the pan to spread the eggs evenly. As the eggs begin to set, shake and rotate the pan back and forth, stirring just the surface to allow the omelet to set. Gently loosen the sides with your spatula. When the center is custardy but not runny, quickly add the pasta mixture and cheese and with your spatula fold ⅓ of the omelet over onto itself. Hold a plate under the pan and shake the omelet onto it, folding it again as you do. (If this is your first omelet, after you have made two or three, you will become a pro at this maneuver.) Serve piping hot.

✿ PER SERVING *Calories: 253, Cholesterol (mg): 7, Saturated fat (g): 3, Total fat (g): 11, Sodium (mg): 360, Total fiber (g): 1*

❦

Plum Focaccia

MAKES 12 THREE-INCH SERVING SLICES

FRESH, DARK PLUMS, SWELLING WITH NATURAL SUGAR *top this pizza-cum-pastry. Our tasters gave this a four-star rating, both those who worry that the earth will run out of sugar in their lifetime and those who never touch the stuff. The key to pleasing both camps is to use tree-ripened fruit and a small amount of butter in the pastry. Note that we use a baking dish rather than a pizza stone, as recommended for our savory Basic Focaccia (page 338–39). This controls the dripping fruit juices and forces them into the dough rather than onto the floor of your oven.*

> 1 package active dry yeast
> ½ cup plus ½ teaspoon sugar
> 1 cup minus 1 tablespoon lukewarm water (105 to 115 degrees F)
> 3 cups unbleached, all-purpose flour plus extra
>   for work surface
> 1 teaspoon salt
> ½ stick (4 tablespoons) butter, melted and cooled
> ¼ cup canola oil
> Butter-flavored vegetable spray for baking dish
> ¼ cup raspberry preserves
> 2 or 3 tablespoons cold water
> 1 pound sweet, firm plums, pitted and sliced

1. Mix the yeast, ½ teaspoon of sugar and the lukewarm water in a measuring cup and set it aside for 3 to 5 minutes until it foams.

2. Combine the flour, the remaining ½ cup sugar and the salt in the bowl of a food processor and pulse several times until well blended.

3. Pour in the dissolved yeast, melted butter and canola oil and process for 1 minute until smooth and elastic. Remove the blade and knead by hand on a floured surface for 15 seconds.

4. Place the dough in a deep bowl and cover it with a wet tea towel. Pull the towel tight, sticking the ends under the bowl if necessary so it doesn't rest on the dough. Set the bowl in a warm spot until the dough doubles in bulk, about 1 hour.

5. Punch down the dough. Preheat the oven to 400 degrees F.

6. On a lightly floured surface, roll the dough out in a rectangle. Coat a 2½-quart rectangular glass baking dish with a film of butter-flavored vegetable spray. Press the dough into the bottom and sides of the dish. Blend the raspberry preserves and the cold water and brush on the dough. Cover with the plums, brush them with the remaining glaze and bake for 25 minutes or until golden and puffed at the edges. Serve warm or allow to cool to room temperature.

❀ PER SERVING *Calories: 293, Cholesterol (mg): 10, Saturated fat (g): 3, Total fat (g): 9, Sodium (mg): 218, Total fiber (g): 2*

Breakfast Cheese Pizza

SERVES 1

A PRACTICE OF KEEPING A ROASTED PEPPER, ONION AND EGGPLANT *in the refrigerator will pay off with this fragrant pizza. Commercially bottled peppers contain more acetic acid than home-roasted peppers and can be very high in sodium. A quick solution when you need a smoky pepper is to slice it almost paper thin, spread it in one layer on a piece of foil and run it under the broiler while you are assembling the rest of the pizza. If you have toasted garlic and/or eggplant, spread them on the pita first, then continue layering.*

> 1 pita round
> 1/4 cup nonfat cottage cheese
> 1 tablespoon freshly grated Parmesan cheese
> 1 teaspoon minced fresh basil
> 1 or 2 sun-dried tomatoes (not packed in oil),
>   plumped in hot water and diced
> 2 tablespoons coarsely shredded part skim-milk
>   mozzarella cheese
> 2 thin slices tomato
> 1/4 red or green bell pepper, roasted (page 280)

1. Place the pita round on a broiler tray. In a blender, purée the cottage cheese, Parmesan cheese, basil and sun-dried tomatoes until smooth. Spread this mixture on the pita round. Cover with half of the mozzarella cheese, then the tomatoes and pepper and sprinkle on the remaining mozzarella.

2. Broil until hot and bubbly, about 2 minutes. Watch it carefully so that it doesn't scorch. Enjoy immediately.

❋ PER SERVING *Calories: 296, Cholesterol (mg): 18, Saturated fat (g): 1, Total fat (g): 6, Sodium (mg): 820, Total fiber (g): 2*

Basic Breakfast Sausage

SERVES 8, MAKES APPROXIMATELY SIXTEEN 3-INCH PATTIES

HOMEMADE LOW-FAT SAUSAGES *are as easy as assembling a hamburger and much leaner than pork links. The fat-tracking tip is the same for all chicken sausages: Substitute turkey breast for chicken to lower the fat count even further. To speed the preparation time (though none of these takes longer than a few minutes to blend), buy ground turkey breast and fold in the seasonings by hand. For economy's sake, however, you may prefer to buy cheaper, whole breast meat and grind it in the food processor. Note that the instructions call for steaming the sausage before panfrying. Low-fat sausage can dry out in the intense prolonged heat generated by skillet cooking. Steaming keeps them moist, and the quick panfrying gives them a delectable crusty finish. An alternate method of preparation is to wrap individual link-size portions or several larger links in plastic wrap and simmer in boiling water for 5 to 8 minutes or until firm and white. Unwrap and slice larger links into individual portions before serving. Use any of the following sausages in any recipe calling for sausage.*

> 2 pounds boned chicken breast, all skin and fat removed
> ½ onion, coarsely chopped
> 2 small garlic cloves
> 1 tablespoon minced fresh parsley
> 1 tablespoon extra-virgin olive oil
> Pinch of cayenne
> 1 teaspoon salt
> Pinch of white pepper
> Vegetable spray or regular olive oil for coating skillet

1. Place the chicken, onion and garlic in a food processor and pulse briefly until you have a coarse-textured mixture. Don't overprocess or purée it or you will lose the "toothiness" of the texture. Alternatively, you can feed the mixture through the tube of a meat grinder fitted with a medium blade into a large mixing bowl. After you have made the sausage two or three times, you will recognize the coarseness you prefer. Stir in the remaining ingredients by hand.

2. Test small samples for seasoning by heating a small amount of oil or vegetable spray in a skillet and cooking a tablespoonful of sausage until it is firm and white. Taste and make adjustments to the raw mixture, adding more pepper, salt or herbs, then retesting until you have a desired blend. Stir additional seasonings in by hand rather than continuing to process by machine or you will end up with chicken paste rather than sausage. Make notes about the amount of seasoning you add or subtract to avoid trial-and-error testing each time you make the sausage.

3. Form the sausage into 3-inch patties. About 4 to 5 minutes before serving, steam the patties on a rack over boiling water in a covered saucepan. Or cover the sausages with paper toweling and microwave them 4 to 5 minutes depending on their size. Coat a skillet with a light film of vegetable spray or olive oil. Turn the heat very high and when a spray of water dances on the surface, add the sausage. Cook over high heat for 30 seconds on each side or until each patty is crisp and golden, then remove them from the pan immediately to prevent them from drying out. If you prefer completely panfried sausages, coat the skillet with oil or vegetable spray and when hot, add the sausage, spaced just far enough apart so you can maneuver a spatula around them. Prepare in several batches if you only have a small skillet. Turn frequently for 3 to 4 minutes or until cooked through. Serve immediately.

❀ PER SERVING *Calories: 160, Cholesterol (mg): 72, Saturated fat (g): 1, Total fat (g): 5, Sodium (mg): 329, Total fiber (g): Trace*

Southwest Sausage
SERVES 8, MAKES APPROXIMATELY SIXTEEN 3-INCH PATTIES

HOT. HOT. HOT. *Some consider this best of show, but if the mixture is too fiery for you, adjust the heat downward by using less jalapeño.*

2 pounds boned chicken breast, all skin and fat removed
2 tablespoons extra-virgin olive oil
1/2 *each* green and red bell pepper, seeded and coarsely chopped
1/2 small red sweet onion (such as Bermuda), coarsely chopped
2 small garlic cloves, minced
2 tablespoons minced fresh sage
1 teaspoon powdered ancho chili (page 281)
Pinch of dried crushed red peppers
Pinch of cayenne
2 tablespoons tomato paste
1 small fresh jalapeño pepper, seeded and minced
1 teaspoon ground cumin
Salt and freshly ground pepper

Following the instructions for Basic Breakfast Sausage (page 321) process the chicken with the oil, peppers, onion and garlic. Stir in the remaining ingredients and test and cook as directed.

❀ PER SERVING *Calories: 183, Cholesterol (mg): 72, Saturated fat (g): 1, Total fat (g): 7, Sodium (mg): 74, Total fiber (g): 1*

Hot Italian Sausage with Fennel

SERVES 6, MAKES APPROXIMATELY 1 DOZEN 3-INCH PATTIES

IN THE ABSENCE OF FAT, *we added apple to the mixture to give some needed moisture, and in the process discovered that it served to bind the flavors of chicken, veal and fennel beautifully. Again, we mix lean and fattier cuts. If you prefer a milder sausage, substitute a teaspoon of* herbes de Provence *or a mixture of oregano, thyme, marjoram and savory in place of the hot pepper.*

2 shallots
1 garlic clove
¾ pound boned chicken breast, all skin and fat removed
¼ pound boned dark chicken, all fat and skin removed
½ pound lean veal
¼ cup white wine
1 teaspoon extra-virgin olive oil
¼ tart green apple, peeled and cored
1½ teaspoons fennel seeds
¼ teaspoon dried crushed red pepper or to taste
Pinch of cayenne
½ teaspoon salt
½ teaspoon coarsely ground pepper
½ teaspoon sugar
¼ teaspoon ground allspice

1. In a food processor with the machine running, add the shallots and garlic. Next, add the chicken and veal, wine, oil and apple, and pulse briefly until you have a coarse purée. Or put through the fine blade of a meat grinder the shallots, garlic, chicken, veal and apple. Place the mixture in a medium-size bowl and blend in the remaining ingredients thoroughly by hand. Test for seasoning as described in the recipe for Basic Breakfast Sausage (page 321). When the mixture is seasoned to your satisfaction, roll into a log shape and wrap tightly in plastic wrap for at least 1 hour to "age." Cook within 3 days or freeze for longer storage.

2. About 5 minutes before serving, shape into 3-inch patties, ½ inch thick. Cook as directed in the recipe for Basic Breakfast Sausage (page 321).

❋ PER SERVING *Calories: 177, Cholesterol (mg): 83, Saturated fat (g): 1, Total fat (g): 6, Sodium (mg): 249, Total fiber (g): Trace*

Turkey Sausage with Apple and Sage

SERVES 6, MAKES APPROXIMATELY 1 DOZEN 3-INCH PATTIES

RECIPES HAVE LONG CALLED FOR *a pinch of this and a pinch of that. Imprecise? Yes, but very small amounts of strongly flavored seasonings, such as cloves, nutmeg and cinnamon can overpower a delicate dish. Most measuring spoons start at ¼ teaspoon increments. Half of that, ⅛ teaspoon, is often too much in dishes where you want just a hint of cayenne or clove, so the cook reaches into the spice jar and whatever is gathered between thumb and forefinger goes into the dish, an amount too small to be measured any other way. In other words, a pinch.*

1½ pounds boned turkey breast, all skin and fat removed,
 or commercially ground turkey breast
½ onion
1 medium-size apple, peeled, cored and shredded
2 tablespoons canola oil
1 tablespoon fresh sage or 1 teaspoon dried
2 tablespoons fresh parsley
1 teaspoon salt
¼ teaspoon white pepper
Small pinch *each* of ground cloves, allspice, nutmeg and mace
2 tablespoons fine bread crumbs
1 egg white

1. In a meat grinder or food processor, process the turkey with the onion, apple and oil as described in the recipe for Basic Breakfast Sausage (page 321) briefly until you have a coarse purée.

2. Stir in the remaining ingredients by hand. Continue testing and cooking as in the recipe for Basic Breakfast Sausage.

❋ PER SERVING *Calories: 184, Cholesterol (mg): 71, Saturated fat (g): 1, Total fat (g): 5, Sodium (mg): 424, Total fiber (g): 1*

CHAPTER 29

Breads

Baked items, like no other set of recipes, *will cause fat-tracking chefs to pull out their hair by the handful. If you need a reason for butter to exist on the planet, they will say, it is a biscuit. And they don't just mean a pat of Wisconsin's finest melting into a hot-from-the-oven biscuit, either. Some pretty rigorous kitchen chemistry demands exact portions of flour and fat to produce tender, flaky and appetizing quick breads, muffins, scones, cakes and, of course, biscuits. However, simply switching to vegetable oil, an able substitute when you want to saute onions without butter, will turn your delicate biscuit into a rock-hard lethal weapon. So in this chapter we have already done the hair-pulling for you by investigating the pitfalls in low-fat baking and offering you the triumphs.*

Our baked goods recipes call for very little butter, margarine or whole eggs, though you may prefer to make additional substitutions. We have found that instead of butter, a combination of oil and soured milk (either the low or nonfat versions of yogurt, buttermilk or milk soured with vinegar) produces a delicate texture in muffins and scones. Sometimes we add extra baking powder for additional leavening power. Our goal in developing these recipes was to produce the best results with the lowest fat possible, rather than see how much fat we could get away with. We leave it up to you to decide if you want to add extra fat to some items on occasions. In place of butter, we might use applesauce or other fruit purée, though contrary to what some food writers claim, a one-for-one substitution doesn't always work: A small amount of oil in addition to the fruit purée can mean the difference between a truly successful result, and something that merely tastes like it is good for you. (Of course, these substitutions work well for pastries, too.) In some quick breads (and desserts, too), we find that using margarine or a blend of margarine and oil works better than using oil alone. Margarine, with its trans-fatty acid problem, is still a better choice for your heart than butter. Unless otherwise mentioned, we use only nonfat yogurt and nonfat cottage cheese. We choose low-fat, 1 percent or nonfat milk, depending on the needs of the recipe. We use low-fat buttermilk exclusively, rather than the higher-fat buttermilk identified as churned or sweet cream buttermilk.

Bread and Olive Oil

Instead of including the ubiquitous bread and butter with your meals, adopt the Mediterranean custom of serving partially sliced, hot, fragrant bread with a spoonful of your best extra-virgin olive oil on the plate. And, if you desire, include a spoonful of good Balsamic vinegar. Each person dips a piece of bread in the oil and vinegar, adding salt and pepper or not, if desired. The amount of fat per serving will depend on how much oil you allow the bread to soak up. For each slice of bread, allow no more than 1 teaspoon of oil (only 4.5 grams of fat, 0.6 of it saturated). If you serve a bread flavored with herbs, honey or naturally sweet, crunchy grains, such as millet, you may find that you don't need any oil at all. Compare those numbers with a pat of butter loaded with 12 grams of fat—7 of it saturated.

Herb and Cheese Biscuits

MAKES APPROXIMATELY 3 DOZEN BISCUITS, SERVING SIZE 1 BISCUIT

INCREDIBLY RICH, THESE SAVORY BISCUITS *go well with any entrée. The next time you fix a nourishing chili serve them as a change from the predictable corn bread. You can also substitute Asiago cheese, one of the lower-fat varieties with a pleasantly sharp bite, in place of Parmesan.*

> Vegetable spray for baking sheet
> 2 cups unbleached all-purpose flour, plus extra for work surface
> 1 tablespoon baking powder
> 1 teaspoon salt
> 2 teaspoons finely chopped chives
> 1 tablespoon minced fresh herbs (such as parsley, thyme, marjoram or a mix of herbs)
> 1 ounce Parmesan cheese, freshly grated (about 1/3 cup)
> 1/4 cup low-fat sour cream
> 1/4 cup nonfat plain yogurt
> 1/2 cup 1% milk
> 5 tablespoons olive oil

1. Preheat the oven to 450 degrees F. Lightly coat a baking sheet with a thin film of vegetable spray. In a large bowl, mix together the flour, baking powder, salt, chives, minced herbs and cheese until thoroughly blended.

2. Lightly beat together the sour cream, yogurt, milk and olive oil in a measuring cup until smooth. Stir this mixture into the flour, beating quickly until the dough forms a loose ball. If necessary, moisten the dough with a few spoonfuls of milk until it forms a ball and pulls away from the sides of the bowl. At this point the dough should feel velvety rather than gluey.

3. Place the dough on a lightly floured work surface, dust with a light coating of flour and roll it out to a circle 3/4 inch thick. Add a pinch or 2 of flour to the work surface as necessary to keep the dough moving easily. Use a light touch as you work with the dough, handling it just enough to make it smooth and pliable, but do not mash or compress it or the biscuits won't reach their full height in the oven. If the dough seems too moist at any point, just dust it with a little flour and brush away the excess. The dough should slide easily on the work surface at this point.

4. Use a 2-inch round cutter or small glass to make the biscuits. Space them closely but not touching on the prepared baking sheet. Bake for 12 to 15 minutes or until the tops turn a pale gold. They're best served right out of the oven.

❋ PER SERVING *Calories: 49, Cholesterol (mg): 1, Saturated fat (g): Trace, Total fat (g): 2, Sodium (mg): 106, Total fiber (g): Trace*

Cranberry Bran Muffins

MAKES 1 DOZEN MUFFINS, SERVING SIZE 1 MUFFIN

MANY OTHERWISE HEALTHFUL BRAN MUFFIN RECIPES *end up tasting more like a prescription than a breakfast treat. The dried cranberries in these nourishing muffins will give you a tart and tasty wake-up call. We developed the robust texture you expect of a dense, wheaty bran muffin, but with a delicious, fruity flavor, which isn't the least bit medicinal. In place of some or all of the bran cereal, you can vary this basic morning starter with quick or rolled oats. Add a few ground walnuts if you like. Because this recipe produces a very moist muffin, allow the muffins to rest for a few minutes to set properly before serving them hot out of the oven. We give you the option of using grapeseed oil, a nice light oil for baking.*

Vegetable spray and liners, optional, for muffin tins
1 cup whole wheat flour
½ cup unbleached all-purpose flour
½ cup bran cereal flakes
½ cup whole bran cereal threads
½ cup nonfat dry milk powder
1 teaspoon baking soda
1 tablespoon baking powder
1 teaspoon salt
1½ teaspoons ground cinnamon
1 teaspoon ground allspice
½ cup firmly packed brown sugar, measured then sifted
3 tablespoons granulated sugar
¾ cup dried cranberries or yellow raisins
1 cup unsweetened applesauce
2 tablespoons fresh orange juice
2 teaspoons grated orange zest
½ cup liquid egg substitute
⅓ cup grapeseed oil or canola oil
½ cup 1% milk
1 teaspoon vanilla extract

1. Preheat the oven to 425 degrees F. Lightly coat regular or miniature muffin tins with a thin film of vegetable spray, or fit them with paper or aluminum foil liners and spray them lightly as well. Place the flours, bran cereals, dry milk powder, baking soda and powder, salt, spices and the sugars in the bowl of a food processor or blender, and pulverize them. Pour this mixture into a large mixing bowl and add the dried cranberries. Toss thoroughly.

2. In a large measuring cup, combine the applesauce and remaining ingredients and whisk until thoroughly blended. Pour the wet ingredients into the cereal mixture and stir lightly until you have a moist and slightly lumpy batter. *Do not overbeat.*

3. Ladle the batter into the prepared muffin tins and bake for 25 minutes or until golden and a knife inserted in the center of a muffin comes out clean. If they appear cooked but too moist, let them rest briefly before serving.

❀ PER SERVING *Calories: 233, Cholesterol (mg): 1, Saturated fat (g): 1, Total fat (g): 7, Sodium (mg): 458, Total fiber (g): 2*

Orange Poppy Seed Muffins

MAKES 1 DOZEN MUFFINS, SERVING SIZE 1 MUFFIN

LOVERS OF ORANGE POPPY SEED CAKE *gravitate toward these moist muffins. You can substitute caraway for poppy seeds for an altogether different and intriguing taste.*

Vegetable spray and liners, optional, for muffin tins
1½ cups unbleached all-purpose flour
½ cup oat bran
1 tablespoon baking powder
½ teaspoon salt
¾ cup sugar
2 tablespoons poppy seeds
Coarsely grated zest from 1 orange
½ cup fresh orange juice
½ cup low-fat buttermilk
¼ cup canola oil
½ cup liquid egg substitute

1. Preheat the oven to 425 degrees F. Lightly coat regular or miniature muffin tins with a thin film of vegetable spray; or fit them with paper or aluminum foil liners and spray them lightly as well. Place the flour, oat bran, baking powder, salt and sugar in a mixing bowl and blend in thoroughly the poppy seeds and orange zest.

2. Combine the remaining ingredients in a measuring cup and beat until thoroughly blended. Stir into the dry mixture until you have a moist but slightly lumpy batter. *Do not overbeat.*

3. Ladle the batter into the prepared muffin tins and bake for 30 minutes or until pale and golden and a knife inserted in the center of a muffin comes out clean. Serve while still hot.

❉ PER SERVING *Calories: 181, Cholesterol (mg): Trace, Saturated fat (g): 1, Total fat (g): 6, Sodium (mg): 210, Total fiber (g): 1*

Red Pepper Muffins

MAKES 1 DOZEN MUFFINS, SERVING SIZE 1 MUFFIN

SPECKLED WITH JEWEL-LIKE NUGGETS *of fresh red pepper, these whole wheat gems use whole wheat pastry flour for a finer texture. If you are unable to find it in your market, just sift whole wheat flour and discard the bran.*

> Vegetable spray and liners, optional, for muffin tins
> 1 cup yellow cornmeal
> 1 cup whole wheat pastry flour
> 1/4 cup sugar
> 1 1/2 tablespoons baking powder
> 1 teaspoon salt
> 1/4 teaspoon freshly ground pepper
> Small pinch of cayenne
> 1/3 cup olive oil
> 1/4 cup liquid egg substitute
> 1 cup nonfat milk
> 1/2 cup minced and seeded red bell pepper
> 1/4 cup minced green onions
> 2 tablespoons minced fresh cilantro

1. Preheat the oven to 425 degrees F. Lightly coat regular or miniature muffin tins with a thin film of vegetable spray; or fit them with paper or aluminum foil liners and spray them lightly as well. Stir together the cornmeal, flour, sugar, baking powder, salt, pepper and cayenne in a mixing bowl until thoroughly blended.

2. In a measuring cup whisk together the olive oil, egg substitute, and milk and stir lightly into the dry ingredients until you have a moist but slightly lumpy batter. *Do not overbeat.* Stir in the remaining ingredients.

3. Ladle the batter into the prepared muffin tins and bake for 20 minutes or until golden and a knife inserted in the center of a muffin comes out clean. Serve while still hot.

❋ PER SERVING *Calories: 158, Cholesterol (mg): Trace, Saturated fat (g): 1, Total fat (g): 6, Sodium (mg): 335, Total fiber (g): 1*

Persimmon and Chutney Muffins

MAKES 1 DOZEN MUFFINS, SERVING SIZE 1 MUFFIN

A TRICK OF NATURE, *Hachiya persimmons, the pear-shaped variety, are at their prettiest and most inviting when firm and unbearably astringent. But let them get almost soupy with blackened, blemished skins and they are pure heaven eaten with a spoon or frozen like a popsicle. Here, however, we use the small, hard and sweet Fuyu persimmons, which you can safely bite into when they are firm. Do not substitute the soft persimmon or you will destroy the texture of the muffin. Use any fruit chutney you like (such as apple, ginger, peach, or mango) and cut up the large pieces of fruit. These muffins only need a spoonful of Sweet Yogurt Cream (page 559), if anything at all. But for a real indulgence, spread with a dab of Sweet Cheese (page 309).*

Vegetable spray and liners, optional, for muffin tins
1¾ cup unbleached all-purpose flour
¼ cup whole wheat flour
½ cup granulated sugar
¼ cup firmly packed brown sugar, measured then sifted
2 tablespoons baking powder
¼ teaspoon baking soda
½ teaspoon salt
½ teaspoon ground cinnamon
¼ teaspoon ground allspice
½ cup yellow raisins
½ cup finely chopped walnuts or cashews
2 small firm Fuyu persimmons, peeled and diced
¼ cup chutney (with any large pieces of fruit chopped)
¾ cup 1% milk
¼ cup canola oil
½ cup liquid egg substitute
Grated zest of 1 orange

1. Preheat the oven to 400 degrees F. Lightly coat regular or miniature muffin tins with a thin film of vegetable spray; or fit them with paper or aluminum foil liners and spray them lightly as well. Stir together in a mixing bowl until thoroughly blended the flours, sugars, baking powder and soda, salt, cinnamon and allspice. Add the raisins and nuts, tossing them with the flour to ensure they will remain evenly distributed throughout and won't sink to the bottom as they bake.

2. In a large measuring cup lightly beat together the remaining ingredients. Pour over the dry ingredients and blend quickly until you have a moist, lumpy batter.

3. Ladle the batter into the prepared muffin tins and bake for 20 minutes or until golden and a knife inserted in the center of a muffin comes out clean. Serve hot.

✻ PER SERVING *Calories: 268, Cholesterol (mg): 1, Saturated fat (g): 1, Total fat (g): 8, Sodium (mg): 328, Total fiber (g): 1*

Whole Wheat Corn Muffins

MAKES 1 DOZEN STANDARD-SIZE MUFFINS OR 2 DOZEN MINIATURE MUFFINS, SERVING SIZE 1 STANDARD-SIZE MUFFIN

IF YOU HAVE A DECORATIVE CAST-IRON MUFFIN PAN *in corn, star or other festive shapes, keep it handy because these muffins will become a favorite. The added vanilla gives a welcome body to these pleasantly sweet, low-fat nuggets.*

> Vegetable spray and liners, optional, for muffin tins
> 1 cup white cornmeal
> ½ cup whole wheat flour
> ½ cup unbleached all-purpose flour
> 1 tablespoon baking powder
> ¾ teaspoon salt
> ¼ cup sugar
> ¼ cup liquid egg substitute
> ⅓ cup olive oil
> 1 cup low-fat milk
> ½ teaspoon vanilla extract

1. Preheat the oven to 425 degrees F. Lightly coat standard-size or miniature muffin tins with a thin film of vegetable spray; or fit them with paper or aluminum foil liners and spray them lightly as well. In a mixing bowl, combine the cornmeal, flours, baking powder, salt and sugar, and stir until thoroughly blended.

2. In a measuring cup, lightly beat together the remaining ingredients. Stir them into the dry ingredients just until you have a moist but slightly lumpy batter. *Do not overbeat.*

3. Ladle the batter into the prepared muffin tins and bake for 25 minutes or until golden and a knife inserted in the center of a muffin comes out clean. Bake miniature muffins 10 to 15 minutes. Serve hot.

✻ PER SERVING *Calories: 163, Cholesterol (mg): 1, Saturated fat (g): 1, Total fat (g): 7, Sodium (mg): 244, Total fiber (g): 1*

Curried Corn Fingers

MAKES APPROXIMATELY 2 DOZEN FINGER-SHAPED MUFFINS,
SERVING SIZE 1 MUFFIN

THESE ARE A HANDS-DOWN FAVORITE. *The ideal amount of curry is a matter of preference, so adjust this intense spice mixture up or down as you desire, from 3/4 teaspoon to 1 tablespoon. More curry not only adds warmth, but it deepens the color to a rich, mustardy glow. If you don't have "finger" molds, bake in miniature or even standard-size muffin pans and extend the cooking time by five to eight minutes. They won't have the same airy texture, but the switch won't harm the complex spicy taste. Make sure you sift the curry powder into the flour mixture (a small tea strainer works well). Otherwise, it can form small lumps, an unpleasant surprise to the palate.*

Vegetable spray for muffin molds
1/2 cup yellow cornmeal
1/4 cup unbleached all-purpose flour
1/4 cup whole wheat flour
2 1/2 tablespoons sugar
1 1/2 teaspoons baking powder
1/2 teaspoon salt
Generous pinch of cayenne
1 teaspoon curry powder
1/4 cup olive oil
2/3 cup low-fat buttermilk
1 tablespoon liquid egg substitute
2 egg whites

1. Preheat the oven to 425 degrees F. Lightly coat miniature muffin tins or corn molds with a thin film of vegetable spray. Combine the cornmeal, flours, sugar, baking powder, salt and cayenne in a mixing bowl. Sift the curry powder into the bowl to distribute it evenly.

2. Blend the oil, buttermilk and egg substitute in a measuring cup and stir into the dry mixture, blending thoroughly.

3. In another bowl, beat the egg whites until soft and fold them into the batter. Pour into the prepared muffin cups and bake for 15 minutes or until golden. Best served hot.

❈ PER SERVING *Calories: 52, Cholesterol (mg): Trace, Saturated fat (g): Trace, Total fat (g): 2, Sodium (mg): 80, Total fiber (g): Trace*

Connemara Scones

OUR PERSONAL FAVORITES, *these scones should not be stored until they have cooled completely, or they will steam and loose their wonderfully crumbly texture. If you find the dough too moist, add flour by the tablespoon until you have a round of dough that glides easily on a floured surface.*

> Vegetable spray for baking sheet
> 1 cup unbleached all-purpose flour, plus extra for work surface
> 1 cup whole wheat flour
> 1½ tablespoons baking powder
> ¼ teaspoon baking soda
> 1 teaspoon salt
> Grated zest of 1 orange
> ¼ cup raisins or currants
> 1 tablespoon caraway seeds
> ½ stick (4 tablespoons) margarine, melted
> ¾ cup low-fat buttermilk
> ¼ cup liquid egg substitute
> 1 teaspoon vanilla extract

1. Preheat the oven to 375 degrees F. Lightly coat a baking sheet with a thin film of vegetable spray. Stir the flours, baking powder and soda, salt, orange zest, raisins and caraway seeds in a mixing bowl until thoroughly blended.

2. Lightly beat the remaining ingredients in a measuring cup and add to the dry mixture. Beat the dough with a fork until it forms a ball and pulls away cleanly from the sides of the bowl. If necessary, add flour or water by small spoonfuls until you have a workable dough.

3. Sprinkle a light coating of flour on a work surface and knead the dough for 15 or 20 seconds. Set aside to rest for 1 minute. Divide the dough into 2 balls and with a rolling pin, gently shape each ball into a circle 1 inch thick, flouring the surface as necessary to keep them from sticking. Place the rounds next to each other on the prepared baking sheet.

4. With the tip of a knife, score each round ¼ inch deep into 8 pie-shaped wedges. Bake for 25 minutes or until a light golden brown. Do not overcook or they will get hard. Cool only slightly. Cut through the scoring, separate the wedges and serve.

❋ PER SERVING *Calories: 100, Cholesterol (mg): Trace, Saturated fat (g): 1, Total fat (g): 3, Sodium (mg): 313, Total fiber (g): 1*

Whole Wheat Herb Scones

MAKES 16 SCONES, SERVING SIZE 1 SCONE

Do not let an absence of fresh herbs *deter you from making these excellent scones; dried herbs will also work and the finished product will immeasurably enhance brunch, lunch, afternoon tea, early supper, late supper or a midnight snack.*

Vegetable spray for baking sheet
1¼ cups whole wheat flour
¾ cup unbleached all-purpose flour, plus extra for work surface
¼ cup oat bran
1½ tablespoons baking powder
1 ounce freshly grated Parmesan cheese (about ¼ cup)
2 tablespoons mixed fresh herbs (such as basil, oregano, thyme,
    marjoram or savory) or 2 teaspoons dried
1 large garlic clove, minced
2 tablespoons chopped fresh chives
½ cup low-fat buttermilk, low-fat plain yogurt or low-fat milk
    soured with 1 tablespoon vinegar
Salt and freshly ground pepper to your taste
⅓ cup olive oil or canola oil
¼ cup liquid egg substitute
Juice of ½ lemon

1. Preheat the oven to 375 degrees F. Lightly coat a baking sheet with a thin film of vegetable spray. Stir the flours, oat bran, baking powder, cheese and herbs in a mixing bowl until thoroughly blended.

2. Lightly beat the remaining ingredients in a measuring cup and add to the dry mixture. Beat the dough with a fork until it forms a ball and pulls away cleanly from the sides of the bowl. If necessary, add flour or water by small spoonfuls until you have a workable dough.

3. Sprinkle a light coating of flour on a work surface and knead the dough for 15 or 20 seconds. Set aside to rest for 1 minute. Divide the dough into 2 balls and with a rolling pin, gently shape each ball into a circle 1 inch thick, flouring the surface as necessary to keep them from sticking. Place the rounds next to each other on the prepared baking sheet.

4. With the tip of a knife, score each round ¼ inch deep, into 8 pie-shaped wedges. Bake for 15 to 20 minutes or until light golden brown. Do not over-cook or they will get hard. Cool only slightly before serving. Cut through the scoring and separate the wedges and serve.

✿ PER SERVING *Calories: 115, Cholesterol (mg): 2, Saturated fat (g): 1, Total fat (g): 5, Sodium (mg): 147, Total fiber (g): 1*

✿

Herb Cheese Bread with Leeks

MAKES 1 LOAF WITH APPROXIMATELY 16 HALF-INCH SLICES,
SERVING SIZE 1 SLICE

THIS MOIST, QUICK BREAD *has a yeast-raised texture, which is intensely fragrant and answers the need for a bread flavorful enough to enjoy on its own, without the addition of buttery spreads. Because we use liquid egg substitutes, low-fat buttermilk, and only a small amount of olive oil, the Parmesan cheese adds a richness to this bread without hiking up the overall fat content.*

> Vegetable spray for loaf pan
> 1¾ cups unbleached all-purpose flour
> ½ cup whole wheat flour
> 2 teaspoons baking powder
> ¼ teaspoon baking soda
> 1½ teaspoons salt
> 1 tablespoon ground walnuts
> 2 tablespoons fresh mixed herbs or 2 teaspoons dried mixed herbs or
>   *herbes de Provence*
> 4 ounces Parmesan cheese, freshly grated (about 1⅓ cup)
> ¼ cup finely minced leek (white part only)
> ⅓ cup liquid egg substitute
> 1 cup low-fat buttermilk
> 2 tablespoons olive oil
> ¼ teaspoon very coarse sea salt mixed with 1 teaspoon olive oil

1. Preheat the oven to 350 degrees F. Prepare a loaf pan by lightly coating it with a thin film of vegetable spray. In a large mixing bowl, blend together the flours, baking powder and soda, salt, walnuts and herbs. Then blend in the Parmesan.

2. Combine the leeks, egg substitute, buttermilk and olive oil in a measuring cup and beat until thoroughly blended. Pour this mixture into the dry ingredients and stir until thoroughly blended.

3. Pour the batter into the prepared loaf pan and bake for 45 minutes. Brush with the salt and olive oil mixture and bake another 10 to 15 minutes or until a knife inserted in the center comes out clean. Cool for at least 15 minutes before slicing.

❉ PER SERVING *Calories: 120, Cholesterol (mg): 5, Saturated fat (g): Trace, Total fat (g): 4, Sodium (mg): 404, Total fiber (g): Trace*

Quick Oatmeal Caraway Bread with Currants

MAKES 1 LOAF WITH APPROXIMATELY 16 HALF-INCH SLICES,
SERVING SIZE 1 SLICE

CHOOSE THIS LIGHT CARAWAY LOAF *to dress up a simple soup and salad supper. Or toast a thin slice and enjoy it with a cup of herbal tea when you need a pick-me-up.*

Vegetable spray for loaf pan
1 cup unbleached all-purpose flour
½ cup whole wheat flour
¾ cup rolled oats
2 tablespoons baking powder
¼ teaspoon baking soda
1 teaspoon salt
2 tablespoons caraway seeds
⅓ cup liquid egg substitute
1 cup low-fat buttermilk
2 tablespoons olive oil
2 tablespoons currants

1. Preheat the oven to 350 degrees F. Lightly coat a loaf pan with a thin film of vegetable spray. In a mixing bowl, mix the flours, oats, baking powder and soda, and salt until thoroughly blended. Stir in the caraway seeds by hand.

2. Combine the egg substitute, buttermilk and olive oil in a measuring cup and beat until blended. Pour this mixture into the dry ingredients and stir until thoroughly blended. Stir in the currants by hand.

3. Pour into the prepared loaf pan and bake for 55 to 60 minutes or until a knife inserted in the center comes out clean. Cool for at least 15 minutes before slicing.

❉ PER SERVING *Calories: 87, Cholesterol (mg): 1, Saturated fat (g): Trace, Total fat (g): 2, Sodium (mg): 315, Total fiber (g): 1*

Basic Focaccia

MAKES 1 DOZEN THREE-INCH SLICES

ORIGINALLY BAKED ON HOT STONES *before the invention of ovens, this flat, leavened bread is found in endless varieties throughout Italy. Focaccia resembles pizza, but do not confuse the two. This chewy bread dressed with herbs, onions or other savories serves as an accent for the meal, whereas pizza as we know it, layered with sauces, meats, vegetables and cheeses, is the meal. A pizza peel eases the job of transferring the dough from counter top to oven and a pizza stone bakes it perfectly. If you don't have this equipment, though, we include alternative directions. Though you can omit the step, using a plastic spray bottle to spritz the oven with a spray of cold water two or three times during baking creates a crisper crust. Don't aim for the hot oven light, though, or it may explode. Make individual focaccias for a party and cut the baking time slightly, depending upon their size.*

> 1 package active dry yeast
> ½ teaspoon sugar
> 1 cup minus 1 tablespoon lukewarm water (105 to 115 degrees F)
> 3 cups bread flour
> 1 teaspoon salt
> ¼ cup olive oil plus 1 tablespoon for topping
> Salt and freshly ground pepper
> Additional toppings, optional (suggestions follow)
> Cornmeal for pizza stone or baking sheet
> Spray bottle filled with cold water for spritzing the oven

1. Mix the yeast, sugar and the lukewarm water in a measuring cup and set it aside for 3 to 5 minutes or until it foams.

2. Combine the flour and salt in the bowl of a food processor and pulse several times to blend. Pour in the dissolved yeast and then add ¼ cup olive oil. Process for 1 minute until smooth and elastic. Remove the blade and knead by hand against the side of the bowl for 15 seconds. Or, combine the flour and salt in a mixing bowl and pour in the dissolved yeast and olive oil. Beat with an electric mixer at high speed for 5 to 6 minutes or by hand for 10 to 12 minutes or until it forms a smooth, elastic ball. If you use a mixer, knead by hand against the side of the bowl for 30 seconds.

3. Place the dough in a large bowl lightly coated with a film of vegetable spray and cover it with a damp tea towel. Set in a warm spot until the dough doubles in bulk, about 1 hour.

4. If you have a pizza stone, place it in the oven before preheating it. Preheat the oven (with or without a pizza stone) to 500 degrees F. Turn the dough onto a floured work surface and punch it down. Roll out the dough into a 12-inch circle. Brush with the remaining tablespoon of olive oil, salt and pepper and any other desired topping. If you are using a pizza stone, sprinkle it with cornmeal and slide a pizza peel under the focaccia. Working carefully, shift the dough onto the hot pizza stone with rapid jerking motions. Or, roll the dough in a 9 x 12-inch rectangular shape and place it on a large baking sheet (it does not have to be an exact fit, the baking sheet can be larger) sprayed with vegetable oil and dusted with cornmeal. Place the baking sheet directly on the hot stone, or in its absence, directly on the oven rack. Reduce the heat to 475 degrees F and spray the bottom of the oven (away from the light bulb) with cold water and bake for 15 to 20 minutes or until golden and puffed at the edges. Spray the bottom of the oven at least once more during baking. Cool only slightly before slicing and serving.

❄ PER SERVING *Calories: 176, Cholesterol (mg): 0, Saturated fat (g): 1, Total fat (g): 6, Sodium (mg): 179, Total fiber (g): 1*

Suggested Toppings for Focaccia

You can simply brush the basic focaccia dough with olive oil, a favorite herb and coarse salt; or dress it up with one of the combinations suggested below. Better yet, consider the dough a canvas that waits for your own bold stroke. As you peruse your supermarket, look for particularly inviting or colorful combinations and when inspiration strikes, create an original. Bake as for Basic Focaccia.

- Toss 1 thinly sliced red onion with 2 tablespoons shredded zucchini. Sauté briefly in 2 tablespoons olive oil until just barely softened. Spread on top of the focaccia, dot with fresh rosemary, salt and pepper, and bake as directed.
- Toss 1 thinly sliced red onion in a skillet over medium-high heat with 2 tablespoons olive oil until barely softened. Sprinkle with 1/2 teaspoon sugar and 1 teaspoon white wine. Toss well and continue cooking over low heat for 15 minutes, stirring frequently and watching carefully to make sure the mixture doesn't scorch. Brush the focaccia with any of our pestos, top with the onions and bake as directed.
- Dice Canadian bacon, green onions, artichoke hearts, green olives and sage; arrange on the dough and bake as directed.
- Toss paper-thin slices of fresh red bell pepper, chopped sun-dried tomatoes, minced garlic, shredded basil leaves and grated Parmesan cheese together. Spread on the dough and bake as directed.
- Sprinkle basic dough with whole sage leaves or rosemary and coarse salt, and bake as directed.

CHAPTER 30

Appetizers

THE TERM "APPETIZER" HAS LONG BEEN AN EXCUSE *for pulling out the high-fat stops, towering trays of cheese nibbles on fat-ridden crackers, sour cream-drenched chips, greasy meatballs and deep-fried this and that. Sophisticated parties offer imported versions of the above, most likely adding rich cholesterol-laden pâtés to the menu. At an early-recipe tasting to celebrate the start of work on this book, Dr. Victor Dzau, Chief of Stanford's Cardiovascular Medicine Division and Chairman of the Department of Medicine, sampled appetizers destined for this chapter—White Bean Pâté (page 345), Stanford Guacamole (page 354), Spiced Chicken Nuggets with Hot Mango Purée (page 358–59), Herb Cheese Bread (page 336–37), grilled scallops with Cilantro Cream (page 294) among others—and looked up in amazement. "You invited me to a party for a heart book," he said. "I was expecting the usual carrot sticks." His comment got straight to the heart of this book: Good food, good living and good health can and must go hand-in-hand.*

In this chapter we have taken the term "appetizer" literally, and offer a collection of tidbits (and some larger bites) that will whet the appetite, soothe the appetite, calm the appetite and spark the appetite, depending on its demands. Some recipes, such as Oven-Baked Tortilla Chips (page 348) and Quick Black Bean Dip (page 355), will become snacking favorites around the TV, others such as our stunning opener, Tuna Tartare (page 342), might announce a formal dinner, while Red Potatoes with Salmon Pâté (page 348–49) could surprise your guests accustomed to picking their way in vain through a holiday hors d'oeuvre tray filled with liver pâtés and expensive cheeses with a delicious and heart-healthy morsel.

Tuna Tartare

SERVES 4

EACH ELEMENT OF THIS MINIMALIST DISH — *pear for texture, sesame oil for fragrance, soy to harmonize the whole and cilantro for surprise — precisely balances the clean taste of fresh ahi tuna. Heart healthy because of its omega-3 fatty acids, ahi is a tuna of incomparable sweetness. The same dish made with another variety of tuna (such as tombo), while good, does not have the same velvety smoothness. You may find that you prefer a drop or two more soy sauce or a little less sesame oil, but don't go too far afield from the amounts listed. While in small amounts they blend perfectly with the rich ahi, too much of one or the other will overpower it. Though this spread is very low in fat, it is quite rich. Small portions suffice. As with any raw fish, be absolutely sure the ahi was caught within 24 hours of serving. If you are unsure, choose a recipe that cooks the tuna and save this preparation for another day.*

> ¼ pound ahi tuna
> ½ teaspoon Asian sesame oil
> ½ teaspoon low-sodium soy sauce
> 2 tablespoons minced Bosc pear
> 6 or 7 leaves cilantro, minced
> 4 crisp lettuce leaves or water crackers

1. With a very sharp knife trim away any white membranes from the tuna (a dull knife will shred the tuna and ruin the appearance of the tartare). Finely mince the ahi, place in a bowl, add the oil and toss gently. Blend in the soy, pear and cilantro ingredients in the order given. Taste a small morsel and adjust the flavoring, adding by drops slightly more sesame oil or soy if you desire.

2. Mound the tartare on lettuce leaves or water crackers and serve immediately.

❉ PER SERVING *Calories: 43, Cholesterol (mg): 13, Saturated fat (g): Trace, Total fat (g): 1, Sodium (mg): 38, Total fiber (g): Trace*

Eggplant Caviar

MAKES APPROXIMATELY 3 CUPS, SERVING SIZE 1 TABLESPOON

ASSEMBLED ON YOUR COUNTER, *the ingredients for this fragrant vegetable mélange resemble a Renaissance still life, capturing the colors and flavors of the Mediterranean: the deep purple eggplant, the regal reds of tomato and pepper, the vibrant green herbs and zucchini, the olive oil glistening gold in its decanter. The pleasures are more than visual, though. The traditional approach to eggplant in this type of dish is to sauté it in olive oil. However, this vegetable can sponge up enormous quantities of oil before it is completely cooked, so we sidestep that fatty pitfall and roast it (or grill, if you prefer) first. The resulting caviar—a first cousin to main course ratatouille—is smooth tasting, very low in fat and absolutely irresistible. Because the caviar needs time to mellow, at least 24 hours and up to three days if desired, this savory spread is ideal for a party menu. Don't worry if you have some left over. Fill pita pockets with it for a snack or quick lunch or use it as a base for Breakfast Cheese Pizza (page 320). If you can't find the dense pumpernickel bread packaged in thin slices, substitute crackers, cocktail rye or warm corn tortillas.*

> 1 large eggplant
> 3 tablespoons extra-virgin olive oil
> 1 large onion, diced
> 1/2 *each* green and red bell pepper, seeded and diced
> 2 to 4 garlic cloves, minced
> 1/2 cup diced zucchini
> 2 large tomatoes, peeled, seeded and chopped
> 2 teaspoons salt
> Freshly ground pepper
> 1 tablespoon minced mixed fresh herbs (such as oregano,
>   thyme, marjoram, savory, chervil)
> 2 tablespoons minced fresh Italian parsley
> Westphalian pumpernickel bread, cut into quarters

1. Preheat the oven to 425 degrees F. Place the eggplant on a baking sheet and bake for 30 to 45 minutes or until soft and blistered. When cool enough to handle, peel and discard the skin and coarsely chop the pulp.

2. While the eggplant roasts, heat the oil in a large nonreactive skillet and add the onion, bell peppers and garlic. Sauté over low to medium heat for 10 to 15 minutes or until softened. Add the cooked eggplant, zucchini, tomatoes and salt, and season to your taste with pepper. Stir over high heat until the mixture boils. Reduce the heat immediately to a simmer, cover and cook slowly for 30 minutes or until the mixture thickens. Uncover and continue cooking for another 15 minutes or until most of the liquid has evaporated.

3. Add the herbs and adjust the seasoning to your taste. Mix well and simmer uncovered for 2 more minutes. Remove from the heat, cover and refrigerate for at least 24 hours. If liquid accumulates on the surface, stir thoroughly before placing it in a serving bowl, sprinkle with the parsley and surround it with the pumpernickel before serving.

FAT TRACKING TIP: Reduce the oil to 1 or 1½ tablespoons and cook the onions over low heat.

❉ PER SERVING (INCLUDES 1 PUMPERNICKEL SQUARE) *Calories: 33, Cholesterol (mg): 0, Saturated fat (g): Trace, Total fat (g): 1, Sodium (mg): 144, Total fiber (g): Trace*

White Bean Pâté

MAKES APPROXIMATELY 2 CUPS, SERVING SIZE 1 TABLESPOON

IN TODAY'S BUSY WORLD, *we might pass up this rich purée if we had to mash the beans with a mortar and pestle. So we are grateful for the high-tech ability to toss the beans and flavorings in a food processor or blender and purée a fabulous pesto in just a few seconds. But when you have time, there is nothing quite like the sensation of rocking a sharp chef's knife back and forth over fresh basil and parsley, and inhaling the heavenly fragrance until they are reduced to a fine, moist mince. Purée the bean mixture until smooth and silky, or if you prefer, stop when it is slightly chunky with a recognizable piece of bean here and there. As with most bean dishes, the salt harmonizes the complexities of flavoring. If you have a high-quality olive oil that you reserve for special dishes, definitely show it off in this pâté. Also, consider this as an appetizer for one of your vegetarian menus—the combination of beans and Melba toast forms a complete protein. If you use canned beans, rinse and drain them well first. Though their taste is satisfactory (not as good as beans you prepare yourself), they will produce a thinner consistency if you don't drain them well before using. The pâté will last several days in the refrigerator.*

2 cups cooked white beans
¼ cup fruity extra-virgin olive oil
2 tablespoons fresh lemon juice
1 tablespoon champagne vinegar or other good white wine vinegar
¾ teaspoon salt
Freshly ground pepper to your taste
Pinch of cayenne
¼ cup *each* fresh minced basil and Italian parsley
2 tablespoons nonfat plain yogurt
Melba toast

1. Several hours before serving, purée the beans in a blender or food processor with the olive oil, lemon juice, vinegar, salt, pepper, cayenne, basil and parsley. Stir in the yogurt and adjust the seasoning to your taste. Cover and refrigerate for several hours before serving.

2. Place the pâté in a serving bowl and surround with squares of Melba toast.

FAT TRACKING TIP: Reduce the olive oil to 2 tablespoons and add 2 tablespoons of the liquid from the beans.

❋ PER SERVING (INCLUDES 1 SQUARE OF TOAST) *Calories: 47, Cholesterol (mg): 0, Saturated fat (g): Trace, Total fat (g): 2, Sodium (mg): 82, Total fiber (g): 1*

Heart-Healthy Hummus

MAKES APPROXIMATELY 2 CUPS, SERVING SIZE 2 TABLESPOONS

ALONG WITH PROVIDING A DELICIOUS SPREAD *for crackers or vegetable sticks, garbanzos supply a dose of water-soluble fiber, which helps to lower cholesterol levels. To keep the fat count down, we use the liquid from the garbanzos (also known as chickpeas or ceci) to make this Middle Eastern specialty both smooth and low in fat. You can make this 24 hours ahead and allow the beans to absorb the tartness of the lemon so that the mixture is tangy, rather than acidic. Tahini, carried in health food stores and specialty markets, is a paste of sesame seeds similar to peanut butter. It has a delicious, mildly toasted flavor that makes this purée distinctive, and the combination of seeds and legumes (garbanzos) enhances the protein count. Old-fashioned peanut butter (that is, without hydrogenated oil), is an alternative if you can't find the sesame paste. Though it has no saturated fat, tahini, like peanut butter, unfortunately is very high in total fat, or we would use it more liberally in our recipes.*

HUMMUS
2 cups canned or cooked garbanzo beans
2 tablespoons tahini or peanut butter
1½ tablespoons extra-virgin olive oil
Juice of ½ lemon
1 large garlic clove
1 teaspoon ground cumin
Salt and freshly ground pepper
½ cup nonfat plain yogurt

ACCOMPANIMENTS
½ cup Salsa Fresca (page 357) or commercial red salsa, optional
Spiced Yogurt (page 291) or nonfat plain yogurt smoothed with a
 tablespoon of nonfat sour cream or low-fat milk, optional
6 rounds of pita bread, each cut into 6 triangles

1. Drain the garbanzo beans and reserve the liquid; then purée them with the remaining hummus ingredients in a blender or food processor. Add as much of the reserved liquid as necessary to make a smooth purée. Taste for seasoning, adding salt, pepper and lemon juice as desired. If you don't plan to serve it immediately, cover and refrigerate. Bring to room temperature before serving.

2. If you have a very coarse salsa, pulse it briefly in a blender to smooth it slightly. Serve the hummus, salsa and yogurt in separate bowls. Accompany the hummus with a basket of warm pita triangles.

FAT TRACKING TIP: Omit some or all of the olive oil and thin with the liquid from the beans.

❊ PER SERVING (INCLUDES ⅙TH PITA ROUND, DOES NOT INCLUDE YOGURT OR SALSA)
Calories: 83, Cholesterol (mg): Trace, Saturated fat (g): Trace, Total fat (g): 3, Sodium (mg): 181,
Total fiber (g): 1

Janet Fletcher's Tabbouleh

SERVES 6

THIS LEMONY, MINTY SALAD *came to us from one of Stanford's distinguished
culinary alumni—Janet Fletcher, San Francisco Bay Area food columnist, restaurant critic and cookbook author. She suggests serving this classic Middle
Eastern whole grain salad with yogurt and pita bread as an appetizer and cautions that, though it doesn't require much oil, don't skimp on the parsley and
mint, tabbouleh's trademark herbs. You can find room for tabbouleh on many
menus, especially one that includes Heart-Healthy Hummus (page 346–47)
and grilled eggplant, though we feel its highest and best use is as a salad for our
Grilled Chicken with Hot Mint Marinade (page 505–6). Note that if your
menu includes legumes, you will have a complete protein that is very low in fat.*

1 cup bulgur (cracked wheat)
2 cups boiling water
2 cups minced fresh parsley
1½ cups seeded and chopped tomato
¼ cup minced green onion
2 to 3 tablespoons chopped fresh mint
1 garlic clove, finely minced
1 tablespoon extra-virgin olive oil
¼ cup or more fresh lemon juice
Salt and freshly ground pepper
Optional garnishes: Greek olives, hearts of romaine
    or wedges of pita bread, low-fat or nonfat plain yogurt

1. Place the bulgur in a medium-size bowl. Add the boiling water, allow to stand
   for 15 minutes and fluff with a fork. If any liquid remains, drain the bulgur
   thoroughly, place it in a double thickness of cheesecloth and squeeze dry
   before fluffing it.

2. Add the remaining ingredients except salt and pepper and garnishes. Toss the
   mixture with a fork until thoroughly blended. Season to your taste with salt and
   pepper. Cover and refrigerate for at least 2 hours. Before serving, taste it once
   more and add more salt, pepper and/or lemon juice if desired. Surround the
   tabbouleh with olives and serve hearts of romaine or wedges of pita bread for
   scooping. Pass a bowl of yogurt separately, if desired.

❊ PER SERVING: (NOT INCLUDING OPTIONAL GARNISHES) Calories: 118, Cholesterol (mg): 0,
Saturated fat (g): Trace, Total fat (g): 3, Sodium (mg): 21, Total fiber (g): 6

Red Potatoes with Salmon Pâté

SERVES 8

Top STEAMED NEW RED POTATOES *with this rich and elegant pâté for an easy but stunning appetizer that adds heart-healthy complex carbohydrates (in the potatoes) and omega-3 fatty acids (in the salmon) to your menu. You can halve or double the recipe easily. And you can use the pâté to dress up a barbecue by coating grilled tuna or other fish with it. We use nonfat yogurt to smooth the pâté, and then top it with reduced fat sour cream just for the rich silkiness of it. You can prepare this at the last minute, but for ease at serving time, have the potatoes cooked and chilled and the pâté ready hours ahead; then assemble minutes before serving. Note that canned salmon does not work well here.*

8 red potatoes (the size of a golf ball or smaller) unpeeled,
    steamed until tender (page 266) and chilled

SALMON PÂTÉ
6 ounces cooked boneless salmon
1 garlic clove
¼ inch slice of onion
¼ cup coarsely chopped fresh Italian parsley
2 tablespoons fresh lemon juice
2 tablespoons capers
1 teaspoon green peppercorns
¼ medium-size red bell pepper, seeded and chopped
3 or 4 fresh basil leaves
2 tablespoons extra-virgin olive oil
Salt and freshly ground pepper
½ cup nonfat plain yogurt

¼ cup low-fat sour cream, optional, for garnish
Minced fresh chives for garnish

1. Trim a thin slice from the top and bottom of each potato so they won't rock on the serving platter and slice the potatoes in thirds crosswise.

2. Place the salmon in the bowl of a food processor or blender. With the machine running, drop the remaining pâté ingredients through the feed tube and process until smooth. Adjust the seasoning to your taste, then chill.

3. Arrange the potatoes on a serving platter. Spread a spoonful of the salmon pâté on top of each slice. Add a dab of sour cream, if desired, sprinkle with chives and serve.

Fat Tracking Tips: Double the yogurt in the pâté and eliminate the sour cream topping. Use nonfat sour cream.

❀ PER SERVING *Calories: 136, Cholesterol (mg): 11, Saturated fat (g): 1, Total fat (g): 5, Sodium (mg): 27, Total fiber (g): 1*

Oven-Baked Tortilla Chips with Tomato Orange Salsa

MAKES APPROXIMATELY 66 CHIPS,
SERVING SIZE 1-OUNCE (APPROXIMATELY 4 CHIPS) AND 1 TABLESPOON SALSA

WE LOVE CHIPS AS MUCH AS ANYONE, *especially when they are as fat free as these—perfect for spooning up salsas and dips. Compare them with commercial brands that weigh in at 165 calories and 8 grams of fat per ounce. Give the chips a spark by sprinkling with Cajun Seasoning (page 496) or an herb blend. Or spritz them with Garlic Oil (page 296), kept handy in a plastic spray bottle. Choose tortillas made only with lime and salt, rather than those with added fat.*

> Tomato Orange Salsa (recipe follows)
> 1 pound corn tortillas
> Olive oil–flavored vegetable spray
> Sea salt, optional

1. Prepare the salsa and chill thoroughly. Preheat the oven to 425 degrees F.

2. Stack 6 or 8 tortillas on top of each other and cut into 6 wedges. Continue with the remaining tortillas.

3. Lightly coat a baking sheet with a thin film of vegetable spray. Spread the cut tortillas loosely and evenly on the sheet to allow the heat to circulate and crisp them. Coat them lightly with the vegetable spray and salt. If you like, at this point add other seasonings suggested in the introduction to this recipe. Spread another layer, allowing them to overlap only slightly, spray and salt again. Don't have them tightly packed or they won't bake evenly. Bake for 25 minutes or until the chips are crisp and toasty.

4. Check the chips often, spreading them apart if they stick together. Give them another light salting if desired at the end and cool. Serve in a bowl and pass the salsa separately. Store remaining chips in a tightly sealed plastic bag.

❀ PER SERVING *Calories: 66, Cholesterol (mg): 0, Saturated fat (g): Trace, Total fat (g): 1, Sodium (mg): 46, Total fiber (g): Trace*

Tomato Orange Salsa
Makes approximately 1 cup, serving size 1 tablespoon

As a change from the familiar blend of hot peppers, lime and cilantro in Mexican salsa, we turned to that favored Mediterranean pairing of tomato and basil for our version and added the surprise of orange for a truly addictive salsa. Try it also on grilled fish or chicken or with white beans or tossed with shredded lettuce for a fat-free salad dressing.

> 1 large tomato, finely diced
> 2 tablespoons minced green onions
> 2 tablespoons fresh orange juice
> 1 tablespoon prepared sweet mustard
> 1/4 cup chopped fresh basil leaves
> Salt and freshly ground pepper

Place all the ingredients in a bowl and toss until thoroughly blended. Adjust the seasoning to your taste. Serve chilled. Cover and refrigerate any remaining salsa for two to three days.

❋ PER SERVING *Calories: 3, Cholesterol (mg): 0, Saturated fat (g): 0, Total fat (g): 0, Sodium (mg): 13, Total fiber (g): Trace*

Yogurt Dips

As a departure from spreads and dips based on sour cream, the following are some delectable recipes using Drained Yogurt (page 290–91) as a base for low-fat dips. In addition you can jazz up plain yogurt simply by adding salt and pepper, grated onions, garlic, chutney and/or a mixture of favorite herbs. We have used nonfat yogurt in these recipes, but you can also use low-fat yogurt, if you prefer, though you can achieve a creamy texture and round flavor without the extra fat. Serve these dips and creams with oil-free or oil-reduced chips, fresh or lightly steamed vegetables or toast fingers. For a refreshing change and a reduction in calories, forego baked goods and chips and serve with slices of chilled melon, jícama or slices of steamed red potatoes. You can also use these creamy sauces as accompaniments to grilled poultry and fish. Do not purée yogurt in a blender or food processor or it will liquefy. If the dip does become too thin, refrigerate for several hours to thicken it.

Salsa Cream

Makes approximately 2 cups, serving size 1 tablespoon

1 cup Tomato Orange Salsa (page 350) or your favorite salsa,
    drained of excess liquid
1 cup nonfat plain yogurt, drained of excess liquid

In a bowl, stir the salsa into the yogurt and serve immediately. This will become watery if you let it stand too long.

❀ PER SERVING *Calories: 18, Cholesterol (mg): 1, Saturated fat (g): Trace, Total fat (g): Trace, Sodium (mg): 21, Total fiber: Trace*

Cucumber Cream With Dill

Makes approximately 1¼ cups, serving size 1 tablespoon

½ medium-size cucumber, peeled, seeded and chopped
1 green onion (white part only), chopped
¾ cup drained nonfat yogurt (page 290–91)
Salt and freshly ground pepper to your taste
½ teaspoon dill seed, dried dill weed or fresh dill

Mince together the cucumber and onion in a food processor or blender. Stir in the remaining ingredients by hand. Serve immediately or cover and chill briefly.

❀ PER SERVING *Calories: 7, Cholesterol (mg): 0, Saturated fat (g): Trace, Total fat (g): Trace, Sodium (mg): 8, Total fiber: 0*

Minted Cucumber Cream

Makes approximately 1¼ cups, serving size 1 tablespoon

½ medium-size cucumber, peeled, seeded and chopped
¾ cup drained nonfat yogurt (page 290–91)
Salt to taste
3 or 4 large fresh mint leaves, minced

Mince cucumber in a food processor or blender. Stir in the remaining ingredients by hand. Serve immediately or cover and chill briefly.

❋ PER SERVING *Calories: 7, Cholesterol (mg): Trace, Saturated fat (g): Trace, Total fat (g): Trace, Sodium (mg): 8, Total fiber: Trace*

Curried Carrot Cream

Makes approximately 1½ cups, serving size 1 tablespoon

½ onion, quartered
⅓ pound carrots, sliced
½ cup drained nonfat yogurt (page 290–91), mixed with ½ cup nonfat
   sour cream
Salt and freshly ground pepper to your taste
½ to 1 teaspoon curry powder

As directed on page 266, steam onion and carrots 10 minutes or until tender. Purée them in a food processor or blender and stir in remaining ingredients. Cover and refrigerate for 30 minutes before serving to allow the flavors to mellow.

❋ PER SERVING *Calories: 10, Cholesterol (mg): Trace, Saturated fat (g): Trace, Total fat (g): Trace, Sodium (mg): 11, Total fiber: Trace*

Onion Cream

Makes approximately 1 cup, serving size 1 tablespoon

½ small onion, unpeeled and halved
A few drops of olive oil
¾ cup drained nonfat plain yogurt (page 290–91)
¼ cup nonfat sour cream
2 tablespoons freshly grated Parmesan cheese
Salt and freshly ground pepper to your taste

Brush cut end of onion with olive oil. Roast or grill it until it is browned (but not burned) and soft. Remove the outer skin and cut in quarters. With the machine running, drop the onion into a food processor or blender and mince. In a small bowl, stir the onion into the remaining ingredients. Blend well, cover and refrigerate for 30 minutes before serving to allow the flavors to mellow.

❀ PER SERVING *Calories: 19, Cholesterol (mg): 1, Saturated fat (g): Trace, Total fat (g): Trace, Sodium (mg): 32, Total fiber: Trace*

Potato–Red Pepper Cream

Makes approximately 3 cups, serving size 1 tablespoon

1 pound boiling potatoes, peeled and quartered
½ cup minced red bell pepper
¼ cup minced green onions
1 cup Drained Yogurt (page 290–91) *or* ½ cup nonfat plain yogurt
    and ½ cup nonfat sour cream
Salt and freshly ground pepper to your taste

As directed on page 266, steam potatoes 8 to 10 minutes or until very tender. Put them through a ricer or mash them in a large bowl. Stir in remaining ingredients. Depending on the moisture in the potatoes, you can add more yogurt if necessary to lighten the purée. Stir in the remaining ingredients and serve while still warm.

❀ PER SERVING *Calories: 12, Cholesterol (mg): 0, Saturated fat (g): Trace, Total fat (g): Trace, Sodium (mg): 4, Total fiber: Trace*

Stanford Guacamole

MAKES 1¼ CUPS, SERVING SIZE 1 TABLESPOON

SWEET AND HOT AND INTENSELY GREEN, *the seasonings in this knockout dip might remind you of the avocado–sour cream original, which inspired it, but the calories, cholesterol and fat are wonderfully lean. Serve with Oven-Baked Tortilla Chips (page 348) or crisp or lightly steamed vegetables.*

> 1 cup fresh or frozen green peas, thawed
> ¼ cup chopped red onion
> 2 medium-size garlic cloves
> 1 tablespoon olive oil or canola oil
> 1 tablespoon nonfat sour cream
> 1 tablespoon nonfat plain yogurt
> Several drops Tabasco or other hot pepper sauce to your taste
> ½ fresh jalapeño pepper, seeded and minced (use more or less
>   as desired)
> Salt and white pepper to your taste
> ¼ cup peeled and mashed avocado
> Juice of 1 lime

1. If you use fresh peas, steam or boil them for 1 minute. Do not allow them to overcook or they will lose the fresh taste and bright color that distinguishes this dip.

2. In a food processor or blender jar, combine the peas with all the ingredients, except the lime juice. Purée until smooth; the peas will retain a slight texture.

3. Add half the lime juice, taste, then add more until you have a desirable piquancy. If you ordinarily like tame seasonings, try experimenting with more heat by increasing the Tabasco and/or jalapeño, as the sweetness of the peas accommodates quite a bit of fiery pepper without exacting too much pain in return. If possible, cover and refrigerate for several hours before serving to allow the flavors to blend thoroughly.

FAT TRACKING TIP: Eliminate the avocado. Decrease or eliminate the oil.

❋ PER SERVING *Calories: 16, Cholesterol (mg): Trace, Saturated fat (g): Trace, Total fat (g): 1, Sodium (mg): 1, Total fiber (g): Trace*

Quick Black Bean Dip

MAKES 1 CUP, SERVING SIZE 1 TABLESPOON

SIMPLE BLACK BEANS *make a delicious fat-free dip for Oven-Baked Tortilla Chips (page 348) or raw or lightly steamed vegetables. Top with one of the salsas listed in the index, or serve your favorite commercial fresh brand of salsa from the dairy case.*

> 1½ cups cooked Basic Black Beans (page 426–27) or canned beans with 2 tablespoons of liquid
> 1 small garlic clove, minced
> ½ teaspoon ground cumin
> ¼ cup fresh cilantro leaves
> 2 tablespoons *each* nonfat plain yogurt and nonfat sour cream
> ½ cup nonfat plain yogurt mixed with 2 teaspoons minced fresh onion
> Salt and freshly ground pepper
> ⅓ cup salsa of choice for topping
> Fresh cilantro leaves for garnish

1. Place the beans, garlic, cumin and cilantro leaves in a blender or food processor and purée. Transfer to a serving bowl. Stir in the 2 tablespoons each yogurt and sour cream. Cover and chill thoroughly.

2. In a separate bowl, stir together the ½ cup yogurt and onion mixture and season to your taste with salt and pepper. Set aside until you are ready to serve.

3. Spoon the salsa over the bean dip and then top with the yogurt mixture. Garnish with cilantro leaves.

❋ PER SERVING *Calories: 29, Cholesterol (mg): Trace, Saturated fat (g): Trace, Total fat (g): Trace, Sodium (mg): 12, Total fiber (g): 1*

Crab with Salsa Fresca in Lettuce Cups

MAKES 1 DOZEN APPETIZERS, SERVING SIZE 1 FILLED LETTUCE CUP

SOME SAY THE BEST THING *about living in the San Francisco Bay Area is our Dungeness crab. The season begins in the autumn with the blessing of the fleet, and all of us who love the sweetness of Dungeness with sourdough bread and a good olive oil–based salad make our own silent wish for a bountiful catch. The familiar presentation for crab—Dungeness, king or other types—calls for a bowl of melted butter or mayonnaise plus a bowl for the discarded shells. We offer a spicy, fat-free salsa that enhances the flavor as well or better than a buttery or eggy bath. Then we dispense with the shells before serving and wrap the crab in lettuce. Even if we didn't have to defend our strategy on health grounds, we would urge you to try the crab cups for the simple reason that they are so delicious. When crab is out of season, substitute chopped cooked bay shrimp or prawns.*

> Chilled iceberg lettuce leaves
> 1 pound cooked, shredded crab meat
> Salsa Fresca (recipe follows) or Tomato Orange Salsa (page 350)
> Fresh cilantro sprigs for garnish

1. At least an hour before serving, place the lettuce leaves in ice water for 5 minutes. Dry them on paper towels, patting them to remove excess water. Remove the thick stems and trim large leaves to palm-sized cups. Wrap them in paper towels and store in a plastic bag or covered container until serving time.

2. In a small bowl, stir the crab into the Salsa Fresca, cover and chill for at least an hour. Spoon the mixture into 12 lettuce cups and arrange on a serving platter. Garnish with sprigs of cilantro.

❋ PER SERVING *Calories: 48, Cholesterol (mg): 29, Saturated fat (g): Trace, Total fat (g): 1, Sodium (mg): 159, Total fiber (g): Trace*

Salsa Fresca

MAKES APPROXIMATELY 1 CUP, SERVING SIZE 1 TABLESPOON

A SIMPLE, CRISP SALSA, *easily assembled, for dipping chips, for spreading on grilled fish or poultry or for topping hummus (page 346–47). Use anytime a recipe calls for fresh salsa.*

> 1 large tomato, finely diced
> 3 large green onions, finely diced
> Juice of 1 lime
> ½ cup seeded and finely diced red bell pepper
> ¼ cup chopped fresh cilantro leaves
> 1 teaspoon minced fresh jalapeño pepper, optional
> Salt and freshly ground pepper

Place all the ingredients in a bowl and toss until thoroughly blended. Adjust the seasoning to your taste. Serve chilled.

❋ PER SERVING *Calories: 4, Cholesterol (mg): 0, Saturated fat (g): 0, Total fat (g): 0, Sodium (mg): 14, Total fiber (g): Trace*

Spiced Chicken Nuggets with Hot Mango Purée

MAKES APPROXIMATELY 2 DOZEN NUGGETS

SOMETHING THIS EASY SHOULDN'T BE THIS GOOD, *but try it and see for yourself. For parties, prepare the Hot Mango Purée and the sesame coating for the chicken the day before. Roll the chicken in the coating early in the day, cover and refrigerate; then bake just minutes before serving (have a supply of toothpicks close by). And, instead of picking up chicken nuggets soaked in saturated fat at a take-out place, tuck these morsels into a picnic basket for a tailgate party or beach outing. You can also bake chicken breasts with the spiced mixture for an easy entrée. This recipe doubles easily for large crowds and would also serve two as an entrée.*

Hot Mango Purée (recipe follows)

SPICED PEANUT COATING
1 tablespoon sesame seeds
2 tablespoons dry roasted peanuts
Pinch of cayenne
1/4 teaspoon ground cinnamon
1/2 teaspoon grated orange zest
1/4 teaspoon curry powder
1/4 teaspoon salt

1 whole chicken breast, boned and skinned, cut into 2 x 1/2-inch strips
Vegetable spray for baking sheet

1. Preheat the oven to 450 degrees F. Prepare the mango purée, place in a serving bowl and refrigerate.

2. Spread the sesame seeds on a baking sheet and bake them for 8 to 12 minutes or until golden. Check frequently to make sure they don't scorch.

3. In a blender or food processor, pulse the peanuts until they are approximately the size of sesame seeds. This only takes seconds; watch them carefully or you will have peanut butter instead of crushed peanuts. In a small bowl, combine the peanuts with the sesame seeds and the other coating ingredients and blend thoroughly.

4. Toss the chicken in the peanut mixture, coating it thoroughly. Lightly coat a baking sheet with a thin film of vegetable spray. Arrange the chicken in 1 layer on the baking sheet and bake in the preheated 450 degree F oven for 8 to 12 minutes or until the chicken is springy to the touch and appears cooked through. Turn once or twice during this time so the pieces will cook evenly. Arrange the nuggets on a serving platter next to a bowl of Hot Mango Purée and a small bowl of toothpicks.

Fat Tracking Tip: Use turkey breast instead of chicken.

❈ PER SERVING (INCLUDES 3 NUGGETS AND 1 ½ TABLESPOONS HOT MANGO PURÉE) *Calories: 67, Cholesterol (mg): 18, Saturated fat (g): Trace, Total fat (g): 2, Sodium (mg): 169, Total fiber (g): 1*

Hot Mango Purée
Makes ¾ cup, serving size 1 tablespoon

You will find many uses for this peppery tropical sauce; coating broiled fish and poultry come easily to mind. But for a refreshing and unique snack, spoon it over an arrangement of bananas and fresh summer fruit. If you like white-hot food, add the full half teaspoon of peppers at once. Otherwise, start cautiously and taste as you go.

> 1 mango, peeled, seeded and puréed
> 2 tablespoons red wine vinegar
> ¼ teaspoon salt
> 1 teaspoon or more fresh lime juice
> 1 to 3 teaspoons grated fresh ginger
> A pinch to ½ teaspoon dried crushed red peppers

Purée the mango, vinegar, salt and lime juice in a blender or food processor until smooth. Begin adding the ginger and peppers in small amounts and continue until the sauce is as hot and fruity as you desire.

❈ PER SERVING *Calories: 12, Cholesterol (mg): 0, Saturated fat (g): 0, Total fat (g): 0, Sodium (mg): 46, Total fiber (g): Trace*

Miniature Black Bean Burritos

MAKES 10 APPETIZERS, SERVING SIZE 1 BURRITO

HAVE THE BEANS VERY HOT *so the shreds of jack cheese will melt easily. Make full-sized versions of these delicious little bean sandwiches for lunch or supper (beans and tortillas provide low-fat complete protein). You can vary the flavor by substituting our Black Bean Chili (page 428) for Orange-Flavored Black Beans.*

> ¼ cup Salsa Fresca (page 357)
> Orange-Flavored Black Beans (page 431), without the cilantro
> ½ ounce reduced-fat Monterey Jack cheese, coarsely grated
>   (about 3 tablespoons)
> 5 large flour tortillas, cut in half
> ½ cup minced fresh cilantro
> Fresh cilantro for garnish

1. Prepare the salsa and beans (omitting the cilantro) and keep the beans hot until ready to serve.

2. Sprinkle a scant teaspoon of cheese onto each tortilla half. Spoon a small mound of beans and a teaspoon of salsa in the center of the tortilla. Sprinkle with cilantro. Fold the bottom third of the tortilla over the bean mixture and fold the sides over in thirds so that you have a papoose shape with the top open. Arrange on a platter and garnish with cilantro. Serve immediately.

FAT TRACKING TIP: Use only a few shreds of cheese per serving, or none at all.

❋ PER SERVING *Calories: 138, Cholesterol (mg): 1, Saturated fat (g): Trace, Total fat (g): 2, Sodium (mg): 96, Total fiber (g): 2*

🌿

CHAPTER 31

Soups

KING ARTHUR'S KNIGHTS *dined on "soups of all sorts."* Larousse Gastronomique, *the famed French encyclopedia of food, lists instructions for almost 300 varieties of soup. And at formal banquets in China, a special soup is so prized that it is served in magnificently and extravagantly carved melons. Yet, with this great culinary tradition behind soup, there are still those who think it comes only in red and white cans. Soups are commonly touted as welcome restoratives for the afflictions of the common cold; they are warming and comforting in the dead of winter and an easy solution for a no-fuss supper. Yes, they are all these wonderful things. But even better, as we will show you, they can perform their tricks unencumbered by harmful fats. In fact, soups, even rich, creamy varieties, are perhaps the easiest recipes to lighten up, thanks to some of our fat-tracking tricks.*

For creamy soups, use vegetable purées smoothed with milk, buttermilk or even yogurt instead of cream. For example, creamy, filling Double Garlic Soup with Red Pepper Purée (page 373–74) eliminates saturated fat ingredients, but then adds an extra dimension of flavor with a swirl of a rich red pepper purée made with heart-healthy oil. Pumpkin and Winter Vegetable Soup (page 368) is a model of ingenuity that strips harmful fats by simmering vegetables in a rich stock rather than frying them in butter. Spicy Black Bean Soup with Garlic-Shrimp Guacamole (page 362–63) incorporates high-fat ingredients, such as avocado, in a low-fat soup so that the whole (total fat count) is less than some of the parts, and happily so.

To paraphrase an old saw, if you want to eat in haste, cook at your leisure. This is especially true for soups, some of which involve several hours of simmering. In this vein, we encourage you to use our homemade chicken, beef, fish and vegetable stocks as the bases for all your soups. Not only are the flavors superior to commercial broths, but canned products can be quite salty, particularly important if you need or want to curb sodium in your diet. Having your own store of low-fat, low-sodium stock also means you can more quickly turn a fresh vegetable into, say, Curried Broccoli Soup (page 372–73), which can simmer while you fix the rest of the meal. A word of caution about puréeing hot soups: Always remember to cover the processor spout or blender jar and purée hot mixtures at low speeds to start, then gradually increase the power to prevent the hot liquid from exploding out of the top.

Spicy Black Bean Soup
with Garlic-Shrimp Guacamole
SERVES 8

WE PUSHED THE FLAVORING ELEMENTS *to the outer limits here and developed a delicious match of seasoned beans and creamy topping. As with all bean soups, this one stores well and you can make it 24 hours ahead for a sensational party menu. Both components are easy to prepare, and the Garlic-Shrimp Guacamole also makes a wonderful spread for the crusty bread you will want to serve with this soup.*

> 1 tablespoon extra-virgin olive oil
> 1 medium-size onion, diced
> 2 large or 4 small garlic cloves, minced
> 1 teaspoon ground cumin
> 1 bay leaf
> 2 cups black beans, washed, soaked and drained
>   (see Basic Black Beans page 426–27)
> 6 cups cold water
> 5 cups Beef Stock (page 288–89) or canned low-sodium,
>   low-fat beef broth
> 1 can (28 ounces) crushed tomatoes
> 1 small fresh jalapeño pepper, seeded and minced
> Salt and freshly ground pepper to your taste
> Chopped fresh cilantro for garnish
> Garlic-Shrimp Guacamole (recipe follows) for topping

1. Heat the oil in a large nonreactive pot over low-medium heat, then add the onion and garlic. Stir thoroughly for 1 minute, then partially cover the pot and, stirring frequently, cook slowly for 4 to 5 minutes or until the onion has softened. Stir in the cumin and add the bay leaf, beans and the cold water. Bring to a boil, then reduce the heat and simmer uncovered for 1 hour or until the beans have begun to soften.

2. Add the remaining soup ingredients. Bring to a boil, reduce the heat to a simmer, and cook for another 1 to 1½ hours or until the beans are very tender. Taste for seasoning, adding salt and pepper as you desire. For a thicker soup, purée 1 cup of the soup and stir it back into the pot.

3. Ladle the soup into 8 bowls and serve hot. Sprinkle with chopped cilantro and pass the Garlic-Shrimp Guacamole separately.

FAT TRACKING TIP: Serve with nonfat plain yogurt instead of the Garlic-Shrimp Guacamole.

❀ PER SERVING (INCLUDES 2½ TABLESPOONS GARLIC-SHRIMP GUACAMOLE) *Calories: 232, Cholesterol (mg): 8, Saturated fat (g): 1, Total fat (g): 4, Sodium (mg): 281, Total fiber (g): 5*

Garlic-Shrimp Guacamole

Makes approximately 1¼ cups, serving size 1 tablespoon

You may want to serve this with other bean soups or side dishes, though keep an eye on the fat in them. By itself, this is a high-fat topping, even though it contains very little saturated fat.

> ½ ripe avocado, peeled and diced
> ¼ cup nonfat plain yogurt
> ¼ cup reduced-fat sour cream
> 1 small garlic clove, minced
> 1½ green onions (white part only), chopped
> ½ tomato, peeled, seeded and chopped
> ½ small fresh jalapeño pepper, optional, minced
> 2 tablespoons chopped fresh cilantro
> Juice of ½ lime
> ¼ cup chopped cooked bay shrimp
> Salt and freshly ground pepper to your taste

For the guacamole, purée the avocado in a food processor or blender, or mash it in a medium-size bowl. Fold in the remaining ingredients, adding salt and pepper as you desire. Serve immediately. If you like, you can prepare the guacamole without the shrimp several hours ahead, cover and refrigerate it, and add the shrimp just before serving.

FAT TRACKING TIPS: Use all nonfat plain yogurt and omit or reduce the sour cream. Use ¾ cup nonfat plain yogurt and use ¼ cup reduced-fat sour cream. Use fat-free sour cream. Savings in saturated and total fat will be slight per serving with each reduction, but would allow larger servings.

❀ PER SERVING *Calories: 16, Cholesterol (mg): 3, Saturated fat (g): Trace, Total fat (g): 1, Sodium (mg): 20, Total fiber (g): Trace*

Curried Red Lentil Soup

SERVES 4

SALMON-COLORED LENTILS TURN A FIERY YELLOW, *mimicking the heat of the sun in this wonderful, highly seasoned soup. This is one of those recipes that makes us wish we could step out from the pages of the book, offer you a taste and say, "See how good heart-healthy food is!"*

> 2 tablespoons extra-virgin olive oil
> 1 cup diced onion
> 1 garlic clove, minced
> 1 cup red lentils
> 4 cups Chicken Stock (page 285–86) or canned low-fat,
>   low-sodium chicken broth
> 1 tablespoon minced fresh serrano or jalapeño pepper, seeded
> 1 teaspoon curry powder
> Pinch of cayenne
> ¼ teaspoon ground turmeric
> Salt and white pepper
> 1 tart green apple, peeled and diced
> 1 red bell pepper, seeded and diced
> ½ cup chopped fresh cilantro
> ½ cup nonfat plain yogurt

1. In a large, heavy-bottomed saucepan, heat the olive oil over low-medium heat and add the onion and garlic. Stir for 2 to 3 minutes until they begin to soften. Reduce the heat, cover the pan and allow the onions to "sweat" for 10 to 15 minutes or until they are very soft. Stir occasionally to make sure they don't scorch.

2. While the onions cook, rinse the lentils several times in cold water. Add the lentils and chicken stock to the cooked onions and bring the mixture to a boil. Reduce the heat and simmer uncovered for 20 to 25 minutes or until the lentils are tender but not mushy.

3. Stir in the serrano pepper, curry powder, cayenne, turmeric, and season to your taste with salt and pepper. Cook for another 5 minutes. In a blender, purée half the soup and stir it back into the saucepan.

4. Ladle the hot soup into 4 bowls and garnish with the diced apple, red pepper, cilantro and a dollop of yogurt. Serve while still hot and the apple and pepper are still crisp.

FAT TRACKING TIP: Eliminate the oil and simmer the onions in stock until they soften.

❄ PER SERVING *Calories: 314, Cholesterol (mg): 1, Saturated fat (g): 1, Total fat (g): 7, Sodium (mg): 41, Total fiber (g): 9*

Jennifer Schroeder's
Instant Black Bean Soup

SERVES 4

THIS EXCITING SOUP DEFEATS THE MYTH *that healthy food is hard to prepare, doesn't taste very good, makes baby food seem spicy by comparison and other nonsense about low-fat food not measuring up. The soup also rebels at refrigeration and reheating (the individual flavors of cumin, garlic and beans become pallid and muddy), so prepare the soup just before you plan to serve it. You can double or halve the recipe quite easily. Use fresh salsa from the deli case of your supermarket, if you don't have homemade salsa on hand; these bright sauces are more versatile, more interesting and often lower in fat than the canned salsas. Homemade beans will lower the sodium count.*

> 2 cups canned black beans, with ¼ cup of their liquid
> 2 tablespoons extra-virgin olive oil
> 1 small garlic clove, minced
> 2 teaspoons ground cumin
> ½ cup fresh cilantro leaves
> 2 tablespoons minced onion
> ¾ cup nonfat plain yogurt
> Juice of ½ lime
> 1 teaspoon grated lime zest
> Salt and white pepper
> Salsa Fresca (page 357) or other fresh salsa, optional
> Fresh cilantro leaves for garnish

1. Put the beans, olive oil, garlic, cumin, cilantro and onion in a saucepan and heat until bubbly. You can also heat it in a microwave. Purée in a food processor or blender until smooth.

2. Stir in ½ cup of the yogurt, the lime juice and grated zest, and season to your taste with salt and pepper. Ladle into 4 bowls and top each with a tablespoon of the remaining yogurt. Serve immediately with a garnish of salsa if you are including it and a sprig of fresh cilantro.

FAT TRACKING TIP: Eliminate the olive oil.

❄ PER SERVING (SALSA FRESCA NOT INCLUDED) *Calories: 247, Cholesterol (mg): 1, Saturated fat (g): 1, Total fat (g): 9, Sodium (mg): 644, Total fiber (g): 11*

White Bean and Tomato Soup
with White Bean Pesto

SERVES 6

THE WHITE BEAN PESTO *adds an irresistible layer of flavor to this filling soup. You can also make the pesto separately and coat grilled chicken with it, or use it instead of butter or margarine as a saturated fat-free spread for hot, crusty bread. Canned white beans work quite well in both the soup and the pesto. In the summertime, shred a few fresh mint leaves onto the soup for a sparkling contrast.*

> 2 cups cooked white beans or canned cannellini
>   (Italian white) beans
> 1 onion, sliced
> 2 large garlic cloves, mashed
> 4 cups Chicken Stock (page 285–86) or canned low-fat,
>   low-sodium chicken broth
> 4 medium-size tomatoes, peeled, seeded and coarsely chopped
> ½ cup chopped fresh basil leaves
> Salt and freshly ground pepper
> 2 small garlic cloves, minced
> 2 tablespoons crushed walnuts, toasted as on page 300
> 2 tablespoons extra-virgin olive oil

1. Combine the beans, onion, garlic and stock in a large nonreactive saucepan. Bring to a boil, then reduce the heat and simmer for 30 minutes. Reserve ½ cup of the beans for the pesto. Add the tomatoes to the saucepan, raise the heat slightly and allow the soup to bubble gently for 5 minutes, stirring from time to time. Add half the basil and simmer for 1 more minute; then purée the soup in a blender or a food processor until smooth. Season lightly with salt and pepper to your taste.

2. To make the pesto, process the reserved beans, remaining basil, garlic and walnuts in a blender or food processor until you have a smooth purée. Slowly pour in the oil until thick and smooth, and season lightly with salt and pepper.

3. Ladle the soup into 6 bowls. Serve hot with a dollop of the pesto on top. Pass the remaining pesto separately.

FAT TRACKING TIPS: Stir the pesto into an equal amount of nonfat plain yogurt to further dilute the concentration of oil; serve half of this mixture with the soup and save the remaining pesto for another menu. Reduce or omit the walnuts.

✳ PER SERVING *Calories: 173, Cholesterol (mg): 0, Saturated fat (g): 1, Total fat (g): 7, Sodium (mg): 14, Total fiber (g): 4*

Carrot, Leek and Fennel Soup

SERVES 6

USE THIS VERY ELEGANT SOUP *to get a holiday feast off to a memorable start. For the sake of convenience, you can make the soup early in the day and reheat with the milk before serving. The pronounced flavor of raw fennel mellows as it cooks.*

> 1 tablespoon extra-virgin olive oil
> 1 bulb fennel, trimmed and sliced
> 1 pound leeks (white part only), sliced
> 1 pound carrots, chopped
> 6 cups Chicken Stock (page 285–86) or canned low-fat,
>   low-sodium chicken broth
> 1 cup low-fat milk
> Salt and freshly ground pepper to your taste

1. Heat the olive oil in a large saucepan. Add the fennel and leeks and stir over low-medium heat for 3 to 4 minutes or until the leeks have softened. Continue cooking, stirring frequently but not continuously, for 10 minutes or until the vegetables are wilted. Watch them carefully so they don't scorch.

2. Stir in the carrots and stock. Over high heat bring to a boil and cook for 30 seconds. Reduce the heat and simmer for 30 minutes or until the carrots are quite soft.

3. Purée soup in a blender and stir in the milk. Season to your taste with salt and pepper and serve hot in 6 individual bowls.

FAT TRACKING TIPS: Use skim or 1% milk instead of low-fat milk. Omit the oil and sauté/sweat (page 271) or braise/sweat (page 273) the fennel and leek.

❋ PER SERVING *Calories: 120, Cholesterol (mg): 3, Saturated fat (g): 1, Total fat (g): 3, Sodium (mg): 85, Total fiber (g): 5*

Pumpkin and Winter Vegetable Soup

SERVES 6

USE EITHER THE LARGE PUMPKIN OR THE SMALL MINIATURES, *sometimes referred to as "Darling" pumpkins, which have recently gained popularity. Follow this soup with a light pasta or consider Chicken Roasted with Pears, Fennel and Red Onion (page 509–10) for a formal meal. If fresh pumpkin is out of season, use unsweetened canned pumpkin.*

2 tablespoons extra-virgin olive oil
1 onion, diced
1 small garlic clove, minced
½ cup white wine
½ pound carrots, chopped
1 small white turnip, peeled and chopped
2 cups cubed fresh pumpkin
6 cups Chicken Stock (page 285–86) or canned low-fat,
    low-sodium chicken broth
Generous pinch of cayenne
Salt and freshly ground pepper to your taste
6 slices French bread

1. Heat the oil in a large nonreactive saucepan until a spray of water dances on the surface. Then add the onion and garlic and stir for 2 or 3 minutes or until they wilt. Add the wine and bring to a boil. Reduce the heat slightly and continue cooking until the liquid reduces to 2 tablespoons, stirring frequently to make sure the onions don't scorch. This reduction makes the onions more flavorful than if you simply add wine to the soup.

2. Add the carrots, turnip, pumpkin, stock and cayenne. Bring to a boil, reduce the heat and simmer for about 40 minutes or until the vegetables are quite tender. Purée half the mixture in a blender or food processor and stir it back into the soup. Reheat if necessary and season to your taste with salt and pepper. Lightly toast the bread and cut it into diagonal quarters. Serve in bowls and tuck the toast around the edge.

FAT TRACKING TIPS: Eliminate the oil and cook the onions and garlic with the soup. Eliminate the cheese.

❦ PER SERVING *Calories: 178, Cholesterol (mg): 3, Saturated fat (g): 1, Total fat (g): 6, Sodium (mg): 270, Total fiber (g): 2*

Potato and Red Pepper Soup

SERVES 6

OUR VERSION *of the classic* potage Parmentier *(potato leek soup) is still rich —
rich in flavor, not butter and cream. Reserve a few pieces of potato before
puréeing to give added texture to the soup (red potatoes make a lighter soup
that complements the peppers, but they do not have the starch that makes
traditional potato soup luxuriously thick). The cooked peppers contribute a
splash of color which signals the late summer harvest, as well as a delightful
contrasting sweetness.*

> 1 tablespoon olive oil
> 1 bunch leeks (white part only), chopped (about ¾ pound)
> 1 cup water
> 4 cups Chicken Stock (page 285–86) or canned low-fat,
>   low-sodium chicken broth
> 1½ to 2 pounds red or new potatoes, unpeeled and quartered
> 3 red bell peppers, seeded and sliced
> 1 cup low-fat milk
> Salt and freshly ground pepper
> ½ cup nonfat sour cream or plain yogurt

1. Heat the oil in a large saucepan over medium heat and add the leeks and
   1 tablespoon of the water. Reduce the heat to a simmer. Cover and cook for
   5 minutes or until the leeks have softened. Check once or twice to make sure
   they don't scorch, adding a little more water if necessary to keep the pan moist.

2. Add the chicken stock, the remaining water, potatoes and red pepper and bring
   to a boil. Reduce the heat to a simmer and cook uncovered for 20 to 25 minutes
   or until the potatoes are tender. With a slotted spoon, remove the peppers and
   several pieces of potato to a separate dish and purée the remaining soup in a
   blender.

3. Reheat and stir in the milk until thoroughly blended. Taste for seasoning,
   adding salt and pepper as desired.

4. Dice the reserved potato and return it, with the peppers, to the soup. Heat thoroughly and serve in 6 individual bowls while still hot. Garnish with a heaping
   spoonful of sour cream or yogurt.

FAT TRACKING TIPS: Substitute vegetable spray for the oil. Use 1 percent or skim
milk in place of low-fat milk.

✷ PER SERVING *Calories: 197, Cholesterol (mg): 3, Saturated fat (g): 1, Total fat (g): 3,
Sodium (mg): 65, Total fiber (g): 5*

Yellow Pea, Butternut Squash and Carrot Soup with Lemon

ROASTING RATHER THAN SAUTÉING THE VEGETABLES *allows you to make this soup without a trace of oil. We can't think of a more delicious way to get the important antioxidant, beta-carotene, than in this filling, golden and extremely low-fat (8 percent!) soup. Remember that diets high in vegetables that contain antioxidants and beta-carotene (found in yellow vegetables) may reduce the risk of heart disease as well as certain cancers. Accompany the soup with pita rounds. The match of yellow peas from the legume family and grains (wheat) in the pita bread yields a complete protein, qualifying the combo as a nutritious but low-fat 2 + 2 vegetarian meal.*

> 1 onion
> Vegetable spray for baking pan
> 1 butternut squash (about 2½ pounds)
> 1 cup yellow split peas
> ¾ pound carrots, chopped
> 8 cups Chicken Stock (page 285–86) or canned low-fat, low-sodium
>   chicken broth or Vegetable Stock (page 289)
> Salt and freshly ground pepper
> Pinch of ground cloves
> Juice of ½ lemon or more
> 1 teaspoon grated lemon zest
> 1 cup nonfat plain yogurt

1. Preheat the oven to 350 degrees F. Peel the onion and slice it in half. Coat a small baking pan with a light film of vegetable spray and place the onion, cut side down, in the pan. Make several incisions in the squash, place it in the pan as well and bake for 40 minutes or until the vegetables are soft. The squash is done when it is fork tender. Cool the squash and onion slightly and when you can handle it, split the squash in half, scoop out the seeds and fibers and chop the pulp.

2. In a large pot, combine the peas, carrots, roasted onion and chicken stock. Season lightly with salt and pepper and bring to a boil. Reduce the heat and simmer the soup for 1 hour or until the peas are soft.

3. When the soup is thick and the peas are soft, add the chopped squash pulp, cloves and lemon juice and bring to a boil. Reduce the heat and simmer for 5 minutes. Taste the soup for seasoning and add more salt and lemon juice if you like. Purée half the soup in a blender or food processor and stir it back

into the pot. Then purée half of it again and blend it back into the soup. Ladle the soup into individual bowls and sprinkle each with a little of the lemon zest. Spoon the yogurt on top and serve while the soup is still hot.

✿ PER SERVING *Calories: 242, Cholesterol (mg): 1, Saturated fat (g): Trace, Total fat (g): 1, Sodium (mg): 77, Total fiber (g): 10*

Fresh Pea Soup with Mint
SERVES 6

IT'S HARD TO IMAGINE *a more refreshing start to a summer meal than this vibrant, minty chilled soup with more than a suggestion of orange. It is especially sweet with fresh peas, but you won't be disappointed if you use frozen.*

> 1 teaspoon canola oil
> ¼ cup chopped green onion
> ¼ cup chopped zucchini
> 1 cup Chicken Stock (page 285–86) or canned low-fat, low-sodium chicken broth
> 1 cup water
> 2 cups fresh or frozen and defrosted green peas
> 1 cup low-fat buttermilk
> 2 tablespoons shredded fresh mint
> Salt and freshly ground pepper
> ½ cup fresh orange juice

1. Heat the oil in a large saucepan and add the onion and zucchini. Stir over medium heat 2 to 3 minutes or until the onion has softened. Stir in the stock and water and bring to a boil. Reduce the heat to medium and cook for 5 to 7 minutes or until the zucchini is tender but not mushy.

2. Add the peas and cook for 2 minutes or until tender. If you use frozen peas, defrost them and cook *just* until heated through, or they will overcook and darken.

3. Purée the soup in a blender with the buttermilk and 1 tablespoon of the mint. Add salt and pepper to your taste, cover and chill thoroughly. Before serving stir in the orange juice and remaining tablespoon mint. Divide among 6 individual bowls and serve.

FAT TRACKING TIP: Use vegetable spray instead of oil.

✿ PER SERVING *Calories: 79, Cholesterol (mg): 1, Saturated fat (g): Trace, Total fat (g): 1, Sodium (mg): 45, Total fiber (g): 2*

Curried Broccoli Soup

SERVES 10

MAKE THIS FOR A CROWD *or cut the recipe in half for a smaller group. This soup uses the tender broccoli florets only. Because potatoes become gummy in a food processor, use a blender to purée the soup. Otherwise, remove the potatoes and mash them by hand or pass them through a ricer before returning them to the soup. The texture may be somewhat coarser than a blender-puréed version, but it will still be quite edible compared to the library-paste texture that food processors give to potatoes.*

> 3 tablespoons extra-virgin olive oil
> 1 leek (white part only), sliced (about 1/4 pound)
> 1 *each* yellow, white, and red onion, chopped
> 3 garlic cloves, minced
> 1 pound white boiling potatoes, peeled and diced
> 8 cups Chicken Stock (page 285–86) or canned low-fat,
>   low-sodium chicken broth
> Florets from 2 bunches broccoli
> 1 1/2 teaspoons curry powder
> 1/2 teaspoon dry mustard
> 1 teaspoon ground cumin
> 1/2 teaspoon coarse ground pepper
> 1 cup 1% milk
> Salt
> Juice of 1 lime
> Grated zest of 1 lime
> 10 tablespoons nonfat plain yogurt for garnish

1. Heat the oil in a large saucepan over medium heat and add the leek, onions and garlic. Stir briefly until they are coated with the oil, then reduce the heat slightly, cover and cook for 10 minutes or until the onions are soft, stirring occasionally. Add the potatoes and chicken stock and bring to a boil. Reduce heat and simmer for 20 to 25 minutes or until the potatoes are tender.

2. Add the broccoli to the soup mixture and stir in the curry powder, mustard, cumin, pepper and milk. Cook for 5 to 6 minutes or until the broccoli is barely tender and still bright green. Purée 2 to 3 cups of the soup at a time in a blender (don't use a food processor) on high speed until smooth, returning each batch of puréed soup to the saucepan and reblending the puréed batch with the unpuréed for the smoothest texture.

3. Season to your taste with salt, the lime juice and grated zest. Serve hot divided among 10 individual bowls with a spoonful of yogurt on each.

Fat Tracking Tips: Eliminate the oil and simmer the leeks, onions and garlic in chicken stock until soft. Use nonfat milk.

✿ PER SERVING *Calories: 133, Cholesterol (mg): 1, Saturated fat (g): 1, Total fat (g): 5, Sodium (mg): 37, Total fiber (g): 3*

Double Garlic Soup with Red Pepper Purée
SERVES 6

THIS IS ONE OF OUR FAVORITE SOUPS, *with a rich silky texture that has the texture and feel of real cream, the work of a highly seasoned garlic purée. A garnish of smoky peppers singing with garlic echoes the theme. As a change from potatoes, you can also substitute a mix of carrots, rutabaga and parsnips. If the garlic in the purée is too bold for your palate or digestive tract, reduce or eliminate it or substitute Garlic Purée (page 284). You can make the soup ahead and even freeze it, then add the purée before serving.*

    1 tablespoon plus 1 teaspoon extra-virgin olive oil
    1 large onion, chopped
    14 medium-size garlic cloves, crushed
    1½ pounds potatoes, thickly sliced
    ½ pound carrots, sliced
    4 cups Chicken Stock (page 285–86) or canned low-fat,
        low-sodium chicken broth
    1 small red bell pepper
    ½ cup 1% milk
    Salt and freshly ground pepper

1. Preheat the oven to 425 degrees F. Heat 1 tablespoon of the oil in a large saucepan and stir in the onion and all but 2 garlic cloves. Stir over medium heat until they begin to soften, then add the potatoes, carrots and chicken stock. Bring to a boil, then reduce the heat and simmer for 30 minutes or until the vegetables are very soft.

2. Meanwhile, place a red pepper on a baking sheet and roast in the oven until the skin softens and blisters. Set aside the pepper in a bowl until cool enough to handle. Slip off the skin and remove and discard the seeds and stem. Purée the pepper in a blender with the remaining 2 crushed garlic cloves and teaspoon of oil. Season lightly with salt and pepper. This can be made 2 to 3 days ahead and stored, covered, in the refrigerator.

3. When the soup has finished cooking, add the milk and purée until smooth in a blender. Taste for seasoning, but remember that the red pepper purée will add seasoning, so use a light hand if you add salt and pepper at this point.

4. Before serving, ladle the hot soup into 6 individual bowls. Then stir the purée into the hot soup, in a colorful swirling pattern, but do not blend completely.

FAT TRACKING TIPS: Use skim milk in place of 1% milk. Omit the oil and sauté/sweat (page 271) the onion and garlic.

❋ PER SERVING *Calories: 179, Cholesterol (mg): 1, Saturated fat (g): 1, Total fat (g): 3, Sodium (mg): 43, Total fiber (g): 4*

Eggplant Soup
with Red Pepper Chutney
SERVES 6

YOU CAN SERVE THIS *as soon as you have puréed the eggplant to a smooth, creamy texture, while your kitchen still radiates the warmth and intoxicating aroma of roasting peppers and eggplant. Or you can cover and refrigerate it for up to 24 hours, and just reheat it before serving. The red pepper chutney, which you can prepare ahead as well, demonstrates yet another way to intensify the flavors of "creamed" soups without resorting to overpowering amounts of butter, cream and eggs. Even though the chutney increases the total fat, harmful, saturated fat is kept to a minimum. Serve with a light pasta, such as Fettuccine with Smoked Salmon Goat Cheese and Chives (page 459), a hot baguette and a green salad, and you still have a lean menu. Keep in mind that the goal is a daily low-fat total. If you served this with items that brought the total for the meal to 40 percent or even 50 percent fat calories, you can still achieve a low-fat total for the day if you chose lean breakfast and lunch foods.*

    1 eggplant
    1 red bell pepper
    Vegetable spray for baking sheet
    2 tablespoons extra-virgin olive oil
    1 onion, sliced
    2 garlic cloves, quartered
    3 cups Chicken Stock (page 285–86) or canned low-fat,
       low-sodium chicken broth
    ½ cup low-fat milk
    Salt and freshly ground pepper
    6 kalamata olives
    1 tablespoon minced fresh parsley

1 teaspoon fresh marjoram or basil or ½ teaspoon dried
1 tablespoon crumbled feta cheese

1. Preheat the oven to 375 degrees F. Make several small slits in the eggplant and place it and the bell pepper on a baking sheet lightly coated with a thin film of vegetable spray. Roast them for 45 minutes or until the eggplant is soft but not mushy and the pepper is blistered. Place the pepper in a small bowl and set aside. Meanwhile, peel and discard the skin of the eggplant and chop the pulp coarsely.

2. While the vegetables roast, heat the oil in a large saucepan over medium heat, add the onion and garlic and stir for 2 to 3 minutes or until they soften.

3. Add the eggplant and chicken stock to the saucepan. Bring to a boil, then reduce the heat and simmer for 30 minutes. Purée with the milk in a blender or food processor and season to your taste with salt and pepper. The soup may be prepared ahead to this point and reheated again before serving.

4. Prepare the chutney by discarding the skin, stem and seeds of the roasted pepper and chopping it finely. Smack the olives with a mallet or cleaver just until they crack. Discard the pits and chop the olives. In a small bowl, blend the pepper, olives, parsley, marjoram and feta.

5. Reheat the soup if necessary and ladle into 6 bowls. Spoon equal portions of the chutney on top of each and serve while still hot.

FAT TRACKING TIPS: Replace the olive oil with vegetable spray and 1 tablespoon of water. Use nonfat milk.

❀ PER SERVING *Calories: 93, Cholesterol (mg): 2, Saturated fat (g): 1, Total fat (g): 6, Sodium (mg): 158, Total fiber (g): 1*

Cold Sweet and Sour Beet Soup

SERVES 6

PALE ROSE IN COLOR, THIS IS A PRETTY SOUP *to serve at a summer brunch.*
Because of its delicate hue, we suggest it for any romantic celebration—
weddings, special anniversaries, intimate birthday dinners. But for those with
a passion for sweet beets, make any day an occasion to indulge yourself; beets
are one of the crucial antioxidant vegetables, meaning they are good for your
heart and the hearts of your loved ones.

1 pound baby beets
1 tablespoon extra-virgin olive oil
1 onion, chopped
½ pound carrots, sliced
1 cup low-fat buttermilk or nonfat plain yogurt
1 cup 1% milk
1 tablespoon sugar
½ cup fresh orange juice
2 tablespoons raspberry vinegar or white wine vinegar
2 tablespoons fresh lemon juice
½ teaspoon salt
1 teaspoon fresh tarragon
1 cup nonfat plain yogurt

1. Preheat the oven to 400 degrees F. Trim the greens from the beets, leaving a 1-inch stalk. Wash the beets, but do not pierce the skins. As directed on page 266–67, steam or microwave the beets for 10 to 12 minutes, depending on their size, or until they are very tender. Cool slightly, trim the stalk and root ends and peel them.

2. While the beets cook, heat the oil in an ovenproof skillet over low-medium heat and add the onion. Stir for 2 to 3 minutes or until the pieces are completely coated with oil. Place the skillet in the oven for 10 minutes or until the onion is wilted. Stir occasionally so the onion will cook evenly; do not allow it to scorch.

3. Steam or microwave the carrots for 4 minutes or until they are very tender.

4. When the vegetables are ready, purée the beets, carrots and onion in a blender or food processor with the buttermilk, 1% milk, sugar, orange juice, vinegar, lemon juice and salt. Stir in the tarragon, cover and chill completely. At serving time, ladle the soup into 6 bowls and garnish each with 2½ tablespoons of the yogurt before serving.

❀ PER SERVING *Calories: 138, Cholesterol (mg): 4, Saturated fat (g): 1, Total fat (g): 3, Sodium (mg): 332, Total fiber (g): 3*

Melon and Cucumber Soup

SERVES 4

As WELCOME AND COOLING *as a frosty glass of lemonade during a heat wave, this versatile soup is a great way to kick off a summer barbecue or serve as a refreshing alternative to ice cream when you need a snack on a hot day. Because of the fibrous nature of both cucumber and melon, expect a somewhat pebbly, slightly crunchy texture when you purée the soup. A few grains of salt heighten the flavors, but don't overdo it or the soup will lose its crisp taste.*

> ½ honeydew melon
> 2 large cucumbers, peeled, seeded and coarsely chopped
> 2 cups nonfat plain yogurt or low-fat buttermilk
> Juice of 1 lime
> Salt to your taste
> A few sprigs of fennel or mint and very thin slices of lime for garnish

1. Remove and discard the seeds from the melon. Cut the flesh away from the rind. In a food processor or blender, purée the melon, cucumber and yogurt until smooth. Add the juice of the lime and add the salt a few grains at a time, tasting until the flavors are bright and slightly tart, but don't add more than ¼ teaspoon salt or the flavor of the melon won't shine. Chill thoroughly.

2. Taste for seasoning again before serving as chilling may have blunted the flavors. Add more lime juice if necessary. Serve very cold in 4 bowls garnished with the fennel or mint and slices of lime.

FAT TRACKING TIP: Use nonfat yogurt.

❋ PER SERVING *Calories: 111, Cholesterol (mg): 2, Saturated fat (g): 0, Total fat (g): 0, Sodium (mg): 92, Total fiber (g): 1*

Minestrone

SERVES 8

DOES THIS HEARTY, VEGETABLE STEW *really need an introduction? Part of its charm is that it is so wonderfully relaxed about its requirements. You can make it with or without meat; choose your seasonings from a vast array of what cooks in Italy refer to as* odori—*savory vegetables, herbs and seasonings; make it thick as mortar or turn it into a delicate broth in which you suspend a few fresh vegetables and herbs and at least a few beans. If you travel to Italy to trace the roots of this soup, you will get lost in a maze of traditions; each region has its own variation. Some regions replace beef with sausage, while in Tuscany you find rice or thick slices of bread added instead of pasta. We fill our minestrone with vegetables, fiber and antioxidants and serve it as an entrée with bread and salad. It also adapts to busy schedules. You can start the soup early in the afternoon and have it simmering for the rest of the day. Or you can leave the pot quietly bubbling on the back burner during the evening, then refrigerate it for the next day's meal. The latter is our favorite method, for the flavor improves as it sits and it makes skimming the fat very easy.*

2 tablespoons extra-virgin olive oil

2 onions, sliced

3 garlic cloves, mashed

3 stalks celery, diced

3 carrots, diced

1 chicken (3 to 4 pounds), cut up with all skin and fat removed

4 to 5 cups water

4 cups Chicken Stock (page 285–86) or canned low-fat,
    low-sodium chicken broth

1 cup chopped cabbage

4 tomatoes, chopped

1 red or green bell pepper, seeded and diced

Salt and freshly ground pepper

1 bay leaf

3 or 4 large sprigs fresh parsley

1 tablespoon fresh oregano or 1 teaspoon dried

2 cups diced summer vegetables (such as zucchini,
    green beans, peas)

1 potato, diced

1/2 cup cooked or canned white beans

1/2 cup small dried pasta (such as orzo, short fusilli,
    ditalini, anellini)

2 tablespoons *each* minced fresh Italian parsley and basil
1 teaspoon fresh or dried thyme
1 ounce Parmesan cheese, freshly grated (about ⅓ cup)

1. Heat the oil in a nonreactive large saucepan or Dutch oven over medium heat until a spray of water dances on the surface. Add the onions, garlic, celery and carrots and toss for 4 to 5 minutes or until the onions have softened.

2. Add the chicken and turn frequently for 5 to 8 minutes or until the pieces brown lightly on all sides. Add the water, stock, cabbage, tomatoes and bell pepper. Season lightly with salt and pepper and add the bay leaf, parsley sprigs and oregano. Bring to a boil, reduce heat and simmer for 1½ hours. Skim away any foamy material that accumulates on the surface and do not allow the soup to boil rapidly.

3. If possible, cover and chill overnight and, about 45 minutes before serving, skim off all fat that has accumulated on the surface. Reheat before continuing. If you plan to serve it the day you make it, continue by adding the summer vegetables, potato, beans, pasta, minced parsley, basil and thyme. Cook for 40 minutes or until the potato is tender and the pasta has softened. Then skim away all fat from the surface of the soup. Ladle into 8 bowls and divide the cheese among the servings.

FAT TRACKING TIPS: Eliminate the oil; roast the onions and garlic before adding them to the stock. Skip the cheese.

�֍ PER SERVING *Calories: 294, Cholesterol (mg): 59, Saturated fat (g): 3, Total fat (g): 11, Sodium (mg): 202, Total fiber (g): 4*

Seafood Soup-Stew

SERVES 8

COOKBOOK AUTHOR BARBARA KAROFF, *who gave us this recipe, calls her savory, filling dish a "soup-stew." Unlike other fish soups, this one improves with a day's stay in the refrigerator. Halibut, sole and snapper work best, but you can choose any firm-fleshed fish. This is definitely a main course dish, appealing both in summer and winter. For a party, make a double batch and provide your guests with an abundance of fresh, hot bread, tossed greens with Mustard Vinaigrette (page 382–83) and frozen yogurt with fresh summer fruit, or stewed and sweetened winter fruits.*

2 tablespoons extra-virgin olive oil
¾ cup chopped onions
2 garlic cloves, minced
¼ cup seeded and diced red or green bell pepper
¾ cup diagonally sliced celery
2 cans (16 ounces each) chopped tomatoes with liquid
1 can (8 ounces) tomato sauce
3 potatoes, peeled and diced
Salt and freshly ground pepper
1 tablespoon fresh oregano or 1 teaspoon dried
1 tablespoon minced fresh basil
2½ cups Rich Fish Stock (page 287) or clam juice
1 pound halibut, cut into bite-size pieces
½ pound sole, cut into bite-size pieces
½ pound snapper, cut into bite-size pieces
½ cup minced fresh parsley

1. Heat the oil in a nonreactive Dutch oven and add the onions, garlic, bell pepper and celery. Toss over medium heat until tender, about 10 minutes.

2. Add the tomatoes, tomato sauce, potatoes, salt and pepper to your taste, oregano, basil and stock. Bring to a boil and then reduce the heat and simmer for 20 minutes or until the potatoes are quite tender.

3. Add the fish, cover and simmer for 5 to 8 minutes more or until the fish is white, firm and just cooked. Do not overcook the fish or allow it to disintegrate. Ladle into 8 bowls and sprinkle with parsley before serving.

FAT TRACKING TIP: Reduce or eliminate the oil and cook the onions in vegetable spray.

✿ PER SERVING *Calories: 210, Cholesterol (mg): 37, Saturated fat (g): 1, Total fat (g): 6, Sodium (mg): 618, Total fiber (g): 1*

CHAPTER 32

Salads

A SALAD CAN BE AS EASY AND REFRESHING *as a bowl brimming with crisp greens, a favorite dressing glistening like dew drops on its leaves. Or robustness may be the order of the day, when your salad plate groans under the weight of vegetables and beans and poultry and croutons and nuts and anything else you can filch from your pantry. It is not so much the ingredients of a salad that concern us, but the dressing that tops it. By definition this dressing is loaded with oil, and even if you use only healthy olive oil or canola oil, as you know, the fat calories mount up.*

The salads that follow don't stint on flavor, complexity, freshness or dressing. But they have been developed to include sufficient calories in the form of carbohydrates and protein so that the salad comprises a significant part of your meal—if not the meal in itself. The oil in the dressing doesn't just moisten greens, the least filling part of a meal, but it adds fat calories to a meal already full of them. We have included croutons, toast points, beans, potatoes, chicken and fish. Thus the oil in our salads coats a hefty portion of vegetable and protein calories as well. Do include these items when they are listed, for they are intended to give you more nourishing and filling food with less fat. With more carbohydrate calories in the salad to fill you up, you don't have to reach for a second helping of high-fat protein or smear your bread with butter to feel satisfied.

Dressings for Green Salads

When you do have a salad of tossed greens and an oil and vinegar dressing, use our low-fat Mustard Vinaigrette. But when you want a creamy dressing, prepare the following heart-healthy Roquefort Dressing instead of a higher-fat bottled ranch-style or cheese dressing. On the occasions when you have a heavily oiled dressing on salad greens, make sure you don't add cheese, olives, nuts or other high-fat items without including the fat grams in your total for the day.

Roquefort Shallot Dressing
Makes approximately 1 cup, serving size 1 tablespoon

The inspiration for this dressing actually started with the shallot and tarragon mixture that is the prelude to the eggy, béarnaise sauce. When we reached for buttermilk instead of butter we had our perfect Roquefort Shallot Dressing with no saturated fat and only one gram of total fat per serving. Use this rich dressing on salads or serve it as a dip with lightly steamed, crisp vegetables instead of a cheesy, sour cream-based concoction. Roquefort Shallot Dressing will last in the refrigerator up to the expiration date for the buttermilk. If you don't find *herbes de Provence* with lavender in your market, use regular *herbes de Provence*, a popular herb mixture with tarragon, or just add fresh or dried tarragon.

> 1/4 cup white wine
> 1 tablespoon red wine vinegar
> 1 teaspoon dried *herbes de Provence* with lavender, or herb mixture
>   with tarragon or plain tarragon
> 1 shallot, finely diced (about 2 tablespoons)
> 1 tablespoon extra-virgin olive oil
> 2 tablespoons low-fat sour cream or sour half-and-half
> 1/2 cup low-fat buttermilk
> 2 tablespoons crumbled Roquefort or blue cheese
> Salt and freshly ground pepper

1. Bring the white wine, vinegar, herbs and shallot to a boil in a small nonreactive saucepan and cook over high heat for 2 to 3 minutes or until the shallot softens and the liquid has reduced by about 1/3.

2. Remove from the heat and whisk in the olive oil. Add the remaining ingredients, seasoning lightly with salt and pepper, and whisk until smooth. For a very creamy texture, purée the dressing in a blender or with a hand processor. Allow the dressing to rest for at least 1/2 hour before serving to infuse the flavors. Shake vigorously before adding to your salad.

FAT TRACKING TIP: Use nonfat sour cream.

❋ PER SERVING *Calories: 19, Cholesterol (mg): 2, Saturated fat: Trace, Total fat (g): 1, Sodium (mg): 26, Total fiber (g): 0*

Mustard Vinaigrette
Makes approximately 1/2 cup, serving size 2 tablespoons

A light, tasty dressing for mixed greens, steamed vegetables, fish or grilled poultry. You can make this in double or triple batches if you wish.

½ cup fresh orange juice
1 tablespoon sherry vinegar
1 generous teaspoon whole-grain Dijon mustard
1 teaspoon olive oil, hazelnut oil or walnut oil
Salt and freshly ground pepper

In a measuring cup, whisk the ingredients together, seasoning to your taste with salt and pepper. Store covered in the refrigerator for up to a week.

❀ PER SERVING *Calories: 25, Cholesterol (mg): 0, Saturated fat (g): Trace, Total fat (g): 1, Sodium (mg): 7, Total fiber (g): Trace*

Stanford Salad
SERVES 6

A GREEN SALAD WITH A PERFECTLY BALANCED VINAIGRETTE *is considered to be the perfect ending to a meal. Our salad could be the meal and includes a selection of items typical of those Mediterranean foods that brought the attention of early researchers to the importance of a heart-healthy diet—greens, a selection of lower-fat cheeses, beans, peppers and olives as well as olive oil— bound together with a smashing dressing. The total fat content is high, so, as needed, choose leaner items for the rest of your meal. Or you can serve small portions if you are concerned about calories or consider the Fat Tracking Tips at the end as a further alternative to limiting total fat when necessary.*

STANFORD VINAIGRETTE
½ cup olive oil
3 tablespoons red wine vinegar
1 tablespoon prepared sweet mustard
1 garlic clove, smashed
Grated zest from ½ lemon or orange
1 tablespoon minced fresh herb (such as oregano or marjoram)
Salt and freshly ground pepper to your taste

6 cups mixed salad greens (romaine, butter, red leaf, exotic mixture)
½ cup chopped fresh basil leaves
¼ cup chopped walnuts, toasted as on page 300
¾ ounce Parmesan Reggiano cheese, shaved (about ¼ cup)
    or 1 ounce feta, crumbled
2 tomatoes, peeled, seeded and chopped
½ cup cooked white beans
1 red bell pepper, seeded and sliced into thin rings
4 kalamata olives, chopped

1. Whisk together all the ingredients for the dressing in a small bowl and set aside to mellow. Remove garlic before serving. Cover and refrigerate if you make it ahead and bring to room temperature before serving.

2. Place greens in a bowl and toss with a few tablespoons of the dressing. Add the basil, walnuts and Parmesan cheese, and toss. Add the tomatoes and white beans and toss again. Arrange the red bell pepper slices on top, sprinkle with the olives and feta cheese and serve.

FAT TRACKING TIPS: Use only as much dressing as needed to moisten salad ingredients. Do not add so much dressing that it puddles in the bottom of the bowl. Use remaining dressing another time. Reduce or eliminate the walnuts, cheese and/or olives.

❀ PER SERVING (INCLUDES APPROXIMATELY 1½ TABLESPOONS STANFORD VINAIGRETTE) *Calories: 205, Cholesterol (mg): 3, Saturated fat: 3, Total fat (g): 17, Sodium (mg): 123, Total fiber (g): 2*

Warm Broccoli, Orange and Walnut Salad with Walnut Vinaigrette
SERVES 6

THE FLAVOR OF ORANGE *always tempers the bite of broccoli, especially in this salad. Sweet red potatoes make it filling enough for a main course lunch dish or an accompaniment to grilled fish for an easy weekend menu.*

WALNUT VINAIGRETTE
2 tablespoons walnut oil
1 tablespoon extra-virgin olive oil
2 teaspoons raspberry vinegar
2 tablespoons fresh orange juice
1 teaspoon grated orange zest
Salt and freshly ground pepper

⅓ pound red potatoes, cubed
1½ pounds broccoli florets, trimmed to 1-inch branches
1½ tablespoons finely chopped walnuts
6 slices dense, multigrain bread, toasted
3 oranges, peeled and sliced
1 sweet red onion, thinly sliced

1. Whisk together the dressing ingredients in a measuring cup, seasoning lightly with salt and pepper to your taste.

2. As directed on page 266, steam the potatoes for 6 or 7 minutes or until tender. Steam the broccoli for 3 minutes or until it is just barely tender, then toss the potatoes and broccoli with the walnuts and half of the dressing.

3. Cut the toast in half diagonally. Arrange the toast on individual salad plates so that the points meet in the center and form a butterfly. Spoon the salad on the toast. Arrange the oranges and onion on top and spoon remaining dressing over the oranges. Serve immediately while still warm.

❋ PER SERVING *Calories: 237, Cholesterol (mg): 0, Saturated fat: 1, Total fat (g): 9, Sodium (mg): 185, Total fiber (g): 6*

Serpentine Salad with Chutney Dressing
SERVES 4

A CLOUD OF VIVID SHREDDED VEGETABLES, *colorful as a New Year's Eve party and just as scintillating, is an antioxidant marvel. But that is not the only reason to love this vibrant mix. The sweet and spicy dressing perfectly sets off the crunchy mix that is at once hot and mellow, sharp and smooth. For an incomparable combination, arrange this salad on a platter with grilled chicken or beef and allow the juices to seep into the dressing. Prepare the vegetables ahead and store in plastic bags to speed last-minute preparations, but do not let the salad sit in the dressing too long or the vegetables will become soggy.*

1 large zucchini
2 carrots
¼ head red cabbage
1 bulb fennel
½ red bell pepper, halved and seeded
½ yellow bell pepper, halved and seeded
1 Bartlett pear

CHUTNEY DRESSING
⅓ cup plus 1 tablespoon fresh orange juice
1 tablespoon mango chutney
1 tablespoon walnut oil
1 tablespoon raspberry vinegar
1 tablespoon prepared sweet mustard

Pinch of salt

1. With the finest *shredding* blade of a food processor or vegetable shredder, shred the zucchini and carrots and transfer them to a large bowl. With the finest *slicing* blade, shred the cabbage and add it to the other vegetables. Using a salad spoon and large fork, toss the vegetables together until they are well blended. Use the fork to scoop the shredded vegetables up and literally shake them into the air to separate the strands of carrot and zucchini and mix the colors and flavors. With the same slicing blade, finely slice the fennel bulb and stalks, and then the peppers. Toss the salad again until everything is well blended.

2. Core the pear but do not peel it. Slice it in very thin strips and toss with the salad.

3. Place the dressing ingredients in a blender or food processor and purée. Pour the dressing over the salad, add a pinch of salt and toss thoroughly once more. Allow the salad to stand for a few minutes before serving so it will absorb the dressing. Serve immediately.

❉ PER SERVING *Calories: 79, Cholesterol (mg): 0, Saturated fat (g): Trace, Total fat (g): 3, Sodium (mg): 49, Total fiber (g): 2*

🍮

Corn Salad with Sautéed Garlic Buds
SERVES 6

GARLIC BUDS, MILDER AND SWEETER *than the cloves, are harvested from the tip of the stalk late in the season just before the plant flowers. During their brief season, you can add the buds to stir-fry dishes or any sautéed vegetable, chicken or meat. You can find garlic buds in farmers markets or organic produce markets, but when they are not available, substitute roasted garlic cloves in this hearty, main course salad.*

> 1 cup fresh corn kernels (approximately 3 large ears)
> 1 small red bell pepper, seeded and diced
> 1/4 cup diced red onion
> 6 pea pods
> 1/4 pound Kentucky Blue green beans
> 2 medium-size red potatoes, diced into 1/2 inch-cubes
> 2 medium-size tomatoes, peeled, seeded and chopped
> 1/2 cup diced jícama

GARLIC BUD DRESSING

⅓ cup olive oil

12 garlic buds, excess stalk trimmed, or 12 cloves garlic, roasted
   (page 265)

3 tablespoons tarragon champagne vinegar

¼ teaspoon sugar

Salt and freshly ground pepper to your taste

1 banana chili pepper (yellow wax) or other mild chili,
   seeded and minced

½ cup minced fresh basil leaves

2 tablespoons minced fresh chives for garnish

1. As directed on page 266–67, steam or microwave the corn for 1 minute and place it in a salad bowl. Add the red bell pepper and onion and toss gently.

2. Plunge the pea pods in boiling water for 30 seconds, then immediately run cold water over them to stop the cooking. Set them aside for garnish.

3. As directed on page 266, steam the green beans for 1 minute and run cold water over them. Slice the beans diagonally into 2-inch pieces and add them to the corn mixture.

4. Steam the potatoes for 4 minutes or until tender, but not mushy. Add the potatoes to the salad bowl with tomatoes and jícama and toss the salad again.

5. To prepare the dressing, warm the oil in a skillet and add the garlic buds. Toss gently over medium heat for 7 or 8 minutes or until they are pale gold and the sheath along the bud begins to burst. For roasted cloves, toss gently in the oil just until heated through. Remove the garlic buds or roasted cloves (but not the oil) and add them to the corn mixture. Blend the remaining dressing ingredients in a measuring cup and whisk in the oil from the skillet.

6. To serve, pour the dressing over the salad and toss well. Arrange pea pods in a sunburst on top and sprinkle with the chives.

❀ PER SERVING *Calories: 349, Cholesterol (mg): 0, Saturated fat: 2, Total fat (g): 14, Sodium (mg): 35, Total fiber (g): 8*

Melon-Chili Salad
with Blackberry Vinaigrette
SERVES 6

USE THIS MOUTH WATERING, *chili-spiked but easy salad as an excuse to make Blackberry Vinegar and serve it the next time you present a fiery entrée, such as Sea Bass Grilled with Cilantro and Jalapeño Marinade (page 483). The mustard in the dressing cuts what would otherwise be a cloying sweetness in the dressing. If a serrano chili is too hot for your taste, choose a mild banana (yellow wax) chili, Fresno chili or a moderately hot jalapeño.*

BLACKBERRY VINAIGRETTE
1 pint fresh blackberries
2 tablespoons rice bran oil or canola oil
2 tablespoons Blackberry Vinegar (page 299), or other fruit
    or white wine vinegar
1 teaspoon mustard seeds, toasted (page 300) and crushed
    or ½ teaspoon dry mustard
1 teaspoon brown sugar
¼ teaspoon salt
White pepper to your taste
Fresh lemon juice, optional

1 large honeydew melon, about 5 pounds, or choose a combination
    of casaba, pink honeydew or Persian melons
Salad greens
1 or 2 serrano peppers, seeded and minced fresh
½ red onion, cut into paper-thin slices
1 small bunch watercress
Edible flowers for garnish
1 hard red apple, halved, cored and sliced into thin wedges

1. Purée the berries in a blender or with a whisk and press them through a fine-mesh sieve set over a mixing bowl to remove the seeds. Stir in the oil and blend well. Add the vinegar, crushed mustard seeds or dry mustard, brown sugar, salt and pepper. Taste and adjust the seasoning, adding more mustard if you desire. If you find the dressing too sweet, add a little fresh lemon juice. Cover and chill until serving time. You can make this several hours ahead.

2. Cut the melon in half and remove the seeds and strings. Cut each half into 3 wedges and cut away the rind. Slice the wedges into thirds again, then into 4 slices about ½ to ¾ inches at the thickest edge. Cover and refrigerate the melon until serving time.

3. Arrange the greens on individual plates or a large platter. Add the melon, overlapping the slices to form a spiral. Spoon half the dressing over the melon slices. Scatter the minced serrano, onion and watercress on top and tuck a few fresh flowers among the melon's glistening curves. Arrange the apple slices around the edge. Drizzle the remaining vinaigrette over the salad and serve immediately.

❀ PER SERVING *Calories: 150, Cholesterol (mg): 0, Saturated fat: 1, Total fat (g): 5, Sodium (mg): 109, Total fiber (g): 5*

❀

Curried Tomato, Melon and Cucumber Salad
SERVES 6

SERVE THIS IN THE HEIGHT OF THE TOMATO HARVEST *using a fat, sweet melon. A favorite salad with grilled fish, it would also make a light lunch accompanied with a basket of corn bread or Whole Wheat Herb Scones (page 335–36).*

> 1 small cantaloupe
> 6 plump tomatoes, sliced
> 2 cucumbers, sliced very thin
>
> **CURRY AND CILANTRO DRESSING**
> 1/4 cup olive oil
> 1 1/2 tablespoons red wine vinegar
> 1 1/2 teaspoons curry powder
> 1/4 teaspoon ground cumin
> 1/2 teaspoon *each* salt and sugar
> Pinch *each* of cayenne and white pepper
> 1/2 fresh jalapeño pepper or milder chili (such as Anaheim), optional, seeded and finely diced
> 1/4 cup minced fresh cilantro or mint
> Fresh cilantro or mint leaves for garnish

1. Cut the melon in half and discard the seeds. Cut it in smaller wedges and peel and discard the rind. Slice the melon into wedges 1/2 inch thick at the outside edge.

2. Arrange the tomatoes, cucumbers and melon in a circle on a serving platter, starting with a slice of tomato and then overlapping it slightly with a slice of cucumber, and then a slice of melon.

3. Combine the dressing ingredients in a small bowl or covered jar and whisk or shake until thoroughly blended. Pour the dressing over the tomatoes and cucumbers, cover with plastic wrap and chill thoroughly. Strew the cilantro leaves over the salad before serving.

❋ PER SERVING *Calories: 191, Cholesterol (mg): 0, Saturated fat: 1, Total fat (g): 10, Sodium (mg): 238, Total fiber (g): 4*

Red and Yellow Beets
with Orange Jalapeño Dressing

SERVES 6

WHEN IT COMES TO BEETS, *the smallest are the sweetest, so look for baby beets. The contrast of chili pepper and delicate beet works very well, but reduce the amount of jalapeño if you are wary of spicy hot food. When blood oranges are in season, use some of these as well as regular oranges to give added color to the plate.*

1 pound red beets
1 pound yellow beets

ORANGE JALAPEÑO DRESSING
¼ cup fresh orange juice
2 tablespoons red raspberry vinegar
¼ cup canola oil
1 to 2 tablespoons minced fresh jalapeño pepper, seeded
1 teaspoon prepared sweet mustard
¼ cup chopped fresh Italian parsley
¼ teaspoon dried crushed red peppers or to taste
1 teaspoon crushed red peppercorns
Salt and freshly ground pepper to your taste

1½ cups mixed salad greens or more
1 bunch green onions (white part only), chopped
3 oranges, peeled and sliced
1 small bunch radishes, sliced
6 slices French bread

1. Scrub the beets, but do not break the skin or they will bleed. Trim the greens from the beets, leaving no more than an inch of stalk; do not trim the root end. Reserve the beet greens. As directed on page 266–67, steam or microwave the beets for 16 to 20 minutes or until they are very tender. Their size will determine the precise cooking time. When they are cool enough to handle, peel and slice them ¼ inch thick and place each color in a separate bowl.

2. While the beets cook, blend the dressing ingredients in a measuring cup, taste for seasoning and set aside. You can make this several hours ahead of time. Spoon 2 tablespoons of the dressing and half the onions on each bowl of beets and toss well. Chill thoroughly.

3. Just before serving, arrange the salad greens on a serving plate. Strew the onions on the greens. Arrange the red beets on one side and the yellow beets on the other. Arrange the oranges and radishes on top of the beets. (When in season, use blood oranges for the yellow beets, yellow oranges for the red beets.) Drizzle the remaining dressing over the oranges and beets. Toast the French bread on both sides, cut slices into diagonal quarters and arrange around the salad. Serve immediately.

❋ PER SERVING *Calories: 258, Cholesterol (mg): 0, Saturated fat: 1, Total fat (g): 10, Sodium (mg): 287, Total fiber (g): 7*

Potato Salad
with Cabbage and Tarragon
SERVES 8

USE YOUR BEST QUALITY *extra-virgin olive oil for this delicious and unusual potato salad.*

> 3 pounds unpeeled red potatoes, cut into 1-inch cubes
> 1/2 teaspoon extra-virgin olive oil
> 1 pound napa cabbage

> **DIJON YOGURT DRESSING**
> 1/2 cup nonfat plain yogurt
> 1/2 cup low-fat mayonnaise
> 2 teaspoons grated orange zest
> 2 tablespoons fresh orange juice
> 2 tablespoons champagne vinegar or white wine vinegar
> 2 tablespoons whole-grain Dijon mustard
> 2 tablespoons extra-virgin olive oil
> Salt and freshly ground pepper

> 1/3 cup minced green onions
> 1/3 cup minced freshly ground Italian parsley
> 1 1/2 tablespoons minced fresh tarragon or 2 teaspoons dried

1. As directed on page 266–67, steam or microwave the potatoes until they are very tender. Drain and toss them in a bowl with 1/2 teaspoon olive oil just to keep them from becoming sticky. Cool to room temperature.

2. Slice the cabbage lengthwise on a cutting board. Without disturbing the arrangement of the slices, rotate the cutting board 90 degrees and slice the strips crosswise into 1/2-inch diced pieces. As directed on page 266–67, steam or microwave the cabbage for 3 minutes or until it is just wilted. The cabbage should retain a

pronounced crispness. Drain it into a colander and allow it to continue to drain until it has thoroughly cooled. If the cabbage still seems damp, drain it on paper toweling until it is free of moisture. You can prepare the potatoes and cabbage ahead and keep them wrapped and chilled until you are ready to assemble the salad.

3. While the vegetables cook, blend the yogurt and mayonnaise in a small bowl. Stir in the orange zest, orange juice, vinegar and mustard, blending well after each addition. Gradually whisk in 2 tablespoons oil and season to your taste with salt and pepper.

4. When the vegetables have cooled, toss the potatoes and cabbage with the green onions and the dressing in a large bowl, coating the vegetables thoroughly. Add the Italian parsley and tarragon and toss gently until the ingredients are well blended. Cover and chill thoroughly before serving.

❀ PER SERVING *Calories: 252, Cholesterol (mg): 5, Saturated fat: 1, Total fat (g): 8, Sodium (mg): 97, Total fiber (g): 4*

Grilled Chicken Salad
with Mango Sesame Dressing
SERVES 8

THIS SPRIGHTLY SALAD *comes from Tina Dreyer, a Stanford alumna and owner of Grand Cru Vineyards in Sonoma, California. We can recommend the lush mango dressing on simply poached salmon, sole and chicken when you don't feel like firing up the grill. Note that the chicken must be marinated at least four hours.*

½ cup low-sodium soy sauce
½ cup Chinese oyster sauce
¼ cup fresh orange juice
1 teaspoon grated orange zest
1 teaspoon grated fresh ginger
2 pounds boned chicken breasts, all skin and fat removed
4 cups assorted salad greens or mesclun mixture
1 red bell pepper, seeded and slivered
1 yellow bell pepper, seeded and slivered
Mango Sesame Dressing (recipe follows)
Chive blossoms, optional, for garnish

1. In a large measuring cup, combine the soy sauce, oyster sauce, orange juice, orange zest and ginger. Arrange the chicken breasts in a shallow bowl and pour the marinade over them, turning them once or twice to completely immerse them. Cover and refrigerate for at least 4 hours or overnight. Turn the chicken breasts once or twice during this time.

2. Prepare the grill as directed on page 264. Drain the chicken breasts and grill 6 to 8 minutes depending on their size or until the meat is springy to the touch and no longer pink in the center. Remove to a cutting board and slice across the grain in 2-inch pieces.

3. Place the greens in equal portions on individual plates, then cover with the slivers of pepper. Arrange the chicken slices on top and drizzle the Mango Sesame Dressing on top. Garnish with chive blossoms if available and serve immediately.

❈ PER SERVING (INCLUDES 2 TABLESPOONS MANGO SESAME DRESSING) *Calories: 188, Cholesterol (mg): 77, Saturated fat: 1, Total fat (g): 6, Sodium (mg): 639, Total fiber (g): 2*

Mango Sesame Dressing
Makes approximately 1 cup, serving size 1 tablespoon.

2 mangoes (preferably Hayden variety)
2 tablespoons Asian sesame oil
2 tablespoons balsamic vinegar or unseasoned rice vinegar
1/2 teaspoon salt
Juice of 1/2 lemon

Peel, seed and purée the mangoes in a blender or food processor. Add the oil, vinegar and salt. Blend well. Squeeze the lemon juice into the dressing, tasting from time to time until seasoned to your taste.

❈ PER SERVING *Calories: 32, Cholesterol (mg): 0, Saturated fat: Trace, Total fat (g): 2, Sodium (mg): 67, Total fiber (g): 1*

Herbed Rice Salad

SERVES 6

USE A SELECTION OF BITTER GREENS *and sweet red lettuce in this herb-scented rice salad. Note that you do not need a great deal of oil to quickly cook the greens; the moisture from the lemon juice and vinegar will wilt them in the hot skillet. You can also use orange or grapefruit juice in place of lemon juice for the tangy hot dressing.*

4 cups cooked white rice (page 438)
3 tablespoons plus 1 teaspoon extra-virgin olive oil
2½ tablespoons champagne vinegar

HERBED SALAD SEASONINGS
½ teaspoon grated orange zest
Small pinch of sugar
2 tablespoons *each* minced fresh basil and mint
1 tablespoon *each* minced fresh Italian parsley and chives
1 teaspoon *each* minced fresh thyme and chervil
Salt and freshly ground pepper

Vegetable spray for salad molds
1 tablespoon coarsely chopped sunflower seeds
4 cups mixed salad greens
Juice of 1 lemon (preferably Meyer)

1. Place the cooked rice in a large bowl and add the 3 tablespoons olive oil, 1½ tablespoons of the vinegar and the salad seasonings, and toss thoroughly. Season to your taste with salt and pepper. Divide the mixture into 4 portions. Lightly coat ramekins, cups or other small molds with a thin film of vegetable spray and fill them with the rice mixture. Chill thoroughly, up to 24 hours ahead.

2. In a small to medium-size cast-iron skillet over medium heat, toss the sunflower seeds briefly until they become fragrant. Add 1 teaspoon oil and warm it gently. Do not allow the oil to smoke or steam. Add the greens and very quickly toss them in the heated oil. As they begin to soften, add the lemon juice and remaining tablespoon vinegar. Work quickly at this point and toss the greens vigorously but briefly until they are wilted but not completely shrunken, adding a little salt and a generous sprinkling of pepper as you turn the greens. Immediately arrange the wilted greens on individual dinner plates. Place the salad molds upside down on the greens and tap the bottom and sides lightly until the rice slips out. Serve immediately.

❋ PER SERVING *Calories: 250, Cholesterol (mg): 0, Saturated fat (g): 1, Total fat (g): 8, Sodium (mg): 5, Total fiber (g): 1*

White Bean and Chicken Salad
with Basil and Fennel

SERVES 4

WHITE BEANS NEED AGGRESSIVE SEASONING *to come to life. Anise-flavored fennel seeds and fresh fennel provide the perfect contrast in this very elegant, nourishing salad. On a sultry evening serve it with a cooling soup, such as Fresh Pea Soup with Mint (page 371), Melon and Cucumber Soup (page 377) or Cold Sweet and Sour Beet Soup (page 376), each low enough in calories and fat to balance the higher totals in the salad. In the fall, choose the more hearty Potato and Red Pepper Soup (page 369) and an assortment of grilled vegetables drizzled with balsamic vinegar.*

6 tablespoons extra-virgin olive oil
1½ tablespoons red wine vinegar
Juice of 1 lemon
Salt and freshly ground pepper

8 ounces chicken breast, all skin and fat removed, cooked and diced
2 cups cooked white beans
⅔ cup seeded and diced red bell pepper
½ cup diced fresh fennel bulb
¼ cup diced green onions
¼ cup chopped fresh basil
1 to 2 teaspoons fennel seeds
4 slices French bread

1. In a small bowl, whisk together the olive oil, vinegar and lemon juice and season to your taste with salt and pepper. Set the dressing aside for 30 minutes.

2. Combine the chicken, beans, red bell pepper, fresh fennel and onions in a mixing bowl and toss thoroughly. Add the dressing, basil, fennel seeds, salt and pepper. Toss gently and season to your taste, applying the pepper liberally.

3. Preheat the broiler. Toast both sides of the French bread under the broiler about 30 seconds or just until golden. Slice each piece in quarters diagonally and place them on individual salad plates with the points arranged in the shape of a star. Mound the salad in the center and serve.

FAT TRACKING TIP: Use cooked turkey breast instead of chicken.

❋ PER SERVING *Calories: 486, Cholesterol (mg): 48, Saturated fat: 3, Total fat (g): 23, Sodium (mg): 206, Total fiber (g): 5*

Salmon Salad with Tangerines and Cucumber in Ginger-Lemon Dressing

SERVES 6

IF POSSIBLE USE HONEY TANGERINES *for their sweetness or Darcy tangerines, the ones that shrink inside their skins. You can prepare the dressing, cucumber and red bell pepper ahead of time and keep covered in the refrigerator 24 hours ahead, bringing it to room temperature at least 20 minutes before serving. You can serve the salmon warm or cook it ahead and serve chilled.*

1 pound salmon fillet or steaks, poached and chilled

GINGER-LEMON DRESSING
2 tablespoons fresh lemon juice
1 teaspoon champagne vinegar or white wine vinegar
Pinch of cayenne
1 teaspoon chopped fresh ginger
¼ cup olive oil
Salt and freshly ground pepper

1 cucumber
¼ cup fresh cilantro leaves
3 green onions (white part only)
1 small red bell pepper, seeded and diced
2 tangerines or fresh Mandarin oranges, peeled and segmented

1. Remove the skin and bones from the salmon and set aside.

2. In a mixing bowl, combine the lemon juice, vinegar, cayenne and ginger; dribble in the oil and whisk until smooth. Season with salt and pepper to your taste.

3. Peel the cucumber and slice in half lengthwise. With a spoon, scoop out the seeds, dice the cucumber and toss in a serving bowl with the cilantro, onion and red bell pepper.

4. Flake the salmon and gently toss it in a medium-size bowl with the tangerines and cucumber-pepper mixture. Add the dressing, toss gently until well blended and serve on individual salad plates.

FAT TRACKING TIP: Decrease the olive oil.

❀ PER SERVING *Calories: 221, Cholesterol (mg): 36, Saturated fat: 3, Total fat (g): 16, Sodium (mg): 37, Total fiber (g): 1*

CHAPTER 33

Vegetables

WHAT MORE CAN WE SAY *about vegetables except to stress the importance of including them in your diet at every turn and maybe give you a few tips for preparing them. Most people who have spent even minimal time in the kitchen can adequately steam, boil or roast a given vegetable. But these basic preparations barely hint at the possibilities. The care with which a cook treats a lowly turnip indicates the care that will be given to the most important ingredients in a meal. While we couldn't find room for every vegetable this time, we treated the ones we have chosen carefully.*

The cardinal rules are first, don't *overcook* delicate vegetables, such as green beans, peas and broccoli, and second, don't *undercook* sturdy types such as potatoes, turnips and winter squashes. Beyond that, you can stuff them, stew them, dress them, undress them, mix and match them or munch on them freshly picked from the garden. On preparing vegetables, in this fiber-conscious age, we discover that peeling vegetables is a waste of fiber. Wash all vegetables before preparing, but don't peel carrots and the like unless absolutely necessary. Scrub root vegetables thoroughly. Rinse gritty vegetables, such as spinach and mushrooms (and fruit such as strawberries), in a bath of abundant cold water and a splash of distilled vinegar (its cheapest), then rerinse thoroughly. The vinegar causes sand and grit to slide right off, a second rinse (or in the case of really grimy spinach, a third or fourth), gets rid of any vinegar taste. We launch our vegetable recipes with an important fat-tracking tip for sautéing vegetables.

Basic Stir-Fries for Tender Green Vegetables

Use the following three basic recipes for any tender green vegetables that don't require long cooking, such as those listed below. You can prepare these vegetables in combination, such as a stir-fry of green beans, mushrooms and onions; or colorful peppers, zucchini, matchstick carrots and shallots; and don't forget winter broccoli, onions, peppers and napa cabbage. On the other hand, when a seasonal favorite is at its peak, you can spotlight a single vegetable in one of these sauces.

Suggestions for Quick-Cooking Vegetables
- Asparagus, thick end of stalk trimmed as necessary, peeled and left whole or cut into diagonal 2-inch slices
- Beans, green, ends trimmed as necessary, left whole or cut into diagonal 2-inch slices
- Broccoli and cauliflower, thick end of stalk trimmed as necessary, florets cut from stalk and trimmed into individual branches, stalk peeled and cut into diagonal 2-inch slices
- Brussels sprouts, end trimmed as necessary, left whole or shredded
- Cabbage (including red, green and napa), end trimmed as necessary, quartered, quartered again and coarsely shredded or chopped
- Carrots, tips and ends trimmed, peeled, cut in matchsticks
- Greens (including spinach and chard), rinsed in vinegar bath and rinsed again in clear water to remove sand, ends trimmed as necessary and chopped
- Mushrooms, ends trimmed as necessary, rinsed in vinegar bath and rinsed again in clear water to remove sand, dried immediately on paper towels and sliced, quartered or left whole
- Onions, green onions or shallots, outer layers removed as necessary, sliced or chopped
- Peas, shelled
- Peppers (bells), halved, stem, seeds and ribs removed, sliced
- Summer squash (pattypan, yellow crookneck, zucchini), stem and ends trimmed, sliced

Vegetables Stir-Fried with Shallots and Wild Mushrooms
Serves 4

> 1 pound quick-cooking vegetables (see above), trimmed as directed
> ¼ cup sliced fresh wild mushrooms or 2 to 3 ounces dried wild mushrooms (cepes, shiitakes) or white mushrooms
> 1 teaspoon Basil Oil (page 296) or extra-virgin olive oil
> ¼ cup minced shallots
> Chicken Stock (page 285–86) or canned low-fat, low-sodium chicken broth or water as needed
> 1 teaspoon minced fresh herbs (blend of thyme, parsley, marjoram or savory)
> Salt and freshly ground pepper

1. As directed on page 266–67, microwave or steam the vegetables until they are barely tender, 2 to 4 minutes depending on the vegetables. Don't overcook them and, as soon as they are done, transfer them to a separate dish to stop the cooking. Clean fresh mushrooms; soak dried mushrooms in a small amount of hot water for 20 minutes (reserve the liquid to add to the vegetables when you add the mushrooms).

2. In a skillet or wok, heat the oil until a spray of water dances on the surface. Add the shallots and stir over low-medium heat for 2 minutes or until they begin to soften. If they begin to scorch at all, add a small amount of chicken stock or water and reduce the heat immediately.

3. Add the mushrooms with their liquid, if any, and the herbs and stir for 1 minute. Immediately stir in the cooked vegetables and season lightly with salt and pepper. Add a little more stock or water if the pan remains dry, but don't add any more than is necessary to keep the vegetables from scorching or the sauce will be weak and watery. Toss briefly until everything is heated through. Taste for seasoning and serve immediately.

❈ PER SERVING *Calories: approximately 52, Cholesterol (mg): 0, Saturated fat (g): Trace, Total fat (g): 1, Sodium (mg): approximately 30, Total fiber (g): approximately 4*

Vegetables Stir-Fried with Chicken Stock, Garlic, Olive Oil and Lemon
Serves 4

⅓ cup Chicken Stock (page 285–86) or canned low-fat, low-sodium chicken broth
1 garlic clove, minced
1 pound quick-cooking vegetables (page 398), trimmed as directed
1 teaspoon extra-virgin olive oil
Juice of ½ lemon
Salt and freshly ground pepper

1. Heat the chicken stock in a wok or covered skillet and add the garlic. Bring to a boil and add the vegetables. Toss them in the hot stock briefly, then reduce the heat to low-medium, cover and cook for 2 to 3 minutes or until barely tender. Uncover the pan, raise the heat to a boil and toss the vegetables briefly until liquid has reduced to 2 to 3 tablespoons.

2. Drizzle the olive oil and lemon juice over the vegetables and toss well. Season to your taste with salt and pepper and add more lemon for more piquancy if you like. Serve immediately before the olive oil begins to cook.

❈ PER SERVING *Calories: approximately 44, Cholesterol (mg): 0, Saturated fat (g): Trace, Total fat (g): 1, Sodium (mg): approximately 30, Total fiber (g): approximately 4*

Vegetables Stir-Fried with Citrus Vinaigrette
Serves 4

CITRUS VINAIGRETTE
Juice of 1 orange or 1 tangerine or ½ lemon
1 teaspoon grated zest from the preceding fruit
1 tablespoon raspberry vinegar or other fruit vinegar
   or white wine vinegar
1 teaspoon brown sugar
1 teaspoon prepared sweet or Dijon mustard

1 pound quick-cooking vegetables (page 398), trimmed as directed
2 teaspoons extra-virgin olive oil
¼ cup diced onion or shallot
1 garlic clove, optional, minced
½ pound white mushrooms, sliced
Salt and freshly ground pepper

1. Blend together the vinaigrette ingredients in a measuring cup and set aside.

2. As directed on page 266–67, microwave or steam the vegetables until they are barely tender, 2 to 4 minutes depending on the vegetables. Don't overcook them and as soon as they are done, transfer them to a separate dish to stop the cooking. Heat the oil in a wok or skillet over low-medium heat and add the onion and garlic, if using. Stir for about 2 minutes or until the onions are soft. Add the cooked vegetables, mushrooms and the citrus vinaigrette and stir over very high heat until the vegetables are heated through and glazed with the sauce. Season to your taste with salt and pepper and serve immediately

❀ PER SERVING *Calories: approximately 87, Cholesterol (mg): 0, Saturated fat (g): Trace, Total fat (g): 3, Sodium (mg): approximately 50, Total fiber (g): approximately 5*

Spiced Sauté of Broccoli Stalks, Carrots and Potatoes

SERVES 4

WHAT DO YOU DO WITH LEFTOVER STALKS OF BROCCOLI *when you have used the florets in a pasta dish? Sauté them with a mix of carrots and potatoes in highly seasoned oil for a dose of antioxidants, an important part of your heart-healthy life plan. If you don't have the Asian Spiced Oil or Garlic Oil on hand, simply sauté the vegetables in olive oil or canola oil, add a clove or two of garlic and toss in a pinch of crushed dried red peppers. This blend of oils gives a mildly peppered flavor; use all Asian Spiced Oil if you prefer more bite.*

½ pound broccoli stalks (approximately)
1 pound carrots
1 large boiling potato
2 teaspoons Asian Spiced Oil (page 297)
2 teaspoons Garlic Oil (page 296)
Salt and freshly ground pepper

1. Trim the root end of the broccoli and peel the stalks. Trim and peel the carrots. Slice both the broccoli and carrots on the diagonal about ⅛ inch thick. Peel the potato and quarter it lengthwise. Slice each quarter into pieces about ⅛ inch thick. Try to cut the vegetables in uniform slices so they will cook evenly.

2. As directed on page 266–67, steam or microwave the potato slices for 4 minutes or until soft but not mushy. Steam or microwave the carrots for 2 minutes; they should retain a slight crunch. Steam or microwave the broccoli for 1 minute.

3. Heat the oils in a skillet large enough to hold the vegetables in a fairly shallow layer. Add the potatoes and turn them in the oil until they are thoroughly coated. Repeat with the carrots and finally the broccoli. Season to your taste with salt and pepper. Stir quickly over moderately high heat for 2 to 3 minutes or until the vegetables are heated through and the potatoes and carrots have begun to crisp. Turn onto a large platter and serve piping hot.

❋ PER SERVING *Calories: 147, Cholesterol (mg): 0, Saturated fat (g): 1, Total fat (g): 5, Sodium (mg): 57, Total fiber (g): 6*

Stir-Fry of Green and White Beans
with Ginger

SERVES 4

A FINAL TOSS WITH SOME SHREDDED GINGER *brings this blend of summer and winter beans to life with stunning piquancy. This dish demonstrates the fat-tracking strategy of keeping a supply of cooked beans in the freezer (for storage suggestions see Basic Beans, page 425–26) so you can quickly add robustness and low-fat protein to your meals. Canned white beans will work here, but beans you have cooked and seasoned yourself will have more character. As with traditional stir-fry dishes, make the minutes before you pull your entire menu together hassle-free by assembling the dressing ingredients and trimming the vegetables before you begin. Use a skillet large enough to hold the vegetables in one layer so that you can toss them with the dressing quickly without overcooking them.*

CITRUS-MUSTARD DRESSING
2 tablespoons fresh lemon juice
¼ cup fresh orange juice
2 tablespoons champagne vinegar or white wine vinegar
2 teaspoons prepared sweet mustard
½ teaspoon sugar
Salt and white pepper to taste

1 pound green beans, trimmed and cut into 2-inch lengths
1½ tablespoons extra-virgin olive oil
½ small red bell pepper, seeded and thinly sliced
½ small red onion, sliced
1 small garlic clove, minced
⅔ cup cooked white beans
1 teaspoon grated fresh ginger

1. Whisk together the dressing ingredients in a measuring cup or small bowl, seasoning lightly with salt and white pepper. You can make this ahead, cover and refrigerate it until you need it.

2. As directed on page 266–67, steam or microwave the green beans for 2 minutes. They should retain quite a bit of crunch. As soon as they are done, transfer them to a separate dish to stop the cooking.

3. Heat the olive oil over medium heat in a skillet, add the red bell pepper, onion and garlic and stir for 1 minute. Stir in the green beans. Add the reserved dressing and the white beans and raise the heat slightly, stirring and tossing the vegetables just until the dressing glazes the beans and everything is thoroughly heated.

4. Remove the skillet from the heat. Add the ginger (you can grate it directly over the vegetables if you like) and toss it with the beans. Let them rest for a moment before tasting to allow the ginger to permeate the beans. Add a little more ginger if you like, but don't overdo it. The ginger should highlight the citrus flavors and cause an occasional gingery explosion on your taste buds, but not dominate the whole dish. Serve immediately while still hot.

❋ PER SERVING *Calories: 140, Cholesterol (mg): 0, Saturated fat (g): 1, Total fat (g): 5, Sodium (mg): 53, Total fiber (g): 3*

Brussels Sprouts with Lemon and Garlic

SERVES 4

SHREDDED, BRUSSELS SPROUTS TAKE ON *an entirely different character than the usual whole sprouts. They more easily absorb the tangy dressing and may become a winter habit.*

> Juice of ½ lemon
> 1 garlic clove, chopped
> 1 tablespoon extra-virgin olive oil
> 1 tablespoon water
> 1 pound Brussels sprouts
> Salt and freshly ground pepper

1. Combine the lemon juice, garlic, oil and water in a small bowl and let stand for 15 minutes.

2. Trim any rough stems from the Brussels sprouts and shred them into slices ⅓ inch wide, starting at the tip and working down to the stem. As directed on page 266–67, steam or microwave the shredded sprouts for 1 minute or until just limp. Do not overcook them. Place them in a serving bowl and immediately toss them with the lemon and garlic mixture. Season to your taste with salt and pepper and serve while still hot.

FAT TRACKING TIP: Eliminate the oil and add an extra tablespoon of water.

❋ PER SERVING *Calories: 76, Cholesterol (mg): 0, Saturated fat (g): 1, Total fat (g): 4, Sodium (mg): 24, Total fiber (g): 5*

Spiced Cauliflower and Peppers

SERVES 4

THE PIQUANT SAUCE *delivers a two-tiered burst of flavor as the heat of the pungent Asian Spiced Oil takes hold after the initial lemony tartness fades. This dish is equally delicious served chilled as part of a cool summer menu or offered as a steaming companion to roast chicken or whole, poached fish.*

> 1 medium head cauliflower, trimmed and cut into florets
> 1/3 cup fresh orange juice
> 1 tablespoon fresh lemon juice
> 1 tablespoon rice vinegar
> 1 teaspoon cornstarch
> 2 teaspoons Asian Spiced Oil (page 297)
> 1 small red or yellow bell pepper, seeded and cut into matchstick strips
> Salt and freshly ground pepper
> 1 tablespoon fresh cilantro, optional

1. As directed on page 267, microwave the cauliflower on high for 4 minutes or steam for 6 to 8 minutes.

2. In a measuring cup or small bowl, blend the juices, vinegar and cornstarch until smooth.

3. Heat the Asian Spiced Oil in a skillet and add the peppers and cooked cauliflower. Toss thoroughly and add the juice mixture. Toss over high heat for 1 minute or until the sauce has thickened slightly. Season to your taste with salt and pepper and add the cilantro if desired. Serve immediately.

❋ PER SERVING *Calories: 54, Cholesterol (mg): 0, Saturated fat (g): Trace, Total fat (g): 2, Sodium (mg): 20, Total fiber (g): Trace*

Green Beans with Sesame Seeds

SERVES 4

SERVE THESE CRISP, AROMATIC *beans whole. And to capitalize on the nutty flavor of toasted sesame seeds, plan to have the seeds ready to come out of the oven as soon as the beans are done.*

> 2 teaspoons sesame seeds
> 1½ pounds green beans, ends trimmed
> 2 teaspoons peanut oil or canola oil
> 1 teaspoon Asian sesame oil
> 1 teaspoon balsamic vinegar
> Salt and freshly ground pepper

1. Preheat the oven to 500 degrees F. Spread the sesame seeds on a baking sheet and bake for 6 to 8 minutes or until the seeds are toasted and golden. Watch them carefully because once they start to toast, the high heat can quickly scorch them beyond salvaging. As soon as they are done, remove them from the oven and set them aside.

2. As directed on page 266–67, steam or microwave the beans for 2 minutes. Heat the oils in a skillet and add the hot beans. Toss them vigorously until they glisten and add the balsamic vinegar and salt and pepper to your taste. Stir the mixture thoroughly and add the seeds. Toss well so that the seeds are distributed evenly. Serve immediately.

FAT TRACKING TIP: Replace the peanut oil with ¼ cup Chicken Stock (page 285–86) or canned low-fat, low-sodium chicken broth. The seeds won't cling to the beans as well and the flavor will be less robust, but still quite good.

❋ PER SERVING *Calories: 98, Cholesterol (mg): 0, Saturated fat (g): 1, Total fat (g): 5, Sodium (mg): 6, Total fiber (g): 3*

Sweet and Spicy Spinach
with Shiitake Mushrooms

SERVES 4

SPINACH STUDDED WITH RAISINS *is not new. Italian and Middle Eastern cooks discovered that match long ago. In this spinach dish, raisins perfectly balance fiery oil in an exquisite blend of sugar and spice. Serve with an uncomplicated grilled or broiled entrée, such as Grilled Turkey Breast with White Wine and Herbs (page 521–22).*

> 1 pound spinach
> Distilled vinegar for washing spinach
> 1½ tablespoons Asian Spiced Oil (page 297)
> 2 tablespoons seedless yellow raisins
> 6 dried shiitake mushrooms, soaked in cold water
> for 20 minutes and sliced
> Salt and freshly ground pepper

1. Swish the spinach in a bowl of water with a few spoonfuls of white vinegar. Drain well and steam 2 to 3 minutes until wilted, but do not overcook. Gently squeeze out excess water (using a ricer is an easy way to do this).

2. While the spinach cooks, heat the oil in a skillet over low-medium heat. Add the raisins and stir briefly until they are coated with the oil. Add the mushrooms and stir for 1 minute until they begin to soften. Stir in the spinach and toss gently until it is thoroughly coated with the oil. Season to your taste with salt and pepper and serve while still hot.

✿ PER SERVING *Calories: 102, Cholesterol (mg): 0, Saturated fat (g): 1, Total fat (g): 5, Sodium (mg): 90, Total fiber (g): 4*

Roasted Carrots
with Fennel and Orange

SERVES 4

WE SO LIKED THE PAIRING OF FENNEL AND CARROT *in Carrot, Leek and Fennel Soup (page 367) that we matched them up again, this time using the seeds of the licorice-scented fennel, instead of the plant. You could slice fresh fennel, however, and use it in place of some or all of the carrot. This is fantastic as finger food for a buffet (served with toothpicks) or as a companion to a grilled or roast chicken.*

¼ cup fresh orange juice
1 tablespoon raspberry vinegar or other fruit vinegar
½ teaspoon fennel seeds
1 pound carrots, sliced diagonally ½ inch thick
Vegetable spray for baking sheet
Salt and freshly ground pepper

1. Blend the orange juice, vinegar and fennel seeds in a shallow bowl large enough to hold the carrots. Add the carrots and toss thoroughly until the fennel seeds cling to the carrots. Let stand for 30 minutes.

2. Preheat the oven to 400 degrees F. Coat a baking sheet with a light film of vegetable spray and arrange the carrots in a single layer. Spoon any remaining juice and seeds over the carrots. Bake in the oven for 15 minutes and turn the carrots so they will brown evenly. If there is any juice remaining in the bowl, brush it over the carrots. Continue cooking for another 10 minutes or until the carrots are tender and glazed. Season very lightly with salt and pepper. Serve hot or cold. If you plan to serve these carrots as an appetizer, serve with toothpicks.

✿ PER SERVING *Calories: 59, Cholesterol (mg): 0, Saturated fat (g): Trace, Total fat (g): Trace, Sodium (mg): 34, Total fiber (g): 4*

Cabbage and Red Grapes

SERVES 4

TO AN AUTUMN MENU *of grilled Garlic Roasted Chicken with Wilted Greens (page 510–11) and oven-roasted potatoes, add a dish of this delicate sweet and sour cabbage. Red Flame grapes have the full-bodied flavor that holds up well with cabbage—and no seeds, which makes them ideal cooking grapes.*

> 1 small head cabbage (about 1 1/4 pounds)
> 1 tablespoon canola oil
> 1 shallot, minced
> 3 tablespoons white wine
> 1 cup seedless Red Flame grapes
> Salt and white pepper

1. Cut the cabbage in quarters and remove the white core at the root end. Shred the cabbage coarsely and plunge into boiling water for 45 seconds or until it just begins to wilt. Drain immediately.

2. Heat the oil in a skillet over low-medium heat and add the shallot and white wine. Stir for 3 to 4 minutes or until the shallot is soft. Add the cabbage and grapes and toss well. Cover and simmer for 3 minutes. Remove the cover and continue cooking for another 10 minutes or until the grapes are very soft and the cabbage is tender. Stir occasionally. Season with a little bit of salt and a liberal dose of pepper and serve immediately.

❀ PER SERVING *Calories: 88, Cholesterol (mg): 0, Saturated fat (g): Trace, Total fat (g): 4, Sodium (mg): 27, Total fiber (g): 3*

Baby Pumpkins with
Apple, Grape and Walnut Stuffing

SERVES 6

IF YOU'D LIKE TO CELEBRATE AUTUMN *with a pumpkin dish, but balk at the idea of cooking one of the monsters that appears at Halloween, choose minia- ture pumpkins, ideal for single servings, and fill them with this savory and fruity stuffing. Serve with roasted chicken or surround your Thanksgiving bird with a ring of these colorful squashes. As you may have discovered, hazelnut oil is a luxury. If you have some on hand, stir a spoonful into the stuffing mixture before filling the pumpkins. The dab of Drained Yogurt in the bottom of each pumpkin is a velvety touch that adds no saturated fat. If you make the stuffing ahead of time, wrap it in foil and reheat it in the oven for 15 minutes until it is steaming.*

6 miniature pumpkins (approximately 6 or 7 ounces each)
¼ cup water

STUFFING
1½ tablespoons extra-virgin olive oil
½ cup finely diced red onion
½ cup finely diced green apple
2 tablespoons minced celery
12 chopped seedless red grapes
2 tablespoons white wine
2 tablespoons Chicken Stock (page 285–86) or canned low-fat,
    low-sodium chicken broth
½ cup coarse bread crumbs
1½ tablespoons finely chopped walnuts
1 sage leaf or ¼ teaspoon minced dry sage
⅛ teaspoon white pepper
1 teaspoon hazelnut oil or Vanilla Oil (page 298), optional
Salt and freshly ground pepper

¼ cup Drained Yogurt (page 290–91) or nonfat plain yogurt

1. Preheat the oven to 375 degrees F. Place the pumpkins in a baking dish and add ¼ cup water. Cover with aluminum foil and bake 45 to 50 minutes or until tender when pierced with the tip of a knife.

2. Meanwhile, heat the olive oil in a small skillet. Add the onion and stir over medium heat for 2 to 3 minutes or until softened slightly. Add the apple, celery, grapes, wine and chicken stock and bring to a boil. Reduce the heat to medium immediately and, stirring occasionally, cook for 5 minutes or until most of the liquid has evaporated. Add the remaining stuffing ingredients and season to your taste with salt and pepper. Set aside until the pumpkins are cooked. You can make this stuffing several hours ahead, cover and refrigerate it until you need it.

3. When they are done, remove the pumpkins from the oven. With the tip of a small, sharp knife, cut a 2½-inch circle around the stem, remove the "cap" and set it aside. Scoop out and discard the seeds and stringy pulp. Spoon 2 teaspoons of Drained Yogurt into the bottom of each hot pumpkin and sprinkle with a few grains of salt. Divide the stuffing into 6 equal portions and fill the pumpkins. If the pumpkins have cooled, place them on a baking sheet and reheat them briefly. Serve with the reserved pumpkin cap perched rakishly on top.

✿ PER SERVING *Calories: 119, Cholesterol (mg): Trace, Saturated fat (g): 1, Total fat (g): 5, Sodium (mg): 95, Total fiber (g): 2*

Palo Alto Pipérade

SERVES 4

OF BASQUE ORIGIN *where it is traditionally made with pimientos, pipérade is commonly assumed to be an omelet with a side of peppers. Not necessarily. We have it on good authority (Julia Child) that pipérade is merely the garnish for eggs. We have appropriated this healthful (high in antioxidants) dish for our own purposes. While you certainly can serve this with a yolkless omelet, we present here its other face, a stand-alone vegetable dish. Look for other opportunities to serve this zesty sauté, such as a topping for pizza with Cilantro Pesto (page 293), as a filling for a burrito stuffed with slivers of grilled London broil or salmon, or even over pasta. Better yet, grace your holiday table with this colorful mix of peppers sparkling with bright flavors. If your market doesn't carry yellow peppers, substitute a red bell pepper.*

> 1 tablespoon extra-virgin olive oil
> 1 *each* yellow, red and green bell peppers, cut into matchstick strips
> 3 green onions, slivered lengthwise
> 3 garlic cloves, minced
> 1 tablespoon *each* minced fresh oregano and thyme,
>   or 1 teaspoon of each dried
> 1 teaspoon red raspberry vinegar or other fruit vinegar
> 1 cup red or yellow cherry tomatoes
> Salt and freshly ground pepper
> 1 tablespoon minced fresh Italian parsley

1. Heat the olive oil over medium heat in a heavy skillet and add the peppers, onions and garlic. Stir constantly for 1 minute, then reduce the heat slightly and cook for 5 minutes or until the peppers have softened slightly. Stir from time to time to make sure the vegetables don't scorch.

2. Add the oregano, thyme, vinegar and tomatoes. Season lightly with salt and pepper and continue cooking, stirring occasionally, until the tomatoes have softened, about 1 to 2 minutes depending on their size. Sprinkle with the Italian parsley and serve.

❋ PER SERVING *Calories: 58, Cholesterol (mg): 0, Saturated fat (g): Trace, Total fat (g): 4, Sodium (mg): 7, Total fiber (g): 2*

Purée of Beets and Cranberries
SERVES 8

MOUTH-PUCKERING CRANBERRIES *normally require a lot of sugar, but we use the natural sweetness of beets and orange juice to mellow this fat-free purée. This is an obvious choice for fall and holiday menus, but since cranberries freeze well, stock up in November and you can enjoy this in any season. Make sure you wash the cranberries thoroughly and remove all the stems before you begin.*

> 2 pounds baby beets
> 1 pound cranberries
> ¼ cup sugar
> ½ cup fresh orange juice
> 1 tablespoon raspberry vinegar

1. If attached, trim the greens from the beets, leaving a 1-inch stalk. Wash the beets thoroughly, but do not trim the root end or pierce the skins or they will bleed uncontrollably. As directed on page 266–67, steam or microwave the beets until they are very tender, from 12 to 17 minutes depending on their size. When they are cool enough to handle, cut off the stem and root end, peel and quarter the beets.

2. While the beets cook, place the cranberries in a saucepan and cover with cold water. Bring to a boil, reduce the heat and simmer gently for 20 to 25 minutes or until they all pop and are soft. Drain thoroughly.

3. Place the cranberries, sugar, orange juice and vinegar in a blender or food processor and purée until smooth. Add the beets and pulse briefly until you have a coarse mixture. Taste for seasoning, adding a little more vinegar if they are too sweet, and a little more orange juice or sugar if they are too tart. You can make this up to 24 hours in advance. Serve hot or cold.

❋ PER SERVING *Calories: 109, Cholesterol (mg): 0, Saturated fat (g): Trace, Total fat (g): Trace, Sodium (mg): 82, Total fiber (g): 6*

Oven-Baked French Fries

SERVES 1

CONVENTIONAL FRIES *crisp in a hot oil bath. Though they are the bane of a fat-tracking program, they are loved by almost everyone. The relatively cooler, drier air in your oven can do wonderful things with a potato, but not produce a crunchy exterior and tender center simultaneously without a little help. Nothing approximates the texture of deep-frying, but you can definitely achieve an amazingly crisp knockoff, which—as far as that soul-satisfying taste of fried food is concerned—will make you feel as though you have to eat them in the closet. Before proceeding with this recipe, read the following tips for Oven-Baked French Fries.*

> 1 potato per person
> Vegetable spray (flavored with olive oil or butter)
> Salt and freshly ground pepper
> Paprika

1. Place the rack on the highest rung of the oven and preheat to 525 degrees F. Coat a large baking sheet with a film of vegetable spray.

2. Slice the potatoes into rounds, ¼ inch thick. Cut the rounds into strips, ¼ inch wide. If the cuts are larger, don't worry, they will just take a little longer to bake. Consistency of size (so they will cook evenly) is more important than actual size. Plunge the slices into a bowl of cold water, drain and dry on paper towels. Season lightly with salt and pepper and sprinkle the paprika over them in an even, light cloud. Don't overdo it, just add enough to color them.

3. Place the prepared baking sheet in the hot oven for 30 to 45 seconds. When it is hot, add the potatoes in one layer and lightly spritz with the vegetable spray. You don't need a lot of it. Bake for 5 minutes, turn the potatoes and spritz them for the last time. Bake for 5 minutes, turn the potatoes again, bake for another 5 minutes, turn them, and then check them every 2 to 3 minutes until they are golden on the outside and tender inside. Serve immediately; they lose their crispness as they cool.

❋ PER SERVING *Calories: 110, Cholesterol (mg): 0, Saturated fat (g): 0, Total fat (g): Trace, Sodium (mg): 275, Total fiber (g): 2*

Tips for Oven-Baked French Fries

- First, have the potatoes evenly sliced using a vegetable slicer or slicing blade of a food processor. The thinner the cut, the crisper the fry.
- Cook in one layer on a very hot surface in a very hot oven. Check and turn them frequently; the browning intensifies every time they hit a hot surface.
- A large, flat baking sheet, which allows the potatoes to release and disperse moisture, works best. A cast-iron skillet, for example, with higher sides than a baking sheet, makes adequate though not superior fries.
- Coat the potatoes with vegetable spray twice for the most satisfying fried potato taste. They will begin to taste greasy if you use more. If you cook several batches, you may notice that the surface remains oiled, and you will not have to respray before you begin the next batch. The texture will vary with the type of potato you use.
- The cold water bath, long used to prepare potatoes for frying, removes the surface starch that accumulates during slicing and does produce a more deeply colored and crisper fry.
- An old family trick, deepening the color of fried potatoes with paprika and lightly seasoning with salt and pepper at the beginning, holds up with these fries. They turn golden brown and absorb the seasoning as they cook, requiring much less salt at the table.
- Before cooking, sprinkle with Cajun Seasoning (page 496), a ground herb mixture or grated orange or lemon zest to add excitement to your fries. Or, instead of coating the potatoes with vegetable spray, use a brush to very lightly coat them with Garlic Oil (page 296), Basil Oil (page 296) or Asian Spiced Oil (page 297).

Oven-Baked Potato Chips

Slice the potatoes into paper-thin rounds and then follow the directions in the preceding recipe for Oven-Baked French Fries. You will have delicious oven-baked potato chips.

Home-Fried Potatoes

Home fries are a favorite treatment of leftover boiled or roast potatoes, cooked in large amounts of butter or oil in a hot skillet. You will not be able to taste the difference when you oven-fry them with a small amount of vegetable spray or seasoned oil such as Garlic Oil (page 296) or Asian Spiced Oil (page 297) brushed on them before cooking. Follow the preceding instructions for Oven-Baked Fries, but substitute cooked potatoes, sliced into rounds approximately ½ inch thick, then cut into halves or quarters, depending on their size, and omit the water bath before seasoning them.

Oven-Fried Yams with Spiced Yogurt

SERVES 4

YAMS AND SWEET POTATOES *(which you can substitute here if you prefer them)* *are among the vegetables highest in antioxidants. Look for ways to include them in your menus as often as possible. They lend themselves to many presentations, even desserts. However, in this change from the usual sugary treatment of yams, the pungency of cumin and mustard seed offsets their natural sugar. Don't be afraid of dealing with whole spices. We explain how to toast them on page 300.*

> 1 teaspoon mustard seeds, toasted (page 300)
> 2 teaspoons cumin seeds, toasted (page 300)
> 2 tablespoons extra-virgin olive oil
> 2 tablespoons minced onion
> 3 garlic cloves, minced
> Pinch of salt and freshly ground pepper
> 1 large yam, thinly sliced (about 2 cups)
> Vegetable spray for baking sheet
> 1/4 cup Spiced Yogurt (page 291)

1. Preheat the oven to 475 degrees F. Crush the spices as described in the toasting instructions, add the olive oil and return the skillet to the heat. Stir over low-medium heat and when the oil is warm and fragrant, add the onion, garlic and salt and pepper. Add the yams and toss them until they are thoroughly coated with the oil and seasonings.

2. Coat a baking sheet lightly with a thin film of vegetable spray. Turn the yams onto the sheet and bake 30 minutes or until the yams are crisp and golden. Turn them once or twice so they will cook evenly. Serve with the Spiced Yogurt while the yams are hot and fragrant.

❊ PER SERVING (INCLUDES 1 TABLESPOON YOGURT) *Calories: 114, Cholesterol (mg): Trace, Saturated fat (g): 1, Total fat (g): 2, Sodium (mg): 87, Total fiber (g): 2*

Roasted Potatoes, Onions and Sausage

SERVES 6

THIS RIB-STICKING, ONE-DISH MEAL *assembles quickly but cooks slowly to give you time to prepare a vegetable salad, such as Warm Broccoli, Orange and Walnut Salad with Walnut Vinaigrette (page 384–85), and to heat whole grain rolls or French bread. Use your favorite, zesty, spicy sausage if you don't use our homemade version, but make sure it is made with low-fat chicken or turkey breast.*

> 2 pounds boiling potatoes, peeled and sliced ½ inch thick
> 2 tablespoons extra-virgin olive oil
> 1 garlic clove, minced
> 1 onion, chopped
> 1 teaspoon dried oregano
> Salt and freshly ground pepper
> 1 pound Hot Italian Sausage with Fennel (page 323)
>   or a low-fat commercial sausage
> Vegetable spray or regular olive oil for skillet

1. Preheat the oven to 425 degrees F. As directed on page 266–67, steam or microwave the potatoes for 3 minutes. Toss and separate the slices to make sure they cook evenly and continue cooking for another 3 minutes.

2. Pour the oil into a baking dish. If the dish tolerates stovetop cooking, heat the oil, add the garlic and onion, and stir over medium heat for 2 minutes. Otherwise, toss the onions with the oil to coat thoroughly and place them in the hot oven for 2 to 3 minutes. Add the partially cooked potatoes, oregano and a light sprinkling of salt and pepper. Toss the mixture thoroughly to coat everything with the oil. Place the dish in the preheated oven for 10 minutes, then reduce the heat to 375 degrees F. Cook for 20 to 25 minutes, turning the mixture in the oil occasionally so the potatoes will brown evenly and the tips of the onions won't scorch. Continue cooking for 20 to 30 minutes or until the potatoes are crispy and golden on the outside and tender in the center.

3. Shortly before serving, steam or microwave the sausages 4 to 5 minutes depending on their size. (See Basic Breakfast Sausage, page 321–22.) Coat a skillet with a light film of vegetable spray or olive oil. Turn the heat very high and when a spray of water dances on the surface, add the sausage. Cook over high heat for 30 seconds on each side or until crisp and golden, then remove them from the pan immediately to prevent them from drying out. Mound the potatoes onto a serving platter. Arrange the sausage around the potatoes and serve immediately.

❈ PER SERVING *Calories: 377, Cholesterol (mg): 53, Saturated fat (g): 2, Total fat (g): 13, Sodium (mg): 75, Total fiber (g): 4*

Potatoes with Garlic and Lemon

SERVES 4

TEXTURE AS MUCH AS FLAVOR *draws us back again and again to a favorite dish. For example, the creaminess of tender new potatoes. You can add another favorite herb instead of chives, such as oregano, rosemary, thyme or a mix of delicate herbs. Just make sure the potatoes get a final splash of your best olive oil. If your potatoes are small, you may want to halve or quarter them, depending on their size.*

> 1 pound unpeeled red potatoes, sliced
> 1 tablespoon plus 1 teaspoon extra-virgin olive oil
> 1 garlic clove, minced
> 2 tablespoons fresh lemon juice
> 2 tablespoons chopped fresh chives
> Salt and freshly ground pepper

1. As directed on page 266–67, steam or microwave the potatoes for 7 to 10 minutes or until they are very tender.

2. Heat 1 tablespoon of the olive oil in a medium-size skillet and add the garlic. Stir over low heat for 2 to 3 minutes or until soft. Add the potatoes and turn them until they are well coated with the oil. Sprinkle the potatoes with the lemon juice and toss thoroughly, then drizzle with the remaining oil. Toss the mixture gently but thoroughly once more with the chives and season to your taste with salt and pepper before serving.

❀ PER SERVING *Calories: 166, Cholesterol (mg): 0, Saturated fat (g): 1, Total fat (g): 5, Sodium (mg): 9, Total fiber (g): 3*

Potatoes and Brussels Sprouts with Mustard, Rosemary and Chive Vinaigrette

SERVES 4

LIKE SO MANY OTHER POTATO-CABBAGE MATCHES, *this combination of spuds and sprouts is a winner (and easy, to boot). This dish has transformed confirmed Brussels sprouts haters into champions of this important, antioxidant vegetable. If you cook the sprouts quickly and uncover them as soon as they are done, you won't end up with any offensive odor.*

1 pound unpeeled red potatoes
½ pound Brussels sprouts

VINAIGRETTE
2 tablespoons extra-virgin olive oil
1 tablespoon sherry vinegar
½ tablespoon prepared sweet mustard
½ teaspoon honey
½ teaspoon chopped fresh rosemary
1 tablespoon minced fresh chives
½ teaspoon green peppercorns, chopped

1 tablespoon or more fresh lemon juice
Salt and freshly ground pepper

1. As directed on page 266–67, steam or microwave the potatoes until they are tender, about 10 minutes. Trim any rough stems from the Brussels sprouts and shred them into slices ⅓ inch wide, starting at the tip and working down to the stem. Then steam or microwave the shredded sprouts for 1 minute or until just limp. Do not overcook them.

2. While the vegetables cook, combine the vinaigrette ingredients in a measuring cup. Blend thoroughly. When the potatoes are done, place them and the Brussels sprouts in a serving bowl and toss well with the vinaigrette. Add more lemon juice, salt and pepper to your taste and serve while hot.

❀ PER SERVING *Calories: 209, Cholesterol (mg): 0, Saturated fat (g): 1, Total fat (g): 7, Sodium (mg): 21, Total fiber (g): 5*

Mashed Potatoes with Fennel

SERVES 4

THE BLEND OF POTATO AND FENNEL *yields an uncommon richness, the type of flavor combination you seek if you are used to a great deal of butter, milk or even cream in mashed potatoes. Olive oil enriches the purée, and the yogurt lightens it.*

> 3 large russet potatoes, peeled and sliced
> 1 bulb fennel
> ¼ cup Chicken Stock (page 285–86) or canned low-fat,
>   low-sodium chicken broth
> ¼ cup 1% milk
> Salt and freshly ground pepper
> 1 tablespoon extra-virgin olive oil or Vanilla Oil (page 298)
> ¼ cup nonfat plain yogurt, optional

1. Boil or steam the potatoes until they are very soft. Do not microwave them; they will be hard to purée.

2. Trim the fronds and the root from the fennel and chop the bulb and tender stalks. As directed on page 266–67, steam or microwave the fennel about 10 minutes just until it is tender. Don't overcook it.

3. Put the potatoes through a ricer or mash them in a large bowl until they are smooth. Do not use a food processor for this step, or the potatoes will become gluey. Purée the fennel with the chicken stock, however, in a food processor or blender and add to the potatoes. Stir in the milk, season to your taste with salt and pepper, and whisk the potatoes with the olive oil until they are very fluffy. Stir in the yogurt and reheat the potatoes if necessary before serving.

❊ PER SERVING *Calories: 125, Cholesterol (mg): 1, Saturated fat (g): 1, Total fat (g): 4, Sodium (mg): 25, Total fiber (g): 2*

Skordalia

SERVES 6

NOT FOR THE FAINT-HEARTED, *this rich, garlic-infused potato purée should be served in small dabs. It has Greek origins and can do double duty, either as a vibrant partner for grilled foods, such as Grilled Lamb Kabobs with Skordalia and Eggplant (page 531–32), or as a spread or dip for crisp vegetables and crackers. A touch of vinegar adds tang. Add it or not as you prefer.*

> 1 pound boiling potatoes, peeled and diced
> 3 garlic cloves, minced (add more or less according to your tolerance)
> 1 teaspoon salt
> 5 teaspoons extra-virgin olive oil
> 1 teaspoon white wine vinegar, optional
> ¼ cup nonfat plain yogurt

1. As directed on page 266–67, steam the potatoes for 8 to 9 minutes or until they are very tender. Put the potatoes through a ricer or mash them in a large mixing bowl. (Do not use a food processor.)

2. With a mortar and pestle or in a small bowl with the back of a spoon, mash the minced garlic with the salt to a smooth paste. Add olive oil, 1 tablespoon at a time, beating briefly but thoroughly after each addition until you have a consistency similar to mayonnaise. Beat the garlic purée into the potatoes, then blend in the vinegar if using and yogurt and serve hot.

❋ PER SERVING *Calories: 123, Cholesterol (mg): 0, Saturated fat (g): Trace, Total fat (g): 4, Sodium (mg): 368, Total fiber (g): 2*

Roasted Winter Vegetables
with Persillade
SERVES 8

To form a crisp crust *on tender root vegetables, cooks usually roast them in pan drippings from a roast beef or chicken—too much saturated fat for a Fat Tracker. Instead, we seal vegetables in foil to steam them slightly, then cover the entire pan with a second lid to intensify the heat during the first part of the cooking. Later we remove the coverings to crisp the softened vegetables in a hot oven. A medley of these vegetables topped with a piquant parsley and bread crumb topping makes a very filling centerpiece for an informal meal, in place of a meaty entrée. With dinner rolls and a hefty salad which includes white or black beans you have a thoroughly nourishing and satisfying meal. You can roast small batches of vegetables, or double or triple the recipe for a party buffet. You can add a turnip, subtract a parsnip or mix your own favorites any way you like, but use at least ½ pound of root vegetables per person. If you have any leftover vegetables, you can slice them and heat them in a little olive oil for your next day's lunch.*

Persillade (recipe follows)

ROOT VEGETABLES
2 large sweet potatoes, peeled and diced into 1-inch squares
2 large white potatoes, peeled and cubed
4 carrots, diagonally sliced ¼ inch thick
1 large parsnip, diagonally sliced ¼ inch thick
1 medium-size rutabaga, peeled and cubed
1 onion, cut into eighths
1 head of garlic
1 tablespoon extra-virgin olive oil
2 tablespoons balsamic vinegar
1 tablespoon fresh oregano or 1 teaspoon dried
½ teaspoon sugar
Pinch of salt
Freshly ground pepper to your taste

1. Preheat the oven to 425 degrees F. Prepare and bake the Persillade, then set aside. Place all of the prepared root vegetables in a baking dish or roasting pan large enough to hold them in a fairly shallow layer. Bury the onion wedges among the vegetables.

2. Remove 12 to 14 of the large outer cloves from the garlic head. Smash each clove with a mallet or the bottom of a small pan just hard enough to loosen the skin. Some of them may crack slightly, but do not mash or crush them. Squeeze each clove gently over the vegetables; it will pop out of the skin easily. Sprinkle the oil over the vegetables and toss thoroughly, trying to coat as many of the vegetables as possible, though it is not necessary that each has a film of oil. Add the vinegar, oregano, sugar, salt and pepper and toss thoroughly again.

3. Cover the vegetables tightly with aluminum foil, pressing it down around them and making as tight a seal as possible. Cover the pan with a lid or another piece of foil, making a second tight seal. Place the pan in the oven, reduce the heat to 350 degrees F and bake for 30 minutes. Remove all the foil and toss the vegetables; raise the heat to 400 degrees F and bake uncovered for another 20 to 30 minutes or until the vegetables are very tender inside and crisp and golden on the outside. Toss them once or twice during this last period so they will brown evenly without sticking to the pan.

4. Turn the vegetables into a serving dish and sprinkle the Persillade on top. Serve while still hot.

❋ PER SERVING (INCLUDES 2 TABLESPOONS PERSILLADE) *Calories: 161, Cholesterol (mg): 0, Saturated fat (g): 1, Total fat (g): 3, Sodium (mg): 50, Total fiber (g): 4*

Persillade

IN FRENCH COOKING, persillade *refers to mixtures of parsley sautéed with various other ingredients. This version uses fresh bread crumbs (they require less oil to toast) as a very low-fat topping for steamed vegetables such as broccoli or carrots, or to dress broiled chicken or prawns.*

> 2 slices fresh whole grain bread
> 1 teaspoon grated lemon zest
> ¼ cup fresh parsley sprigs
> ¼ cup fresh cilantro, mint or basil leaves
> 1½ teaspoons extra-virgin olive oil
> Salt and freshly ground pepper to your taste

1. Tear the bread into a few pieces and place them in a food processor or blender. Add the lemon zest, parsley and cilantro and process into coarse crumbs. Turn off the machine and using a fork stir in the oil, salt and pepper; toss lightly until the mixture is well blended. You can do this well ahead and store the mixture in a plastic bag.

2. Preheat the oven to 425 degrees F. Spread the crumbs on a shallow baking dish and bake for 5 to 8 minutes or until the crumbs are crisp and browned. Stir them once during this time so they will bake evenly. Watch them carefully and don't allow them to scorch. Use as directed in recipe.

✵ PER SERVING *Calories: 25, Cholesterol (mg): 0, Saturated fat (g): Trace, Total fat (g): 1, Sodium (mg): 33, Total fiber (g): Trace*

CHAPTER 34

Legumes and Grains

BEANS AND GRAINS GROW IN ENDLESS VARIETY *throughout the world and together (especially eaten together) they are among our healthiest foods, providing abundant fiber, protein and other nutrients. Sometimes the byproduct is more familiar than the original grain—popcorn and oatmeal cookies, for example. And, at least in the case of popcorn, easier to prepare. But it is the whole grain we will focus on here, as in polenta, wild rice and couscous. And we will give the humble bean its due, as well.*

Of the hundreds of types of beans harvested worldwide, we use surprisingly few with any regularity. Recipes for the commonly known kidney beans, black-eyed peas, or lima beans don't even begin to describe the legume's repertoire. Beans come in brilliant shades of magenta and deep burnished chestnut, while others are black as coal, pristine white, speckled, spotted and striated. Their names are as evocative as their meat is nourishing: Appaloosa, Black Valentines, rattlesnake, China yellows, Wren's Eggs, cranberries, Scarlet Runners, Jacob's cattle, all heirlooms (rediscovered native strains, newly harvested). You don't like the hard outer shell of a kidney bean? Then purée a cup of meaty cannellinis to a rich, velvety smooth White Bean Pâté (page 345). Or stew a pot of gigandes until they are as fluffy as mashed potatoes. Beans differ in taste, as well as texture, and they meld with highly flavored ingredients. You can make them sweet, hot, herbal or garlicky, depending on your mood. With all this variety and with the importance of legumes as a source of cholesterol-lowering fiber, almost fat-free protein (when combined with grains, nuts or seeds) and all-around nutrition and economy, you owe it to yourself to experiment with bean dishes until you find one you like. And don't forget, when you pair legumes with grains, such as rice or wheat (as in bread) in the same meal, you have a complete protein. You will find suggestions for combining beans and grains throughout this chapter.

Keeping a supply of cooked beans on hand can be a boon to a busy Fat Tracker. Set dried beans to simmer or soak when you have other things to do, and let them cook as long as they need. Refrigerate them when they are tender to add them to chilies, soups, stews, salads or other dishes on subsequent evenings. Or toss cooked flageolets or other favorite beans with a tablespoon of olive oil and freeze in small batches. While you prepare dinner, thaw a package at room temperature to scatter over a salad or into vegetable soups. Or place the frozen beans in a bowl over a slightly larger bowl of hot water to thaw before adding to a stew of eggplant and tomatoes or a simple pasta with vegetables.

Tips on Cooking Beans

Beans vary in moistness and quality, so cooking times are approximate. Beans that have been stored in a warehouse for long periods of time are drier and require longer cooking, for example. The only way to be certain that beans are done is to taste them. Some strains of carefully bred and dried beans have a higher moisture content and more delicate flavor; you can find them in specialty food shops or health food stores. Because they don't dry out on shelves for years in plastic packaging they can cook in half the time of commercial beans.

Dried legumes become edible first by absorbing large amounts of water, which softens them — either during cooking or in a precooking soak. Covered with cold water, they will swell to their maximum in four to six hours. Just as a submerged sponge will only absorb so much water, longer soaking will not benefit them. But it will not hurt them, so adapt the soaking period to your schedule, for example setting them to soak before you go to bed at night or leave for work in the morning. Older beans benefit more from soaking, but soak all legumes, if possible, except lentils and split peas. It softens them and helps speed up the cooking time. If you do not soak, plan to cook beans longer. Discard beans that float to the top of the water as they soak. There is no moisture in them and they will be tough. Soaking also helps remove certain starch compounds that cause gas. Though baking soda speeds up cooking time and reduces these compounds, it does so at great cost to the final product, turning it to mush, and we do not recommend this treatment. Eating beans more frequently helps your digestive tract tolerate them.

Some cautions about cooking beans: Add salt to beans after they have cooked or you will retard the softening process. Do not try to flavor beans with vinegar, lemon, chili peppers, tomatoes, molasses or any other acidic ingredient before they are tender, because even if you cook them into eternity, the presence of acid aborts the chemical reaction necessary to produce tender beans. On the other hand, if they reach the required stage of doneness before you are ready to proceed with a recipe, add a little vinegar or lemon juice to stop the cooking and prevent the beans from turning to mush.

You can cover cooked beans and refrigerate up to 4 days, then reheat thoroughly and refrigerate for another four days. If you still haven't used them, freeze them.

Jazzing Up Canned Beans

Of the more than 30 varieties of legumes available, you can find many in cans or in the frozen food section of your market. Canned beans offer many of the virtues of legumes—nutrition, water-soluble fiber and economy—and some of them have acceptable flavor and, unfortunately, lots of sodium. Some canned varieties are easy to find—garbanzos (also known as chickpeas and ceci), pintos and kidney beans. Others such as cannellini (Italian white beans) or black beans may take some searching. To enhance the flavor of canned beans, drain them and add 1 cup chicken stock, a pinch of dried sage, ½ teaspoon dried oregano or a bay leaf, ½ cup sliced onion and 1 minced garlic clove. Bring to a boil then reduce the heat and simmer for 20 minutes. Use as directed in your recipe.

Basic Beans

SERVES 4

USE THIS RECIPE *for cooking dried red, pink, pinto, kidney, navy, white or cranberry beans. (The basic recipe for black beans follows.) Nothing is more basic and simple than cooking beans, but the directions include some tips that will help you add interesting seasonings and avoid the very few problems that beans present to the cook (in a word, don't let the pot dry out). Stewing the beans with onion and garlic adds flavor, even if you plan to add other season-ings to your finished dish. However, you can omit this step with no harm to the final result. If you are planning to use the beans in another recipe, omit the spices. You can also enrich the recipe by toasting and grinding the spices as directed on page 300. Stir beans occasionally while they cook to prevent the ones on the bottom from overcooking before the ones at the top, further away from the intense heat of the burner, have a chance to soften.*

> 2 cups dried beans
> 1 large onion, chopped
> 1 garlic clove, chopped
> 3 to 4 cups cold water
> 3 to 4 cups unsalted Chicken Stock (page 285–86) or low-fat,
>   low-sodium canned chicken broth or Vegetable Stock (page 289)
> ½ bay leaf
> 1 teaspoon crushed, dried oregano
> ¼ teaspoon freshly ground pepper
> 1 teaspoon cumin seeds or ½ teaspoon ground cumin, optional
> ¼ teaspoon coriander seeds or ground coriander, optional
> Small pinch of ground cinnamon, optional
> Salt and freshly ground pepper

1. Pick over the dried beans to remove any foreign material, such as pebbles and twigs. Rinse the beans, place them in a bowl and add enough cold water to cover them by an inch. Set them aside to soak for 4 to 6 hours or overnight. Alternatively, you can quick soak them: Place them in a pot uncovered, cover them with water and bring them to a boil. As soon as they boil vigorously, remove them from the heat and set them aside for 1 hour.

2. Drain, but do not rinse the soaked beans. Place them in a heavy-bottomed Dutch oven or large pot. Add the onion, garlic, 3 cups of water, 3 cups of stock, and the remaining ingredients, except salt and pepper. Bring to a boil, stir well, reduce the heat and simmer uncovered for about 1 hour or until the beans are barely tender. Check frequently, adding water and/or stock as necessary to keep the level an inch above the beans; otherwise the liquid may evaporate and you will end up with burned beans and a badly scorched pot.

3. After the beans have softened initially (1 to 2 hours depending on the type and age of the beans), you can add salt and pepper to your taste. Continue cooking until they are tender but not mushy.

✿ PER SERVING *Calories: 300, Cholesterol (mg): 0, Saturated fat (g): Trace, Total fat (g): 1, Sodium (mg): 6, Total fiber: 10*

🐛

Basic Black Beans
SERVES 8

THIS RECIPE HAS JUST ENOUGH SEASONING *to offset the natural sweetness of the beans and is the base for many of our dishes: Black Bean Breakfast Cakes (page 302–3), Black Beans with Yellow Pepper Purée with Cilantro and Ginger (page 430), Quick Black Bean Dip (page 355), Jennifer Schroeder's Instant Black Bean Soup (page 365), Miniature Black Bean Burritos (page 360). Use this recipe in any other black bean dish. Or, serve the hot beans sprinkled with chopped cilantro and a squeeze of fresh lime juice. Add a hefty ladleful of Salsa Ranchero (page 303), then crown them with a dollop of creamy nonfat yogurt and serve with a basket of Whole Wheat Corn Muffins (page 332) or slices of grilled Basic Polenta (page 445). You can double the recipe or cut it in half to suit your needs. Black beans require more water than other varieties. If you don't keep the water level high enough, you will end up with a thick chili type of consistency, which in itself is not bad, especially if you plan to use them for Black Bean Breakfast Cakes. However, they will not be suitable for a recipe that requires whole beans.*

> 4 to 6 cups water
> 4 to 6 cups unsalted Chicken Stock (page 285–86) or canned low-fat, low-sodium chicken broth

2 cups dried black beans, soaked as directed in Basic Beans (page 425–26)
1 small onion, coarsely chopped
1 large carrot, coarsely chopped
2 garlic cloves, chopped
1 teaspoon ground cumin
½ bay leaf
¼ teaspoon *each* dried oregano and thyme
Pinch of cinnamon
¾ teaspoon salt
A few twists of a peppermill

1. In a Dutch oven or large heavy-bottomed pot, bring the water and stock to a rolling boil. Add all the remaining ingredients except the salt and pepper. Bring to a boil again, reduce the heat and simmer for 1½ to 2 hours or until the beans are tender, but not mushy. Add more water and/or stock from time to time as necessary to keep the water level at least an inch above the beans.

2. When the beans are tender, discard the bay leaf and season with salt and pepper to your taste. Use as directed in recipe.

❄ PER SERVING *Calories: 152, Cholesterol (mg): 0, Saturated fat (g): Trace, Total fat (g): 1, Sodium (mg): 28, Total fiber: 5*

Jazzed-Up Canned Black Beans
SERVES 6

WHEN YOU DON'T HAVE TIME *to prepare black beans from scratch, use the well-flavored beans as they are, or use them in any of our black bean recipes in place of dried beans. Note, however, the increase in sodium when you use canned products.*

2 cans (15 ounces each) black beans
½ small onion, coarsely chopped
1 small carrot, coarsely chopped
1 garlic clove, chopped
½ teaspoon ground cumin
Pinch *each* of dried oregano, dried thyme and ground cinnamon
¼ teaspoon salt
A few twists of a peppermill

Place the beans, their liquid and the remaining ingredients in a medium-size saucepan and bring to a boil. Reduce the heat and simmer for 30 minutes. Serve or continue as directed in your recipe.

❄ PER SERVING *Calories: 117, Cholesterol (mg): 0, Saturated fat (g): Trace, Total fat (g): 1, Sodium (mg): 500, Total fiber: 8*

Black Bean Chili with Cilantro Pesto

SERVES 8

WHEN THE SUN IS HELD HOSTAGE *by dreary midwinter skies, warm your spirits with this exuberantly seasoned chili. The list of ingredients is long, but the actual work is minimal. Once you sauté the onions and flavorings, you simply add the remaining ingredients at the appropriate time and check occasionally to make sure the chili simmers with the proper vigor: not too rapidly or the chili will dry up and scorch; not too gently or the beans won't cook. Use this chili to make spicy versions of Black Bean Breakfast Cakes (page 302–3), Black Bean Chili Pizza (page 480) and Miniature Black Bean Burritos (page 360). Be sure to savor the burst of smoky fragrance when you add the dried chipotle chili pepper; there is nothing like it. If your markets don't carry it, however, use one of our recommended substitutes. The chili won't have quite the same flavor, but it will still be well spiced. For a milder version, eliminate the dried peppers, or for an incendiary pot, add some of the jalapeño seeds.*

> 1 pound dried black beans, soaked as directed
>   in Basic Beans (page 425–26)
> 8 cups cold water
> ½ yellow onion, diced
> 1 shallot, minced
> 2 tablespoons extra-virgin olive oil
> ½ red onion, diced
> 4 garlic cloves, chopped
> 2 carrots, diced
> 1 stalk celery, diced
> ½ red bell pepper, seeded and diced
> ½ fresh jalapeño pepper, seeded and minced (use more pepper
>   and leave in some seeds for extra heat)
> ¼ cup dry white wine
> 1 teaspoon *each* cumin and coriander seeds, toasted and crushed
>   (page 300) *or* 1 teaspoon *each* ground cumin and coriander
> Pinch of cayenne
> ¼ cup chopped fresh cilantro
> 1 bay leaf
> 1 small dried chipotle chili pepper seeded; *or* a generous pinch
>   of powdered ancho chili (page 281); *or* a generous pinch
>   of crushed dried chili powder (more or less to your taste)
> 4 cups Chicken Stock (page 285–86) or canned low-fat, low-sodium
>   chicken broth or Vegetable Stock (page 289) or water
> 1 can (28 ounces) crushed tomatoes and liquid

1 teaspoon salt
Freshly ground pepper
1 teaspoon *each* fresh oregano and thyme
Grated zest of 1 lime
¼ cup Cilantro Pesto (page 293)
¼ cup nonfat plain yogurt
Nonfat plain yogurt for garnish, optional

1. Drain the soaked beans and place them in a nonreactive Dutch oven or large pot. Add the water, making sure it covers the beans by an inch. Bring to a boil, reduce the heat and add the yellow onion and shallot. Simmer for 1 hour, stirring occasionally. Adjust the heat as necessary to keep the liquid gently bubbling.

2. Meanwhile, heat the olive oil in a nonreactive medium-size skillet and add the red onion, garlic, carrot, celery, red pepper and jalapeño, and toss over low-medium heat until the onion softens. Do not allow it to scorch. Add the wine, bring to a boil and then reduce the heat slightly. Simmer 3 to 4 minutes or until the wine almost evaporates, stirring frequently. Remove the skillet from the heat and set it aside while the beans cook.

3. When the beans have begun to soften, add the onion mixture, cumin, coriander, cayenne, cilantro, bay leaf, chipotle, chicken stock, tomatoes, salt and a few twists of pepper. Stir thoroughly, bring to a boil, reduce the heat and simmer until the beans are tender and the chili is thick and flavorful, about an additional 1 to 1½ hours. Stir frequently. If at any time the beans cook too quickly and the liquid evaporates or the chili becomes too thick, add more stock or water as necessary. Add the oregano and thyme during the last 15 minutes of cooking.

4. Adjust seasoning to your taste and just before serving, add the grated zest and stir. In a small bowl blend the Cilantro Pesto with the ¼ cup yogurt. Serve the beans in individual bowls with the pesto on top. If you like, garnish with a dab of plain yogurt.

FAT TRACKING TIP: Decrease the olive oil to 1 tablespoon and cook the onions and garlic slowly. Further dilute the blend of Cilantro Pesto and yogurt with an equal amount of nonfat yogurt.

✳ PER SERVING (INCLUDES ½ TABLESPOON OF THE PESTO-YOGURT MIXTURE) *Calories: 297, Cholesterol (mg): Trace, Saturated fat (g): 1, Total fat (g): 9, Sodium (mg): 478, Total fiber: 6*

Black Beans with Yellow
Pepper Purée with Cilantro and Ginger

SERVES 8

PROPER SEASONING BRINGS OUT THE NATURAL SWEETNESS *of black beans, also called turtle beans. Yellow Pepper Purée with Cilantro and Ginger elevates humble beans to a stunning dish. For an easy, informal party menu, prepare the beans two to three days ahead and then purée them the day before. We developed Whole Wheat Corn Muffins (page 332) specifically to accompany this dressed-up bean. Use this fantastic pepper purée on any of our bean dishes, float a spoonful on a vegetable soup or spread it on hot bread. If you use a very fresh pepper, this purée will keep covered in the refrigerator for several days.*

Basic Black Beans (page 426–27)

YELLOW PEPPER PURÉE
1 large or 2 small yellow bell peppers, roasted,
    peeled and seeded (page 280)
Juice of 1/2 lemon
Juice of 1/2 lime
1 teaspoon minced fresh ginger
Generous pinch of cayenne
1/3 cup or more fresh cilantro leaves
2 peeled garlic cloves
1/3 cup extra-virgin olive oil
Salt and freshly ground pepper

1. Prepare the Basic Black Beans. Place the yellow pepper, lemon and lime juice, ginger, cayenne, cilantro and garlic in a blender jar or food processor and pulse until you have a coarse mixture. With the motor running, slowly dribble in the oil until smooth. Season to your taste with salt and pepper and add more lime juice if desired. Store the purée in a covered bowl and refrigerate until serving time.

2. Heat the beans and ladle them into individual bowls and top each serving with equal portions of the yellow pepper purée.

FAT TRACKING TIP: Fold the purée into an equal amount of nonfat plain yogurt to dilute the oil.

✳ PER SERVING *Calories: 262, Cholesterol (mg): 0, Saturated fat (g): 1, Total fat (g): 10, Sodium (mg): 209, Total fiber: 6*

Orange-Flavored Black Beans

SERVES 6

THIS VARIATION HIGHLIGHTS *the natural sweetness of black beans. Serve also with a menu of Herb Crusted Oven-Fried Chicken (page 500–1), warm corn tortillas, fresh corn and Melon-Chili Salad with Blackberry Vinaigrette (page 388–89).*

> 1 can (15 ounces) black beans
> 1 tablespoon brown sugar
> 2 green onions, diced
> ½ cup fresh orange juice
> ½ teaspoon ground cumin
> Pinch of ground cinnamon
> Salt and freshly ground pepper to your taste
> 3 tablespoons minced fresh cilantro

Combine all the ingredients except the cilantro in a nonreactive medium-size saucepan and bring to a boil. Reduce the heat and simmer for 15 minutes. Adjust seasoning with salt and pepper. Serve hot with a sprinkling of fresh cilantro.

❋ PER SERVING *Calories: 72, Cholesterol (mg): 0, Saturated fat (g): Trace, Total fat (g): 1, Sodium (mg): 206, Total fiber (g): 4*

Pinto Beans with Caramelized Onions and Thyme

SERVES 4

THIS DISH IS EASY AND UNBELIEVABLY GOOD, *even with humble pintos. Start your meal with Eggplant Soup with Red Pepper Chutney (page 374–75) and dab a spoonful of honey on a slice of rye potato or mixed grain bread as a nice contrast to the beans. These pintos are wonderful hot, or for a cold buffet dish stir in a teaspoon of raspberry vinegar. To measure fresh thyme, pull the stalks through your pinched thumb and forefinger and pile the small leaves loosely in a tablespoon.*

> 1 cup dried pinto beans, soaked as directed in Basic Beans (page 425–26)
> 1 bay leaf
> 1 garlic clove, minced
> 1/4 yellow onion, chopped
> 2 tablespoons extra-virgin olive oil
> 2 large red onions, thinly sliced
> Pinch of sugar
> Salt and coarsely ground pepper
> 1 to 1 1/2 tablespoons fresh thyme
> Nonfat plain yogurt, optional

1. Place the drained beans in a large saucepan and add water, making sure it covers them by at least an inch. Add the bay leaf, garlic and yellow onion. Bring to a boil and reduce the heat to a simmer. Cook for 1 1/2 hours or until tender. As the beans cook, add water as necessary to keep them submerged; do not allow them to boil dry.

2. While the beans cook, heat 1 tablespoon of the olive oil in a small skillet and add the red onions. Cook over medium heat for about 20 minutes or until they are soft and translucent, tossing frequently but not constantly. Add the sugar, toss well and continue cooking another 8 to 10 minutes or until the onions are caramelized and golden. Set them aside until the beans have finished cooking. You may store these in the refrigerator at this point and rewarm before adding to the beans as a topping.

3. When the beans are tender but not mushy, drain their liquid into a measuring cup and pour about 1/2 cup of the liquid back into the beans, just enough to keep them moist but not watery. Add the remaining 1 tablespoon olive oil and toss thoroughly. Season to your taste with salt and pepper. Refrigerate them if you don't plan to continue with the recipe at this time.

4. Reheat the beans if necessary, then add the fresh thyme and stir once more. Serve topped with the reserved caramelized onions and a dollop of yogurt if desired.

Fat Tracking Tips: In place of caramelizing the onions in oil, roast the onions until they are very soft, slice them and top the beans with them. Omit the final tablespoon of oil.

❋ PER SERVING *Calories: 243, Cholesterol (mg): 0, Saturated fat (g): 1, Total fat (g): 7, Sodium (mg): 5, Total fiber: 9*

Red Bean Stew with Basil Purée

SERVES 6

FOR THE BEST FLAVOR, *make this robust stew the day before and serve it as a vegetarian 2 + 2 entrée with a crisp salad and Whole Wheat Herb Scones (page 335–36); moisten the scones with a spoonful of the Basil Purée instead of butter or margarine. Follow with Gingerbread with Ginger Cream (page 544–45) for a winter dessert or an assortment of frozen desserts such as Raspberry Sherbet (page 564) and Pear Mousse with Blueberries (page 563).*

Basil Purée (recipe follows)
1 cup dried red kidney beans, soaked as directed
    in Basic Beans (page 425–26)
1½ tablespoons extra-virgin olive oil
1 onion, chopped
2 garlic cloves
½ cup *each* diced potato, carrot, zucchini and red bell pepper
½ cup dry white wine
1 bay leaf
1½ cups canned crushed or chopped tomato or 4 fresh tomatoes,
    seeded and chopped
½ cup chopped spinach leaves, loosely packed
¼ cup chopped fresh parsley
5 to 6 fresh basil leaves
1 sage leaf or pinch of dried sage
1 tablespoon fresh oregano or 1 teaspoon dried
⅛ teaspoon dried crushed red peppers, optional
¼ teaspoon coarsely ground pepper
6 cups Chicken Stock (page 285–86) or canned, low-fat,
    low-sodium chicken broth
Salt and freshly ground pepper
½ cup dried penne (small tube pasta)

1. Prepare the Basil Purée, cover and refrigerate. Drain the beans and place them in a nonreactive Dutch oven or stockpot and add water, making sure it covers them by at least an inch. Bring to a boil, then reduce the heat and simmer for 1 hour.

2. While the beans cook, heat the olive oil in a medium-size skillet over low-medium heat and add the onion and garlic. Stir 3 to 4 minutes until the onion begins to soften. Add the potato, carrot, zucchini and bell pepper, partially cover the pot and continue cooking over low heat for 15 minutes or until the vegetables are soft and golden. Stir from time to time so they will cook evenly.

3. Add the white wine and bay leaf to the vegetables and bring to a boil. Reduce the heat slightly and stir until all but a teaspoon of the liquid has evaporated; then remove from the heat.

4. When the beans have cooked for an hour (they will still be firm), stir in the wine-cooked vegetables with the tomatoes, spinach, parsley, basil, sage, oregano, crushed red pepper (if using), coarsely ground pepper and chicken stock. Bring to a rolling boil for 30 seconds, then reduce the heat until the surface bubbles gently. Cook uncovered for 1 hour or until the beans and vegetables are tender. Season to your taste with the salt and pepper and add the penne. Cook for another 30 minutes. If necessary, thin the stew with more stock. Or if you prefer it thicker, purée 1 cup of the beans and vegetables in a blender and stir the purée back into the soup. Continue cooking for 15 minutes or until the stew has thickened to your satisfaction. Remove the bay leaf before serving.

5. Ladle the stew into 6 serving bowls and spoon a dollop of the Basil Purée on top of each. Serve immediately.

FAT TRACKING TIPS: Reduce the oil. Use nonfat yogurt in the Basil Purée.

❋ PER SERVING (INCLUDES ABOUT 1⅔ TABLESPOONS BASIL PURÉE) *Calories: 257, Cholesterol (mg): 2, Saturated fat (g): 1, Total fat (g): 5, Sodium (mg): 174, Total fiber: 6*

Basil Purée
Makes approximately ⅔ cup, serving size 1 tablespoon

Use this in place of mayonnaise, butter or margarine on sandwiches and dinner rolls.

> ½ cup loosely packed fresh basil leaves
> ¼ cup *each* loosely packed lettuce leaves and fresh Italian parsley
> 1 very small garlic clove
> 1 green onion (white part only)
> Salt and freshly ground pepper to your taste
> ½ cup low-fat plain yogurt
> 1 tablespoon fresh orange juice

Purée the basil, lettuce, parsley, garlic, onion, salt and pepper in a blender. Place the yogurt in a small bowl and add the purée and orange juice. Stir by hand, cover and refrigerate. This will last several days in the refrigerator.

❋ PER SERVING *Calories: 10, Cholesterol (mg): 1, Saturated fat (g): Trace, Total fat (g): Trace, Sodium (mg): 9, Total fiber: 0*

Flageolets with Tarragon

SERVES 4

IF THE PINTO, NAVY BEAN AND LIMA *are the common beans, the flageolet is royalty. Diminutive and delicately flavored, its pale green color has an almost Victorian delicacy. And often dried flageolets (such as those from Phipps Ranch in Pescadero, California) are of such good quality that they do not require pre-soaking; check the package directions or ask your grocer about soaking requirements. Yet this bean holds up during cooking without turning mushy, as will some varieties of white beans. Flageolets also do not need elaborate recipes and, because of their delicate flavor, can give other dishes a boost of unobtrusive, low-fat protein. Here the cooked beans are given a simple reduction with white wine and fresh tarragon, perfect with roast chicken or any grilled entrée. As with all beans, after cooking, use enough salt and lots of pepper to bring out their flavor.*

> 1 cup dried flageolets, soaked if necessary (see above note)
> About 3 cups cold water
> ½ onion, diced
> 3 garlic cloves, chopped
> 1 tablespoon extra-virgin olive oil
> 1 shallot, minced
> Salt and freshly ground pepper
> ⅓ cup dry white wine
> 1 tablespoon minced fresh tarragon

1. Place the beans in a saucepan with their soaking liquid and enough cold water to cover them by at least an inch. Stir in the onion and garlic. Bring to a boil, reduce the heat and simmer uncovered for 1 to 1½ hours or until the beans are tender but not mushy. As they cook, add water as necessary to keep them submerged, as described in the Basic Beans recipe (page 425–26), taking care not to let the pot boil dry. When the beans are done, drain the liquid into a measuring cup and reserve it for the next step. If you don't plan to continue with the recipe at this time, toss the beans with a spoonful of olive oil, cover and refrigerate or freeze them. Cover and store the reserved liquid in a separate container.

2. Heat the olive oil in a small nonreactive skillet and add the shallot. Stir over medium heat 3 to 4 minutes or until soft and translucent. Add the beans, ½ cup of their cooking liquid and season to your taste with salt and pepper. Add the white wine and bring to a boil. Stir continuously until the liquid has reduced by about a third. Add a little more of the reserved liquid if it cooks down too quickly and the beans get too dry. You can prepare the flageolets up to this point, cover and store in the refrigerator and reheat before serving.

3. To serve, reheat beans if necessary, add the tarragon and adjust seasoning to your taste. Serve them, hot, steaming and fragrant.

✴ PER SERVING *Calories: 196, Cholesterol (mg): 0, Saturated fat (g): Trace, Total fat (g): 2, Sodium (mg): 5, Total fiber: 6*

❧

White Bean and Vegetable Chili with Grilled Chicken

SERVES 6

MOST OFTEN, CHILI IS SERVED *with mounds of grated cheese. We substitute succulent grilled chicken breast, which sharply reduces the fat and cholesterol. For a meatless entrée, omit the chicken and complete the protein by serving corn bread or whole wheat baguettes.*

1 tablespoon olive oil
1 large yellow onion, finely chopped
2 garlic cloves, minced
3 large carrots, diced
1 large red bell pepper, seeded and finely chopped
1 pound Great Northern white beans, soaked as directed
  in Basic Beans (page 425–26)
5 to 6 cups Chicken Stock (page 285–86) or canned low-fat,
  low-sodium chicken broth
½ teaspoon ground cumin
1 tablespoon fresh minced oregano or 1 teaspoon
  dried and crushed
1 fresh Anaheim or other mild chili pepper,
  seeded and finely chopped
½ to 1 fresh jalapeño chili pepper, optional, seeded
1 generous pinch of cayenne
Salt and freshly ground pepper
1 cup *each* finely diced assorted summer squash
  (zucchini, pattypan, crookneck) and fresh green beans
1 cup fresh peas (about 1 pound in shells)
¼ cup minced fresh parsley
¼ cup minced fresh cilantro, optional
½ pound boneless chicken breast, all skin and fat removed
Salsa Fresca (page 357) or Tomato Orange Salsa (page 350)
Nonfat plain yogurt, optional
Chopped green onions for garnish

1. Heat the oil in a Dutch oven or large heavy-bottomed saucepan over low-medium heat and add the yellow onion, garlic, carrots and red pepper. Stir until the onion has softened but not browned. Add the beans, chicken stock, cumin and oregano. Bring to a boil and then reduce the heat and simmer uncovered for 1½ hours. Check the beans regularly to make sure they are not cooking too slowly or too quickly. The liquid should bubble very gently.

2. When the beans have softened considerably, add the chili and cayenne. Season lightly with salt and pepper. Continue cooking for another 20 minutes. You can refrigerate the chili at this point and reheat thoroughly before continuing with the remaining steps shortly before serving time.

3. Prepare the grill as directed on page 264 or preheat the broiler. Add the squash, green beans, peas, parsley and cilantro to the hot chili beans. Grill or broil the chicken breast and carve in ½-inch slices across the grain. When the fresh vegetables are barely tender, taste for seasoning, adding more salt if necessary. Ladle into 6 soup bowls with slices of grilled chicken and pass the salsa, yogurt (if using) and green onions separately.

FAT TRACKING TIPS: Use turkey breast instead of chicken breast. Omit poultry entirely.

❈ PER SERVING *Calories: 350, Cholesterol (mg): 24, Saturated fat (g): 1, Total fat (g): 4, Sodium (mg): 52, Total fiber: 12*

Cooking Rice: White, Basmati and Brown

Achieving perfectly cooked rice depends as much on the pot as it does on the ratio of water and time. Rice cookers consistently produce uniform grains and are a good investment for rice fanatics. If rice is a sometime thing on your menu, experiment with saucepans and when you get a batch of rice perfectly cooked, use that pot and no other for all time. Use the specifications we give as a guideline, and be prepared to fine-tune cooking times and water amounts depending on your cookware and the type of rice you use (there are thousands of varieties grown throughout the world). Also, rice that has been on the shelf for a long time will be drier and take longer to cook. *One cup of raw rice yields approximately 3 cups cooked rice.*

WASHING RICE As a general rule, imported rice requires a great deal of washing and domestic rice hardly any at all. You can almost see the starch clinging to imported rice (often sold in bulk) and your rice will be gluey unless it is removed before cooking. Place the raw rice in a large bowl of cold water and swish it until the water becomes cloudy. Rinse and add more cold water. Continue this step until the water is clear. The number of washings will be determined by individual batches of rice, but expect to do this at least three or four times. Purists wash for many minutes. Packaged and boxed rice as well as converted rice (a processed rice) require no washing at all. Rice, depending on the variety, has between 110 and 130 calories per half cup serving size, negligible fat and fiber ranging from 1/2 gram for white rice to 2 grams for brown rice. Sodium amount varies depending on how much salt is added to the water.

STEAMING RICE By steamed rice we refer to cooking rice in a covered saucepan over low heat. Some general rules will help you achieve perfect results.

- Do not stir rice as it cooks or it will become gummy.
- Keep the pot covered as it cooks and, especially for brown rice, remove it from the heat and allow it to stand 5 minutes or more before uncovering.
- Use the correct amount of liquid: too little and the rice will be uncooked; too much and it will be gummy.
- Bring water to a boil, add rice and cover. Cook, then fluff rice with a fork before serving. If rice is ready before you are, remove the lid, place a tea towel over the top of the pan and replace the lid. Rice will remain fluffy.

LONG-GRAIN WHITE RICE For 1 cup raw white rice (washed as necessary), use 2 cups of water and a pinch of salt. Bring water and salt to a boil, add the rice, raise the heat until the water reaches the boil again, reduce the heat to a simmer, cover and cook 15 to 17 minutes. Remove from the heat and allow to stand for 10 minutes before uncovering. Fluff with a fork before serving.

SHORT- OR MEDIUM-GRAIN WHITE RICE For 1 cup raw rice (washed as necessary), use 1¾ cups water and a pinch of salt. Bring water and salt to a boil, add the rice, raise the heat until the water reaches the boil again, reduce the heat to a simmer, cover and cook 15 to 17 minutes. Remove from the heat and allow to stand for 10 minutes before uncovering. Fluff with a fork before serving.

BROWN RICE For 1 cup brown rice (washed), use 2½ cups water and a pinch of salt. Bring the water and salt to a boil, add the rice, raise the heat until the water reaches the boil again, reduce to a simmer, cover and cook for 45 to 50 minutes. Remove from the heat and let stand for 5 to 10 minutes before uncovering. Fluff with a fork and serve.

BASMATI RICE For 1 cup basmati rice (washed as necessary), use 2 cups water and a pinch of salt. Bring water and salt to boil, add the rice, raise the heat until the water reaches the boil again, reduce the heat to a simmer, cover and cook 17 to 20 minutes or until tender. Remove from the heat and allow to stand for 10 minutes before uncovering. Fluff with a fork before serving.

Brown Rice with
Tofu and Mushroom Stir-Fry

SERVES 4

THOUGH TOFU IS NOT NOTABLY LOW IN TOTAL FAT, *it has very little saturated fat. Our friend Shirley Ingalls, an inveterate Fat Tracker, gave us this recipe. She suggests that steamed broccoli and carrots make a colorful presentation with this healthy dish.*

8 ounces regular tofu
1 tablespoon olive oil
½ cup diced green onion
1 garlic clove, minced
½ pound fresh mushrooms, sliced
3 dried mushrooms, soaked in warm water until softened
½ red bell pepper, seeded and diced
½ cup water
1½ tablespoons soy sauce
2 tablespoons Chinese oyster sauce
¼ cup white wine
1 tablespoon sugar
¾ tablespoon arrowroot or cornstarch

ACCOMPANIMENTS
4 cups cooked brown rice (page 439)
¼ cup chopped green onions
¼ cup chopped peanuts
¼ cup raisins

1. Cut the tofu into 1-inch cubes and drain in a colander for ½ hour.

2. Heat the oil in a wok or skillet over medium heat and add the diced green onions, garlic, fresh and soaked mushrooms and red bell pepper. Toss briefly; then add the tofu and cook, stirring and turning the tofu frequently for 8 minutes or until lightly browned.

3. In a bowl, combine the remaining ingredients except the accompaniments, and stir into the tofu. Bring to a boil, reduce the heat and cook until slightly thickened. Serve over brown rice and sprinkle with the chopped green onions, peanuts and raisins.

❋ PER SERVING (INCLUDING ACCOMPANIMENTS) *Calories: 377, Cholesterol (mg): 0, Saturated fat (g): 2, Total fat (g): 12, Sodium (mg): 677, Total fiber (g): 5*

Basmati Rice with
Orange-Mustard Dressing and Currants

SERVES 4

BASMATI IS SWEET ENOUGH *to serve without any added flavoring, but we could not resist gilding the lily. Serve as a grain dish or as a hearty salad on a buffet table.*

3 cups cooked basmati rice (page 439)

ORANGE-MUSTARD DRESSING
1 tablespoon canola oil
1 tablespoon raspberry vinegar
3 tablespoons fresh orange juice
1 tablespoon fresh lemon juice
1 tablespoon prepared sweet mustard
1 tablespoon cold water
Pinch of white pepper
Pinch of salt, optional

2 tablespoons finely diced green onion
2 tablespoons currants

1. Prepare the basmati rice and allow it to stand for 10 minutes.

2. While the rice cooks, stir together all the dressing ingredients in a measuring cup. Pour the dressing over the cooked rice and toss thoroughly. Add the onion and currants and toss again. Serve warm or chilled.

❋ PER SERVING *Calories: 208, Cholesterol (mg): 0, Saturated fat (g): Trace, Total fat (g): 4, Sodium (mg): 19, Total fiber (g): 1*

Hot Red Rice Salad

SERVES 4

INCREDIBLY SWEET AND NUTTY, *red rice deserves its growing popularity (aided we hope by this plug). The best by far is called Christmas Rice, grown by Lundberg Family Farms in northern California. Though red rice takes a little longer to cook than conventional brown rice, it is definitely worth the wait. This short, russet grain is delicious right out of the pot and even better served with grilled poultry, the better to absorb tasty marinades and cooking juices. Add it to vegetable soups in place of regular brown rice, use it for stuffings, or transform it into a salad, as we do here. We found the range of doneness was a matter of taste. Longer cooking will produce a softer (though still quite chewy) grain, but we also liked the crunchy quality when we experimented with shorter cooking times.*

1 cup red rice
2¼ cups cold water
Pinch salt
1 teaspoon olive oil
1 shallot, finely diced
1 small tomato, peeled, seeded and chopped
¼ cup *each* seeded and diced red and green bell peppers
1 teaspoon red wine vinegar
Salt and freshly ground pepper to your taste

1. Preheat the oven to 400 degrees F. Rinse the rice briefly in cold water and place in a medium-size saucepan. Add the water and salt. Bring to a boil, reduce the heat, cover and simmer for 45 minutes. Remove from the heat and allow to stand for 10 minutes.

2. While the rice cooks, heat the olive oil in a medium-size nonreactive ovenproof skillet until a spray of water dances on the surface. Add the shallot, stir for 30 seconds and place in the oven for 8 to 10 minutes or until the shallot softens.

3. Handling carefully with potholders, remove the skillet from the oven and stir in the chopped tomato and peppers. Cook over low-medium heat for 2 to 3 minutes until just heated through. Set aside until the rice is ready. This can be done ahead of time and reheated just before serving.

4. Fluff the rice with a fork (you will notice the color has deepened) and stir the cooked vegetables into the rice. Stir in the vinegar and season to your taste with salt and pepper. Serve hot.

✱ PER SERVING *Calories: 195, Cholesterol (mg): 0, Saturated fat (g): Trace, Total fat (g): 3, Sodium (mg): 6, Total fiber (g): 3*

Wild Rice with Pecans

SERVES 6

THE NAME WILD RICE IS DECEIVING. *Actually, it is not rice at all, but a grain in its own right. Hence, it requires presoaking to soften the grains. Delicious both hot and cold, this nutty dish is excellent with turkey, chicken and fish, but it especially complements veal.*

> 1 cup wild rice
> 4 cups Chicken Stock (page 285–86) or canned low-fat,
>   low-sodium chicken broth
> 1 tablespoon canola oil
> 2 tablespoons diced onion
> ½ cup very finely diced celery
> ¼ cup chopped pecans
> Salt and freshly ground pepper

1. Soak the wild rice in a bowl of cold water for ½ hour then drain it thoroughly.

2. Place the rice in a saucepan with the chicken stock and bring it to a boil. Allow the rice to boil for 5 minutes, then reduce the heat, cover and simmer over low heat for 50 minutes. Remove it from the heat and without uncovering, allow the rice to sit undisturbed for 10 minutes.

3. While the rice is cooking, heat the oil in a small skillet over medium heat and add the onion and celery. Stir the mixture until the onion begins to soften and partially cover the skillet. Continue cooking over low heat until the onion and celery have wilted. Add the pecans and season lightly with salt and pepper. Set aside until the rice has finished cooking.

4. Fluff the rice with a fork. If any liquid remains in the bottom of the saucepan, heat the rice over high heat and toss it continuously until it evaporates. Stir in the onion mixture and season to your taste with salt and pepper. Serve hot or chilled.

FAT TRACKING TIP: Instead of ¼ cup, use 2 tablespoons pecans.

✽ PER SERVING *Calories: 148, Cholesterol (mg): 0, Saturated fat (g): 3, Total fat (g): 6, Sodium (mg): 11, Total fiber (g): 1*

Polenta with Roasted Eggplant, Rosemary and Two Cheeses

SERVES 6

HEARTY ENOUGH FOR A MAIN COURSE DISH, *this fits into a prepare-ahead schedule if you make the polenta and eggplant sauce one or even two days ahead. Assemble with the cheeses and bake just before serving.*

Basic Polenta (recipe follows)
1 red onion
Vegetable spray for baking sheet
1 eggplant
1 red, yellow or green bell pepper
2 tomatoes, peeled, seeded and chopped
1 or more tablespoons fresh rosemary
Salt and freshly ground pepper
½ cup skim-milk ricotta cheese
¾ ounce part-skim-milk mozzarella cheese, freshly shredded
(about ¼ cup)

1. Prepare the polenta and spread in a shallow baking dish, as directed in the recipe. You may do this the day before and store it covered in the refrigerator.

2. Preheat the oven to 400 degrees F. Slice off the stem of the onion and peel the papery outer layers down to the root. Pull them away but do not cut off the root. Place cut side down on a baking sheet lightly coated with a thin film of vegetable spray. Score the eggplant several times and place it and the pepper on the baking sheet as well. Roast for 45 minutes or until tender.

3. Lightly coat a small nonreactive skillet or saucepan with a thin film of vegetable spray and add the tomatoes. Bring to a boil, reduce the heat and cook about 20 minutes or until slightly thickened and no longer watery. Stir from time to time and check the heat to make sure they don't scorch.

4. When the vegetables are done, remove from oven and raise the temperature to 425 degrees F. When the pepper is cool enough to handle, peel and discard the skin and seeds. Peel the eggplant and cut off the root end of the onion. Place all the vegetables in a food processor or blender and process until very chunky. Stir in the tomatoes and rosemary, and season to your taste with salt and pepper.

5. Spread the ricotta cheese over the polenta and spoon on the eggplant mixture. Sprinkle on the mozzarella. Bake at 425 degrees F for 15 minutes, cut into 6 squares and serve.

✿ PER SERVING *Calories: 191, Cholesterol (mg): 13, Saturated fat (g): 2, Total fat (g): 3, Sodium (mg): 463, Total fiber (g): 2*

Basic Polenta
Serves 6

Southerners call it "fried cornmeal mush," the Italians know it as "polenta," while in our Southwest many corncake recipes bear a friendly resemblance to this increasingly popular cornmeal pudding. We call it "wonderful" and vary the presentation by sometimes dousing it with maple syrup, other times spooning a piquant salsa or spiced applesauce on top. Polenta cooked in skim milk is more satisfying and rich than polenta cooked in water, the most common preparation, and the milk adds an easy dose of calcium.

> 3 cups skim milk
> 1 package butter granules, optional
> 1 teaspoon salt
> 1 cup polenta or yellow cornmeal
> Vegetable spray for baking dish

1. In a medium-size saucepan, bring the skim milk to a boil over medium-high heat and add the butter flavoring and salt, blending well. Add the polenta in a slow stream, stirring constantly until it has thickened and absorbed all the liquid. You must keep stirring for about 5 minutes until smooth or you will end up with a lumpy mess if you abandon it while it is cooking.

2. Lightly coat an 8-inch square baking dish with a film of vegetable spray. Spread the cooked polenta in the dish and allow to cool. Use as directed in recipe. Or, to serve as an accompaniment, cut into squares and grill or broil briefly until toasted. Serve hot.

✿ PER SERVING *Calories: 127, Cholesterol (mg): 2, Saturated fat (g): Trace, Total fat (g): 1, Sodium (mg): 419, Total fiber (g): 1*

Corn and Polenta Soufflé
with Cilantro Cream
SERVES 6

THE COMBINATION OF POLENTA (CORNMEAL) AND EGGWHITES *produces a deceptively delicate-looking puff, which is full of nourishing and filling carbohydrates and warmed by our Cajun Seasoning. It is richly doused with low-fat Parmesan cheese, enough to make it creamy, not enough to make much of a dent in your fat account. Serve this with Orange-Flavored Black Beans (page 431) when you are planning one of your twice weekly vegetarian menus (polenta and beans form a complete protein) or with Grilled Turkey Breast with White Wine and Herbs (page 521–22) for a casual supper party.*

> 6 tablespoons Cilantro Cream (page 294)
> Vegetable spray for soufflé dish
> 2 teaspoons extra-virgin olive oil
> 1 cup diced onion
> ½ cup seeded and finely diced red bell pepper
> 2 cups cold water
> Pinch of salt and white pepper
> 1 cup polenta or yellow cornmeal
> 2 cups fresh corn kernels (from about 4 ears)
> 2 tablespoons fine yellow cornmeal
> 2 cups nonfat milk
> 2 tablespoons butter granules, optional
> 1 teaspoon or more Cajun Seasoning (page 496)
> 3 ounces Parmesan cheese, coarsely grated (about 1 cup)
> ½ cup liquid egg substitute
> 4 egg whites
> Pinch *each* of cream of tartar and salt

1. Prepare the Cilantro Cream and set aside. Preheat the oven to 500 degrees F. Coat an 8-cup soufflé dish with a light film of vegetable spray and set aside.

2. Heat the olive oil in a large ovenproof skillet over low-medium heat and add the onion and red bell pepper. Stir until the vegetables are well coated with the oil and place the skillet in the oven for 20 minutes or until the vegetables are soft. Stir them from time to time to make sure they don't scorch.

3. While the vegetables roast, bring the cold water and salt and pepper to a boil in a large saucepan. Stirring constantly, whisk in the polenta and continue to stir over medium heat until thick, about 5 minutes. Remove from the heat and set aside to cool, but do not chill.

4. Handling it very carefully, remove the skillet from the oven and reduce the heat to 375 degrees F. Stir in the corn kernels and fine cornmeal and stir until well blended. Whisk in the milk, butter granules (if using), Cajun Seasoning, and salt to your taste and bring to a boil, stirring vigorously. Stir this mixture into the polenta and lightly beat the mixture until well blended. If any lumps appear, continue to stir until they smooth out. Beat in the cheese and liquid egg substitute.

5. In a large bowl, beat the egg whites with the cream of tartar and salt until soft peaks form. Do not overbeat. Add ⅓ of the egg whites to the polenta mixture and fold gently to lighten the base. Add the remaining egg whites and fold carefully until just blended. Do not overmix or the soufflé will not rise as high. Using a light touch, pour the mixture into the prepared dish and place in the lower third of the oven. Bake for 50 minutes or until golden and firm and a knife inserted in the center comes out with just a few droplets of moisture. Serve immediately with a tablespoon of Cilantro Cream topping each portion.

✿ PER SERVING *Calories: 421, Cholesterol (mg): 15, Saturated fat (g): 5, Total fat (g): 22, Sodium (mg): 471, Total fiber (g): 3*

Couscous with Spiced Vegetables
SERVES 6

DESPITE THE LENGTH OF THE RECIPE, *this stew of vegetables simmered in a spicy broth and served over couscous is quite easy to prepare. Couscous, a grain used extensively in Moroccan cookery, adapts to many stewlike preparations. The couscous (grain) and beans (legume) form a complete protein, which makes this hearty, delicious dish an ideal vegetarian entrée. This recipe calls for the quick-cooking couscous, though you can also serve this stew over white or brown rice, bulgur wheat or cooked barley. Serve smaller portions if you plan it as an accompaniment to a grilled fish or poultry entrée.*

> 1 tablespoon olive oil
> 1 large onion, sliced
> 1 garlic clove, minced
> 1 pound carrots, diced
> 1 red bell pepper, seeded and diced
> 2 large tomatoes, chopped
> 1 pound yams, peeled and cut into cubes
> 2 cups cooked or canned garbanzo beans (chickpeas) or 1 cup
>   garbanzo beans and 1 cup white or kidney beans
> 4 cups Chicken Stock (page 285–86) or canned low-fat, low-sodium
>   chicken broth or Vegetable Stock (page 289)

SPICE MIXTURE

¼ teaspoon *each* ground cinnamon and ground allspice
⅛ teaspoon *each* curry powder and ground turmeric
Pinch *each* of ground nutmeg and ground cloves
Salt and freshly ground pepper to your taste

1 large zucchini, diced
⅓ cup currants or raisins
2¼ cups cold water or stock used with vegetables
2 cups quick-cooking couscous
3 bananas, optional, peeled and halved
¼ cup fresh minced parsley
2 or 3 leaves fresh basil or cilantro, optional, minced
6 tablespoons nonfat plain yogurt or Spiced Yogurt (page 291)

1. Heat the oil in a large nonreactive Dutch oven or heavy-bottomed saucepan over medium-low heat. Add the onion and garlic and stir until coated with the oil. Cook for 5 to 7 minutes or until softened. Stir frequently.

2. Add the carrots, bell pepper, tomatoes, yams, garbanzos, chicken stock and the spice mixture. Stirring well, bring to a boil. Reduce the heat and simmer for 30 minutes. Check frequently to make sure the soup bubbles but does not boil dry. Add more stock if it evaporates too rapidly. The stew should remain quite liquid. Add the zucchini and currants and continue cooking about 40 minutes or until the vegetables are tender.

3. To prepare the couscous, bring the cold water to a boil in a medium-size saucepan and add a pinch or two of salt. Stir in the couscous, cover and remove from the heat. Let stand for at least 5 minutes and fluff it with a fork before serving.

4. If you desire, before serving, broil the bananas for 2 to 3 minutes until golden but not mushy. Remove them to a separate dish and cover to keep warm.

5. Stir the parsley and, if desired, the basil, into the vegetables. Taste for seasoning. Spoon the couscous into bowls and serve the vegetables and broth on top. Garnish with the grilled bananas or a sprig of parsley. Pass the yogurt separately.

✿ PER SERVING (INCLUDES 1 TABLESPOON YOGURT) *Calories: 481, Cholesterol (mg): Trace, Saturated fat (g): Trace, Total fat (g): 4, Sodium (mg): 59, Total fiber (g): 14*

🐚

Pasta and Pizza

THOUGH WE ASSOCIATE PASTA WITH ITALIAN FOOD, *its history takes us on a world tour and back in time to at least ancient China. Food buffs like to speculate that Marco Polo had something to do with the introduction of pasta to Italy. But in truth, pasta, though by different names, traveled the globe more widely and much earlier than even that intrepid explorer. Dried and fresh noodles appear in one form or another in cuisines around the world, from the Japanese soba (buckwheat noodle), to the soybean and rice threads of China, to the spaetzle and Nudel of Germany. And like its Italian-born cousin, pizza, pasta has become as American as, well, that other well-known pie, with contemporary chefs using garnishes from herbs and garlic to exotic vegetables and even flowers.*

Definitely budget friendly, pasta is praised—and prized—for its taste, its texture and its delicious interaction with foods of all types. We coat it with pungent sauces, salad dressings and stocks. We float it in savory broths and soups. We layer it with meats and cheeses. We stuff it. We color it. We twist it. We stretch it. We roll it. We dry it. We love it. But we also look to pasta to balance our diet, to replace excessive animal protein and fat with healthful complex carbohydrates and to increase the fiber in our foods. Pasta fits the bill on all counts.

Pasta Perfect: Do's and Don'ts

Texture, not cooking time, determines the doneness. Marcella Hazan, premier Italian food writer, claims that eating overcooked pasta is like eating soggy bread, and we agree. Many factors influence cooking time: amount of water in the pot, relative dryness of the pasta (if it has it been on your grocer's shelf for a long time it may need a few extra minutes), variety of wheat used and the shape of the pasta. Dried pasta takes between 5 and 9 minutes, depending on the type and thickness of the noodles. Thin strands of capellini or angel hair cook more quickly, for example, than fat linguini. Here are some do's and don'ts for making perfect pasta.

- *Do* sample it as it cooks, starting as soon as it can hang over your wooden spoon; when the pasta resists your teeth slightly, not too mushy, not too crunchy, it's done—al dente.
- *Don't* rely on package directions for timing.
- *Do* bring the water to a rolling boil.
- *Don't* skimp on water or crowd it into a small pot. Pasta will absorb all the water and get soggy.
- *Do* add 1 teaspoon of salt. Unsalted pasta is quite bland and, for the sodium-conscious cook, much of the salt gets thrown out with the water.
- *Don't* add oil to the water to keep strands from sticking together. Remember, oil and water don't mix; the oil merely pools on the surface of the water instead of coating the pasta.
- *Do* add all the pasta at once (it will not cook evenly if you add it to the water in batches) and stir thoroughly to separate the strands.
- Unless you have a monster bathtub-sized pot, *don't* cook more than 2 pounds of pasta at a time.
- *Do* keep your noodles long if you like to roll nests of them in your spoon.
- *Don't* if you don't.
- *Do* cover the pot to bring the water back to a boil after you add the pasta, since the temperature of the pasta will reduce the temperature of water.
- *Don't* add pasta to anything less than rapidly boiling water.
- *Do* undercook pasta ever so slightly. It will continue to cook in its own heat and the heat of its sauce before it gets to your mouth.

- *Don't* overcook pasta.
- *Do* drain pasta as soon as it is cooked.
- *Don't* soak pasta in water or allow it to sit in water before draining it after it has finished cooking or it will swell and become an inedible, waterlogged, gluey mess.
- *Do* drain cooked pasta into a colander immediately.
- *Don't* rinse cooked pasta unless you fear it has seriously overcooked. In which case, add to hot sauce immediately after rinsing.
- *Do* shake the colander a few times to remove excess water, but allow some cooking water to adhere to it. Pasta drained too thoroughly can become sticky and will absorb sauce like a sponge, rather than have a delicious coating of it.
- *Don't* let drained pasta get too dry.
- *Do* make oil or a sauce containing oil the first ingredient that coats cooked pasta.
- *Don't* allow milk products to coat pasta first or it will congeal into an inedible mess.

Master Pasta Recipe

Have a large pot of rapidly boiling water ready approximately 10 minutes before you are ready to serve. Use approximately 4 quarts of water for each pound of pasta. Add no more than 2 pounds of pasta to the water. For larger crowds cook the pasta in 2 pots. Immediately add a teaspoon of salt, stir vigorously and cover. When the water returns to a boil, reduce the heat slightly and check the pasta frequently for doneness. Stir if the noodles appear to clump together. Taste when the noodles appear to soften and when they are done, drain immediately, allowing some water to cling to the noodles, transfer to a bowl and add the desired sauce. Serve while still hot. Note that because fresh pasta is most often made with whole eggs, we do not recommend using it on a regular basis and have not included any homemade or fresh pasta recipes. However, if, on occasion, you do use fresh noodles, they cook in under 2 minutes and are done as soon as they begin to hang over a wooden spoon.

Rosamarina with Lemon and Herbs

SERVES 4

EASIER TO COOK *than even a boiled potato (no peeling)! Serve rosamarina pasta with this simple sauce of lemon, flavored oil, fresh herbs and a little cheese. Rosamarina resembles a long flattened grain of rice and actually can be used in place of that grain for rice salads. It is also a little easier to manage than long pasta and therefore ideal for quick pasta dishes. Follow this quick pasta with Curried Tomato, Melon and Cucumber Salad (page 389–90) to add a zesty contrast to a summer menu. Also, think of this quick pasta when you want to round out a meal of grilled fish.*

½ pound dried rosamarina (oblong grain-shaped pasta)
1 lemon
1 tablespoon Basil Oil (page 296) or Vanilla Oil (page 298)
2 tablespoons fresh thyme, marjoram, chervil, dill or other fresh,
     delicate herb
½ cup minced fresh Italian parsley
Salt and freshly ground pepper
1 ounce Parmesan cheese, freshly grated (about ⅓ cup)

1. Have a large pot of lightly salted boiling water ready and add the rosamarina 7 to 9 minutes before serving. Cook as directed on page 451. With a vegetable peeler, remove a 2-inch strip of the thin, colored zest of the lemon peel, no white rind. Mince the zest.

2. Heat the oil in a skillet and add the lemon zest. Stir over low-medium heat for about 2 minutes and then add the fresh herbs and parsley. Stir until their green color intensifies, about 1 minute. Season with salt and a lot of pepper, and taste. Add another squirt of lemon juice or more as necessary, until the sauce tastes bright and lively.

3. Pour the drained pasta in a bowl and add the sauce. Toss the mixture until it is completely coated with oil and herbs. Add the cheese and toss again. Serve immediately while hot and fragrant.

FAT TRACKING TIP: Use less cheese.

✻ PER SERVING *Calories: 275, Cholesterol (mg): 5, Saturated fat (g): 2, Total fat (g): 6, Sodium (mg): 141, Total fiber (g): Trace*

Linguine with Quick Roasted Tomato Sauce

SERVES 4

SIMPLE, SIMPLE, SIMPLE. *You may be tempted to roast all of your tomatoes after tasting this easy sauce. It also doubles and triples easily.*

> 1 large onion, peeled and sliced in half lengthwise
> Vegetable spray for baking sheet
> 1 pound dried linguine
> 2 tablespoons extra-virgin olive oil
> 1 tablespoon fresh oregano or 1 teaspoon dried
> 3 pounds roasted tomatoes (page 282)
> Salt and freshly ground pepper
> 1½ ounces Parmesan cheese, freshly grated (about ½ cup)

1. Preheat the oven to 400 degrees F. Place the onion cut side down on a baking sheet coated with a light film of vegetable spray. Roast it in the oven for 35 to 40 minutes or until very soft. Chop the onion coarsely.

2. Have a large pot of lightly salted boiling water ready and add the linguine 7 to 9 minutes before serving. Cook as directed on page 451.

3. Heat the olive oil over low heat in a medium-size nonreactive skillet. Add the oregano and stir for 1 minute until it is fragrant. Add the onion and stir until it is heated through and coated with oil. Add the tomatoes and season lightly with salt and freshly ground pepper. Simmer 4 or 5 minutes, stirring frequently until the tomatoes just begin to release their juices.

4. Pour the drained linguini into a large serving bowl. Purée the tomatoes and onion mixture in a blender until smooth. Season to your taste with salt and freshly ground pepper and immediately pour the puréed sauce over the linguine. Pass the cheese separately.

FAT TRACKING TIP: Reduce the oil to 1 tablespoon.

✿ PER SERVING (INCLUDES 1½ TABLESPOONS GRATED CHEESE) *Calories: 615, Cholesterol (mg): 8, Saturated fat (g): 3, Total fat (g): 13, Sodium (mg): 238, Total fiber (g): 5*

Fusilli al Radicchio Rosso

SERVES 4

THIS UNUSUAL TREATMENT *of Italy's famed purplish red leaf was sent to us by our friend and gifted cook and writer, Pamela Shaver, while she worked as a pastry chef in Italy. This dish calls for a lot of cheese. To keep your total fat intake in line, we suggest you start your meal with Carrot, Leek and Fennel Soup (page 367) and follow the pasta with a green salad and light dressing. While this pasta is somewhat higher in fat than some of our other recipes, note that it is still well under the fat count of just one slice of apple pie made according to a typical, old-fashioned recipe that has 20 grams of fat, 10 of them saturated!*

> 2 tablespoons extra-virgin olive oil
> 1 large onion, thinly sliced
> 1 head radicchio, shredded
> 1 cup white wine
> Salt and freshly ground pepper
> ¾ pound dried fusilli (*rotini* or corkscrew pasta)
> 4 ounces Parmesan cheese, shredded or shaved (about 1⅓ cups)

1. Heat the oil in a large skillet. Add the onion and cook over very low heat until softened and almost caramelized, about 20 minutes. Do not allow the onion to scorch.

2. Add the radicchio, cover and cook over low-medium heat, stirring occasionally for 4 or 5 minutes or until the radicchio has wilted slightly. Add the white wine, cover and cook over low-medium heat about 15 minutes or until the liquid has almost completely evaporated. Season lightly with salt and freshly ground pepper.

3. Meanwhile, have a large pot of lightly salted boiling water ready and add the fusilli 7 to 9 minutes before serving. Cook as directed on page 451.

4. Pour the drained fusilli into a large bowl. Toss with the cooked radicchio and Parmesan cheese. Serve immediately.

FAT TRACKING TIP: Reduce the amount of cheese to 3 ounces.

❋ PER SERVING *Calories: 560, Cholesterol (mg): 22, Saturated fat (g): 6, Total fat (g): 17, Sodium (mg): 540, Total fiber (g): 1*

Spaghetti with Broccoli in White Wine

SERVES 6

WE RARELY RECOMMEND USING MARGARINE *because of concern about trans-fatty acids boosting lethal* LDL *levels and lowering healthy* HDL. *But when the ingredients of a dish are as low in fat as this rich pasta, you can add a small amount to further smooth the sauce. Or, you can make the trade-off of using butter and eliminating transfatty acids but increasing the cholesterol slightly.*

1 bunch broccoli
2 tablespoons extra-virgin olive oil
1 medium-size onion, chopped
3 garlic cloves, minced
1 cup dry white wine
1 pound dried spaghetti
1 tablespoon margarine
Salt and freshly ground pepper
1½ ounces Parmesan cheese, freshly grated (about ½ cup)

1. Trim the stalks from the broccoli florets. Peel and dice the florets and cut them into 1-inch pieces.

2. Heat the olive oil in a large nonreactive skillet. Add the onion and garlic and stir over medium heat for 3 or 4 minutes or until the onion is soft and transparent. Do not allow it to scorch. Add the wine and broccoli and bring to a boil. Reduce the heat and simmer for 10 to 12 minutes or until the wine has reduced by half and the broccoli is slightly tender. Do not cover the broccoli or it will discolor. Stir occasionally.

3. Have a large pot of lightly salted boiling water ready and add the spaghetti 7 to 9 minutes before serving. Cook as directed on page 451.

4. Pour the drained spaghetti into a large serving bowl. Stir the margarine into the broccoli and season to your taste with salt and freshly ground pepper. Pour the broccoli and sauce over the spaghetti and toss thoroughly before serving. Pass the cheese separately.

FAT TRACKING TIP: Omit the margarine.

❋ PER SERVING (INCLUDES ABOUT 2 TABLESPOONS GRATED CHEESE) *Calories: 422, Cholesterol (mg): 5, Saturated fat (g): 2, Total fat (g): 10, Sodium (mg): 175, Total fiber (g): 2*

Orecchiette with Cauliflower and Currants

SERVES 6

LOVE OF PASTA *has spanned not only centuries, but millennia in southern Europe. Long before the poet Horace, who lived from 65 to 8 BC, lauded pasta, the ancient Etruscans made noodles using tools, such as cutting wheels, that are not too different from those we rely on today. Renaissance cooks paired savory broths and sauces with fruit, and raisins and honey found their way into main courses, setting the stage for our presentation of orecchiette with currants. Translated, this pasta means "little ears," perfect little dishes that collect the delightful currant-flecked cauliflower and sauce. If you cannot find this small, round shape, you can substitute pasta wheels or short tube pasta.*

2 tablespoons dried currants
¼ cup very hot water
1 pound dried orecchiette (dish-shaped pasta)
2 tablespoons extra-virgin olive oil
1 onion, finely diced
1 tablespoon pine nuts
1 head cauliflower, finely chopped
½ cup dry white wine
Salt and freshly ground pepper
2 tablespoons minced fresh Italian parsley
1 ounce Parmesan cheese, freshly grated (about ⅓ cup)

1. Preheat the oven to 400 degrees F. Place the currants in the hot water and let stand for 10 minutes or until plumped. Drain and dry on paper towels.

2. Have a large pot of lightly salted boiling water ready and add the orecchiette 8 to 10 minutes before serving. Cook as directed on page 451.

3. Heat the olive oil in a large ovenproof skillet and add the onion. Toss well for about a minute, then place in the oven for 8 to 10 minutes or until softened. While the onion cooks, place the pine nuts in a dry heavy skillet and toss over medium-high heat for 1 minute until they are fragrant and toasty. Or, place them on a baking sheet and toast in the oven for 5 minutes. Watch them carefully to prevent them from scorching. Set them aside.

4. As directed on page 267, steam or microwave the cauliflower for 3 minutes. Add it to the wilted onions and toss thoroughly. Add the wine and stir over high heat until it has reduced by half, 3 or 4 minutes. Stir in the pine nuts and currants. Season to your taste with salt and freshly ground pepper. Place the drained orecchiette in a serving bowl, add the cauliflower sauce and parsley, and toss thoroughly. Serve and pass the Parmesan cheese in a separate bowl.

FAT TRACKING TIP: Use less cheese.

❋ PER SERVING (INCLUDES A SCANT TABLESPOON GRATED CHEESE) *Calories: 396, Cholesterol (mg): 4, Saturated fat (g): 2, Total fat (g): 8, Sodium (mg): 110, Total fiber (g): 2*

Penne with Anchovy and Garlic
SERVES 2

DOUBLE OR TRIPLE THIS QUICK PASTA *if your guest list suddenly expands. Serve with lots of bread and a salad of greens and mushrooms dressed with our low-fat Mustard Vinaigrette (page 382–83) to compensate for the added fat in the anchovy paste.*

> 6 ounces dried penne (short tube pasta)
> 1 tablespoon Garlic Oil (page 296) or extra-virgin olive oil
> 3 garlic cloves, minced
> 3 tablespoons anchovy paste
> 1 tablespoon fresh lemon juice
> 1 tablespoon chopped fresh basil, Italian parsley or cilantro
> Salt and freshly ground pepper
> 1 ounce Parmesan cheese, freshly shredded or shaved (about ⅓ cup)

1. Have a large pot of lightly salted boiling water ready and add the penne 7 to 9 minutes before serving. Cook as directed on page 451.

2. Heat the oil in a skillet and add the garlic. Stir over low-medium heat for 30 seconds, then add the anchovy paste. Stir until it dissolves and blends into the oil. Add the lemon juice and chopped herbs and season to your taste with salt and freshly ground pepper.

3. Pour the drained penne into a serving bowl, add the sauce and toss gently until the kernels of pasta are completely coated. Sprinkle with the cheese and serve immediately.

FAT TRACKING TIP: Reduce the cheese by half.

❋ PER SERVING *Calories: 481, Cholesterol (mg): 10, Saturated fat (g): 4, Total fat (g): 12, Sodium (mg): 271, Total fiber (g): 1*

Vanilla-Scented Butter Beans
with Orecchiette
SERVES 4

OUR VANILLA OIL *puts a luxurious contemporary twist on the classic peasant dish, pasta and beans. Capitalizing on the natural sweet creaminess of fresh butter beans, the Vanilla Oil, lemon zest and nutmeg create an exquisitely perfumed and easy sauce. Don't add too much pasta or it will overwhelm the delicate flavors. Serve this as a side dish with poached salmon or Chicken Roasted with Pears, Fennel and Red Onions (page 509–10). This is not intended to be a cheesy sauce, only a few shreds are necessary to fine-tune the finished dish. You can make this with olive oil or canola oil, but it will not have the same richness that the Vanilla Oil imparts.*

> 1½ tablespoons Vanilla Oil (page 298)
> ½ shallot, minced
> 2-inch strip lemon zest
> 1 cup fresh butter beans or lima beans
> 1 cup cold water
> Salt and freshly ground pepper
> 1 cup dried orecchiette (little ears pasta), about 3½ ounces
> Pinch of nutmeg
> 1 teaspoon fresh thyme or ½ teaspoon dried
> 2 teaspoons freshly grated Parmesan cheese

1. Heat the oil in a small saucepan. (Don't use a large pan or the water will evaporate before the beans finish cooking.) Add the shallot and lemon zest and stir over low-medium heat 2 or 3 minutes until the shallot softens.

2. Add the beans and the water and bring to a boil. Reduce the heat to a simmer, season lightly with salt and freshly ground pepper and partially cover the pan. Checking frequently, cook until the beans soften and the water has almost, but not totally evaporated. As soon as the beans lose their firmness, pierce them with the tip of a knife so the centers will cook. Continue cooking for a total of about 25 minutes, stirring often or until the beans are soft but not mushy. Do not overcook them or allow the pan to dry out. The flavored broth that cooks the beans becomes the basis for the sauce. If the water cooks down too fast, reduce the heat and add another half cup or so.

3. Have a large pot of lightly salted boiling water ready and add the orecchiette 10 to 12 minutes before serving. Cook as directed on page 451.

4. Pour the drained pasta into a bowl. When the beans are done, remove and discard any skins that slip off easily and add the nutmeg and thyme. Season to

your taste with salt and freshly ground pepper. Pour over the orecchiette, sprinkle with the cheese and serve.

❋ PER SERVING *Calories: 207, Cholesterol (mg): 1, Saturated fat (g): 1, Total fat (g): 6, Sodium (mg): 10, Total fiber (g): 4*

Fettuccine with Smoked Salmon, Goat Cheese and Chives

SERVES 4

PROOF THAT YOU DON'T HAVE TO SACRIFICE *elegant food to protect your heart, this lush pasta is both chic and light. Because the olive oil is kept to a minimum, you can enjoy both sour cream and goat cheese and still keep the fat at a mere 16 percent. Especially good paired with fresh asparagus in the early spring.*

1 teaspoon extra-virgin olive oil
1 shallot, finely diced
½ cup white wine
½ cup Rich Fish Stock (page 287) or bottled clam juice
1 red bell pepper, seeded and thinly sliced
½ cup reduced-fat sour cream
Salt and freshly ground pepper
½ pound dried fettuccine
½ pound smoked salmon, cut into 1-inch-wide slivers
2 tablespoons crumbled goat cheese
¼ cup minced fresh chives

1. Preheat the oven to 400 degrees F. Heat the oil in a nonreactive ovenproof skillet and add the shallot. Toss thoroughly and place in the oven for 10 minutes or until the shallot is soft. Stir once or twice during this time.

2. Using potholders on the hot skillet handles, add the wine, fish stock and red pepper and bring to a boil. Reduce the heat to a simmer and cook for 15 minutes or until the pepper has softened, stirring occasionally. Add the sour cream and stir until smooth. Season lightly with salt and freshly ground pepper.

3. Have a large pot of lightly salted boiling water ready and add the fettuccine 7 to 9 minutes before serving. Cook as directed on page 451.

4. Pour the drained fettuccine into a serving bowl, add the sauce and toss gently. Strew the salmon over the pasta, then follow with the goat cheese and chives. Serve immediately while the sauce is still hot.

❋ PER SERVING *Calories: 347, Cholesterol (mg): 18, Saturated fat (g): 1, Total fat (g): 6, Sodium (mg): 492, Total fiber (g): 2*

Fettuccine with Scallops
in Asian Spiced Sauce
SERVES 4

KEEP OUR ASIAN SPICED OIL ON HAND *and you can always create an instant sauce with a slight charge of electricity, such as this piquant mix of fresh herbs and sweet scallops. Lacking our special oil, substitute peanut oil. Both large ocean scallops or small bay scallops, rinsed free of all sand, work equally well. This pasta cries out for something green to accompany it—steamed broccoli, wilted greens, barely cooked green beans or sweet peas. Or, treat yourself to a riot of healthful antioxidants and have a little of each!*

1 pound scallops
½ pound dried fettuccine, linguine or spaghetti
2 tablespoons Asian Spiced Oil (page 297)
1 garlic clove, minced
1 red bell pepper, seeded and finely diced
1 large tomato, seeded and finely diced
¼ cup chopped fresh basil, cilantro or mint,
    plus whole leaves for garnish
Salt and freshly ground pepper

1. Cut large scallops into approximately 1-inch pieces.

2. Have a large pot of lightly salted boiling water ready and add the fettuccine 7 to 9 minutes before serving. Cook as directed on page 451.

3. Heat the oil in a nonreactive medium-size skillet over low-medium heat and add the garlic and bell pepper. Stir for 2 minutes or until the pepper softens slightly. Add the tomato and scallops and turn them in the oil for 4 or 5 minutes or until the scallops are firm and white. Don't overcook them or they will become rubbery.

4. Add the basil, season with salt and freshly ground pepper to your taste and toss gently.

5. Place the drained pasta in a serving bowl and add the scallops and sauce. Toss gently and garnish with the leaves of mint or cilantro. Serve immediately.

❈ PER SERVING *Calories: 386, Cholesterol (mg): 45, Saturated fat (g): 1, Total fat (g): 9, Sodium (mg): 230, Total fiber (g): 3*

Spaghetti with Sardines and Capers

SERVES 4

A QUICK BUT ROBUST PASTA *to warm you on chilly nights. The combination of raisins, pine nuts and garlic comes by way of Sicily, where the mix of sweet and savory has a long history as elsewhere in southern European cooking. By the way, because you eat the small bones, sardines are high in calcium.*

> 1 tablespoon yellow raisins
> 1 tablespoon pine nuts
> ½ pound dried spaghetti
> 4½ ounces sardines canned in olive oil
> 2 garlic cloves, minced
> 2 tablespoons capers, drained
> 2 tablespoons minced fresh Italian parsley
> 1 teaspoon fresh lemon juice
> Freshly ground pepper to your taste
> 2 tablespoons freshly grated Romano or pecorino cheese

1. Preheat the oven to 400 degrees F. Place the raisins in a small bowl and cover with hot water for 10 minutes until plumped. Drain and dry on paper towels. Spread the pine nuts on a baking sheet and toast in the oven for 6 or 7 minutes or until fragrant. Check them frequently and if they appear to scorch, remove them immediately.

2. Have a large pot of lightly salted boiling water ready and add the spaghetti 7 to 9 minutes before serving. Cook as directed on page 451.

3. In a medium-size skillet, place the sardines and 1 tablespoon of their oil. Add the garlic and stir over low-medium heat for 2 minutes or until the garlic is fragrant and soft. Add the remaining ingredients except the cheese and quickly stir until heated through.

4. Pour the drained spaghetti into a serving bowl and add the sardines and sauce. Toss gently and serve immediately. Pass the cheese separately.

FAT TRACKING TIP: Use less cheese.

✽ PER SERVING (INCLUDES ½ TABLESPOON GRATED CHEESE) *Calories: 363, Cholesterol (mg): 47, Saturated fat (g): 2, Total fat (g): 11, Sodium (mg): 199, Total fiber (g): 1*

Linguine with Crab and Peas

SERVES 4

THE SAN FRANCISCO BAY *is the favorite breeding ground for a local treasure, Dungeness crab, which is beautifully showcased in this elegant pasta. Other varieties of hard-shell crab, though, will work just as well, for all of them are low in fat, especially saturated fat. While it is not customary to add cheese to fish pastas, a little Parmesan adds a needed savory flourish to this creamy sauce. Pay close attention to the timing after you add the crab. As it is already cooked, it only needs reheating. Overcooking will rob it of its sweet tenderness.*

> 1 pound dried linguine
> 2 teaspoons canola oil
> 1 shallot, minced
> 2 cups fresh peas (about 2 pounds in shells)
>   or tiny frozen peas without butter
> 2 tablespoons water
> 1 pound cooked crab meat
> Salt and freshly ground pepper
> 1 cup Red Pepper Sauce for Fish (recipe follows)
> 1 ounce Parmesan cheese, freshly grated (about ⅓ cup)

1. Have a large pot of lightly salted boiling water ready and add the linguine 7 to 9 minutes before serving. Cook as directed on page 451.

2. Heat the oil in a small skillet and add the shallot. Stir over low heat for 3 or 4 minutes or until soft and transparent; do not allow it to scorch. Add the peas and 2 tablespoons water and bring to a boil. Reduce the heat, cover and cook for 2 minutes. Add the crab and stir just until heated through, about 1 minute. Season to your taste with salt and freshly ground pepper.

3. Place the drained linguine in a serving bowl and add the crab mixture. Toss with the Red Pepper Sauce for Fish, sprinkle with the Parmesan cheese and serve very hot.

❀ PER SERVING *Calories: 650, Cholesterol (mg): 71, Saturated fat (g): 2, Total fat (g): 8, Sodium (mg): 460, Total fiber (g): 3*

Red Pepper Sauce for Fish
Makes approximately 1 cup, serving size 1/4 cup

You can add a film of this incredibly rich and creamy sauce to any fish such as poached sole or salmon. To use with poultry dishes, such as grilled or poached chicken breast, substitute chicken stock for the Rich Fish Stock. For a sauce that is slightly less tart, you can substitute half-and-half for the sour cream.

> 1 teaspoon olive oil
> 1 tablespoon chopped shallot
> 1 large garlic clove, minced
> 1/2 cup Rich Fish Stock (page 287) or bottled clam juice
> 1 red bell pepper roasted (page 265)
> 3 fresh basil leaves
> 1 tablespoon low-fat sour cream
> Salt and freshly ground pepper

1. In a small skillet, heat the olive oil and add the shallot and garlic. Stir over low heat for 2 to 3 minutes or until they soften. Add the fish stock, bring to a boil, then reduce the heat and simmer for 10 minutes. Add the roasted pepper and just bring to the boil.

2. Place roasted pepper mixture and basil in a blender and purée until smooth.

3. Stir in the sour cream and season to your taste with salt and pepper. Serve immediately as directed with pasta or over grilled, broiled, poached or baked seafood. Cover and refrigerate any remaining sauce. It will last for 2 to 3 days.

FAT TRACKING TIP: Use nonfat sour cream in place of the low-fat sour cream.

✿ PER SERVING *Calories: 67, Cholesterol (mg): 1, Saturated fat (g): 1, Total fat (g): 2, Sodium (mg): 6, Total fiber (g): 1*

Radiotore with Chicken, Mushrooms, Peppers and Fresh Basil

SERVES 4

IF YOU CAN'T FIND RADIOTORE, *the curved pasta with a frilly edge, substitute any short shape such as orecchiette (little ears), penne, fusilli (corkscrew) or ziti. In this quick hybrid preparation—not quite a salad, yet not a traditional sauce—fresh mushrooms and sweet peppers, barely warmed by the hot pasta, soak up a sauce sweetened with basil and spiced with cayenne. Though mushrooms do not exactly brim with nutrients, peppers are high on the list of heart-healthful antioxidant vegetables.*

> 1 pound fresh white mushrooms
> Distilled vinegar, optional
> 3/4 pound dried radiotore (curved frilly-edged pasta)
> 1 *each* small yellow and red bell pepper, cut into matchstick strips
> 8 ounces cooked shredded chicken breast, all fat and skin removed
> 1/2 cup coarsely chopped fresh basil
> 3 tablespoons extra-virgin olive oil or Basil Oil (page 296)
> Coarsely ground pepper
> Juice of 1 lemon
> 1/2 teaspoon salt
> 1/4 teaspoon cayenne
> 1/4 ounce Parmesan cheese, freshly grated (about generous
>   1 tablespoon)

1. If the mushrooms are gritty, add a splash of vinegar to a bowl of cold water. Swish the mushrooms briefly in the vinegar bath, then immediately rinse and roll them in paper toweling until dry or they will become soggy. Never let mushrooms sit in water or on the counter undrained and undried. Slice the mushrooms (you can use a food processor with the thick blade) and place them in a salad bowl.

2. Have a large pot of lightly salted boiling water ready and add the radiotore 7 to 9 minutes before serving. Cook as directed on page 451.

3. Add the peppers to the mushrooms, follow with the shredded chicken and toss lightly. Add the basil, oil, a heavy dose of black pepper and the juice from half of the lemon. In a small bowl blend the salt and cayenne to distribute the hot pepper evenly and add it to the salad. (If you add it all at once, the cayenne may cling to a mushroom or two and give one of your diners a fiery surprise.) Toss thoroughly.

4. Add the drained pasta to the salad and toss gently until everything is coated with the dressing. Toss once more with the cheese and taste for seasoning. Add enough of the lemon to give a sprightly flavor. Serve immediately.

❀ PER SERVING *Calories: 545, Cholesterol (mg): 49, Saturated fat (g): 2, Total fat (g): 14, Sodium (mg): 349, Total fiber (g): 2*

❦

Spaghetti with Chicken, Garlic and Salsa
SERVES 6

AN EASY DISH FOR A GROUP OF SIX, *although you can double or triple this for a bigger family or party crowd. Scout specialty cheese shops for low-fat cheeses; they often have better success acquiring truly delicious varieties from small producers than do large supermarkets.*

> 1½ pounds boned chicken breasts, all skin and fat removed
> 1 pound dried spaghetti
> 3 tablespoons extra-virgin olive oil
> 6 garlic cloves, minced
> 1 cup chopped fresh basil
> Salt and freshly ground pepper
> 3 cups Salsa Fresca (page 357) or Tomato Orange Salsa (page 350), or your favorite salsa
> 1 ounce reduced-fat Monterey Jack cheese, freshly shredded or shaved (about ⅓ cup)

1. Wash and dry the chicken and cut it into ½-inch slices. Have a large pot of lightly salted boiling water ready and add the spaghetti 7 to 9 minutes before serving. Cook as directed on page 451.

2. Heat the oil in a skillet over medium heat and add the garlic. Stir until it becomes fragrant, about 1 minute, and add the chicken. Toss the mixture for 2 minutes or until chicken is springy to the touch and the juices run clear.

3. Add the basil, salt and freshly ground pepper to your taste and cook for another 30 seconds. Pour the cooked spaghetti into a large bowl and add the sauce. Toss thoroughly and serve. Pass the salsa and cheese separately.

FAT TRACKING TIP: Use turkey breast instead of chicken.

❀ PER SERVING (INCLUDES ½ CUP SALSA AND ½ TABLESPOON CHEESE) *Calories: 526, Cholesterol (mg): 74, Saturated fat (g): 2, Total fat (g): 12, Sodium (mg): 180, Total fiber (g): 1*

Fettuccine with Lemon Chicken and Red Pepper Pesto

SERVES 4

NO DOUBT YOU WILL FIND OTHER USES *for the red pepper pesto that laces this zesty pasta: as a sandwich spread, a dip for crisp vegetables or a sauce for poultry or fish. Instead of mayonnaise, drizzle it on cold, steamed red potatoes for a stunning, quick potato salad. Serve with a basket of breadsticks at a week-end lunch or with a hearty bowl of Minestrone (page 378–79) for a more filling supper menu.*

½ pound boned chicken breast, all skin and fat removed
2 tablespoons extra-virgin olive oil
Juice of ½ lemon
1 teaspoon fresh thyme or a pinch dried
1 whole bulb garlic
1 large red bell pepper, roasted, peeled and seeded (page 280)
1 cup fresh basil leaves
1 large garlic clove
Salt and freshly ground pepper
¾ pound dried fettuccine
¾ ounce Parmesan cheese, freshly grated (about ¼ cup)

1. Preheat the oven to 400 degrees F. Wash and dry the chicken. In a small bowl, blend 1 teaspoon of the olive oil and all but 1 teaspoon of the lemon juice and brush this mixture over the chicken. Sprinkle with the thyme. Cover and refrigerate for at least 30 minutes.

2. To make the red pepper pesto, cut the garlic bulb in half crosswise and brush the cut sides with a few drops of olive oil. Press the cut sides together and wrap tightly in aluminum foil. Place in the oven for 30 minutes. Then unwrap and set aside to cool.

3. Place the roasted pepper in a blender. Squeeze the roasted garlic into it as you would a tube of toothpaste, scooping out any resistant cloves with a spoon. Add the basil, fresh garlic and all but a teaspoon of the remaining olive oil (about 1¼ tablespoons) and purée until smooth. Stir in ½ teaspoon of lemon juice and season to your taste with salt and freshly ground pepper and a few more drops of lemon juice if you wish. You can make this up to 24 hours ahead cover and store it in the refrigerator, but bring the pesto to room temperature before serving. You can also make this with a food processor or hand processor, but the purée may not be as smooth.

4. Have a large pot of lightly salted boiling water ready and add the fettuccine 7 to 9 minutes before serving. Cook as directed on page 451.

5. Preheat the broiler. Broil the chicken for 4 or 5 minutes on each side or until it is springy to the touch and the juices run clear. Do not overcook it. Shred the chicken coarsely.

6. Place the drained fettuccine in a serving bowl, toss with the remaining olive oil and then add the chicken. Add the red pepper pesto, toss thoroughly and serve immediately. Pass the cheese separately.

FAT TRACKING TIPS: Omit the cheese. Reduce the oil to 1 tablespoon.

❋ PER SERVING (INCLUDES 1 TABLESPOON GRATED CHEESE) *Calories: 492, Cholesterol (mg): 41, Saturated fat (g): 3, Total fat (g): 12, Sodium (mg): 150, Total fiber (g): Trace*

Spicy Noodles with Chicken

SERVES 4

EASY, EASY, EASY. *Our Asian Spiced Oil, which we consider a kitchen staple, makes quick work of providing a subtle and delicious seasoning for the noodles. You can use chili oil or hot oil, recognizable by the distinctive red hue from the hot peppers that fire it, or an infusion of peanut oil and hot peppers instead, but it is not as interesting. Fish sauce, along with soy sauce, is an inexpensive condiment produced in China, Thailand and Vietnam and available in Asian markets as are the Japanese noodles. As you can see from this recipe, soy sauce and fish sauce are the types of salty flavorings that boost the sodium content of a dish. If you are salt-sensitive, you may need to pass up this recipe. Definitely use low-sodium chicken stock. In place of chicken you can add firm-fleshed fish, such as salmon, snapper or halibut, or other vegetables, such as broccoli or carrots. You can also pour this over rice instead of pasta.*

> ½ pound boned chicken breast, all skin and fat removed
> 1 pound dried Japanese *soba* (buckwheat) or *udon* (wheat flour) knoodles
> ½ cup rice vinegar
> ½ cup Asian fish sauce or light soy sauce
> ½ cup Chicken Stock (page 285–86) or canned low-fat, low-sodium chicken broth
> 1 tablespoon Asian Spiced Oil (page 297)
> 1 scant teaspoon Asian sesame oil
> 2 carrots, peeled and cut into long, thin shreds
> ½ cup chopped green onions
> ½ cup shredded bok choy, green cabbage or spinach
> 2 tablespoons coarsely chopped fresh basil or cilantro

1. Cut the chicken in long, thin shreds. This may be done several hours ahead, covered and refrigerated.

2. Have a large pot of lightly salted boiling water ready and add noodles 7 to 9 minutes before serving. Cook as directed for pasta on page 451.

3. In a medium-size nonreactive saucepan combine the vinegar, fish sauce, chicken stock, Asian Spiced Oil and sesame oil. Bring just to a boil, then reduce the heat immediately. Add the chicken, carrots, onions and bok choy and simmer 3 or 4 minutes until the chicken is white and firm. Do not overcook. Stir in the basil.

4. Pour the drained soba into a bowl. Add the chicken and vegetables with the liquid and toss lightly. Serve immediately.

❀ PER SERVING *Calories: 258, Cholesterol (mg): 36, Saturated fat (g): 1, Total fat (g): 6, Sodium (mg): 1,495, Total fiber (g): 5*

Lean Meat Sauce over Spaghetti
MAKES 6 CUPS SAUCE, SERVING SIZE 1 CUP

HERE IS EVERYONE'S FAVORITE PASTA, *a classic Italian tomato and meat sauce that requires a long, slow cooking to develop its rich flavor. Though based on the classic Bolognese meat sauce, we cut the amount of beef usually called for in the original version to lower the saturated fat count. We use milk and wine to tenderize the meat and beef stock to deepen the flavor. Use only olive oil here; canola and vegetable oils do not have enough body. You can make the sauce one or two days ahead, cover and refrigerate it for an even richer flavor. This sauce freezes very well. Use in any recipe that calls for meat sauce.*

LEAN MEAT SAUCE
2 tablespoons extra-virgin olive oil
1 cup diced onion
5 garlic cloves
½ cup finely diced carrot
¼ pound ground beef (top round)
1 cup white wine
¼ cup low-fat milk
2 pounds fresh tomatoes, peeled, seeded and coarsely chopped
1 can (28 ounces) crushed tomatoes
Pinch of ground nutmeg
Salt and freshly ground pepper to your taste
1 tablespoon minced fresh oregano or 1 teaspoon dried
1 tablespoon minced fresh basil or 1 teaspoon dried

1 cup Beef Stock (page 288–89) or canned low-fat, low-sodium
   beef broth or water
1 pound fresh mushrooms, chopped

1 pound dried spaghetti

1. Heat 1 tablespoon plus 2 teaspoons of the olive oil in a large nonreactive skillet or Dutch oven. Add the onion and 2 of the garlic cloves and cook partially covered over low heat for 5 minutes, stirring once or twice. Add the carrot and cook for 4 to 5 more minutes or until the onions are limp. Stir occasionally and lower the heat if the vegetables begin to scorch.

2. Add the ground beef and stir until it just begins to color. Add the wine to the skillet, bring to a boil, reduce the heat and gently boil until the wine has reduced to about 2 tablespoons, stirring frequently. Add the milk and cook over medium-high heat until the liquid has almost completely evaporated, but do not allow the pot to dry out or the mixture to burn.

3. Add the tomatoes, nutmeg, salt and freshly ground pepper, oregano, ½ tablespoon of the basil and the beef stock and bring to a boil. Immediately reduce the heat to the slowest simmer and cook for 2 hours, giving it an occasional stir. If the sauce doesn't bubble now and then, it has stopped cooking, so raise the heat a little. However, don't let it bubble too rapidly, or the liquid will evaporate before the flavors have a chance to cook thoroughly and mellow the sauce. You can interrupt the cooking at any time from now on, if necessary, refrigerate and resume cooking at your convenience.

4. After the sauce has simmered 2 hours, sauté the remaining 3 garlic cloves in the 1 teaspoon of olive oil in a small skillet. Add the mushrooms and sauté over high heat for 1 minute. Stir them into the sauce and continue cooking uncovered 1 or 2 more hours or until the sauce is very thick and flavorful. If during cooking the sauce appears too thick, thin with a mixture of half water and half beef stock until you have a desirable consistency. When cooked, stir in the remaining ½ tablespoon basil. If you are not using the sauce immediately, cover and refrigerate for future use or freeze either in a large container or single-serving batches.

5. Have a large pot of boiling water ready and add the spaghetti 7 to 9 minutes before serving. Cook as directed on page 451. Place the drained spaghetti in a large bowl and add the sauce. Toss thoroughly before serving.

✽ PER SERVING *Calories: 467, Cholesterol (mg): 12, Saturated fat (g): 1, Total fat (g): 8, Sodium (mg): 350, Total fiber (g): 3*

Pasta Shells Stuffed with
Winter Squash and Four Cheeses

SERVES 6

Use pumpkin or butternut squash *for this delicious one-dish pasta. The shells are easy to manage and can be assembled ahead, refrigerated, then baked before serving. You will only need two cups of cooked squash. Put the remainder in a soup or stew or freeze it for future use.*

> 1 small butternut squash or pumpkin (approximately 1½ pounds)
> Vegetable spray for baking sheet
> 2 tablespoons extra-virgin olive oil
> 1 onion, chopped
> ½ cup nonfat cottage cheese
> ½ cup part skim-milk ricotta cheese
> 1 ounce low-fat mozzarella cheese, freshly grated (about ⅓ cup)
> 2 ounces Parmesan cheese, freshly grated (about ⅔ cup)
> 3 egg whites
> Salt and freshly ground pepper to your taste
> 1 pound jumbo pasta shells
> 3 cups Tomato Pepper Purée (recipe follows) or Sun-Dried Tomato
>   Sauce (page 476)

1. Preheat the oven to 350 degrees F. Pierce the squash in several places with the tip of a knife. Place it on a baking sheet coated with a light film of vegetable spray and bake for 45 or 60 minutes or until tender. Cool slightly and peel. Cut in half and scrape away and discard the strings and seeds. Chop 2 cups of pulp coarsely, saving any remaining for another dish. Alternatively, you can microwave the squash for 20 to 25 minutes, depending on the size.

2. Heat the olive oil in a medium-size skillet and add the onion. Stir occasionally and cook over low-medium heat for 5 minutes or until soft and transparent.

3. In the bowl of a food processor, combine the cooked squash, onion, cheeses, egg whites, salt and freshly ground pepper, and purée until smooth. You can blend this by hand, if you wish, or with a blender or hand processor.

4. Have a large pot of lightly salted boiling water ready and add the shells 7 to 9 minutes before you are ready to fill them. Cook as directed on page 451.

5. Coat a large baking dish (or 2 small ones) with a light film of vegetable spray. Drain the shells and arrange them on the baking sheet, separating any that cling together. Fill each shell evenly with the squash mixture. As you fill the empty shells and they begin to press together in the pan, the shells will close slightly and hold the filling. Spread the mixture evenly in the shells, rather than mounding it all in the middle. Cover the baking dish tightly with a sheet of aluminum and bake in the 350 degree F oven for 30 minutes. Drizzle the Tomato and Pepper Purée over the shells and serve.

❉ PER SERVING *Calories: 549, Cholesterol (mg): 17, Saturated fat (g): 4, Total fat (g): 12, Sodium (mg): 322, Total fiber (g): 6*

Tomato Pepper Purée
Makes approximately 3 cups, serving size ½ cup

Make this purée in double or triple batches and freeze in half-cup size portions to flavor soups and pasta sauces. You can use this whenever a recipe calls for tomato sauce or purée, for it is far superior to canned brands.

> 1 teaspoon olive oil
> 1 shallot
> 1 small garlic clove, minced
> 1 teaspoon fresh thyme or marjoram
> 1 can (28 ounces) tomato purée (without citric acid if possible)
> 4 red bell peppers, roasted (page 280)
> Salt and freshly ground pepper
> ¼ cup fresh basil leaves

1. Preheat the oven to 400 degrees F. Heat the olive oil in a nonreactive oven-proof saucepan or skillet. Add the shallot and garlic and stir over low heat for 1 minute. Place in the oven for 8 to 10 minutes or until the shallot begins to wilt.

2. Using potholders, carefully transfer the pan from the oven to the stovetop and add the thyme, tomato purée, red peppers and season with salt and pepper. Bring to a boil, stirring frequently and reduce the heat until the sauce bubbles gently but continuously. Cook for 15 minutes, stirring frequently. Purée in a blender or food processor with the basil, taste and add a little more salt and pepper if necessary. If you don't use it at once, freeze small amounts in ice cube trays, then pop out and store in a tightly sealed plastic bag.

❉ PER SERVING *Calories: 92, Cholesterol (mg): 0, Saturated fat (g): Trace, Total fat (g): 1, Sodium (mg): 30, Total fiber (g): 4*

Lasagna with Cheese
SERVES 8

NEVER A LEAN ENTRÉE, *family-style lasagna calls for some ingenuity before it will qualify for regular appearances on your heart-healthy menus. In addition to streamlining the white sauce by keeping margarine to a minimum and using 1 percent milk, we have used a variety of low-fat cheeses to give the sauce lots of flavor. Our Lean Meat Sauce further lightens this favorite dish, but note that it must simmer for three or four hours or make a day in advance.*

> 3 cups Lean Meat Sauce (page 468–69)
> 1 teaspoon margarine
> 2 tablespoons potato flour
> 1 cup 1% milk
> Salt and white pepper
> ½ cup nonfat cottage cheese
> ½ cup skim-milk ricotta cheese
> 3 ounces mozzarella cheese, freshly shredded (about 1 cup)
> Vegetable spray or oil for baking pan
> ½ pound lasagna (approximately)
> 1 red or yellow bell pepper, roasted, peeled and seeded (page 280)
> 1 tablespoon freshly grated Parmesan cheese

1. Prepare the meat sauce or, if made in advance, reheat it in a nonreactive Dutch oven or large saucepan.

2. In a small saucepan, melt the margarine over low heat and add the potato flour, stirring for 1 minute until it is smooth. Add the milk and stir over medium heat until the mixture just begins to bubble. Immediately remove from the heat. Or, blend the potato flour and milk in a microwave-safe container and heat on high for 1 minute. Stir and cook for another minute, then stir in the margarine. Season to your taste with salt and freshly ground pepper. If you do not use this immediately, place a piece of plastic wrap directly on the surface of the sauce to prevent a skin from forming.

3. Blend the cottage cheese, ricotta and ¾ cup of the shredded mozzarella. This may be done ahead of time and stored covered in the refrigerator for several hours.

4. Preheat the oven to 350 degrees F. Lightly coat an 11 x 7-inch baking dish with a thin film of vegetable spray or oil. Have a large pot of lightly salted boiling water ready and add the lasagna 7 to 9 minutes before you are ready to begin layering the ingredients. When the pasta is tender but not mushy, working quickly, dip the strips of pasta in a bowl of cold water and drain on paper towels. Spread out the strips so they do not overlap or they will stick together.

5. Dice the red pepper and stir it into the meat sauce, blending thoroughly. Spread 2 or 3 tablespoons of meat sauce on the bottom of the baking dish, and arrange a layer of pasta on top, allowing the sheets to extend up the sides of the dish at both ends. Dot with some of the cheese mixture and spread it loosely over the pasta; it does not have to cover it completely. Smooth a thin layer of white sauce over the pasta and cheese and then top with the meat sauce. Continue layering in this manner until you have used all the sauces and cheese mixture. Finish with a layer of pasta and some of the white sauce. Then sprinkle on the reserved mozzarella and the Parmesan cheese. Bake for 30 minutes or until bubbly and golden. Cool briefly before serving.

FAT TRACKING TIP: Substitute Sun-Dried Tomato Sauce or other meatless tomato sauce.

✿ PER SERVING *Calories: 291, Cholesterol (mg): 21, Saturated fat (g): 3, Total fat (g): 8, Sodium (mg): 389, Total fiber (g): 3*

Lasagna with Fennel, Artichokes and Sun-Dried Tomato Sauce

SERVES 8

ARTICHOKES AND SWEET FENNEL, *exotically scented with anise, lavish so much flavor in this lasagna that no one will notice the absence of fat. Sometimes called Florentine or Roman fennel, this bulb figures importantly in many Italian dishes and is also delicious raw (as in our White Bean and Chicken Salad with Basil and Fennel, page 395). You can slice it lengthwise to retain its lovely architectural shape, as we suggest here, or simply chop the bulb and stalks, as you would celery. Potato flour gives a silkier texture to low-fat white sauces, although you can substitute unbleached white flour. Also, if you use homemade pasta rolled very thin, the first layer of pasta can overlap the edge of the dish with no danger of the finished lasagna becoming too doughy, as it can become with thicker, commercial lasagna. Because our recipe is less "juicy" than heavily sauced lasagnas, we recommend you lay the pasta flat.*

> Sun-Dried Tomato Sauce (recipe follows)
> 1 bulb fennel
> 2 carrots
> 1 zucchini
> 2 shallots or 1 medium-size onion or 1 medium-size leek
> Vegetable spray or oil for baking sheet and dish
> 1 package (9 ounces) frozen artichoke hearts
> 1 teaspoon margarine
> 2 tablespoons potato flour
> 1 cup 1% milk
> ¼ cup Chicken Stock (page 285–86) or canned low-fat, low-sodium chicken broth
> Salt and white pepper
> 1 cup nonfat cottage cheese
> ¼ cup skim-milk ricotta cheese
> 3 ounces mozzarella cheese, freshly shredded (about 1 cup)
> 1 ounce Parmesan cheese, freshly grated (about ¼ cup)
> ½ pound dried lasagna

1. Prepare the Sun-Dried Tomato Sauce and set aside or cover and refrigerate until ready to use. Preheat the oven to 425 degrees F.

2. Slice the stalks from the fennel and set the bulb aside. Trim off the tops of the stalks and chop the bottoms. Trim away and discard about ¼ inch of the root end, leaving the bulb intact. Standing the bulb upright, make lengthwise slices (⅓ inch thick) from the top down through the root. Slice the carrots and

zucchini into long diagonal slices ¼ inch thick. Chop the shallot or onion; if you use a leek, slice it lengthwise half way through to the center, swish it in a bowl of cold water with a splash of vinegar, rinse thoroughly to remove all grit and then chop.

3. Place the fennel stalks and bulb, carrots, zucchini and shallots on a baking sheet lightly coated with a thin film of vegetable spray or oil and roast in the oven for 30 to 45 minutes, removing each vegetable as it becomes very tender. Turn the vegetables once or twice as they cook. (Alternatively, you can grill the vegetables if you wish, but chop the shallots, onion or leek when done, not before cooking.) Steam the artichoke hearts briefly until they are thawed. To save time, you can microwave or steam the vegetables (see directions on page 266–67), but they won't be as deeply flavored or aromatic as roasted or grilled vegetables.

4. While the vegetables cook, in a small saucepan, melt the margarine over low heat and add the potato flour, stirring for 1 minute until it is smooth. Add the milk and chicken stock and stir over medium heat until the mixture just begins to bubble. Or, blend the potato flour, milk and chicken stock in a microwave-safe container and heat on high for 1 minute. Stir and cook for another minute, then stir in the margarine. Season to your taste with salt and pepper. If you do not use this immediately, place a piece of plastic wrap directly on the surface of the sauce to prevent a skin from forming.

5. In a medium-size bowl, blend the cottage cheese, ricotta and ¾ cup of the mozzarella. In a small bowl, blend the remaining mozzarella with the Parmesan cheese. This may be done ahead of time, covered and stored in the refrigerator for several hours.

6. Reduce the oven to 350 degrees F. Have a large pot of lightly salted boiling water ready and add the lasagna 7 to 9 minutes before you are ready to begin layering the ingredients.

7. Lightly coat an 11 x 7-inch baking dish with a thin film of vegetable spray or oil. When the pasta is done, drain and, working quickly, dip the strips of pasta in a bowl of cold water and drain on paper towels. Spread out the strips so they do not overlap or they will stick together.

8. Lay the pasta strips flat on the bottom of the prepared baking dish. Then create layers alternating the ingredients in the following order: vegetables, white sauce, cottage cheese mixture, grated cheeses, tomato sauce and another layer of pasta. Continue until all the ingredients are used. Finish with pasta, white sauce and a final sprinkling of mozzarella and Parmesan. It is not necessary to coat each layer thickly from corner to corner. If you dot the cheese and sauces uniformly, they will all melt together beautifully as the lasagna bakes. Bake for 35 to 40 minutes or until bubbly and golden. Cool briefly before serving.

❄ PER SERVING *Calories: 303, Cholesterol (mg): 16, Saturated fat (g): 3, Total fat (g): 6, Sodium (mg): 403, Total fiber (g): 5*

Sun-Dried Tomato Sauce
Makes 3½ cups, serving size ½ cup

Take advantage of an abundant tomato harvest to make enough of this sauce to carry you through the winter months. As a variation, you can add several cloves of roasted garlic instead of the fresh garlic clove for a deeper flavor. Make this sauce in double or triple batches and freeze in ice cube trays or half-cup portions and use to flavor soups, for pasta or chicken or to add to other sauces.

> 1 teaspoon olive oil
> 1 shallot
> 1 small garlic clove, minced
> 2 pounds fresh tomatoes
> 10 sun-dried tomatoes, softened in hot water to cover for 10 minutes
> 1 teaspoon fresh thyme or marjoram
> ½ teaspoon salt
> Freshly ground pepper

1. Preheat the oven to 400 degrees F. Heat the olive oil in a nonreactive large ovenproof skillet or small Dutch oven. Add the shallot and garlic and stir over low heat for 30 or 40 seconds until well coated with the oil. Place in the oven for 8 to 10 minutes or until the shallot and garlic are soft. Stir at least once during this time.

2. Slice the fresh tomatoes in half and squeeze out the seeds, then chop them coarsely. Add the fresh and dried tomatoes and remaining ingredients to the shallot mixture and cook over medium heat for 15 or 20 minutes or until the tomatoes are very soft, stirring occasionally. Purée in a blender or food processor and season to your taste with pepper and another pinch of salt if you wish. If you don't use it at once, freeze small amounts in ice cube trays, then pop out and store in a tightly sealed plastic bag.

❄ PER SERVING *Calories: 48, Cholesterol (mg): 0, Saturated fat (g): Trace, Total fat (g): 1, Sodium (mg): 207, Total fiber (g): 2*

Eggplant and Red Onion Pizza

MAKES 1 DOZEN 3-INCH SLICES, SERVING SIZE 1 SLICE

PIZZA REIGNS AS ONE OF AMERICA'S FAVORITE FOODS. *Loaded with the typical greasy meats and extra cheese, it also reigns as America's number one heartbreaker—unless you make one of our mouthwatering pies. When the gang calls for pizza, start with our Basic Pizza Dough (page 478–79), add a full-flavored tomato sauce as a base, get out your favorite low-fat toppings, such as the eggplant and chili suggestions that follow, and give them what they want.*

> 1 recipe Basic Pizza Dough (recipe follows)
> ¼ cup chopped oil-packed sun-dried tomatoes, drained
> ¼ cup shredded fresh basil leaves, loosely packed
> 1 cup shredded fresh spinach, loosely packed
> ¼ cup Mustard Vinaigrette (page 382–83)
> 1 red onion, sliced
> 3 Japanese eggplants, thinly sliced lengthwise
> Cornmeal for sprinkling dough
> ½ cup Tomato Pepper Purée (page 471) or other rich tomato sauce
> 1 ounce Parmesan cheese, finely grated (about ⅓ cup)

1. As directed in the recipe, prepare the pizza dough, allow it to rise and preheat the oven and pizza stone, if using; preheat the broiler or grill.

2. In a medium-size bowl, toss the sun-dried tomatoes, basil and spinach with 1 tablespoon of the Mustard Vinaigrette and marinate until ready to use.

3. Brush the onion and eggplant slices with the Mustard Vinaigrette and broil or grill for 5 minutes just until softened. Turn and broil the other side for 2 minutes. Watch them carefully so they do not burn.

4. Punch down and roll out the pizza dough as directed in recipe, and coat it with a light sprinkling of cornmeal. Brush the dough with the Tomato Pepper Purée and cover with the spinach mixture. Arrange the broiled eggplant and onions on top and sprinkle with the cheese. Bake as directed in the pizza dough recipe.

FAT TRACKING TIP: Substitute sun-dried tomatoes without oil and soften them in hot water.

❋ PER SERVING *Calories: 130, Cholesterol (mg): 2, Saturated fat (g): 1, Total fat (g): 4, Sodium (mg): 49, Total fiber (g): 1*

Basic Pizza Dough
Makes one 12- to 14-inch pizza crust, about 1 dozen 3-inch slices

The food processor takes all the work out of making pizza dough. Prepare several batches and freeze each after the first rising. Allow it to defrost and rise the second time before baking. Look for the designation "rapid rising yeast," as distinguished from active dry yeast, on the package. Rapid rising yeast also speeds up the preparation.

> 1 tablespoon rapid rising yeast
> ¾ cup lukewarm water
> 1 teaspoon sugar
> 2 cups unbleached all-purpose flour or bread flour,
>   plus extra for work surface
> 2 tablespoons olive oil, plus extra for bowl
> Cornmeal for work surface
> Vegetable spray for baking sheet

1. Combine the yeast, ½ cup of the lukewarm water, the sugar and ½ cup of the flour in the bowl of a food processor or heavy-duty electric mixer. Allow to rise in a warm place for 20 minutes.

2. If using a processor, when the yeast mixture is bubbly, add the olive oil and the ¼ cup lukewarm water and 1½ cups flour. Process until a smooth ball forms, 30 to 40 seconds. If using an electric mixer add the oil and remaining water to the yeast mixture and then gradually beat in the remaining flour until a smooth ball forms, about 1 minute.

3. Turn out the dough onto a lightly floured surface and knead by hand 10 times. Place in a large bowl lightly coated with olive oil, cover with a clean, damp cloth, and allow to rise until doubled in bulk, about an hour, depending on the amount of warmth in the rising area. Punch down and allow to double once more, 30 to 40 minutes.

4. If using a pizza stone, place it in a cold oven. Preheat the oven to 500 degrees.

5. Punch down the dough and form into a ball. With a rolling pin, roll out to a 12- to 14-inch circle on a surface coated with a little flour and cornmeal. Place the dough on a pizza peel or the underside of a baking sheet coated with a film of vegetable spray and dusted with cornmeal.

6. Dress the pizza with your choice of sauce and toppings and slide it in jerked motions onto the stone. (If you have difficulty getting the dough to slide onto the stone, you can bake the pizza on a baking sheet as described above, placing the sheet over the hot stone, which will help crisp the crust.) If you don't have a pizza stone simply place the baking sheet on the oven rack. After you have made pizza several times this technique will get easier. Cook for 15 to 20 minutes or until puffed and slide the pizza onto a serving platter. Slice and serve.

✽ PER SERVING (1 SLICE WITHOUT TOPPINGS) *Calories: 100, Cholesterol (mg): 0, Saturated fat (g): Trace, Total fat (g): 2, Sodium (mg): Trace, Total fiber (g): 1*

Black Bean Chili Pizza

MAKES 1 DOZEN 3-INCH SLICES

NEXT TIME YOU MAKE OUR BLACK BEAN CHILI, *freeze one cup to make this delicious pizza. You can also use Jazzed-Up Canned Black Beans.*

   1 recipe Basic Pizza Dough (recipe precedes)
   ½ cup Sun-Dried Tomato Sauce (page 476) or Tomato Pepper
      Purée (page 471)
   1 cup Black Bean Chili (page 428) or Jazzed-Up Canned Black
      Beans (page 427), well drained
   1 small red bell pepper, seeded and cut into matchsticks
   ½ cup thinly sliced red onion
   ¼ cup Cilantro Pesto (page 293)
   2 ounces reduced-fat Monterey Jack cheese, freshly shredded
      (about ⅔ cup)
   1 ounce reduced-fat mozzarella cheese, freshly shredded
      (about ⅓ cup)

1. As directed in the recipe, prepare the pizza dough, let it rise, preheat oven and pizza stone, punch down dough, roll it out to a circle and place on pizza wheel. (Steps 1 through 5.)

2. Brush the Sun-Dried Tomato Sauce in a circle to within 1 inch of the edge of the dough.

3. Chop the chili or drained canned beans in a blender or food processor until coarse but not puréed. Then spread on top of the sauce.

4. In a bowl, toss the red bell pepper and red onion in the Cilantro Pesto and spread on top of the chili. Drizzle any remaining pesto over the top. Sprinkle on the cheeses.

5. Bake as directed in Basic Pizza Dough.

❋ PER SERVING *Calories: 182, Cholesterol (mg): 2, Saturated fat (g): 1, Total fat (g): 8, Sodium (mg): 88, Total fiber (g): 2*

CHAPTER 36

Fish and Shellfish

IN THE DAYS OF FIFTEEN-COURSE DINNERS *at the turn of the century, fish bones invariably littered the route to the main course, a huge slab of meat. Always included but never the star attraction, oysters or trout, a stuffed fillet of sole or a whole lobster would whet gargantuan appetites, not satisfy them. We have weaned ourselves away from food orgies in the style of Diamond Jim Brady, humbled perhaps by his early demise at 61. (So prodigious was his appetite that some say he made it to that age only due to his lifelong habit of drinking barrelfuls of orange juice daily—not to mention downing dozens of oysters!) But today, sadly, some people have thrown out the fish with the baron of beef.*

The Stanford 25 Gram Plan urges you to put fish at the head of your menu—in place of, not in addition to, red meat. To sing the praises of fish as healthful—low in fat, negligible saturated fat, high in important omega-3 fatty acids—is not to detract from its pleasurable aspects. Flavors range from incomparably sweet—fresh mussels, delicate petrale sole, raw or rare-cooked ahi tuna—to robust—mackerel and anchovies. Nevertheless, some health-conscious fish lovers step warily around shellfish because of its high cholesterol levels. However, the saturated fat count is so low and omega-3 fatty acids are so abundant that you can welcome to your table all manner of crustaceans, mollusks, cephalopods and bivalves: clams, mussels, shrimp, lobster, abalone, crab, crayfish, squid and all their relatives.

We hear many people say, "I love fish, but I don't know how to cook it." Take it from us, fish could not be more user-friendly. All fish demand brief cooking times, so what could be more perfect for the harried cook? Actually, the trick to perfect fish lies in selecting it as much as cooking it. Find yourself a reliable fishmonger and follow his or her guidelines.

Tips on Buying and Cooking Fish and Shellfish

Select fish with clear eyes, a sweet but briny smell, and a smooth feel to flesh or skin and gills. Unpleasant odors and slimy texture signal fish past its prime; throw it out. Whenever possible choose fresh fish over frozen. Freezing (even the best method, freezing quickly at extremely low temperatures) wreaks havoc with the muscle fibers, rendering them dry and tough during cooking. Crustaceans, such as whole crab and lobster, are available either live (to be prepared at home) or already cooked. Discard as toxic any shelled creatures, such as clams and mussels, that are open before cooking or remain tightly closed after cooking. Like all fish, shellfish should have a bracing sea smell that is refreshing, not off-putting. Always make absolutely sure that fish or shellfish that you intend to eat raw is no more than 24 hours out of the water. The rule is: If in doubt, don't. If you are not sure about species to serve raw, as for sushi dishes, check with a reliable fish market in your area.

The cardinal rule for fish cooking is: Don't overcook it! This applies to all fish, regardless of any recipe that instructs to cook fish until it flakes. Overcooking dries out fish and toughens it. Small white pellets appear on the surface of overcooked fish, a sure sign to remove the fish from the heat immediately, not to remedy the damage—you can't—but to prevent further destruction. Perfectly cooked fish is opaque through to the center, the color of a frosted light bulb. Undercooked fish, on the other hand, is translucent with a jellied appearance. Slightly undercooked fish, however, is not a bad thing; it can continue to cook to perfection in its own heat as it travels from stove to table.

Some oily fish, such as tuna, are delicious served rare as beef, though you must take the same precautions as for raw fish: Make sure it is absolutely fresh. And even robust fish (such as tuna) are more delicately fleshed than land animals and require more temperate cooking. Don't throw them into a white hot frying pan (they don't benefit from searing and browning the way meat does) or have them too close to the coals on a grill. The old rule about cooking fish 10 minutes per inch of thickness is not quite accurate, but makes the point that the thicker the fish the longer the cooking time. How much longer will depend on the size of your particular species.

A fish on the fire can tolerate a certain amount of poking to test for doneness. Insert the tip of a knife in the center of a fillet or next to the bone. If you can just separate the layers without their falling apart, the flesh appears uniformly white with perhaps just a strip of slightly undercooked meat, and if the fish is springy to the touch, like the pad of your thumb, not the back of your hand, it is done. Test it quickly with the tip of your finger or with the flat blade of a knife. More specific times are included in the recipes. Times vary for species, but generally, serve shellfish either raw if you like, as for clams and oysters, or fully cooked rather than rare, though not overcooked, or it will turn rubbery.

Sea Bass Grilled with Cilantro and Jalapeño Marinade

SERVES 6

WHITE SEA BASS, *closely related to grouper, is extremely low in fat, leaner even than black sea bass, which is also an excellent choice. Try this peppery oil-free marinade on scallops or salmon, as well. If your food philosophy is the hotter the better, use serrano chilies instead of jalapeño. On the other hand, if you have fragile taste buds, choose the relatively cooler banana (yellow wax) chilies. Reserve 1/3 of the prepared marinade to brush on the grilled fish just before serving to heighten the flavor, as the heat may dull some of the jalapeño's fire.*

1 1/2 pounds sea bass steaks or fillets

JALAPEÑO MARINADE
1/4 cup white wine
1/4 cup white vinegar
1/2 teaspoon salt
Pinch of sugar
1 small garlic clove, minced
1 green onion, diced
3 tablespoons minced fresh cilantro
2 fresh jalapeño peppers, seeded and diced

Salad greens
Slivered green onions and sprigs of fresh cilantro for garnish

1. Rinse and dry the fish and place it in a nonreactive baking dish.

2. Combine the marinade ingredients in a covered jar and shake thoroughly. Reserve 1/3 of the marinade in a separate bowl, cover and refrigerate until serving time. Pour the remaining marinade over the fish, turning the sea bass to coat it thoroughly. Cover and refrigerate for at least 30 minutes and up to several hours.

3. Prepare the grill as directed on page 264. When the coals are ready, place the fish in a hinged grilling basket. Arrange the greens on a platter, then grill the sea bass 3 to 4 minutes on each side, depending on its thickness. Brush it often with the marinade to keep it moist. Arrange the grilled fish on the greens and drizzle with the reserved marinade. Scatter the green onions and cilantro over the sea bass before serving.

❋ PER SERVING *Calories: 117, Cholesterol (mg): 45, Saturated fat (g): 1, Total fat (g): 2, Sodium (mg): 259, Total fiber (g): 0*

Grilled Prawns with Spiced Fresh Plum Sauce

SERVES 4

WE PAINT THIS FAT-FREE MARINADE ON PRAWNS, *but chicken or turkey breast would also benefit from a coating of this tart plum sauce before grilling. The variety of plum you use determines the relative sweetness of the sauce. Leave the skins on; they all but disintegrate as they cook. Leftover sauce (which has not touched fish or poultry) will keep covered and refrigerated for a week. This recipe doubles easily if you are cooking for a larger crowd. Steamed basmati rice (page 439) and Warm Broccoli, Orange and Walnut Salad with Walnut Vinaigrette (page 384–85) complete a favorite summer menu. For one pound of unshelled prawns you need only buy two or three extra ounces. Unlike other shellfish such as clams or crab, the shells are quite thin and weigh very little.*

SPICED FRESH PLUM SAUCE
1 pound firm, fresh purple or red plums, pitted and chopped
¼ cup red wine
2 tablespoons red wine vinegar
¼ cup fresh orange juice
1 teaspoon grated orange zest
½ cup loosely packed brown sugar
¼ cup minced green onion
2 tablespoons minced fresh ginger or 1 teaspoon ground ginger
⅛ teaspoon cayenne
Pinch of salt

1 pound shelled and deveined raw prawns (see preceding note)

1. To make the plum sauce, place all the sauce ingredients in a nonreactive saucepan and bring to a boil. Reduce the heat and simmer gently for 1 hour or until the sauce is syrupy. Stir from time to time. Makes approximately 1 cup. Reserve half the sauce, cover and chill until serving time.

2. Prepare the grill as directed on page 264. Place the prawns in a shallow bowl. Brush the remaining sauce on the prawns; cover and refrigerate them for at least 15 minutes or up to 3 hours. Shake as much excess sauce from the prawns as possible; a too-thick coating of a sweet sauce invites the flames to flare up and scorch the sugar (and anything else it clings to) more than is desirable. Place the prawns in a hinged grill basket and grill them from 3 to 5 minutes, turning them frequently. As soon as they turn pink, remove them from the grill. Glaze the prawns lightly with the reserved sauce and divide the remainder of the chilled sauce equally among the servings.

✳ PER SERVING *Calories: 271, Cholesterol (mg): 166, Saturated fat (g): Trace, Total fat (g): 2, Sodium (mg): 211, Total fiber (g): 3*

Grilled Lemon-Pepper Monkfish
and Lemon-Garlic Rouille

SERVES 6

THE SPICY ROUILLE OF PROVENCE, *thickened with bread crumbs, inspired our lemon and garlic sauce. Made without the traditional egg yolks, it still has a creamy mayonnaiselike texture and happily is free of cholesterol. Add more or less garlic as you desire, though the delicious monkfish is robust enough to handle a potent sauce (you can substitute bass, snapper or other firm-fleshed cold water fish). You will no doubt find many uses for this intriguing bright and quick sauce: as a spread on cold chicken or turkey sandwiches, as a dip with Oven-Baked Tortilla Chips or as a topping for lightly steamed vegetables. Leftover sauce will keep up to the expiration date of the yogurt. Expect more than usual shrinkage from monkfish (which, like snapper, is exceedingly low in fat), and increase the portion size accordingly. Don't use stale bread or bread crumbs in this recipe or the texture will be grainy; remove the crusts if they are too hard and add another small slice of soft bread.*

LEMON-GARLIC ROUILLE
3 or more garlic cloves, minced
4 thick slices fresh French or Italian bread (see note above)
    torn into small pieces
½ cup fresh Italian parsley leaves
1 tablespoon white wine vinegar
2 tablespoons fresh lemon juice
½ teaspoon salt or to taste
⅓ cup extra-virgin olive oil
1 cup nonfat plain yogurt
Salt and freshly ground pepper
1 tablespoon fresh orange juice
1 tablespoon cold water, optional

1½ pounds monkfish fillets
Juice of 1 lemon
1 teaspoon white pepper
Lemon slices and dill sprigs for garnish

1. To make the rouille, place the garlic, bread, parsley, vinegar, lemon juice and salt in a blender or food processor and process until crumbly. With the machine running, drizzle in the olive oil. Continue processing until you have a smooth paste.

2. Place the sauce in a small serving bowl and stir small amounts of the yogurt into it until you have a smooth mixture. Season to your taste with salt and pepper, and stir in the orange juice. Taste and if you find that it is too tart, stir in the cold water. Cover and chill until serving time. This may be made several hours ahead.

3. Prepare the grill as directed on page 264. Rinse and dry the fish. Sprinkle with the lemon juice and pepper and place in a hinged grill basket. Grill the fillets 4 to 6 minutes per side, depending on their thickness, until firm and opaque at the center. Arrange the cooked monkfish on a serving platter and garnish with lemon slices and sprigs of dill. Serve with a spoonful of Lemon-Garlic Rouille and pass the remaining sauce separately.

FAT TRACKING TIP: Use a small serving of Lemon-Garlic Rouille.

❀ PER SERVING (INCLUDES 3 TABLESPOONS LEMON-GARLIC ROUILLE) *Calories: 263, Cholesterol (mg): 28, Saturated fat (g): 2, Total fat (g): 14, Sodium (mg): 343, Total fiber (g): 0*

Grilled Halibut with Cherry Tomato Salsa
SERVES 6

OF COURSE FAT TRACKERS EAT STEAK. *Especially when it is rich, lean and moist such as halibut, considered by many to be aquatic royalty. You can use your favorite salsa recipe or a good commercial fresh salsa here, but we like this mild, but well-seasoned, relish, made with cherry tomatoes. Look for tomatillas at Latino markets or some supermarkets. You will recognize them by the husk that covers the small, tomatolike fruit. If you can't locate them, substitute green tomatoes (sometimes even harder to come by unless you have access to a vegetable garden) or double the cherry tomatoes. The salsa will not have quite the same refreshing tartness, however.*

CHERRY TOMATO SALSA
½ pound tomatillos
1 tablespoon extra-virgin olive oil
½ cup chopped onion
3 garlic cloves, minced
1 green bell pepper, seeded and diced
3 tablespoons cold water
½ pound cherry tomatoes
½ teaspoon ground cumin
1 tablespoon or more fresh lime juice
Salt and freshly ground pepper
½ cup minced fresh cilantro

1½ pounds halibut steaks
1 tablespoon lime juice
½ teaspoon ground cumin
Freshly ground black pepper

1. Remove and discard the husks from the tomatillos. Wash them in cold water, then quarter them, cutting larger pieces in half again.

2. Heat the oil in a nonreactive medium-size skillet and add the onion, garlic and green pepper. Stir 2 to 3 minutes, or just until the onion begins to wilt. If the pan dries out, add water by the tablespoon to provide enough liquid to cook the vegetables. Add the tomatillos, cherry tomatoes, cumin, 1 tablespoon lime juice and season to your taste with salt and pepper. Raise the heat just until the salsa begins to bubble, then reduce the heat and simmer for 10 to 12 minutes or until the vegetables are soft. Taste, adding more lime juice if desired. When the salsa has cooled slightly, stir in the cilantro and place in a small serving bowl. Cover and chill thoroughly. You can prepare this up to 24 hours before serving.

3. Prepare the grill as directed on page 264. Rinse and dry the halibut. Blend the remaining lime juice, cumin and lots of pepper and rub both sides of each steak with this mixture. You may do this several hours ahead and cover and refrigerate the fish until serving time. Place the halibut in a hinged grill basket and grill the halibut 5 to 8 minutes per side or until it is firm but not flaking. Arrange the fish on a serving platter and surround with the salsa. Serve while the fish is still hot, dividing the salsa equally for each portion.

❋ PER SERVING *Calories: 174, Cholesterol (mg): 35, Saturated fat (g): 1, Total fat (g): 5, Sodium (mg): 67, Total fiber (g): 1*

Stir-Fried Snapper with Ginger and Peppers

SERVES 4

TART AND GINGERY, *this pungent dish has great color. Notice also the low calorie count (165) for this entrée. Snapper is extremely lean and we use a combination of oil and water for frying, rather than the large quantities of oil some stir-fry recipes insist you need. Slice the peppers very thin so they will cook quickly and serve steamed rice to absorb the tangy sauce.*

2 tablespoons dry sherry
1 tablespoon light soy sauce
3 tablespoons cold water
1/4 teaspoon Asian sesame oil
2 teaspoons red wine vinegar
1/2 teaspoon salt
1/2 teaspoon sugar
1 teaspoon cornstarch
1 tablespoon peanut oil
1 red bell pepper, seeded and thinly sliced
6 green onions, slivered
2 teaspoons minced fresh ginger
1 pound red snapper fillets, cut into 2-inch slices
2 tablespoons finely chopped fresh cilantro

1. Blend the sherry, soy sauce, 1 tablespoon of the water, sesame oil, vinegar, salt and sugar in a small bowl. Blend the cornstarch with a tablespoon of the water until well mixed; set aside.

2. Heat the oil and 1 more tablespoon water in a wok or skillet and add the red pepper, green onions and ginger. Toss them over high heat for 2 minutes. Add a little more of the remaining cold water if necessary to keep the pan moist. Add the red snapper and cook 2 to 4 minutes or until the fish is white and firm. Do not allow the snapper to cook to the point of flaking, as it will continue to cook as the sauce progresses.

3. Add the sauce mixture and toss gently for 15 seconds. Stir the cornstarch mixture for a moment until it is again well blended and add it to the fish, stirring constantly and turning the snapper for about 1 minute or until the sauce thickens, the fish is cooked through and the vegetables glisten. Arrange the fish on a serving platter and spoon the vegetables and sauce over it. Sprinkle with the cilantro and serve while still hot.

❋ PER SERVING *Calories: 165, Cholesterol (mg): 40, Saturated fat (g): 1, Total fat (g): 5, Sodium (mg): 472, Total fiber (g): 0*

Poached Red Snapper
with a Purée of Peas and Tangerines
SERVES 6

WHEN THE WINTER HARVEST *sends honey tangerines to the market, use their juice to poach snapper and add sparkle to the accompanying bright green purée. Serve with fettuccine moistened with a little olive oil, basmati rice or steamed red potatoes and a huge salad of greens burgeoning with crisp green beans, white beans, lightly steamed carrots, and shredded red cabbage dressed with Mustard Vinaigrette (page 382–83).*

PEA AND TANGERINE PURÉE
1¼ cup fresh or frozen (without butter or salt) baby green peas
¼ cup chopped green onions
½ cup freshly squeezed tangerine juice
2½ tablespoons extra-virgin olive oil or canola oil
½ teaspoon salt
⅛ teaspoon white pepper
Fish stock, water or nonfat milk, optional
Salt and freshly ground pepper

1 cup Rich Fish Stock (page 287) or water
¼ cup white wine
½ cup freshly squeezed tangerine juice
Large pinch each of fresh thyme and Italian parsley
1 yellow onion, sliced
1½ pound snapper fillets

1. As directed on page 266–67, steam or microwave the peas for 2 minutes or until they are cooked through, tender but not mushy. If you cover the peas, do not re-cover the pot once you have lifted the lid to check them or they will darken and sabotage the brilliant color of the purée.

2. Drain the peas, place in a blender or food processor and purée with the remaining purée ingredients. If the purée is too thick, add some fish stock, water or nonfat skim milk to thin it to a smooth consistency. Season to your taste with salt and pepper. Reheat briefly if necessary, uncovered.

3. Place the fish stock in a large, nonreactive skillet with the remaining ingredients, except the snapper. Bring to a boil, reduce the heat and simmer for 5 minutes. Add the snapper and raise the heat slightly to maintain a gentle simmer. Continue cooking for 5 minutes or until the fish is white and firm to the touch. Do not overcook and reduce the heat if the liquid begins to boil.

4. Arrange the snapper on individual plates and spoon a little of the cooking liquid over them. Divide the purée into 6 portions, mound on top of fish and serve immediately.

❀ PER SERVING *Calories: 205, Cholesterol (mg): 40, Saturated fat (g): 1, Total fat (g): 7, Sodium (mg): 228, Total fiber (g): 1*

🌿

Poached Salmon with Spiced Melon Sauce

SERVES 6

WHEN MELONS ARE FAT AND SWEET *and the weather is hot and sticky, serve this chilled, creamy but essentially fat-free sauce on fresh salmon. You can serve the salmon cold or grill it outside to keep your kitchen cool as you prepare this simple and spectacular dish. For variation, use cucumbers instead of melon or coat chicken breasts or snapper with the sauce. Serve with grilled summer vegetables and garlic bread.*

> ¼ small to medium-size honeydew melon
> 1 cup Spiced Yogurt (page 291)
> 4 cups Rich Fish Stock (page 287) *or* 2 cups cold water
>   *and* 2 cups bottled clam juice
> 1 onion, coarsely chopped
> 1 large bunch fresh parsley
> 1 small bay leaf
> Pinch of saffron, optional
> 1½ pounds salmon fillets

1. Scrape away the seeds of the melon and cut the pulp from the rind. Purée the pulp in a food processor or blender (the hand processor does not work well here) until it is as smooth as possible; the mixture will be coarse but you should not have any chunks of melon. In a small bowl, stir the melon into the yogurt and chill until serving time. Alternatively, you can purée the melon several hours ahead, then cover and refrigerate it until you need it. Just before serving, drain any excess moisture from the melon, and stir the Spiced Yogurt into the purée.

2. In a large skillet, bring the fish stock to a boil, add the onion, parsley, bay leaf and saffron (if you are using it) and reduce the heat. Simmer for at least 15 minutes. This can also be made ahead and refrigerated until it is time to poach the salmon.

3. Add the salmon to the hot stock and immediately reduce the heat to a simmer. Do not allow it to boil. Simmer uncovered for approximately 8 minutes or until the salmon is firm and the center is uniformly pink (in contrast to undercooked salmon, which has a jellied appearance). Spoon a little of the melon sauce on individual serving plates. Arrange the salmon on top of the sauce and spoon the remainder over the salmon. Serve immediately.

FAT TRACKING TIP: Serve small portions of the Spiced Yogurt.

❋ PER SERVING *Calories: 220, Cholesterol (mg): 43, Saturated fat (g): 2, Total fat (g): 10, Sodium (mg): 199, Total fiber (g): 1*

Cilantro Citrus Prawns

SERVES 4

PRAWNS POACHED IN A TANGY CITRUS BATH *crown sweet basmati rice. The sauce looks innocent too, with its sunny colors of saffron and red pepper—until the surprise burst of Cajun warmth hits and gently settles on your taste buds like the afterglow of a sunset. Don't skimp on the cilantro or you will probably say, "It's good, but something's missing." If you find the Cajun Seasoning too intense, use less.*

CITRUS SAUCE
1 cup fresh orange juice
¼ cup white wine
¼ cup chopped green onion
¼ cup diced and seeded red or yellow bell pepper
2 teaspoons or more diced and seeded fresh jalapeño pepper
2 slices (the size of a quarter) fresh ginger, minced
½ teaspoon *each* grated orange and lime zest
Pinch of sugar
Salt and freshly ground pepper
1 teaspoon Cajun Seasoning (page 496), more or less as desired,
    or a generous pinch of cayenne

1 pound prawns, shelled and deveined
2 cups cooked basmati rice (page 439)
3 tablespoons *each* minced fresh mint and cilantro

1. Combine the sauce ingredients (except salt, pepper and Cajun Seasoning) in a medium-size saucepan and bring to a boil. Reduce the heat and simmer for 15 or 20 minutes. Do not allow the mixture to evaporate. It should bubble very slowly. Season to your taste with salt and pepper and Cajun Seasoning.

2. Add the prawns and bring to a boil. Reduce the heat and simmer for 5 to 8 minutes, depending on their size, or until they turn bright pink. Do not overcook the prawns or they will become rubbery.

3. Place the rice on a serving platter, arrange the prawns on top and spoon the sauce over them. Sprinkle with the mint and cilantro and serve immediately.

❋ PER SERVING *Calories: 245, Cholesterol (mg): 175, Saturated fat (g): Trace, Total fat (g): 2, Sodium (mg): 234, Total fiber (g): 1*

Coquilles Provençal

SERVES 4

THIS PRESENTATION OF SCALLOPS *remains anchored in French tradition, but unlike the coquilles usually blanketed under a cream and butter sauce, these are given the flavors of Provence—garlic, tomatoes, a mix of onions and a distinctive curl of orange zest. Different from the haute cuisine treatment, but equally special, they have much less cholesterol and saturated fat. Each serving works out to approximately 30 percent fat. Serve with hot crusty bread.*

> 3 cups cooked basmati rice (page 439)
> 3 tablespoons extra-virgin olive oil
> 1 large yellow onion, sliced
> 1 bunch green onions, chopped
> 1 leek, chopped
> 1 shallot, chopped
> 3 garlic cloves, minced
> ¼ cup white wine
> 3 tomatoes, peeled, seeded and chopped
> 1-inch strip of orange zest
> ¼ cup minced fresh parsley
> Salt and freshly ground pepper
> Juice of 1 lemon
> 1 pound sea scallops

1. Prepare the rice and let it stand at least 15 minutes. While the rice cooks, heat the olive oil in a large nonreactive skillet. Add the yellow and green onions, leek, shallot and garlic and sauté over low to medium heat until soft and transparent.

2. Add the wine to the skillet, raise the heat slightly and boil until the wine has reduced to about 1 tablespoon. Add all the remaining ingredients except the scallops. Simmer gently for 10 to 15 minutes or until the tomatoes have softened.

3. Add the scallops and cook for 5 minutes or until they are white and firm, but do not overcook, or they will become rubbery.

4. Just before serving, discard the orange zest, taste the scallops and adjust the seasoning if necessary. Uncover and fluff the rice with a fork. Serve the rice on individual plates and spoon the scallops and sauce over it.

❋ PER SERVING *Calories: 354, Cholesterol (mg): 45, Saturated fat (g): 1, Total fat (g): 12, Sodium (mg): 243, Total fiber (g): 3*

New England Fish Cakes and Tartar Sauce

SERVES 4

IN FISHING COMMUNITIES ALONG THE EASTERN SEABOARD, *fish cakes and crab cakes are a staple. They are a happy addition to inland menus as well, especially our version which is moistened with some mayonnaise but cooked in a minimum of oil to offset the total fat in the recipe. If you have them on hand, leftover cooked potatoes and/or fish that has been previously seasoned will give your fish cakes more character. (We prefer russet potatoes, small creamer or Yellow Finns for their fluffy, cooked texture.) Because the amount of moisture in the fish and potatoes will determine the precise amount of yogurt and mayonnaise you will need, add the latter in small increments until you have a mixture that you can form easily into cakes. The patties shouldn't fall apart in your hand as they would be difficult to maneuver as they cook. Nor should they be too stiff (they flip easily in a skillet but are not as light and delicate tasting). Use trout, sole, salmon, cod or other firm-fleshed, but not oily, fish.*

> 1½ cups cooked firm-fleshed fish (see above)
> 1 pound russet potatoes, peeled and sliced, or cooked potatoes
> ¼ cup minced green onion
> 2 tablespoons Chicken Stock (page 285–86) or Rich Fish Stock
>   (page 287) or bottled clam juice
> 1 tablespoon whole-grain Dijon mustard
> Up to ⅓ cup *each* nonfat plain yogurt and low-fat mayonnaise
>   (see instructions before adding)
> 1 cup dry bread crumbs
> Salt and freshly ground pepper
> 2 tablespoons extra-virgin olive oil
> ¼ cup Tartar Sauce (recipe follows) or Spiced Yogurt (page 291)

1. In a large mixing bowl, break up the cooked fish with a fork until it is finely flaked.

2. Steam the potatoes until they are very soft, about 8 to 10 minutes. Put the potatoes through a ricer. If you are using leftover potatoes, mash them thoroughly.

3. Gently mash the potatoes and onions into the fish with a fork until you have a coarse, dense mixture. Don't aim for a perfectly puréed texture.

4. Add the chicken or fish stock and mustard. And then add, a tablespoon at a time, equal amounts of yogurt and mayonnaise until you have a light and workable texture. If you have finished assembling the cake mixture and find it is too loose, add just enough of the bread crumbs until the mixture is manageable. Season lightly with salt, heavily with pepper.

5. Spread the remaining bread crumbs in a shallow bowl. With your hands, form patties of the fish mixture, 2½ inches in diameter and about ½ inch thick. Dredge the patties in the bread crumbs, coating them completely. You can make the cakes up to this point; then cover and refrigerate them for several hours.

6. In a medium-size skillet, heat 1 tablespoon of the olive oil and add half the cakes. Cook them about 1 to 2 minutes on each side or until they are steaming and golden on both sides. Remove them to a serving platter to keep warm and cook the second batch. (A larger skillet may accommodate all the cakes at once.) Serve immediately plain or with Tartar Sauce or Spiced Yogurt.

FAT TRACKING TIPS: Cook them in less oil or use vegetable spray. Use nonfat mayonnaise.

✿ PER SERVING (INCLUDES 1 TABLESPOON TARTAR SAUCE) *Calories: 478, Cholesterol (mg): 62, Saturated fat (g): 2, Total fat (g): 15, Sodium (mg): 428, Total fiber (g): 3*

Tartar Sauce
Makes approximately 1¾ cups, serving size 1 tablespoon

Tartar sauce often comes as a fast mix of equal parts pickle relish and bottled mayonnaise, plunked down in a paper container as a dunk for greasy fried fish (and often equally greasy fried potatoes). But with a few quick additions to a blend of mayonnaise (preferably homemade) and yogurt, you can enjoy a superior version of this favorite condiment on any grilled firm-fleshed fish, with far fewer grams of fat. If you wish, you can alter the mix of mayonnaise and yogurt to reduce the fat content even more, blending ¼ cup mayonnaise with ¾ cup low-fat or nonfat yogurt. Use sweet or sour pickles as you prefer. You can serve this tartar sauce immediately, but the flavor improves if you assemble and chill it several hours ahead.

> ½ cup low-fat mayonnaise
> ½ cup nonfat plain yogurt or Drained Yogurt (page 290–91)
> ½ cup finely chopped sweet gherkins or dill pickle
> 2 tablespoons minced shallots or green onion
> 2 tablespoons minced fresh Italian parsley
> 1 tablespoon minced fresh herbs (such as basil
>   or tarragon) or 1 teaspoon dried
> 1 tablespoon capers
> 1 tablespoon fresh lemon juice
> 2 teaspoons Dijon mustard
> Large pinch of cayenne
> Salt and freshly ground pepper to your taste

Combine the mayonnaise and yogurt in a small bowl until smooth. Stir in the pickles, onions and remaining sauce ingredients. Blend well, transfer to a serving bowl, then cover and refrigerate for several hours if possible. This makes approximately 1½ cups.

FAT TRACKING TIP: Use low-fat or nonfat mayonnaise.

❈ PER SERVING *Calories: 20, Cholesterol (mg): 1, Saturated fat (g): Trace, Total fat (g): 1, Sodium (mg): 51, Total fiber (g): Trace*

Spicy Grilled Scallops with Hot Melon Salsa
SERVES 4

THE ELEGANT SCALLOP SHELL *has become a cultural icon, inspiring works of art from Botticelli's paintings to Philadelphia's Early American furniture to a modern oil company's logo. Inside the beautiful fan-shaped shell is a muscle that the scallop uses to propel itself through cold waters, making it especially lean and healthful and inspiring several of our own artful dishes. Here we emulate the crusty succulence of panfried fish by coating scallops (or any other delicate fish) with our zesty Cajun coating before grilling or broiling them. Not just a source of heat, this coating has as much flavor as it does flame, and the cooling salsa is a comfort after the fiery scallops. Instead of the hot salsa, however, you can serve slices of fresh chilled melon brushed with Cilantro Pesto (page 293). Serve with grilled red potatoes, ears of fresh corn, a simple green salad and, of course, hot, crusty bread. Note that the Cajun Seasoning is high in sodium. However, although you add a full recipe to the coating, not all of it will cling to the scallops. We have adjusted the calculations to reflect the amount you will consume.*

Hot Melon Salsa (recipe follows)

CAJUN COATING
Cajun Seasoning (recipe follows)
½ teaspoon grated lemon zest
1 teaspoon fresh lemon juice
1 tablespoon extra-virgin olive oil
2 to 3 tablespoons cold water

1 pound sea scallops
Wooden skewers soaked in cold water
Salt

1. Prepare the melon salsa and chill. Prepare the grill as directed on page 264.

2. In a small bowl, blend the coating ingredients and stir with just enough water to make a paste that clings easily to the scallops.

3. Cut large scallops into 1- to 1½-inch pieces and place them in a shallow bowl. Pour the coating mixture over them, turning them until they are completely coated. Thread the scallops on skewers and grill 4 to 6 minutes or until they are firm and white in the center. Do not overcook them or they will become rubbery. With a fork, gently nudge the scallops off the skewers and arrange them on a serving platter. Take a pinch of salt between your fingers and sprinkle a few grains over the scallops, but don't overdo it; they don't need very much salt at this point, just enough to marry the flavors of the spices and juices of the scallops. Pass the Hot Melon Salsa separately.

✿ PER SERVING (INCLUDES ½ CUP HOT MELON SALSA) *Calories: 168, Cholesterol (mg): 45, Saturated fat (g): Trace, Total fat (g): 5, Sodium (mg): 498, Total fiber (g): 1*

Cajun Seasoning
Makes about 3 tablespoons, serving size 1 teaspoon

Don't be alarmed by the excessively high sodium count. Remember that the seasoning gets diluted in a larger recipe and, like salt, the actual amount you consume per serving is much, much less.

> 2 teaspoons paprika
> 1 teaspoon salt
> 1 teaspoon *each* garlic powder and onion powder (do not use onion or garlic salt)
> 1 tablespoon *each* fresh thyme and oregano or 1 teaspoon dried
> 1 teaspoon finely minced fresh basil
> ½ teaspoon cayenne
> ¼ teaspoon *each* ground cinnamon and white pepper
> 1 teaspoon grated lemon zest

Blend all of the ingredients and store in a tightly covered container.

✿ PER SERVING *Calories: 4, Cholesterol (mg): 0, Saturated fat (g): 0, Total fat (g): 0, Sodium (mg): 252, Total fiber (g): 0*

Hot Melon Salsa
Makes approximately 2 cups, serving size 1 tablespoon

On hot days, serve this with cold or grilled poultry or tuck it into the pocket of a pita for a quick, snappy snack. You can increase the crunch by adding ¼ cup finely diced celery, cucumber and/or jícama. This salsa will keep for several days covered and refrigerated.

> ½ small honeydew or other melon (not cantaloupe)
> 1 small green or red bell pepper, seeded and diced
> ¼ cup diced green onions
> Juice of ½ lime

Juice of 1 orange
2 tablespoons raspberry vinegar or white wine vinegar
1/2 small, fresh jalapeño, seeded and finely diced
1/4 cup minced fresh basil, Italian parsley or cilantro
Salt and freshly ground pepper

1. Cut the melon into quarters, remove seeds and trim away the rind. Finely dice the melon and place it in a small bowl.

2. Add the remaining ingredients, toss thoroughly and season to your taste with salt and pepper. Cover and chill until serving time.

✿ PER SERVING *Calories: 4, Cholesterol (mg): 0, Saturated fat (g): 0, Total fat (g): 0, Sodium (mg): 0, Total fiber (g): Trace*

Snapper en Papillotte with Tomatoes, Cilantro and Lime-Speckled Rice
SERVES 6

COOKING FISH en papillote *(tightly wrapped in parchment paper or foil), steams the fish and requires no fat. The seasoning comes from the additions you tuck inside the packet; quick-cooking combinations work best. Also, choose mixtures that retain the sea-fresh taste of the fish, such as the tomato and lime combination we use here, which keeps snapper, flounder, sole or salmon sweet and tender. If you want a change of taste on some occasions, substitute parsley and lemon for cilantro and lime. Be sure to dunk crusty French bread in the wonderfully flavored broth.*

3 cups cooked basmati rice (page 439)
1/2 teaspoon grated lime zest
1 1/2 pounds red snapper fillet, cut into 6 equal portions
2 large garlic cloves, minced
6 green onions, chopped
Juice of 2 limes
Salt and freshly ground pepper
1 pound tomatoes, seeded and chopped
1/2 cup fresh cilantro leaves
Chopped fresh cilantro for garnish

1. Prepare the rice and allow it to stand for at least 15 minutes. Uncover and fluff the rice with a fork. Stir in the grated zest.

2. While the rice cooks, preheat the oven to 400 degrees F. Cut 6 pieces of parchment paper or aluminum foil large enough to wrap around individual portions of the fish and vegetables, including an edge of about 1 inch to fold over and provide a tight seal.

3. Place 1 portion of snapper on each piece of parchment or foil. Scatter the garlic and onions over the fish, squeeze the lime juice over everything, then season to your taste with salt and pepper. Dot with the tomatoes and cilantro. Bring the edges of the packet together and fold down at least twice to seal the edges tightly.

4. Place a small amount of water in the bottom of a 9 x 3-inch baking dish to prevent the bottom of the dish from scorching, and add the fish packets. Bake for 20 minutes.

5. Place the rice on individual plates and garnish with the fresh cilantro. Add the fish packet. Instruct each person to open the packet carefully to avoid the initial burst of steam, then inhale the fragrance before spooning the broth over the rice.

❋ PER SERVING *Calories: 191, Cholesterol (mg): 40, Saturated fat (g): Trace, Total fat (g): 2, Sodium (mg): 58, Total fiber (g): 1*

CHAPTER 37

Poultry

BRILLAT-SAVARIN, *the 19th-century French philosopher of food and manners,*
wrote that "poultry is to the cook, what canvas is to the painter." Chicken is
the invalid's restorative, the breadwinner's day-before-payday salvation, the
imaginative cook's inspiration and, of course, the Fat Tracker's mainstay. For a
heart-healthy source of protein, look to white meat of poultry to replace frequent
servings of red meat. Dark poultry meat, on the other hand, contains almost as
much saturated fat as red meat and should be restricted to twice-a-week entrées.
Duck and goose, even skimmed of the rivers of fat that ooze forth during cooking,
must remain occasional treats. Wild game, deprived of the pampering that ten-
derizes and fattens domestic birds, tends to be well muscled and, therefore, lower
both in cholesterol and fat.

But instead of always relying on the ubiquitous chicken, turn to turkey, especially white meat, which is the leanest of the lean. No longer do you have to buy
the whole bird when all you want is turkey with just a few of the trimmings. Whole
and sliced turkey breasts, as well as other parts, are now widely available, and for
small families or singles, are a smart alternative to cooking a huge turkey and facing
a week of leftovers. Recipes for chicken breast are numerous, but turkey recipes don't
receive as much attention. For that reason, we have showcased turkey dishes, and as
a boon to the harried cook, most of them are quick fixes. But in fact, recipes for
any white meat poultry are interchangeable, so use chicken or turkey as your taste
dictates. For recipes calling for ground turkey, we recommend that, if possible, you
buy ground breast meat with 1 percent fat or grind it yourself in a food processor
or meat grinder. Commercially packaged ground turkey meat often has lots of fat
and fatty dark meat added.

Remove all fat and skin from poultry before serving and ideally before cooking, except, of course, when you cook whole birds. Regardless of the size of your bird, for the purpose of the nutritional calculations, we have assumed a serving size of 3.5 cooked ounces.

Poultry Safety Tips

It is common knowledge these days that large-scale poultry production practices promote the spread of bacteria among birds. To prevent the spread of salmonella or other bacteria, we offer the following important tips. We urge you to follow them whenever you cook and handle poultry.

- As you prepare poultry for cooking, do not allow raw meat and skin to come in contact with serving pieces or dinnerware before cooking. Spread plenty of paper towels or other disposable covering on your work surface and discard after use. Wash with hot, soapy water all knives, utensils, cutting surfaces, sink and counter areas and any bowls or containers that have been used to store or marinate raw poultry. And wash your hands after touching it.
- Discard any marinade used on uncooked poultry because it will contaminate anything else it touches. We recommend that if you want to use a marinade as a sauce or baste poultry with it after cooking, separate and reserve some marinade for that use. If you brush marinade on poultry as it grills or broils, remember that you are applying possibly contaminated marinade on cooked, healthy food. Allow food to cook thoroughly after the last application.
- Store poultry below 40 degrees F and no longer than 1 to 2 days before cooking. Refrigerate 3 to 4 days except when covered with broth or gravy, then use in 1 to 2 days.

<hr/>

Herb Crusted Oven-Fried Chicken

SERVES 6

SEVERAL ELEMENTS MAKE THIS *a highly successful dish. First, the chicken marinates in yogurt, which tenderizes it. A highly seasoned mix of herbs, spices and cheese guarantees rich flavor. And finally, it has all of the crusty deliciousness of fried chicken with a fraction of the fat. Be sure to cook the chicken on a rack; it allows the heat to circulate around the pieces and crisp them. Remember that because of the dark meat in the chicken, we recommend you include this as one of your 2 + 2 entrées when you plan your weekly meals.*

COATING MIX

3/4 cup nonfat plain yogurt
1 teaspoon grated lemon zest
1/4 cup fresh lemon juice
1 teaspoon olive oil
2 shallots, minced
1 tablespoon *each* minced fresh oregano, thyme and Italian parsley
1/2 teaspoon salt
Freshly ground pepper to your taste
1/2 teaspoon cayenne
Pinch of ground cinnamon

1 chicken (3 to 4 pounds), cut up with all skin and fat removed
2/3 cup yellow cornmeal
1/2 cup coarse bread crumbs
1/3 ounce Parmesan cheese, freshly and finely grated (about 1/4 cup)
3 egg whites
2 tablespoons ice water
Juice of 1/2 lemon

1. Combine the ingredients for the coating mix in a bowl and blend thoroughly.

2. Arrange the chicken in a shallow dish in one layer. Cover with the coating mixture and turn the pieces until they are thoroughly coated. Cover and refrigerate for at least 4 hours or overnight if desired.

3. Blend the cornmeal, bread crumbs and cheese in a shallow bowl and the egg whites, the water and lemon juice in another.

4. Dip the chicken in the egg white mixture and then in the crumb mixture. Arrange the pieces on a rack set in a baking sheet, cover and refrigerate for at least 30 to 40 minutes. This step can be done early in the day and the chicken refrigerated until cooking time.

5. Preheat the oven to 425 degrees F. Bake the chicken for 40 to 60 minutes or until golden and the juices run clear when you pierce the chicken with the tip of a knife or long-tined fork. Serve hot or cold.

FAT TRACKING TIP: Use chicken or turkey breast instead of a whole chicken.

✿ PER SERVING *Calories: 362, Cholesterol (mg): 105, Saturated fat (g): 3, Total fat (g): 11, Sodium (mg): 478, Total fiber (g): 1*

Thai Minced Chicken

SERVES 6

SWEET AND HOT, TANGY AND REFRESHING — *this quick dish is irresistible on many counts. Serve it as the centerpiece of a small buffet with Heart-Healthy Hummus (page 346–47) and warm pita bread cut into triangles, Janet Fletcher's Tabbouleh (page 347) and Curried Tomato, Melon and Cucumber Salad (page 389–90). Or tuck spoonfuls of this spicy, mint-scented chicken into a pita pocket for a picnic lunch. If you have leftover grilled, broiled or poached chicken, use it here for an almost instant entrée.*

1 pound boned chicken breasts, all skin and fat removed

HOT CHILI DRESSING
½ teaspoon dried crushed red peppers
Juice of 1 lemon
1 tablespoon very cold water
1 tablespoon rice vinegar
1 tablespoon canola oil
1 scant teaspoon sugar

¼ cup finely diced onion
12 cilantro leaves, chopped
12 mint leaves, chopped
1 head iceberg lettuce, shredded

1. Prepare the grill as directed on page 264 or preheat the broiler. Grill or broil the chicken breasts until the chicken is springy to the touch, white in the center and the juices run clear. Cover and refrigerate until cool.

2. Finely mince the cooked chicken. If you use a food processor, pulse it several times until you have a fine mince; check it frequently and don't overprocess it or it will turn into a paste.

3. In a small bowl, combine the hot chili dressing ingredients and blend well.

4. Toss the chicken, chili dressing, onion, cilantro and mint in a mixing bowl until everything is thoroughly blended. Mound the shredded lettuce on individual plates and spoon the chicken mixture on top. Serve immediately.

❁ PER SERVING *Calories: 132, Cholesterol (mg): 48, Saturated fat (g): 1, Total fat (g): 4, Sodium (mg): 51, Total fiber (g): 1*

Chicken Breasts Poached in Tomato, Orange, Mustard and Basil

SERVES 6

SIMMERED CHERRY TOMATOES AND ORANGE JUICE *yield a refreshing poaching medium for chicken breasts. Sweet mustard thickens it into a quick, smooth, fat-free sauce. You can also make the sauce up to the point of adding the chicken breasts and serve it with roasted, grilled or broiled chicken, garnished with the final addition of basil.*

> 2 cups cherry tomatoes
> 3 tablespoons fresh orange juice
> 1 tablespoon prepared sweet mustard
> 2 tablespoons minced green onion
> 2 tablespoons shredded fresh basil
> Salt and freshly ground pepper
> 1½ pounds boned chicken breasts, all skin and fat removed

1. Place the cherry tomatoes in a covered saucepan or skillet large enough to hold the chicken in one layer. Add the orange juice and bring to a boil. Reduce the heat to a simmer and cover. Cook 3 to 4 minutes or until the tomatoes begin to soften and release their juices.

2. Add the mustard, green onion and 1 tablespoon of the basil and stir until the juices thicken. Season lightly with salt and pepper and immerse the chicken breasts in the sauce. Spoon the sauce over the chicken so that it is covered as completely as possible. Raise the heat until the sauce bubbles, then immediately lower it to a simmer. Press a piece of aluminum foil directly onto the chicken and seal the edges around the pan. Cover the pan and cook over low-medium heat for 8 to 10 minutes or until the chicken is springy to the touch, white in the center and the juices run clear.

3. Stir in the remaining basil and serve immediately, spooning the sauce over each portion.

FAT TRACKING TIP: Use turkey breast or fillet of sole or other delicate fish instead of chicken.

❋ PER SERVING *Calories: 163, Cholesterol (mg): 72, Saturated fat (g): 1, Total fat (g): 3, Sodium (mg): 101, Total fiber (g): 1*

Chicken Breasts with Tangerines and Chutney

SERVES 6

VARY THE FLAVOR OF THIS QUICK CHICKEN *with different types of chutney.*
Experiment with mango, peach or plum, nut and fruit combinations or your
own homemade recipe. Rice bran oil has a light taste that is especially
appealing in this dish, but you can substitute olive or peanut oil if you prefer.
Complete the meal with basmati rice flecked with a bit of grated tangerine
rind and Green Beans with Sesame (page 405). Satsuma tangerines, a seedless
variety, are easiest to work with, but honey tangerines provide the sweetest
flavor for the poaching liquid.

> 6 tangerines
> 1½ pounds boned chicken breasts, all skin and fat removed
> Salt and freshly ground pepper
> 1 tablespoon rice bran oil
> ½ teaspoon curry powder
> Generous pinch of cayenne
> 2 tablespoons chutney
> 1 tablespoon reduced-fat sour cream
> Fresh herbs for garnish (such as Italian parsley, mint
>   or flowering thyme)

1. Preheat the oven to 375 degrees F. Grate and set aside ½ teaspoon of zest from
   1 tangerine. Squeeze ¾ cup juice (this will take about 3 tangerines). Peel the
   remaining 3 tangerines and separate them into segments, discarding any white
   membranes.

2. Lightly dust the chicken breasts with salt and pepper. Heat the oil over medium heat in a nonreactive ovenproof skillet large enough to hold the chicken
   in one layer. Add the chicken breasts and turn them in the pan until the flesh
   turns white on all sides. This will take only a minute or so. Add the tangerine
   juice and raise the heat until it just begins to bubble. Immediately remove
   the pan from the heat. Press a piece of aluminum foil or waxed paper over the
   chicken, sealing the edges and completely enclosing it in the liquid. Cover the
   pan with a lid and place it in the oven for 10 minutes or until the chicken is
   springy to the touch, white in the center and the juices run clear. Remove the
   chicken from the pan, arrange it on a serving dish and cover to keep warm.

3. Over medium-high heat, bring the pan juices to a boil and cook rapidly until
   the liquid has reduced to approximately ½ cup. Add the curry powder, cayenne
   and chutney. Stir over high heat briefly until the chutney dissolves. Reduce the
   heat, stir in the sour cream and blend well. Add the grated zest a little at a time

until it suits your taste. Add the reserved tangerine segments and stir until the sauce is thoroughly heated, but don't overcook it or the tangerines will disintegrate. Pour the sauce over the chicken breasts, garnish with the fresh herbs and serve immediately.

FAT TRACKING TIPS: Reduce the oil to 1 teaspoon. Use fat-free sour cream.

❀ PER SERVING *Calories: 214, Cholesterol (mg): 73, Saturated fat (g): 1, Total fat (g): 6, Sodium (mg): 66, Total fiber (g): 2*

❧

Grilled Chicken with
Hot Mint Marinade and Tabbouleh
SERVES 6

MINT IS FAVORED BY COOKS AROUND THE WORLD *in cuisines as diverse as Hindi, Middle Eastern and English. In this zesty citrus marinade, one of our favorites, mint leaves cool the fire of hot peppers and are reprised in that classic whole grain salad, tabbouleh. Make the tabbouleh hours ahead for an easy, summertime menu and grill an assortment of summer vegetables along with this luscious chicken. For a smaller crowd, make the full recipe for the marinade, which yields about ³/₄ cup, use what you need for the chicken and cover and store the remainder in the refrigerator for another time.*

> Janet Fletcher's Tabbouleh (page 347)
> 1½ pounds boned chicken breasts, all skin and fat removed
> ¼ teaspoon dried crushed red peppers
> ¼ teaspoon salt
> 1 teaspoon sugar
> 2 tablespoons minced onion
> 1 garlic clove, minced
> 2 tablespoons extra-virgin olive oil
> Juice and grated zest of ½ lime, ½ lemon *and* ½ orange
> ¼ to ½ cup minced fresh mint
> Whole fresh mint leaves for garnish

1. Prepare the tabbouleh, cover and refrigerate for at least 2 hours.

2. Rinse and dry the chicken and place it in a shallow bowl. Blend the remaining ingredients, except the whole mint leaves, in a small bowl. Reserve ¼ cup of the marinade to brush on the chicken after it has cooked. Pour the remaining marinade over the chicken, then turn it several times to coat it thoroughly. Cover and refrigerate for at least 1 hour, longer if possible, turning the chicken once or twice during this time.

3. Meanwhile, prepare the grill as directed on page 264. About 10 minutes before serving, shake any excess marinade from the chicken (do not discard the marinade yet; use it to brush on the chicken during cooking). Then grill the chicken for 5 to 8 minutes on each side or until the meat is firm and white and the juices run clear. Turn frequently, brushing with the remaining marinade once or twice during cooking. Discard the marinade that was used to cook the chicken after the last application and cook the chicken for at least 1 more minute. Transfer the chicken to a serving platter and brush the chicken with the reserved ¼ cup of marinade. Garnish with the whole mint leaves and serve with the tabbouleh.

✿ PER SERVING (INCLUDES ½ CUP TABBOULEH) *Calories: 277, Cholesterol (mg): 72, Saturated fat (g): 1, Total fat (g): 6, Sodium (mg): 204, Total fiber (g): 6*

Yakitori
SERVES 6

YAKITORI IS A MOUTHWATERING JAPANESE BARBECUE *in which morsels of food are grilled over a hibachi. Rice is a must with this succulent smoky chicken, and though steamed white rice is traditional, nutty brown rice with an assortment of steamed or grilled vegetables also nicely accents this Japanese favorite. Keep the menu simple; you don't want the yakitori sauce to compete with any other highly flavored sauces. If you wish, you can reserve a few tablespoons of the sauce and brush it on the cooked vegetables, then grill them briefly before serving. A word about soy sauce, an essential ingredient that can send the sodium count through the roof. We specify low-sodium soy sauce and use Kikkoman, a Japanese soy sauce, available in a low-sodium version. It is most often our soy sauce of choice. Called shoyu, Japanese soy sauce is lighter, sweeter and less salty than the Chinese version. Tamari, another soy product, is an acceptable substitute. All of these products are high in sodium, though you do not consume the whole amount that is used for the marinade. Persons who must curb their intake of sodium should approach this type of recipe with caution.*

1½ pounds boned chicken breasts, all skin and fat removed
Wooden skewers soaked in cold water
6 green onions, cut into 1-inch diagonal pieces

YAKITORI SAUCE
½ cup low-sodium soy sauce
¾ cup sake
¾ cup mirin (Japanese sweet rice wine) or cream sherry
1 teaspoon sugar
2 tablespoons minced fresh ginger

3 cups cooked white or brown rice (page 438)

1. Prepare the grill as directed on Page 264. Rinse and dry the chicken and cut it into 3 x 1-inch strips. Thread the chicken onto small skewers, alternating with a piece of green onion.

2. Combine the sauce ingredients in a small saucepan and bring to a boil. Reduce the heat to medium and simmer slowly for 5 minutes. Place half the sauce in a small serving bowl.

3. Brush the chicken thoroughly with the remaining sauce and grill 3 to 4 minutes or until the chicken is firm and white. Brush frequently on all sides with the marinade and cook the chicken for at least 1 minute after your last application. Serve immediately with the rice; spoon the reserved sauce on the cooked chicken and over the rice.

❋ PER SERVING (INCLUDES ½ CUP RICE) *Calories: 284, Cholesterol (mg): 72, Saturated fat (g): 1, Total fat (g): 3, Sodium (mg): 323, Total fiber (g): 1*

Chicken Breasts Stuffed with Tarragon and Mustard
SERVES 6

IN FRENCH COOKING, *tarragon is most notably associated with chicken. Its slender anise-scented leaves have a perfume like no other herb and, in our opinion, are underutilized in American kitchens. We hope this fat-reduced, pungent stuffing flecked with tarragon will change that. Because the chicken requires little oil, the simple sauce has a hint of cream for a rich, satisfying finish. Note that some tarragon sold in supermarkets has very little tarragon aroma and is quite bland. Look for French tarragon, or buy a seedling (tarragon does not start from seeds very well) and set it to grow on your kitchen counter.*

MUSHROOM STUFFING
1½ tablespoons extra-virgin olive oil
1 shallot, minced
¼ cup minced fresh mushrooms
2 tablespoons minced fresh tarragon
3 tablespoons whole-grain mustard
½ cup fine bread crumbs
Juice of ½ orange
Salt and freshly ground pepper

1½ pounds whole chicken breasts, all fat and skin removed
Vegetable spray for baking dish
1 teaspoon extra-virgin olive oil
¼ cup dry white wine
1 tablespoon half-and-half or reduced-fat sour cream

1. To make the stuffing, heat the oil over low-medium heat in a small nonreactive skillet and add the shallot. Stir for about 2 minutes or until it softens. Add the mushrooms and raise the heat to high. (If the heat is too low, the mushrooms will render too much liquid for the stuffing.) Toss the mushrooms furiously but briefly just until they begin to wilt. Stir in the remaining stuffing ingredients, seasoning lightly with salt and pepper. You can make this ahead, cover and store it in the refrigerator for several hours.

2. Rinse and dry the chicken. Slice whole chicken breasts in half along the center seam and place them between sheets of waxed paper. Then pound them with a mallet or small skillet until they are approximately ⅓ inch thick. You can do this early in the day, then cover and refrigerate them.

3. Preheat the oven to 400 degrees F. Divide the reserved stuffing into 6 equal portions and spoon onto the center of each chicken breast, spreading it very slightly toward the edges. Starting at one end, roll up each chicken breast, tucking any stray stuffing inside. Lightly coat a flameproof baking dish with a thin film of vegetable spray. Place the chicken, ends down, in the baking dish. Brush the teaspoon of olive oil over the tops of the chicken and pour the wine into the bottom of the dish.

4. Cover the chicken with aluminum foil and tuck it around the edges of the dish to form a seal. Bake for 25 to 30 minutes or until the chicken is springy to the touch, white in the center and the juices run clear when you pierce it with the tip of a knife. Remove from the oven and preheat the broiler.

5. Spoon the pan juices over the chicken and place it under the broiler for 45 seconds or just until the surface is lightly browned. Arrange the chicken on individual plates. Add the half-and-half to the pan juices and stir briefly over medium heat just until the sauce is smooth. Season to your taste with salt and pepper. Spoon the sauce over the chicken and serve immediately.

❀ PER SERVING *Calories: 243, Cholesterol (mg): 72, Saturated fat (g): 2, Total fat (g): 8, Sodium (mg): 224, Total fiber (g): Trace*

Chicken Roasted with Pears, Fennel and Red Onions

SERVES 6

OUR DISCOVERY THAT WHOLE SWEET PEARS ROAST *to a melt-in-your-mouth, almost buttery purée led to this delectable but uncomplicated dish. You can serve the luscious trio of roasted pears, fennel and onion with grilled or broiled chicken breasts, but roasting a whole chicken produces wonderful natural juices for a simple, fat-free sauce that binds all the flavorful elements together. For the best flavor, serve the pears piping hot. Firm pears, such as Bosc, will roast to the same sweetness, but not the desirable, soft texture of tender pears, such as Bartlett and D'Anjou. Whatever kind you use, make sure the skins remain intact or the pears will not have the desired custardy texture.*

> 1 roasting chicken (about 4 pounds)
> Salt and freshly ground pepper
> 1 orange, unpeeled and quartered
> 1 yellow onion, peeled and quartered
> Metal skewers for chicken cavity
> ¼ cup cold water or chicken stock
> 3 sweet red onions, cut in half lengthwise
> Balsamic vinegar for brushing onions
> 3 bulbs fennel
> Vegetable spray for baking dish
> 6 D'Anjou or Bartlett pears, stems removed, unpeeled
> 2 teaspoons red wine vinegar mixed with 3 tablespoons cold water

1. Preheat the oven to 475 degrees F. Rinse and dry the chicken. Trim all visible fat and excess skin from around the cavity. Lightly salt and pepper the cavity and outside of the chicken and stuff the cavity with the orange and onion quarters and close the cavity with metal skewers. Do not truss the chicken or tie the legs to the body or it will not cook evenly. Place the chicken on a rack and set it in a roasting pan. Roast the chicken in the preheated oven for 15 minutes. Then add ¼ cup water or chicken stock to the pan juices to prevent them from scorching.

2. While the chicken cooks, brush the cut sides of the onions with balsamic vinegar. Trim ¼ inch from the root end of the fennel, cut away the stalks and fronds, and cut the bulbs in half lengthwise. Lightly coat an ovenproof dish or pie plate with a film of vegetable spray, and place the onions and fennel cut side down on the dish.

3. When the chicken has been in the oven for 15 minutes, reduce the heat to 375 degrees F, place the dish of vegetables in the oven and continue roasting for 40 to 50 minutes or until the juices run clear when you pierce a chicken thigh with the tip of a knife or long-tined fork. Do not add the vegetables to the pan juices or they will absorb too much fat from the chicken.

4. About 30 minutes before you expect the chicken to be done, add the whole pears to the fennel and onions. Continue cooking until the pears shrink and all the vegetables are fork tender.

5. Remove the chicken from the roasting pan and set it aside for about 10 minutes before you begin carving the meat. Pour the fat and pan juices into a fat skimmer or chilled bowl, as described in Garlic Roasted Chicken with Wilted Greens (page 510–11), and allow the fat to separate from the juices and rise to the surface. Pour off the fat and return the juices to the roasting pan. Add the vinegar and cold water and over medium-high heat scrape up the coagulated juices and stir until smooth. Season very lightly with salt and pepper. Pour this mixture into a measuring cup and allow it to stand while you attend to the last minute assembling.

6. Trim and discard all the skin from the chicken. Remove and discard the onion and oranges from the cavity of the chicken. Carve the meat and arrange it on a serving platter. Arrange the whole pears, onions and fennel around the chicken. Skim off any remaining fat that has accumulated on the surface of the pan juices and pour them into a small serving bowl. Serve the chicken, giving each person a whole pear and an onion and half of a fennel bulb. Spoon the pan juices over the chicken and pears (don't worry that the volume is small; they will be adequately flavored) and serve while the pears are very hot.

❀ PER SERVING *Calories: 368, Cholesterol (mg): 101, Saturated fat (g): 2, Total fat (g): 9, Sodium (mg): 98, Total fiber (g): 6*

Garlic Roasted Chicken with Wilted Greens

SERVES 4

THOUGH THE FINAL RESULT IS NOT AT ALL FRUITY, *the oranges and onions stuffed into the cavity of this simple chicken produce an exceptionally moist and flavorful bird. If you don't have a fat separator or skimmer, follow our directions for skimming the fat from the pan juices any time you roast a chicken. Serve with either Mashed Potatoes with Fennel (page 418) or pasta tossed with a small amount of olive oil. For an easy next-day lunch, put slices of leftover chicken on focaccia with a slice of sweet red onion, fresh basil leaves and the wilted greens (if you have any left) and run under the broiler briefly.*

1 roasting chicken (about 4 pounds)
Salt and freshly ground pepper
4 to 6 large garlic cloves, minced
1 teaspoon extra-virgin olive oil
1 teaspoon dried oregano
1 onion, peeled and quartered
1 orange, unpeeled and quartered
Metal skewers for chicken cavity
1/4 cup cold water
3 cups tightly packed mixed greens (such as beet, mustard,
  rocket, chard and sorrel)
1 cup tightly packed spinach leaves

1. Preheat the oven to 475 degrees F. Rinse and dry the inside and outside of the chicken. Remove any excess skin and fat from around the cavity, then lightly salt and pepper the cavity and skin. Place the garlic in a small bowl and whisk in the olive oil and oregano.

2. Create a pocket between the chicken's skin and breast meat by inserting your finger or a spoon under the skin and work it back and forth sideways until the skin has separated from the breast meat. Spread the garlic mixture evenly inside this pocket. Insert 1 onion quarter and all of the orange quarters in the cavity and close the cavity with metal skewers. Separate the layers of the remaining onion quarters and scatter on the bottom of a roasting pan. Place the chicken on a rack, set it in the roasting pan and roast in the preheated oven for 15 minutes. Then add 1/4 cup of water to prevent the pan juices from scorching. Reduce the heat to 375 degrees F and continue roasting for 40 to 50 minutes or until the juices run clear when you pierce the thigh with the tip of a knife or long-tined fork. Meanwhile, if you don't have a fat separator, 15 minutes before the chicken is ready to come out of the oven, place a metal bowl in the freezer.

3. Transfer the cooked chicken to a separate dish and cover lightly with aluminum foil to keep warm. Remove the fat if you have a fat separator, otherwise strain the pan juices into the metal bowl and swirl them around until they no longer steam, then return the bowl to the freezer for 10 minutes or until the fat congeals on the surface. Skim and discard the fat.

4. Heat the defatted pan juices in a medium-sized skillet. When they just begin to bubble, add the greens, spinach, a pinch of salt and some pepper and toss continuously for 30 seconds or so, coating the greens thoroughly until they just begin to wilt. Pour the greens and juices onto a serving platter. Carve the chicken, discarding all skin, and arrange the chicken over the greens. Serve immediately while very hot.

❋ PER SERVING *Calories: 240, Cholesterol (mg): 101, Saturated fat (g): 2, Total fat (g): 10, Sodium (mg): 112, Total fiber (g): 1*

Turkey Piccata

SERVES 4

THIS VARIATION ON VEAL PICCATA *translates easily to turkey because its texture mirrors that of veal and has a similarly mild flavor to contrast the sharpness of caper and lemon. The buttermilk coating holds the key to the turkey's delicacy; it tenderizes the meat and the result is at once velvety and piquant. An elegant, outstanding, yet simple dish.*

> 1 pound turkey breast, thinly sliced
> ½ cup unbleached all-purpose flour
> Salt and freshly ground black pepper
> 1 tablespoon minced fresh thyme or marjoram or 1 teaspoon dried
> ½ cup low-fat buttermilk
> 2 tablespoons extra-virgin olive oil
> Juice of 1 lemon
> 2 tablespoons capers, drained
> Sprigs of fresh flowering thyme, small edible flowers or other delicate
>   greenery for garnish

1. Place the turkey slices between 2 sheets of waxed or parchment paper and pound them lightly and evenly to a ¼-inch thickness. Spread the flour in a shallow bowl or on a large sheet of waxed paper and season lightly with salt and pepper. Stir the thyme and buttermilk into a shallow bowl. Dredge the turkey in the seasoned flour, dip it in the buttermilk and then into the flour once more, shaking off any excess.

2. Heat the oil over medium heat in a nonreactive skillet large enough to hold the turkey slices in one layer and add the cutlets. Squeeze half the lemon over the cutlets and cook them 3 to 5 minutes on each side, depending on their thickness, or until they are firm and the juices run clear. Add the remaining lemon juice a few drops at a time, tasting until the sauce has a refreshing zip without puckering your mouth. Stir in the capers and heat through. Place the turkey slices on individual plates, spoon the sauce over them, garnish and serve immediately.

FAT TRACKING TIPS: Decrease the olive oil to 1 tablespoon. Use vegetable spray in place of the olive oil.

❀ PER SERVING *Calories: 246, Cholesterol (mg): 72, Saturated fat (g): 1, Total fat (g): 8, Sodium (mg): 77, Total fiber (g): Trace*

Turkey Cutlets
with Cranberry-Orange Sauce
SERVES 2

QUICK AND DELICIOUS, *this dish demonstrates yet another elegant sauce that doesn't use butter or cream. If you can't find dried cranberries, substitute yellow raisins, though the sauce will be less tangy. This recipe doubles and triples easily. As an added fillip, stir a spoonful of sherry or Cognac into the sauce before serving.*

> ½ cup dried cranberries
> ½ cup dry white wine
> 1 tablespoon extra-virgin olive oil
> 2 tablespoons minced shallots
> ½ pound turkey breast, sliced into cutlets ¼ inch thick
> 2 tablespoons fresh orange juice
> ¼ teaspoon grated orange zest
> Pinch of salt
> Pinch of cayenne

1. Plump the cranberries in a small bowl of hot water for 15 to 20 minutes. Drain thoroughly. Toss them with the wine and set them aside as you assemble the other ingredients.

2. Heat the oil in a nonreactive skillet large enough to hold the turkey in one layer and add the shallots. Stir over medium heat for 2 to 3 minutes until they soften. Add the turkey and cook for 4 to 5 minutes, turning occasionally, or until the cutlets are firm and white in the center and the juices are clear. Don't overcook the turkey or it will toughen.

3. Remove the cutlets to a separate platter and cover them to keep them warm. Add the wine and berries to the skillet and bring to a boil, stirring to scrape up any coagulated juices sticking to the pan. Cook until the wine has reduced by half. Stir in the orange juice, orange zest, salt and cayenne. Return the turkey to the pan and cook just until the cutlets are heated through. Arrange the cutlets on individual plates and spoon the sauce over them. Serve immediately.

FAT TRACKING TIP: Replace the olive oil with a thin film of vegetable spray.

❋ PER SERVING *Calories: 269, Cholesterol (mg): 71, Saturated fat (g): 1, Total fat (g): 8, Sodium (mg): 49, Total fiber (g): 5*

Citrus Grilled Turkey with Herbed Rice Salad

SERVES 6

A SWEET AND TART MARINADE *balances the sweet herbs in the rice salad.*
Note that in most of our grilled turkey recipes, we recommend thick slices of
breast meat rather than thin cutlets. Because turkey is so low in fat, it will dry
out in the intense dry heat of a grill or broiler. Thicker slices, however, produce
moist fillets. Buy the whole or half breast and slice it yourself for grilling and
use presliced thin cutlets for dishes cooked in a skillet with oil, stock or a sauce
added. Usually we recommend discarding the marinade that has touched
uncooked poultry to prevent contamination with bacteria. However, here we
heat it (to kill any harmful creatures) and turn it into a sauce, a trick you can
use for any of the marinades. Serve with roasted corn on the cob and Curried
Corn Fingers (page 333).

CITRUS MARINADE
Juice of 3 limes
2 tablespoons fresh orange juice
1½ tablespoons fresh lemon juice
3 tablespoons cold water
¼ cup minced green onion
1½ tablespoons canola oil
1½ teaspoons low-sodium soy sauce
1½ teaspoons sugar
1 teaspoon salt
Generous twist of freshly ground pepper
1½ teaspoons *each* dried thyme and oregano
¾ teaspoon ground cumin

Herbed Rice Salad (page 394)
1½ pounds turkey breast, sliced 1 inch thick
Sprigs of fresh herbs or small edible blossoms for garnish

1. Combine the ingredients for the marinade in a measuring cup. Blend thoroughly. You may make this 24 hours in advance, cover and store it in the refrigerator. Also prepare and chill the Herbed Rice Salad, up to a day in advance.

2. Arrange the turkey slices in a shallow bowl and pour the marinade over them, turning the turkey once or twice to coat it thoroughly. Cover and refrigerate for at least 20 minutes or up to 1 hour.

3. While the turkey marinates, prepare the grill as directed on page 264. Finish preparing the Herbed Rice Salad and arrange on individual plates, allowing space for the turkey.

4. Just before serving, grill the turkey 3 to 4 minutes on each side, depending on the thickness of the cutlets. Brush once or twice with the marinade, allowing the turkey to cook for at least 1 minute after the last application. As soon as the cutlets are springy to the touch, white in the center and the juices run clear, transfer them to the plates with the salad. Heat the remaining marinade until it just begins to bubble and spoon 2 tablespoons of the heated sauce on each cutlet. Garnish and serve immediately.

❋ PER SERVING (INCLUDES ½ CUP HERBED RICE SALAD) *Calories: 387, Cholesterol (mg): 71, Saturated fat (g): 2, Total fat (g): 11, Sodium (mg): 203, Total fiber (g): 1*

Grilled Turkey Dijon with Honey-Mustard Peanut Sauce

SERVES 4

THE PEANUT SAUCES OF INDONESIA *inspired us to develop a small collection of recipes to demonstrate the range of sauce-making techniques that are free of saturated fat. We take some fat-trimming liberties with the original idea because, though peanut butter is low in saturated fat, large portions can put you over your total fat limit. However, our addition of nonfat yogurt and hot water dilutes the calories and fat content per serving without interfering with the satisfying creaminess these sauces promise. To further offset the fat in the peanut butter, use the sauce to coat smoky morsels of lean grilled turkey breast, this one marinated in an infusion of mustard, lemon and honey. Use our basic formula for a peanut sauce and use your own culinary imagination to create a battery of innovative and healthy sauces.*

> 1 pound boned turkey breast, all skin and fat removed,
>   cut into slices 1½ inches thick
>
> **HONEY-MUSTARD MARINADE**
> 1 tablespoon extra-virgin olive oil
> 1 tablespoon honey
> 1 tablespoon Dijon mustard
> 1 tablespoon fresh lemon juice
> Large pinch of cayenne

HONEY-MUSTARD PEANUT SAUCE

2 tablespoons creamy, unsweetened old-fashioned peanut butter
2 tablespoons boiling water
2 tablespoons nonfat plain yogurt
1 teaspoon honey
2 teaspoons rice vinegar or 1 tablespoon white wine vinegar
1 teaspoon prepared sweet mustard
6 to 7 drops Tabasco sauce, or to taste

1. Place the turkey in a shallow bowl. Blend the marinade ingredients in a measuring cup and pour it over the turkey, turning it several times until completely coated. Cover and refrigerate for at least 30 minutes.

2. Place the peanut butter in a small serving bowl and stir in the boiling water. Cool slightly, stir in the yogurt, then blend in the remaining ingredients until you have a smooth and creamy mixture. Cover and refrigerate the sauce until serving time. You can prepare this 24 hours ahead.

3. Prepare the grill as directed on page 264. Grill the turkey 3 to 4 minutes on each side, turning several times and brushing both sides at least once with the marinade. When the cutlets are springy to the touch, white in the center and the juices run clear, arrange the grilled slices on a serving platter and serve, passing the Honey-Mustard Peanut Sauce separately.

❀ PER SERVING *Calories: 224, Cholesterol (mg): 71, Saturated fat (g): 1, Total fat (g): 8, Sodium (mg): 199, Total fiber (g): 1*

Curry-Spiked Turkey
with Mango Chutney Sauce
SERVES 6

THIS ALMOST FAT-FREE *but highly seasoned entrée owes its appeal to the blend of curry and citrus in the coating and the unusually zesty sauce. The yogurt marinade both flavors and tenderizes the turkey. For an ample menu, serve steamed rice, Spiced Cauliflower and Peppers (page 404) and follow with fresh fruit drizzled with Hal's Hot Fudge Sauce (page 565–66) and a small scoop of frozen nonfat yogurt for dessert.*

CURRY-CITRUS MARINADE
1½ cups plain nonfat yogurt
2 teaspoons curry powder
⅛ teaspoon cayenne
1 tablespoon fresh lemon juice
2 teaspoons fresh lime juice
½ teaspoon ground cumin
¾ teaspoon salt
1 garlic clove, minced
3 tablespoons minced fresh cilantro
1 teaspoon minced fresh ginger or ¼ teaspoon ground ginger

1 whole boned turkey breast (about 1½ pounds), all skin and fat
   removed and cut into 1-inch-thick slices
1 small, ripe mango
¼ cup nonfat plain yogurt
3 tablespoons mango chutney or Major Grey–type chutney
Sprigs of fresh cilantro for garnish

1. In a small bowl blend the yogurt and remaining marinade ingredients until smooth. Taste and adjust the seasoning, adding more curry powder if desired. If the mixture is too hot for your taste, temper the sauce with a few more tablespoons of yogurt.

2. Place the turkey in a shallow bowl. Pour half the yogurt mixture over it, turning the pieces until thoroughly coated. Cover and refrigerate for several hours, overnight if possible.

3. Over a blender jar, food processor bowl or small mixing bowl to catch the juices, peel the mango and cut the fruit away from the pit. Purée the pulp until smooth. Stir the yogurt in by hand and then the chutney. Spoon the sauce into a serving bowl, cover and chill until serving time. You can make this 24 hours in advance.

4. Prepare the grill as directed on page 264. Place the turkey on the grill and cook 3 to 4 minutes on each side until the cutlets are springy to the touch, white in the center and the juices run clear. When it is done, arrange the turkey on a serving platter garnished with a few sprigs of fresh cilantro. Pass the mango chutney sauce separately.

❀ PER SERVING *Calories: 180, Cholesterol (mg): 72, Saturated fat (g): Trace, Total fat (g): 1, Sodium (mg): 167, Total fiber (g): 1*

Broiled Turkey with Minted Eggplant Purée
SERVES 6

TRY THIS PAIRING OF JUICY, SMOKY CHARRED TURKEY *juxtaposed with a cool and silky vegetable purée refreshed with lemon and mint. On a hot summer's evening vary the presentation by grilling the turkey and dunking wedges of pita into the chilled eggplant purée. Or spoon the purée over grilled onions and zucchini as a vegetable course. If you have leftovers, spread hard rolls with the eggplant, add a slice or two of turkey and stack the sandwich with layers of grilled peppers, onions and zucchini for a Fat Tracker's Crunchy Lunch.*

> Minted Eggplant Purée (recipe follows)
> 2 garlic cloves
> 1½ pounds boned turkey breast, all skin and fat removed,
>   cut into slices, 1 inch thick
> 1½ tablespoons or more fresh lemon juice

1. Prepare the Minted Eggplant Purée.

2. Preheat the broiler. Slice the garlic cloves in half and rub the cut sides over the turkey slices. Squeeze the lemon juice over the turkey, coating all sides. Place the turkey under the broiler about 2 inches from the heat source and broil for 4 to 5 minutes on each side until the cutlets are springy to the touch, white in the center and the juices run clear.

3. While the turkey cooks, reheat the eggplant if you want to serve it hot. Spoon it into a serving bowl and stir in the remaining mint. Arrange the turkey on a serving platter. Spoon a little of the eggplant purée over the top of the turkey and serve immediately. Pass the bowl of the remaining eggplant purée separately.

❀ PER SERVING (INCLUDES ½ CUP MINTED EGGPLANT PURÉE) *Calories: 196, Cholesterol (mg): 71, Saturated fat (g): 1, Total fat (g): 5, Sodium (mg): 48, Total fiber (g): 1*

Minted Eggplant Purée
Serves 6, serving size about ½ cup

The combination of mint and eggplant appears throughout the food of the Mediterranean. This version works as a dip for bread or lightly steamed vegetables on your appetizer tray as well as in this main course accompaniment. Instead of roasting the vegetables, you can grill them for an equally sumptuous purée.

> 2 tablespoons extra-virgin olive oil
> 1 large eggplant
> 1 red onion
> 1 whole bulb garlic
> 2 tablespoons fresh lemon juice
> Salt and freshly ground pepper
> 3 tablespoons chopped fresh mint

1. Preheat the oven to 375 degrees F. Place the olive oil in a small bowl for brushing. Prick the eggplant several times and place it on a baking sheet. Trim the root and stem ends of the onion, then cut it in half crosswise. Brush the cut ends with just enough of the olive oil to moisten them, then place the cut sides down on the baking sheet. Slice the bulb of garlic in half crosswise and drizzle the cut ends of the bulb with a few drops of the olive oil. Face the cut ends together, wrap the bulb tightly in aluminum foil and place on the baking sheet. Roast the eggplant for 35 to 45 minutes, depending on its size, or until it is very soft and the skin has blistered. The garlic is done when the cloves are soft and creamy, approximately 40 minutes. Cook the onion until it is browned and tender, 40 to 50 minutes. As each vegetable finishes cooking, remove it from the oven and set it aside to cool.

2. When the vegetables are cool enough to handle, remove and discard the skin of the eggplant. Chop the pulp coarsely and place it in a food processor bowl, blender jar or bowl to use with a hand processor. Squeeze the soft roasted garlic into the eggplant. Add the onion, remaining olive oil and the 2 tablespoons lemon juice to the mixture and process until smooth. Season to your taste with salt and pepper and add more lemon juice if desired. If you are serving it immediately, blend in all of the mint. If you are preparing it ahead of time, add half the mint. Transfer the purée to a serving bowl. At this point you can cover and chill the purée in the refrigerator for 24 hours, allowing it to come to room temperature about 20 minutes before serving. Alternatively, you can serve it hot.

❁ PER SERVING *Calories: 71, Cholesterol (mg): 0, Saturated fat (g): 1, Total fat (g): 5, Sodium (mg): 3, Total fiber (g): 1*

Turkey Brochettes
with Corn Bread–Cranberry Dressing
SERVES 6

YOU DON'T HAVE TO WAIT FOR THE HOLIDAYS *to enjoy cranberries and turkey with trimmings, nor do you have to make gravy or any of the other fatty and time-consuming side dishes. This flavorful stuffing relies on apples for moisture instead of oceans of melted butter and you can use leftover corn muffins or slivers of corn bread in this easy dressing. Or, buy packaged corn bread crumbs without saturated fat. Finish the menu with grilled baby zucchini and carrots and, instead of gravy, spoon warmed applesauce spiced with ground cinnamon and a little fresh ginger over the turkey.*

½ cup fresh orange juice
3 tablespoons extra-virgin olive oil
Pinch of cayenne
1½ pounds turkey breast, all skin and fat removed
    and cut into 1-inch cubes
½ cup diced onion
1 garlic clove, minced
2½ cups corn bread crumbs
½ tablespoon crumbled dried sage
1 teaspoon *each* crumbled dried thyme and oregano
½ cup finely diced, peeled green apple
½ cup dried cranberries (use yellow raisins if you can't find
    dried cranberries)
½ cup white wine
¼ cup Chicken Stock (page 285–86) or canned low-fat, low-sodium
    chicken broth
Salt and freshly ground pepper
Wooden skewers soaked in cold water
Orange slices, dried cranberries and tufts of fresh parsley for garnish

1. Blend the orange juice, 1 tablespoon of the olive oil and the cayenne in a shallow bowl. Toss the turkey in the juice mixture until it is thoroughly coated, cover and refrigerate for at least 30 minutes.

2. Meanwhile, preheat the oven to 350 degrees F and prepare the grill as directed on page 264. Heat the remaining 2 tablespoons olive oil in a medium-size skillet and add the onion and garlic. Stir over low-medium heat for 1 minute until the onions are well coated with the oil. Partially cover the skillet and, stirring occasionally, cook slowly for 8 to 10 minutes or until the onions are very soft, but do not allow the mixture to scorch. Stir in the corn bread crumbs and remaining ingredients and simmer until the dressing has absorbed the stock, about 15 minutes. Stir frequently.

3. Place the dressing in a baking dish, cover and bake for 15 to 20 minutes or until set. Uncover and bake another 5 minutes or until the top is slightly crusty.

4. While the dressing bakes, thread the turkey onto skewers and grill for 12 to 15 minutes, depending on their distance from the coals, or until the meat is springy to the touch, the center is white and the juices run clear. Baste occasionally with the orange marinade. Spoon the dressing on one side of a serving platter and arrange the turkey brochettes next to it. Garnish with the orange slices, cranberries and parsley. Serve immediately.

❈ PER SERVING *Calories: 364, Cholesterol (mg): 88, Saturated fat (g): 2, Total fat (g): 10, Sodium (mg): 322, Total fiber (g): 1*

Grilled Turkey Breast with White Wine and Herbs

SERVES 6

THIS MARINADE PRODUCES *an incredibly moist and flavorful grilled turkey, and you can also use it for chicken breasts. Start preparations the day before you plan to serve, so the turkey will have a full 24 hours to plump in the herb-scented marinade. Serve the turkey hot or cold with Stir-Fry of Green and White Beans with Ginger (page 402–3), Hot Red Rice Salad (page 442) and French or Italian bread brushed with a cut garlic clove and toasted on the grill. Or, instead of planning a meal around this turkey, you can simply grill it to have on hand for sandwiches, to dice into salads or for a quick, cold slice when you need a substantial but low-fat midnight snack.*

    1 boned turkey breast (about 1½ pounds), all skin and fat removed
    3 garlic cloves, quartered
    1 teaspoon fresh oregano

WHITE WINE MARINADE

½ cup white wine
¼ cup extra-virgin olive oil
1 tablespoon fresh lemon juice
1 teaspoon sugar
¼ cup coarsely chopped fresh Italian parsley
1 tablespoon *each* fresh oregano and thyme
1 crushed bay leaf
3 garlic cloves, minced
½ cup coarsely chopped onion
1 teaspoon salt
Large pinch of cayenne
Scant ⅛ teaspoon white pepper

1. Rinse and dry the turkey breast and make 12 small slits just deep enough to hold a piece of garlic. Insert a piece of garlic and a pinch of oregano in each slit. Place the turkey in a shallow nonreactive baking dish.

2. Combine the marinade ingredients in a measuring cup and blend thoroughly. Pour the marinade over the turkey, turning it once or twice to coat it thoroughly. Cover and refrigerate for 24 hours. Turn the meat 2 or 3 times during this period.

3. Prepare the grill as directed on page 264. Grill the turkey until the meat is springy to the touch, white in the center and the juices run clear when you pierce the flesh with the tip of a knife, about 30 minutes. Brush with the marinade from time to time, allowing it to cook at least 1 minute after the last application. Remove turkey to a platter and slice it before serving.

❀ PER SERVING *Calories: 171, Cholesterol (mg): 71, Saturated fat (g): 1, Total fat (g): 4, Sodium (mg): 164, Total fiber (g): Trace*

CHAPTER 38

Meat

CAN A MEAT EATER FIND HAPPINESS *on The Stanford 25 Gram Plan? He or she certainly can—twice a week. In these fat-conscious days, when people want more sizzle than steak on their plates, others are defensive or apologetic about eating meat. But there is really no reason for guilt if they follow the advice in this book. Throughout we have warned you against the evils of saturated fat and one of its largest repositories: red meat. But now it is time to take a little of the heat off meat, to praise meat, not condemn it. A small steak or a medallion of pork contains all the amino acids for complete protein that your body needs. And a slice of rare, garlic-perfumed, grilled lamb can bring a smile of joy to a care-worn face, as it has since ancient times when lamb was praised by poets, such as Homer, and used as an offering to the gods.*

While we don't hold meat as sacred, we do know that it has a central place in the meal planning of most Americans. If you are one of them, the fact that you eat meat should not concern you, but simply the amount. The healthful portions we recommend in The Fat Tracker's Meal Planning Guide give you ample leeway to enjoy a wide range of grilled, roasted, sautéed and stewed meat entrées, twice a week, every week. And if you heed our call to use leaner cuts, you will find that these portions tend to have more flavor. Also, concern about pesticides and feed additives, such as antibiotics, has spawned ranches that raise their animals on organic feed and allow them to roam free—practices that produce healthier animals with stronger flavor. You pay more for meat so produced (mostly veal) but you also have the assurance of a healthier product all around.

Meat cooking is a culinary specialty. As popular as the backyard barbecue is, you can ruin a piece of beef by attempting simply to grill it or by trying to adorn it with a complicated sauce. The Fat Tracker's Cooking Course (Chapter 26) will advise you on low-fat techniques for sautéing, grilling, roasting, stewing and the like, but here are a few reminders to help you turn out tantalizing meat dishes. Remember the basic rule: Tender and fattier cuts require quick cooking and leaner but tougher cuts take beautifully to long simmers in flavorful sauces. That also means that for best flavor, cook tender cuts of meat (such as London broil) rare and cook tougher cuts (such as bottom round) until well done. Also, when you are cooking tougher cuts for stews, sear the meat first by giving it an initial cooking at very high heat. (This does not so much seal in flavor, as was once commonly thought, as create flavor by encouraging the browning process.) And instead of resorting to buttery sauces, such as steak Diane, search the shelves of specialty markets for fat-free spiced sauces to brush on grilled meat, such as mustard glazes and picante sauces. And, of course, don't overlook the delectable sauces and marinades on the following pages.

Veal Marengo
SERVES 6

THE CULINARY LORE *associated with the original veal Marengo is that Napoleon's chef created the veal and tomato dish to celebrate the victory at Marengue. We celebrate a victory of sorts as well, transforming an overly rich classic dish into a chic, delicious and lean entrée. In this version we cook the veal directly in the stock, rather than giving it an initial sauté in oil—a good technique for preparing lean meat dishes when you must skim every possible gram of fat from your meals. This may be prepared completely the day before and reheated before serving. Serve with noodles or rice.*

> 2 pounds veal loin, cut into 2-inch cubes
> 2 tablespoons minced shallots
> 1 garlic clove, minced
> ½ cup dry white wine
> 3 cups Chicken Stock (page 285–86) or canned low-fat,
>   low-sodium chicken broth
> 1 large sprig fresh Italian parsley
> 1 teaspoon thyme
> 1 bay leaf
> ¼ cup diced celery
> 24 white boiling onions, peeled
> 24 brown or white mushroom caps
> 3 fresh tomatoes, peeled, seeded and coarsely chopped
> Fresh parsley for garnish

1. Place the veal in a large nonreactive saucepan or Dutch oven and cover with cold water. Bring to a boil and drain. There will be a gray foamy material on the surface which you will discard, thus ensuring a clear sauce for the veal.

2. Place the veal, shallots, garlic, wine, 2 cups of the chicken stock, parsley, thyme, bay leaf, and celery in the pot. Bring to a boil, reduce the heat to a simmer and cook uncovered for 1 to 1½ hours or until the veal is tender.

3. Meanwhile, place the onions in a medium-size saucepan with the remaining cup of chicken stock and bring to a boil. Reduce the heat and simmer until the onions are tender.

4. When the veal is just about tender, skim all fat from the surface and add the onions, mushrooms and tomatoes. Continue cooking for another ½ hour. Transfer 1 cup of the vegetables and liquid to a blender and purée until smooth. Stir this back into the sauce. Serve on individual plates garnished with parsley.

❀ PER SERVING *Calories: 298, Cholesterol (mg): 120, Saturated fat (g): 3, Total fat (g): 8, Sodium (mg): 125, Total fiber (g): 4*

Grilled Lemon Veal
with Green Bean and Basil Purée
SERVES 6

THE TART MARINADE FOR THE VEAL *blends perfectly with the natural sweetness of the purée, which you can serve hot or cold.*

LEMON MARINADE
1 teaspoon canola oil
1 teaspoon grated lemon zest
Juice of 1 lemon
2 tablespoons minced fresh Italian parsley
½ teaspoon dried thyme
Pinch of salt and white pepper

1½ pounds veal tenderloin, sliced into thin cutlets
1 tablespoon canola oil
½ cup chopped onion
2 garlic cloves, minced
1 pound green beans
¼ cup nonfat plain yogurt
¼ cup Chicken Stock (page 285–86) or canned low-fat, low-sodium chicken broth
⅓ to ½ cup coarsely chopped, fresh basil
1 teaspoon fresh lemon juice

Salt and freshly ground pepper
Sprigs of fresh thyme, if available, for garnish
3 to 4 thin curls of zest cut from a lemon for garnish

1. In a measuring cup, blend the marinade ingredients. Rinse the veal and pat dry, then place it in a shallow nonreactive dish. Pour the lemon marinade over the veal, turning it at least once to coat it thoroughly. Cover and refrigerate for at least 1 hour.

2. Heat the canola oil in a skillet. Add the onion and garlic and stirring occasionally, cook over low-medium heat for about 10 minutes or until they are soft and transparent. If the pan gets too dry, add a tablespoon of water and as it is absorbed, add another tablespoon and continue until the onions are very soft. Do not allow them to scorch.

3. Meanwhile, set aside for garnish 2 or 3 of the prettiest crisp green beans. Trim the ends of the remaining beans and (as directed on page 266–67) steam or microwave them until they are very tender. Cook them a little longer than you would for crisp beans, or you will have a crunchy rather than a smooth purée. Remove the beans from the heat as soon as they are done. Run them under cold water to halt the cooking and set the color, then drain the beans thoroughly.

4. Place the beans in a blender or food processor. Add the onion mixture, yogurt and chicken stock and purée until the mixture is as smooth as possible. Add the basil and lemon juice and season to your taste with salt and pepper. Purée once more until the basil is absorbed. Cover and chill until serving time, or assemble the purée just before the veal is ready and serve it hot.

5. Prepare the grill as directed on page 264. Grill the veal 2 to 3 minutes on each side, brushing once with the marinade. Don't overcook or it will toughen. Stack the fresh beans, sprigs of fresh thyme (if using) and curls of fresh lemon zest in the center of a serving platter. When the veal is firm and the juices run clear, arrange it on one side of the garnish and spoon the purée on the other side. Serve immediately.

❀ PER SERVING *Calories: 249, Cholesterol (mg): 89, Saturated fat (g): 2, Total fat (g): 9, Sodium (mg): 91, Total fiber (g): 2*

London Broil Teriyaki

SERVES 6

CUT FROM THE ROUND, *London broil is as tender a cut of beef as you could want for grilling, with so much less fat than steaks. Though we have tried many others, we have not found a superior teriyaki sauce to this one. It makes about 1¼ cups and will last in the refrigerator for up to two weeks, so you can make the full recipe and keep it on hand to brush on grilled chicken, fish or meat.*

TERIYAKI SAUCE
1 garlic clove, minced
¾ cup low-sodium soy sauce
¼ cup water
¼ cup white wine
½ teaspoon grated fresh ginger
2 teaspoons sugar

1½ pounds London broil

1. In a small bowl, combine all the sauce ingredients and blend well. Store covered in the refrigerator for at least 30 minutes before using to balance the flavors.

2. Place the beef in a shallow nonreactive bowl and pour at least ⅓ cup of the teriyaki sauce over it. Turn once to coat thoroughly, cover and set aside for at least 30 minutes.

3. Meanwhile preheat the broiler or prepare the grill as directed on page 264. Pour ⅓ cup of the reserved teriyaki sauce into a small bowl for basting the meat. (Discard any teriyaki left in the bowl after basting; it could carry bacteria from the raw meat.) Broil or grill the beef for 7 to 8 minutes on each side, depending on the desired degree of doneness. Brush often with the teriyaki sauce. Allow to stand for 5 to 10 minutes for tenderness, slice and serve.

❋ PER SERVING *Calories: 200, Cholesterol (mg): 46, Saturated fat (g): 4, Total fat (g): 9, Sodium (mg): 389, Total fiber (g): 0*

Moroccan Beef with Couscous

SERVES 6

LIKE ALL STEWS, *it is best not to have your eye on the clock when you are preparing it. The cooking time of two to three hours is approximate. It needs at least two hours for the flavors to begin to meld, and it is done only when the beef is tender and the stew is thick, spicy and fragrant. The stew is quite watery at first, but the acorn squash thickens it and adds a subtle sweetness, which is surprisingly delectable and unexpected in a beef dish.*

> 1 tablespoon olive oil
> 1 pound bottom round of beef, cubed
> 2 onions, chopped
> 2 carrots, finely chopped
> 1 red bell pepper, seeded and sliced
> 2 garlic cloves, minced
> 1 cup cold water
> 2 cups Beef Stock (page 288–89) or Chicken Stock (page 285–86)
>   or canned lowfat, low-sodium beef or chicken broth
> 3/4 cup red wine
> Salt and freshly ground pepper
> 1 acorn squash
> 1 can (28 ounces) tomatoes with juice
> 1/4 teaspoon *each* ground cinnamon and cloves
> Generous pinch of cayenne
> 1 1/2 cups cooked or canned garbanzo beans (chickpeas)
> 1/2 pound yams, peeled and cut in 3/4 inch cubes
> 1/4 cup *each* minced fresh parsley and cilantro
> 2 cups quick-cooking couscous
> 1 3/4 cups boiling water

1. Heat the olive oil in a large nonreactive Dutch oven. Add the beef and toss over moderate heat until the meat browns on all sides.

2. Add the onions, carrots, bell pepper and garlic, and stir frequently over moderate heat until the onions have softened. Add the water, stock and wine and bring to a boil. Reduce the heat and season lightly with salt and pepper. Partially cover and simmer for 2 hours. Check from time to time to make sure the liquid continues to bubble gently and stir the stew as well.

3. Meanwhile, preheat the oven to 350 degrees F. Pierce the acorn squash several times and bake for 40 minutes or until tender but not mushy. Set aside until cool enough to handle. Slice the squash in half, scoop out and discard the seeds, remove the skin and cut the pulp into 2-inch chunks.

4. After the beef has cooked 2 hours, add the tomatoes, cinnamon, cloves, cayenne and garbanzo beans. Continue cooking for 1 hour or until the beef is tender.

5. Boil the yams for 12 to 15 minutes or until tender but do not overcook them or allow them to become mushy. When the beef is done add the yams, acorn squash, parsley and cilantro to the stew and stir thoroughly. Simmer just until everything is heated through.

6. Place the couscous in a mixing bowl, add the boiling water and a pinch of salt and stir. Let stand for 5 minutes. If the couscous does not absorb all the water, press through a sieve or wring in several layers of cheesecloth. Fluff with a fork. Arrange the couscous on individual dinner plates and cover with the stew.

❄ PER SERVING *Calories: 626, Cholesterol (mg): 55, Saturated fat (g): 2, Total fat (g): 9, Sodium (mg): 384, Total fiber (g): 13*

Curried Beef in a Bowl
with Lentils and Chutney
SERVES 8

BEEF IS MORE THAN WELCOME *at a Fat Tracker's table when it contains as little fat as this hearty, highly seasoned main course soup. A slow simmer makes it thick, and spicy chutney seeps into the stock to give it an unexpected charge. This dish would star as a main course for a casual supper with Red Pepper Muffins (page 330). This zesty soup improves with age, and, because it freezes well, you can store it in small batches in plastic containers, ready to pop into the microwave when you need quick nourishment. Ask your butcher to cut the bottom round from the wide end of the round, which will not disintegrate in slow, moist heat.*

2 teaspoons extra-virgin olive oil
1 onion, diced
3 garlic cloves, minced
1 leek (white part only) diced
1 pound carrots, diced
2 stalks celery, diced
1 pound bottom round of beef, cut in 1½-inch cubes
8 cups water
7 cups Beef Stock (page 288–89) or canned low-fat, low-sodium
   beef broth
3 cups dried green lentils, picked of stones and rinsed
½ teaspoon *each* ground cinnamon and allspice
1 teaspoon *each* ground cumin, mace, ginger and white pepper
Salt to your taste
¼ cup minced fresh Italian parsley
1 teaspoon dried oregano
1 cup peach chutney
1 cup nonfat plain yogurt
¼ cup minced fresh cilantro leaves

1. Heat the oil in a large heavy saucepan or Dutch oven over low-medium heat and add the onion, garlic, leek, carrots and celery. Stir the vegetables to coat them with the oil, then partially cover the pan and cook for 5 minutes, stirring frequently so they don't scorch. Reduce the heat even further if the onions begin to scorch and add 1 or 2 tablespoons of the water or beef stock to keep them moist. Remove the vegetables to a separate dish.

2. Add the beef to the pan and raise the heat slightly. Do not add any additional oil. Turn the beef constantly for 3 to 4 minutes or until it is brown on all sides. Return the vegetables to the pan and add the water. Raise the heat until the mixture boils and immediately lower the heat to a simmer. Skim away any foam that rises to the surface. Continue simmering, uncovered, for 1½ hours, skimming as necessary.

3. Add the stock, lentils and the remaining ingredients except the yogurt and cilantro and bring to a boil. Immediately reduce the heat to a simmer again and cook for an additional 30 to 40 minutes or until the beef is tender and the soup is thick. Stir occasionally and adjust the heat as necessary to make sure the bottom doesn't scorch.

4. When the beef is tender and the soup thick, ladle it into bowls and garnish each with 2 tablespoons yogurt and ½ tablespoon cilantro. Serve very hot.

✿ PER SERVING *Calories: 508, Cholesterol (mg): 42, Saturated fat (g): 1, Total fat (g): 5, Sodium: 121, Total fiber: 8*

Grilled Lamb Kabobs
with Skordalia and Eggplant
SERVES 6

LAMB, ALWAYS HIGHER IN FAT THAN BEEF, *can fit into your meal planning as a twice-a-week entrée if you thread small cubes on a skewer and grill it in our excellent wine marinade. Serve it with filling portions of heady Skordalia (a purée of garlicky potatoes) and another Greek lamb tradition, eggplant, as a complete menu. Serve these accompaniments hot or at room temperature. Use this marinade for any grilled or roasted lamb, such as boned and butterflied leg of lamb for a large group. Note that even though you use one quarter cup of oil in the marinade, very little of it clings to the lamb once you cook it.*

> 1½ pounds lean, boneless loin lamb, cut into approximately 1-inch
>   cubes
> ½ cup sliced onion
>
> **RED WINE MARINADE**
> ½ cup red wine
> ¼ cup extra-virgin olive oil
> ¼ cup coarsely chopped fresh parsley
> 2 bay leaves
> 1 teaspoon fresh thyme
> 1 garlic clove, minced
> 1 tablespoon sugar
> 1 teaspoon salt
> Coarse ground pepper
>
> Skordalia (page 419)
> Minted Eggplant Purée (page 519)
>   or a whole roasted eggplant
> Wooden skewers, soaked in cold water
> 3 red bell peppers, seeded and cut into eighths
> 2 sweet red onions, cut into eighths
> Fresh mint and parsley sprigs for garnish
> 6 pita rounds, cut into quarters

1. Place the lamb in a large nonreactive baking dish and cover with the onions. Whisk the marinade ingredients together in a measuring cup and pour over the lamb, turning the cubes several times to coat thoroughly. Cover with aluminum foil or plastic wrap and refrigerate for 12 to 24 hours, turning the lamb 2 or 3 times during this period.

2. Prepare the Skordalia and Minted Eggplant Purée.

3. Up to an hour before cooking, thread the lamb on skewers, alternating with the bell peppers and red onion slices. Brush the lamb lightly with the marinade. Prepare the grill as directed on page 264. Grill the lamb for 5 to 8 minutes or until it achieves the desired degree of doneness, turning it frequently and moving the skewers away from the center of the grill as necessary to keep them from scorching.

4. Reheat the Skordalia and Minted Eggplant Purée if desired. Arrange the kabobs on a large serving platter and spoon the purées around them. Garnish with large tufts of fresh parsley and mint and serve with pita bread for scooping up the two purées.

❀ PER SERVING (INCLUDES MINTED EGGPLANT PURÉE, SKORDALIA AND 1 PITA ROUND) *Calories: 470, Cholesterol (mg): 74, Saturated fat (g): 4, Total fat (g): 16, Sodium (mg): 476, Total fiber (g): 2*

Pork Roast with Prunes

SERVES 6

IN RESPONSE TO A DEMAND, *pork is coming to market leaner and leaner these days. Loin, as we present it here with a covering of fruit simmered in port to keep it moist and succulent, is not as lightweight as tenderloin, but still a fat-tracking bargain. Tuck slices of leftover cold pork between halves of a french roll brushed with sweet prepared mustard.*

> 6 ounces *each* dried, pitted prunes, apricots and pears
> 1 cup port wine
> 1 cup fresh orange juice
> 1 teaspoon grated orange zest
> 1 boned pork loin (about 3 pounds)
> Salt and freshly ground pepper
> 1 tablespoon olive oil
> ½ cup Chicken Stock (page 285–86) or canned low-fat, low-sodium chicken broth
> 1 tablespoon potato starch or cornstarch
> 1 tablespoon red currant jelly

1. Place the dried fruit in a nonreactive saucepan, cover with the port and ½ cup of the orange juice and the zest and set aside for 1 hour. Then bring to a boil, immediately reduce the heat to low and simmer for 30 minutes or until the fruit has softened. Cook it slowly or the port will evaporate. Cool slightly before using. You can prepare this several hours ahead.

2. Preheat the oven to 350 degrees F. Cut 4 pieces of kitchen string each approximately 10 inches long. Arrange them about 2 inches apart. Lay the pork roast on top of the string. Lightly salt and pepper the pork. Arrange ⅓ of the fruit mixture down the center of the pork and, making sure the fruit is tucked well inside, roll it into a long cylinder. Tie each piece of twine to make a tight roll.

3. Heat the olive oil in a large skillet over medium high heat until a spray of water dances on the surface and add the pork. Turn in the oil for 3 to 4 minutes until the pork has browned evenly on all sides. Place the pork on a rack set in a roasting pan and arrange one third of the remaining fruit over the top of the pork. Roast the pork for approximately 1 hour or 20 to 22 minutes per pound. A meat thermometer should read 155 to 160 degrees F. Transfer to a serving platter and keep warm.

4. Skim the fat from the roasting pan. Over medium-high heat, add the chicken stock and bring to a rapid boil, stirring constantly to scrape up the coagulated juices. Stir in the potato starch and blend until smooth. Strain the remaining juices from the fruit into the pan and add the remaining orange juice and red currant jelly. Stir until the jelly has dissolved and add a little water if necessary to make a smooth consistency. Add the remaining fruit and stir just until heated through. Set aside and keep warm.

5. Cut and discard the strings from the pork. Slice and arrange on a serving platter. Spoon some of the sauce over the top and divide the rest and the remaining fruit into equal portions. Serve hot.

❀ PER SERVING *Calories: 518, Cholesterol (mg): 52, Saturated fat (g): 4, Total fat (g): 13, Sodium (mg): 68, Total fiber (g): 7*

Island Stew with Pork

SERVES 4

AN OLD-FASHIONED STEW *with the zing of tropical spice and the distinctive mix of fruit and meat that we expect from Caribbean cuisine. Yams and rice add heft to this dish, spices capture the attention of your taste buds and the pork adds richness and flavor, but very little fat. Very easy to assemble, this stew appears quite liquid, but the addition of yams thickens it nicely by the time you are ready to serve it over fragrant basmati rice.*

SEASONED FLOUR
¼ cup unbleached all-purpose flour
½ teaspoon *each* salt, ground ginger and cinnamon
¼ teaspoon *each* ground cloves and nutmeg
Pinch of cayenne

1 pound pork tenderloin, cubed
4 teaspoons olive oil
1 onion, chopped
2 garlic cloves, minced
1 red or yellow bell pepper, seeded and sliced
1 tablespoon or more minced fresh jalapeño pepper
1 teaspoon minced fresh ginger
2 cups Chicken Stock (page 285–86) or canned low-fat,
    low-sodium chicken broth
1 cup white wine
1 pound carrots, sliced
2 tablespoons tomato paste
½ bay leaf
1 teaspoon grated orange zest
1 pound yams, peeled and diced
½ cup raisins
Salt and freshly ground pepper
3 cups cooked basmati rice (page 439)

1. Put the flour and seasonings in a medium-size bowl and blend with a whisk or fork. Add the pork and toss until completely coated with the seasoned flour. Shake off any excess.

2. Heat 2 teaspoons of the oil in a large nonreactive skillet or Dutch oven over medium heat until a spray of water dances on the surface. Add the pork and toss until browned, scraping the bottom of the pot to keep the floured meat from sticking and scorching. Transfer the pork to a separate dish for a few moments. Add the remaining 2 teaspoons olive oil, the onions, garlic, bell pepper, jalapeño and fresh ginger and toss over medium heat until well coated. Reduce the heat and cook for 1 minute, stirring frequently. Adjust the heat so the vegetables don't scorch. Add the pork, chicken stock, wine, carrots, tomato paste and bay leaf and bring to a boil, stirring constantly. Reduce the heat to a gentle simmer and cook uncovered for 45 minutes.

3. Add the orange zest, yams and raisins and taste for seasoning, adding salt and pepper to your taste. Continue cooking for 20 to 25 minutes or until both the yams and pork are tender. Stir frequently, the sauce will thicken as the yams release their starch.

4. While the pork cooks, prepare the rice. Place the rice on a large serving platter and arrange the stew on top. Remove the bay leaf and serve hot.

❋ PER SERVING *Calories: 640, Cholesterol (mg): 69, Saturated fat (g): 4, Total fat (g): 15, Sodium (mg): 404, Total fiber (g): 5*

Pork Medallions with Two Marmalades
SERVES 6

THE TWO MARMALADES *— onion-champagne and red cabbage–apricot — are two of the easiest showstoppers for accompanying fowl we can think of. Let them mellow in the refrigerator overnight, thus eliminating a lot of last-minute preparation. You can certainly serve them separately, but we like to present them side by side, encouraging people to savor the tastes individually and then discover their blended pleasure.*

ONION-CHAMPAGNE MARMALADE
2 onions, thinly sliced
1 cup Champagne or white wine
1/3 cup red raspberry vinegar
1 tablespoon honey
1/4 cup yellow raisins

RED CABBAGE–APRICOT MARMALADE

1½ pounds red cabbage, shredded
1½ tablespoons red raspberry vinegar
3 tablespoons apricot preserves
3 tablespoons chopped dried apricots
3 tablespoons margarine
½ teaspoon sharp dry mustard
Pinch of dried ginger
Very small pinch of cayenne

PORK TENDERLOIN

2 teaspoons olive oil
½ cup finely diced shallots
1½ pounds pork tenderloin, thinly sliced
Salt and freshly ground pepper
2 tablespoons white wine
1 tablespoon Chicken Stock (page 285–86)
   or canned low-fat, low-sodium chicken broth
1 teaspoon margarine

1. To make the onion-champagne marinade, place the ingredients in a nonreactive saucepan and bring to a boil. Reduce the heat to a simmer and cook for 45 to 60 minutes or until the liquid has been absorbed and the mixture is quite thick. Check frequently, stirring so it does not scorch. Chop coarsely in a blender or food processor. This can be made several days ahead and stored covered in the refrigerator. Rewarm before serving.

2. To make the red cabbage–apricot marinade, place the cabbage with water to cover in a large saucepan, bring to boil and cook for 20 minutes or until tender but not mushy. Drain well and place in a smaller nonreactive saucepan. Stir in the remaining marmalade ingredients and heat thoroughly. This, too, can be made several hours or days ahead, covered and refrigerated. Rewarm before serving.

3. Heat the oil in a large heavy-bottomed skillet and add the shallots. Sauté briefly over medium heat, add the pork and a light dusting of salt and pepper. Sauté for 3 to 4 minutes or until the juices are clear, not pink, turning frequently. Arrange the medallions on a serving platter and keep warm.

4. Working quickly, add the wine and stock to the skillet and bring to a boil. Stir until the sauce has reduced by about half, then stir in the margarine. Pour over the pork and place each marmalade on opposite sides of the platter. Serve immediately, dividing both marinades into equal portions.

✿ PER SERVING *Calories: 421, Cholesterol (mg): 69, Saturated fat (g): 5, Total fat (g): 17, Sodium (mg): 167, Total fiber (g): 3*

CHAPTER 39

Desserts

TO SOME OF US, HEAVEN IS A PLACE *where butter and sugar are good for you, and if you don't eat your vegetables, you have to eat chocolate. To make waiting for that celestial pastry shop bearable, we set out to prove that healthy desserts are no longer a challenge. Imaginative reduced-fat frozen desserts abound in the supermarket freezers to help you create exotic sundaes topped with passion fruit, fresh strawberries, raspberries or pineapple, perhaps steeped in Champagne and strewn with mint. But the supermarket and produce stand are not the only places you can find healthful goodies. For the cook, we have assembled a selection of cakes, creams, parfaits, soufflés, tarts and even a knockout fudge sauce to delight you and yours. In this chapter you will learn some new techniques for baking cakes, no-fail pie crusts and cheesecakes without harmful fats. In addition, though, you will discover that you can still count on old standbys, such as soufflés, to produce sensational sweets for the Fat Tracker.*

We give you updated tips for all these desserts. For example, did you know that in the old days, some cooks were known to snap a bristle from the kitchen broom and stick it into a cake to test its doneness? The proliferation of plastic brooms (to say nothing of a justifiable obsession with sanitation) has led modern cooks to prefer a knife, toothpick, or in our case, a long-tined fork (it gives you two samples of batter). When a recipe indicates a cake is ready when a knife inserted in the center comes out clean, it means that no uncooked batter or clusters of partially baked crumbs streak the blade. It simply slides in and out easily and cleanly. Evidence of moisture is sometimes appropriate, though, as you will find with any cheesecake or crumb cake that substitutes fruit purées for some or all of the shortening.

We start our collection of recipes with a favorite trick for intensifying the flavor of your desserts and baked goods—flavored sugars. Use these sugars in place of all or part of the sugar for any of your sweet recipes or stir them into coffee or hot chocolate made with nonfat milk to enrich the taste.

Vanilla Sugar

An easy way to give desserts and baked goods more depth—especially when you limit butter, oil and whole-milk products—is to increase flavorings such as lemon and orange zest and spices such as cinnamon, ginger, and, most especially, vanilla. To this end, keep a 5- or 10-pound bag of sugar reserved for dessert making and baking, and bury a whole vanilla bean in it. Replace the sugar as you use it, the bean will continue to flavor subsequent batches. Replace the bean when it loses its aroma. Use the lovely vanilla-scented sweetener whenever a sweet recipe calls for regular sugar. No adjustment in the amount of sugar or vanilla called for in your recipe is necessary. You can even stir vanilla sugar into your coffee. Note that you would not use this sugar for savory dishes that call for a pinch of sugar, such as salad dressings, tomato sauces and the like.

Orange Sugar

Following the same strategy as for vanilla sugar, peel the thin outer zest of 2 oranges and place on a piece of foil or a baking sheet. Place in a preheated 250 degree F oven for 20 minutes. Cool completely and bury the peel in a canister of sugar.

Walnut Brownies

MAKES 16 BROWNIES, SERVING SIZE 1 BROWNIE

THERE ARE THOSE WHO CLAIM *that a good brownie is the mark of a highly evolved society. The truth is that a* healthy *brownie, which does not compromise the hearts of its citizens, is the mark of a truly advanced society. This one wins on all counts. Don't overbake or you will have a cakey rather than fudgy brownie. For an interesting twist, omit the walnuts and make raspberry brownies by puréeing ¾ cup of raspberries with 3 tablespoons of sugar and swirl the purée into the batter before putting it into the oven.*

> Vegetable spray for baking pan
> ¼ cup plus 2 teaspoons liquid egg substitute
> 1 cup brown sugar
> 2 tablespoons vanilla sugar (page 538) or granulated sugar
> ½ cup applesauce
> 1 tablespoon canola oil
> 2 teaspoons vanilla extract
> ½ cup unsweetened cocoa powder
> 1½ cups unbleached all-purpose flour
> 1 teaspoon baking powder
> ½ teaspoon salt
> ¼ teaspoon baking soda
> ⅓ cup chopped walnuts

1. Preheat the oven to 350 degrees F. Lightly coat an 8-inch square baking pan with a film of vegetable spray and wipe the excess with a paper towel. Line the bottom with parchment or waxed paper. Spray the paper and set the pan aside.

2. In a large bowl, combine the egg substitute, both sugars, applesauce, oil and vanilla extract. Sift in the cocoa and beat until thick and smooth.

3. Sift together the flour, baking powder, salt and baking soda. Add the flour mixture to the chocolate mixture in two portions, mixing thoroughly after each addition just until everything is incorporated. Fold in the nuts.

4. Pour the batter into the prepared pan and bake for 22 to 25 minutes or until the crumbs on a knife or long-tined fork inserted in the center come out moist but cooked. Slice into quarters and then quarter each square. Slice and cool thoroughly in the pan before serving.

❉ PER SERVING *Calories: 141, Cholesterol (mg): 0, Saturated fat (g): Trace, Total fat (g): 3, Sodium (mg): 125, Total fiber (g): 1*

Buttermilk Brandy Spice Cake

MAKES ONE 10-INCH CAKE, 1 DOZEN 3-INCH SERVING-SIZE SLICES

MOIST, SPICY, ADDICTIVE. *Serve this wonderful, fine-crumbed cake at a festive brunch, to a gathering of friends for an afternoon tea or coffee party or as a sweet dessert following Garlic Roasted Chicken with Wilted Greens (page 510–11) and Spiced Sauté of Broccoli Stalks, Carrots and Potatoes (page 401).*

Vegetable spray for cake pan
2½ cups cake flour
1 teaspoon baking powder
¼ teaspoon baking soda
1 teaspoon salt
1 teaspoon ground cinnamon
¾ teaspoon ground cloves
½ teaspoon ground allspice
¼ teaspoon ground ginger
Pinch of ground nutmeg
⅔ cup canola oil
¾ cup vanilla sugar (page 538) or granulated sugar
½ cup brown sugar
1 teaspoon grated orange zest
¾ cup liquid egg substitute
1 teaspoon vanilla extract
¾ cup low-fat buttermilk
¼ cup Cognac or brandy

TOPPING
¼ cup low-fat buttermilk
¼ cup vanilla sugar (page 538) or granulated sugar
¼ teaspoon baking soda
¼ teaspoon vanilla extract
1 teaspoon grated orange zest

1. Preheat the oven to 350 degrees F. Lightly coat a 10-inch Bundt pan with a thin film of vegetable spray and wipe the excess with a paper towel. To prevent the cake from sticking, cut 2 or 3 strips of waxed or parchment paper 1½ x 5 inches and press them into the bottom of the pan, overlapping the ends to make a circle. Spray the paper lightly and set aside the pan.

2. Measure the flour, then sift it into a medium-size bowl with the baking powder, baking soda, salt, cinnamon, cloves, allspice, ginger and nutmeg. Blend the mixture well and set it aside.

3. In a large bowl beat the oil, vanilla sugar, brown sugar and 1 teaspoon orange zest with an electric mixer (not a food processor) on high speed about 2 minutes or until thick and thoroughly blended. Add the egg substitute, ¼ cup at a time, beating after each addition just until it is incorporated into the batter. Add the vanilla and continue beating for 4 to 5 minutes or until the batter is light and frothy.

4. Sprinkle ⅓ of the flour mixture over the batter and, on low speed, beat it in thoroughly, but stop as soon as the flour is incorporated. With each of the following additions beat gently, thoroughly but quickly and don't overbeat or the texture of the cake will suffer. Scrape the sides of the bowl and add ½ cup of the buttermilk. Beat on low speed just until it is absorbed, add half the remaining flour and beat it in quickly. Keep the speed low at all times. Add the cognac and remaining ¼ cup buttermilk, beat again, and then incorporate the remaining flour.

5. Pour the batter into the prepared pan and bake for 35 to 40 minutes or until a toothpick or long-tined fork inserted in the center comes out dry. Set the cake aside for 8 to 10 minutes before unmolding it.

6. For the topping, combine the ingredients in a small bowl and stir until they are thoroughly mixed. Run a knife between the cake and the pan to loosen it. Place a cake platter over the cake and (using potholders to protect your hands) turn the cake and platter upside down in one swift motion and set it on the counter. Slide the pan up and off the cake. While the cake is still hot, use a skewer or toothpick to poke small holes in several rows 2 inches apart about halfway down into the cake (so the cake will absorb the topping). Pour the topping over the top of the cake, spreading it evenly. Some of it will drip down the sides. Set aside to cool before serving.

❋ PER SERVING *Calories: 324, Cholesterol (mg): 1, Saturated fat (g): 1, Total fat (g): 13, Sodium (mg): 314, Total fiber (g): 1*

Mocha Torte with Apricot Filling

MAKES ONE 9-INCH LAYER CAKE, 10 SERVING-SIZE SLICES

To HAVE YOUR CAKE AND EAT IT TOO, *use reduced-fat sour cream and canola oil, instead of butter or margarine, to produce an elegant, delicate cake for special parties. Similar to a European baking technique that relies on beaten egg whites instead of baking powder for leavening, this cake achieves a rich, chocolatey flavor with unsweetened fat-free cocoa. You can vary the flavor by making very strong coffee with flavored beans, such as chocolate, vanilla or one of the popular blends with a liqueur added. You can also substitute unsweetened apricot purée for the jam if you want to reduce the sugar calories. For a very luxurious center, soak a cup dried apricots in cold water until softened, chop and scatter them over the preserves. Don't let the length of the instructions concern you; this is not a difficult, nor exceedingly time-consuming cake to make.*

Vegetable spray for cake pans
3 cups cake flour
1/2 teaspoon baking soda
1/2 teaspoon salt
1/2 cup canola oil
1 cup reduced-fat sour cream
3/4 cup unsweetened cocoa powder
2 cups vanilla sugar (page 538) or granulated sugar
1 teaspoon vanilla extract
1 cup double-strength coffee (using flavored beans if you like), cooled
5 egg whites (approximately 2/3 cup)
Pinch of cream of tartar
Pinch of salt
1/2 cup unsweetened apricot jam or apricot preserves
    with large pieces cut up
Juice of 1/2 orange
White thread and toothpicks
Powdered sugar for topping
Fresh apricot halves, mint leaves or edible flowers for garnish

1. Preheat the oven to 350 degrees F. Spray the bottom and sides of two 9-inch cake pans with a light coating of vegetable spray and wipe the excess with a paper towel. Place one of the cake pans on waxed paper or parchment, draw an outline with the tip of your scissors and cut 2 rounds of paper. Fit one into the bottom of each cake pan. Lightly coat the paper with vegetable spray and set the pans aside.

2. Sift together the measured flour, baking soda and salt. Put the oil, sour cream, cocoa and 1 1/2 cups of the sugar into a large bowl. With an electric mixer (not

a processor) beat them together on high speed for 2 minutes. In a measuring cup, stir the vanilla extract into the cooled coffee and add to the batter, pouring slowly and beating until it is thoroughly blended. Beat on medium speed for 2 minutes, scraping the sides of the bowl from time to time.

3. With a spatula, stir in the flour (by hand, not with the mixer) in three portions, bringing the spatula to the bottom of the bowl and gently shaking it up through the batter to mix in the flour. Don't overbeat, just blend the ingredients thoroughly.

4. In a clean mixing bowl and with clean dry beaters, whip the egg whites, cream of tartar and salt on high speed until they form a soft mound on the beaters. Don't overbeat them until they are stiff or the egg whites will be hard to fold into the cake batter. In addition, they may dry out and the cake won't rise properly. Add the remaining ½ cup sugar and beat the egg whites just until they are fully absorbed.

5. Add a third of the egg whites to the batter and fold them in as you did the flour, bringing the spatula from the bottom of the bowl up through the batter with a gentle, shaking motion. Give the bowl a quarter turn and repeat. Fold in the remaining egg whites, using the same technique.

6. Divide the batter equally between the two cake pans and place them in the center of the oven. Bake for 30 minutes or until a toothpick or long-tined fork inserted in the center comes out dry. Set the cake pans aside to cool briefly. Loosen the edges of the cake layers with a knife, place a cake rack over each one and turn it upside down. Slide the pan off the cake and cool it thoroughly on the racks.

7. In a small nonreactive saucepan, heat the apricot jam and orange juice, blending it well and set aside.

8. To slice the layers (and to flatten off their uneven tops), wrap a piece of thread a few inches wider than the diameter of the cake around each toothpick and adjust the height of the thread so that it just reaches the top of the layer (at its lowest point). Place one cake layer on a piece of waxed paper on a flat surface. Starting at the edge farthest from you, pull the toothpicks toward you so that you make a thin slice with the thread to smooth the top. Remove the scraps. Lower the thread so that when you pull it toward you this time, you will slice the layer in half. Do not separate the layers yet. Repeat with the other layer so that you have four thin layers. Place a layer on a serving platter and brush with the apricot sauce. Repeat with the remaining layers, stacking them evenly on top of each other and pressing them together slightly. Do not put the apricot sauce on the top of the cake, instead sift powdered sugar over it. Garnish the edge of the cake with slices of fresh apricots, mint leaves or fresh flowers. Slice into 10 thin wedges and serve.

❀ PER SERVING *Calories: 463, Cholesterol (mg): 10, Saturated fat (g): 3, Total fat (g): 15, Sodium (mg): 217, Total fiber (g): Trace*

Gingerbread with Ginger Cream

MAKES EIGHT 2 X 4-INCH SERVING-SIZE SLICES

LIKE MOST OF THE EARLY AMERICAN FOOD TRADITIONS *that survived the Revolution, the history of gingerbread began in Europe. It was popularized by the Pennsylvania Dutch, but in the 1790s Amelia Simmons wrote* American Cookery *and transformed the hard European gingerbread into what she called "soft gingerbread." In doing so, she became the first in a long line of chefs who broke the Old World mold to create something new and uniquely American. In our approach to gingerbread, we dispense with the usual call for butter or sour cream and add applesauce in place of a hefty portion of shortening. It lightens, moistens and mixes with a perfect blend of spices to ensure that gingerbread remains at the healthy heart of American cooking.*

> Ginger Cream (recipe follows)
> Vegetable spray for baking pan
> 1¼ cups unbleached all purpose flour
> ½ cup cake flour
> 1½ teaspoons baking soda
> ½ teaspoon salt
> 1½ teaspoons ground ginger
> ½ teaspoon ground cinnamon
> ¼ teaspoon ground allspice
> Pinch *each* of ground nutmeg, cloves and mace
> ¼ cup liquid egg substitute
> ¼ cup unsweetened applesauce
> ½ cup light molasses
> ½ cup vanilla sugar (page 538) or granulated sugar
> ¼ cup canola oil
> ½ cup boiling water

1. At least 1 hour before serving prepare the Ginger Cream, cover and refrigerate.

2. Preheat the oven to 350 degrees F. Coat an 8-inch square baking pan with a light film of vegetable spray and wipe the excess with a paper towel. Line the bottom with waxed or parchment paper. Lightly spray the paper and set the pan aside.

3. Over a medium-size bowl, sift together both flours, the baking soda, salt and all the ground spices. Stir them together until well blended.

4. In a large bowl, whisk together the egg substitute, applesauce, molasses and sugar until frothy. Fold the dry ingredients into the egg mixture. Add the oil and boiling water and blend thoroughly but do not overbeat. Pour into the prepared pan and bake 45 to 50 minutes or until a knife inserted in the center comes out clean (see chapter introduction, page 537). Remove from the oven, slice into squares and cool thoroughly in the pan. Serve with the Ginger Cream.

❋ PER SERVING (INCLUDES 2 TABLESPOONS GINGER CREAM) *Calories: 307, Cholesterol (mg): 0, Saturated fat (g): 2, Total fat (g): 9, Sodium (mg): 408, Total fiber (g): 1*

Ginger Cream
Makes approximately 1 cup, serving size 1 tablespoon

Cool and creamy with an unexpected snap of ginger that reminds you of the variety of this gnarly root so crucial to Asian stir-fries and so vibrant in Western desserts. Unfrosted cakes, fresh or grilled fruit, dessert fruit soups or other fruit desserts come to life with just a dab of Ginger Cream. As with other yogurt creams, blend by hand, not in a mixer or food processor or it will liquefy. This will keep refrigerated up to the expiration date for the yogurt.

> ½ cup nonfat plain yogurt
> ½ cup reduced-fat sour cream
> 2 teaspoons or more finely minced glacéed ginger or ginger in syrup
> 4 teaspoons vanilla sugar (page 538) or granulated sugar

In a small bowl, blend all the ingredients until smooth. Cover and refrigerate for at least 1 hour before serving.

FAT TRACKING TIP: Use fat-free sour cream.

❋ PER SERVING *Calories: 21, Cholesterol (mg): 3, Saturated fat (g): Trace, Total fat (g): 1, Sodium (mg): 8, Total fiber (g): Trace*

Fresh Plum Pastry Cake

MAKES ONE 11 X 7-INCH CAKE, 1 DOZEN SERVING-SIZE SLICES

A STUNNING CONFECTION *of airy cake which absorbs the nectar of fresh plums as they bake. In place of large amounts of shortening, this mouthwatering pastry uses orange juice and a little canola oil to good advantage. Choose very sweet fruit at the height of its season or you may need to toss the plums in a little more sugar; however, if the plums are especially sweet, do not toss them in any sugar at all. You can substitute peaches or nectarines, but they must be very sweet and ripe.*

> Butter-flavored vegetable spray for cake pan
> 2 pounds sweet, firm plums
> ⅔ cup vanilla sugar (page 538) or granulated sugar plus 1 teaspoon
> 1½ cups unbleached all-purpose flour
> 1½ teaspoons baking powder
> 1 tablespoon butter granules
> ½ teaspoon ground cinnamon
> ½ teaspoon salt
> ¾ cup fresh orange juice
> ¼ cup liquid egg substitute
> 1 teaspoon grated orange zest
> 2 tablespoons canola oil

1. Preheat the oven to 350 degrees F. Liberally coat an 11 x 7-inch baking dish with butter-flavored vegetable spray (a smaller pan produces a cakier pastry) and wipe the excess with a paper towel. Without peeling them, slice the plums in uneven thicknesses to add an interesting texture to the topping. Discard the pits. Place the plums in a bowl and toss them with about 1 teaspoon of sugar, more or less—or none—depending on their sweetness.

2. Sift together the sugar, flour, baking powder, butter granules, cinnamon and salt into a large bowl and stir well to blend the ingredients.

3. In a measuring cup beat together the orange juice, egg substitute and orange zest until well mixed. Blend in the oil. Stir this mixture into the dry ingredients and blend thoroughly but do not overbeat. Pour the batter into the prepared baking dish. Cover with the plums and bake for 55 to 60 minutes or until the cake is golden and the plums soft and juicy. Cool, then slice into 12 pieces before serving.

❋ PER SERVING *Calories: 174, Cholesterol (mg): 0, Saturated fat (g): Trace, Total fat (g): 3, Sodium (mg): 159, Total fiber (g): 2*

Black Cherry Cheese Pie

MAKES ONE 9-INCH CHEESECAKE, EIGHT 3-INCH SERVING-SIZE SLICES

LIKE RUBIES SET ON A VELVET PILLOW, *this dessert looks as rich as it tastes. Ruby red cherries on a velvety cream, that is. This is another example of making pristine creams taste richer than they are with artfully flavored low-fat and nonfat soft cheeses and yogurt. Allow several hours for chilling this pie or make a day ahead.*

> 1 Crunchy Crust (recipe follows)
> Black Cherry Compote (recipe follows)
> 1 pound very low-fat ricotta cheese
> 1 teaspoon vanilla extract
> 1 teaspoon grated orange zest
> ⅓ cup vanilla sugar (page 538), orange sugar (page 538)
>   or granulated sugar
> 1 cup Drained Nonfat Yogurt (page 290–91)
> 1 teaspoon unflavored gelatin dissolved in 1 tablespoon
>   fresh orange juice

1. Prepare and cool or chill the Crunchy Crust and Black Cherry Compote.

2. In a large bowl, beat the ricotta, vanilla extract, orange zest and sugar until smooth. Fold in the yogurt and the gelatin mixture and blend well. Fill the cooled crust with this mixture. Refrigerate for 30 minutes or until the cheese filling has begun to set.

3. Spread the cherry compote on top and refrigerate for at least 2 hours. Slice and serve chilled. Immediately refrigerate any remaining pie.

✽ PER SERVING *Calories: 349, Cholesterol (mg): 9, Saturated fat (g): 1, Total fat (g): 9, Sodium (mg): 104, Total fiber (g): 3*

Crunchy Crust
Makes one 9-inch crust, eight 3-inch serving-size slices

This lean, nutty prebaked crust with a cookielike crunch will hold any unbaked pie filling. Because it doesn't have the 1½ cups of butter that short pastry needs, you may be able to pinch a second slice and still remain under your fat target for the day. You can vary the taste and crispiness with different types of low-fat granola. Or, in place of granola, you can use ground almond cookies, chocolate ice box cookies or graham crackers.

> Vegetable spray for pie pan
> ½ cup rolled oats
> ½ cup unbleached all-purpose flour
> ¼ cup whole wheat flour
> ¼ cup tightly packed brown sugar
> 1 teaspoon ground cinnamon
> ½ cup low-fat granola or muesli without dried fruit
> 3 tablespoons canola oil
> 2½ tablespoons unsweetened applesauce

1. Preheat the oven to 325 degrees F. Lightly coat a 9-inch pie pan with a film of vegetable spray and wipe the excess with a paper towel. Place all the ingredients in a food processor and beat until a moist dough forms that holds together loosely or, beat in a blender, scraping down the sides frequently. Press the dough into the prepared pie pan. Press your knuckle gently into the corners to ease it up along the sides of the pan. As you do, guide the crust with the index finger of your other hand to shape the top edge.

2. Bake the crust for 15 to 18 minutes or until very lightly toasted. Do not overbake it or it will have too much crunch. Cool before filling the crust. You can make this up to 24 hours in advance, cover tightly with plastic wrap or aluminum foil and refrigerate.

❋ PER SERVING *Calories: 200, Cholesterol (mg): 0, Saturated fat (g): 1, Total fat (g): 7, Sodium (mg): 18, Total fiber (g): 2*

Black Cherry Compote
Serves 6

Use plump black cherries to make a luscious sauce for angel food cake, a topping for low-fat or nonfat frozen yogurt or this mouthwatering Black Cherry Cheese Pie. Use fresh cherries in the summer, or frozen when the fresh fruit is out of season. Score each cherry as you remove the stem and you will find it quite easy to remove the pits after they are cooked.

> 1 pound black cherries
> 1 cup cold water
> ½ cup fresh orange juice
> 3 tablespoons vanilla sugar (page 538), orange sugar (page 538)
>   or granulated sugar
> 2 teaspoons cornstarch dissolved in 1 tablespoon cold water
> 2 tablespoons kirsch or orange liqueur, optional

1. Place the cherries in a medium-size nonreactive saucepan with the water, orange juice and sugar. Bring to a boil, then reduce the heat and simmer for 15 minutes or until they are tender. With a slotted spoon, remove the cherries to a small bowl and allow them to cool. When you can handle them comfortably, remove and discard the pits.

2. While the cherries cool, raise the heat under the juices in the saucepan until the liquid bubbles quite rapidly. Simmer vigorously until approximately ¼ to ⅓ cup of juice remains. Stir frequently and lower the heat as necessary to prevent the juices from boiling away completely. Give a stir to the cornstarch mixture, add it to the pan and stir vigorously until the sauce thickens. Stir in the liqueur (if using) as well as the cherries and any juice remaining in the bowl. Chill thoroughly.

❀ PER SERVING *Calories: 91, Cholesterol (mg): 0, Saturated fat (g): 0, Total fat (g): 1, Sodium (mg): Trace, Total fiber (g): 1*

Chocolate-Crusted
Raspberry Cheesecake

MAKES ONE 9-INCH CHEESECAKE, EIGHT 3-INCH SERVING-SIZE SLICES

DECEPTIVELY RICH TASTING, *the smooth texture of this cheesecake comes from vigorous beating that incorporates air into the filling, while whipped egg whites add another lightening strike. Don't strain the seeds from any raspberry purée unless a recipe requires a smooth texture; they provide additional fiber.*

CHOCOLATE CRUST

Vegetable spray for cake pan

12 graham crackers (2 inches square)

3 tablespoons unsweetened cocoa powder

2 tablespoons vanilla sugar (page 538) or granulated sugar

1 tablespoon frozen orange juice concentrate, thawed

1 tablespoon canola oil

CHEESE FILLING

1 pound part-skim ricotta cheese

8 ounces low-fat cream cheese

½ cup liquid egg substitute

½ cup vanilla sugar (page 538) or granulated sugar

2 tablespoons cornstarch

¾ cup evaporated low-fat milk

1 teaspoon grated lemon zest

2 tablespoons fresh lemon juice

2 egg whites

Pinch of cream of tartar

RASPBERRY TOPPING

4 cups fresh raspberries

1 tablespoon cornstarch

2 tablespoons vanilla sugar (page 538), orange sugar (page (538)
   or granulated sugar

Small flowers or mint leaves for garnish

1. Preheat the oven to 350 degrees F. Coat the bottom and sides of a 9-inch cake pan with a thin film of vegetable spray and wipe the excess with a paper towel. Place the crust ingredients in a food processor or blender and grind until thoroughly blended and moist. Press the mixture into a thin layer on the bottom and sides of the prepared pan following the instructions for Crunchy Crust on page 548, and bake for 8 minutes. Remove from the oven to cool. *Reduce the oven temperature to 325 degrees F.*

2. Combine the ricotta cheese, cream cheese, egg substitute, ½ cup sugar, cornstarch and half of the milk (6 tablespoons) in the bowl of an electric mixer and blend well at medium speed. Add the remaining 6 tablespoons milk and beat at high speed for 5 minutes. Add the lemon zest and lemon juice and beat for 1 minute more.

3. In a separate bowl, beat the egg whites with the cream of tartar until very thick and a spoonful falls into a soft mound. Do not overbeat or allow to become stiff or the whites will not blend easily into the cheese mixture. Using a light touch, gently stir ¼ of the beaten egg whites into the cheese mixture and blend thoroughly to lighten the batter. Then carefully fold in the remaining egg whites. Pour into the prepared pan.

4. Bake for 1 hour or until browned on top and a long-tined fork inserted in the center comes out clean. The baked cheesecake will puff up slightly and crack, then deflate a bit as it cools. Chill thoroughly.

5. Before serving, purée 2 cups of the raspberries in a blender and place them in a small saucepan. Add the cornstarch and 2 tablespoons sugar and stir continuously over medium heat until thickened. Cool thoroughly. Spread the purée on top of the cheesecake and arrange the fresh berries on the top in a circular pattern. Tuck the flowers or mint leaves around the bottom edge before serving.

✤ PER SERVING *Calories: 361, Cholesterol (mg): 28, Saturated fat (g): 2, Total fat (g): 14, Sodium (mg): 400, Total fiber (g): 3*

Summer Fruit Tart

MAKES ONE 9-INCH TART, SIX 4-INCH SERVING-SIZE SLICES

FRUIT TARTS ARTFULLY ARRANGED *with the bright colors of the summer harvest draw the eye like an intricate mosaic. Hidden beneath our kaleidoscope of fruit is a heavenly lean pastry cream that lets you enjoy this tart all through the berry season.*

> 2 or more cups unblemished fresh fruit (such as berries or peeled peaches, plums, apricots, nectarines, kiwi fruit, bananas)
> Filo Pastry Crust (recipe follows)
> Heart-Healthy Pastry Cream (recipe follows)
> 2 tablespoons unsweetened apricot preserves
> 2 tablespoons hot water

1. Slice the berries and fruit as necessary to make an artful arrangement on the top of the tart. Mix sliced and whole strawberries, if using. Prepare the pastry cream and pastry crust. In a small bowl mix the preserves and hot water for a glaze.

2. Spread the pastry cream on the bottom of the pastry crust, covering it completely. Arrange the fruit over the pastry cream, for example, starting with an outside row of strawberries or raspberries and filling in with ever smaller alternating circles of peaches, kiwi and plums. Crown the center with a large, perfect strawberry. Make an effort to completely cover the pastry cream. Lightly brush the fruit with the apricot glaze, cover and chill thoroughly before serving.

❋ PER SERVING *Calories: 106, Cholesterol (mg): 3, Saturated fat (g): Trace, Total fat (g): 1, Sodium (mg): 62, Total fiber (g): 1*

Filo Pastry Crust
Makes one 9-inch crust, six 3-inch serving-size slices

Finally, here's an easy and fat-free pastry crust. Filo dough comes frozen in a roll of large sheets. Allow the frozen filo to thaw for about an hour on the counter or until it is just flexible enough to unroll the outer sheets. Carefully unwrap a few sheets from the roll while it's partially frozen, then reseal and return the remaining sheets to the freezer for your next tart. If the roll thaws completely and dries out as you are working with it, you may not be able to reuse it. The thin individual sheets will continue to thaw as you prepare the pastry. Use what you need and, to prevent drying, be careful to keep the unwrapped sheets covered with a damp cloth until they have been moistened with vegetable spray.

Butter-flavored vegetable spray
2 sheets filo dough
1 teaspoon powdered sugar

1. Preheat the oven to 350 degrees F. Spray a 9-inch quiche pan with a removable bottom with a light film of butter-flavored vegetable spray and place ½ sheet of filo on it. Spray lightly again. Sift over the filo the *lightest possible* cloud of powdered sugar. (You will do this with each half sheet, but do not attempt to use the entire teaspoon of sugar for the pastry. Also don't worry about edges overlapping at this point.) Give the pan a half turn, add another sheet, spray as before, dust with powdered sugar and give the pan another half turn. Continue with the remaining sheets. The crisscrossing will ensure that the entire pan is covered with dough. Carefully tuck the filo into the bottom corner and to prevent shrinkage fold the edges over the outside. Use a light touch; it may be unwieldy but don't worry if the filo cracks. Spray and dust again.

2. Bake for 10 to 12 minutes or until the shell is golden. Set aside to cool and then fill as directed in the recipe.

❋ PER SERVING *Calories: 15, Cholesterol (mg): 0, Saturated fat (g): 0, Total fat (g): Trace, Sodium (mg): 16, Total fiber (g): 0*

Heart-Healthy Pastry Cream
Makes 1⅓ cups, serving size 2 tablespoons

We have had friends who foreswear rich desserts actually insist on seeing the recipe before they would believe this was an enlightened pastry. The coup here, of course, is an easy, cholesterol-free pastry cream (and custard sauce as in the variation for Crème Anglaise that follows) made without egg yolks or whole milk. We have developed this heart-healthy pastry cream to use as the foundation for fruit tarts and as fillings for cakes. In addition to filling this Summer Fruit Tart, you can spread it between the layers of Mocha Torte (page 542–43). Anyone who has ever stirred egg yolks and milk for 15 or 20 minutes until they reached a perfect consistency will never return to the original technique after trying this microwaved version. You can make this with whole, low-fat, 1 percent or nonfat milk, depending on your need to streamline the fat. Typically, we use low-fat milk. Nonfat and even 1 percent–fat milk work well as far as consistency is concerned, though, as you might expect, the taste is somewhat thinner. If you use the lighter milk, plan to enrich it with a liqueur or add a little extra vanilla. Caution: Do not add chocolate extract to this sauce or the variation that follows. It turns the sauce a decidedly unappetizing gray. Note that if you use the conventional method for preparing the sauce, you may wish to add a vanilla bean instead of vanilla extract as it cooks. Split a vanilla bean in half lengthwise and add to the milk. Retrieve the bean after cooking. Some tiny dark seeds will remain in the sauce, testifying to the added care you have taken with this delicacy.

1 cup low-fat milk

2½ tablespoons vanilla sugar (page 538) or granulated sugar

1 teaspoon vanilla extract

2 teaspoons butter granules

⅓ cup liquid egg substitute

2 tablespoons flour or cornstarch

2 tablespoons Grand Marnier or other orange liqueur, optional

1. In a microwave-safe bowl, heat the milk with the sugar, vanilla and butter granules for 1 minute on high. Whisk in the eggs and flour. Microwave on high for
40 seconds. *Whisk and stir thoroughly.* Repeat for another 40 seconds. *Whisk and
stir thoroughly.* Microwave for 30 seconds. *Whisk and stir thoroughly.* Repeat
three more times for 10 seconds each and finally microwave for 5 seconds. Set
aside for 4 or 5 minutes. Stir thoroughly. If any lumps occur, strain the cream. Stir
in the Grand Marnier, if using. Place a piece of plastic wrap directly on the surface of the cream if you do not intend to use it right away, and refrigerate.

2. For conventional stoves, place the milk, sugar, vanilla and butter granules in a
small saucepan and heat just until it begins to steam. Do not allow it to come
near a boil. In a small bowl, whisk together the egg substitute and flour until
well blended and stir 2 tablespoons of the heated milk into the egg mixture,
blend well and return the mixture to the saucepan. Stir over low heat until the
sauce thickens. This step may take up to 15 minutes. Stir constantly and keep
the heat low. When the sauce has thickened, immediately remove it from the
heat. If it has any lumps at all, press it through a sieve. Stir in the Grand Marnier
or other flavoring if desired and serve hot or cold.

CHOCOLATE PASTRY CREAM Instead of Grand Marnier, while still warm stir
in 1 scant tablespoon unsweetened cocoa.

FAT TRACKING TIP: Use 1% milk instead of low-fat.

❋ PER SERVING *Calories: 21, Cholesterol (mg): 2, Saturated fat (g): Trace, Total fat (g): Trace,
Sodium (mg): 22, Total fiber (g): Trace*

Crème Anglaise

Makes approximately 1⅓ cups, serving size approximately 2 tablespoons

Whip up this classic sauce to top seasonal berries, Poached Apples in Rum Sauce with Raisins and Dried Blueberries (page 556), Roasted Pears (page 557) or any other dessert that begs for a custard topping. The sauce thickens as it sits, but if you follow the timing instructions it will remain a creamy consistency. Longer cooking results in a thicker texture (almost a custard) which, depending on your use, may be desirable.

> ⅓ cup liquid egg substitute
> 2½ tablespoons vanilla sugar (page 538), orange sugar (page 538)
>   or granulated sugar
> 1 cup low-fat milk
> 1 teaspoon vanilla extract
> 2 tablespoons Grand Marnier or other liqueur, optional

1. In a microwave-safe bowl, blend together the egg substitute and sugar and whisk in the cold milk. Stir in the vanilla and microwave on high for 1 minute. *Whisk and stir thoroughly.* Cook for 1 minute. *Whisk and stir thoroughly.* Cook for 1 minute more. *Whisk and stir thoroughly.* Cook for 30 seconds. Set the bowl aside for 4 or 5 minutes and stir. If the sauce has any lumps, press it through a strainer. Stir in Grand Marnier and serve warm or cold.

2. For conventional stoves, whisk the milk, sugar and vanilla in a small saucepan and heat just until it begins to steam. Do not allow it to come near a boil. In a small bowl, stir 2 tablespoons of the heated milk into the egg substitute, blend well and return the mixture to the saucepan. Stir over low heat until a coating of the sauce clings to the spoon. This step may take up to 15 minutes. Stir constantly and keep the heat low. When the sauce has thickened, immediately remove it from the heat. If it has any lumps at all, press it through a sieve. Stir in the Grand Marinier or other flavoring if desired and serve hot or cold.

❀ PER SERVING *Calories: 42, Cholesterol (mg): 2, Saturated fat (g): Trace, Total fat (g): 1, Sodium (mg): 27, Total fiber (g): 0*

Poached Apples in Rum Sauce
with Raisins and Dried Blueberries
SERVES 6

For something warm and sweet on a crisp fall evening, poach tangy Granny Smiths and let them mellow in the natural sugar of raisins and dried blueberries. You also can keep the apples handy in the refrigerator for a quick spoonful of something rich tasting and fat free now and then. You can also make this ahead of time to allow the apples to sweeten even further as they absorb the syrup, then reheat before serving. Or, to preserve some of the zing of autumn apples, serve as soon as they are tender and glazed with the rum sauce. As still another option, you can spoon the apples over frozen yogurt or top with nonfat plain yogurt, Sweet Yogurt Cream (page 559) or Crème Anglaise (page 555).

> 6 large Granny Smith or Gravenstein apples, cored and sliced
> 2 to 2½ cups cold water
> ½ cup white wine
> ¼ cup vanilla sugar (page 538) or granulated sugar
> ½ cup yellow raisins
> ¼ cup dried blueberries, if available
> ¼ cup firmly packed brown sugar
> ½ teaspoon ground cinnamon
> 2 tablespoons rum

1. Place the apple slices in a nonreactive medium-size saucepan and add the water (just enough to cover), wine and vanilla sugar. Bring to a boil and then reduce to a simmer. Cook uncovered 12 to 15 minutes or until the apples are tender. Use a slotted spoon to scoop them into a bowl.

2. Add the raisins, blueberries (if using), brown sugar and cinnamon to the poaching liquid and bring to a boil. Reduce the heat just slightly and, stirring frequently, cook uncovered until the liquid is syrupy and reduced by about a third. Whisk in the rum and continue simmering for 30 to 40 seconds. Taste and add more cinnamon or rum if desired. Add the apples to the syrup and stir until well blended. Serve warm or cold.

✱ PER SERVING *Calories: 237, Cholesterol (mg): 0, Saturated fat (g): 0, Total fat (g): 1, Sodium (mg): 10, Total fiber (g): 4*

Roasted Pears with Anise Crumbs

WE BELIEVE THAT ANISE IS TO PEARS, *what cinnamon is to apples. The almost custardy texture of roasted pears needs little adornment, but the delicate taste of licorice in the anise crumbs adds an exotic touch. Be sure to handle the pears carefully. The skins must remain intact as they roast to capture the juice and natural sugar, which produces the creamy result. Of the almost 500 catalogued varieties of pears, the soft fleshed types such as Bartlett and D'Anjou work best. But for a special treat, use Comice.*

> Vegetable spray for baking sheet
> 6 Bartlett or D'Anjou pears, unpeeled, stems intact
> 2 tablespoons Anise Crumbs (recipe follows)

1. Preheat the oven to 450 degrees F. Coat a baking sheet with a light film of vegetable spray and wipe out the excess. Arrange the pears on the baking sheet and bake them for 25 to 30 minutes or until they look rumpled and are very tender when you pierce them with the tip of a knife or a long-tined fork. Test them at the end of the cooking time to keep the skins intact.

2. Place the hot pears on individual dessert plates and sprinkle with the Anise Crumbs. Do not slice the pears, but allow each diner to savor the burst of aroma as they break into the pear for the first creamy bite.

❋ PER SERVING *Calories: 110, Cholesterol (mg): 0, Saturated fat (g): 0, Total fat (g): 1, Sodium (mg): 10, Total fiber (g): 5*

Anise Crumbs
> *Makes ½ cup, serving size 1 teaspoon*

Brown sugar and the tease of licorice in aniseed make for a heady blend that can be intoxicating on sweet poached fruit. Use as a sweet sprinkle for broiled grapefruit at breakfast, or scattered on baked apples or poached summer fruits for dessert. The crumbs also are excellent on grilled white Babcock peaches. Though the nuts add fat, it is monounsaturated, and the crumbs are a far better and more creative garnish than a dollop of heavy cream. Stick a slice of bread in your toaster to make the bread crumbs.

¼ cup coarse bread crumbs from toasted honey wheat bread
   or your favorite dense, wheaty bread
2 tablespoons brown sugar
2 tablespoons ground hazelnuts or walnuts
1 teaspoon aniseed

Blend the ingredients in a small bowl. Cover tightly and refrigerate. They will keep for weeks in the refrigerator, longer in the freezer.

Fat Tracking Tip: Reduce the walnuts to 1 tablespoon.

✿ Per serving *Calories: 15, Cholesterol (mg): 0, Saturated fat (g): 0, Total fat (g): 1, Sodium (mg): 10, Total fiber (g): Trace*

Fruit Parfait
with Peaches and Cream
SERVES 6

Even if you were to throw dietary caution to the wind, *you could not find a more satisfying indulgence than ripe berries swelling with natural sugar. Take advantage of the best the summer fruit harvest has to offer and showcase it in this sparkling parfait.*

1 pint fresh strawberries
1 pint fresh raspberries
2 pints fresh blueberries or blackberries
3 large, ripe peaches
1 tablespoon fresh lemon juice or orange juice
1 teaspoon to 2 tablespoons vanilla sugar (page 538)
   or granulated sugar
3 to 4 tablespoons fresh orange juice *or* 2 tablespoons of juice
   and 1 to 2 tablespoons orange liqueur or kirsch
Sweet Yogurt Cream (recipe follows)
Mint leaves or small edible blossoms for garnish

1. Set aside a dozen or so perfect berries for garnish. Peel, pit and slice one of the peaches and gently toss it with all the remaining berries in a large bowl, using a light touch to avoid bruising or mashing the fruit. Add the lemon juice and up to 1 tablespoon of sugar. (If your berries are exceedingly sweet, you may only need a teaspoon to marry the various flavors. The sweetness will increase as the fruit absorbs the juices.) Mix gently and chill for at least 30 minutes and up to several hours.

2. Peel, pit and slice the remaining 2 peaches over a blender jar or food processor bowl to catch the juice. Purée the peaches with the orange juice and liqueur (if using) until you have a thick, smooth sauce. Add the remaining sugar by teaspoonfuls, testing for sweetness in between. In the height of the season, you may not need any sugar at all. If you are not going to use the sauce right away, cover and refrigerate it until serving time.

3. To assemble, spoon some of the fruit and juice into 6 parfait glasses or wine goblets. Drizzle several spoonfuls of the peach sauce over the fruit, then add a small scoop of yogurt cream. Continue layering until the glass is about 2/3 full. Top with a last dollop of the cream and garnish with reserved berries, mint leaves or edible blossoms. Serve immediately.

❋ PER SERVING (INCLUDES 2 TABLESPOONS SWEET YOGURT CREAM) *Calories: 178, Cholesterol (mg): 0, Saturated fat (g): 0, Total fat (g): 1, Sodium (mg): 26, Total fiber (g): 7*

Sweet Yogurt Cream
Makes 3/4 cup, serving size 1 tablespoon

This is our all-purpose dessert cream and topping. For very sweet dishes, you may prefer the slightly acidic taste of unflavored yogurt. Or you may find that naturally tart fresh fruit mixtures beg the sweeter vanilla yogurt. It's your call.

> 1/2 cup nonfat sour cream
> 1/4 cup nonfat plain yogurt or creamy-style nonfat vanilla yogurt
> 1 tablespoon vanilla sugar (page 538) or granulated sugar

In a small bowl, blend all the ingredients until smooth. Cover and refrigerate until needed. If the cream separates on standing, stir well before using. This will keep several days.

❋ PER SERVING *Calories: 12, Cholesterol (mg): 0, Saturated fat (g): 0, Total fat (g): 0, Sodium (mg): 10, Total fiber (g): 0*

Summer Fruit en Papillote

SERVES 6

MOST COMMONLY USED FOR SAVORY DISHES, *the technique of wrapping fruit in a tightly sealed parchment or foil packet and baking it in a hot oven yields an incredible nectar, especially when the fruit is perfectly vine sweetened to begin with. Fabulous by itself, this dessert is sublime with a spoonful or two of Creme Anglaise (page 555).*

> 2 cups mixed fresh berries
> 2 cups mixed, peeled and sliced fruit (peaches, pears, plums,
>   nectarines, pineapple and/or quartered figs)
> 3 tablespoons white wine or Champagne
> 2 teaspoons Triple Sec
> 2 teaspoons vanilla sugar (page 538), orange sugar (page 538)
>   or granulated sugar
> Parchment paper or aluminum foil, cut into six 10-inch sheets
> 1 cup Crème Anglaise (page 555), optional

1. Preheat the oven to 425 degrees F. in a large bowl, mix the berries and fruit with the white wine, Triple Sec and sugar, stirring gently so you don't bruise the berries. Carefully, without puncturing the parchment or foil, make a boat or a box of each sheet by folding up the edges. Divide the fruit and the juice from the bowl equally among the packets. Pull the edges together and fold over several times so that you have a tight seal.

2. Place the fruit packets on a baking sheet and bake for 15 minutes. Set aside briefly to cool. Place each packet on an individual serving plate and open each packet carefully to keep the original shape. Peel the sides back to expose the fruit. Spoon the Crème Anglaise (if using) on top of the fruit, and serve in the packets immediately.

❋ PER SERVING *Calories: 75, Cholesterol (mg): 0, Saturated fat (g): 0, Total fat (g): Trace, Sodium (mg): 1, Total fiber (g): 3*

Tropical Soufflé
with Orange Banana Rum Sauce
SERVES 6

LIGHT AS A CLOUD, *though not as puffy as the traditional soufflé, this will bring a rich, warm glow of the tropics to a winter evening with friends. While elegant enough for holidays, this queen of desserts is simple enough to assemble after a casual pasta and salad supper. Unlike most soufflé batters—ballooning in fat from whole milk, butter and egg yolks—our smooth purée of naturally sweet yams (or sweet potatoes) is thick enough to form its own fat-free custard. You need only give attention to fine-tuning the flavorings and achieving the right, pleasing balance of cinnamon and rum before lightening it with egg whites and sending it into a hot oven for the magical explosion of texture and taste. Serve it with Orange Banana Rum Sauce (recipe follows) or a spoonful of Ginger Cream (page 545) or even completely unadorned.*

> Orange Banana Rum Sauce (recipe follows)
> Vegetable spray for soufflé dish
> ½ cup plus 1 tablespoon vanilla sugar (page 538),
>   orange sugar (page 538) or granulated sugar
> 1 pound garnet yams, peeled and cut into 1-inch cubes
> 1 teaspoon grated orange zest
> ¼ teaspoon ground cinnamon
> 1 tablespoon butter
> 1 tablespoon unbleached all-purpose flour
> ⅔ cup liquid egg substitute
> ¼ cup rum
> 6 egg whites
> Pinch of cream of tartar

1. Prepare the Banana Rum sauce and set aside. Preheat the oven to 375 degrees F. Liberally coat the bottom and sides of a 6-cup soufflé dish with a film of vegetable spray. Sprinkle it with the tablespoon of sugar and rotate the dish several times so that the sugar coats the sides and bottom evenly. Shake the excess sugar onto a piece of waxed paper (you will add it to the egg whites shortly) and set the dish aside.

2. Place the yams in a saucepan and cover with water. Bring to a boil, reduce the heat and cook uncovered for 15 or 20 minutes or until the yams are very soft. Drain thoroughly and peel them. In a food processor or blender, purée the yams with the ½ cup sugar, orange zest and cinnamon until smooth.

3. Over very low heat, melt the butter in a medium-size saucepan. Add the flour and stir for 1 or 2 minutes until well blended. If the mixture lumps, the heat was too high. Remove the pan from the heat immediately and stir until cooled and smooth. Add the puréed yams and stir over high heat just until the mixture is very hot. Remove the pan from the heat and stir in the egg substitute first and then the rum. You can press a sheet of plastic wrap onto the surface, cover the pan and refrigerate it for several hours. Warm thoroughly before continuing.

4. In a large bowl, beat the egg whites and cream of tartar with an electric mixer at high speed, stopping to scrape the sides of the bowl from time to time, until the whites form soft mounds on your spatula. Shake in the excess sugar from the soufflé dish and continue beating just until the peaks can stand upright. Do not overbeat. Working quickly, gently fold about ¼ of the egg whites into the yams, blending until the mixture has lightened. Fold in the remaining egg whites, pulling the spatula along the bottom of the bowl and gently shaking the soufflé up and over itself, giving the bowl a quarter turn and continuing until well blended. Don't overmix the soufflé or you will lose the air you have just beaten into the egg whites.

5. Immediately pour the mixture into the prepared soufflé dish and place in the preheated oven for 40 to 45 minutes or until puffed and golden and a knife or long-tined fork inserted in the center comes out clean. Meanwhile reheat the Orange Banana Rum Sauce, pour into a bowl and serve with the souffle the instant it comes out of the oven.

❋ PER SERVING (INCLUDES APPROXIMATELY 3½ TABLESPOONS SAUCE) *Calories: 308, Cholesterol (mg): 5, Saturated fat (g): 1, Total fat (g): 3, Sodium (mg): 132, Total fiber (g): 2*

Orange Banana Rum Sauce
Makes about 1⅓ cups, serving size 1 tablespoon

Use on crêpes instead of a buttery crêpe suzette sauce, on dessert waffles or angel food cake. Or serve as a very intense sauce on low-fat vanilla frozen yogurt for a very grown up, very sensational sundae.

> 1¼ to 1½ cups fresh orange juice
> 2 tablespoons brown sugar
> 1 tablespoon cornstarch
> 1 tablespoon banana liqueur
> 1 tablespoon rum

Place the orange juice, sugar and cornstarch in a small nonreactive saucepan and whisk briskly over medium-high heat about 1 minute or until it comes to a boil and thickens. Reduce the heat immediately, stir in the banana liqueur and rum, and simmer and stir for 15 seconds. Serve hot or cold. This will keep several days covered and refrigerated.

❀ PER SERVING *Calories: 18, Cholesterol (mg): 0, Saturated fat (g): 0, Total fat (g): 0, Sodium (mg): 1, Total fiber (g): 0*

Pear Mousse with Blueberries

MAKES EIGHT ½-CUP SERVINGS

FABULOUSLY LIGHT AND PURE FRUIT, *this purée yields a soft and custardy mousse with absolutely no fat. For a family dinner that includes children, omit the brandy. The possibilities are endless. Do you like your pears with raspberries? Then serve our mousse with a scoop of Raspberry Sherbet (page 564) or puréed and slightly sweetened fresh berries. Do you long for pears Hélène? Then cap pear mousse with Hal's Hot Fudge Sauce (page 565–66). Don't overlook fruit toppings in the Breakfast chapter, either, such as Dried Blueberry Honey Sauce (page 306) or Strawberry-Peach Sauce (page 308).*

> 4 pears, roasted and cooled (see Roasted Pears, page 557)
> 1 teaspoon vanilla extract
> 1 tablespoon vanilla sugar (page 538) or granulated sugar
> 1 teaspoon unflavored gelatin dissolved in 1 tablespoon boiling water
> 1 to 2 tablespoons pear brandy
> 2 cups fresh blueberries

1. Peel and core the pears and slice into the bowl of a blender or food processor. Add the vanilla extract, sugar and the dissolved gelatin, and purée until smooth. Stir in 1 tablespoon of the pear brandy. Taste and add the remaining brandy if desired. Chill thoroughly.

2. To serve, scoop into wine goblets or small decorative bowls and sprinkle each serving with about ½ cup of blueberries.

❀ PER SERVING *Calories: 67, Cholesterol (mg): 0, Saturated fat (g): 0, Total fat (g): 0, Sodium (mg): 0, Total fiber (g): 3*

Raspberry Sherbet

MAKES EIGHT ¼-CUP SERVINGS

IN A NEAT TRICK OF KITCHEN ALCHEMY, *the grated orange zest conceals its own flavor, but intensifies the taste of the raspberries in this best-ever frozen dessert.*

> 2 cups water
> ½ cup vanilla sugar (page 538) or granulated sugar
> 2 pints fresh raspberries
> Grated zest from 1 orange
> 2 tablespoons heavy cream

1. Place the water and sugar in a saucepan and bring to a boil, reduce the heat slightly and cook for 5 minutes or until syrupy. Chill thoroughly. You can make this up to a week ahead.

2. Mash the raspberries into a bowl through a sieve, which will both purée them and remove the seeds. If you like a textured sherbet (as we do for added fiber), simply whirl the berries in a blender or food processor, or beat with the back of a large spoon to purée. Grate the orange zest into the berries and add the cream, blending well.

3. Follow the manufacturer's instructions for your ice cream maker; or place the sherbet in an ice tray and place in the freezer. Check it frequently and as ice crystals begin to form and it becomes slushy, thoroughly mix the sherbet. Repeat every 20 minutes or so until the mixture is quite slushy. Freeze until firm before serving. If you want a smoother texture, place the almost frozen sherbet in a bowl and, using an electric mixer, beat thoroughly at high speed for 1 minute, then freeze.

FAT TRACKING TIP: Use half-and-half in place of heavy cream.

❊ PER SERVING *Calories: 98, Cholesterol (mg): 5, Saturated fat (g): 1, Total fat (g): 2, Sodium (mg): 4, Total fiber (g): 3*

Hal's Hot Fudge Sauce

MAKES APPROXIMATELY 1 CUP, SERVING SIZE 1 TABLESPOON

WE PROMISED YOU COULD ENJOY RICH, INDULGENT SWEETS *and still take care of your heart, and now we deliver the goods: an indispensable sauce with deep chocolate flavor, the luxuriously thick consistency of fudge, a glossy and expensive-looking sheen, but with only a few crucial grams of fat. We developed this sauce for one of our favorite Fat Trackers, Hal Jennings, by using a bit of kitchen chemistry. The trick is to cook the sugar until it is golden and syrupy, following a few rules for caramelized sugar. First, add a little cream of tartar to prevent crystallization. Second, never turn your back on the sugar; a perfect golden glaze can become a blackened molten rock in a heartbeat. Last, add the milk warm, so the sauce doesn't congeal. If the sauce does harden (and we do mean harden), simply stir it over low-medium heat and it will dissolve beautifully. Once you begin, do not answer the phone, doorbell or anything else except a fire alarm until the sauce is finished. Short of burning the sugar, this is a foolproof and easy sauce. In addition to vanilla and chocolate extract, you can add other flavorings, such as Grand Marnier, grated orange zest, Amaretto, almond extract or a teaspoon of coffee granules. Store any remaining sauce in the refrigerator and rewarm over hot water or in the microwave. It will keep for over a week in the refrigerator (though once you taste it, it may not last that long).*

> ⅔ cup brown sugar
> 2 tablespoons cold water
> Pinch of cream of tartar
> 1 tablespoon butter or margarine
> ½ cup Dutch process cocoa powder
> ½ cup whole milk, warmed
> 1 teaspoon vanilla extract
> 1 teaspoon chocolate extract

1. Place the sugar, water and cream of tartar in a small saucepan and stir until blended. *(Do not stir again until the sugar has finished cooking.)* Place over medium heat. Watch the sugar as it bubbles slowly, then vigorously, then lazily and finally begins to melt into a golden syrup; this will occur in a few minutes at most. If you turn the heat higher it will melt faster, but if this is your first time caramelizing sugar, it is best to go slowly. If one side of the sauce begins to cook faster and color before the other, *without stirring*, simply rotate the pan on the burner, swirling the syrup gently as you do. When the sugar is uniformly golden, wheat-colored, or amber, remove it from the heat *instantly*. The darker the color the more intense caramel flavor you will have, but don't go beyond a rich caramel shade, making sure you stop short of burning it.

2. Immediately remove from the heat and stir in the butter and cocoa. (It will thicken; don't worry.) Stir in the warm milk. If the milk is cold or even cool, the syrup will immediately congeal. Don't worry here, either; return the sauce to medium heat and stir until smooth. Add the vanilla and chocolate extracts and stir until they are blended. Taste a drop and if the flavor of the extracts dominates, cook for another few minutes, stirring at all times. Serve hot or cool.

❋ PER SERVING *Calories: 49, Cholesterol (mg): 3, Saturated fat (g): 1, Total fat (g): 1, Sodium (mg): 12, Total fiber (g): 0*

Stanford Shake

SERVES 4

To OUR LIST OF CALCULATIONS *we add one extra—calcium—with this yummy, almost fat-free, bone strengthening shake. It is hard to find a better calcium bargain than this fruity froth of delicious nutrition: lots of calcium, barely a trace of fat and a minimal expense of calories. As we do here, both haute chefs and country cooks have paired peaches and raspberries in desserts as varied as peach Melba and homey cobblers. If you prefer a different match, add a fresh banana and pineapple sherbet; lots of fresh kiwi, orange sherbet and strawberry yogurt or any other favorite combination that will keep you coming back for more—more luscious heart-healthy flavor for kids, more low-calorie snackability for weight-watchers and most important, more bone-hardening calcium for everyone.*

> 1 cup 1% milk
> 1 cup nonfat vanilla yogurt
> ½ cup nonfat raspberry sherbet or sorbet
> ⅓ cup nonfat dry milk powder
> 1 peach, unpeeled, pitted and quartered
> 3 or 4 ice cubes

Place all the ingredients in a blender and whip on high speed until thick and frothy. Pour into tall glasses and serve immediately.

FAT TRACKING TIP: Use nonfat milk.

❋ PER SERVING *Calories: 130, Cholesterol (mg): 5, Saturated fat: Trace, Total fat: 1, Sodium (mg): 97, Total fiber (g): Trace, Calcium (mg): 246*

The philosophy for this book originated in 1976 when Helen Cassidy Page and Dr. John Schroeder stated in their introduction to *The Whole Family Low Cholesterol Cookbook* (published by Grossett & Dunlap), "life is too short not to eat well—and wisely." In the ensuing years, we have seen wave after wave of scientific research confirm the link between diet and coronary heart disease. Recent reports show that lowering blood cholesterol levels will, indeed, not only lower the risk of heart attack, but reverse the buildup of cholesterol plaque. In view of the fact that John Farquhar, M.D., and his group at the Center for Research in Disease Prevention have pioneered research into the causes and prevention of coronary heart disease, it is only appropriate that the philosophies of the Stanford community be consolidated into *The Stanford Life Plan for a Healthy Heart.* This book opens the door for heart disease prevention to move from the laboratory to the kitchen. In fact, we believe so strongly that diet can positively influence your health, that every patient entering Stanford Hospital, whether for a heart transplantation or an appendectomy, receives dietary guidelines (including The Stanford 25 Gram Plan), which are expanded upon in this book.

We wish to thank the authors for the hard work and commitment that have made this book an important arm of Stanford's campaign against heart disease: John Schroeder, M.D., for his development of the groundbreaking Stanford 25 Gram Plan; Tara Coghlin Dickson for translating the guidelines of the National Cholesterol Education Program into a user-friendly nutritional program; and Helen Cassidy Page, food writer and cooking teacher, whose creativity and insistence on the best are reflected in every single word in this book. To all the readers of this book, we wish you a long and healthy life.

MALINDA MITCHELL
Chief Operating Officer
Stanford Health Services

Index

Buttermilk, 198

Cafés, 255
Cakes: fat tracking, 224, 231; mixes, 224
Calcium, 153–57
Calcium blockers, 37, 71
Calories: counting, 161–67; estimated daily need of, 56; on labels, 173; typical daily consumption of, 162, 166
Canadian bacon, 192
Cancer: antioxidants and, 148–49; aspirin and, 77; breast, 82, 83, 87; colon, 77, 146; lung, 69; smoking and, 69; uterine, 87
Candy, 26, 232
Canned products, 179; fish and shellfish, 191
Canola oil, 115, 135, 214, 218, 277; on labels, 178; smoking point of, 213, 214
Carbohydrates, 96–98; complex, 97, 174; on labels, 174; simple, 96–97
"Carbo loading," 96
Castelli, William, 64–65
Cereals: fat tracking, 224–26; fiber in, 147; serving size of, 134; shopping list for, 228
Chard, 156
Cheese: calcium in, 156; cholesterol in, 206; fat in, 26, 204–6, 278; frequency of, 135; grated, 206; nutritional analysis of, 102; shopping list for, 210; substitutes, 205–6; varieties of, 206
Chestnuts, 219, 230
Chicken: cholesterol in, 189; deep-fried, 241; fat content of, 189; frequency of, 135; on labels, 176. *See also* Organ meats
Children: calcium requirements for,

155; calorie needs of, 56; fat targets for, 56; heart disease and, 35–36, 78–79; low-fat diet for, 78, 88; protein quota for, 99; reduced milk consumption among, 154; secondary smoke and, 69
Chili, 237
Chinese restaurants, 248–49
Chocolate: bars, 105–6, 237; fat tracking, 231; frequency of, 135; grating, 231; on labels, 176; saturated fat in, 26; stearic acid in, 112
Cholesterol: antioxidants and, 148; blood test, 41–42; body production of, 23; definition of, 23; drugs lowering, 37–38; exercise and, 74; in fish, 181; food sources of, 24; "good" and "bad," 23, 25; HDL, 23, 32–33, 64, 74; heart disease and, 16, 32–33; high levels of, in women, 85–86; on labels, 173–74, 175; LDL, 23, 32–33, 63, 148; low levels of, 61, 62–63; in meat, 181, 183–87; national recommendations for, 10; normal levels of, 19; in organ meats, 187; in poultry, 181, 189; quotient, 13, 30; ratio of total to HDL, 64–65; reducing, 65–66, 168; research on, 13–21; saturated fat and, 25, 28–29; smoking's effects on, 70; soluble fiber and, 146; target levels, 61–65, 67; transfatty acids and, 116; triglycerides and, 35; unsaturated fat and, 110; weight and, 161 "Cholesterol free": definition of, 177; misleading claims of, 175
Clams, 191
Cocoa: for chocolate, 231; on labels, 178
Cocoa butter, 176
Coconut, 113; on labels, 176; saturated

105, 240–43; saturated fat in, 27
"Fat free," 177
Fats: American consumption of, 105;
animal, 113; calories in, 162; fake,
117, 218; guide to, 115; hidden, 114;
hydrogenated, 112; on labels,
173–74, 175; monounsaturated vs.
polyunsaturated, 110–12; necessity
of, 105, 106–8; in processed foods,
113–14; product claims regarding,
177; saturated, and cholesterol,
25, 28–29; saturated, foods high
in, 26–27, 114, 125; saturated, recommended levels of, 53–57; saturated, typical consumption of,
7–8; saturated vs. unsaturated,
108–9; shopping list for, 220;
sources of, 113–14; stearic acid, 112;
total, recommended level, 57;
traps, 58–60; vegetable, 113. *See
also* Fat tracking
Fat tracking: baked goods, cereals
and pasta, 221–28; dairy products,
195–210; definition of, 94–95;
desserts and snacks, 229–34; fast
foods, 235–38; Fat Account,
129–30; fats and oils, 211–20; fish
and shellfish, 181, 190–91, 194;
meal-planning guide, 131–43;
meat, 181–87, 192–93, 194; poultry, 181, 188–89, 194; in restaurants, 239–56; success in, 103–4;
in supermarkets, 171–80
FDA, 181
Fiber, 145–48; in breakfasts, 138; in
cereals, 224–25; in grains, 146–47;
heart disease and, 78; insoluble,
146; on labels, 174, 175; legumes,
146; recommended level of, 145;
soluble, 146
Fish: cholesterol in, 191; fat tracking,
181, 190–91, 194; frequency of, 135;
labels for, 181; nutritional analysis

of, 102; omega-3 fatty acids in, 112;
serving size of, 133–34; shopping
list for, 194
Fish oil, 112, 118
Five City Project, 18
Food Guide Pyramid, 131–32
Fortmann, Steven, 6
Four basic food groups, 16–17, 131
Framingham study, 16, 64, 70, 85–86
Free radicals, 148
French diet, 118–19
Frozen yogurt, 208, 209, 255
Fruits: antioxidants in, 150–51;
frequency of, 135; serving size of,
134

Game, 188, 189
Gelato, 208, 209
Goose, 188, 189
Grains: antioxidants in, 150–51;
complementary with legumes and
nuts, 101; fiber in, 146–47;
frequency of, 135; serving size of,
134; variety of, 101
Granola, 26, 113; bars, 223
Grapeseed oil, 178, 214

Half-and-half, 26, 106, 200, 278
Ham, 186, 192
Hazelnut oil, 214, 215
Heart attacks, 33, 35; deaths from, 6,
33; warning signs of, 36
Heart disease: antioxidants and, 78,
148–49; causes of, 20; in children,
35–36, 78–79; diabetes mellitus
and, 75; early symptoms of, 33; in
the elderly, 79; exercise and,
74–75; fiber and, 78; free radicals
and, 148; genetic factors for, 76,
78, 79; in men, 78; oral contraceptives and, 39, 84; prevention of,

of, 135; shopping list for, 194

Sherbet, 208, 209

Shopping lists: for baked goods, cereals and pasta, 228; for dairy products, 210; for desserts and snacks, 234; for fats and oils, 220; for meat, poultry and seafood, 194

Shortening, 115, 211; frequency of, 135; on labels, 176; substitutes for, 212; substitutes for, 217

Shrimp, 24, 25, 191

Shumway, Norman, 15

Smoking: heart disease and, 39, 69–71; passive, 69; quitting, 70–71, 122; women and, 84

Snacks: fat tracking, 229, 230, 233; shopping list for, 234

Sodium: in Asian restaurants, 248; heart disease and, 72–73; on labels, 174, 175; product claims regarding, 177; recommended level of, 72, 174; sources of, 73

Sorbet, 208, 209

Soups, canned, 26, 179, 237

Sour cream: fat tracking, 26, 201, 202, 277; nonfat, 197, 201

Soybean oil, 115, 215, 218; on labels, 178; smoking point of, 214

Spinach, 156

Squid, 191

Stanford Center for Research in Disease Prevention, 18

Stanford 17 Gram Plan: incomplete labels and, 176; timetable for, 123–24

Stanford 25 Gram Plan: calories in, 161–67; frequency table, 135; in complete labels and, 176; meal planning, 132–43; saturated fat in, 53–57; strategy for, 124–27; timetable for, 122–23

Stearic acid, 112

Stress: heart disease and, 39, 75–76; reduction of, 71

Stress test, 37

Strokes, 35

Stuffing mixes, 238

Sunflower oil, 178, 214

Supermarkets, fat tracking in, 171–80

Supplements: calcium, 157; vitamin, 148

Thai restaurants, 248–49

Thiazide diuretics, 71, 75

Three Community Study, 18

Tofu, 102, 156

Tortillas, 102, 251

Trail mix, 230

Transfatty acids, 115–16

Triglycerides, 35, 97

Turkey: cholesterol in, 189; fat content of, 189; frequency of, 135; ground, 189; processed, 193

2 + 2 Dinners, 140

"Two Step Eating Plan," 123

U.S. Department of Agriculture, 131

U.S. Department of Health and Human Services, 131

U.S. Physicians Health Study, 77

Uterine cancer, 87

Veal: cholesterol in, 187; cuts of, 187; fat tracking, 186–87; free-range, 186; shopping list for, 194

Vegetables: antioxidants in, 150–51; calcium in, 156–57; frequency of, 135; frozen, 238; oils, 215, 218; oil spreads, 216; serving size of, 134; without enhancements, 217

Vegetarianism, 100–101, 140

Vietnamese restaurants, 248–49

Vitamins: C, 148–51; E, 148–51; on

labels, 174, 175; supplements, 148

Waffles, 226, 237
Walnut oil, 214, 215
Weight, ideal, 47
Weight control, 73–74; carbohydrates
   and, 97, 98; exercise and, 74, 107;
   fat consumption and, 107; for
   women, 85. *See also* Obesity
Wheatberries, 147
White, Paul Dudley, 17
Women: calcium requirements for,
   155; diabetes and, 84–85; estrogen
   replacement therapy for, 76, 158;
   future studies with, 88; HDL levels
   in, 64; heart disease in, 81–88;
   high blood pressure in, 85; high
   cholesterol levels in, 85–86; ideal
   weight for, 47; menopause in,
   86–87; oral contraceptives and,
   84; osteoporosis and, 154, 158; as
   role models, 88; smoking and, 70,
   84; weight gain in, 85
Wood, Peter, 73, 162

Yogurt: calcium in, 156; fat tracking,
   204, 277; nutritional analysis of,
   102; shopping list for, 210. *See also*
   Frozen yogurt

Recipe Index

Table of Equivalents
AND EQUIVALENTS FOR COMMONLY USED INGREDIENTS

The exact equivalents in the following tables have been rounded for convenience.

US/UK	Metric
oz = ounce	g = gram
lb = pound	kg = kilogram
in = inch	mm = millimeter
ft = foot	cm = centimeter
tbl = tablespoon	ml = milliliter
fl oz = fluid ounce	l = liter
qt = quart	

OVEN TEMPERATURES

Fahrenheit	Celsius	Gas
250	120	½
275	140	1
300	150	2
325	160	3
350	180	4
375	190	5
400	200	6
425	220	7
450	230	8
475	240	9
500	260	10

LIQUIDS

US	Metric	UK
2 tbl	30 ml	1 fl oz
¼ cup	60 ml	2 fl oz
⅓ cup	80 ml	3 fl oz
½ cup	125 ml	4 fl oz
⅔ cup	160 ml	5 fl oz
¾ cup	180 ml	6 fl oz
1 cup	250 ml	8 fl oz
1½ cups	375 ml	12 fl oz
2 cups	500 ml	16 fl oz
4 cups/1 qt	1 l	32 fl oz

WEIGHTS

US/UK	Metric
1 oz	30 g
2 oz	60 g
3 oz	90 g
4 oz (¼ lb)	125 g
5 oz (⅓ lb)	155 g
6 oz	185 g
7 oz	220 g
8 oz (½ lb)	250 g
10 oz	315 g
12 oz (¾ lb)	375 g
14 oz	440 g
16 oz (1 lb)	500 g
1½ lb	750 g
2 lb	1 kg
3 lb	1.5 kg

LENGTH MEASURES

US/UK	Metric
⅛ in	3 mm
¼ in	6 mm
½ in	12 mm
1 in	2.5 cm
2 in	5 cm
3 in	7.5 cm
4 in	10 cm
5 in	13 cm
6 in	15 cm
7 in	18 cm
8 in	20 cm
9 in	23 cm
10 in	25 cm
11 in	28 cm
12 in/1 ft	30 cm

ALL-PURPOSE (PLAIN) FLOUR/DRIED BREAD CRUMBS/CHOPPED NUTS

¼ cup	1 oz	30 g
⅓ cup	1½ oz	45 g
½ cup	2 oz	60 g
¾ cup	3 oz	90 g
1 cup	4 oz	125 g
1½ cups	6 oz	185 g
2 cups	8 oz	250 g

WHOLE-WHEAT (WHOLE MEAL) FLOUR

3 tbl	1 oz	30 g
½ cup	2 oz	60 g
⅔ cup	3 oz	90 g
1 cup	4 oz	125 g
1¼ cups	5 oz	155 g
1⅔ cups	7 oz	210 g
1¾ cups	8 oz	250 g

BROWN SUGAR

¼ cup	1½ oz	45 g
½ cup	3 oz	90 g
¾ cup	4 oz	125 g
1 cup	5½ oz	170 g
1½ cups	8 oz	250 g
2 cups	10 oz	315 g

WHITE SUGAR

¼ cup	2 oz	60 g
⅓ cup	3 oz	90 g
½ cup	4 oz	125 g
¾ cup	6 oz	185 g
1 cup	8 oz	250 g
1½ cups	12 oz	375 g
2 cups	1 lb	500 g

LONG-GRAIN RICE/CORNMEAL

⅓ cup	2 oz	60 g
½ cup	2 ½ oz	75 g
¾ cup	4 oz	125 g
1 cup	5 oz	155 g
1½ cups	8 oz	250 g

ROLLED OATS

⅓ cup	1 oz	30 g
⅔ cup	2 oz	60 g
1 cup	3 oz	90 g
1½ cups	4 oz	125 g
2 cups	5 oz	155 g

RAISINS/CURRANTS/SEMOLINA

¼ cup	1 oz	30 g
⅓ cup	2 oz	60 g
½ cup	3 oz	90 g
¾ cup	4 oz	125 g
1 cup	5 oz	155 g

JAM/HONEY

2 tbl	2 oz	60 g
¼ cup	3 oz	90 g
½ cup	5 oz	155 g
¾ cup	8 oz	250 g
1 cup	11 oz	345 g

DRIED BEANS

¼ cup	1½ oz	45 g
⅓ cup	2 oz	60 g
½ cup	3 oz	90 g
¾ cup	5 oz	155 g
1 cup	6 oz	185 g
1¼ cups	8 oz	250 g
1½ cups	12 oz	375 g

GRATED PARMESAN/ROMANO CHEESE

¼ cup	1 oz	30 g
½ cup	2 oz	60 g
¾ cup	3 oz	90 g
1 cup	4 oz	125 g
1⅓ cups	5 oz	155 g
2 cups	7 oz	220 g